CAMBRIDGE COMPANIONS TO RELIGION
This is a series of companions to major topics
religious studies. Each volume contains speci
international scholars, which provide an accessi
to the subject for new readers and nonspecialis

G000075559

Other Titles in the Series

THE COUNCIL OF NICAECA Edited by Young Richard Kim

APOSTOLIC FATHERS Edited by Michael F. Bird and Scott Harrower

AMERICAN CATHOLICISM Edited by Margaret M. McGuinness and Thomas F. Rzeznik

AMERICAN ISLAM Edited by Juliane Hammer and Omid Safi

AMERICAN JUDAISM Edited by Dana Evan Kaplan

AMERICAN METHODISM Edited by Jason E. Vickers

ANCIENT MEDITERRANEAN RELIGIONS Edited by Barbette Stanley Spaeth

APOCALYPTIC LITERATURE Edited by Colin McAllister

AUGUSTINE'S CITY OF GOD Edited by David Vincent Meconi

AUGUSTINE'S 'CONFESSIONS' Edited by Tarmo Toom

KARL BARTH Edited by John Webster

THE BIBLE, 2nd edition Edited by Bruce Chilton

THE BIBLE AND LITERATURE Edited by Calum Carmichael

BIBLICAL INTERPRETATION Edited by John Barton

BLACK THEOLOGY Edited by Dwight N. Hopkins and Edward P. Antonio

DIETRICH BONHOEFFER Edited by John de Gruchy

JOHN CALVIN Edited by Donald K. McKim

CHRISTIAN DOCTRINE Edited by Colin Gunton

CHRISTIAN ETHICS Edited by Robin Gill

CHRISTIAN MYSTICISM Edited by Amy Hollywood and Patricia Z. Beckman

CHRISTIAN PHILOSOPHICAL THEOLOGY Edited by Charles Taliaferro and Chad V. Meister

CHRISTIAN POLITICAL THEOLOGY Edited by Craig Hovey and Elizabeth Phillips

THE CISTERIAN ORDER Edited by Mette Birkedal Bruun

CLASSICAL ISLAMIC THEOLOGY Edited by Tim Winter

JONATHAN EDWARDS Edited by Stephen J. Stein

EVANGELICAL THEOLOGY Edited by Timothy Larsen and Daniel J. Treier

FEMINIST THEOLOGY Edited by Susan Frank Parsons

FRANCIS OF ASSISI Edited by Michael J. P. Robson

GENESIS Edited by Bill T. Arnold

THE GOSPELS Edited by Stephen C. Barton

THE GOSPELS, SECOND EDITION Edited by Stephen C. Barton and Todd Brewer

(continued after index)

THE CAMBRIDGE COMPANION TO
BIBLICAL WISDOM LITERATURE

Study of the wisdom literature in the Hebrew Bible and in the contemporary cultures of the ancient Near Eastern world is evolving rapidly as old definitions and assumptions are being questioned. Scholars are now interrogating the role of oral culture, the rhetoric of teaching and didacticism, the understanding of genre and the relationship of these factors to the corpus of wisdom writings. The scribal culture in which wisdom literature arose is also under investigation, alongside questions of social context and character formation. This *Companion* serves as an essential guide to wisdom texts, a body of biblical literature with ancient origins that continue to have universal and timeless appeal. Reflecting new interpretive approaches, including virtue ethics and intertextuality, the volume includes essays by an international team of leading scholars. They engage with the texts, provide authoritative summaries of the state of the field and open up to readers the exciting world of biblical wisdom.

Katharine J. Dell is Professor of Old Testament Literature and Theology at the University of Cambridge and Fellow of St Catharine's College. She is the author of *The Book of Proverbs in Social and Theological Context* (Cambridge University Press, 2006), *Interpreting Ecclesiastes: Readers Old and New (Eisenbrauns, 2013)* and *The Solomonic Corpus of 'Wisdom' and Its Influence (Oxford University Press, 2020)*.

Suzanna R. Millar is a Chancellor's Fellow in Hebrew Bible at the University of Edinburgh and assistant director of its Centre for Theology and Public Issues. She is the author of *Genre and Openness in Proverbs* (SBL Press, 2020).

Arthur Jan Keefer is schoolmaster and chaplain in the Divinity Department of Eton College. He is the author of *The Book of Proverbs and Virtue Ethics* (Cambridge University Press, 2020).

THE CAMBRIDGE COMPANION TO

BIBLICAL WISDOM
LITERATURE

Edited by

Katharine J. Dell
University of Cambridge

Assistant Editors

Suzanna R. Millar
University of Edinburgh

Arthur Jan Keefer
Eton College

CAMBRIDGE
UNIVERSITY PRESS

CAMBRIDGE
UNIVERSITY PRESS

University Printing House, Cambridge CB2 8BS, United Kingdom

One Liberty Plaza, 20th Floor, New York, NY 10006, USA

477 Williamstown Road, Port Melbourne, VIC 3207, Australia

314–321, 3rd Floor, Plot 3, Splendor Forum, Jasola District Centre,
New Delhi – 110025, India

103 Penang Road, #05-06/07, Visioncrest Commercial, Singapore 238467

Cambridge University Press is part of the University of Cambridge.

It furthers the University's mission by disseminating knowledge in the pursuit of
education, learning, and research at the highest international levels of excellence.

www.cambridge.org
Information on this title: www.cambridge.org/9781108483162
DOI: 10.1017/9781108673082

© Cambridge University Press 2022

This publication is in copyright. Subject to statutory exception
and to the provisions of relevant collective licensing agreements,
no reproduction of any part may take place without the written
permission of Cambridge University Press.

First published 2022

A catalogue record for this publication is available from the British Library.

Library of Congress Cataloging-in-Publication Data
NAMES: Dell, Katharine J. (Katharine Julia), 1961- editor. | Millar, Suzanna R., editor. |
Keefer, Arthur Jan, 1987- editor.
TITLE: The Cambridge companion to biblical wisdom literature / edited by Katharine J
Dell, University of Cambridge, Suzanna R Millar, University of Edinburgh, Arthur Jan
Keefer, Eton College.
DESCRIPTION: Cambridge, United Kingdom ; New York, NY, USA : Cambridge University
Press, 2022. | SERIES: Cambridge companions to religion | Includes bibliographical
references and index.
IDENTIFIERS: LCCN 2021044796 (print) | LCCN 2021044797 (ebook) | ISBN 9781108483162
(hardback) | ISBN 9781108716475 (paperback) | ISBN 9781108673082 (epub)
SUBJECTS: LCSH: Wisdom literature–Criticism, interpretation, etc.
CLASSIFICATION: LCC BS1455 .C36 2022 (print) | LCC BS1455 (ebook) | DDC 223–dc23
LC record available at https://lccn.loc.gov/2021044796
LC ebook record available at https://lccn.loc.gov/2021044797

ISBN 978-1-108-48316-2 Hardback
ISBN 978-1-108-71647-5 Paperback

Cambridge University Press has no responsibility for the persistence or accuracy
of URLs for external or third-party internet websites referred to in this publication
and does not guarantee that any content on such websites is, or will remain,
accurate or appropriate

Contents

List of Contributors   *page ix*
Acknowledgement   *xi*
List of Abbreviations   *xiii*

Part I   *The Context of Wisdom Literature*

1   Introduction   3
    KATHARINE J. DELL, SUZANNA R. MILLAR AND ARTHUR
    JAN KEEFER

2   The Scope of Wisdom Literature   13
    TREMPER LONGMAN III

3   The Multiple Genres of Wisdom   34
    SUZANNA R. MILLAR

4   The Literary Context(s) and Development of
    Wisdom Literature in Ancient Israel (with
    Special Reference to Proverbs)   57
    KNUT M. HEIM

5   The Scribal World   76
    MARK SNEED

6   Theological Themes in the 'Wisdom
    Literature': Proverbs, Job
    and Ecclesiastes   96
    KATHARINE J. DELL

7   The Solomonic Connection: Solomon and
    Wisdom in Kings and Chronicles   116
    DAVID FIRTH

Part II   *Wisdom Literature in the Hebrew Bible*

8   Proverbs   137
    CHRISTOPHER B. ANSBERRY

9   Job   162
    WILL KYNES

10   Ecclesiastes   184
     METTE BUNDVAD

11   The Song of Songs   200
     JENNIFER L. ANDRUSKA

12   Wisdom Psalms   219
     SIMON CHI-CHUNG CHEUNG

13   Wisdom's Wider Resonance   239
     MICHAEL C. LEGASPI

Part III   *Wisdom Literature beyond the Hebrew Bible*

14   Ben Sira   261
     SETH A. BLEDSOE

15   The Book of Wisdom   283
     JOACHIM SCHAPER

16   Wisdom at Qumran   303
     DAVID A. SKELTON

17   Egyptian Wisdom   323
     MICHAEL V. FOX AND SUZANNA R. MILLAR

18   The Syro-Palestinian Wisdom of the Late
     Bronze Age   344
     NOGA AYALI-DARSHAN

19   Mesopotamian Wisdom   366
     PAUL-ALAIN BEAULIEU

Part IV   *Themes in the Wisdom Literature*

20   Creation in the Wisdom Literature   391
     ZOLTÁN SCHWÁB

21   Reward and Retribution   414
     PETER T. H. HATTON

22   From Rebuke to Testimony to Proverb:
     Wisdom's Many Pedagogies   433
     WILLIAM P. BROWN

23   The Wisdom Literature and
     Virtue Ethics   455
     ARTHUR JAN KEEFER

     Bibliography   475
     Index   511

Contributors

Jennifer L. Andruska
University of Manchester

Christopher B. Ansberry
Grove City College

Noga Ayali-Darshan
Bar Ilan University

Paul-Alain Beaulieu
University of Toronto

Seth A. Bledsoe
Radboud University

William P. Brown
Columbia Theological Seminary

Mette Bundvad
University of Copenhagen

Simon Chi-chung Cheung
China Graduate School of Theology

Katharine J. Dell
University of Cambridge

David Firth
Trinity College

Michael V. Fox
University of Wisconsin–Madison

Peter T. H. Hatton
Bristol Baptist College

Knut M. Heim
Denver Theological Seminary

Arthur Jan Keefer
Eton College

Will Kynes
Samford University

Michael C. Legaspi
Penn State University

Tremper Longman III
Westmont College

Suzanna R. Millar
University of Edinburgh

Joachim Schaper
University of Aberdeen

Zoltán Schwáb
Spurgeon's College

David Skelton
Virginia Tech

Mark Sneed
Lubbock Christian University

Acknowledgement

This volume is the culmination of three years' work in planning, writing, compiling, editing and, at last, publishing a work that the editors hope will be an impressive addition to the fields both of wisdom literature and of Hebrew Bible/Old Testament studies as a whole, not to mention its intersections with many other fields within and outside biblical studies and theology. We would like to thank all the contributors to the volume who have produced material to deadlines and word lengths and who have given us some fascinating and fresh insights into the subject area of wisdom. We are grateful to them and to each other for friendly and efficient editorial interaction. Lastly, we would like to thank Beatrice Rehl at Cambridge University Press for being prepared to take on this project and to take it forward with great efficiency. This is an exciting and timely contribution to the Cambridge Companion series and to the field of biblical wisdom literature.

Abbreviations

AAeg	*Analecta Aegyptiaca*
AB	Anchor Bible
ABRL	Anchor Bible Reference Library
ABS	Archaeology and Biblical Studies
AIL	Ancient Israel and Its Literature
AnBib	Analecta Biblica
AMD	Ancient Magic and Divination
AOAT	Alter Orient und Altes Testament
AOTC	Abingdon Old Testament Commentaries
ASJ	*Acta Sumerologica*
ATANT	Abhandlungen zur Theologie des Alten und Neuen Testaments
AThR	*Anglican Theological Review*
AuOr	*Aula Orientalis*
BBR	*Bulletin for Biblical Research*
BBRSup	*Bulletin for Biblical Research, Supplements*
BCOTWP	Baker Commentary on the Old Testament Wisdom and Psalms
BETL	Bibliotheca Ephemeridum Theologicarum Lovaniensium
BibInt	*Biblical Interpretation*
BJRL	*Bulletin of the John Rylands University Library of Manchester*
BJS	Brown Judaic Studies
BKAT	Biblischer Kommentar, Altes Testament
BZAW	Beihefte zur Zeitschrift für die alttestamentliche Wissenschaft
BZNW	Beihefte zur Zeitschrift für die neutestamentliche Wissenschaft
CANE	*Civilizations of the Ancient Near East*
CBQ	*Catholic Biblical Quarterly*
CBQMS	Catholic Biblical Quarterly Monograph Series

CurBR	*Currents in Biblical Research*
CHANE	Culture and History of the Ancient Near East
ConBOT	Coniectanea Biblica: Old Testament Series
CurBS	*Currents in Research: Biblical Studies*
CSHJ	Chicago Studies in the History of Judaism
CTM	*Concordia Theological Monthly*
CurBR	*Currents in Biblical Research*
CurBS	*Currents in Research: Biblical Studies*
CUSAS	Cornell University Studies in Assyriology and Sumerology
DCLS	Deuterocanonical and Cognate Literature Studies
DSD	*Dead Sea Discoveries*
EJL	Early Judaism and Its Literature
ETL	*Ephemerides Theologicae Lovanienses*
ExpTim	*Expository Times*
FAT	Forschungen zum Alten Testament
FCB	Feminist Companion to the Bible
FOTL	Forms of the Old Testament Literature
FRLANT	Forschungen zur Religion und Literatur des Alten und Neuen Testaments
GBS	Guides to Biblical Scholarship
GTJ	*Grace Theological Journal*
HAT	Handbuch zum Alten Testament
HBM	Hebrew Bible Monographs
HBT	*Horizons in Biblical Theology*
HKAT	Handkommentar zum Alten Testament
HS	*Hebrew Studies*
HSM	Harvard Semitic Monographs
HSS	Harvard Semitic Studies
HThKAT	Herders Theologischer Kommentar zum Alten Testament
HTR	*Harvard Theological Review*
HTS	Harvard Theological Studies
HUCA	*Hebrew Union College Annual*
IB	Interpreter's Bible
IBC	Interpretation: A Bible Commentary for Teaching and Preaching
ICC	International Critical Commentary
IEKAT	Internationaler Exegetischer Kommentar Zum Alten Testament
Int	*Interpretation*
JAJ	*Journal of Ancient Judaism*
JAAR	*Journal of the American Academy of Religion*

content. Surveying Proverbs, Ecclesiastes, Job, Ben Sira and Wisdom of Solomon, Millar discerns four clusters of genres, grouped according to their communicative purpose. Some genres intend to instruct their users (sayings, instructions, diatribe, protreptic and didactic narratives); others engage in reasoning (reflections and wisdom dialogues). These genres are not unexpected in wisdom literature, but the next are more familiar from other biblical corpora: some genres offer praise (either to wisdom, people or God), and others enunciate complaints (laments and legal complaints). These multiple genres combine and interact in complex ways within each wisdom book.

Knut Heim (Chapter 4) then examines the literary and historical contexts of wisdom literature, taking the book of Proverbs as a case study and surveying the work of key scholars in the field. Beginning with literary context, he argues that the sayings are organised into 'clusters' through linguistic and thematic links with their neighbours and that this context has hermeneutical significance. Particularly important is the placement of religious proverbs, which are well integrated with their surroundings. This calls into question the scholarly assumption that religious elements are a late addition to the book and that wisdom was originally a 'secular' endeavour. Rather, elements like the 'fear of the Lord' were already embedded within the sayings collections by the time an editor added chapters 1–9. This has implications for the historical development of Proverbs and, more broadly, of wisdom in Israel.

Next, Mark Sneed (Chapter 5) introduces readers to the world of scribes. Drawing first on some of the earliest developments of Sumerian scribalism, he gives an overview of how scribes trained and worked in the ancient Near East more broadly. In Egypt and elsewhere, scribal training began at an early age and involved a wide range of curricula, including wisdom literature, which scribes copied and memorised, as it played a significant role in scribal education. Although concrete evidence for Israelite schools is lacking, Sneed finds reason to believe that similar scribal practices existed there, where wisdom literature too served technical and ethical purposes. Scribes, then, existed in ancient Israel, and for Sneed could be identified in various ways: as priests, prophets and sages. Behind each of these categories lies the 'scribe' as the one who composed the texts themselves. Thus, Sneed finds far more that is common than different among the biblical materials, wisdom texts included, and conceives of the scribe as holding a wide-ranging professional role in Israel that was not tied down to a single genre of literature.

Katharine Dell's contribution (Chapter 6) explores the question whether there is a distinctive set of theological ideas for the three key wisdom books – Proverbs, Job and Ecclesiastes. After a brief survey of scholarship on this debate over the last century and a half, key themes that the books have in common are explored, with salient examples – the doctrine of retribution, the fear of the Lord, the figure of Wisdom and the attainment of wisdom, the theme of creation, communication and life and death. Although considerable commonality is found, there is also a discovery of difference and of interlinking with other books in the canon. The themes themselves are not confined to these 'wisdom' books, even though they characterise them and they are accompanied by an essential didactic approach.

With his 'Solomonic Connection', David Firth (Chapter 7) observes the man Solomon as he appears in Kings and Chronicles. Solomon is 'paradigmatic' for understanding wisdom in both of these books and yet he is not treated identically therein. Kings and Chronicles offer different portraits of this exceedingly wise king, whether that be his foundational role for wisdom or his problematic relationship with it. Matters of the temple, Solomon's behaviour, Torah and the very conception of wisdom itself all have a place in biblical presentations of Solomon. Firth looks closely at 1 Kings 1–11 and 2 Chronicles 1–9, employing a literary and theological reading that does not let one account determine the other or allow the Solomonic portraits in Proverbs and Ecclesiastes to have all of the attention.

Part II focuses on wisdom literature in the OT/HB. In his chapter on Proverbs, Christopher Ansberry (Chapter 8) provides a refreshing introductory approach to the book, not least because he starts with the history of interpretation rather than letting thematic concerns dominate. He identifies five patterns within the history of the book's interpretation, including a focus on character formation, debates about the nature of its 'wisdom' and place in the canon, interest in its reception via matters of date and authorship, the discovery of comparative ancient Near Eastern material and current, expanding interdisciplinary approaches to the book. A section on the fundamental nature of the book takes on matters of form, genre, poetic features and the idea of a 'collection', whilst granting admiration rather than suspicion to the complexities of the book's sayings. Likewise, the structure of Proverbs, though containing many parts, comes together into a coherent whole, an 'anthology', to which each piece contributes. Ansberry concludes by proposing four 'dominant' themes in the book: the fear of the Lord, a theological orientation that takes on an intensely personal characterisation; wisdom, a skill and holistic product of education, never far from the images of the book; moral order and created order; and retribution and reward. In all of this, Ansberry keeps scholarly alternatives on the surface of discussion without shying away from making the case that some such alternatives are more plausible than others.

Will Kynes (Chapter 9) then introduces the book of Job by asking 'What is the book of Job, and how does that affect how you read it?' This question entails investigation into the book's genre, for genre recognition provides a horizon of expectations which shapes the reader's perspective. Job has traditionally been read as wisdom literature, based on perceived similarities with Proverbs and Ecclesiastes in form, theme and Sitz im Leben. However, this genre grouping leads to Job's unwarranted separation from the rest of the canon, theological abstraction and hermeneutical limitations. Job is an open and ambiguous text which might be placed in multiple genre groupings. Kynes surveys several of these (sifre emet, lament, exemplary sufferer texts, poetry, drama, controversy dialogue, history, epic, didactic narrative, Torah, prophecy, lawsuit and apocalyptic), as well as some meta-generic readings (parody, citation and polyphony). Given this diversity, and recognising that all readings are culturally contingent and only partially appropriate, he advocates a multi-perspectival approach which draws insights from many directions.

Mette Bundvad (Chapter 10) considers Ecclesiastes as a book of contradictions and one that has a peculiar narrator and special thematic concerns. Instead of giving a catalogue of possible or plausible contradictions in the book, Bundvad surveys the ways in which scholars have reckoned with the book's evident tensions. The question that emerges, then, is whether these contradictions are a feature of the book or a 'bug' of sorts. Ecclesiastes' portrayal of its narrator falls under the rubric of these very tensions, exhibiting a man, or men, who wears various guises and no one persona. Bundvad concludes with reflections about the book's treatment of time, a theme that does not resolve every tension but does open up new questions and possible structures.

Jennifer Andruska (Chapter 11) sees close affinities between the Song of Songs and Wisdom Literature. She acknowledges that this is a minority position, surveying the history of reception, which has offered various alternative interpretations (e.g., literal, allegorical, cultic, feminist). She then defines wisdom literature, centralising the forms found in ANE advice literature, the concern for wisdom and the intended character transformation of the audience. All of these are found in the Song. Andruska discusses the mashal (proverb) in 8:6–7 and the intergenerational instructions found in the refrains (2:7, 3:5, 8:4). She argues that the Song offers wisdom about love, didactically advocating one particular vision of love (in contrast to other ANE love songs, which give varied depictions of love). The purpose of the Song is to transform its readers into wise lovers who follow the example of the lovers in the Song.

Next, Simon Cheung (Chapter 12) discusses the scholarship surrounding the 'wisdom psalms', with an eye towards the varied proposals, as well as the grounds for and development of them over the last century. From this, Cheung sets forth his own conception of wisdom psalms. They constitute 'a family of psalms, with varying degrees of membership, that exhibit a wisdom-oriented constellation of its generic elements'. The core traits are likened to DNA, which can be more or less present, and are mainly discerned in theme, tone and intention. 'Wisdom psalms', to some degree, then, feature wisdom, carry an 'intellectual tone' and a pedagogical intent, all of which Cheung inspects in Psalm 34:8–17. Overall, his approach may offer interpreters additional accuracy when considering wisdom and its influence within the Psalter.

In the final chapter of Part II, Michael C. Legaspi (Chapter 13) examines 'Wisdom's Wider Resonance'. It has been common to find the influence of wisdom literature across the canon, but Legaspi outlines the problems with this and takes an alternative approach. He examines the ḥ-k-m ('wisdom') root in parts of the Bible not usually associated with wisdom literature to find overlooked resonances of the concept. Specifically, he examines the idea that wisdom concerns the relationship between human and divine realms (common in Greek and Jewish thought). This understanding is evident in biblical descriptions of sacred spaces, for the lead craftsmen who construct the tabernacle and temple (Bazalel and Hiram respectively) are divinely endowed with wisdom. Equally, wisdom (albeit a corrupted wisdom) proliferates in Ezekiel 28, associated with proximity to and specialist knowledge of the divine and construction of sacred spaces. A similar understanding may also underlie Jeremiah's descriptions of Jerusalem's degraded wisdom. This analysis encourages us to understand 'wisdom' more capaciously than traditional delimitations of 'wisdom literature' allow.

Part III moves to consider wisdom literature beyond the traditional canon of the OT/HB. First, Seth Bledsoe (Chapter 14) introduces the second century BCE wisdom book of Ben Sira. While not forming part of the Tanakh or Protestant Old Testament, Ben Sira appears in the Septuagint (LXX) and subsequently the Roman Catholic and Eastern

Orthodox canons. The book presents itself as the words of a well-educated scribe and draws on both Jewish and Greek traditions. Central to the book is the figure of Wisdom, which is intimately connected to creation, fear of the Lord, Torah and tradition. It also contains advice on practical matters, such as finance (it both respects wealth and advocates generosity) and relations with women (it is in places decidedly misogynistic). Although generally optimistic that good deeds will lead to positive consequences, Ben Sira also grapples with the problems of theodicy and death, concluding that righteous persons can live on through the legacy of a good name.

The somewhat neglected Wisdom of Solomon, or 'Book of Wisdom', contains concepts important not only for understanding wisdom in the rest of the OT but also for understanding how wisdom bridged both testaments. Joachim Schaper (Chapter 15) gives priority to the book's theology and its place in Hellenistic Jewish and early Christian thought. He provides an overview of the book's structure and versions, its intellectual context, its universalistic conceptions of God and humans in history and how the book exhibits a 'spiritual exercise'. Most important here are Wisdom's use of πνευμα ('spirit') and its amalgam of Platonic, Stoic and Egyptian elements. It offers a distinct interpretation of the Exodus, with which Schaper accounts for ideas of liberation and eschatology. As for the book as spiritual exercise, the discussion turns to matters of genre and literary function, disclosing its purpose to fortify religious beliefs and one's self-mastery.

In 'Wisdom at Qumran', David Skelton (Chapter 16) takes stock of the Dead Sea Scrolls and shows that they, in some ways, differ from the wisdom literature of the OT/HB. The Scrolls lack those references to Solomon that seem so characteristic to biblical wisdom; and whilst they exhibit Wisdom as a personification, she is 'toned down' and appears more passive than she does in, say, Proverbs 1–9. Amplified in tone are the Torah-wisdom connection and apocalyptic nature of the Qumran materials, not least the well-known *raz nihyeh* ('the mystery of existence' or 'mystery that is to be'). Skelton also discusses the importance of poverty and hymnody in the Scrolls, to conclude by drawing these many distinctives together, as well as the Hellenistic context, pedagogy and scribal practices, in order to reconsider the notion of 'wisdom literature' and the scholarly consensus surrounding it.

Moving into the wider world of the ancient Near East, Michael Fox and Suzanna R. Millar (Chapter 17) examine Egyptian wisdom literature. They begin with an overview of extant examples from the Old Kingdom to the Late Period and then turn to some major themes and issues. They consider Ma'at (the regulating force of truth/justice), character development (particularly as expressed through polar character types), pedagogy (including the debate about who is capable of learning) and transmission (through the generations in oral and written forms). The second half of the chapter assesses some commonly proposed examples of Egyptian influence on biblical wisdom literature, namely, the influence of the Instruction of Amenemope on Prov 22:17–23:11 and elsewhere in Proverbs, Egyptian parallels to Proverbs 8, Egyptian parallels to Prov 23:12–24:22, an alleged precursor to Job 38–39 in Egyptian onomastica, and connections between Ben Sira and the Demotic Instruction *Phibis*.

Noga Ayali-Darshan (Chapter 18) covers the wisdom works and vernacular sayings of Syria-Palestine from the Late Bronze Age. This material exists in some form of Akkadian, including Sumero-Akkadian and Akkadian-Hurrian, all of which comes from sites at Ugarit and/or Emar. Darshan organises the works into four types: practical wisdom, disputation poems and fables, critical wisdom and righteous sufferer compositions. Much of her chapter introduces readers to the texts themselves, by way of their provenance, language and versions. Additionally, some thematic and particular linguistic reflections are given. In short, this chapter provides an introduction to an emerging, and perhaps neglected, area of wisdom from the biblical world.

Paul-Alain Beaulieu (Chapter 19) examines Mesopotamian Wisdom. While acknowledging that there is no native category of 'wisdom literature' in Mesopotamia, Beaulieu nonetheless finds it a helpful classification. Within this category are texts of several genres: we find disputations which begin with a mythological introduction, progress to a verbal contest between non-human combatants and conclude with the victor pronounced by a god. There are proverbs, found in collections and quoted in letters, as well as fables, often about animals. Instructions and admonitions transmit antediluvian wisdom to postdiluvian generations. Some texts reflect on the problem of theodicy, ruminating on the human-divine relationship and individual divine retribution, while others lament the futility of life and advocate a *carpe diem* attitude. School debates centralise learning and the scribal arts. These texts are linked by intertextual references and shared features, such as their frequent ascription to individual wise figures, assumption of the absolute and inscrutable power of the gods and reflection on the human predicament.

In Part IV, the chapters consider certain important themes and issues in wisdom literature. First, Zoltán Schwáb (Chapter 20) discusses creation in the wisdom literature. He begins with a historical overview, describing how such creation texts became guides for meditation in antiquity, encouragements for science in early modernity and mirrors for liberal ethics in (post)modernity. Scholars have characterised wisdom literature as emphasising 'creation theology' and 'world order', but Schwáb suggests this is misleading. Rather, these texts exhibit 'creator theology' concerned with the God behind the world. Their theology holds in tension the twin themes of power and beauty. As a case study of this, Schwáb turns to Ecclesiastes. Creation is often seen as unimportant in this book, but Schwáb argues the opposite. For example, wind (*hebel, rûaḥ*) infuses the argument throughout. In Ecclesiastes, God creates everything, not just in a single primordial act but in ongoing creative activity – not just in the realm of nature but in the realms of history and culture. Ecclesiastes, then, points us towards the deep things of God's creation, but it concludes that we cannot ultimately comprehend them.

The contribution by Peter T. H. Hatton (Chapter 21) is dedicated entirely to conceptions of reward and retribution in the wisdom literature. He considers how well-placed, and sometimes misplaced, the paradigm can be, namely, that wickedness brings retribution and righteousness brings reward. Such doctrines, he says, remain 'key claims of a dominant interpretive tradition' and have consequently formed a 'pejorative paradigm' that leaves the book of Proverbs out of favour in comparison to more nuanced books of the OT/HB. The seminal work of 1955 by Klaus Koch – 'Gibt es ein Vergeltungsdogma im Alten Testament?' (Is there a Dogma of Retribution in the Old Testament?) – receives special attention, as do subsequent, critical responses to it. Hatton suggests that the moral mechanism of act-consequence is just not that predictable and that in Proverbs, Job and Ecclesiastes the paradigm is principally relational, for 'reward' and 'retribution' are not mechanical but are rather conditioned by one's relationship with the Lord.

William P. Brown (Chapter 22) explores the pedagogy of the wisdom literature. He argues that wisdom is dynamic as it is imparted between individuals and that it finds its *telos* in human character development. This dynamic pedagogy is versatile. Sometimes (especially in Proverbs 1–9) it manifests itself in rebuke, pronounced hierarchically in the matrix of patriarchal authority. Rebuke, though, can also be dialogic; in Proverbs, the wise also impart it amongst themselves. Both models of rebuke are evident in Job, where Job and his friends reciprocally rebuke each other, and God hierarchically rebukes Job. God's rebuke, though, is not simply belittling, rather eliciting wonder through the pedagogy of the Master Poet. These texts also teach through testimony – Qohelet in the book of Ecclesiastes invokes his personal observations and investigations, and Wisdom herself testifies to her role in creation (Proverbs 8). Here, Wisdom comes alongside readers as a playing child, and welcomes them as a gracious host. Finally, proverbs have pedagogical power, revelling in comparison, paradox, irony and metaphor.

Arthur Jan Keefer (Chapter 23) concludes the volume by discussing the relationship of wisdom literature and virtue ethics. Posing questions of both method and substance, the chapter proposes how interpreters might make use of virtue theories for reading biblical wisdom literature. Of foremost importance are precise definitions for concepts of 'virtue', a selection of particular texts that set out an understanding of virtue and an appreciation of traditional methods of biblical interpretation, all of which guards against vague conclusions and artificial comparison. Within the last decade, several scholars have pioneered the study of virtue ethics and wisdom literature, most notably through Proverbs and Job. Keefer presents this work and then suggests some inroads for similar studies of Ecclesiastes and Ben Sira, which have received less attention with respect to virtue. Lastly, he considers how the possibilities of virtue within each of these books link up with notions of 'the good' and provides a teleological orientation for ethics.

2 The Scope of Wisdom Literature

TREMPER LONGMAN III

What is the scope of wisdom literature in the Bible? Is there a category of biblical literature that we might designate 'wisdom literature', and if so, what books or texts might be included in that group? How far does the label 'wisdom' extend in the Bible? At the present moment, scholarly answers to these questions are diverse. While in recent decades most scholars would recognise a core group of three books within the Old Testament/Hebrew Bible (OT/HB) – Proverbs, Job and Ecclesiastes – and two deuterocanonical books – Wisdom of Solomon and Ben Sira – other scholars dispute this designation and challenge the idea that 'wisdom literature' is anything more than a scholarly construct first created in the mid-nineteenth century.

Among those who believe that there is a core group, a further debate is whether the designation might include other books or passages within other books of the OT/HB beyond the core group. Scholars have contended, for example, that various psalms be designated 'wisdom psalms'. Others would also include the Song of Songs. Some portions of historical books have also been nominated for membership, most notably the account of the Fall (Genesis 3), the Joseph narrative (Genesis 37–50), the Succession Narrative (2 Samuel 9–20; 1 Kings 1–2), the book of Esther and the stories found in Daniel 1–6. Still others would include various prophets or parts of prophetic books. In addition, there is a vibrant discussion of the relationship between law and wisdom, particularly centring on a passage like Deut 4:4–8, which clearly intertwines law with the concept of wisdom. With the growing awareness of the role of scribes in the final production of biblical books,[1] there is also the possibility of the sapientialisation of entire books. But

---

[1] See David M. Carr, *Writing on the Tablet of the Heart: Origins of Scripture and Literature* (Oxford, 2005).

at this point the question can be and has been raised, 'if Wisdom can mean anything and everything, then it means nothing'.[2]

However, paradoxically, some of these same scholars have seen wisdom literature as not only permeating the OT/HB but also as a distinct group with its own worldview. Indeed, these scholars argue that wisdom literature produces a theology which is distant from, even 'alien' to or a 'foreign corpus' among,[3] the other traditions found in the OT/HB. These researchers have noted an absence of reference in these core books to redemptive history, like the patriarchs or the exodus, or to the covenant. In addition, they argue, those who produced the wisdom literature did not get their message directly from God (via revelation) but rather through tradition, observation and experience. And furthermore, they are struck by the similarity and openness of the sages, whom they believe produced Proverbs in particular, to the thinking of Egyptian, Mesopotamian and Aramaic wisdom teachers.

To illustrate these different schools of thought, we will focus on representative thinkers of the past half century. We will move from more traditional scholars, those who argue that there is a distinct category that can be designated wisdom, to those who question and even apparently reject the idea that there is such a genre. We will then offer a way forward that recognises a genre of wisdom literature as a viable, but not exclusive, categorisation.

TRADITIONAL VIEW OF WISDOM

The Genre of Wisdom

What we are calling the 'traditional view' of wisdom literature was the dominant view held by scholars working in the area of wisdom from at least the end of World War II up to the turn of the millennium. Some specialists still hold this view, at least in general, and many who are not engaged in research or on the cutting edge of studies in this area still hold some form of this view as a default position.[4] Of course, even

---

[2] Will Kynes makes a forceful case in *An Obituary for 'Wisdom Literature': The Birth, Death, and Intertextual Reintegration of a Biblical Corpus* (Oxford, 2019). See later discussion; quotation is found on p. 39.

[3] Harmut Gese, *Lehre und Wirklichkeit in der alten Weisheit* (Tübingen, 1958). His term is '*Fremdkörper*'.

[4] As can be seen by continued course listings at colleges and seminaries on wisdom literature and the textbooks that support them. The latter includes Daniel J. Estes, *Handbook on the Wisdom Books and Psalms* (Grand Rapids, 2010); Ernest C. Lucas, *Exploring the Old Testament: A Guide to the Psalms and Wisdom Literature*

among the scholars cited here, there was not complete unanimity on all issues, but what I hope to provide is an accurate representation of the thought of the majority of scholars who represent this general perspective on the question of the extent of wisdom literature. In the process, we will also discover that the answer to the scope of wisdom literature also feeds a particular understanding of the nature of wisdom literature, both of which have come under critique in recent years as we will see below.

The first and most fundamental feature of the traditional view of wisdom is that there is a distinct genre of wisdom texts whose core is formed by three books considered canonical by all Christian traditions, namely, Proverbs, Job and Ecclesiastes. Two other books, Ben Sira and Wisdom of Solomon, are of disputed canonical status but are also uniformly considered to be part of the wisdom literature corpus.[5] Our discussion will mainly focus on the three core and widely accepted canonical books.

To say that Proverbs, Job and Ecclesiastes are wisdom literature is, at least in the first place, to make a genre identification. Genres are literary categories and individual texts are thought to be members of a genre based on similarities in content, form, style, purpose or intention. The traditional school of thought works within the parameters of genre theory associated with form criticism as developed at the beginning of the twentieth century.

The work of Hermann Gunkel, commonly considered the founder of form criticism, is foundational to an understanding and application of genre (German *Gattung*) in the field throughout much of the twentieth century. Gunkel himself commendably reached outside his field to develop his understanding of genre by learning from the theory of folklorist scholars, particularly the Grimm brothers.[6]

Gunkel believed that genres had pure forms and those texts that had features from other genres he referred to as *Mischwesen* with the presumption that somehow those texts originally were more consistent

---

(Downers Grove, 2014); Craig G. Bartholomew and Ryan P. O'Dowd, *Old Testament Wisdom Literature: A Theological Introduction* (Downers Grove, 2018); Stuart Weeks, *An Introduction to the Study of Wisdom Literature* (London, 2010).

[5] In other words, the ecclesial traditions, while disagreeing about the canonical status of Sirach and Wisdom of Solomon, all agree that Proverbs, Job and Ecclesiastes are canonical.

[6] As noted by Gene M. Tucker, *Form Criticism of the Old Testament*, GBS (Philadelphia, 1971), 4–5; and Martin J. Buss, 'The Study of Forms', in *Old Testament Form Criticism*, ed. John H. Hayes, TUMSR 2 (San Antonio, 1967), 50.

with their genre and at a later point were merged with another text or adapted with accretions that were detectable against the background of the supposed pure form. Gunkel and his followers believed that texts grew over time from their oral origins to their present literary form, so that in a study of a text one can go from the form in which we have it in the canon and then trace it back to its original form. In other words, Gunkel had a diachronic understanding of genre and a Romantic sense that the original was better or more authentic than the later form.

Another feature of Gunkel's understanding of genre that is influential upon the traditional understanding of wisdom has to do with a text's social location, what he called its Sitz im Leben. Genres have one and only one social location, so he argued. We can see, for instance, a vibrant debate among Gunkel's followers over the Sitz im Leben of the Psalms. Mowinckel posited that psalms emerged in the context of, and were used in, an annual New Year's festival, while Weiser suggested an annual covenant festival and Kraus an annual Zion festival. In the following discussion, we will see that traditional interpreters will argue that wisdom literature has a Sitz im Leben that differs from other biblical literature with a concomitant belief that the genre emerges from a distinct worldview.

Gunkel, in essence, adopted a neoclassical genre theory, which G. N. G. Orsini describes as 'a nineteenth-century phenomenon that held a rigid view of genres as pure and hierarchical'.[7] His approach to genre may be described as taxonomic in that each text ought to be assigned to a specific genre that could be associated with a particular social location.

Such an approach to genre can easily become prescriptive rather than descriptive. The latter simply observes similarities between texts of different types (content, themes, structure, vocabulary, etc.), while the former has a list of essential characteristics that a text must display in order to be a member of a genre. This view of genre is rigid too because it asserts that there is only one right genre for each text, a mistaken view that we will address below with examples.

We now turn our attention to the traditional school's assertion that there is a genre of wisdom literature; we are initially struck by how wisdom's distinctiveness seems defined by contrast or absence of features found in other parts of Scripture. In the first place, Proverbs, Job and Ecclesiastes do not feature the great historical-redemptive moments of biblical history. There are no references to the patriarchs or the exodus, or to the conquest, continuing down through the history of Israel. In connection with this, these

---

[7] G. N. G. Orsini, "Genres," in The Princeton Encyclopedia of Poetry and Poetics (Princeton: Princeton University Press, 1974), 104.

scholars will also argue that there is no real connection to the covenant, featured throughout the redemptive history or to the law.

A second feature that these scholars cite as distinguishing wisdom literature from the rest of the canon is a lack of appeal to revelation. Whereas the law was revealed to Moses on Mount Sinai (Exodus 19–24), and the prophets both cite their divine commissioning (Isaiah 6; Jer 1:6–10; Ezekiel 1–3) and frequently remind their hearers/readers that their message comes directly from God ('thus says the Lord'; 'decree of the Lord'), the sages who produced the wisdom books relied on human experience and observation (Prov 6:6–8; 7:6–13), tradition handed down from previous generations (Prov 4:1–4a) and learning from their mistakes (Prov 10:17; 12:1).[8] In the words of Douglas Miller who is characterising and critiquing this traditional view, the sages represent 'an epistemology rooted in human experience'.[9]

Not only, according to this traditional view, is wisdom literature distinct from the redemptive-historical, covenantal, legal and prophetic traditions, it is also distinct from the priestly realm. There is, in other words, no sustained interest in sacrifice, prayer, the temple, worship, issues of ritual purity and the like.

Indeed, this view often comes with the claim that wisdom literature downplays or even forfeits a distinctive Israelite understanding of God himself, leading some to the verge of characterising Israelite wisdom as secular or at least as holding a rather commonly held view of God. As Otto Eissfeldt put it, 'The basis for the commendation of wisdom and piety is purely secular and rational'.[10] Claus Westermann similarly stated: 'The proverbs as such have a universal character. Proverbs can surface anywhere among humankind ... [Proverbs mentioning God] have no specifically theological foundation in an explicitly theological context. Rather, they speak of God in such a manner as would any person without stepping outside of everyday secular discourse.'[11]

---

[8] For more references and discussion, see Tremper Longman III, *The Fear of the Lord Is Wisdom: A Theological Introduction to Wisdom in Israel* (Grand Rapids, 2017), 111–119.

[9] Douglas B. Miller, 'Wisdom in the Canon: Discerning the Early Intuition', in *Was There a Wisdom Tradition?: New Prospects in Israelite Wisdom Studies*, ed. Mark R. Sneed (Atlanta, 2015), 96.

[10] Otto Eissfeldt, *The Old Testament: An Introduction* (New York, 1965), 47.

[11] Claus Westermann, *Roots of Wisdom* (Edinburgh, 1995), 130. See also Walter Brueggemann, *In Man We Trust: The Neglected Side of Biblical Faith* (Atlanta, 1972), 81–83. The idea that wisdom is fundamentally secular has been effectively critiqued by Lennart Boström, *God of the Sages: The Portrayal of God in the Book of Proverbs* (ConBOT 29, Stockholm, 1990), 36–39; and Zoltán S. Schwáb, *Toward an*

This viewpoint is often supported by the common and widely accepted observation that the type of wisdom found in Proverbs, say, is similar to and often thought to be influenced by broader ancient Near Eastern wisdom.[12] This discussion goes back to at least 1924, when similarities were discovered between the Instruction of Amenemope and Proverbs, particularly in 'the words of the wise' found in Prov 22:17–24:22. Indeed, the fact that Solomon's wisdom was considered 'greater than the wisdom of all the people of the East, and greater than all the wisdom of Egypt' (1 Kgs 4:30) shows that non-Israelite wisdom had significant value.

All of these observations lead to the conclusion that the wisdom literature of the Bible is not only distinct from other traditions within the Bible but also a kind of foreign or alien presence (*Fremdkörper*) in that it is cosmopolitan, universal, ecumenical, secular and non-particular. In short, in the words of William Brown: 'Ancient Israel's sages had no qualms incorporating the wisdom of other cultures. Biblical wisdom seeks the common good along with the common God. Wisdom's international, indeed universal appeal constitutes its canonical uniqueness. The Bible's wisdom corpus is the open door to an otherwise closed canon.'[13] But, in this traditional school of thought, wisdom literature was not only defined by what it isn't but also by what it is. What it is, though, also contrasts with other traditions in the OT/ HB. As opposed to other traditions that were situated in one way or another in redemptive history, Wisdom was thought to be embedded in the theology of creation. As Zimmerli famously stated: 'Wisdom thinks resolutely within the framework of a theology of creation'.[14] God created the world with wisdom (Prov 3:19–20), meaning in an ordered way. We might see this expressed in Qohelet's assertion that God 'has made everything suitable for its time' (Eccl 3:11), leading to his reflection that there is 'a time for everything, and a season for every activity

Interpretation of the Book of Proverbs: Selfishness and Secularity Reconsidered, JTISup 7 (Winona Lake, 2013).

[12] This observation goes back at least to Adolf Erman, 'Eines agyptische Quelle der "Spruche Salomos"', in SPAW 1924), 86–93.

[13] William P. Brown, *Wisdom's Wonder: Character, Creation, and Crisis in the Bible's Wisdom Literature* (Grand Rapids, 2014), 3. See also Paul S. Fiddes, *Seeing the World and Knowing God: Hebrew Wisdom and Christian Doctrine in a Late-Modern Context* (Oxford, 2013) and the summary statement by Leo G. Perdue, *Wisdom Literature: A Theological History* (Louisville, 2007), 344.

[14] Walter Zimmerli, 'The Place and Limit of Wisdom in the Framework of the Old Testament Theology', *SJT* 17 (1964): 148.

under heaven' (Eccl 3:1). The purpose of wisdom is to put one in touch
with God's creation in order to live in a way that maximises a successful
life. Thus, the sages study the creation to see how it works, a way of
knowing that would be accessible to all, including foreign sages.

We earlier commented on the characterisation of wisdom by the
traditional view as secular, in terms of its lack of appeal to revelation or
as having a specific theological foundation. The traditional view of
wisdom also differentiates wisdom from other biblical traditions by
being secular in its focus of interest. Von Rad commented that 'since
the objects of this search for knowledge were of a secular kind, questions about man's daily life, systematic reflection on them was held to
be a secular occupation'.[15] The early Walter Brueggemann similarly
opines: 'I believe it is much more plausible to suggest that in the
wisdom tradition of Israel we have a visible expression of secularization
as it has been characterized in the current discussions. Wisdom teaching
is profoundly secular in that it presents life and history as a human
enterprise.'[16] Reading through Proverbs in particular can give the
impression indeed that what the sages were interested in were practical
matters like wise speech, human relationships, planning, interacting
with authorities and more.

This secular, or at least diminished, theological understanding of
wisdom in the traditional school was also furthered by K. Koch's study
of retribution in wisdom, which he characterised as an act-consequence
connection (*Tun-Ergehen-Zusammenhang*).[17] He argued that, in
wisdom, bad deeds led to their own negative consequences, while good
deeds led to positive results without God's intervention.

The Extent of Wisdom Literature

The traditional view thus asserts that Proverbs, Job and Ecclesiastes
form the core of wisdom literature in the OT/HB and that they present a
distinct genre over against the other genres of biblical literature.
However, with these three books as a base, the category of wisdom grew
over time to include other biblical books or portions thereof. Of
course there is something of a paradox in scholarly thinking here. On
the one hand, wisdom literature is distinct from other genres of the

---

[15] G. von Rad, *Wisdom in Israel* (London, 1972), 57–58.
[16] Brueggemann, *In Man We Trust*, 81–82.
[17] In his influential Klaus Koch, *Um das Prinzip der Vergeltung in Religion und Recht
des alten Testaments* (Darmstad, 1972).

Bible; on the other hand, scholars detected wisdom throughout the rest of the OT/HB.

We should again note that, among scholars representing this traditional view, there is no unanimity about what should be included, and arguments were made over time for the inclusion of a number of other texts from other portions of the canon. We here highlight just a few of the most well-known examples.

Among books containing historical narrative, the Joseph narrative (Genesis 37–50) and Daniel (chs. 1–6) have been identified as wisdom. Both men are presented in their respective narratives as exhibiting the characteristics of wisdom as expressed particularly in the book of Proverbs. Von Rad made the case for Joseph by pointing to examples such as Joseph's rejection of the sexual advances of Potiphar's wife (Genesis 39) in keeping with the warnings of the father to his son in Proverbs 5–7.[18] The story itself explicitly identifies Joseph as a wise person, who is able to navigate the predicaments in which he finds himself and also can guide Pharaoh in his preparations for a severe famine (Gen 41:39–40).[19] Since Daniel has many similarities as a character with Joseph, we are not surprised that Daniel is sometimes thought to be a sage and that the stories in the first part of the book are thought to be wisdom. After all, both are Hebrews who find themselves in a pagan court and both exhibit the behaviour and attitudes of proverbial wisdom. In the case of Daniel, he shows wisdom as he interacts with the king and the court in keeping with Prov 16:14; 22:11 and 25:15. In Daniel 1, as Daniel seeks to avoid eating the food and drink provided by King Nebuchadnezzar, he exhibits patience and calm as advised in Prov 14:17; 14:29; 16:32 and 17:27. And again, the biblical text explicitly describes him as a person with wisdom (see Dan 2:14).

We might also cite other studies that have sought to expand the wisdom label to a number of other historical texts. These include

---

[18] See his full argument in Gerhard von Rad, 'The Joseph Narrative and Ancient Wisdom', in *The Problem of the Hexateuch and Other Essays* (New York, 1966), 292–300.

[19] That traditional scholars do not agree on the particulars of the expansion of the wisdom category may be illustrated by James L. Crenshaw's ('Method in Determining Wisdom Influence', *JBL* 88 [1969]: 129–142) stinging critique of von Rad. See also Donald B. Redford, *Study of the Biblical Story of Joseph (Genesis 37–50)*, VTSup 20 (Leiden, 1970), 100–105.

Genesis 3, the Succession Narrative[20] and Esther.[21] These connections are drawn on the basis of a similar vocabulary as that found in Proverbs, similar concepts or, as with the Joseph and Daniel narratives, the depiction of behaviours and attitudes that conform to the values of Proverbs.

In terms of law, a passage like that found in Deuteronomy asserts that the law is a public expression of wisdom:

> just as the Lord my God has charged me, I now teach you statutes and ordinances for you to observe in the land you are about to enter and occupy. You must observe them diligently, for this will show your wisdom and discernment to the peoples, who when they hear all these statutes will say. 'Surely this great nation is a wise and discerning people!' (4:5–6)[22]

Going back to at least Gunkel and Begrich,[23] many specialists in the book of Psalms have categorised some psalms as wisdom. Indeed, while there are disagreements as to the exact number and identity of wisdom psalms in the collection, Psalms 1, 19 (second half), 37, 49, 73, 112 and 119 provide a consistent core. These psalms share language and themes with Proverbs, Job or Ecclesiastes. For instance, the composer of Psalm 73 struggles with the issue of the suffering of the righteous and the prosperity of the wicked in a spirit similar to Job. Psalm 1 uses the language and the concepts (the way of the righteous and the wicked) that we find in Proverbs. Since Psalm 1 is the opening psalm of the book, and surely occupies that introductory place by intention, some scholars, such as Jacobsen, believe that it turns the book as a whole into a book of instruction. As she puts it, 'the Psalter is also a book of instruction. Psalms are not only prayed and sung; they are also to be read and studied'.[24]

[20] R. Norman Whybray, *The Succession Narrative: A Study of II Samuel 9–20; I Kings I and 2*, SBT 2/9 (London, 1969).

[21] Shemaryahu Talmon, 'Wisdom in the Book of Esther', *VT* 13 (1963): 419–455.

[22] Thomas Krüger ('Law and Wisdom according to Deut 4:5–8', in *Wisdom and Torah: The Reception of the 'Torah' in the Wisdom Literature of the Second Temple Period*, ed. Berndt U. Schipper and D. Andrew Teeter, SJSJ [Leiden, 2013], 35) comments: 'Only here are Wisdom and Torah related to each other in the Pentateuch'.

[23] Hermann Gunkel and Joachim Begrich, *Introduction to Cultic Poetry: The Genres of Religious Lyric of Israel* (1933; repr., Macon, 1998), 293–305.

[24] Diane Jacobson, 'Wisdom Language in the Psalms', in *The Oxford Handbook of the Psalms* (Oxford, 2014), 155.

Other scholars identify the Song of Songs as wisdom literature.[25] The primary connection here has to do with wisdom's practical and ethical nature.[26] The Song's focus on intimate sexual relationships is sometimes related to the teaching of the father in Proverbs that the son find satisfaction in his relationship with 'the wife of your youth' and specifically the teaching found in Prov 5:15–23.

From these examples, we can see how the category of wisdom spread through the rest of the canon. As we will see, recent scholarship argues that there is a fundamental conflict in thinking that wisdom is distinct from the rest of the canon while suggesting that wisdom permeates the different parts of the canon.

The Social Location and Worldview of Wisdom Literature

What we are calling the traditional view often goes beyond putting forward a clear core of books that constitute wisdom literature by expanding the category to many other portions of the OT/HB. Even further, it often posits that these books were produced by a distinct group within Israelite society: the sages, who lived in a world distinct and sometimes in contrast to the world inhabited by the prophets and priests. To those holding such a perspective, Jer 18:18 might operate as a kind of prooftext: 'Come, let us make plots against Jeremiah – for instruction will not perish from the priest, nor counsel from the wise, nor the word from the prophet'.

In the form critical tradition originating in the thought of Gunkel, genres were thought to have a single and distinct sociological setting (Sitz im Leben; see more below). In the case of wisdom literature, that setting was thought to be in the social world of the sage. Often accompanying this perspective was the belief that schools of some sort existed for training sages for their profession and had a distinct worldview that,

---

[25] Examples include Brevard S. Childs, *Introduction to the Old Testament as Scripture* (Philadelphia, 1979), 573–575; Francis Landy, *Paradoxes of Paradise: Identity and Difference in the Song of Songs* (Sheffield, 1983), 33; Michael Sadgrove, 'Song of Songs as Wisdom Literature', in *Papers on the Old Testament and Related Themes*, vol. 1 of *Studia Biblica 1978: Sixth International Congress on Biblical Studies, Oxford, 3–7 April 1978*, ed. E. A. Livingstone, JSOTSup 11 (Sheffield, 1979), 245–248; Nicolas Tromp, 'Wisdom and the Canticle: Ct. 6c–7b', in *La Sagesse de l'Ancien Testament*, ed. Maurice Gilbert (Louvain, 1980).

[26] Though Childs (*Introduction to the Old Testament*) also points to the superscription that associates the book with Solomon (1:1), the paradigmatic sage. In the early modern period, one strand of allegorical reading of the Song, represented by Don Isaac Abravanel in the sixteenth century, takes the woman in the Song as Wisdom, comparable to Woman Wisdom in Proverbs.

as we have already discussed, was rooted in creation theology and was more universal, cosmopolitan, ecumenical and practical than the world-view of other sectors of society that produced biblical literature.

THE CONTEMPORARY REACTION AGAINST THE TRADITIONAL VIEW

The Genre of Wisdom

In the past decade or so, some scholars have mounted a significant challenge to the traditional view of the scope and nature of wisdom literature described above. In the first place, they question whether there is a distinct genre of wisdom literature at all, which, of course, leads to a question concerning the existence of a distinct wisdom trad-ition, worldview or social group. Among those advocating this chal-lenge, we take particular note of the work of Mark Sneed and Will Kynes. These two and others that follow their line of argument do not agree on all the particulars but hold a general consensus that the trad-itional view misrepresents the nature of Proverbs, Job and Ecclesiastes by insisting that they be read as a distinct genre produced by a distinct group within Israel who share a distinct worldview.[27] Our focus will be on the work of Kynes, as the most recent and in some ways the most radical, though other scholars will be included in the discussion.

Kynes announces the death of wisdom[28] as a literary category and makes the claim that the birth of wisdom literature was a scholarly construct of the mid-eighteenth century. He locates the origins of the category with Johann Friedrich Bruch who published *Weisheits-Lehre der Hebräer* in 1851. Kynes finds it significant that wisdom literature's birth was a relatively modern invention that he believes appealed to modern scholars since they thought that this corner of the canon, when judged apart from the other biblical books, was resonant with their own more humanistic bent of thought.

He and other scholars question the utility of separating Proverbs, Job and Ecclesiastes from other books and then differentiating them

---

[27] Mark R. Sneed ('Grasping after the Wind: The Elusive Attempt to Define and Delimit Wisdom', in Sneed, *Was There a Wisdom Tradition?*, 40) points out that the traditional view 'assume[s] falsely that genre can encapsulate a worldview', and he helpfully reminds us that 'the reality is that all the Israelites held the same worldview' (p. 41). In the same volume, Michael V. Fox ('Three Theses on Wisdom', 74) agrees that 'there is no reason to suppose that the authors of Israelite wisdom belonged to a certain school and subscribed to a distinctive ideology'.

[28] As is clearly announced by the title of his book, *An Obituary for 'Wisdom Literature'*.

from other traditions within the Bible. In the first place, all three books resist the prescriptive and rigid conception of genre advanced by Gunkel and employed by the traditional school that leads to the view that wisdom literature is a distinct category in itself.

According to Kynes and other more recent researchers, genres are not pure forms that may be recognised by a list of required shared characteristics. On the contrary, genre categories are fluid and not distinct, having fuzzy boundaries, not distinct lines of demarcation.[29] Texts within genres are never exactly alike, not even necessarily sharing what are considered by some to be essential characteristics. Sneed, for instance, uses the language of family resemblance when he talks about genre.[30] Just as members of a family may bear similarities in their looks and mannerisms, so texts share similarities that draw readers' attention and leads them to read the texts in the light of each other.

Kynes employs a different analogy, though his views share a similar perspective to Sneed. He argues that genre connections are similar to constellations. Constellations are formed by stars that have a perceived pattern that cause the observer to look at them as a set, even though the stars involved may have differences that would cause them to be grouped with another set of stars if judged by other characteristics (say by size). Constellations form groups of stars and genres create groups of texts.

Constellations are dynamic in relationship to space and time. The stars move and die over time and thus obscure or eradicate the pattern. They also may be perceived differently from different locations. The perception of genres is also dynamic, according to Kynes, particularly as viewed over time or from different cultural perspectives. For this reason, researchers must recognise the potential distortion in understanding caused by imposing modern categories on ancient literature. Such a perspective on genre also highlights the need to recognise that a text participates in multiple genres.[31] We will see that this is one of Kynes'

---

[29] Tremper Longman III, 'Israelite Genres in Their Ancient Near Eastern Context', in *The Changing Face of Form Criticism in the Twenty-First Century*, ed. M. A. Sweeney and Ehud Ben Zvi (Grand Rapids, 2003), 183.

[30] Sneed, 'Grasping the Wind', 59. He cites Alistair Fowler, *Kinds of Literature: An Introduction to the Theory of Genres and Modes* (Cambridge, 1982). Katharine J. Dell ('Deciding the Boundaries of "Wisdom": Applying the Concept of Family Resemblance', in Sneed, *Was There a Wisdom Tradition?*, 155–156) also works with the metaphor of family resemblance.

[31] Kynes, *An Obituary for 'Wisdom Literature'*, 141–143.

fundamental insights[32] and shows that his genre theory differs radically from that inspired by Gunkel, where texts have one genre which themselves have one Sitz im Leben.

Kynes is quick to point out that this view of genre does not lead to relativism. After all, he says that 'any genre grouping is constrained by the actual features of the text'.[33] In other words, to suggest that a text participates in a genre of other texts with which it shares no features is wrong. To include texts in a genre requires that the interpreter point to actual similarities between the texts. But again, and this is key to Kynes and others like him, it is a mistake that leads to a distorted understanding of a text to suggest that any text belongs to one and only one genre. As he succinctly puts it, 'arguing that *Pilgrim's Progress* is not an allegory is a misinterpretation, but so is arguing that an allegory is all that it is'.[34]

Kynes' genre theory emerges from his recognition of the vast intertextual relationship between texts. He understands that texts are not able to be understood in strict isolation but need to be read in relationship to each other. He sees genre as an 'intertextual shorthand' that highlights certain significant similarities between texts that lead to a richer reading of the text as long as genres, which he calls 'irrigation ditches',[35] don't become a dam (by suggesting that there is only one genre).

When it comes to wisdom, we need to recognise that, say, the book of Job, may also participate, as Katharine Dell argues,[36] in the category of lament. Kynes goes further, saying that 'as a particularly bright star in the canonical universe, it shines in numerous constellations'.[37] He then goes on to speak about Job's participation 'before "Wisdom Literature"', presumably meaning a broader genre category (sharing fewer traits but with more participants) with the *Sifrei Emet*, poetry, history, Torah, prophecy, drama and epic. Then he goes to speak of Job's relationship to other texts in its ancient Near Eastern context, such as exemplary-sufferer

---

[32] Kynes, *An Obituary for 'Wisdom Literature'*, 140. 'Rejecting the notion of a single correct genre for texts – a single pattern in which they should be read that has emerged from a solitary vantage point – and instead embracing the multidimensional subjectivity of interpretation might actually enable interpreters to produce a *more objective interpretation* by triangulating the text's meaning among a broader array of subjective vantage points.'

[33] Kynes, *An Obituary for 'Wisdom Literature'*, 139.

[34] Kynes, *An Obituary for 'Wisdom Literature'*, 140.

[35] Kynes, *An Obituary for 'Wisdom Literature'*, 110.

[36] Katharine J. Dell, *The Book of Job as Sceptical Literature*, BZAW 197 (Berlin, 1991).

[37] Kynes, *An Obituary for 'Wisdom Literature'*, 159.

Texts, controversy dialogue and didactic narrative. He then concludes by exploring what he calls 'adapted genres', genres of the whole and of parts that he suggests have been 'consistently remolded and repurposed',[38] including lament, lawsuit, metaprophecy and apocalyptic. Finally, he considers 'meta-genres', which are proposals that 'associate the book with other texts that use this same technique' so 'they could also be considered proposals for its genre'.[39] Here he includes parody, citation and polyphony.

Importantly, Kynes does not deny that 'wisdom is certainly an important concept in the debate between Job and his friends, and the book as a whole engages many of the issue central to Proverbs and Ecclesiastes'.[40] We will come back to this point later, since it seems to allow for ongoing discussion of a genre of wisdom literature; but for now, Kynes makes the very significant point, over against traditional interpreters, that it is distorting to the discernment of the meaning of the book of Job to restrict our perspective to one and only one genre. He makes the same case with Proverbs and Ecclesiastes.

The Extent of Wisdom

In our description of the traditional approach to wisdom literature, we detected a tendency to significantly expand the category beyond the core of Proverbs, Job and Ecclesiastes. Various stories in the historical accounts, law, some psalms, Song of Songs and some prophets have been brought into the purview of wisdom.

Kynes complains that if all texts are wisdom, then none are wisdom.[41] He likens this category expansion to the expansion that occurred with the idea of Deuteronomic theology. The first move was to speak of a Deuteronomic or Deuteronomistic history that extends from Joshua through 2 Kings. Then various prophets, most notably perhaps Jeremiah, were read as reflecting Deuteronomic theology. As the category expands, it weakens its distinctive nature. When it comes to wisdom, it diminishes the argument that wisdom is a *Fremdkörper* as well. But the real problem Kynes has with this expansive move is that it sucks everything into the wisdom category. He complains about 'the progression from scholarly consensus to vague definition to

---

[38] Kynes, *An Obituary for 'Wisdom Literature'*, 169.
[39] Kynes, *An Obituary for 'Wisdom Literature'*, 173.
[40] Kynes, *An Obituary for 'Wisdom Literature'*, 177.
[41] See also J. McLaughlin, 'Wisdom Influence', in *The Oxford Handbook of Wisdom and the Bible*, ed. Will Kynes (New York, 2021) 409–422.

chain-reaction extension and consequent dilution of the genre's interpretive significance'.[42] For Kynes, the expansion of the wisdom category
in other parts of the OT/HB shows the vagueness of the definition of
wisdom and thus he advocates abandoning the practice of bringing
nearly everything under the rubric of wisdom.

The Social Location and Worldview of Wisdom

As we observed above, the traditional view argued that wisdom was
produced by a distinct group in Israel, the sages, who did not think like
prophets or priests. They had their own worldview that differentiated
them from these others. They eschewed revelation in favour of personal
experience and observation. They did not think in terms of the history
of redemption but rather did their reflection in the light of a theology of
creation. They focused on everyday life rather on God's acts in history.
In short, according to the traditional view, wisdom was the purview of
the sage whose worldview could be characterised as universal (or international, in that it shared ideas with the broader ancient Near East),
secular and humanistic. In short, wisdom was an alien or foreign presence in the OT/HB.

According to Kynes, Sneed and others, however, this is a distorted
picture of wisdom in the OT/HB, a stereotype that reflected the ecumenical thinking of the scholars who painted this picture of wisdom.
On the contrary, they insist, wisdom was not the result of the thinking
of a distinct group with its separate worldview and institutions in Israel.
Wisdom – far from being universal, secular and humanistic – was particular and deeply theological. Weeks, for instance, points out that 'at
the level of ideas, it is difficult to find anything in the wisdom literature
as a whole which is not found elsewhere as well'.[43]

Sneed argues effectively that the advocates of the traditional view
'assume falsely that genre can encapsulate a worldview',[44] and he helpfully reminds us that 'the reality is that all the Israelites held the same
worldview'.[45] Fox, though in some ways a more traditional thinker,
agrees that 'there is no reason to suppose that the authors of Israelite
wisdom belonged to a certain school and subscribed to a distinctive
ideology'.[46]

---

[42] Will Kynes, 'The Modern Scholarly Wisdom Tradition and the Threat of Pan-
Sapientialism: A Case Report', in Sneed, *Was There a Wisdom Tradition?*, 26.
[43] Stuart Weeks, *An Introduction to the Study of Wisdom Literature*, 142.
[44] Sneed, 'Grasping after the Wind', 40.
[45] Sneed, 'Grasping after the Wind', 41.
[46] Fox, 'Three Theses on Wisdom', 74.

THE WAY FORWARD

The Genre of Wisdom

As we noted above, a tremendous difference exists between the traditional view and its contemporary challenge in the area of genre theory. The former operates with an early nineteenth-century rigid, prescriptive, taxonomic understanding that is sometimes called a realistic approach to genre. In the last quarter of the twentieth century,[47] biblical scholars began to shift their view to what is commonly called a nominalistic approach.

While the former thought in terms of a text having one genre which itself had one sociological setting, the latter rightly thinks that a text can participate in more than one genre and may have more than one setting, which itself does not have to be sociological but literary or historical. While Kynes pronounces the death of the wisdom category based on more sophisticated nominalist genre theory, in reality it provides the grounds for continuing to call Proverbs, Job and Ecclesiastes 'wisdom literature'.

The following argument may be put forward to support the idea that Proverbs, Job and Ecclesiastes do indeed participate in a genre that we might call wisdom. To paraphrase Kynes' statement above about *Pilgrim's Progress*, I believe it is correct to say that arguing that Proverbs, Job and Ecclesiastes are not wisdom literature is a misinterpretation but so is arguing that wisdom literature is all that it is.

What I provide here is simply what might be called the lead argument for such a claim, not a full marshalling of all the similarities. Even so, we are of the opinion that these observations are sufficient to establish that, though not its exclusive genre, these three books may be called 'wisdom literature'. Indeed, we would say that the following observations are why scholars in the modern period[48] have studied these books together. The observation is that all three of these books are in one way or another about wisdom. If it is not a mature theme, it is certainly a significant one.

Proverbs, for instance, announces that wisdom is its main subject in the preamble (1:1–7), where it announces that its purpose is to teach wisdom to both those who are 'simple' and 'young', on the one hand, as

---

[47] See Tremper Longman III, *Fictional Akkadian Autobiography* (Winona Lake, 1991), 3–22. This approach is picked up by Kenton L. Sparks (*Ancient Texts for the Study of the Hebrew Bible: A Guide to the Background Literature* [Peabody, 2005], 5–21) and adopted by Sneed in 'Grasping after the Wind'.

[48] See below on etic (non-native) and emic (native) approaches to genre.

well as the 'wise' and 'discerning', on the other hand (1:4–5). In the
opening three verses of the preamble, we read:

The proverbs of Solomon, son of David, king of Israel:

For learning about wisdom and instruction,
    for understanding words of insight,
For gaining instruction in wise dealing,
    righteousness, justice, and equity.

(1:1–3)

While lots of questions surround the interpretation of Proverbs, the rest
of the book certainly lives up to the billing anticipated in this preamble.

The book of Ecclesiastes also relates to wisdom in that the two
speakers, Qohelet (1:12–12:7) and the frame narrator (1:1–11; 12:8–14),
both style themselves men of wisdom. Qohelet begins his autobiographical reflections by announcing his project to 'seek and search out by
wisdom all that is done under heaven' (1:13). He also claims 'I have
acquired great wisdom, surpassing all who were over Jerusalem before
me; and my mind has had great experience of wisdom and knowledge'
(1:16). Even the frame narrator, who I believe is critical of Qohelet's
conclusion that life is meaningless under the sun, tells his son that
Qohelet is 'wise' (12:9). While the frame narrator never self-identifies
as wise, he seems to represent himself as such as he guides his son away
from an 'under-the-sun' perspective to an 'above-the sun' one (see below
on fear of God).

Kynes and Dell are certainly correct that Job should be studied
in association with books other than Proverbs and Ecclesiastes.
Nonetheless, we should continue to note Job's connection to wisdom.
When we do, we can see that Job is a type of debate, and more precisely,
a debate about wisdom. 'Who is wise?' and 'where is wisdom to be
found?' are two important questions addressed by Job. The book of Job
is a 'thought experiment'[49] where Job's suffering leads to a heated
interaction between Job and his three friends (Job 1–27). Wisdom can
provide a prescription for a problem and offer a remedy, and both Job and
his three friends assert their wisdom to address Job's situation. The
three friends say Job's suffering is a result of his sin; therefore, the
solution to his problem is repentance (see, for instance, Zophar's argument in Job 11). Job resists their interpretation because he knows he has

---

[49] John H. Walton and Tremper Longman III, *How to Read Job* (Downers Grove,
2015), 35.

not sinned. His view is that his suffering is the result of divine injustice and that the only remedy is to meet God and demand justice. Elihu comes in after the disputation between Job and his three friends, claiming a spiritual source for his wisdom (32:8–9), but then ultimately he ends up parroting the three friends' argument that Job is a sinner and needs to repent (34:5–37). Job 28 anticipates the conclusion of the book of Job. At the end, Job gets his wish to meet with God, but it does not go the way he expected it would. Rather than advancing his claim against God, God simply asserts his power and wisdom. Ultimately, Job submits to God and decides to live in God's presence without an explanation for his suffering. If Job is rightly understood to be a debate over who is wise and where wisdom can be found, the answer is none other than Yahweh.

These readings of Proverbs, Job and Ecclesiastes need to be defended in more detail.[50] Nevertheless, if we are on the right track, then we should agree that indeed there is a generic connection between these three books. We will simply highlight another feature that connects them. All three books intend to move their readers to fear God.

Proverbs, of course, communicates this intention by its so-called motto which concludes the preface with 'the fear of the Lord is the beginning of knowledge' (1:7), an observation that echoes throughout the book (1:29; 2:5; 3:7; 8:13; 10:27; 14:2, 26, 27). The book of Ecclesiastes concludes when the second wise man exhorts his son (see 12:10) to 'fear God, and keep his commandments; for that is the whole duty of everyone' (12:13). The book of Job begins with Job already fearing God (1:1), and, when he chooses to suffer in silence at the end of the book, his fear is more mature since it is based on a more intimate knowledge: 'I had heard of you by the hearing of the ear, but now my eye sees you' (42:5). Indeed, in Job 28, often seen as an anticipation of the ultimate conclusion of the book, we read that 'the fear of the Lord, the I wisdom; and to depart from evil is understanding' (Job 28:28).[51]

But what about Kynes' concern that the category of 'wisdom literature' is a mid-nineteenth century construct? Yes, there is a danger that a modern category might prevent us from reading these books in the way the original audience did but not necessarily so. Kynes himself is aware that simply to rule 'out a category because it is modern not ancient is

---

50 As I do in *Proverbs*, BCOTWP (Grand Rapids, 2006); *Job*, BCOTWP (Grand Rapids, 2012); and *Ecclesiastes*, NICOT (Grand Rapids, 1998) as well as *The Fear of the Lord Is Wisdom*.

51 See Longman, *The Fear of the Lord Is Wisdom*.

not a sufficient argument'. He realises that 'the implications of the origin of Wisdom Literature must be interpreted with care, since any conclusions drawn from it run the risk of the genetic fallacy that an idea's origins can be used either to confirm or contradict its truth'.[52]

In my own study over the years,[53] I have found the distinction between emic and etic approaches to language and literature to prove helpful.[54] The emic approach describes native designations and classification of literature. This approach has the advantage of giving the researcher insight into the native consciousness of a particular text and also into the relationship between that text and others bearing the same designation. The etic view of literature imposes a non-native grid or classification scheme, not necessarily defined in their language, and is the result of modern scholarly observation of similarities among texts. To be honest, since we do not have a poetics of ancient Hebrew literature, we can't be sure whether or not the ancients shared our views on the subject, but then again not even authors are necessarily fully conscious of the genre in which they write.

The Extent of Wisdom

As for the expansion of the wisdom category put forward by the traditional approach and challenged by Kynes, we might suggest that both are overreactions. If one argues, for example, that the Joseph Narrative as a whole is wisdom literature, then that is simply an overreaching conclusion. Still, one can't deny that there are wisdom elements in the text, especially in Joseph's characterisation as a wisdom figure.[55] On the other hand, Kynes goes too far when he says 'if Wisdom can mean anything and everything, then it means nothing'.[56] We might push back and say, no one, or at least very few people, argues that everything is

---

[52] Kynes, *An Obituary for 'Wisdom Literature'*, 98.

[53] Going back to Longman, *Fictional Akkadian Autobiography* in chapter 1, 'A Generic Approach to Akkadian Literature' (published in 1991 but finished in 1983).

[54] Kenneth Pike, *Language in Relation to a Unified Theory of Human Behavior* (The Hague, 1967), ch. 2; and Vern S. Poythress, 'Analysing a Biblical Text: Some Important Linguistic Distinctions', *SJT* 32 (1979): 113–137. The emic/etic distinction was first proposed in linguistics, where it was used to distinguish native understanding of language from the analysis of a language by linguists or other outsiders. Pike was the first to generalise the distinction into a principle that could be used in the study of any aspect of culture. Poythress further refined the concept. For the tendency of taking linguistic categories and applying them to other disciplines, see Jonathan Culler, *The Pursuit of Signs* (Ithaca, 1981), 27–39.

[55] See my response to Crenshaw's critique of von Rad in Longman, *The Fear of the Lord Is Wisdom*, 84–85.

[56] Kynes, 'The Modern Scholarly Wisdom Tradition', 21.

wisdom. Even those, for instance, who would argue that the introductory Psalm 1 puts one in a wisdom mindset at the beginning of the psalter would still recognise only a relatively small, discrete number of psalms as wisdom psalms. The others are hymns, laments, thanksgiving, kingship, confidence or some other type of psalm.

But it is precisely in the idea that texts can participate in more than one genre that we have a literary justification for continuing to speak of and study wisdom literature, to posit Proverbs, Job and Ecclesiastes as a core and to suggest that other texts in the OT/HB might also participate in the genre. Kynes himself rightly defines genre 'simply as groups of texts gathered together due to some perceived significant affinity between them'.[57] Our contention is that Proverbs, Job and Ecclesiastes have a 'significant affinity' with each other that justifies the modern perception of them as participating in a genre that has been labelled 'wisdom'. Furthermore, other texts that share these similarities, at least in part, may also be fruitfully studied in relationship to them.

The Social Location and Worldview of Wisdom Literature

This approach to wisdom literature, however, does not subvert what might be seen as Kynes' central project – to demolish the idea that wisdom literature is a *Fremdkörper*, an alien part of the canon definitively distinct from the other traditions as if it does not share a fundamental allegiance to Israel's core commitment to Yahweh. Upon close reading, it appears that Kynes is being provocative and hyperbolic when he speaks of the 'obituary' of wisdom literature. For the category is not dead even in his own thinking. He himself says that 'the Wisdom Literature category, then, is only one of the ways that texts may be grouped together within the OT/HB. It recognizes certain salient affinities between its three core texts'.[58] What Kynes rightly worries about is not that there is a case to be made for wisdom as a generic category but that a sole focus on these books as wisdom leads to a distorted understanding of them and obscures actual relationship with other books within the canon. Wisdom literature, he rightly insists, does not have a completely different worldview than the rest of the OT/HB.

---

[57] Kynes, *An Obituary for 'Wisdom Literature'*, 247. Sneed ('Grasping after the Wind', 62) also acknowledges that 'all the books scholars usually designate as wisdom literature share a family resemblance', though also rightly noting differences between them.

[58] Kynes, *An Obituary for 'Wisdom Literature'*, 248.

CONCLUSION

Kynes, Sneed and others have done the study of wisdom a great service by moving the field away from the traditional view held by some. Not only do some scholars hold the view that these texts were radically different from the rest of the canon, but some also took a diachronic view of the books to argue that any part that shared an affirmation of Yahweh as opposed to a general view of god that could be shared with others was a later addition.

Kynes and others have succeeded in bringing Proverbs, Job and Ecclesiastes back into the canonical fold. They have rightly urged the study of wisdom in its final form and also in relationship to other texts which form different genres with which they also share characteristics. We just need to be cautious against the tendency to overreact by thinking that the category of wisdom literature is actually dead.

Further Reading

Dell, Katharine J. *The Book of Job as Sceptical Literature*. BZAW 197. Berlin: 1991.

Fowler, Alistair. *Kinds of Literature: An Introduction to the Theory of Genres and Modes*. Cambridge: 1982.

Kynes, Will. *An Obituary for 'Wisdom Literature': The Birth, Death, and Intertextual Reintegration of a Biblical Corpus*. Oxford: 2019.

Longman, Tremper III. *The Fear of the Lord Is Wisdom: A Theological Introduction to Wisdom in Israel*. Grand Rapids: 2017.

Von Rad, Gerhard. *Wisdom in Israel*. London: 1972.

Sneed, Mark R. 'Is the "Wisdom Tradition" a Tradition?' *CBQ* 73 (2011): 50–71.

Sneed, Mark R. ed. *Was There a Wisdom Tradition? New Prospects in Israelite Wisdom Studies*. Atlanta: 2015.

Sweeney, Marvin A., and Ehud B. Zvi, eds. *The Changing Face of Form Criticism in the Twenty-First Century*. Grand Rapids: 2003.

Weeks, Stuart. *An Introduction to the Study of Wisdom Literature*. London: 2010.

3 The Multiple Genres of Wisdom

SUZANNA R. MILLAR

INTRODUCTION

Scholars are increasingly uneasy about calling 'wisdom literature' a genre (see Longman, Chapter 2 in this volume). This category is anachronistically constructed[1] and carries scholarly baggage (a tradition, worldview, sociological context and place in Israelite theology). What's more, the texts subsumed by this label are diverse. They are neither wholly cohesive with each other nor wholly distinct from 'non-wisdom' texts. It has accordingly been argued that 'wisdom' constitutes not a genre proper but a 'mode' – a general manner of writing that may incorporate many genres.[2] Wisdom is not one genre but multiple.

Indeed, genres exist at different taxonomic levels.[3] Scholars have separated them into macro- and micro-, supra- and sub-, primary and secondary, large and small. These are, of course, all relative terms, and a simple bifurcation is misleading. For example, 'wisdom literature' may be a macro-genre containing the micro-genre 'instruction'. But 'instruction' is itself a macro-genre containing the micro-genre 'proverb'. A diverse range of smaller genres will be the subject matter of this chapter. First, though, we must consider what genres are and how they are recognised.

Debate simmers in wisdom studies about the nature of genres. At one extreme, genres are considered 'nominal', artificial creations superimposed on texts by scholars.[4] At the other, genres are considered 'real',

---

[1] Will Kynes, *An Obituary for 'Wisdom Literature': The Birth, Death, and Intertextual Reintegration of a Biblical Corpus* (Oxford, 2019).

[2] Mark Sneed, 'Is the "Wisdom Tradition" a Tradition?', *The Catholic Biblical Quarterly* 73.1 (2011): 50–71. Sneed's suggestion of referring to wisdom as a 'mode' has not been widely adopted. I prefer to speak of 'multiple genres'.

[3] For a detailed classification of the genres within wisdom literature, see John G. Gammie, 'Paraenetic Literature: Toward the Morphology of a Secondary Genre', *Semeia* 50 (1990): 41–77.

[4] Sneed, 'Wisdom Tradition', 66.

inherent within texts, later discovered by scholars. Neither is quite right. Rather, as Will Kynes put it, 'genres emerge *between* readers and texts as readers perceive and structure "real" textual relationships'.[5] A further distinction is also important: genres emerge in the text's interaction with communities of both modern scholars and original readers.

The genre categories discerned by modern scholars have heuristic value. They offer intertextual analysis of texts sharing salient properties, which may illuminate overlooked textual features and highlight each composition's genericity and distinctiveness. This approach has pragmatic benefits, allowing comparison between texts that are historically distant from one another and from us. In this volume, Kynes (Chapter 9) demonstrates possible groupings for the book of Job and the insights that emerge from the comparisons.

But genre analysis can go beyond this. Ancient writers had a sense of genre, and used it for their own purposes, to be recognised by original readers. The genre of a text communicates something to the reader. It is, according to Alastair Fowler, 'an instrument not of classification or prescription but of meaning'.[6] It serves as a 'social contract' with the reader, an implicit agreement about what to expect and how to interpret. When I read a scientific treatise, for example, I prepare to encounter facts, data and arguments for analysis. When I read a fairy tale, I wander imaginatively into make-believe realms, receptive to moral lessons. In effect, genre configures the relationship between reader and text. It projects an ideal reader, who will respond in a particular way, and asks the actual reader to adopt this persona. It conveys certain types of truth, which should be received appropriately.[7] Texts also communicate when they deviate from generic conventions or exploit genres in subtle and nuanced ways. In this chapter, we will be sensitive not just to 'what genres?' but to what genres communicate.

To achieve this, we must first recognise genres. Any trait might become salient for genre recognition: for example, form, subject matter, style, perspective, register, structure, motifs, medium, social context. In a genre, a constellation of these features works together to communicate a coherent impression. But there are no necessary and sufficient

---

[5] Kynes, *An Obituary for 'Wisdom Literature'*, 114.

[6] Alastair Fowler, *Kinds of Literature: An Introduction to the Theory of Genres and Modes* (Oxford, 1982), 22.

[7] Carol A. Newsom, *The Book of Job: A Contest of Moral Imaginations* (Oxford, 2009), 12–13.

criteria which define genre membership, no checklists of characteristics to tick off. Characteristics may be shared by certain member texts but not others (like family traits; some members have them, some don't).[8] Characteristics have varying degrees of importance for genre recognition. Some are cognitively central, and strongly provoke recognition, while others are only peripherally relevant.[9] What's more, texts can invoke more than one set of generic conventions. Molly Zahn elucidates: 'texts are no longer seen as "belonging" to a single genre. Instead, we can speak of texts "participating" in genres: dipping into them, employing their elements in modified fashion, combining them'.[10]

In this chapter, I will analyse the multiple genres within wisdom literature. I will focus on the books traditionally labelled 'wisdom' – Proverbs, Job, Ecclesiastes, Ben Sira and Wisdom of Solomon – and show that these consist of not one genre but many. I will cluster these genres according to their main communicative purposes. The first two clusters – genres of instruction and human reasoning – are unsurprising constituents of 'wisdom literature'. The latter two, however – genres of praise and complaint – are more familiar from other biblical corpora. Throughout the chapter, I will ask: What genres do these texts participate in? What constellations of features work together to this end? And, crucially, what does this communicate to the reader?

GENRES OF INSTRUCTION

Sayings

Let us begin, then, with genres whose main communicative purpose is to instruct their readers: sayings, instructions, diatribe/protreptic and didactic narrative. The most basic instructional form may be the saying or proverb. Indeed, these have been used in societies throughout history to pass on traditional wisdom. They are characterised by a recognisable constellation of features: they are short, pithy and self-contained; third

---

[8] A 'family resemblance' model for genre was popularised by Fowler, *Kinds of Literature*, 41–43. It has been applied to wisdom literature by Katharine J. Dell, 'Deciding the Boundaries of 'Wisdom': Applying the Concept of Family Resemblance', in *Was There a Wisdom Tradition? New Prospects in Israelite Wisdom Studies*, ed. M. Sneed, Ancient Israel and Its Literature 23 (Atlanta, 2015), 145–160.

[9] Wright applies this 'prototype theory' to the genre of wisdom texts in the Dead Sea Scrolls, see Benjamin G. Wright III, 'Joining the Club: A Suggestion about Genre in Early Jewish Texts', *DSD* 17.3 (2010): 289–314.

[10] Molly M. Zahn, 'Genre and Rewritten Scripture: A Reassessment', *JBL* 131.2 (2012): 271–288, here 277.

person and observational; stylised through, for example, imagery, word-play and soundplay.[11] Proverbs have a cultural status as indisputable truths. They can cut into conversations, demanding acquiescence without further argumentation. A single proverb is multi-applicable, and the hearer must discern its relevance for her own circumstances. It is also multi-functional, serving as a speech-act to many different ends. Often, proverbs evaluate situations or direct the hearer to action.

It is likely that Israel had a stock of conventional sayings, and we may find examples in narratives and prophetic books.[12] There are also possible examples in Job, both in the dialogues and in the narrative frame, where Job possibly cites traditional, pious sayings about God's providence (1:21 [cf. Eccl 5:14(15); Sir 40:1]; 2:10).[13]

Most closely associated with the proverb genre is (of course) the book of Proverbs (Heb: *mᵉšālîm*).[14] Elsewhere, I have argued that the sayings here do invoke the generic conventions of genuine proverbs and thus communicate their function as conversational tools for evaluation and direction.[15] However, they also have significant differences from folk proverbs. Rather than being single-lined, they typically exhibit stylised two-line parallelism. Rather than employing imaginative imagery, they often use generalised language. Rather than being spoken in conversations, they are written in collections. These features conspire together for a didactic, moralising purpose. Their expanded, generalised, collected form offers a worldview to students – a simple framework of categories and patterns to make sense of life's complexity. Particularly prevalent are character categories and act-consequence patterns, emphasising the importance of being and doing good.

Comparable sayings collections are also found elsewhere: for example, Ben Sira, Tobit, Aramaic *Aḥiqar* and Egyptian and Mesopotamian texts. Also relevant is Ecclesiastes (e.g., 7:1–12; 9:16–10:20). Ecclesiastes, though, uses this genre subversively and sceptically, undermining its conventional conveyance of trustworthy wisdom. This subversion occurs partly through

---

[11] See Neal R. Norrick, 'Subject Area, Terminology, Proverb Definitions, Proverb Features', in *Introduction to Paremiology: A Comprehensive Guide to Proverb Studies*, ed. H. Hrisztova-Gotthardt and M. Aleksa Varga (Berlin, 2015), 7–27.

[12] Carol Fontaine, *Traditional Sayings in the Old Testament* (Sheffield, 1982).

[13] J. J. Burden, 'Decision by Debate: Examples of Popular Proverb Performance in the Book of Job', *OTE* 4.1 (1991): 37–65.

[14] For a thorough analysis of this Hebrew term, see Jacqueline Vayntrub, *Beyond Orality: Biblical Poetry in Its Own Terms* (Oxford, 2019).

[15] Suzanna R. Millar, *Genre and Openness in Proverbs 10:1–22:16* (Atlanta, 2020).

contextualisation. For example, the sayings in 7:1–12 purport to express what is 'good' (*ṭōb*), but they sit in the shadow of the immediately preceding pronouncement that no one knows what is good (6:12). A little later, 10:8a repeats the traditional dictum that 'He who digs a pit will fall into it' (cf. Prov 26:27a). In Proverbs, this expresses the proper working of the act-consequence connection: the pit-digger intends to harm the wayfarer and will be punished accordingly. In Ecclesiastes, though, it becomes a piece of bad luck. It is paralleled with the injuries that befall manual labourers (those who quarry stones and split logs, 10:9) and is thus read as a comparable unfortunate accident.

Instructions

Sometimes, sayings are incorporated into larger texts, dubbed 'instructions'. Across the ancient Near East are found examples of this genre, sharing a constellation of characteristics. It is unclear whether Israelite scribes had access to (m)any of these texts or the linguistic abilities to read them. But certain passages in Proverbs, Ecclesiastes and Ben Sira exhibit the same genre-salient strategies to instruct, so the comparison is fruitful. There are some specific links too: a literary connection is evident between Prov 22:17–24:22 and the Egyptian *Instruction of Amenemope*[16] and dependence has been posited for Ben Sira on the Demotic *Papyrus Insinger*[17] and the *Satire on the Trades* (esp. Sir 38:24–39:11).

In Proverbs, instructions are particularly found in chs. 1–9 and 22–24. In 1–9, several scholars distinguish ten separate instructions (though not always agreeing on their bounds).[18] In Ecclesiastes, this genre is not dominant but may be invoked (e.g., 4:17–5:6 [5:1–7]; 8:1–4; 9:7–10; 11:7–10; 12:12–14),[19] and in Ben Sira it occurs throughout (especially in chs. 3–42). Instructions can be distinguished by their form, voice, style and content, all of which contribute to their communicative purpose.

---

[16]   J. A. Emerton, 'The Teaching of Amenemope and Proverbs XXII 17–XXIV 22: Further Reflections on a Long-Standing Problem', *VT* 51.4 (2001): 431–465.

[17]   Jack T. Sanders, *Ben Sira and Demotic Wisdom* (Chico, 1983).

[18]   E.g., Michael V. Fox, 'Ideas of Wisdom in Proverbs 1–9', *JBL* 116.4 (1997): 613–633; R. Norman Whybray, *The Composition of the Book of Proverbs* (Sheffield, 1994).

[19]   These are amongst the passages identified as instructions by Roland E. Murphy, *Wisdom Literature: Job, Proverbs, Ruth, Canticles, Ecclesiastes and Esther* (Grand Rapids, 1981).

Form-critically, instructions are characterised by imperatives, often supplemented by conditions, motivations and consequences.[20] They give explicit advice with supporting argumentation and exhortations, both commanding and persuading. They directly address the reader, creating a sense of immediacy and demanding obedience. Structurally, the instructions in Proverbs follow a recognisable but flexible pattern. Norman Whybray hypothesises 'a "basic" model of parental instruction' with a stereotyped and fixed structure, later supplemented by diverse additions.[21] It is more likely, though, that variation was inherent from the beginning. Michael V. Fox distinguishes a tripartite structure – exordium, lesson, conclusion – which makes room for diverse internal argumentation.[22]

Common to ancient Near Eastern instructions is the authoritative *voice* with which they are spoken, usually figured as a father's voice advising a son. The speaker thus claims the traditional authority and filial loyalty of the father figure, who signifies the benevolent and trustworthy wisdom of a previous generation. The intergenerational relationship configures the subject position of the reader, who is explicitly addressed as 'my son' (*bᵉnî*). This appellation occurs throughout Proverbs 1–9, intermittently in Ben Sira and once in the epilogue of Ecclesiastes (12:12). This son is silent, exemplary in his acquiescence and assumed receptivity. The ideal reader, too, learns submissiveness.

Many ancient Near Eastern instructions have a narrative context at a moment of succession. The son is nearing adulthood; the father is aging; it is time for the former to adopt the latter's mantle. Leo Perdue suggests that the son inhabits a liminal zone, about to re-enter the social structure with his state fundamentally changed.[23] In Proverbs too, the son is apparently newly entering society, and the father warns him against the dangers he might find there, notably gangs and seductresses. Proverbs, though, diverges from ancient Near Eastern convention here: it allows voices other than the father's to speak.[24] Elsewhere, we encounter a single speaker; here we find various: Lady Wisdom, the strange woman, no-good youths. The son/reader must learn to

---

[20] William McKane, *Proverbs: A New Approach* (London, 1970), e.g., 75–79.

[21] Whybray, *The Composition of the Book of Proverbs*, 56.

[22] Fox, 'Ideas of Wisdom', 614–615.

[23] Leo Perdue, 'Liminality as a Social Setting for Wisdom Instructions', *ZAW* 93.1 (1981): 114–126.

[24] Stuart Weeks, *Instruction and Imagery in Proverbs 1–9* (Oxford, 2007), 42–44.

distinguish righteous from wicked voices, submitting obediently to the former but evading the seduction of the latter.[25]

This is challenging, as each speaks with persuasive and alluring language. Indeed, the *style* of instructions is generally sophisticated – poetic and carefully crafted. Both ancient Near Eastern and Israelite examples employ rare vocabulary, imaginative imagery and aural effects.[26] This high style has rhetorical purpose. It models the fine oratory which is often commended (e.g., Prov 15:23, 26; 16:23–24; 25:11). It trains the readers' intellect and erudition, sharpening their interpretive skills. Moving beyond the cognitive to the aesthetic, it excites the reader's senses and emotions, increasing the appeal of the advice. The beauty of the language is an appropriate – even necessary – vehicle for the profound truths expressed.

These truths, which constitute the instructions' main *content*, amount to traditional societal values. Instructions socialise readers into culturally exalted virtues and form their characters. Miriam Lichtheim surveys these virtues in Egyptian instructions, listing 'honesty and truthfulness; justice, kindness, and generosity; temperance and patience; thoughtfulness, diligence, and competence; loyalty and reliability'.[27] Hebrew instructions exhort very similar morals, though with a notable addition: wisdom. Wisdom does occur in ancient Near Eastern instructions (notably in Papyrus Insinger), but it is only one virtue amongst many. In the Israelite examples, wisdom is a meta-virtue. Attain wisdom and other virtues will follow; it is to be desired above all else (e.g., Prov 4:7; 8:11; 16:16). In form, voice, style and content, then, the instruction genre is powerful in its pedagogy.

Diatribe and Protreptic

Our consideration of instructions has drawn on ancient Near Eastern parallels; now we look to Greece. This is particularly relevant for later wisdom books, which may have been composed in Hellenistic environments. The genres described here – diatribe and protreptic – are hortatory like instructions. But the imagined audience is no longer a naïve child who will obey – rather, a reasonable interlocutor who might object.

---

[25] J. N. Aletti, 'Séduction et Parole En Proverbes I–IX', *VT* 27.2 (1977): 129–144.

[26] Weeks, *Instruction and Imagery*, 57–60.

[27] Miriam Lichtheim, 'Didactic Literature', in *Ancient Egyptian Literature: History and Forms*, ed. A. Lopriendo, Proleme Der Ägyptologie (Leiden, 1996), 243–262, here 261.

Diatribe is usually associated with the Cynics and Stoics. It incorporates rhetorical techniques and conventional themes to offer moral exhortation and ethical philosophy for daily life. It was probably intended for the public assembly, where its fine oratory would persuade the masses. It does not have a fixed form but incorporates a cluster of conventional characteristics which work together to its rhetorical ends. Several of these characteristics have been found in Ecclesiastes.[28] Whether or not we can posit actual influence from Greek texts, the comparison highlights features with communicative impact.

The most commonly cited feature is a dialogue with an imagined interlocutor. This can make sense of the abrupt shifts and apparently contradictory voices in Ecclesiastes. Curtis Giese explains how, in a diatribe, a discursive section is often interrupted unexpectedly by a direct address to the interlocutor.[29] Thus, Epictetus interrupts his discussion about how 'people' (third person) respond to philosophers with the imperative: 'consider first what your business is!'[30] Similarly, Qohelet[31] follows his third-person generality – 'the patient in spirit is better than the proud in spirit' – with a command: 'Be not quick in your spirit to become angry!' (7:8–9). The imagined interlocutor remains present in subsequent verses, where erroneous words are ascribed to them (7:10), and they are asked a rhetorical question (7:13). Giese also cites other features reminiscent of diatribes: short, simple sentences; repetition of key words; illustrations (1:3–7; 4:7–8; 5:13–14; 9:13–16); analogies (7:1, 19); ironic commands (9:7–9; 11:9) and rhetorical questions.[32]

If Ecclesiastes has been likened to diatribe, Wisdom of Solomon finds connections with *protreptic*.[33] Protreptic is a genre combining philosophy and rhetoric, usually associated with the Sophists. It offers didactic, hortatory discourse, highly rhetorically charged to persuade hearers to a particular course of action. Connections to protreptic are most notable in 1:1–6:21. This section purports to be addressed to the

---

[28] Curtis Giese, 'The Genre of Ecclesiastes as Viewed by Its Septuagint Translator and the Early Church Fathers' (PhD diss., Hebrew Union College, 1999). Giese argues that features resembling diatribe are already present in the Hebrew text and are recognised as such by later translators and interpreters.

[29] Giese, 'The Genre of Ecclesiastes', 51–55.

[30] Epictetus, *Discourses* 3.15.8–9, cited in Giese, 'The Genre of Ecclesiastes', 53.

[31] In this chapter, I use 'Ecclesiastes' to refer to the book, and 'Qohelet' to refer to the speaking persona.

[32] Giese, 'The Genre of Ecclesiastes', 55–64.

[33] James M. Reese, *Hellenistic Influence on the Book of Wisdom and Its Consequences* (Rome, 1970).

'rulers of the earth', claiming grandeur and universality for its advice. It establishes a polar opposition of righteous and wicked lifestyles, incentivising the former while warning against the latter. Its carefully constructed argument incorporates rhetorical techniques common to protreptic. We find, for example, *diptychs* (contrasting images of the righteous and wicked, chs. 3–4), *prosōpopoiia* (imaginary speeches put in the mouths of the wicked, chs. 2 and 5) and *soritēs* (chains of reasoning in which the conclusion of one proposition becomes the premise of the next, 6:17–20). Viewing Ecclesiastes and Wisdom through the lenses of diatribe and protreptic respectively can alert us to the sophisticated persuasiveness of their rhetoric.

Didactic Narrative

Instructions, diatribe and protreptic are explicit in their communicative intention to advise. But didacticism needn't be overt. Indeed, every teacher knows the pedagogical value of a good story. From Jesus to Aesop, teachers have used parables, fables and allegories whose arresting images and memorable plots covey didactic messages. We find scattered examples in the Hebrew Bible – fantastical accounts of trees, birds and animals, offered to explain particular situations (e.g., Judg 9:8–15; 2 Sam 12:1–4; 2 Kgs 14:8–10; Ezekiel 15, 17, 19, 31).[34] There are surprisingly few such tales within the wisdom books, save a few vignettes about hardworking ants (Prov 6:6–8), dilapidated vineyards (24:30–34), city sieges (Eccl 9:13–16) and wise paupers and foolish kings (4:13–16).

Longer narratives with didactic intent have also been found throughout the Hebrew Bible.[35] Hans-Peter Müller distinguished the genre of '*weisheitliche Lehrerzählung*' (wisdom didactic narrative) in the prose tale of Job, Joseph, Daniel, Esther, Tobit and Aramaic *Aḥiqar*.[36] He claimed the genre could be recognised by an inventory of scenes revolving around a virtuous protagonist who is tested and rewarded. How well these narratives fit into his schema is debatable.

---

[34] Kevin J. Cathcart, 'The Trees, the Beasts and the Birds: Fables, Parables and Allegories in the Old Testament', in *Wisdom in Ancient Israel: Essays in Honour of J. A. Emerton*, ed. John Day, R. P. Gordon, and H. G. M. Williamson (Cambridge, 1995), 212–221.

[35] These are sometimes questionably considered products of 'wisdom influence'. Suzanna R. Millar, 'History and Wisdom Literature', in *The Oxford Handbook of Wisdom and the Bible*, ed. Will Kynes (New York, 2021), 441–458.

[36] Hans-Peter Müller, 'Die Weisheitliche Lehrerzählung Im Alten Testament Und Seiner Umwelt', *Die Welt Des Orients* 9.1 (1977): 77–98.

But they – particularly Job – exhibit a constellation of features with particular pedagogical impact.[37]

The virtuous characters are paragons for the reader. Job is immediately extolled as 'blameless and upright, fearing God and turning from evil' (1:1). He exhibits hyper-scrupulous piety, regularly offering preemptive sacrifices (1:5), and when all he has is taken, wholly submitting to God's will (1:20–22). His character in the prologue lacks complexity and his moral choices are presented as unambiguous. This simplicity (conveyed also through the basic syntax and vocabulary) makes the narrative straightforward and accessible. There is a story-like, fabulous tone. Long ago and far away, the protagonist lives in hyperbolic grandeur, with livestock in extraordinary and symbolically perfect numbers (1:3). The narrative is repetitive and balanced, with scenes alternating between heaven and earth. The genre creates a world of clarity, simplicity and symmetry; as Carol Newsom puts it, 'a world of utterly unbreachable wholeness'.[38] Such a story projects a particular kind of reader whose relationship with the narrator is figured around 'the submerged metaphor of parent-child'.[39] The narrator's voice is supremely authoritative but also benevolent. The reader takes the subject position of a child absorbing moral lessons.

The genres considered here – sayings, instructions, diatribe/protreptic and didactic narrative – share the primary communicative purpose of instructing. Each is characterised by a distinctive constellation of textual features which work together to exhort and advise.

GENRES OF HUMAN REASONING

Reflection

We move now to a second set of genres, whose purpose is not to instruct but to reason, to cause the reader not to do but to think. We will consider two examples: the reflection and the wisdom dialogue.

Several scholars have distinguished a genre of first-person reasoning, dubbed the 'reflection'. It is loosely defined and occurs predominantly in just one text: Ecclesiastes.[40] It has few obvious precedents in ancient Near Eastern or Israelite texts (notwithstanding a few first-person contemplations; e.g., Prov 7:6–23; 24:30–34; Job 4:8; 5:3), so

---

[37] See Newsom, *The Book of Job*, 32–71.
[38] Newsom, *The Book of Job*, 53.
[39] Newsom, *The Book of Job*, 45.
[40] E.g., Friedrich Ellermeier, *Qohelet I/1* (Herzberg am Harz, 1967), 89–92.

we might be wary of understanding it as a conventionalised and easily recognisable genre. The categorisation does highlight, though, a coalescence of features with particular impact.

Qohelet's reflections are structured broadly around an observation, progression of thought and conclusion. In the observation, Qohelet notes something he has 'seen' (1:14; 2:13, 24; 3:16, 22 etc.). From the observation, thought progresses, suggesting an empirical epistemology different from, for example, the tradition-based reasoning of instructions.[41] The reasoning is often narrated as an internal dialogue between Qohelet and his 'heart' (lēb), conveying interiority, introspection and reflexivity. The reader has the sense of overhearing something private and attains psychological intimacy with the speaking persona. The presence of the heart as a discursive partner also makes room for other partners and catches the reader up in the dialogue.

Qohelet's thoughts are not static. Friedrich Ellermeier noted that there is often a development from ideas which seem negative to those which seem positive or vice versa. Using this development as his criterion, he subdivided reflections into: unitary (einheitlich; negative ideas are followed by negative ideas; e.g., 6:1–6); broken (gebrochene; positive followed by negative; e.g., 4:13–16) and reverse broken (umgekehrt gebrochene; negative followed by positive; e.g., 4:4–6).[42] However, this glosses over the sheer variety of reflections, which do not conform to simple patterns. Indeed, the reflections are non-linear, turning subjects over from multiple perspectives. As Michael V. Fox, puts it, Qohelet 'bares his soul in all its twistings and turnings, ups and downs, taking his readers with him on a sometimes arduous journey to knowledge – a knowledge that turns out to be very incomplete'.[43] And indeed, inbuilt in the reflections is uncertainty. Their conclusions are rarely conclusive; Qohelet often picks up on earlier conclusions and reflects on them again in a contradictory manner.

Wisdom Dialogue

These apparent contradictions in Ecclesiastes have led some to posit that the book represents a dialogue between interlocutors. Indeed, Theodore Perry argues that the whole book constitutes a debate

---

[41] Michael V. Fox, 'Qohelet's Epistemology', HUCA 58 (1987): 137–155.
[42] Ellermeier, Qohelet I/1, 88–92.
[43] Michael V. Fox, Ecclesiastes: The Traditional Hebrew Text with the New JPS Translation (Philadelphia, 2004), xliii.

between the Presenter (P) and Kohelet (K).[44] P offers the traditional wisdom of faith, while K speaks the sceptical voice of experience. Every verse can be ascribed to one speaker or the other. Ultimately, P controls the dialogue, and frames it with third-person narration. Perry's hypothesis is ingenious but, with no text-internal indications of the changes of speaker, stretches credulity.

A much clearer case of dialogue occurs in Job 4–27, in which Job argues with his three friends. They debate about Job's present affliction and broader questions of suffering, God and the order of the cosmos. Job's friends are rooted in traditional retributive theology and aver that Job must have sinned. Job maintains his innocence and rails against God for afflicting him. Several comparable texts exist from Mesopotamia, in which speakers offer sophisticated examinations of alternate sides to an existential problem: for example, the Sumerian *A Man and His God*, *Ludlul bel nemeqi*, a Dialogue between a Man and his God and the Babylonian Theodicy.[45]

The wisdom dialogue genre has a particular impact on readers and privileges a certain way of confronting reality. The alternating opinions convey lack of satisfaction with traditional wisdom but unwillingness to dispense with it entirely.[46] Both sides are taken seriously. Though readers might prefer one or the other, neither is straightforwardly privileged. The genre inherently acknowledges contradictions and indeed focuses relentlessly on them. There is little room for compromise or agreement, and the dialogues prove irresolvable. This is strikingly demonstrated in Job through the notorious breakdown of the third cycle of argumentation (chs. 24–27). As Carol Newsom puts it, 'at the end, two incommensurable ways of apprehending and engaging the world remain simply juxtaposed, both requiring acknowledgment'.[47] The genre, finally, assumes a particular reader. Its sophisticated form, style and content require erudition and intellect. And though the dialogue purports to be between characters in the text, the reader too must enter the fray.

---

[44] Theodore Anthony Perry, *Dialogues with Kohelet: The Book of Ecclesiastes* (University Park, 1993).

[45] Newsom, *The Book of Job*, 79.

[46] Karel van der Toorn, 'The Ancient Near Eastern Literary Dialogue as a Vehicle of Critical Reflection', in *Dispute Poems and Dialogues in the Ancient and Mediaeval Near East: Forms and Types of Literary Debates in Semitic and Related Literatures*, ed. G. J. Reinink and H. L. J. Vanstiphout (Leuven, 1991), 59–76, here 68–69.

[47] Newsom, *The Book of Job*, 85.

GENRES OF PRAISE

Praise of Wisdom

That genres of instruction and human reasoning are found in sapiential discourse is unsurprising. More surprising, perhaps, are the genres of praise also found therein. These are common to the Psalms, more often associated with the 'cult' than the 'school'. Nonetheless, the wisdom books sing praises – praises of wisdom, of people and of God.

Several passages offer praises to the figure of Wisdom. They display shared traits which may distinguish them as a coherent genre. With sweeping, sophisticated poetry, they lyricise about Wisdom, often personified as a female. They frequently employ rich creation imagery to express her place in the cosmos and her relationship with God and humanity. Some passages emphasise her immanence and accessibility (Proverbs 8; Ben Sira 24; Wisdom 7–10), others her transcendence and inaccessibility (Job 28; Bar 3:9–4:4; 1 Enoch 42).

Praises of Immanent Wisdom

Wisdom is personified into a female figure to adore. The adoration is expressed in Proverbs 8 and Ben Sira 24 by Wisdom herself and in Wisdom 7–10 by King Solomon (who is also extolled in the process). The origins of this personification are debated. The figure may be a poetic embellishment, a hypostasis of God or a (semi-)divine person. Some claim that she originated in a Canaanite wisdom goddess[48] or in the Egyptian deity Ma'at.[49] Often, she is connected with the Egyptian goddess Isis.

The Isis cult was widespread amongst Egyptians and (in the Hellenistic period) amongst Greeks. Wife of Osiris and mother/wife of the Pharaoh, she was worshipped for her healing and protective powers. Often, this worship was conducted through à specific literary genre: the *aretalogy*. The aretalogy exalts the deity by listing her *aretai* (virtues) and *dunamis* (power). Though second and third-person examples exist, it is often a first-person genre – a self-praise of the goddess, structured by the anaphoric repetition of the pronoun 'I'. There are numerous extant aretalogies in Greek, most significantly the Kyme-Memphis

---

[48] Bernhard Lang, *Wisdom and the Book of Proverbs: A Hebrew Goddess Redefined* (New York, 1986).

[49] Christa Bauer-Kayatz, *Studien Zu Proverbien 1–9: Eine Form- Und Motivgeschichtliche Untersuchung Unter Einbeziehung Ägyptischen Vergleichsmaterials* (Neukirchen-Vluyn, 1966).

inscription (first century BCE).[50] Self-praises of Isis also occur in Egyptian hieroglyphic texts, notably the Metternich magical Stela (fourth century BCE).[51]

Parallels have been found with the biblical praises of Wisdom. For example, in these inscriptions and in Proverbs 8, the female figure is associated with life, knowledge and righteousness/justice; she participates in creation and law-giving; she is the daughter of the supreme deity and is intimate with human kings.[52] Ben Sira 24 has been found to share a structure with the Kyme-Memphis inscription, beginning with Wisdom's/Isis' nature (vv. 3–4), then her power (vv. 5–11), then her works (vv. 12–17).[53] Johannes Marböck further observes similarities between Ben Sira 24 and aretalogies from Ios and Nysa, regarding the woman's cosmological function, claim to power, cultic function and connection with law.[54] In Wisdom of Solomon 7–10, the trifold pattern of nature-power-works has also been observed,[55] and, what's more, Wisdom is depicted as a bride of the king and a saviour. These characteristics may have little precedent in biblical tradition but much in the Isis aretalogies.[56]

Others, however, have been sceptical of the connection. The aretalogies are probably too late to have influenced Proverbs 8. Many of the thematic connections are general, explicable without recourse to extrabiblical texts. Furthermore, the 'I-form' of self-praise, which has been the starting point for comparison, is quite common amongst ancient Near Eastern kings and deities. In the Metternich Stela, we find not only Isis but Thoth and Min engaging in self-praise,[57] and in a Mesopotamian text, the goddess Gula sings in self-exaltation.[58]

[50] Gail Corrington Streete, 'An Isis Aretalogy from Kyme in Asia Minor, First Century B.C.E', in *Religions of Late Antiquity in Practice*, ed. R. Valantasis, Princeton Readings in Religions (Princeton, 2000).

[51] Constantin Emil Sander-Hansen, *Die Texte Der Metternichstele. the Text, with a German Translation and Commentary*, AAeg 7 (København, 1956).

[52] Lady Wisdom in Proverbs is connected with Isis by Michael V. Fox, 'World Order and Ma'at: A Crooked Parallel', *JANESCU* 23 (1995): 37–48; Leo G. Perdue, *The Sword and the Stylus: An Introduction to Wisdom in the Age of Empires* (Grand Rapids, 2008), 92–93, 111–112.

[53] Johannes Marböck, *Weisheit Im Wandel: Untersuchungen Zur Weisheitstheologie Bei Ben Sira* (Berlin, 1999).

[54] Marböck, *Weisheit Im Wandel*, 47–54.

[55] Reese, *Hellenistic Influence*, 43.

[56] John S. Kloppenborg, 'Isis and Sophia in the Book of Wisdom', *HTR* 75.1 (1982): 57–84.

[57] Thoth: Ll.138, 245; Min: Ll.84–86. Sander-Hansen, *Die Texte Der Metternichstele*.

[58] B. R. Foster, *Before the Muses: An Anthology of Akkadian Literature* (Bethesda, 2005), 583–591.

Regardless of the direct connection, the comparison highlights a communicative constellation of features. The I-form removes mediating voices, bringing directness and immediacy. It assumes a high level of authority: she herself is the speaker most worthy to sing her praises. The virtues, powers and deeds pile up, evoking her overwhelming majesty. The hymn-like exaltations teach the reader to revere her almost as they would revere God. Directness combines with grandeur to create a productive tension between Wisdom's immanence and transcendence, keeping readers ever searching after her.

Isis aretalogies, however, are not the only generic connection posited for these praises. Wisdom of Solomon 7–10 is sometimes labelled an *encomium* – a Greek rhetorical form which praises a person, virtue or thing and inspires admiration from the audience. In fact, the passage may be a 'double encomium' for both Wisdom and Solomon.[59] Andrew T. Glicksman highlights eight structural elements conventional for encomia: introduction, ancestry, birth, youth, way of life, deeds, comparison, epilogue. Each of these he finds reflected in the passage.[60]

A further comparison is offered by *love poetry*. In Wisdom of Solomon 7–10, the marital language is explicit (8:2), and Solomon lavishes praise on his betrothed. But even when inexplicit, the language of love bubbles through. Anne Stewart posits this connection for Proverbs, noting the prevalence of desire.[61] Wisdom is compared adoringly with gold and fine jewels (Prov 3:14–15; cf. Song 1:10–11; 5:11, 14–15) and the young man is exhorted to 'Love her ... adore her ... embrace her' (Prov 4:6, 8; Stewart's translation). Lady Wisdom, though, vies with Lady Folly for the man's attention. Just as the lover in the Song of Song sometimes finds herself unrequited (Song 3:2), so too does Lady Wisdom call out (Prov 1:20–21) but remains unanswered (1:24). Similarly, Ben Sira 24 evokes the language of love. Martti Nissinen explores its connections with Song of Songs and Mesopotamian love poetry, particularly in the sensual imagery employed.[62] Across these works, the readers' senses are delighted by gardens and trees, fruit and honey, scents and spices.[63]

---

[59] Andrew T. Glicksman, *Wisdom of Solomon 10 a Jewish Hellenistic Reinterpretation of Early Israelite History through Sapiential Lenses* (Berlin, 2011).

[60] Glicksman, *Wisdom of Solomon 10*, 80–88.

[61] Anne W. Stewart, *Poetic Ethics in Proverbs: Wisdom Literature and the Shaping of the Moral Self* (New York, 2016), 61–69.

[62] Martti Nissinen, 'Wisdom as Mediatrix in Sirach 24: Ben Sira, Love Lyrics, and Prophecy', *Studia Orientalia Electronica* 106 (2015): 377–390.

[63] Song of Songs itself has sometimes been considered wisdom literature. See Andruska, Chapter 11 in this volume.

Praises of Hidden Wisdom

These texts find wisdom immanent and accessible. Others, though, employ similar generic conventions to express transcendency and inaccessibility. Job 28 breaks away from the fraught dialogue preceding it with a meditative lyric on wisdom. As in other wisdom poems, wisdom here is close to God, has pre-eminence in the cosmos and is sought by humans. However, the search is no longer successful. Wisdom no longer speaks nor appears directly to humanity. Indeed, the central refrain is 'Where can wisdom be found?' (28:12, 20). The sweeping, cosmic scope makes readers feel they are glimpsing something far beyond themselves.

The poem concludes that wisdom is not to be sought like an object. Proverbs had compared wisdom to fine jewels (Prov 3:15; 8:11), but Job declares such comparisons inadequate (Job 28:15–19). Wisdom is found in activity, pre-eminently in God's activity in creation (28:23–27). Humanity's access is therefore through activity, through their morals and piety (28:28). The poem has taken readers on a journey of cosmic speculation, only to arrive back at the humdrum of everyday ethics, imbuing them with new significance.[64]

Job's themes are picked up in hidden wisdom poems of later apocalyptic authors. Baruch 3:9–4:4 too employs cosmic language and rhetorical questions to muse on the quest. The text asks 'who has found wisdom?' (3:15, 29–30) and answers 'no one' (3:20, 23, 31) – apart from God (3:32–36). Humanity's access to her comes only through the commandments (3:37–4:1). Similarly, 1 Enoch 42 stresses wisdom's hiddenness. She found no place to dwell amongst humankind, so instead resides amongst angels in heaven.

Overall, the constellation of traits shared by these texts exalts wisdom into a near-divine and transcendent figure. But this is not just exaltation for exaltation's sake. Unlike in most aretalogies, encomia or love songs, the praise is to didactic ends. Proverbs 8, Ben Sira 24 and Wisdom of Solomon 7–10 are contextualised by didactic exhortation. Wisdom appears to humans in order to change the way they live. In Sir 24:23 and Bar 4:1, this is given specificity, as wisdom is equated with Torah. In Job 28 and Bar 3:9–4:4, the inaccessibility of cosmic wisdom means that humans must instead exhibit the wisdom of piety.

---

[64] As it is so different from the preceding poem, Job 28:28 is sometimes considered to be a later addition. See Newsom, *The Book of Job*, 169–170, 181.

Praise of People

Some texts invoke genres which praise not wisdom but human beings. We will consider two examples: Ben Sira's 'Praise of the Ancestors' and Ecclesiastes' royal self-praise. Ben Sira 44–49 extensively describes heroes of biblical history, from Enoch to Nehemiah, and culminates (ch. 50) with an exaltation of Simon Son of Onias – probably the high priest Simon II, with whom Ben Sira was likely acquainted.[65] Recitations of history are not uncommon in biblical tradition (e.g., Ezek 20:4–44; Neh 9:6–37; Psalms 78; 105; 106; 135; Jdt 5:5–21; Wis 10:1–12:27; 1 Macc 2:51–64), but none are so lengthy nor so exuberant about key individuals. Scholars have therefore looked elsewhere for comparisons.

Thomas R. Lee has influentially argued that this is an encomium for Simon II.[66] He distinguishes four main structural features in encomia and finds them represented here: *prooemium* (introduction; 44:1–15); *genos* (genealogy; 44:16–49:16); *praxeis* (deeds and virtues; 50:1–21); epilogue (50:22–24). The text's purpose is to celebrate the recently deceased Simon and to encourage his son (Onias III) to follow his example. This proposal has, however, been challenged.[67] The structure Lee delineates is debateable, both for encomia and for Ben Sira 44–50 (notice that Glicksman offered a different structure for the alleged encomium for wisdom discussed above). Lee's hypothesis is Simon-centric, ch. 50 being climactic and essential. However, ch. 50 has been seen by some as a mere 'appendix',[68] and Simon is not mentioned at all before this point. The historical recitation might have significance beyond simply introducing him. Burton L. Mack, for example, suggests that it functions as a 'mythic etiology of Second Temple Judaism'.[69]

Quite a different genre of human praise is found in Ecclesiastes. Ecclesiastes 1:12–2:24 has been likened to ancient Near Eastern royal autobiographies, typically monumental inscriptions intended as political propaganda to glorify and praise the king. Comparative texts have been adduced amongst Assyrian inscriptions and Egyptian testaments.[70]

---

[65] See discussion in Lindsey A. Askin, 'Beyond Encomium or Eulogy: The Role of Simon the High Priest in Ben Sira', *JAJ* 9.3 (2018): 344–365.

[66] Thomas R. Lee, *Studies in the Form of Sirach 44–50* (Atlanta, 1986).

[67] Askin, 'Beyond Encomium'.

[68] Patrick W. Skehan and Alexander A. Di Lella, *The Wisdom of Ben Sira: A New Translation, with Notes* (New York, 1987), 499.

[69] Burton L. Mack, *Wisdom and the Hebrew Epic: Ben Sira's Hymn in Praise of the Fathers* (Chicago, 1985), 6.

[70] Yee-Von Koh, *Royal Autobiography in the Book of Qoheleth* (Berlin, 2006).

Tremper Longman influentially suggested a comparison with 'fictional Akkadian autobiographies'.[71] Analysing fifteen texts alongside Ecclesiastes, he discerned a shared structure: self-identification, first-person account of accomplishments, conclusion. However, this structure is dubious, and Longman has been criticised for arbitrary classification of Akkadian texts and unpersuasive analysis of Ecclesiastes.[72]

Perhaps the most striking similarity is with West Semitic royal inscriptions.[73] These generally begin with a formulaic self-announcement: 'I [name] am king over [place]' (cf. Eccl 1:12). There follow stereotyped boasts of royal achievements, including building works and prosperity (2:4–8). The whole is hyperbolic and bombastic, peppered with exaltations of the speaker above his predecessors (1:16; 2:7, 9). These comparisons are revealing. The texts apparently share a royal ideology and pool of literary conventions. Significantly, the autobiographies generally function as propaganda and self-praise for the king. In Ecclesiastes, however, this is subverted, for the king's greatness and wisdom ultimately prove to be vanity (e.g., 1:17, 2:11, 15).

Praise of God

Finally, some sapiential texts (notably Ben Sira and Job) contain genres of praise to God. Ben Sira often draws on psalmic motifs and incorporates hymns. Ben Sira 18:1–7 exults that no one is able to fathom God's wonders; 39:12–35 avers that God created everything with a purpose; 51:1–12 thanks God for deliverance from enemies; and the Hebrew of ch. 51 includes further praises with incessant refrains modelled after Psalm 136.

In Job too, we find hymns of praise. Eliphaz (Job 5:8–13), Zophar (11:7–12) and Bildad (25:2–3) all employ conventional psalmic tropes. Job himself also draws on the genre but with subversion and parody.[74] The themes which traditionally elicit praise now convey terror, helplessness and indignation. For example, God's attention to humankind brings ecstatic wonder in Ps 8:5[4], but bitterness in Job 7:17–18. Like many psalms, Job cites the works of creation as evidence of God's supreme power (9:5–10). But this power is not to be celebrated. Rather, it reminds Job of his helplessness before his malevolent God (9:2–4,

[71] Tremper Longman III, *Fictional Akkadian Autobiography: A Generic and Comparative Study* (Winona Lake, 1991).
[72] Koh, *Royal Autobiography*, 107–112.
[73] Koh, *Royal Autobiography*.
[74] Katharine J. Dell, *The Book of Job as Sceptical Literature* (Berlin, 1991).

14–16). In the Psalms, birds, beasts, plants and fish are exhorted to praise God for his works (Ps 148:7–10). In Job too, they witness his works (12:7–10), but now these works are destructive and terrifying. Recognising the genre here can help us understand how Job twists it.

Genre manipulation is also evident in passages which invoke both psalmic and instructional genres; for example, the 'sapiential hymns' of Job 36:24–37:13 (a speech of Elihu) and Sir 42:15–43:33.[75] These passages contain elements conventional for hymns of praise: an exhortation to the self or others to praise (Job 36:24; Sir 42:15, 43:30), declarations of God's greatness (Job 36:26; Sir 43:5, 29), rhetorical questions (Job 36:29; Sir 42:25; 43:3, 28, 31), descriptions of God's mighty works (*passim*). They also contain elements familiar from instructional genres. The exhortations to praise assume an audience whom the speaker is instructing. Ben Sira begins by offering himself as a model of praise (42:15) and ends with detailed instructions to follow his example (43:30). Elihu's exhortation has a hint of warning: 'remember to extol' (36:24) rather than just 'extol'. It is conventional for praise hymns to follow the exhortation with *kî* ('because') and a reason (Exod 15:21; Ps 33:1–4; 81:1–4; 95:1–3; 96:1–4; 98:1; 149:1–4). Elihu offers an exhortation (Job 36:24) and reason (36:27) but between them interjects sapiential reflections.[76] Moreover, the theme of wisdom is prevalent. Elihu's hymn is prefaced by God as a teacher (36:22) and culminates with the disciplinary rod (*šēbet*; 37:13). In between, it muses on humanity's lack of understanding (36:26, 29; 37:5). Ben Sira extols God's all-surpassing knowledge (42:18–21) and concludes that 'to the godly he has given wisdom' (43:33b).

The hymns focus on God's majesty revealed through creation – a theme common to both psalms of praise (e.g., 104 and 148) and sapiential texts. The reader is exhorted to attend to creation (Job 37:2; Sir 43:11), and is treated to lavish, exuberant descriptions of cosmic occurrences. This brings an aesthetic dimension to human reflection on God. The contemplation engenders awe and wonder, in turn giving rise to praise. Carol Newsom even describes such contemplation as a 'spiritual discipline'.[77] Through a sophisticated mixing of genres, then, these poems become both 'an act of instruction and an act of praise'.[78]

---

[75] Newsom, *The Book of Job*, 220–233.
[76] Harold-Martin Wahl, *Der Gerechte Schöpfer: Eine Redaktions- Und Theologiegeschichtliche Untersuchung Der Elihureden – Hiob 32–37* (BZAW 207. Berlin, 2015), 113–114, n.94.
[77] Newsom, *The Book of Job*, 224, 231.
[78] Newsom, *The Book of Job*, 229.

GENRES OF COMPLAINT

Lament

If sapiential texts invoke praise, so too do they invoke lament. Ben Sira and Job again draw on psalmic genres but now to quite a different end. Ben Sira incorporates motifs reminiscent of lament psalms, noting that human life is transient (14:17–19; 18:8–10; cf. Pss 39:5–7[4–6]; 90:3–10) and that the dead cannot praise God (17:27–28; cf. Pss 6:6[5]; 30:10[9]; 88:11–13[10–12]). A more extended passage in 22:27–23:6 resembles psalms of individual lament (whilst also retaining sapiential flavour). The speaker petitions his 'God and Father' (Sir 23:4; cf. Ps 89:27[26]) to help him avoid sins, particularly desiring a guard on his mouth (Sir 22:27; cf. Pss 39:2[1]; 141.3) and defence against wrongful passions (Sir 23:6; cf. Ps 119:133). Assuming that sin brings hardship and defeat, he depicts his enemies rejoicing over him (Sir 23:3; cf. Pss 13:5[4]; 38:17[16]).

A later passage, 36:1–22, is similar to communal laments. The speaker urgently calls on God, opening with the abrupt imperative: 'Save us!' (cf., e.g., 54:1, 56:1, 140:1). He prays for the downfall of other nations (Sir 36:1–12; cf. Pss 79:6–7; 83) and concomitant exaltation of the chosen people (36:13–22), including a prayer for the holy city (36:18–19; Pss 51:20[18]; 74:2). God must act again as in Israel's past (Sir 36:4, 16, 20), to the end of his universal glorification (Sir 36:22; Ps 83:19[18]). Incorporating laments shifts Ben Sira's momentum from the cerebral to the emotional. The passages function as speech-acts, enacting psychological release for the speaker, engendering solidarity from the listener and provoking God's attention.

Lament is also found throughout Job and is sometimes considered determinative for its overall genre. Harmut Gese described Job as a 'paradigm of answered lament' (Klageerhörungsparadigma).[79] He argued that the original folktale of Job (retained in the prologue and epilogue) showed this paradigm operating via the act-consequence connection, in a basic pattern of distress, lament, response and restoration. The dialogues, however, complicate this and replace mechanical retribution with God's transcendence.

Claus Westermann considered Job a dramatisation of lament – not a reflection on suffering but an outpouring of it.[80] Job's words begin and

---

[79] Hartmut Gese, *Lehre und Wirklichkeit der alten Weisheit: Studien zu den Sprüchen Salomos und zu dem Buche Hiob* (Tübingen, 1958).
[80] Claus Westermann, *Der Aufbau des Buches Hiob* (Stuttgart, 1978).

end with laments (chs. 3 and 29–31), and his intervening speeches are dominated by the form. Westermann distinguished three parts in a lament – self-lament, lament about enemies, lament directed to God – all of them found in Job. The self-lament is an expression of sufferings, for example, descriptions of disease (7:4–6 and 30:27–30) and reflections on human finitude (7:6–10; 9:25–31; 10:18–22; 14:1–15). Job's human enemies are his erstwhile friends – both those with whom he altercates and his wider acquaintances. These enemies do not attack Job but disdain and reject him (6:14–20; 19:13–19; 30:1–15). Job does have an attacker, though: God. In a striking subversion of the genre, the lament directed to God becomes an accusation against God, the enemy (6:4; 7:12–21; 9:17–18; 16:9–17; 19:7–12). Other conventional features of lament psalms, viz., the affirmation of trust and vow to praise, make scarce appearance.

Legal Complaint

The complaints in Job evoke not just the cultic sphere of psalms but also the legal court. According to Heinz Richter, 'The all-pervasive basis of the drama of Job are the genres taken from law'.[81] Others confirm this pervasiveness through close linguistic studies of legal terminology[82] and comparison with ancient Near Eastern judicial texts.[83] Read as a lawsuit, a complex web of litigation emerges, in which God, Job and the friends are all periodically accuser and accused. The heavenly adversary (śāṭān) accuses Job of blasphemy and implicitly accuses God for blessing a blasphemer (1:9–11). When God removes Job's blessings, it seems from an earthly perspective that he has accused Job of wrongdoing. The friends (8:3–4; 11:6; 22:5–9) and Elihu (33:9–12; 34:5–12; 35:2–8) support these accusations, while Job asserts his innocence (27:2–6; 31). Job accuses God for launching false accusations and demands a trial (9:14–20; 13:3, 15–24; 23:2–17), with an arbiter to handle the case (9:33, 16:18–22, 19:25–27). When God does appear, Job concedes defeat (42:3–6), but God finally vindicates Job and accuses the friends (42:7–8).

Legal genres are invoked throughout Job. Such passages become performative – high-stakes speech acts with convulsive implications. Avi Schveka and Pierre van Hecke read Job 22:5–9 as

---

[81] Cited in Roland E. Murphy, *Wisdom Literature*, 17.
[82] Sylvia Scholnick, 'Lawsuit Drama in the Book of Job' (PhD diss., Brandeis University, 1976).
[83] F. Rachel Magdalene, *On the Scales of Righteousness: Neo-Babylonian Trial Law and the Book of Job* (Providence, 2007).

official litigation.[84] Here, Eliphaz files criminal charges against Job – a serious action in a legal system which heavily penalised false accusations. Job 31 presents an extensive oath of innocence, in which Job enumerates crimes and offers himself willingly for punishment if he has committed them, culminating with a plea for fair legal proceedings (vv. 35–37). Based on comparison with Akkadian legal texts, Michael Brennen Dick argues that this chapter 'follows the pattern of the defendant's appeal for a civic trial after pre-trial arbitration has failed'.[85] Choon Leong Seow compares it to a Hebrew inscription from Meṣad-Ḥashavyahu, in which the writer declares his innocence and recounts injustice he has suffered from a powerful adversary.[86] Framed as legal genres, these texts intend themselves as performative acts within the story-world. One might even say they turn the reader into a juror, forced to weigh the evidence.

CONCLUSION

This chapter has examined the multiple genres found in Proverbs, Job, Ecclesiastes, Ben Sira and Wisdom of Solomon. These genres are not just heuristic groupings of texts but communicative tools, positioning the reader vis-à-vis the text and providing conventions for interpretation and expectations about content. Sometimes texts subvert these expectations with communicative impact. The genres are signalled by constellations of features, working together to particular ends.

We have considered four clusters of genres, each with a different communicative intent. Genres of instruction (sayings, instructions, diatribe/protreptic and didactic narratives) persuade the reader to a particular course of action and develop their character. Genres of human reasoning (reflections and wisdom dialogues) catch the reader up in the intellectual process, entangling them in complex thought. Genres of praise (towards wisdom, humans and God) orientate readers outwards, uplifting them into admiration and exaltation. And genres of complaint (laments and legal complaints) ask readers to share with the speakers in anguish and adjudicate the injustice they see. Each book examined here incorporates a variety of these genres, which interact as

---

[84] Avi Shevka and Pierre van Hecke, 'The Metaphor of Criminal Charge as a Paradigm for the Conflict between Job and His Friends', *Ephemerides Theologicae Lovanienses* 90.1 (2014): 99–119.

[85] Michael Brennan Dick, 'The Legal Metaphor in Job 31', *CBQ* 41.1 (1979): 37.

[86] Choon Leong Seow, *Job 1–21: Interpretation and Commentary* (Grand Rapids, 2013), 60.

parts within a whole. Different books combine different genres in different proportions and different ways. We have considered the individual
genres here; it is the task of future research to analyse their interaction
in more detail.

Further Reading

Gammie, John G. 'Paraenetic Literature: Toward the Morphology of a Secondary
    Genre'. *Semeia* 50 (1990): 41–77.
Kynes, Will. *An Obituary for 'Wisdom Literature': The Birth, Death, and
    Intertextual Reintegration of a Biblical Corpus*. Oxford: 2019.
Murphy, Roland E. *Wisdom Literature: Job, Proverbs, Ruth, Canticles,
    Ecclesiastes and Esther*. Forms of the Old Testament Literature. Grand
    Rapids: 1981.
Nel, P. J. 'The Genres of Biblical Wisdom Literature'. *JNWSL* 9 (1981): 129–142.
Newsom, Carol A. 'Spying out the Land: A Report from Genology'. Pages
    437–450 in *Seeking out the Wisdom of the Ancients: Essays Offered to
    Honor Michael V. Fox on the Occasion of His Sixty-Fifth Birthday*. Edited
    by Ronald L. Troxel, Kelvin G. Friebel and Dennis Robert Magary. Winona
    Lake: 2005.
    The Book of Job: A Contest of Moral Imaginations. Oxford: 2009.
Perdue, Leo G. *The Sword and the Stylus: An Introduction to Wisdom in the
    Age of Empires*. Grand Rapids: 2008.
Weeks, Stuart. 'Wisdom, Form, and Genre'. Pages 161–180 in *Was There a
    Wisdom Tradition? New Prospects in Israelite Wisdom Studies*. Edited by
    M. Sneed. Ancient Israel and Its Literature 23. Atlanta: 2015.

4 The Literary Context(s) and Development of Wisdom Literature in Ancient Israel (with Special Reference to Proverbs)

KNUT M. HEIM

The three core books making up the so-called wisdom literature of the OT/HB are traditionally designated Proverbs, Job and Ecclesiastes. In a recent monograph, Will Kynes has however demonstrated that the very notion of the so-called Wisdom Literature is a relatively recent scholarly convention that can in fact be dated to the publication of Johann Friedrich Bruch's *Die Weisheits-Lehre der Hebräer* in 1851.[1] Kynes has shown that Bruch's own convictions and interests influenced his identification and characterisation of Israelite 'wisdom' as secular. Bruch held to 'the rationalist commitment to Protestant liberty, which involved the freedom to examine critically all truths, including religious ones, and suspicion of ecclesiastical authority'.[2] Such sentiments guided liberals like Bruch as they 'sought to address contemporary cultural and intellectual questions in order to demonstrate religion's continuing relevance' and so Bruch's 'description of "the wise" and the literature that they produced, particularly free thought and distaste for religious authority', contributed to his efforts to defend the relevance of religion in his own day.[3] Therefore, Bruch's characterisation of the wise reflects philosophical ideals of his own time remarkably well: 'the *non-theocratic spirit*, blowing already in multiple texts of the Old Testament, ought to have made one aware that ... there was no lack of men who found *no satisfaction in the religious institutions* of their nation. These men therefore sought other ways – namely, *the way of free thinking* – to gain answers about the questions that moved them'.[4] Bruch's historical reconstruction

---

[1] Johann Friedrich Bruch, *Weisheits-Lehre der Hebräer: Ein Beitrag zur Geschichte der Philosophie* (Strasbourg, 1851). See Will Kynes, *An Obituary for 'Wisdom Literature': The Birth, Death, and Intertextual Reintegration of a Biblical Corpus* (Oxford, 2019), 82–98.

[2] Kynes, *An Obituary for 'Wisdom Literature'*, 86.

[3] Kynes, *An Obituary for 'Wisdom Literature'*, 86.

[4] The quote is from Kynes' translation; see Kynes, *An Obituary for 'Wisdom Literature'*, 95, emphases added. The German is given in Kynes, *An Obituary for 'Wisdom Literature'*, 95–96, n.23.

of the emergence of wisdom thought in Israel identifies Solomon's example
of 'indifference to the theocratic institutions of the nation, aversion to its
exclusive particularism, and patience with foreigners' as the inspiration for
a 'new class of wisdom men' to develop Israel's wisdom tradition.[5]

Kynes' historical meta-criticism exposes that secularising tenden-
cies in nineteenth-century Europe prompted an interpretation of the
books of Proverbs, Job and Ecclesiastes as the product of an Israelite
wisdom tradition which conveniently reflected ideals and values that
were popular at the time.[6] Our survey below will demonstrate that this
influence extended also to scholarly reflections on the origin and thus
the literary context and development of the wisdom tradition and its
representative literature, notably in Proverbs. The first section of this
chapter then will explore literary contexts within and between the
various parts of the book(s) of Proverbs (focusing on the nature of the
proverbial sayings of chapters 10–29), looking at the phenomenon and
significance of proverbial clusters. These evaluations in turn influence
conclusions as to theological developments across the book of
Proverbs and beyond into other wisdom literature. A clear pattern
emerged in twentieth-century scholarly work: the literary contexts
in which the so-called wisdom literature arose were secular; in its
early manifestations, such literature was secular; it only acquired its
present theological contents at a later time, through lengthy literary
developments. This model held the field for a long time but has been
challenged in recent years as will be shown, leading to fresh paradigms
in the current debate.

LITERARY CONTEXTS AND PROVERBIAL CLUSTERS
IN PROVERBS

The materials in the proverb collections of the book of Proverbs (chapters 10–29) at first glance seem to consist of self-contained individual
proverbs which appear to have been added randomly one after another.
Consequently, there does not seem to be any literary context or development of thought in these chapters. Nonetheless, from the second half
of the twentieth century onwards, there has been a lively debate
regarding whether or not such literary contexts exist and what their

---

[5] Kynes, *An Obituary for 'Wisdom Literature'*, 97, with reference to Bruch, *Weisheits-
    Lehre*, 47–48.
[6] Kynes, *An Obituary for 'Wisdom Literature'*, 98–99.

significance for interpretation should be,[7] a debate which continues to the present day.[8] A number of studies appeared in the second half of the last century which argued for the existence of literary contexts and their significance for interpretation in the book of Proverbs. Such arguments typically favoured one particular kind of structural arrangement, such as (a) chapter divisions,[9] (b) educational sayings,[10] (c) paronomasia and catchwords,[11] (d) theological reinterpretations,[12] (e) proverbial

---

[7] Cf. the review of the relevant secondary literature until the year 2000 in Knut M. Heim, *Like Grapes of Gold Set in Silver: An Interpretation of Proverbial Clusters in Proverbs 10:1–22:16* (Berlin, 2001), 7–19, 27–66.

[8] Cf. Christine Roy Yoder, *Proverbs* (Nashville, 2009), 110; with Bernd Ulrich Schipper, *Proverbs 1–15: A Commentary on the Book of Proverbs 1:1–15:33* (Minneapolis, 2019), 354.

[9] For examples, see Ruth Scoralick, *Einzelspruch und Sammlung* (Berlin; New York: 1995), 96–97, nn.15–18 and 147–156. Cf. also the discussion in Heim, *Like Grapes of Gold*, 27–28. Cf. also Patrick William Skehan, 'A Single Editor for the Whole Book of Proverbs', *CBQ* 10 (1948), 115–130; John Goldingay, 'The Arrangement of Sayings in Proverbs 10–15', *JSOT* 61 (1994), 75–83; R. Norman Whybray, *The Composition of the Book of Proverbs*, JSOTS 168 (Sheffield, 1994). More recently, the chapter divisions have also been accepted by Bernd Schipper (*Proverbs 1–15*: esp. 343–344).

[10] Luis Alonso Schökel et al., *Proverbios* (Madrid, 1984), 255–257, 299, 326, but cf. 335; Arndt Meinhold, *Die Sprüche*, 2 vols. (Zürich, 1991); Crawford Howell Toy, *A Critical and Exegetical Commentary on the Book of Proverbs* (New York, 1899); Gerrit Wildeboer, *Die Sprüche* (Freiburg, 1897), 31, 39. Cf. Heim, *Like Grapes of Gold*, 28–30. See also Hans-Jürgen Hermisson, *Studien zur israelitischen Spruchweisheit* (Neukirchen-Vluyn, 1968), 174–179. Hermisson included 12:1 and 14:2 among such introductory educational sayings. R. Norman Whybray, 'Thoughts on the Composition of Proverbs 10–29', in *Priests, Prophets and Scribes*, ed. Eugene Ulrich et al. (Sheffield, 1992), 112–114. Goldingay, 'The Arrangement of Sayings in Proverbs 10–15', 75–83.

[11] G. Boström, *Paronomasi i den äldre hebraisca Maschalliteraturen* (Lund, 1928); Hermisson, *Studien zur israelitischen Spruchweisheit*, 171–183; Steven Perry, 'Structural Patterns in Prov 10:1–22:16' (PhD diss., University of Texas at Austin, 1987); Jutta Krispenz, *Spruchkompositionen im Buch Proverbia*, Bd 349 (Frankfurt am Main; New York, 1989). For a critique, see Heim, *Like Grapes of Gold*, 30–33.

[12] The following scholars took a diachronic perspective: Hans Heinrich Schmid, *Wesen und Geschichte der Weisheit: Eine Untersuchung zur altorientalischen und israelitischen Weisheitsliteratur* (Berlin, 1966); William McKane, *Prophets and Wise Men* (London, 1983); William McKane, *Proverbs: A New Approach* (Philadelphia, 1970). By contrast, other scholars argued that theological statements created a hermeneutically significant literary context for the interpretation of individual proverbs: R. Norman Whybray, 'Yahweh-Sayings and Their Contexts in Proverbs 10,1–22,16', in *La sagesse de l'Ancien Testament*, ed. Gilbert, vol. 51 of *Bibliotheca Ephemeridium Theologicarum Lovaniensium* (Leuven, 1979), 153–165; Magne Saebø, 'From Collections to Book – A New Approach to the History of Tradition and Redaction of the Book of Proverbs', in *Proceedings of the 9th World Congress of Jewish Studies, Jerusalem, Aug 1985*, eds. Moshe Goshen-Gottein and David Assaf (Jerusalem, 1986), 99–106.

pairs[13] and (f) proverbial strings.[14] The influence of these studies became increasingly visible in commentaries written on the book of Proverbs, notably in those by R. van Leeuwen (1997),[15] where he pays particular attention to literary contexts in Proverbs 25–29, and D. Garrett (1993),[16] who argues that emphasis should be placed on the forms of the proverbial sayings rather than on their thematic content.[17]

The most comprehensive exploration of literary contexts in Prov 10:1–22:16 is found in Heim's monograph on proverbial clusters from 2001.[18] Heim's monograph made three distinct contributions to the debate. First, he developed a theory of reading proverbs in a collection, with the idea that a collection provides a *literary performance context* with hermeneutical impact.[19] Second, he closed a gap in the literature by providing a methodologically consistent and carefully argued basis for what until then had been an intuitive assumption: that characterisations like wise and righteous, on the one hand, and fool and wicked, on the other, are 'coreferential'; they refer to one and the same kind of person, even though they may be evaluated with different criteria – intellectual evaluation in the case of wise and fool, moral criteria in the case of righteous and wicked.[20] Third, he built on previous work to establish more integrated yet flexible criteria for determining literary contexts, which he titled 'proverbial clusters'.[21]

Heim illustrated his approach with an analogy. The interpretation of intentional groupings of proverbs is like eating a bunch of grapes: the cluster of grapes (= proverb cluster) forms an organic whole which is

---

[13] Theodore A. Hildebrandt, 'Proverbial Pairs: Compositional Units in Proverbs 10–29', *JBL* 107 (1988), 207–224.

[14] Theodore A. Hildebrandt, 'Proverbial Strings: Cohesion in Proverbs 10', *GTJ* 11.2 (1990), 171–185.

[15] Raymond C. Van Leeuwen, 'The Book of Proverbs', in *New Interpreter's Bible* (Nashville, 1997), 19–264.

[16] Duane A. Garrett, *Proverbs, Ecclesiastes, Song of Songs* (Nashville, 1993).

[17] Otto Plöger, *Sprüche Salomos* (Neukirchen-Vluyn, 1984), xix–xx, cf. 118. Cf. also Otto Plöger, 'Zur Auslegung der Sentenzensammlungen des Proverbienbuches', in *Probleme biblischer Theologie: Gerhard von Rad zum 70. Geburtstag*, ed. Wolff (Munich, 1971); Alonso Schökel et al., *Proverbios*, 255. Meinhold, *Sprüche*; Garrett, *Proverbs, Ecclesiastes, Song of Songs*; Roland E. Murphy, *Proverbs* (WBC 22 Nashville, 1998); Leo G. Perdue, *Proverbs* (IBC. Louisville, 2000). For detailed reviews of these, see Heim, *Like Grapes of Gold*, 36–49.

[18] Heim, *Like Grapes of Gold*. The study by Scoralick, which has similar aims to those of Heim, only covers Proverbs 10–15 (Scoralick, *Einzelspruch und Sammlung*).

[19] Heim, *Like Grapes of Gold*, 69–75. Cf. Barbara Kirshenblatt-Gimblett, 'Toward a Theory of Proverb Meaning', *Proverbium* 22 (1973), 821–827.

[20] Heim, *Like Grapes of Gold*, 77–103.

[21] Heim, *Like Grapes of Gold*, 105–108.

more than the sum of the individual parts, linked by small twiglets
(= linking devices), yet each grape (= proverb) can be consumed individu-
ally. Although grapes contain juice from the same vine, each tastes
slightly different, and so it does not matter in which sequence the grapes
are consumed. Yet eating them together enhances the flavour of each
and enriches the culinary experience. For this reason, Heim prefers the
term 'proverb cluster' rather than more traditional designations like
group, section, unit, etc., in order to indicate the organic rather than
linear arrangement within given groupings of proverbs.[22] The twiglets
which connect them are repetitions in the textual environment, such as
repetitions of consonants, word roots, words and synonyms. Heim's
volume then provides interpretations of proverbial clusters in Prov
10:1–22:16.[23] He ends his study with the recommendation that the
printed editions of modern Bibles should adopt a new layout which
reflects the proverbial clusters he identified.[24]

The most comprehensive critique of Heim's proposal is that of
Michael Fox. In a six-page review,[25] he presented a sustained and comprehensive critique of Heim's theory in which he accused Heim of bias,
idiosyncrasy and esotericism and of a Christian preacherly hermeneutic.[26] These points were, in turn, countered by Ernest Lucas.[27] Fox
also noted that the proverbs collections cover a limited number of
subjects: and for this reason; the kinds of repetitions that Heim
employed as arguments for the existence of clusters are so frequent that
it is easy to find correspondences between proverbs even when these
may have been completely unintended. Heim himself was aware of this
danger,[28] as Lucas noted, and adopted 'linking devices' rather than
boundary markers as criteria for delimitation.[29] Fox also argued that
the history of scholarly interpretation of Prov 10:1–22:16 goes against
Heim's identification of numerous clusters, and yet scholarly biases and
trends change and a growing number of scholars were beginning to see

---

[22] Heim, *Like Grapes of Gold*, 107.
[23] Heim, *Like Grapes of Gold*, 111–311.
[24] Heim, *Like Grapes of Gold*, 316–319.
[25] Michael V. Fox, 'Like Grapes of Gold Set in Silver: An Interpretation of Proverbial
Clusters in Proverbs 10:1–22:16', *HS* 44 (2003), 267–272.
[26] Fox maintained his position in his 2009 commentary on Proverbs 10–31, being critical
of 'totalizing approaches to the question of literary context in the proverb collections
and preferring "a sweet disorder"' in the materials, despite some groupings (Fox,
Proverbs 10–31, 477–478).
[27] Cf. also Ernest C. Lucas, *Proverbs* (Grand Rapids, 2015), 19–21.
[28] Heim, *Like Grapes of Gold*, 55–57, 107–108, etc.
[29] Lucas, *Proverbs*, 20.

intentional editorial links in these materials even before Heim's work appeared.[30]

Many scholars however took up Heim's views or variants on them in commentaries which appeared between 2004 and 2019. Bruce Waltke's two-volume commentary (2004; 2005), for example, adopted Heim's proposal that the main characterisations in the book of Proverbs – 'wise and righteous', on the one hand, and 'fool and wicked', on the other – are coreferential.[31] His criteria for identifying literary contexts are those identified by others, such as inclusio, catchwords, structural patterns like chiasm, as well as logical and thematic connections.[32] As Lucas has observed, Waltke's subunits in Prov 10:1–22:16 'more-or-less correspond to what Heim calls "clusters"'.[33] Waltke's overall approach to the interpretive significance of literary contexts is encapsulated in the following programmatic statement: 'Construing Solomon's memorable aphorisms as originally intended to stand on their own two feet and secondarily to be collected as literature giving them contexts, I interpret them both ways.'[34]

Waltke differed from Fox in his 2009 commentary in finding hermeneutically significant literary contexts almost everywhere, while for Fox these were quite rare. Fox found a 'fair number of proverb pairs', but not all of them are hermeneutically significant.[35] Similarly, while proverbial clusters are 'the most important principle of grouping in Prov 10–29', the clusters Fox talks about are *thematic* clusters,[36] and again these are few in number; and even so, these proverb clusters are rather loose literary arrangements which emerge from an editor or compiler's 'associative thinking', and this 'accounts for most of the phenomena sometimes thought to indicate editorial designs'.[37] Fox regularly commented on the train of thought where such associative thinking takes

---

[30] Another critique of Heim's proposal was made by Tremper Longman III, *Proverbs* (Grand Rapids, 2006), 38–42. He claimed that 'twice-told' proverbs (sayings which occur in two slightly different forms at two points in the book of Proverbs) were randomly placed, against which Heim argued in a subsequent monograph on variant repetitions in Proverbs (See Knut M. Heim, *Poetic Imagination in Proverbs: Variant Repetitions and the Nature of Poetry*, BBRSup 4, [Grand Rapids, 2013], 157–161). He also stressed the subjectivity of the exercise of finding groupings and questioned the hermeneutical significance of proverbial clusters, to which Heim also responded in his monograph.

[31] Waltke, *Proverbs 1–15*, 93–94.

[32] Bruce K. Waltke, *The Book of Proverbs: Chapters 1–15* (Grand Rapids, 2004), 47.

[33] Lucas, *Proverbs*, 16.

[34] Waltke, *Proverbs 1–15*, 21; cf. 46–47.

[35] Fox, *Proverbs 10–31*, 478.

[36] Fox, *Proverbs 10–31*, 478–479.

[37] Fox, *Proverbs 10–31*, 480.

place, but this is a far cry from the hermeneutical significance which other recent commentators assign to literary contexts. Rather, he rejected construals of larger structures with intricate designs that are considered hermeneutically significant.[38] The following illustration is worth including for its evocative beauty: 'A proverb is like a jewel, and the book of Proverbs is like a heap of jewels. Indeed, it is a heap of different *kinds* of jewels. Is it really such a loss if they are not all laid out in pretty, symmetric designs or divided into neat little piles? The heap itself has the lushness of profusion and the charm of a "sweet disorder in the dress"'.[39]

In spite of Fox's insistence on glorious disorder in the proverb collections of the book of Proverbs, however, there are occasions where literary context is of at least some hermeneutical significance. This is also and especially true for religious proverbs (which will be central to our discussion below).[40] In fact, Fox went even further and drew attention to the circumstance that the contextual interplay created through the inclusion and placement of 'Yahweh' proverbs has a hermeneutical impact not only on their immediate literary context but also beyond, even to the level of whole collections and the book as a whole. Nonetheless, they are 'but part of the natural effort of the compilers to provide a balanced selection of counsels and principles'.[41]

Christine Yoder's 2009 commentary by and large treats the material in Prov 10:1–22:16 as a collection of randomly arranged individual proverbs.[42] The material in Proverbs 25–27 contains some intentional arrangements, mostly two or three verses in length, without overarching structural progress.[43] The same is largely true for Proverbs 28–29, apart from the circumstance that there is a thematic concern for just government.[44] Nonetheless, Yoder made a distinctive contribution to the debate over context by drawing attention to the significance of a more diffuse kind of literary context for interpretation; she claimed, 'the extent to which the proverbs seem for the most part disconnected from literary and oral contexts sharpens the significance and effects of context itself'.[45] Consequently, such 'decontextualized' proverbs require

---

[38] Fox, *Proverbs 10–31*, 481.
[39] Fox, *Proverbs 10–31*, 481. The quotation is from the opening line of Robert Herrick's poem 'Delight in Disorder'.
[40] Fox, *Proverbs 10–31*, 482.
[41] Fox, *Proverbs 10–31*, 481.
[42] Yoder, *Proverbs*, 110.
[43] Yoder, *Proverbs*, 245–246.
[44] Yoder, *Proverbs*, 263–264.
[45] Yoder, *Proverbs*, 110.

readers 'to imagine appropriate contexts of use'.[46] Borrowing a meta-phor from E. B. White, she illustrated such a reader-oriented construc-tion of context with the image of a mosaic,[47] a helpful comparison to which I will return.

The 2015 commentary by Ernest Lucas follows Heim and Waltke in identifying numerous proverbial clusters throughout Prov 10:1–22:16.[48] Ryan O'Dowd's 2017 commentary also adopts Heim's proposal to take literary contexts in Prov 10:1–22:16 as hermeneutically significant.[49] Variant repetitions, by contrast, evoke in him the impression of 'sense-less repetition'.[50] In Proverbs 10–29, there are 'many places where proverbs have been gathered in pairs or smaller groups, usually around common sounds or common themes. The editing style appears light-handed, so to speak, like the work of a careful and mature artist', and he identifies 'many of these signs of artistry' in Prov 10:1–22:16.[51] In Proverbs 25–29, he identifies 'a breadth and variety of sayings that seems random at the same time that the chapters show numerous signs of artistry, careful editing, and repetition'.[52]

The first volume of Bernd Schipper's 2018 commentary, translated into English in 2019, also assigns hermeneutical significance to literary contexts.[53] Drawing on the work of Snell (1993) and Heim (2013), variant repetitions play an essential role in Schipper's reconstruction of the composition of these chapters: 'twice-told proverbs reflect a literary process in which individual proverbs were applied to different contexts', a method of contextualisation which used small changes to integrate repeated proverbs with their new contextual environments.[54] And since Yahweh-sayings have been integrated into units of two, three and more sayings, and since it is impossible to detect diachronic devel-opments in these arrangements, 'it is *no longer* possible to speak of a

---

[46] Yoder, *Proverbs*, 110.

[47] Yoder, *Proverbs*, 111.

[48] Lucas, *Proverbs*, esp. 15–22.

[49] Ryan O'Dowd, *Proverbs* (Grand Rapids, 2017), 31.

[50] 'Variant repetitions' refer to proverbs which occur in slightly different forms in two or more places in the book of Proverbs; see, e.g., O'Dowd, *Proverbs*, 175.

[51] O'Dowd, *Proverbs*, 176.

[52] O'Dowd, *Proverbs*, 179.

[53] Bernd Ulrich Schipper, *Sprüche (Proverbia) 1–15* (Göttingen, 2018); Schipper, *Proverbs 1–15*.

[54] Schipper, *Proverbs 1–15*, 342–344, quotation on page 352. Twice-told proverbs belong to an elaborate and extensive editorial technique of variant repetitions that permeates the entire book of Proverbs, as Daniel C. Snell, *Twice-Told Proverbs and the Composition of the Book of Proverbs* (Winona Lake, 1993); and Heim, *Poetic Imagination*, have shown.

later "theologizing" of older material or even of a theological redaction of Proverbs 10–15',[55] and the same is true for the collection as a whole. Theological concerns were present from the start.[56] The artful combination of individual proverbs in Prov 10:1–22:16 formed them into a masterful literary composition.[57] What is more, the individual chapters in Prov 10:1–22:16 and the collection as a whole are 'masterful compositions that do not readily reveal prior stages of literary development'.[58]

These comments by Schipper lead to the second section of this overview which is to do with the debate over the secular/theological development of the proverbial sayings. However, to conclude this section, I wish to revisit Yoder's illustration of proverb collections as literary mosaics, distinguishing the different pieces (proverbs) not only by colour, as she does, but also by shape and placement.[59] Viewing the literary mosaic (= proverb collection) up close, we focus on each proverb, then on those immediately around it, noting the ways in which the shapes and colours are distinct from one another and observing how they interact. From a step or two back, however, we notice parts of the mosaic that contain pieces which are both different and alike. They are alike in that they share the same colour (corresponding to shared contextual features like linking devices at the literary level). They are different because they are cut into different shapes (corresponding to different thematic contents at the literary level). Yet once we take another step or two back, we eventually gain a perspective where we recognise that individual proverbs of the same colour cluster together. They have been placed into the same areas (corresponding to proverbial clusters at the literal level), so that the bits of polished colour blur into larger portions and begin to form distinguishable parts of an entire scene, different from what any of the pieces standing alone resemble, yet together making vital contributions to the literary mosaic.

THE DEVELOPMENT OF (SECULAR/THEOLOGICAL) IDEAS IN PROVERBS AND BEYOND

The mid-1960s saw ideas about the so-called wisdom literature's secular origin influence all manner of scholarly proposals regarding its social context and literary development. Our first example is H. H. Schmid's

---

[55] Schipper, *Proverbs 1–15*, 343. The phrase in italics has been slightly adapted to reflect Schipper's German more closely.
[56] Schipper, *Proverbs 1–15*, 343.
[57] Schipper, *Proverbs 1–15*, 352–354.
[58] Schipper, *Proverbs 1–15*, 354.
[59] Yoder, *Proverbs*, 111.

influential monograph *Wesen und Geschichte der Weisheit* from 1966. He posited that in its early phase, 'genuine' wisdom had understood the connection on the basis of historical events observed within the context of a belief in an ordered world. It remained flexible, depending on actual historical circumstances. In a second phase, however, such observations were systematised into scholastic and dogmatic beliefs which divorced the connection from historical points of reference and transformed wisdom itself into an unhistorical system of rules without exceptions. For Schmid, the perception of a connection between attitudes and their consequences in Israelite wisdom has at times become an axiomatic doctrine that demands absolute consent, as, for example, in Proverbs 10–15, which he saw as part of this late systematising stage: 'The juxtaposition of 184 verses which almost exclusively mention positive consequences for the righteous and bad consequences for the wicked appears to suggest that their compiler, at least, held to a doctrine of retribution'.[60] Positing an 'older wisdom' in Proverbs 10–29 overall, he identifies Proverbs 25–27 as the oldest stratum in the book, which he characterises as 'the most worldly' or secular of the sub-collections.[61] By contrast, Proverbs 1–9 and Proverbs 10–15 represent wisdom thought in its second stage, which theologised the connection between deeds and their consequences.[62] In Schmid's reconstruction, the tendency to recast the 'genuine wisdom-oriented insights and formulations' of the first stage of wisdom thinking into a 'systematizing doctrine of wisdom' at its second stage inevitably led to a 'crisis of wisdom' that eventually pro-voked an 'open conflict' that can be seen in the wisdom-critical writings of the books of Job and Ecclesiastes, which represent the third stage of wisdom's development:[63] 'this kind of wisdom is no longer genuine wisdom …. It is against this rigid worldview that Qoheleth reacts'.[64]

Our second example comes from the work of William McKane. In his volume *Prophets and Wise Men* from 1965, he assumed a secular origin of wisdom in Israel at the royal court in Jerusalem: 'The Israelite wisdom literature is, for the most part, a product not of full-time men of letters or academics, but a production of men of affairs in high places of state.'[65] He developed his views in his Proverbs commentary

---

[60] Schmid, *Wesen und Geschichte der Weisheit*, 164.
[61] Schmid, *Wesen und Geschichte der Weisheit*, 145–146.
[62] Schmid, *Wesen und Geschichte der Weisheit*, 146–149, 49–63.
[63] Schmid, *Wesen und Geschichte der Weisheit*, 173–196, here 173.
[64] Schmid, *Wesen und Geschichte der Weisheit*, 194.
[65] McKane, *Prophets and Wise Men*, 44. Cf. R. Norman Whybray, *The Book of Proverbs: A Survey of Modern Study* (Leiden, 1995), 21, 22.

of 1970.[66] Here he argued for the secular origin and subsequent theological reinterpretation of Proverbs 1–9: 'the Instruction which is originally, in Egypt if not in Israel, a means of educating officials, becomes in Israel a method of generalized mundane instruction and thereafter a way of inculcating Yahwistic piety'.[67] With regard to most of the 'sentence literature' of Proverbs 10–29, which he considered the oldest stratum in the book, he developed a three-class system of proverbs which originate in subsequent historical phases and also display a development from secular to theological. He identified Class A sentences as the earliest proverbs which 'are set in the framework of old wisdom and are concerned with the education of the individual for a successful and harmonious life'. Subsequently, Class B sentences were introduced, and these are proverbs which have an ethical orientation and are concerned with the community. For the most part, they describe the harmful effect of anti-social behaviour on the community. Finally, Class C sentences were added, and these are proverbs with God-language or other vocabulary 'expressive of a moralism which derives from Yahwistic piety'. He explained: 'class C material represents a reinterpretation of class A material and a later stage in the history of the Old Testament wisdom tradition'.[68] McKane's reconstruction highlights the secular nature and contextual origin of Israel's early wisdom and its gradual theological development, visible in distinct literary forms. In this reconstruction, he did not consider the literary arrangement of the proverbs; in fact, his commentary reorders them according to his own scheme.

The general trend then in the study of the so-called wisdom literature has followed the patterns of Schmid and McKane, positing that wisdom in Israel was originally irreligious or derived from non-Israelite religious convictions and arose in a secular social location. It then underwent a theological development that can be read off of a variety of literary and conceptual developments that have been proposed.[69] In the following paragraphs, I will review the work of four scholars who have departed from this pattern.

Until recently, a rare exception to the debate concerning the theological component of the pattern has been the work of Leo Perdue,

---

[66] McKane, *Proverbs*.
[67] McKane, *Proverbs*, 10.
[68] McKane, *Proverbs*, 10.
[69] See Norman Whybray's magisterial survey of the modern study of the book of Proverbs in which he identifies similar trends across the work of approximately twenty-five scholars (Whybray, *Proverbs*).

beginning with a 1977 monograph entitled *Wisdom and Cult*.[70] He
dated Proverbs 1–9 and 10–31 in the pre-exilic period[71] and concluded
from an analysis of Prov 3:9–10 that it is 'obvious' that 'the sage and his
students are seen as functioning members of the cultic community'.[72]
In his discussion of Proverbs 10–31, he analysed references to sacrifice
and prayer (15:8, 29; 17:1; 21:3; 21:27; 28:9), concluding that, though few
in number, they nonetheless offer reliable information on the views of
the sages regarding the cultic aspects of their religion.[73] This led him to
conclude that 'the traditional wise regarded the realm of the cult to be
an important compartment within the orders of reality', and for this
reason it 'merited sapiential scrutiny and demanded sagacious participation'.[74] In subsequent publications, Perdue also sought to demonstrate the importance of theology in the wisdom literature,[75] but his
work remained an outlier in scholarly debates. Whybray correctly noted
that 'Perdue's work deserves more consideration than it has received',[76]
and it is now becoming clear why Perdue's contribution has been neglected. His insights did not align with the scholarly paradigm of wisdom
literature's secularity.

The only book-length study of the compositional history of the book
of Proverbs, Norman Whybray's *The Composition of the Book of
Proverbs*, from 1994,[77] departs from the literary development component of the pattern. His investigation led him to conclude that 'it is not
possible to date different parts of the book by their contents, points of
view, theology or literary form'.[78] Furthermore, he also noted that it is
now generally acknowledged that 'the individual proverb and the longer
wisdom poem were two distinctive genres which continued to be
employed simultaneously in the ancient Near East from early until
quite late times'.[79] In his review of scholarly literature on the dates of
the various parts of the book of Proverbs, he therefore concluded that 'to

---

[70] Leo G. Perdue, *Wisdom and Cult: A Critical Analysis of the Views of Cult in the
Wisdom Literatures of Israel and the Ancient Near East* (Missoula, 1977).
[71] Perdue, *Wisdom and Cult*, 143–144.
[72] Perdue, *Wisdom and Cult*, 146.
[73] Perdue, *Wisdom and Cult*, 155–165.
[74] Perdue, *Wisdom and Cult*, 362.
[75] Leo G. Perdue, *Wisdom and Creation: The Theology of Wisdom Literature* (Nashville,
1994); Leo G. Perdue, *Wisdom Literature: A Theological History* (Louisville, 2007).
[76] Whybray, *Proverbs*, 135.
[77] Whybray, *The Composition of the Book of Proverbs*.
[78] Whybray, *The Composition of the Book of Proverbs*, quoted in slightly adapted form
in Whybray, *Proverbs*, 156.
[79] Whybray, *The Composition of the Book of Proverbs*, 164.

judge this instructional material as late because of its form is mistaken: there is evidence from other wisdom literatures that instructions did not necessarily succeed sentence literature chronologically but could be contemporary with it'.[80] His results challenge many of the various relative dates that have been assigned to different parts of the book of Proverbs in order to posit literary developments in the book. They also challenge the idea that theological re-interpretations can be read off such literary developments.

The most extensive exploration of the social and theological context of the book of Proverbs is Katharine Dell's monograph *The Book of Proverbs in Social and Theological Context* (2006),[81] which combines the concerns raised in the work of Perdue and Whybray. She explores wisdom's social context, its theological identity and its relationship with other parts of the Old Testament.[82] In relation to the secular/theological debate, Dell examined how integrated religious materials were with other materials, especially in Proverbs 1–9. An analysis of the figure of personified wisdom, references to Yahweh and the religious concept of the fear of Yahweh suggested that 'structural integrity was imparted by the often interchangeable figures of Yahweh and Wisdom, and religious elements were seen to exist comfortably alongside more general ethical and educational concerns'.[83] The purposeful distribution of Yahweh proverbs in Proverbs 10–31, for example, their juxtaposition to sayings about the king, also suggested that 'the religious elements were integral, probably belonging to a formative stage of the material rather than to a later redaction'.[84]

In her review of the scholarly debate over the place of theology in wisdom thought, Dell found the ideas of creation and order to be key ingredients, with creation theology providing a strong link with the theology of other parts of the Old Testament.[85] Dell also found sufficient evidence of legal, cultic and prophetic influences to conclude that, from the start, wisdom may have been more integrated with the rest of

---

[80] Whybray, *Proverbs: A Survey*, 156–157.
[81] Katharine J. Dell, *The Book of Proverbs in Social and Theological Context* (Cambridge, 2006).
[82] Dell, *Proverbs in Social and Theological Context*, 2–3.
[83] Dell, *Proverbs in Social and Theological Context*, 90–124, quotation from the chapter summary on page 92.
[84] Dell, *Proverbs in Social and Theological Context*, esp. 108–117, quotation from the chapter summary on page 92.
[85] Dell, *Proverbs in Social and Theological Context*, 125–154; cf. summary on page 93.

the Old Testament than commonly recognised.[86] In conclusion, 'Wisdom represents a mainstream tradition within Old Testament life and thought. Both the social context(s) and theology of the book of Proverbs can be successfully integrated in relation to other known contexts of social functions and theological expression'.[87] Dell's work presents the most sustained critique of the aspect of the literary and theological development in the scholarly pattern we have observed. Her proposal that the ethical concerns raised in the book of Proverbs indicate 'a wider educational context' makes another important contribution.[88]

Finally, Heim's monograph *Poetic Imagination in Proverbs* (2013) is the most comprehensive study of poetic parallelism and variant repetitions in the book of Proverbs. His focus was not on questions of social context, dating, theology or literary development, but several insights resulting from his work are relevant. The repetition of similar verses in slightly altered form is a pervasive feature of the book involving more than 223 of its 915 verses, almost a quarter of the material. With very few exceptions, these repeated proverbs were contextualised, that is, they were adapted to link them with their various contextual environments.[89] An exploration of their literary contexts enables 'an analysis of what may have prompted their placement or repetition in their present locations and what may have shaped a particular variant differently from another'.[90] Particularly instructive are 'incidents in which features that distinguish one variant from others in a set find echoes in the surrounding materials'.[91] Heim presented a table which lists all sets of variant repetitions in the book of Proverbs and indicates the likely direction of borrowing based on these criteria.[92] Their distribution reveals important insights into the redaction of Proverbs 1–9.[93] Since, with the exception of the first wisdom poem, the introduction of every section in Proverbs 1–9 has one or more variant repetitions, it appears that the editor used them 'to forge the entire subcollection Proverbs 1–9 into a coherent whole consisting of lectures, Wisdom interludes, and some miscellaneous materials'.[94] Furthermore, since

---

[86] Dell, *Proverbs in Social and Theological Context*, 155–187, 93–94.
[87] Dell, *Proverbs in Social and Theological Context*, 200.
[88] Dell, *Proverbs in Social and Theological Context*, 33.
[89] Heim, *Poetic Imagination*.
[90] Heim, *Poetic Imagination*, 35.
[91] Heim, *Poetic Imagination*, 35.
[92] Cf. the explanation in Heim, *Poetic Imagination*, 627. The list is on pages 629–633.
[93] Heim, *Poetic Imagination*, 624–627.
[94] Heim, *Poetic Imagination*, 624.

there is such a high concentration of repeated verses in the introductions to the lectures and the interludes about personified wisdom, 'we can conclude that both kinds of material – lectures and interludes – are integral to the editorial scheme for which variant repetitions is such an important instrument'.[95] This evidence counters the broad consensus that the wisdom interludes are significantly later than the rest of Proverbs 1–9.

Their distribution also reveals that the editor used variant repetitions 'to link various subunits of Proverbs 1–9 – and thus the entire subcollection – to the rest of the book of Proverbs'.[96] Particularly instructive is the placement of the variants 1:7 // 9:10 // 15:33a, which mention the fear of the Lord. The first two variants in the set frame Proverbs 1–9 and provide it with a hermeneutical key that highlights the fundamentally religious nature of wisdom. They were created and placed when the subcollection reached its final design to function as the introduction to Proverbs 10–31. According to Heim, the third verse in the variant set, 15:33, inspired its first two verses. His reconstruction reveals that

> this hermeneutical key is not the product of a relatively unimportant afterthought but the crowning achievement of a careful, extended, competent editorial scheme that shaped the entire book of Proverbs and its diverse subcollections in profound ways. As far as the final editor(s) of the book are concerned, fear of the Lord is *the* hermeneutical key to the book, and competent reading of Proverbs is impossible without it.[97]

Even before the editorial work which combined Prov 10:1–22:16 with its introduction in Proverbs 1–9, therefore, the important theological concept of the fear of the Lord in 15:33 was an integral part of this subcollection, which is commonly assumed to be the oldest part of the book of Proverbs.[98] The introductory Proverbs 1–9, then, did not introduce theological content and concepts into earlier material but already found them there. Heim's work demonstrates that literary developments in the book of Proverbs did indeed happen, but it also demonstrates that there is no need for the assumption that such developments extended over long

---

[95] Heim, *Poetic Imagination*, 626.
[96] Heim, *Poetic Imagination*, 625.
[97] Heim, *Poetic Imagination*, 626–627.
[98] For a full analysis, see Heim, *Poetic Imagination*, 51–61.

periods of time. It also shows that the book reflects theological concerns in line with other parts of the Hebrew Bible from the start.

These monographs have pointed the way towards a change in perspective towards the nature of the wisdom literature, as evidenced in recent commentaries such as those mentioned above – those of Waltke, Fox and Schipper. Waltke followed the trend of assigning a long period of development to the book's composition, but he departed from the pattern by ascribing its theological materials to the earliest phase of the book's composition and integrating it fully with other parts of the Hebrew Bible.[99]

Fox's commentaries on Proverbs appeared in 2000 and 2009.[100] He presented a detailed analysis of the evolution of the wisdom concept alongside his reconstruction of the book's literary development. This happened in three stages and extended over centuries.[101] First, in Proverbs 10–29, wisdom is practical and leads to 'an inclination to *do* what serves one's goals'. Ethical and religious concerns are not at play.[102] Sayings with ethical and/or religious content, such as Prov 22:12 or Prov 15:33, do not contradict this view:[103] 'It is not that these things are untrue of the wise man. It is just that they are not what the concept of wisdom, in its early sense, is *about*.'[104] Although Fox contrasted his approach from that of McKane discussed above,[105] his position is in reality remarkably similar. At the next stage of wisdom's development, represented by Proverbs 1–9, Fox identified a thoroughly religious and ethical tone. It is now 'religious at its very foundations',[106] and the Lectures introduce 'the *intellectualization* of moral virtue'.[107] Stage 3 in Fox's sketch is reached with the Wisdom Interludes (Prov 1:20–33; 3:13–20; 8:1–35; 9:1–18). Here wisdom 'transcends the human mind and permeates all space and all time'.[108]

Schipper's reconstruction of the compositional history of Prov 10:1–22:16 is strikingly different from other proposals. The purposeful and contextualised repetition of the same or similar proverbs plays an

---

[99]   Waltke, *Proverbs 1–15*, 63–133.
[100] Fox, *Proverbs 1–9*; Fox, *Proverbs 10–31*.
[101] Fox, *Proverbs 10–31*, 923–933.
[102] Fox, *Proverbs 10–31*, 925–928.
[103] Fox, *Proverbs 10–31*, 929–930.
[104] Fox, *Proverbs 10–31*, 929, emphasis original.
[105] Fox, *Proverbs 10–31*, 924, with reference to McKane, *Proverbs*, 10–22.
[106] Fox, *Proverbs 10–31*, 930, with reference to Prov 3:5, 7, 9, 11, 12; 2:6; and 1:7.
[107] Fox, *Proverbs 10–31*, 932.
[108] Fox, *Proverbs 10–31*, 932.

essential role.[109] Diachronic developments cannot be demonstrated, and the contextualisation of Yahweh-sayings led him to reject 'a later "theologizing" of older material'.[110] Theological concerns were present from the start.[111] The chapters in Prov 10:1–22:16 'are masterful compositions that do not readily reveal prior stages of literary development'.[112] They reflect a 'discursive wisdom'.[113] This creates 'a "critical dialogue" which reflects a process of critical ethical reflection', promoting an advanced wisdom.[114] In fact, all of Prov 10:1–22:16 form a masterful composition, suggesting that it, or at least a large portion of it, is the work of a single author.[115] Schipper believes that literary and theological developments across the book of Proverbs happened quickly and that all parts of the book were theological from the beginning. In contrast with earlier developmental schemes, Schipper's reconstruction of the redaction history of the book suggests that 'already the earliest literary stratum in Proverbs 1–9 contains a discursive contrast between different concepts of wisdom', and the same 'discursive' character prevails in Proverbs 10–22: 'The redactional history of Proverbs 1–9 reflects what is characteristic of the composition of chaps. 10–22 from the outset: the conceptually open, discursive character of sapiential instruction is abandoned in favor of an orientation toward Yhwh.'[116] Schipper has challenged the traditional position among scholars over the last century: 'the line of thought found in the book of Proverbs leads not to a "crisis of wisdom" but to a "critical wisdom" that ultimately points to the divine dimension of sapiential knowledge'.[117] It is somewhat ironical that due to Schipper's late dating of all of the materials in the book of Proverbs, the period which he designates as the *beginning* of wisdom in Israel is in fact that same period which the majority of scholars have identified as the *final* stage of development in the wisdom thought of Israel.

In relationship to the books of Job and Ecclesiastes, Schipper rejects the traditional construal of a crisis of wisdom prompted by the book of

---

[109] Schipper, *Proverbs 1–15*, 342–344.
[110] Schipper, *Proverbs 1–15*, 343. The phrase in italics has been slightly adapted to reflect Schipper's German more closely.
[111] Schipper, *Proverbs 1–15*, 343.
[112] Schipper, *Proverbs 1–15*, 354.
[113] Schipper, *Proverbs 1–15*, 354–356.
[114] Schipper, *Proverbs 1–15*, 355.
[115] Schipper, *Proverbs 1–15*, 357.
[116] Schipper, *Proverbs 1–15*, 37.
[117] Schipper, *Proverbs 1–15*, 36.

Proverbs' apparently simplistic worldview. Here is a selection of illus-
trative statements. The book of Proverbs exemplifies 'a type of thinking
that is characteristic of the book of Qohelet', notably Eccl 5:13–14a.[118]
Its critical reflection on traditional wisdom 'leads to a form of sapiential
reflection similar to that found in the books of Qohelet, Job, and
Sirach'.[119] For example, Prov 15:11 reflects similar sentiments in the
book of Job: 'What is inscribed in the divine speeches in the book of Job
as the creator's knowledge is described in Prov 15:11 through the motif
of the afterlife.'[120] And the emphasis on the fear of God in Prov
10:1–22:16 belongs to the same line of thinking as the phrase 'Fear
God, and keep his commandments' (Eccl 12:13) in the epilogue to the
book of Ecclesiastes.[121]

    In conclusion, I have five proposals regarding future work on the
literary contexts and development of wisdom literature. First, the theological and ethical contents of the books of Proverbs, Ecclesiastes and
Job need to be taken more seriously. They were present from the start
(with Schipper) and probably at an early date (with Dell). Second, the
late dates assigned to various parts of the book of Proverbs need to be
reconsidered. As Whybray has reminded us, the books of Proverbs, Job
and Ecclesiastes contain next to no specific information that indicates
historical dates. In the book of Proverbs, 'there are no references to Israel
and its political or religious history, and few to its institutions; no
Israelite proper names occur in it apart from those of Solomon and
Hezekiah ... it is difficult to pinpoint its religious thought in the
context of any particular stage in the development of Yahwistic theology'.[122] In the absence of other signposts for dating, the two we
actually do have should therefore count all the more. The reference to
Hezekiah's men in 25:1, which many scholars find credible, refers to
editorial work occurring during the eighth century, and it also refers to
material from the early monarchy. The mention of Solomon in 1:1, 10:1
and 25:1 does not necessitate a direct ascription of the materials they
introduce to him, although his figure pervades the 'wisdom' canon.[123]

---

[118] Schipper, *Proverbs 1–15*, 35.
[119] Schipper, *Proverbs 1–15*, 40.
[120] Schipper, *Proverbs 1–15*, 36.
[121] The reference to advanced students of wisdom ('Weisheit für Fortgeschrittene') only
       appears in the German version of the commentary; cf. Schipper, *Sprüche (Proverbia)
       1–15*, 605 with Schipper, *Proverbs 1–15*, 357–358.
[122] Whybray, *Proverbs*, 150.
[123] See Katharine J. Dell, *The Solomonic Context of 'Wisdom' and Its Influence*
       (Oxford, 2020).

Even so, the trend to date parts of the book of Proverbs, including Proverbs 1–9, into the Persian or Hellenistic period should be abandoned, unless new evidence can be found. Third, the literary contexts and social locations in which the books of Proverbs, Job and Ecclesiastes were developed and used may well have included the same circles which produced and used other parts of the Hebrew Bible, and this would have included the temple. Fourth, the idea of a 'crisis of wisdom', including the theory that the books of Job and Ecclesiastes somehow object to a supposedly unrealistic worldview in the book of Proverbs, should be laid to rest. Fifth, the books of Proverbs, Job and Ecclesiastes and their theological and ethical contributions should be more integrated with other parts of the Hebrew Bible.

Further Reading

Bruch, Johann Friedrich. *Weisheits-Lehre der Hebräer: Ein Beitrag zur Geschichte der Philosophie.* Strasbourg: 1851.

Dell, Katharine J. *The Book of Proverbs in Social and Theological Context.* Cambridge: 2006.

Fox, Michael V. *Proverbs 1–9: A New Translation with Introduction and Commentary.* Anchor Bible, 18A. New York: 2000.

Proverbs 10–31: A New Translation with Introduction and Commentary. Anchor Yale Bible, 18B. New York: 2009.

Heim, Knut M. *Poetic Imagination in Proverbs: Variant Repetitions and the Nature of Poetry.* BBRSup, 4. Grand Rapids: 2013.

Kynes, Will. *An Obituary for 'Wisdom Literature': The Birth, Death, and Intertextual Reintegration of a Biblical Corpus.* Oxford: 2019.

Schipper, Bernd Ulrich. *Proverbs 1–15: A Commentary on the Book of Proverbs 1:1–15:33.* Hermeneia. Minneapolis: 2019.

Sneed, Mark R., ed. *Was There a Wisdom Tradition? New Prospects in Israelite Wisdom Studies.* Ancient Israel and Its Literature, 23. Atlanta: 2015.

Waltke, Bruce K. *The Book of Proverbs: Chapters 1–15.* The New International Commentary on the Old Testament. Grand Rapids: 2004.

The Book of Proverbs: Chapters 16–31. The New International Commentary on the Old Testament. Grand Rapids: 2005.

Weeks, Stuart. *An Introduction to the Study of Wisdom Literature.* T&T Clark Approaches to Biblical Studies. London: 2010.

Whybray, R. Norman *The Composition of the Book of Proverbs.* JSOTSup, 168. Sheffield: 1994.

5 The Scribal World

MARK SNEED

The biblical wisdom literature is intricately connected to the scribal world since this is its matrix. Wisdom literature is a mode of literature (a categorisation broader than a genre, such as a *folk* epic or *pastoral* poetry)[1] that is found among the curricula and preserved literature of ancient Near Eastern scribal schools or archives, from Egypt to Mesopotamia and from Canaan to Anatolia. Thus, modes would be represented by legal material, omen texts, prophetic literature, erotica, liturgical literature, historical narratives, etc. Genres would include hymns, oracles and instructions. Unfortunately, we do not have extant library archives, either from schools or royal contexts, for the ancient Israelites because their scribes wrote on perishable material such as vellum or papyrus scrolls. However, by utilising a comparative method, one can safely postulate that the biblical wisdom literature represents the same type of scribal literary tradition as the world that surrounded them. In fact, it represents one of several types of curricular, literary traditions (legal, prophetic, erotic, epic, etc.) found throughout the ancient Near East.

The categorisation 'wisdom literature' is in fact a modern notion (with its origin in nineteenth-century Germany, with *'Weisheit-Lehre'*, penned by Johann Bruch),[2] but a majority of biblical and ancient Near Eastern scholars believe that it is a helpful category. The books are what one could describe as folk-philosophical, in that they treat the domains of philosophy, such as ethics (Proverbs) and the problem of evil (Job and Ecclesiastes). This philosophical categorisation of the wisdom literature can be traced back to Origen, who viewed Proverbs and Ecclesiastes as types of philosophical literature,[3] with Job also sometimes connected

---

[1] See Mark Sneed, 'Is the "Wisdom Tradition" a Tradition?', *CBQ* 73 (2011): 50–71.
[2] See Will Kynes, *An Obituary for 'Wisdom Literature': The Birth, Death, and Intertextual Reintegration of a Biblical Corpus* (Oxford, 2019), 4.
[3] See Kynes, *An Obituary for 'Wisdom Literature'*, 70.

with this category, specifically as a type of natural philosophy, itself a medieval category, with its focus on animals, plants and the natural world.[4]

With the discovery of other ancient Near Eastern texts, beginning in the nineteenth century, scholars began to note that there were striking resemblances between the biblical 'wisdom' books and several such texts, many of which were used for scribal, educational purposes. For example, the Egyptian instructions, collections of topical, parenetic material (paragraphs of ethical and social exhortations) which are much older than the biblical wisdom literature, were perceived as resonating formally and topically with Proverbs 1–9; 22:17–24:22; and 30–31. These texts are often identified as authored by famous sages, like Ipuwer, but sometimes also specifically identified as scribes (a royal scribe: *Instruction of Any*) or even a Pharaoh, who lectures his son (e.g., *Instruction of Merikare*).[5] Most of the instructions are most likely pseudepigraphal, and the ascription to a famous sage or king is for the purpose of legitimation.[6] It is likely that Egyptian instructions developed, as a genre, from the Egyptian tomb biographies wherein the deceased boasts that he was virtuous and pious in life and avoided the typical vices.[7] This, incidentally, points to one of the main functions of ancient Near Eastern wisdom literature: the enculturation or reinforcement of ethical and social norms in the context of piety. Even such an instruction as that of *Ptahhotep*, which ostensibly claims to instruct concerning the vizierate, is focused on the common moral values of the Egyptian Old Kingdom elite.[8] In the following, I discuss briefly what we know about ancient Near Eastern scribalism (the institution that ancient Near Eastern governments created to enhance their administrative roles) and the role that wisdom literature played in its formation and maintenance and how this relates to biblical wisdom literature.

---

[4] See Peter Harrison, *The Fall of Man and the Foundations of Science* (Cambridge, 2007), 112.

[5] Interestingly, Stuart Weeks does not see Proverbs 1–9 fulfilling that function (*Instruction and Imagery in Proverbs 1–9* [Oxford, 1994], 177–179). Jacqueline Vayntrub ('The Book of Proverbs and the Idea of Ancient Israelite Education', *ZAW* 128 [2016]: 96–114) argues that, as an essentially poetic text, the book of Proverbs itself cannot directly be used to extrapolate ancient Israelite pedagogy. However, this does not mean that Proverbs must be precluded from having served as a part of an apprentice scribal curriculum.

[6] See Miriam Lichtheim, *Ancient Egyptian Literature*, 3 vols. (Berkeley, 1973–1980), 1:6–7.

[7] See Lichtheim, *Ancient Egyptian Literature*, 1:1, 5.

[8] See Lichtheim, *Ancient Egyptian Literature*, 1:7.

SUMERIAN SCRIBALISM

Scribalism's birth can be traced back to the very first civilisation, ancient Sumer. Scribalism emerged originally to deal with the organisation and management of the canal system for the rivers of the Tigris and the Euphrates (late fourth/early third millennium BCE). In order to manage the burgeoning city-states in ancient Sumer, the profession of scribe was created to serve as the lubrication of the political system that enabled the states to run smoothly and efficiently. Scribalism could not have arrived until the emergence of the various social classes. With the abundance of crops, due to irrigation, some families naturally became wealthier than others, transcending the subsistence level of existence. Over time, some persons were able to live off this surplus labour in the form of the pursuit of leisure and ceased to become actual productive members of the society. Their function was then to govern the manual labourers.

With increased social stratification in ancient Sumer emerging, a powerful priesthood emerged that would need the aid of scribes to ensure that the surplus goods, enabled by the irrigation system, would flow to the temples. This, in turn, would enable the king to display ostentatious wealth to legitimate his own reign but also to ensure that the needs of the governing class were met. The king and priests needed scribes as administrators, who could produce records and inventories to ensure that the taxes were collected and distributed accordingly. Writing (not literature as yet) was necessary for that to happen. The first type of writing was inventory lists, which were necessary for the temples to keep up with the tax revenue, in the form of goods, like grain or olive oil. The very first scribes in Sumer, then, were essentially accountants. After a couple of centuries, literature emerged as another form of writing. Literature is a significant cultural artefact, and, in their role as copyists of this literature, scribes became responsible as the repositories of culture in whatever respective society they served. In fact, at this time their social roles began to proliferate from accountant to keepers of cultural traditions to serving as notaries, witnesses to contracts and surveyors, to various other administrative roles that often involved the central government. This included serving as ambassadors or delegates, due to their usually multilingual capability, as well as judges, though scribes could also work in private businesses.

Since they represented the tiny percentage of persons who could effectively read and write in their respective societies, this made their roles extremely valuable, which served to increase their social status within these societies.[9] However, they usually wielded little power or else they held power that was derived from their superiors. This is because scribes formed part of the retainer class of their respective societies.[10] Retainers were the persons whose role was to serve the governing class. But this should not be described as a middle class. For in the ancient world, there were only retainers and merchants who occupied what might be described as a middle layer.[11] Retainers included soldiers, military officers, butlers and bakers, etc. Some retainers would eventually become part of the governing class and attain real power, such as military officers. Retainers experienced many benefits being attached to the governing class, including an improved lifestyle over against that of the peasants – the social class to which most Israelites belonged.

ANCIENT NEAR EASTERN SCRIBAL CURRICULA

Though we have little direct evidence of the ancient Israelite scribal curriculum, we have plenty of evidence for not only Egypt and Mesopotamia but more significantly, the Western Periphery (of Mesopotamia), which includes Ugarit, and, it can be argued, represents Canaan, Israel's neighbour. In ancient Egypt, during the Old Kingdom (2650–2135 BCE), novice scribes were often taught by their fathers in an apprenticeship system.[12] The first scribal school is mentioned during the Intermediate Period (2135–2040 BCE). During the Middle Kingdom, a school in Memphis existed that enrolled both elite and less-advantaged boys.

During the New Kingdom (1550–1080 BCE), a boy started scribal school at age 10.[13] The student would study the *Book of Kemit*, which included the phraseology of letters and tomb biographies. Then students would copy works like *Satire on the Trades*, which is an apology for the trade of scribalism, and the *Instruction of Khety*, more obviously a wisdom text. Eventually, the instructor would recite texts orally and

---

[9] See Christopher Rollston, *Writing and Literacy of Ancient Israel: Epigraphic Evidence from the Iron Age*, Archaeology and Biblical Studies 11 (Atlanta, 2010).

[10] On the nature of retainers, see Gerhard Lenski, *Power and Privilege: A Theory of Social Stratification* (New York, 1966; repr. Chapel Hill, 1984), 243–248.

[11] See Mark Sneed, 'A Middle Class in Ancient Israel?', in *Concepts of Class in Ancient Israel*, ed. Mark Sneed, South Florida Studies in the History of Judaism: The Hebrew Scriptures and Their World 301 (Atlanta, 1999), 53–69.

[12] For the following, see Edward F. Wente, 'The Scribes of Ancient Egypt', in *Civilizations of the Ancient Near East 4*, ed. Jack Sasson (New York, 1995), 2215.

[13] For the following, see Wente, 'Scribes', 2215–2216.

the student would copy and later memorise them. Their elementary
education lasted for four years, and instructors focused on their students'
learning of the classics of the Middle Kingdom. After this, the student had
to decide on a specialisation such as administration, the priesthood or the
military. This stage lasted twelve years. They had to learn Late Egyptian
and studied mathematics, accounting, geometry, surveying and engineer-
ing. Students had to copy model texts from their masters, including
miscellanies that contained a diversity of genres. Word lists (a taxonomy
of related terms) were memorised and represent the birth of encyclo-
paedic knowledge. Those students who chose to become priests studied
at the House of Life at a temple where they copied old religious and
magical texts. At the House of Life, future physicians, astronomers,
magicians and oneiromancers were also trained. During the New
Kingdom, because priests had to manage large temple estates, they had
to be trained as administrators and ritualists as well.

In Mesopotamia, the situation was similar. In the Old Babylonian
period (2000–1600 BCE), young scribes at Nippur were trained in two
phases.[14] In the first phase, students copied lexical texts; this activity
imparted the writing system and introduced Sumerian vocabulary. At
the end of the first phase, tablets with proverbs were used, and their
contents prepared students for studying Sumerian in the second phase,
which involved the reading of texts. In fact, Sumerian tablets have been
found containing lexical lists on one side and matching proverbs on the
other.[15] This, by the way, is the only concrete evidence for how wisdom
genres, here a proverb, functioned within a scribal context.

As for Canaan (Syria), in the Western Periphery, the curriculum was
essentially Mesopotamian.[16] Students first became familiar with cuneiform and the tablets on which it was written. Next, students learned
lexical lists that introduced them to different domains of their world
(names of gods, objects, professions, etc.). Memorisation and the copying
of phrases and sentences further reinforced their learning of cuneiform but
also introduced them to literary texts that would help to enculturate them.
Next, literature was studied and parts of it memorised, such as liturgical
texts (hymns), mythical narratives, wisdom texts and 'scientific' texts

---

[14] For the following, see Nick Veldhuis, 'Sumerian Proverbs in Their Curricular
Context', *JAOS* 210 (2000): 383–387.

[15] Bendt Alster, *Proverbs of Ancient Sumer: The World's Earliest Proverb Collections*
(Bethesda, 1997), 1:xviii.

[16] See Yoram Cohen, *Wisdom from the Late Bronze Age*, Writing from the Ancient
World 29 (Atlanta, 2013); *The Scribes and Scholars of the City of Emar in the Late
Bronze Age*, HSS 59 (Winona Lake, 2009).

(omen texts). Also, more practical texts like model letters, inscriptions and business contracts were copied. Finally, apprentice scribes specialised in training for divination, medicine or the priesthood.

In general, then, in the ancient Near East, wisdom literature appears to have been viewed as highly significant for training scribal apprentices. This type of literature was studied especially during the early stages of their education. Of all the differing types of literature studied by young scribes, wisdom literature broadly defined (proverbs, dialogues, debates, satires, fables, instructions, theodicy literature, etc.) was always part of the curriculum, as indicated by its representation at schools, like at Emar, and in archives. The Sumerian tablets mentioned above provide the only clear-cut evidence for how this type of literature was used in the training of scribes. In this case, it is clearly for linguistic proficiency in Sumerian. Beyond this clear case, we have to speculate, and yet we can do so with some degree of confidence. In New Kingdom Egypt, apprentice scribes were required to copy texts like the *Instruction of Khety* and *Satire of the Trades*, both being what one could describe as sapiential texts.[17] We can see why the *Satire* would be helpful for young scribes, spurring them on to study hard to become scribes. But what function did the instructions have for scribes? To reinforce morality or social mores, it appears. Miriam Lichtheim emphasises that the scribes of the New Kingdom copied what were considered classic literature, as well as 'basic genres such as letters, hymns, prayers, and of course, instructions in wisdom'.[18] She also notes that the didactic texts 'would help to form the characters of the young scribes'.[19] Whatever its specific purposes, at least we know the copying of instructions formed part of Egyptian training of scribes and was one genre among many used to train them.

ISRAELITE SCRIBALISM AND CURRICULUM

Though we have never discovered an ancient Israelite archive or 'school', we can still postulate that the Israelite scribal curriculum was similar to that of the rest of the ancient Near East. This is because the biblical modes of literature and genres have striking corollaries to other ancient Near Eastern modes and genres that were used to train scribes. In fact, David Carr has recently argued that part of or at least a large segment of the Hebrew Bible represents a scribal curriculum.

[17] Wente, 'Scribes', 2215.
[18] Lichtheim, *Ancient Egyptian Literature*, 2:167.
[19] Lichtheim, *Ancient Egyptian Literature*, 2:167.

Carr compares the scribal curricula of ancient Mesopotamia, Egypt, Greece and ancient Israel and finds striking similarities in terms of curriculum and sequence of educational stages. He believes the scribal curriculum was primarily intended to enculturate the young scribes and the elite to prepare for governmental service and leadership roles.[20] He argues that the very first corpus of school texts may have been the wisdom literature, specifically the book of Proverbs, with other genres studied as well.[21] Later came the Deuteronomistic History, which he describes as an alternative curriculum.[22] The prophetic corpus, in turn, became even a counter-curriculum. He believes the Hebrew Bible canon was largely set during the days of the Hasmonean dynasty, which had its own library and was influenced by Greek models.[23] Carr also argues that apprentice Israelite scribes recited many of their written texts and memorised them as part of their training.

Similarly, Karel van der Toorn argues that the Hebrew Bible was originally scribal literature, written by scribes, for scribes, but he does not believe it formed a scribal curriculum for training scribes.[24] Rather, it represents general, scribal literature.[25] For him, this is because so many of the genres in the Hebrew Bible are not paralleled in the Mesopotamian curriculum, particularly the technical divinatory (e.g., omen texts) and exorcism texts.[26] But this is simply semantics. Perhaps both Mesopotamia and Israel feature divinatory literature, one of a deductive type, the other inspired divination. So, the significant question is, why would apprentice Israelite scribes not have benefitted from studying divinatory texts?

Speaking of the correlation of ancient Near Eastern genres, some Assyriologists do not agree that one can properly speak of wisdom literature in Mesopotamia, mainly because in this literature there are no lexical-semantic cognates or equivalents to the sapiential vocabulary concentrated in the biblical wisdom literature (e,g., *byn*, *yd'*, *ḥkm*, etc.) or because there is no focus on the notion of wisdom that these imply. Georgio Buccellati, for example, argues that there is no Mesopotamian wisdom

---

[20]   David Carr, *Writing on the Tablet of the Heart* (Oxford, 2005), 119, 126.

[21]   Carr, *Writing*, 126–134.

[22]   Carr, *Writing*, 134–142.

[23]   Carr, *Writing*, 253–272.

[24]   Karel van der Toorn, *Scribal Culture and the Making of the Hebrew Bible* (Cambridge, 2007), 247.

[25]   Cf. Stuart's Weeks' view of Proverbs 1–9 (*Instruction and Imagery in Proverbs 1–9* [Oxford, 2007]).

[26]   Weeks, *Instruction*, 247.

corpus per se, because wisdom themes are too diffused throughout a variety of Mesopotamian genres.[27] Rather, he sees a sapiential cultural phenomenon reflected by the literature but distinct from it. However, Buccellati's notion of genres is out of date, not reflecting recent trends in prototype theory that allow for more flexible identifications of genre. Paul-Alain Beaulieu also sees no concept or category of wisdom literature for Babylonian literature, yet this does not prevent him from employing the term 'Babylonian wisdom literature'.[28] W. G. Lambert, however, is fine with the term for describing a corpus of Babylonian literature, while recognising its liabilities.[29] Similarly, among Egyptologists, Miriam Lichtheim prefers the term 'didactic literature' to 'wisdom literature' because the corollary Egyptian literature rarely makes the terms or concept of wisdom its focus,[30] though Kenneth Kitchen sees no problem with it.[31] Again, a more up to date and sophisticated notion of genre allows for an identification of wisdom literature outside of ancient Israel.

Surely Israel had some similar scribal system with a curriculum and some kind of schools?[32] Even James Crenshaw admits that there had to be schools in ancient Israel by the eighth century BCE, simply based on the epigraphic evidence from inscriptions.[33] Chris Rollston pushes this back a century to the ninth because the epigraphic evidence shows that the Hebrew language had become standardised by then.[34] Perhaps these 'schools' were more like the Koranic madrasa that did not require actual buildings and were more informal with a father teaching a son and other boys.[35] And surely wisdom literature was only one genre (or, preferably, mode of literature) that Israelite scribes studied among several others (legal material, divination [prophetic] texts, hymnic literature, erotica, etc.).

---

[27] Georgio Buccellati, 'Wisdom and Not: The Case of Mesopotamia', *JAOS* 101 (1981): 35–47.

[28] Paul-Alain Beaulieu, 'The Social and Intellectual Setting of Babylonian Wisdom Literature', in *Wisdom Literature in Mesopotamia and Israel*, ed. Richard Clifford, Symposium Series 36 (Atlanta, 2007), 3.

[29] W. G. Lambert, *Babylonian Wisdom Literature* (Oxford, 1960; repr. Winona Lake, 1996), 1.

[30] Miriam Lichtheim, 'Didactic Literature', in *Ancient Egyptian Literature: History and Forms*, ed. Antonio Loprieno, PAe 10 (Leiden, 1996), 243–262.

[31] Kenneth Kitchen, 'Proverbs and Wisdom Books of the Ancient Near East: The Factual History of a Literary Form', *TynBul* 28 (1977): 69–114.

[32] I speculate on this in my *The Social World of the Sages: An Introduction to Israelite and Jewish Wisdom Literature* (Minneapolis, 2015), 179–191.

[33] James Crenshaw, *Education in Ancient Israel: Across the Deadening Silence*, ARL (New York, 1998), 112.

[34] Rollston, *Literacy of Ancient Israel*, 157–158.

[35] See André Lemaire, 'Sagesse et écolés', *VT* 34 (1984): 278.

THE SCRIBAL SIGNIFICANCE OF STUDYING/COPYING WISDOM LITERATURE

Besides the linguistic proficiency function that we discussed earlier, three more have been suggested: rhetorical, enculturation and moral formation. Bendt Alster argues that studying Sumerian 'proverbs' not only taught literary skills but also rhetorical ones.[36] He maintains that the 'proverb' collections functioned as a source for rhetorical phrases used in debates. Similarly, today African proverbs are commonly used in court trials and can be effective rhetorical tools.[37] This assumes, of course, that the maxims are indeed folk proverbs current within the contemporary society. But even if this is not so, the study of literature in general, whether epigrams or other genres, would naturally enable a person to become a better speaker.

As Carr has argued, the practice of requiring apprentice scribes to study various genres is primarily meant to enculturate them, to train them in their nation's literature and lore, and that would serve to make them better scribes and governmental functionaries.[38] This shows that most parts of the Hebrew Bible could have served this purpose originally because most of the genres and modes of literature have scribal-curricular parallels. It also points to the fact that scribes received a training much broader than simply learning the technical skills of copyists. Israelite scribes, like other ancient Near Eastern scribes, were expected to have breadth, culturally. The notion is that a cultured scribe makes for a better scribe!

Another function has recently been persuasively argued by Anne Stewart. In her book *Poetic Ethics in Proverbs*, she combines literary and philosophical strategies by arguing that the aesthetic sophistication of the sayings and longer poems in Proverbs was intentional to facilitate moral formation. She maintains that poetry, pedagogy and ethos are all intertwined in Proverbs.[39] She points out that poetry in Proverbs would be more difficult for students to read than narrative but that its difficulty is intentional in order to hone skills in moral discernment.[40]

---

[36] Alster, *Proverbs of Ancient Sumer*, 1:xix.

[37] J. Messenger, 'The Role of the Proverb in a Nigerian Judicial System', *Southwestern Journal of Anthropology* 15 (1959): 64–73.

[38] Carr, *Writing*.

[39] Anne Stewart, *Poetic Ethics in Proverbs: Wisdom Literature and the Shaping of the Moral Self* (Cambridge, 2016), 1–8. On how African proverbs are used to teach young people morality, see E. Arera and A. Dundes, 'Proverbs and the Ethnography of Speaking Folklore', *American Anthropologist* 66.6 (1954): 70–85.

[40] Stewart, *Poetic Ethics*, 41–43.

As opposed to narrative, Proverbs, she argues, does not simply etch out the correct moral path for the student to take: it helps develop general moral discernment so that when the student matures socially and morally, he will be prepared to make the best moral decision required by the situation.[41] Stewart has also published a recent article using the theorisation of Mark Johnson to argue that Proverbs employs various metaphors involving prototypes. According to that theory, those proto-types are deliberately flexible and generic so as to aid the reader in imagining moral possibilities that will serve him in ethical decision-making in the future.[42]

SCRIBES AND SENTENCE LITERATURE

The type of literature represented by biblical wisdom literature also reveals another function of it. The scribes who composed the wisdom literature focus more on form than content. For example, in the book of Proverbs, the sentences, the smallest genre in the book, are structured according to a bicolon form, where the meaning of the second colon resonates in some way with the first. This structure is absent from the folk proverbs one finds in the Hebrew Bible (Judg 8:21; 1 Sam 24:13; 2 Sam 5:6; 1 Kgs 20:11). For example, when Gideon tells his son to slay Zeba and Zalmunna, he is hesitant because of his youth. In response, the two men proclaim, 'As the man, so is his strength', only two words (kə'îš gəbûrātô) in Hebrew and certainly not in bicolon form. As typical of proverbs in English, this one is short and sweet and to the point. Its moral is similar to our own cliché: 'Don't get a boy to do a man's job'! In contrast, in the very first sentence in Prov 10:1 we find:

bēn ḥākām yəśamaḥ-' āb ûbēn kəsîl tûgat' immô

A wise son will bring joy to the father,
Whereas a foolish son is the grief of his mother.

This contains two cola that resonate with each other. And its meaning is totally dependent on the relationships between the cola. It also contains eight words, four times the number of the folk proverb. Unlike the proverb cited by Zeba and Zalmunna, this maxim is rather

---

[41] See Stewart, *Poetic Ethics*, 50, 55, 59, 66–69.
[42] Stewart, 'Wisdom's Imagination: Moral Reasoning and the Book of Proverbs', *JSOT* 40 (2016): 351–372.

banal. It simply teaches the most fundamental principle of an honour/ shame culture: honorable children only bring honor to their respective families, or more basically it exhorts: be honorable! So, the focus is not on the content but on the aesthetics of the proverb.

These nuances of aesthetics are in the following features of the text. This maxim follows what is known as antithetical parallelism. Significant words in the second colon are the opposite of those found in the first colon, yet the two lines together express the same sentiment: 'foolish' for 'wise', 'mother' for 'father', 'grief' (a noun this time) for 'bring joy' (verb). The second colon also expresses what Robert Alter calls specification.[43] '*His* mother' is more specific than simply '[the] father' of the first colon. Thus, the parallelism is doublefold here: opposite terms at the first level of aesthetics and different parts of speech at the second. And the third level of aesthetics is the specification. So, we have a threefold form of aesthetics not present in the simple proverb of Judges 8. That proverb simply reflects terseness, which is typical of poetry and represents the only aesthetic element the proverb contains.

Now, these nuances are not the kind that Israelite peasants would necessarily catch, or if they did, appreciate, especially if these maxims were never meant to be cited in public generally. Public citation would make them real proverbs, which are always current in a particular society as a whole. Not that they were not possibly cited orally among scribes, especially in a class or pedagogical setting. Yet, they were not likely to have circulated beyond a small circle of elite scribes. This means these proverbs are not real proverbs but more like epigrams as in the English language. This is further supported by the superscriptions attached to the collections of aphorisms in Proverbs: 1:1; 10:1; 22:17; 24:23; 25:1; 30:1; 31:1. If these collections had simply been collections of proverbs, which modern paremiologists produce today, then there would be no need for the superscriptions, where they are identified with famous people or categories ('wise men').

Thus, the focus here in Prov 10:1 on form and aesthetics, and less so on content, is typical of elite intellectuals. This fits the perspective and social position of a scribe. By developing high literary skills that require sophisticated training to perceive nuances, the scribes of ancient Israel separate themselves from both the king and nobility and also the peasantry. Since they represented the only truly literate social group in ancient Israel, they were naturally elevated in status and held skills that

---

[43]   Robert Alter, *The Art of Biblical Poetry*, new and rev. ed. (New York, 2011), 20.

few other people had. Though a couple of Mesopotamian kings appear to have been literate (e.g., Shulgi) and even prided themselves in having scribal skills, most kings were illiterate, like the rest of their respective societies. This was also true for ancient Israel. King Josiah was apparently illiterate because he required the reading by the scribe of the scroll found in the temple during remodelling (2 Kgs 22:10). So, while the Israelite nobility might have been distinct in their tastes for luxury items and expensive cuisine that often included meat, something peasants apparently rarely ate, the scribes distinguished themselves from them with their literary expertise and artistry.

As mentioned earlier, the Israelite scribes were part of the retainer class, which put itself at the behest of the governing class (royal family, court, chief priests and administrative officers) but also above the peasants, who could be very poor on the one hand or wealthy enough to become noblemen on the other. Because social classes often overlap in terms of values and mores, it makes it difficult to demonstrate any specific class location definitively just by examining the literature.[44] The best one can do is look for hints of class location that are at least compatible with a particular class perspective, here that of retainers. The book of Proverbs contains such hints. There are several warnings about keeping a distance from the king's anger and use of power, which would at least point to a lack of substantial power among the scribes. For example:

> The wrath of the king is a messenger of death,
> And a wise man will propitiate for it.
> (Prov 16:14; cf. 25:1–7)

There are also maxims that depict the sorry lot of the poor, as if the authors were neither rich, nor poor:

> The wealth of the rich is a city of strength for him,
> And their poverty is the ruin of the poor.
> (10:15)

Similarly, here is an aphorism that neutrally observes benefits to being both wealthy and poor:

> By his wealth, a man can ransom his life,
> Whereas the poor don't have to listen to rebuke.
> (13:12)

---

[44] See Mark Sneed, 'The Class Culture of Proverbs: Eliminating Stereotypes', *SJT* 10 (1996): 296–308.

And, finally, here is an epigram that reveals that the scribes, though well-to-do, were sympathetic to the plight of the poor:

> The generous person ('good eye') is blessed,
> For he gives his food to the poor.
>
> (22:9)

The fixation on morality in the book of Proverbs and within the wisdom literature more generally reveals a curriculum that novice scribes could have used to hone their skills in morality and to increase their piety to the patron deity. This not only would have made them better scribes who often served as governmental officials. It also gave them a political advantage, a bit of leverage that might help them out when dealing with either the masses or the king and his high officials. The masses would respect their piety, making them popular, whereas the governing class would have to fear this popularity and hesitate to treat them abusively.

PRIESTS, PROPHETS, SAGES AND SCRIBES

Many wisdom experts and other biblical scholars point to Jer 18:18 as evidence of three professional groups which are the collectives largely responsible for our current Hebrew Bible, for the legal, sapiential and prophetic literature, especially. The context is the opposition of the Judean leadership to Jeremiah's words of judgement against Jerusalem:

> Then they said, 'Come, let us devise plots against Jeremiah, for instruction (tôrâ) will not cease from the priest, nor advice ('ēṣâ) from the wise (ḥākām), nor an oracle (dābār) from the prophet. Come, let us smite him by tongue and let us not listen to all his words'.

Compare these words of Ezekiel:

> They will seek a vision (ḥāzôn) from the prophet; instruction (torah will perish from the priest, and counsel ('ēṣâ) from the elders. (7:26)

Biblical scholars apparently confuse the references to the 'sage' in these passages with the 'sages' in the superscriptions in Proverbs (e.g., 'words of the wise [ḥăkāmîm] [22:17]) and with Qoheleth himself ('besides being wise' [ḥākām] [12:9]). There are numerous problems with doing that. First, the passages in these prophetic texts do not seem to refer to these categories as authors.[45] Rather, they are described in their role as

---

[45] Interestingly, Joseph Blenkinsopp identifies these 'sages' as legal scribes, distinct from priests, though perhaps part of the clergy; see *Wisdom and Law in the Old Testament:*

public officials, as leaders. This does not necessarily exclude their role as authors outside of this context; it is just that the context does not suggest this particular role. In both prophetic passages (Jeremiah and Ezekiel), the 'counsel', 'instruction' and 'oracle' all assume an oral context where each professional in view (prophet, priest and sage) communicates the will of the deity, with an implied inspiration in all cases.[46] The parallel between 'elders' (Ezekiel) and 'the wise' (Jeremiah) especially suggests such a context. Royal elders were consulted by the king for what would have been considered inspired advice or at least as good as inspired advice. Remember that Ahithophel, David's courtier, a wise man, was said to offer advice every bit as inspired as that of a prophet's word (2 Sam 16:23).[47] He is never identified as a scribe, however. 'Instruction' from the priest was apparently oral information gleaned from God,[48] perhaps through the Urim and Thummim or through some other divinatory means.

Second, the designation 'sage' (ḥākām) is too ambiguous for such a conflation. Apparently, there was more than one category of 'sages' in ancient Israel.[49] So, simply conflating the 'sages' from the passages in Jeremiah and Ezekiel with the references to 'sages' in the superscriptions of Proverbs is highly problematic. Unlike the prophet and priest, who could be readily identified because of their idiosyncratic roles, and even clothing in the case of the priest, the sage could represent anyone who had some skill that could be designated as 'wise', including a smith or craftsman (e.g., Bezalel [Exod 31:1-3]). But this, of course, does not mean there was no professional group of sages in ancient Israel,[50] only that one must be cautious in identifying what kind of group may be in mind and avoid simple conflations, such as the one presently discussed.

Third and finally, the word for 'counsel' or 'advice' ('ēṣâ) is never used specifically as a designation for literary genres. The word can

---

The Ordering of Life in Israel and Early Judaism, Oxford Bible Series (Oxford, 1983), 8–10; and Sage, Priest, Prophet: Religious and Intellectual Leadership in Ancient Israel, LAI (Louisville, 1995), 39–40; whereas Lester Grabbe refuses to identify them (Priests, Prophets, Diviners, Sages: A Socio-Historical Study of Religious Specialists in Ancient Israel [Valley Forge, 1995], 154).

[46] Cf. John Bright, Jeremiah: A New Translation with Introduction and Commentary, AB 21 (Garden City, 1965), 124, n.18.

[47] In fact, prophetic 'advice' ('ēṣâ) assumes the same inspired status: 'advice of his messengers' (Isa 44:26).

[48] BDB 435, s.v. תּוֹרָה.

[49] See Sneed, Social World of the Sage, 20–80, 161–172.

[50] Contra R. Norman Whybray, The Intellectual Tradition in the Old Testament, BZAW 135 (Berlin; New York, 1974).

certainly be used broadly as a designation for oral advice (a father to his son [Prov 1:25]; the kind the wise listen to [Prov 12:15]) but not for any of the literary genres represented in the wisdom literature, such as a maxim (māšāl), a figure (məlîṣâ), 'words of wisdom', and a 'riddle' (ḥîdâ) (Prov 1:6). Of course, one could say that in a general way, all wisdom literature is 'advice', but if a literary genre is what was in mind for the scribe who coined Jer 18:18, he would have a used a different term; 'ēṣâ is more compatible with the notion of oral, political advice given by sages to the king and, specifically, advice considered to be divinely inspired. To see 'wisdom literature' as intended here is a rather large stretch, indeed.

So, if the professional groups listed in Jer 18:18 (priests, prophets and sages) are not to be identified as the authors of Scripture (or the bulk of it), then who are? The answer is simple: the scribes. While the Hebrew Bible certainly may reflect the viewpoints of various types of persons and statuses, such as kings, priests, sages, prophets or even peasants at times, it is scribes who actually created the texts themselves, who actually penned the scrolls. This is not to suggest that scribes were a monolithic, homogeneous body, that they never disagreed among themselves. In fact, they were never like a political party or reflected a single viewpoint or perspective or even theology. But they did share a common worldview and similar training. But ascribing the Hebrew Bible to scribes acknowledges an important facet of the nature of the biblical text, that is, its essentially scribal character.

So, then, who were the 'wisdom writers', that is, the term often used by biblical scholars for the authors of the wisdom literature? I have already answered this question above: scribes. This fits a growing awareness among scholars (e.g., van der Toorn, Carr) of the importance of scribes in the composition of the Hebrew Bible (the Dead Sea Scrolls and New Testament as well).[51] Even prophetic literature is now recognised as ultimately being the product of scribes, even if prophetic oracles could be traced back to actual prophets who were once important intellectual figures in their respective societies.[52] What is important is that scribes have

---

[51] See also William M. Schniedewind, *How the Bible Became a Book: The Textualization of Ancient Israel* (Cambridge, 2004).

[52] See Martti Nissinen, *Ancient Prophecy: Near Eastern, Biblical, and Greek Perspectives* (Oxford, 2018); Rannfrid Thelle, 'Reflections of Ancient Israelite Divination in the Former Prophets', in *Israelite Prophecy and the Deuteronomistic History: Portrait, Reality, and the Formation of History*, ed. Mignon R. Jacobs and Raymond F. Person Jr., AIL 14 (Atlanta, 2013), 7–33.

produced the prophetic *literature* that we have now in the Hebrew Bible. Baruch is an example for Jeremiah.

The fact that the Hebrew Bible was written by scribes does not mean, of course, that priests and prophets or wise courtiers[53] are not important to consider when studying the formation of the canon and that some of their ideas are not reflected in this literature and in the wisdom literature in particular. But they were not the authors of our biblical texts per se, at least not in these roles. It would have only been in their role as scribes.

The actual authors of the Hebrew Bible were scribes before they were anything else. It is the most significant social variable to consider when trying to understand their identity and how they would have identified themselves and how this might be reflected in the biblical texts they authored. They might also have been priests (e.g., Ezra) or employed by them (e.g., Temple scribes) or even closely associated with prophets or employed by them (e.g., Baruch). They might have been courtiers or viziers and associated with the royal family (e.g., Shaphan). But it is their scribal identity that is most significant for understanding their particular worldview and political perspective. Just as one could speak of a Western Periphery scribal subculture, where scribes even had their own patron scribal deities, like Nisaba, Nabû and Ea,[54] one could speak of an Israelite scribal subculture and even a worldview. The Israelite subculture would, of course, only have had one primary deity, YHWH or Elohim, as their scribal patron. Its worldview would have largely overlapped with that of the Israelites en masse, except that it would be more elitist, though not completely aligned with the governing class. It shared the same ancient supernatural worldview of the Israelite masses. The issue up for debate back then was not whether prophecy was a legitimate form of knowledge but whether one claiming

---

[53] Michael Fox ('The Social Location of the Book of Proverbs', in *Texts, Temples, and Traditions: A Tribute to Menachem Haran*, ed. Michael Fox et al. [Winona Lake, 1996], 234–239) argues that Proverbs 10–29 was originally intended for royal courtiers (or better, 'the king's men'), whereas Christopher Ansberry (*Be Wise, My Son, and Make My Heart Glad: An Exploration of the Courtly Nature of the Book of Proverbs*, BZAW 422 [Berlin, 2011], 49, 69–70, 184–190) believes this for the book as a whole. This is mainly because of the 'courtly' material in it (e.g., 23:1–8; 25:1–7). Fox (236), in fact, rejects scribes as in view and understands the Hebrew word for scribe (*sōpēr*) as 'clerk or scholar', because '*sopher* was not in itself a profession' but merely a requirement for further specialisation, a rather bizarre notion. Ezra was from a priestly family, yet the status that is emphasised is that 'he was a scribe (*sōpēr*) skilled (*māhîr*) in the Law of Moses' (Ezra 7:6).

[54] See Sneed, *Social World of the Sages*, 111–146

to be a prophet spoke for YHWH or not. But to get at this worldview one must look at all the various modes of literature represented in the Hebrew Bible: legal material, mythic and historical narratives, hymnic and poetic literature, erotica, prophetic and apocalyptic literature (a later development and representing a different social location) and wisdom literature. One could not simply examine one type of literature to discern this worldview.

This is why, while one can speak legitimately of a scribal subculture represented by the Hebrew Bible, one cannot do the same for a supposed worldview of the wisdom writers, as if this is distinct from the world-view reflected by the other types of literature.[55] The wisdom literature no more reflects a complete worldview than does any of the other modes of literature (legal, historical narrative, prophetic, etc.). To speak of a distinctive worldview of the wisdom writers is to illegitimately and artificially separate this literature from the other scribal modes of lit-erature. How could the wisdom literature reflect a complete worldview when it only treats morality and the problem of evil and focuses mainly on the concerns of the individual?[56] This separation creates bizarre and anomalous effects. It meant that earlier scholars and even more recent ones, like Joseph Blenkinsopp, viewed the earlier wisdom writers as secular (how anachronistic!), essentially non-cultic (also anachronistic!) and only later becoming more theologically oriented.[57] It means for James Crenshaw that the biblical wisdom writers are not even Yahwistic![58] Even Qoheleth, whom one might characterise as non-Yahwistic (I disagree), cannot legitimately be characterised as non-cultic or anti-divinatory. He cites the Mosaic law as authoritative (4:17–5:6 Hebrew). His scepticism concerns reckless cultic behaviour, not cultic behaviour carte blanche or the notion of divination.

The biblical wisdom literature is simply the product of Israelite and Jewish scribes who engaged in the literary modal conventions of sapien-tial literature at the time of writing. At other times, they might engage

---

[55] See James Crenshaw, *Old Testament Wisdom: An Introduction* (Louisville, 2010), 24–25, 34, 243; Blenkinsopp, *Sage, Priest, Prophet*, 4.

[56] A complete worldview involves the following components, according to worldview expert, Ninian Smart: doctrinal, mythical, ethical, ritual, experiential and social (*Worldviews: Crosscultural Explorations of Human Beliefs* [New York, 1983], 7–8).

[57] Blenkinsopp, *Sage, Priest, Prophet*, 9, 32–34, 42.

[58] Crenshaw, *Old Testament Wisdom*, 243. In contrast, other scholars, who see a sapiential worldview as compatible with Yahwism include Gerhard von Rad, *Wisdom in Israel* (London, 1972; repr. Nashville, 1988), 316–317; Katharine J. Dell, 'I Will Solve My Riddle to the Music of the Lyre (Psalm XLIX 4[5]): A Cultic Setting for Wisdom Psalms', *VT* 54 (2004): 445–458.

other modes, like copying or composing legal material or historical narrative. A scribe was proficient to engage a vast number of modal and generic conventions, all with differing rules and parameters – they even broke these rules, on purpose, at times! A scribe who composed an epigram one day, could easily compose a psalm or love poem another day.

Again, this does not mean that all the biblical scribes who composed the Hebrew Bible agreed theologically on everything. They obviously did not. But they never expressed these theological differences via literary modes or genres alone. It was the content of the genres that expressed the differences. The literary mode was chosen depending on the need and purpose of the text. That biblical authors disagreed within the same literary mode confirms this notion. The authors of Proverbs and Qoheleth engage the sapiential mode of literature and its genres, such as the sentence, but they obviously differ on the doctrine of retribution, that is, they differ theologically while engaging the same type of literary mode and genres: wisdom literature and the sentence.

There is no reason why a royal scribe could not compose a hymn, a wisdom text or even a legal text. Such a scribe might have trouble composing a text like Leviticus, of course, but it is not out of the question. Likewise, there is no reason why a Temple scribe could not do the same.[59] In fact, the Egyptian scribes who composed the instructions were often simultaneously (lector) priests (*Instruction of Amenemope, The Complaints of Khakheperre-sonb, Instruction of Ankhsheshonq*). Similarly, during the Late Bronze Age, Syrian scribes composed or copied wisdom literature and simultaneously served as diviners, priests or exorcists (e.g., Madi-Dagan, of Emar, was the chief municipal scribe and *apkallu* priest, who practiced magic and medicine). Any wisdom expert who wants to argue that ancient Israel represents an anomaly to this picture has the burden of proof to contend with.

SUMMARY

One cannot really understand the biblical wisdom literature without fundamental knowledge about ancient Near Eastern scribalism. The wisdom literature clearly reveals features that resonate with the training of scribes throughout the rest of the ancient Near Eastern world. Though there is no epigraphic evidence because it has long

---

[59] Cf. Grabbe, *Priests, Prophets, Diviners, Sages*, 170.

disappeared, by comparing the extra-biblical scribal literature and curricula, one can reasonably speculate on how the wisdom literature functioned for apprentice Israelite scribes. First, it helped Israelite scribes learn Hebrew and hone their linguistic skills. Second, it most likely helped them rhetorically, which would have been of great benefit to the typical career of scribes. Third, it enculturated them. Fourth, it also contributed to their moral formation. An ethical scribe was a good scribe. Their piety and elite scribal skills in turn served to provide an advantage for scribes who occupied the retainer class, enabling them to distinguish themselves from the nobility and royalty, as well as the peasantry.

But wisdom literature was not the only mode of literature they studied. They studied all the types that are represented by the other ancient Near Eastern curricula and classics. The study and copying of all these different types served to make scribes broadly cultured, which would serve them well in their careers. The sages who composed the wisdom literature were most likely engaged in the production of the other modes of literature found in the Hebrew Bible. That is why it makes no sense to speak of a particular worldview of the wisdom writers. They shared the same supernatural worldview the rest of the Israelites held, though certainly elitist, but not completely aligned with the governing class, since they were retainers. Biblical wisdom literature cannot represent a complete worldview because it only treats the ethical realm. It correlates with what one might describe as folk philosophical literature, treating ethics and the problem of evil.

One could also rightly speak of an Israelite, scribal subculture, which is what unites all the authors of the Hebrew Bible, even if they might simultaneously be priests or courtiers or have served alongside prophets. This does not mean that they agreed theologically on everything. They differed on many matters, sometimes drastically, but this does not justify speaking of different worldviews. And they never expressed these differences along modal (types of literature) or generic lines.

Further Reading

Carr, David M. *Writing on the Tablets of the Heart*. Oxford: 2005.

Cohen, Yoram. *The Scribes and Scholars of the City of Emar in the Late Bronze Age*. HSS 59. Winona Lake: 2009.

Wisdom from the Late Bronze Age. Writing from the Ancient World 29. Atlanta: 2013.

Davies, Philip R., and Thomas Römer, eds. *Writing the Bible: Scribes, Scribalism and Script*. Bible World. New York: 2015.

Rollston, Christopher A. *Writing and Literacy of Ancient Israel: Epigraphic Evidence from the Iron Age*. Archaeology and Biblical Studies 11. Atlanta: 2010.

Schmidt, Brian B., ed. *Contextualizing Israel's Sacred Writings: Ancient Literacy Orality, and Literary Production*. AIL 22. Atlanta: 2015.

Sneed, Mark. 'Is the "Wisdom Tradition" a Tradition?' *CBQ* 73 (2011): 50–71.

—— *The Politics of Pessimism in Ecclesiastes: A Social-Science Perspective*. AIL 12. Atlanta: 2012.

—— *The Social World of the Sages: An Introduction to Israelite and Jewish Wisdom Literature*. Minneapolis: 2015.

—— ed. *Was There a Wisdom Tradition? New Prospects in Israelite Wisdom Studies*. AIL 23. Atlanta: 2015.

—— 'A Taste for Wisdom: Aesthetics, Moral Discernment, and Social Class in Proverbs'. Pages 111–126 in *Imagined World and Constructed Differences in the Hebrew Bible*. Edited by Jeremiah W. Cataldo. LHBOTS 677. London, 2019.

—— 'Inspired Sages: *Massa'* and the Confluence of Wisdom and Prophecy'. In *Scribes as Sages and Prophets*. Edited by Jutta Krispenz. BZAW 496. Berlin: 2020, 15–32.

Stewart, Anne. *Poetic Ethics in Proverbs: Wisdom Literature and the Shaping of the Moral Self*. Cambridge: 2016.

Toorn, Karel van der. *Scribal Culture and the Making of the Hebrew Bible*. Cambridge: 2007.

6 Theological Themes in the 'Wisdom Literature': Proverbs, Job and Ecclesiastes

KATHARINE J. DELL

With the current focus on the problems that beset an attempt to define the limits of 'wisdom literature' in the HB/OT, it is hard to move on from matters of definition and literary genre to those of 'theology'.[1] Theological ideas imbue all parts of the Bible and, in a sense, this is the key function of scripture, that is, to describe and transmit the relationship between God and the world through his 'word'. The question becomes whether there is a distinctive set of theological ideas for a certain group of books, such that they can be separated in terms of classification. The edges of such an attempt are however quite blurred and much recent work has shown the integration of 'wisdom' ideas in varied parts of the canon.[2] It is a question of the extent of a distinctive emphasis, set of vocabulary, presuppositions and focus on certain themes, and it is this that I shall try to trace here. Although I have argued elsewhere that Job is the more distant partner to Proverbs and Ecclesiastes when it comes to defining the scope of the wisdom literature,[3] for the purposes of this chapter I shall look to all three books to see what is distinctive to all three in the first instance and hence test the theory that there is a special theological identity running through this

---

[1] This debate was initiated by Mark Sneed's seminal paper 'Is the Wisdom Tradition a Tradition?', *CBQ* 73 (2011): 50–71; and taken up by Stuart Weeks in, 'Is "Wisdom Literature" a Useful Category?', in *Tracing Sapiential Traditions in Ancient Judaism*, ed. Hindy Najman, Jean-Sébastien Rey and Eibert J. C. Tigchelaar (Leiden, 2016), 3–23; and most fully by Will Kynes, *An Obituary for 'Wisdom Literature': The Birth, Death, and Intertextual Reintegration of a Biblical Corpus* (Oxford, 2019). A volume on the definition of wisdom resulted also from this debate, Mark R. Sneed, ed., *Was There a Wisdom Tradition?: New Prospects in Israelite Wisdom Studies*, AIL (Atlanta, 2015).

[2] Donn F. Morgan, *Wisdom in the Old Testament Traditions* (Atlanta, 1981); and taken up by many others.

[3] Katharine J. Dell, 'Ecclesiastes as Mainstream Wisdom (without Job)' in *Goochem in Mokum/Wisdom in Amsterdam: Papers on Biblical and Related Wisdom Read at the Fifteenth Joint Meeting of The Society of Old Testament Study and the Oudtestamentisch Werkgezelschap, Amsterdam July 2012*, ed. George J. Brooke and Pierre Van Hecke, *OtSt* 68 (Leiden, 2016), 43–52.

literature. Whilst other articles in this volume have included Ben Sira in this evaluation, adding this book would introduce further theological themes as well as extending those already identified and so, largely in the interest of lack of space, I choose to except it here. Its inclusion though would illustrate the point that the goalposts of theological theme tend to change with questions of definition.[4]

The nomenclature of 'wisdom literature' and presupposition that it is a distinctive corner of the OT/HB has early roots in nineteenth-century scholarship[5] and has been a presupposition of a century and a half of scholarly work and so deserves to be given serious consideration. It is of interest to me how trends within the wider field of biblical studies have influenced these decisions alongside trends within the study of wisdom literature itself.[6] For example, the nineteenth- and early twentieth-century analysis was dominated by source-critical findings that led to conclusions about the coming together of wisdom books that are still widely held today.[7] Theological evaluations were often a key part of these conclusions; for example, the conclusion that Proverbs 1–9 was later than the rest of Proverbs was largely based on its more developed theology;[8] ideas about later theological developments influenced which parts of Job were seen as later, for example, the Satan parts of the Prologue (i.e., the heavenly scenes) were seen by some as later additions because they aligned with Persian dualistic ideas and aligned more closely with late books such as Daniel and Zechariah;[9] and in Ecclesiastes, the Epilogue (Eccl 12:8–14) was seen as later because of its emphasis on the fear of the LORD and mention of 'commandments'.[10]

---

[4] Kynes, *An Obituary for 'Wisdom Literature'*, helpfully uses the imagery of clusters of constellations in the heavens and the way they are viewed from earth from various angles to describe the way a different hermeneutic or way of classifying material leads to a new set of conclusions.

[5] Notably Johann Friedrich Bruch, *Weisheits-Lehre der Hebräer: Ein Beitrag zur Geschichte der Philosophie* (Strasbourg, 1851).

[6] As I have shown recently in relation to Proverbs in my *The Theology of the Book of Proverbs*, OTT (Cambridge, forthcoming).

[7] E.g., Job was divided into a three-stage production by Norman H. Snaith, *The Book of Job: Its Origin and Purpose* (London, 1968); Ecclesiastes was subjected to a Pentateuch style redaction by G. A. Barton, *Ecclesiastes*, ICC (Edinburgh, 1908) amongst many others of his time.

[8] Although the presence of different genres, instruction and poetry, also dominated these source-critical conclusions.

[9] E.g., L. W. Batten, 'The Epilogue to the Book of Job', *AThR* 15 (1933): 125–128.

[10] Ideas of three possible stages even of redaction of the Epilogue were mooted on source-critical grounds that found different redactional levels.

There was considerable interest in theological aspects of the three books from this period. They tended to be dated late within the canon, at least in their final form, and they were often aligned with intertexts such as Deuteronomy, Genesis 1–11 and Psalms and usually seen to have been influenced by those books rather than doing the influencing themselves.[11]

Tracing trends can be a subjective enterprise, but one point of objective discovery was the Egyptian Instruction of Amenemope in the 1920s which closely aligned with a part of Proverbs (22:17–24:22) and with instruction texts within Proverbs 1–9.[12] This opened up a fresh interest in the ANE world and its links to 'wisdom literature'[13] and also in questions of literary genre and social context. Wisdom literature came to be seen as closer to foreign parallels than to literature within the OT/HB and so seemed more theologically distinct (often seen as theological inferior) than ever before.[14] Some even dared to think that Proverbs was largely 'secular', particularly in the sayings sections;[15] that Job with its setting in Uz was not a strictly Israelite piece,[16] and with its links to Mesopotamian sufferer genres, closer to that culture;[17] and that Ecclesiastes was a philosophical treatise full of personal musings and rather outside mainstream OT/HB literature[18] – after all, its entry to the canon itself had been questioned by the Rabbis.[19] The ANE often became

[11]   See Katharine J. Dell, 'Studies of the Didactical Books of the Hebrew Bible/Old Testament', in *Hebrew Bible/Old Testament: The History of Its Interpretation*, ed. Magne Saebø (Gottingen, 2012), 3.1:603–624.

[12]   E. W. Budge, *The Teaching of Amen-Em-Apt, Son of Kanekht* (London, 1924). See R. Norman Whybray, *The Book of Proverbs: A Survey of Modern Study* (Leiden, 1995), who uses this discovery as the starting point of modern scholarly study of Proverbs. See also Knut Heim's overview of twentieth-century trends in wisdom scholarship in 'The Phenomenon and Literature of Wisdom', in *Hebrew Bible Old Testament: The History of Its Interpretation*, ed. M. Saebø (Göttingen, 2015), 3.2:559–593.

[13]   Typified by W. G. Lambert, *Babylonian Wisdom Literature* (Oxford, 1960).

[14]   G. E. Wright, *God Who Acts: Biblical Theology as Recital*, SBT 8 (London, 1952), provides a good example of this older scholarly view that saw the salvation history as the beating heart of the Old Testament.

[15]   E.g., W. McKane, *Proverbs: A New Approach*, OTL (London, 1970), found in Proverbs 1–9 a Yahwistic reinterpretation of an older, empirical more mundane wisdom.

[16]   Uz is normally identified with Edom.

[17]   Job and Mesopotamian parallels to the suffering lamenter figure are well known. See overview and comparison in Katharine J. Dell, *Job: Where Shall Wisdom Be Found?*, T & T Clark Study Guides to the Old Testament (London, 2016).

[18]   Closer to French philosophy, e.g., Pascal's pensées; see Eric S. Christianson, *Ecclesiastes through the Centuries*, Blackwell Bible Commentary (Oxford, 2007).

[19]   See Katharine J. Dell, 'Ecclesiastes as Wisdom: Consulting Early Interpreters', *VT* 44 (1994): 301–332.

the starting point for defining 'wisdom' or 'wisdom literature' before moving onto the biblical material,[20] even though, ironically, there was no such category in these cultures and, in circular fashion, their 'wisdom texts' tended to be isolated on the basis of biblical parallels.

Texts generally started to be dated earlier in this period and seen as having older roots, and hence as having possibly influenced other books in the canon, including, in particular, the eighth-century prophets and Deuteronomic law;[21] but there was also a dominating interest in social context that came to a head in the mid-twentieth century.[22] Again, Egyptian and Mesopotamian social and literary models held great sway in these debates, but the net was also cast around other parts of the OT/HB to find 'wise' types such as Joseph and Daniel and other 'wisdom literature' such as wisdom psalms and narratives. There was a concern to define wisdom literature separately though – these other relatives were either in the wisdom family or not.[23] There was a particular interest in reconstructing the social location of sages and scribes, the role of the court and the place of schools in the educational task.[24] There was also much interest in theological themes in the three books and yet attempts to integrate them into visions of 'Old Testament theology' were pretty thin. It was not until the later twentieth century that 'wisdom theology' found a stronger voice in such 'Old Testament theology' assessments, although even then there was still the feeling that salvation history, narrative, covenant themes and the promised land were where Israel's true heart beat and that notions of God as creator were secondary and often later theological developments.[25] One of the key reasons for hiving these three books off from others in the first place was the noted lack of interest in national events and key moments in Israelite history and

---

[20] As does Stuart Weeks in his wisdom introduction: *An Introduction to the Study of Wisdom Literature*, Approaches to Biblical Studies (London; New York, 2010).

[21] Eighth-century prophecy in particular was seen to have been influenced by wisdom. See H. W. Wolff's various commentaries on Amos, Hosea and Micah in the Hermeneia series. Also on Deuteronomy, the classic work is M. Weinfeld, *Deuteronomy and the Deuteronomic School* (Oxford, 1972).

[22] A dominating interest in this aspect and the question of who 'the wise' were. Cf. Eric W. Heaton, *The School Tradition of the Old Testament* (Oxford, 1994).

[23] James L. Crenshaw has always maintained wisdom's essential separateness as a classification with clear parameters; see his collection of articles in *Urgent Advice and Probing Questions: Collected Writings on Old Testament Wisdom* (Macon, 1995).

[24] A. Lemaire, *Les écoles et la formation de la Bible dans l'ancien Israel*, OBO 39 (Fribourg; Göttingen, 1981).

[25] Walter Brueggemann, *Theology of the Old Testament: Testimony, Dispute, Advocacy* (Minneapolis, 1997).

major theological themes such as covenant. So it seems that a theological evaluation of wisdom literature might be just as much about what these books do not contain as what they do feature!

In the twenty-first century, with its hermeneutical questions and focus on the reader, on the canon, on final form, on the feminine and on intertextuality (to name but a few modern trends), new questions have arisen, not least whether the grouping of 'wisdom literature' is ultimately a subjective readerly one.[26] Other alignments have been suggested, including a Solomonic one that brings the Song of Songs into the frame.[27] This inclusion would change the parameters of theological discussion too. However, partly through the interest in final form and books as they stand in the canon of scripture, there has been a rise in interest in the theology of 'wisdom'. A number of recent works have sought to find key dominating themes – Wisdom and Creation,[28] Woman Wisdom,[29] the fear of the LORD,[30] character ethics in Wisdom[31] and so on. Commentaries and monographs have also been written with quite a theological emphasis.[32] Whilst Job and Ecclesiastes more naturally evoke a theological evaluation, it is interesting that Proverbs, with its less obvious theological nature (at least outside Proverbs 1–9), has been brought into this theological trend.[33] There are many maxims that have no theological content but are

[26] It is a subjective evaluation at the end of the day – see discussion in Kynes, *An Obituary for 'Wisdom Literature'.*

[27] Roland E. Murphy, *The Tree of Life: An Exploration of Biblical Wisdom Literature*, 2nd ed. (Grand Rapids, 1996); Katharine J. Dell, 'Does the Song of Songs Have Any Connections to Wisdom?', in *Perspectives on the Song of Songs*, ed. Anselm C. Hagedorn, BZAW 346 (Berlin, 2005), 8–26.

[28] Leo G. Perdue, *Wisdom and Creation: The Theology of Wisdom Literature* (Nashville, 1994).

[29] Claudia V. Camp, *Wisdom and the Feminine in the Book of Proverbs*, BLS 11 (Sheffield, 1985); B. Lang, *Wisdom and the Book of Proverbs: An Israelite Goddess Redefined* (New York, 1986).

[30] Tremper Longman III, *The Fear of the Lord Is Wisdom: A Theological Introduction to Wisdom in Israel* (Grand Rapids, 2017).

[31] William P. Brown, *Character in Crisis: A Fresh Approach to the Wisdom Literature of the Old Testament* (Grand Rapids, 1996).

[32] E.g., on Proverbs, Ernest C. Lucas, *Proverbs*, THOTC (Grand Rapids, 2015); on Job, the influential liberation theology reading of Gustavo Gutiérrez, *On Job: God-Talk and the Suffering of the Innocent* (Maryknoll, 1987); and, e.g., on Ecclesiastes, Longman, *The Book of Ecclesiastes*, NICOT (Grand Rapids, 1998); and readings from ecological and feminist perspectives, such as that of Elsa Támez, *When the Horizons Close: Rereading Ecclesiastes* (Maryknoll, 2000).

[33] Christine Roy Yoder, 'Objects of our Affections: Emotions and the Moral Life in Proverbs 1–9', in *Shaking Heaven and Earth: Essays in Honor of Walter Brueggemann and Charles Cousar*, ed. C. R. Yoder, K. M. O'Connor, E. E. Johnson and S. P. Saunders (Louisville, 2005).

essentially observations about a whole range of aspects of life, but they are often put into a cluster where mention of Yahweh frames the set, hence there is an implicit theological framework even in the sayings collections. None of these books, though, displays one straightforward theological position, with dialogue and debate between opposing views being at the heart of the wisdom enterprise. There are nowadays some resonances of nineteenth-century concerns with more integration across books in the canon and a generally later dating preferred. It is into this current debate that I primarily step as I now turn to the three traditionally named 'wisdom books' and look for common theological themes. As I say, while I have written quite extensively on why I think that Job is the outlier of the three on many counts, including the genres used and the attitudes taken, for the purposes of this chapter, I will attempt to draw the three wisdom books together.

KEY THEMES IN COMMON

The Doctrine of Retribution

At the most basic level, an interest in the doctrine of retribution is at the heart of 'wisdom', offering two choices of behaviour with their automatic reward or punishment consequences. Becoming wise involves a choice between two paths of behaviour and hence between their inevitable outcomes, and this binary pattern is found throughout these works. In a sense, the opposite classifications of righteous/wicked, good/evil, rich/poor, industrious/lazy, wise/fool and so on represent extremes of behaviour or character 'types' that have little reality in the complexities of a real human being. And yet, this is the framework that seems to be basic to the wisdom worldview: that it is by discovering character types that decisions about appropriate behaviour can be taken and the consequences of that behaviour judged. Let us consider three random verses from Proverbs, where this pattern is first set down, reinforced by the form of the two-line saying:

> Prov 3:33: 'The LORD's curse is on the house of the wicked, but he blesses the abode of the righteous.'
> Prov 5:22: 'The iniquities of the wicked ensnare them, and they are caught in the toils of their sin.'
> Prov 24:1: 'Do not envy the wicked, nor desire to be with them.'

In the first of these proverbs, the traditional contrast is drawn between the wicked and the righteous, and we could multiply with many examples. This is the basic theological idea that God blesses the

righteous but curses the wicked. They are not simply ingrained charac-
teristics; rather they are theological virtues/evils led by God's purpose.
God reinforces the binary characters in that once they are established
God metes out suitable reward or punishment. This is the 'doctrine of
retribution' – that is, it is about reward and punishment for behaviour.
This is what scholars have called the 'act-consequence' relationship in
Proverbs – every action has a consequence that can be known.[34] On one
level, it is mechanistic and yet individual actions make up a network of
actions that then impact on a whole characterisation of someone as
either righteous or wicked.[35] Once the choices for good or bad have been
made, God reinforces the behaviour by punishment or reward.[36] This is
an antithetical proverb, contrasting the two paths of behaviour with
'but' indicating two options. The second proverb here concerns the
wicked only and the second line simply reinforces the first. Here the
wicked ensnare themselves and God is not immediately present. This
reinforces the idea that it is human action that is primarily to blame for
the predicaments in which humans find themselves. It is a characteristic of the wicked that once set upon this path, they tend to go on
entangling themselves, deeper and deeper. The third proverb here opens
up a hint of contradiction in the scheme. The question is raised in the
reader's mind, why would anyone envy the wicked or want to be like
them? This suggests that all is not quite so straightforward in the world
of righteous and wicked – why would the righteous wish to emulate the
wicked? Of course, this desire is condemned (e.g., Prov 17:15; 18:5), but

---

[34] First coined by K. Koch, 'Is There a Doctrine of Retribution in the Old Testament?', in
Theodicy in the Old Testament, ed. James L. Crenshaw (Philadelphia; London, 1983),
57–87. Koch thought that there was a mechanical outcome for most proverbs, not the
result of God stepping in to administer punishment and reward. Many since him have
found it more nuanced (see overview in Tova Forti, 'The Concept of "Reward" in
Proverbs: A Diachronic or Synchronic Approach?', *CurBR* 12 [2014]: 128–144); and see
God as an important part of the picture, e.g., Peter Hatton, *Contradiction in the Book
of Proverbs: The Deep Waters of Counsel*, SOTSMS (Aldershot, 2008), has argued that
two causal phenomena can be identified in Proverbs, one divine, the other human and
that they are in tension. Timothy Sandoval, *The Discourse of Wealth and Poverty in
the Book of Proverbs* (Leiden, 2005), argues against a mechanistic order, preferring to
speak of 'a symbolic construction of the world within which the values and virtues of
the sages make sense' (p. 94, n.48).

[35] Lucas (*Proverbs*) rephrases the act-consequence relationship in terms of character
formation rather than individual actions and so prefers to speak of a 'character-
consequence nexus' (p. 204).

[36] Lucas (*Proverbs*) prefers to take a theological view that roots this nexus in the
character and will of God and suggests that while it works most of the time, God's
purposes are not fully known by humans.

the very fact that it is mentioned indicates that such an attitude was present. Proverbs tantalises us with such a possibility but does not afford much more detail. For example, Prov 24:15–16 mentions the possibility that, threatened by a wicked person, the righteous may 'fall' seven times, but it is then affirmed that they will arise again whereas the wicked will stumble and Prov 25:26 warns the righteous person not to give way to the wicked, suggesting that powerful forces seek to thwart those on the righteous path (cf. Prov 28:28). It is up to Job and Ecclesiastes to explore this further.

It is clear that the dialogue between Job and his friends in the book of Job is reliant upon the same scheme.[37] Whilst the friends tend to uphold the status quo, Job too indicates that he knows the scheme when he says: 'Yet the righteous hold to their way, and they that have clean hands grow stronger and stronger' (17:9). Eliphaz could not put it more strongly when he says that 'The wicked writhe in pain all their days' (Job 15:19a). And yet that note of uncertainty found in Proverbs echoes more strongly in Job, especially when Bildad says in a passage about the 'godless' (implying 'the wicked') that, 'their shoots spread over the garden' (Job 8:16). Here we have the answer to why people might wish to emulate the wicked – they seem to prosper! In fact, they seem to prosper at the expense of the righteous. The friends also ask deep questions 'Can mortals be righteous before God?' (Eliphaz in Job 4:17a) and 'Is it any pleasure to the Almighty if you are righteous?' (Eliphaz in Job 22:3a). Job picks up these same questions and intensifies them. Here is a righteous man who is suffering bitterly – he is questioning the doctrine of retribution at its source – the fair/unfair treatment of human beings by God. If God 'directs the steps' of a person's path (Prov 16:9), then he must be to blame if a person on the righteous path receives the opposite to the expected reward – punishment. And yet Job goes further in his bitterness and despair to question the whole premise of the doctrine of retribution when he says: 'It is all one; therefore I say, he [God] destroys both the blameless and the wicked' (Job 9:22). Here Job is not simply worrying about the seeming mismatch in the fates of righteous and wicked, but he is questioning the very premise that God treats them differently. If God destroys both, God is equally capable of

[37] The doctrine of retribution is the main theological theme of the dialogue section of Job. Disinterested righteousness characterises the Prologue and Epilogue whilst the God-human relationship dominates the God speeches and Job's replies; see Katharine J. Dell, *The Book of Job as Sceptical Literature*, BZAW 197 (Berlin, 1991).

upholding both – in the end the treatment is arbitrary and God is not playing according to the rules.[38]

In Ecclesiastes, we find verses that straightforwardly uphold the doctrine of retribution, as found in Proverbs: 'I said in my heart, God will judge the righteous and the wicked, for he has appointed a time for every matter, and for every work' (Eccl 3:17). This is one of this author's more affirmative statements in contrast with his musings on the vanity of human life in general. Of course, this could hint that, although God is in charge, human beings have no knowledge of God's choices in individual cases. How predestined are these outcomes?[39] The author of Ecclesiastes makes it clear that there is much injustice in the world such that opposite fates to what would be expected occur to both righteous and wicked. So he says 'in my vain life I have seen everything; there are righteous people who perish in their righteousness, and there are wicked people who prolong their life in their evil-doing' (Eccl 7:15). Here he is reinforcing what is said by Job, but only slightly hinted at in Proverbs, that the system seems to be going wrong. In this case, being righteous doesn't lead to the expected prosperity and longevity that is assumed for them, and those blessings are seemingly bestowed on the wicked. And yet, there is an underlying sense in Ecclesiastes, following Proverbs more closely, that the doctrine is alive and well at the end of the day, accompanied by a requisite piety: 'but it will not be well with the wicked, neither will they prolong their days like a shadow, because they do not stand in fear before God' (Eccl 8:13). Once again, God comes into the picture, with the nuance here that a human attitude of 'fear' before God may make all the difference. It is interesting that this echoes a key phrase of Proverbs: 'the fear of the LORD is the beginning of wisdom' (Prov 9:10). It is also echoed in Job: 'And he [God] said to humankind, "Truly, the fear of the LORD, that is wisdom"' (Job 28:28), admittedly in a section most think of as a separate poem and not words from the mouth of Job.

---

[38] The more profound issue of theodicy is thus raised – how can a good God allow such evil? See James L. Crenshaw, *Defending God: Biblical Responses to the Problem of Evil* (Oxford, 2005). See also R. Norman Whybray, 'Wisdom, Suffering and the Freedom of God in the Book of Job', in *In Search of True Wisdom: Essays in Old Testament Interpretation in Honour of Ronald E. Clements*, ed. E. Ball, JSOTS 300 (Sheffield, 1999), 231–245.

[39] This is a well-known debate in Ecclesiastes studies. For an overview of key scholarly issues in the book, see R. Norman Whybray, *Ecclesiastes* (Sheffield, 1989).

The Fear of the LORD

Mention of 'the fear of the LORD' brings us onto a second theological theme that is often found in common to wisdom books.[40] It accompanies the doctrine of retribution, but it goes further to say that even if all the answers to life's mysteries are not available, a basic attitude of trust in God will ensure a return to the right path, the path of good that leads to life. It is noticeable that in Job this phrase is reserved for a separate poem in Job 28. One could argue that Job's whole life is lived in the fear of the LORD – he never abandons faith in God, however much he may waver and protest – and he is pictured as one who 'feared God' in the opening line of the book (1:1, cf. 1:8–9; 2:3), clearly a model of piety in the opening prologue. The friends echo this: 'Is not your fear of God your confidence?' asks Eliphaz (Job 4:16) and Bildad accuses Job of 'doing away with the fear of God' (15:4). Yet it is not such a prominent theme in this book. Nor is it so prominent in Ecclesiastes, although the author does recommend it a few times (3:14; 5:7; 7:18).[41] It is used to reinforce the doctrine of retribution 'Though sinners do evil a hundred times and prolong their lives, yet I know that it will be well with those who fear God, because they stand in fear before him' (Eccl 8:12; cf. 8:13). Perhaps the most famous mention of the fear of God is in the epilogue to Ecclesiastes, possibly by a different hand, which concludes the book with 'Fear God and keep his commandments' (12:13), an unusual alignment of this piety with mention of the commandments (possibly of the law).

The phrase comes up many times in Proverbs, normally in conjunction with good and bad choices. The wicked are indicted 'because they hated knowledge and did not choose the fear of the LORD' (Prov 1:29). This again shows the tension between fates already pre-ordained and the choices that humans might make. Once on the path to good and bad, it is hard to change course. The fear of the LORD is often paired with

---

40 Longman, *The Fear of the Lord*. It may have its origins in the awed response of the people in Exod 14:31; 19:16; 20:18–21 and it is formulated in covenant terms in Deuteronomy. Michael V. Fox (*Proverbs 1–9*, AB 18a [New York, 2000]) argues that there is still an element of dread when the phrase is used in Proverbs, e.g., 14:27; 24:21–22. However, he acknowledges that it seems to have become more of a motivation for moral behaviour in the context of Proverbs.

41 Longman argues that Qohelet is advocating not the kind of fear that leads to obedience but the kind of fear that would lead a person to run away and hide. Longman, 'The "Fear of God" in the Book of Ecclesiastes', *BBR* 25 (2015): 13–22. I am not personally convinced that there is such a different meaning from Proverbs here.

knowledge (e.g., Prov 2:5; 9:10).[42] As well as being 'the beginning of wisdom' (9:10; cf. 1:7) or 'instruction in wisdom' (15:33), it also accompanies long life (Prov 10:27; 14:26) and is described as a 'fountain of life' in contrast to the 'snares of death' (Prov 14:27; 18:4). It is even equated with 'life' (Prov 19:23) which is, in turn, wisdom's 'reward' (Prov 22:4). It is closely linked to a third theological theme, that of the benefits of wisdom, both with a small 'w' but also of Wisdom herself, a female personification of the attribute who is inextricably linked in relationship to God, mediating between the divine and human realms, which I shall go on to discuss in the next section.

Wisdom/wisdom

Wisdom in Proverbs is both the attribute to be attained and the gift on offer from a personification of the quality in feminine terms, Woman Wisdom. The opening verses (1:1–7) speak of 'learning about wisdom' as the goal of the book; and as we just saw, wisdom springs from the fear of God (9:10). In that sense, it is inextricably linked to the divine. In Prov 1:20, we are introduced to the figure of Wisdom who 'cries out in the street' about the wisdom that she has on offer. Whilst this is a poetic/rhetorical device,[43] its effect is to present wisdom as a gift on offer from God via this figure of Wisdom, freely available for all who will 'make your ear attentive' (Prov 2:2). It is in Proverbs 1–9 that this figure features, in the more theological section of the book, and there is more reflection in this section on the benefits wisdom brings. In fact, it is clearly stated that 'the LORD gives wisdom, from his mouth come knowledge and understanding' (Prov 2:6; cf. 24:3). These other two qualities often accompany wisdom closely (cf. Prov 1:1–7; 2:10). Linked to the doctrine of retribution too, wisdom is 'for the upright' (Prov 2:7) and there are many exhortations to 'Get' it, for example,

---

[42] Raymond Van Leeuwen, *Proverbs*, NIB V (Nashville, 1997) sums up the meaning of the phrase in Proverbs as '*religion* in the comprehensive sense of life in its entirely devoted to God's service. Here *all* activities are undertaken in the light of God's presence and purposes in the world' (p. 33, his italics).

[43] A poetical device is the majority view, although Wisdom has been seen as a hypostasis of God (as in the apocryphal Wisdom of Solomon). The idea that it springs from the Egyptian idea of Ma'at ('world order') is widely acknowledged; see Christa Bauer-Kayatz, *Studien zu Proverbien 1–9. Eine form- und motivgeschichtliche Untersuchung unter Einbeziehung Ägyptischen Vergleichmaterials*, WMANT 22 (Neukirchen-Vluyn, 1966).

Prov. 4:5, 7; 7:4 (paired with 'insight').[44] It is taught by parent to child (4:11) and the parent calls on the child, in the instruction texts of Prov 1–9, to pay attention to it as a key quality (Prov 5:1). One of the key benefits of wisdom is happiness (Prov 3:13) – it is also one's ticket to future happiness (Prov 19:20). Wisdom is not personified in the sayings collections but is a quality to be pursued and refined, inextricably linked to the righteous, the humble, those who listen and understand. 'How much better to get wisdom than gold!' says Prov 16:16, echoing the description of Woman Wisdom as more priceless than jewels in Prov 8:11. It is in Prov 3:13 that we get the first indication that there is a connection between Wisdom and the creative work of God and this is a key theological leap: 'The LORD by Wisdom founded the earth; by understanding he established the heavens.' We now learn that Wisdom is part of the creation, a means by which God created in that she precedes the establishing of the heavens. Wisdom is built into the structure of the world in a profound way but also linked inextricably to the divine will and intention. This leads on to another key theme of this literature – the presupposition of God as creator, to which I will proceed shortly. It is in Proverbs 8, though, from verse 22 onwards, that we have a fuller description of Woman Wisdom's role in creation which I will describe below.

Neither Job nor Ecclesiastes feature Woman Wisdom, but Job does have a poem to wisdom in chapter 28 that seems to personify the attribute that it is hidden to all except God. As the wonders of the earth, and the efforts of miners to find the earth's hidden treasures, are enumerated, the question is repeatedly asked 'where shall wisdom be found? And where is the place of understanding?' (Job 28:12, 20; the same pairing of these two attributes as in Proverbs). This hiddenness of wisdom contrasts with the availability of wisdom in Proverbs. Only at the end of the wisdom hymn is wisdom on offer to the one who fears the LORD (28:28). Elsewhere in Job, wisdom is mentioned as an attribute in much the same way as in Proverbs. It is a quality that the friends claim to have and that they are sure the wicked do not have (Job 4:21). The friends warn Job of not limiting God's wisdom 'For wisdom is many-sided. Know then that God exacts of you less than your guilt deserves' (Job 11:6). This is a part of the friends' argument that there are deeper aspects to Job's suffering, and hence for them his presumed guilt, than

---

[44] See my own Wisdom introduction, Katharine J. Dell, *Get Wisdom, Get Insight: An Introduction to Israel's Wisdom Literature* (London, 2000), where I took this common phrase as my title.

Job realises and that he is limiting God's wisdom in his claims to unfair
treatment. Job accuses them of the same – 'do you limit wisdom to
yourself?' (Job 15:8). Job too knows that 'With God are wisdom and
strength' (Job 12:13, 16). There is also a debate about who is qualified
to be wise – do you have to be aged to be wise? (Job 12:12). Not according
to the fourth 'young' friend Elihu. Job badgers the friends for their
wisdom – 'If you would only keep silent', he says, 'that would be your
wisdom!' (Job 13:5). In the God speeches too, the subject of wisdom
comes up – it is God who has 'put wisdom in the inward parts' of
humans (38:36). God is the source of all wisdom and he holds the kind
of wisdom that humans cannot aspire to – the knowledge of how many
clouds there are, the ability to make it rain (38:37), understanding of the
ways of animals and birds. This is the wisdom of God in creating and
sustaining the world, chiming with the God as creator theme I shall go
on to discuss.

In Ecclesiastes, the author has an ambivalent attitude to the acquisition of wisdom. On the one hand, it is the ground of this work, his goal
in life (Eccl 1:13) but, on the other, he realises that it is ultimately
unattainable by humans. God is the one who has all wisdom and yet
there seems to be no system to whether he reveals it or not or to how
reward and punishment are meted out. When he takes on the persona of
Solomon for one and a half chapters (Eccl 1:12–2:26), he is deliberately
becoming the wisest king ever known (cf. 1 Kings 4:29–34). The
Solomonic quest is 'to know wisdom' but it turns out to be a worthless
chase. It may lead to great wealth and power but does it ultimately lead
to satisfaction?: 'For in much wisdom is much vexation, and those who
increase knowledge increase sorrow' (Eccl 1:18). Wisdom helps to guide
this author's mind and choices and he values it above all else, and yet he
cannot attain it (Eccl 7:23) and the quest is causing him grief (Eccl 8:16).
He swings on a proverbial pendulum of seeing wisdom as great as light
(Eccl 2:13) or life itself (Eccl 7:12), to seeing it as a burden and a toil (Eccl
2:21) and a vain thing.[45]

Creation

The next theme I wish to consider is that of creation. There is no doubt
that the conception of God as creator (and not as saviour or redeemer of
Israel, nor even as covenant partner) dominates this literature.[46] There

---

[45] For more discussion, see Katharine J. Dell, 'A Wise Man Reflecting on Wisdom:
Qoheleth/Ecclesiastes', *TynBul* 71 (2020): 137–152.
[46] Perdue, *Wisdom and Creation*.

is an implicit monotheism here too.[47] Scholars have debated whether creation is the key theme or whether it is a sub-theme.[48] Certainly, from a theological angle, it is a presupposition about God that he is the creator and sustainer of the world. This is agreed upon by all three of these wisdom books. In Prov 8:22–31 'The LORD created me at the beginning of his work, the first of his acts of long ago' (8:22). As in Proverbs 3, Wisdom is created (here in chapter 8, though, *qanah* lit. 'purchased' is used) by God at the start and she is the means through which creation has structure and meaning. There follows a marvellous description of creation – she watched with delight as God shaped, made, established, drew a circle, made firm and assigned boundaries. She was beside God, delighting and rejoicing in the world and in the human race. This is the strongest statement of God as creator in the book, but it is presupposed in the sayings too, for example, Prov 20:12 'The hearing ear and the seeing eye – the LORD has made them both'. Ultimately, 'The LORD has made everything for its purpose' (16:4a).

In Job, Job himself recognises God as creator – in 9:9 God 'made the Bear and Orion, the Pleiades and the chambers of the south' and on a personal level 'Your hands fashioned and made me' (10:8a). Furthermore, in Job 26:3, 'by his wind the heavens were made fair; his hand pierced the fleeing serpent' indicates a reference to the myth of the serpent conquered by God at creation. This is all taken up in much more depth in the speeches of God where we find four chapters of description of God's creation of the world, focusing particularly on the wild animals. God reveals that he made the Leviathan and the Behemoth (Job 40:15) too, whether these be real animals or mythical beasts or even fictional. These speeches are often described as a paean of praise to God the creator and form a central expression of this doctrine, not just within the wisdom literature but within the whole Hebrew Bible, in interesting ways an alternative starting point to Genesis 1–3.[49]

Ecclesiastes contains less about the process of creation itself,[50] although there is an explicit acknowledgement of this action in 11:5, 'Just as you do not know how the breath comes to the bones in the mother's womb, so you do not know the work of God, who makes

---

[47] Some have found a goddess consort in the figure of Woman Wisdom, but that is a minority view. See Lang, *Wisdom and the book of Proverbs*.

[48] Most recently Weeks, *An Introduction to the Study of Wisdom Literature*.

[49] Terence E. Fretheim, *God and World in the Old Testament: A Relational Theology of Creation* (Nashville; Edinburgh, 2005).

[50] See Schwáb, Chapter 20 in this volume, for discussion of the creation theme in Ecclesiastes.

everything.' An interest in the creation of humans and of animals (3:21) comes through here. God makes physical entities and he makes each day 'the day of prosperity' and the 'day of adversity' (7:14). If God decides to 'make crooked' no one can straighten it, and the irony is that human beings cannot find out the future (or what God has planned for their future) (7:13–14). It is certainly presupposed in the same way as the other books that God is creator rather than in any other theological guise. This author is certainly aware of the patterns of nature's cycles, expressing the stability of repetitive natural occurrence. In 1:4–7, the changes of a cyclical nature are compared to human generations and are stable acts of God's creation, like the earth itself.

Communication

A rather more subtle theme that is arguably not so explicitly theological is that of communication. This theme has not been emphasised by scholars to the extent that it should be, in my view. This involves issues of relationship between humans and between humans, the natural world and God, but it is specifically about how that is communicated. The words that are communicated give us insights into the character and emotions and priorities of the speakers. Many communication proverbs contain no mention of God, but the ones that do are of interest to our theological emphasis here. In Prov 30:5, 'every word of God proves true'. By contrast 'lying lips are an abomination to the LORD' (Prov 12:22). This links up with wider issues about the use of body imagery in Proverbs, but lips, tongue, mouth are all explicitly linked with word and communication. Lips are the guardians of the mouth, enabling the wise to judge when to speak 'noble things' and 'what is right' (Prov 8:6) and helping them to judge when to keep silent (Prov 5:2). Woman Folly, by contrast, has 'lips' that 'drip honey' (5:3) and once spoken 'the utterance of your lips' is a snare (Prov 6:2).[51] The king is known for his 'righteous lips' (Prov 16:10, 13) and as God's representative conveys the centrality of the need for the wisdom that lies behind the 'inspired decisions' uttered by those lips (16:10).

In Job, one of Job's key qualities at the opening of the book is that 'Job did not sin with his lips' (2:10), with body language again a feature of Job (e.g., lips in Job 8:21; 11:5; 13:6; 15:6; 16:5; 23:12; 27:4; 32:20; 33:3). In 4:12–16, 'a word' comes 'stealing' to the ear of Eliphaz, a word of

---

[51]   On Woman Folly, see Claudia V. Camp, *Wise, Strange and Holy: The Strange Woman and the Making of the Bible*, JSOTSup 320 (Sheffield, 2000).

vision from God, suggesting a communication plane beyond the strictly rational. Later, the friends cite God's word of consolation 'that deals gently with you' (Job 15:11) – are these not enough for Job? The finale has God speaking words that seem to settle the debate in Job 42:7, expressing anger at the friends and supporting Job – 'for you [the friends] have not spoken of me what is right as my servant Job has'. Again, the spoken word is key. But communication is not simply about words – the 'hand' of the LORD is prominent in Job – God's smiting hand is blamed by Job for his ills.

Ecclesiastes with its character as a 'pensée' by an individual author features the communication theme less, but he does quote a proverb in Eccl 10:12 that sounds familiar: 'Words spoken by the wise bring them favour, but the lips of fools consume them'. He too speaks of the 'hand of God' that controls the deeds of the righteous but 'whether it is love or hate one does not know' (9:1). God is at all times behind the quest to gain wisdom, but here the author expresses doubt that humans can know God's will. The inner dialogue of this author as expressed through changing sentiments and opposing ideas is an effective method of communication in itself.

Life and Death

Ecclesiastes comes into its own though on the subject of death! For this author, death is the great relativiser of life. The quest to succeed becomes pointless in the light of this common human fate. The striving for wealth is empty if one has no one to leave one's money to, and even if one has, why should another enjoy everything for which one has striven? Work too is all too often an empty reward, given one's ultimate fate. Ecclesiastes 8:8 expresses the author's view well, 'No one has power over the wind to restrain the wind, or power over the day of death; there is no discharge from the battle, nor does wickedness deliver those who practice it.' Only God wields this power and even God cannot in this worldview reverse the natural human ending to life. For this author, life is short (Eccl 2:3b) and often hateful (Eccl 2:17) and yet there is also a profound affirmation of the need for enjoyment whilst one is here in Ecclesiastes – 'eat drink and find enjoyment in all the toil' he says, but with the caveat 'for the few days of the life God gives us, for this is our lot' (Eccl 5:18). He uses the imagery of a shadow to express the brevity of life (Eccl 6:12) and he often describes life as 'vain'. And yet 'life under the sun' is all that humans have and so 'I commend enjoyment' (Eccl 8:15), not just eating and drinking (Eccl 10:19) but also enjoying one's partner in life (Eccl 9:9). I would argue, against those who see Ecclesiastes as very optimistic,[52] that he always tempers his 'life' statements with a melancholy tone and so he clearly shows the balance between the two opposites.

For Proverbs, death is simply the opposite to life and the path of wickedness leads to death. Proverbs is more optimistic about wisdom being the route to life in the fullest sense. Woman Wisdom offers life, her counterpart Folly's way 'leads down to death and her paths to the shades' (2:18) and 'her feet go down to death; her steps follow the path to Sheol' (5:5); indeed, 'her house is the way to Sheol, going down to the chambers of death' (7:27). By contrast, 'in the path of righteousness there is life, in walking its path there is no death' (Prov 12:28). The imagery of a fountain of water is used to describe life (Prov. 13:14), also linked with the fear of the LORD which is sometimes described as a fountain (Prov 14:27). Linking up with the communication theme 'death and life are in the power of the tongue' (Prov 18:21). A long life is an ideal of Proverbs (e.g., Prov 9:11) and this is on offer from Wisdom: 'Long life is in her right hand; in her left hand are riches and honour' (Prov 3:16). Wisdom is also described as a 'tree of life' (3:18).[53] Wisdom is life-giving and nourishing to the soul as well as to the intellect. This is explicitly linked to finding God; for example, in Prov 8:35, Wisdom speaks and says 'Whoever finds me finds life and obtains favour from the LORD'. Life is the path that is on offer to the would-be wise.

All three books presuppose that Sheol is the place of the dead, from whence there is no return and where there is no further contact with God.[54] It is portrayed as a house (Job 30:23) or as a pit (Job 33:22) with gates (Job 38:17). Job is frightened that he may die and hence go to Sheol before he has finished his conversation with God. The death theme for Job is more of a death-wish, for example, 'I would choose strangling and death rather than this body' (Job 7:15). At one point in the book – Job 28:22 in the hymn to wisdom – Death and Abaddon (another name for the place of the dead) are personified as saying that they have heard a 'rumour' of wisdom's location but no more than that. For Job, 'life' is firmly in God's hand – 'in his hand is the life of every living thing and the breath of every human being' (12:1). Life and light are often aligned (e.g., Job 33:28–30). In the epilogue, Job receives the blessings of wisdom:

---

[52] R. Norman Whybray, 'Qoheleth, Preacher of Joy', *JSOT* 23 (1982): 87–98; Eunny P. Lee, *The Vitality of Enjoyment in Qoheleth's Theological Rhetoric* (Berlin, 2005).

[53] The title of Murphy's introduction to the wisdom literature – *The Tree of Life* – which also includes the Song of Songs.

[54] Philip Johnston, *Shades of Sheol: Death and Afterlife in the Old Testament* (Leicester, 2002).

restored health, progeny and a long life that enables him to see four generations of his family going forward.

CONCLUSION

I could go on with further themes,[55] but I think it will be helpful to round this essay off with an assessment of these findings. Although I have attempted to bring these books together thematically, I think I have also demonstrated how different the books are too, not perhaps in overarching theological terms but in relation to the way they set out these messages. The genres in the three are very different. They also interlink intertextually with books outside this narrow group and this belies any attempt to draw narrow boundaries. All three link up with Deuteronomic influence, and with the Psalms, not just wisdom psalms but the themes link well beyond those. Proverbs 1–9 shows some close affinity with Deuteronomic precepts, for example, 'bind the command-ments' and the social ethics of Deuteronomy comes to influence its pages too.[56] Sentiments in the dialogue of Job in particular have been linked to Deuteronomic ideas, for example, widow and orphan.[57] Ecclesiastes less so, but some have suggested Deuteronomic influence in the Epilogue.[58] Wisdom psalms are an amorphous group in that they are generally defined on the basis of links with these three 'wisdom' books.[59] The book of Job, in particular, seeks to subvert psalmic lament in the speeches of Job.[60] But looking at the theological themes listed above, many of them could be equally applied to the psalter – the final two themes that I discussed, life and death and communication, for example. These are grand themes that permeate biblical literature which brings us back to the point of what characterises a theology of

---

[55]   Wealth and poverty might be another theme, along with other specific topics such as work, education and family relationships, but these veer off from being strictly theological in nature. See Sandoval, *The Discourse of Wealth and Poverty*.

[56]   See the recent article by Bernd U. Schipper, '"Teach Them Diligently to Your Son!": The Book of Proverbs and Deuteronomy', in *Reading Proverbs Intertextually*, ed. Katharine Dell and Will Kynes, LHBOTS 629 (London, 2019), 21–34.

[57]   Susannah Ticciati, *Job and the Disruption of Identity: Reading beyond Barth* (London, 2005).

[58]   Deuteronomic influence in the Epilogue of Ecclesiastes was recently argued for, e.g., by Craig G. Bartholomew, *Ecclesiastes*, BCOTWP (Grand Rapids, 2009).

[59]   On a broad definition, the following psalms are contenders for the 'wisdom psalm' category in my view: Psalms 1, 14, 19, 25, 32, 33, 34, 36, 37, 39, 49, 51, 53, 62, 73, 78, 90, 92, 94, 104, 105, 106, 111, 112, 119, 127 and 128.

[60]   See Will Kynes, *'My Psalm Has Turned into Weeping': Job's Dialogue with the Psalms*, BZAW 437 (Berlin, 2012).

'wisdom' from themes outside it.[61] Whilst the key themes are the doctrine of retribution, the fear of the LORD, the quest for wisdom/ Wisdom and the doctrine of creation, these themes are not confined to these books and yet they are present in large part. The other two themes of communication and life and death are also much broader but are particularly characteristic of at least sections of this literature. However, the purpose of this 'wisdom' literature is as important as its theology. At the end of the day, it is not just a selection of themes, it is also the 'didactic' approach of these books that seeks to teach and educate, to inspire ethical behaviour and to personalise it such that each and every reader can enter into the simplicity (and yet profundity) of the quest for wisdom. The Epilogue to Ecclesiastes sums it up well: 'Besides being wise, the Teacher also taught the people knowledge, weighing and studying and arranging many proverbs. The teacher sought to find pleasing words and he wrote words of truth plainly' (Eccl 12:9–10). It should not be forgotten though that this is a practical quest behind which stands God, the creator and sustainer, who is in essential relationship with humans and the world and so a theological evaluation is at the heart of the wisdom worldview.

Further Reading

Brown, William. *The Ethos of the Cosmos: The Genesis of Moral Imagination in the Bible*. Grand Rapids: 1999.
   Wisdom's Wonder: Character, Creation, and Crisis in the Bible's Wisdom Literature. Grand Rapids: 2014.
Brueggemann, Walter. *Theology of the Old Testament: Testimony, Dispute, Advocacy*. Minneapolis: 1997. Notably, chapter 24 on the sages of Israel.
Crenshaw, James L., ed. *Theodicy in the Old Testament*. Philadelphia; London: 1983.
   Defending God: Biblical Responses to the Problem of Evil. Oxford: 2005.
Dell, Katharine J. *Job: Where Shall Wisdom Be Found?* T & T Clark Study Guides to the Old Testament. London, 2016.
   The Theology of the Book of Proverbs. OTT. Cambridge: forthcoming.
Fretheim, T. E. *God and World in the Old Testament: A Relational Theology of Creation*. Nashville; Edinburgh: 2005.

---

[61] Creation is a good example – we can overdo comparisons to Genesis 1–11 – see my article advising caution: Katharine J. Dell, 'Exploring Intertextual Links between Ecclesiastes and Genesis 1–11', in *Reading Ecclesiastes Intertextually*, ed. Katharine Dell and Will Kynes, LHBOTS 587 (London, 2014), 3–14.

Longman, Tremper III. *The Fear of the Lord Is Wisdom: A Theological Introduction to Wisdom in Israel.* Grand Rapids: 2017.

Lucas, Ernest C. *Proverbs.* THOTC. Grand Rapids: 2015.

Murphy, Roland E. *The Tree of Life: An Exploration of Biblical Wisdom Literature.* 2nd ed. Grand Rapids: 1996.

Perdue, Leo G. *Wisdom and Creation: The Theology of Wisdom Literature.* Nashville: 1994.

Támez, Elsa. *When the Horizons Close: Rereading Ecclesiastes.* Maryknoll: 2000.

Weeks, Stuart. *An Introduction to the Study of Wisdom Literature.* Approaches to Biblical Studies. London; New York, 2010.

Whybray, R. Norman. 'Wisdom, Suffering and the Freedom of God in the Book of Job'. Pages 231–245 in *In Search of True Wisdom: Essays in Old Testament Interpretation in Honour of Ronald E. Clements.* Edited by E. Ball. JSOTS 300. Sheffield: 1999.

7 The Solomonic Connection: Solomon and Wisdom in Kings and Chronicles

DAVID FIRTH

INTRODUCTION

The figure of Solomon is fundamental to the Old Testament's conception of wisdom. Whether or not we can identify 'wisdom' as a literary genre,[1] we can speak of Old Testament literature which is particularly interested in wisdom as a concept,[2] most notably Job, Proverbs and Ecclesiastes. The concept is explored more widely than just these books, but they remain central. Although Job does not mention Solomon, both Proverbs and Ecclesiastes reference him. For Proverbs, this is explicit, with Solomon named at 1:1, 10:1 and 25:1, each introducing new sections of the book. Ecclesiastes does not name Solomon directly, though the introduction of the Teacher (qōhelet) in the book's introduction (1:1) alludes to him by using the description 'son of David, king in Jerusalem'. Whether taken as a claim for Solomonic authorship or as part of the literary frame constructed for reading the book, it is still agreed that a reference to Solomon is intended.[3] Job's setting in the patriarchal period excludes the possibility of allusion to Solomon.

Solomon's importance for these works is no surprise when we trace his presentation in Kings and Chronicles. For both, he is paradigmatic for understanding wisdom, the one whose wisdom exceeds all others. Yet, although they have much in common, a close reading of the main Solomon narratives (1 Kings 1–11; 2 Chronicles 1–9) shows some significant differences. Each sees Solomon as foundational for any wisdom

---

[1] See Will Kynes, *An Obituary for 'Wisdom Literature': The Birth, Death, and Intertextual Reintegration of a Biblical Corpus* (Oxford, 2019).

[2] Tremper Longman III, *The Fear of the Lord Is Wisdom: A Theological Introduction to Wisdom in Israel* (Grand Rapids, 2017), 276–282.

[3] Katharine J. Dell, 'Reading Ecclesiastes with the Scholars', in *Exploring Old Testament Wisdom: Literature and Themes*, ed. David G. Firth and Lindsay Wilson (London, 2016), 85. The Song of Songs has some interest in wisdom themes, and it too references Solomon (Song 1:1, 3:7–9). See R. Clarke, 'Seeing Wisdom in the Song of Songs', in Firth and Wilson, *Exploring Old Testament Wisdom*, 100–112.

tradition, but each problematises his relationship to that wisdom in distinct ways. For Kings, wisdom is shown to be a multivalent concept, something that can be positive or negative, and only some aspects of Solomon's wisdom are evaluated positively. Although the temple is central to Kings' presentation of Solomon, it is the part of his reign where wisdom is downplayed. By contrast, for Chronicles, the temple is central to Solomon's wisdom, and though it too has some criticisms of Solomon's wisdom, these are more muted than those of Kings. To explore this, the wisdom motif will be traced through the main Solomon narratives within their larger settings. Although Kings is here assumed to be the earlier text, and so read first, as Cook has recently argued, Chronicles must first be read in its own terms and not simply in terms of its variations from Kings.[4] As such, a reading of each is provided because each creates a coherent narrative in its own terms. From this it will be seen that although both present Solomon as foundational for wisdom, that wisdom can be interpreted differently.

SOLOMON IN KINGS

Readers know very little about Solomon when he first comes to prominence in Kings. His birth is recounted in 2 Sam 12:24–25, though it was already flagged in 2 Sam 5:13. Beyond this, he is not mentioned in 2 Samuel. Nevertheless, the fact that his mother was Bathsheba picks up on information from 2 Samuel. Likewise, although Bathsheba and Nathan might seem an unlikely pair to work together (given Nathan's prior pronouncement of the death of David and Bathsheba's first child), it was Nathan who brought the message from Yahweh that indicated that Solomon was also to be called Jedidiah, 'beloved of Yahweh' (2 Sam 12:25). This factor is probably enough to ensure that readers who have moved from Samuel to Kings expect him to play a significant role when he is reintroduced to the narrative. This background material becomes important when David's sons begin to jostle for the throne once it is apparent that he was old and seemingly infirm (1 Kgs 1:1–10). Solomon's importance to the question of succession is evident from that fact that when his brother Adonijah began to promote himself for this purpose, he was careful not to invite him (1 Kgs 1:8–10). The process of Solomon's accession is complex, featuring considerable conflict within

---

[4] Sean E. Cook, *The Solomon Narratives in the Context of the Hebrew Bible: Told and Retold*, LHBOTS 638 (London, 2017), 10–14.

the royal family. Yet, perhaps surprisingly, these events provide the crucial background to the first reference to Solomon's wisdom.

The first two chapters of Kings are often treated as the conclusion to a putative Succession Narrative; but when we read the book in its final form, it becomes clear that the association of Solomon with wisdom transcends the source-critical distinctions that have been applied.[5] Indeed, attention to this shows that as readers move through 1 Kings 1–11, we encounter different modes of wisdom that are applied to Solomon.[6] Each mode of wisdom explores the relationship between Solomon and the wisdom tradition while also preparing for his turning away from Yahweh in 1 Kings 11, a chapter where wisdom language is notably lacking until its mention in the summary of his reign (1 Kgs 11:41). Although scholars differ over where Solomon's ultimate failure begins,[7] wisdom is presented as a bookend to his reign, covering his achievements and his failures.

The motif of wisdom emerges in Kings when the dying David instructed Solomon about how to act once he succeeded him as king. This is presented as a charge for Solomon to adhere to the Torah since this was the means by which Solomon would succeed:

> Be strong, be courageous, and keep the charge of the Lord your God, walking in his ways and keeping his statutes, his commandments, his ordinances, and his testimonies, as it is written in the law of Moses, so that you may prosper in all that you do and wherever you turn. (1 Kgs 2:2b–3)

The focus on Torah and the language of success (śkl) evokes Yahweh's charge to Joshua following Moses' death (Josh 1:7). The verb is translated 'prosper' by the NRSV, but it is elsewhere associated with wisdom (Prov 1:3), while in Ps 119:99 it is also associated with Torah. The success of which David speaks emerges from prudence which is expressed in walking in the ways of Torah. Wisdom that is submitted

---

[5] On some of the general problems with the theory of a Succession Narrative, see David G. Firth, *1 and 2 Samuel: A Kingdom Comes* (London, 2017), 46–48.

[6] This adopts the proposal of David S. Williams ('Once Again: The Structure of the Narrative of Solomon's Reign', *JSOT* 86 [1999]: 49–66), that 1 Kings 1–11 is written as an integrated unit that should be read as a whole.

[7] Compare the different approaches of K. I. Parker, 'Solomon as Philosopher King? The Nexus of Law and Wisdom in 1 Kings 1–11', *JSOT* 53 (1992): 75–91; J. Daniel Hays, 'Has the Narrator Come to Praise Solomon or to Bury Him?: Narrative Subtlety in 1 Kings 1–11', *JSOT* 28 (2003): 149–174; and John W. Olley, 'Pharaoh's Daughter, Solomon's Temple and the Palace: Another Look at the Structure of 1 Kings 1–11', *JSOT* 27 (2003): 355–369.

to Torah will emerge as the key concept in Kings' account of Solomon, and it is on this point that he ultimately fails. Although Solomon himself is not called 'wise' at this point, the concept is being introduced. Yet when David has issued this charge, he directs Solomon to repay a range of people with whom he had been in conflict by executing them, save for the descendants of Barzillai (2 Kgs 2:5–9). David had earlier promised Shimei ben Gera that he would not execute him, and so he passed this task on to Solomon. Strikingly, David describes Solomon as a 'wise man' (2 Kgs 2:9); therefore, he would know how to ensure Shimei's death.

The commencement of Solomon's reign thus deploys concentrated language associated with wisdom. Faithfulness to the Torah is presented as 'prudence', a means of prospering. We might associate this prosperity with the broader term for 'wisdom' introduced by David (ḥkm) given its positive place in the introduction to Proverbs (1:1–7). However, such wisdom is commonly presented more negatively in Samuel, especially within the royal court. For example, in 2 Samuel 13 we encounter Jonadab, a friend of David's son Amnon, who is said to be 'very wise' (2 Sam 13:3).[8] It soon becomes clear that his 'wisdom' is employed to enable Amnon to enter into an illicit sexual relationship with his sister Tamar. Ultimately, Tamar was raped by her brother, but Jonadab's only other involvement was to reassure David that her brother Absalom had only killed Amnon, not his other sons, in revenge several years later. This background shows that, within Joshua–Kings, wisdom can be regarded negatively, a means to manipulate others (even to acts contrary to Torah). Pointing to Solomon's wisdom while proposing that he find a way to work around a promise hardly suggests that such wisdom is regarded positively. Rather, it fits within a pattern in the royal court where the wise manipulate others to achieve much darker goals. The wisdom Solomon deploys in following David's instructions and securing the kingdom in the balance of 1 Kings 2 might therefore be better translated as 'craftiness'. The narrative refrains from making an explicit judgement on Solomon at this point,[9] preferring instead to show him following David's charge. But the chapter's closing note (1 Kgs 2:46b) shows that he has benefitted from doing this – and we

---

[8] NRSV renders it 'very crafty' to stress the negative ways in which he will deploy his wisdom, thus masking the connection to Solomon in 1 Kgs 2:9. On the more negative portrayal of wisdom in the books of Joshua–Kings, see Firth, 'Worrying about the Wise: Wisdom in Old Testament Narrative', in Firth and Wilson, *Exploring Old Testament Wisdom*, 155–173.

[9] See Cook, *Solomon Narratives*, 26.

might think that a crafty person would see this possibility. There thus
exists a rift between the prudent wisdom which is consistent with
Torah and the craftiness which is content to manipulate people to
achieve a desired outcome.[10]

The material in 1 Kings 2 is thus essential background to the events
of 1 Kings 3, where a much more positive portrayal of wisdom is made –
though a rather different species of wisdom emerges here. Apart from
1 Kgs 3:1-2, the whole chapter has wisdom as a central motif. These
opening verses raise key questions that become more important later in
Solomon's story. First Kings 3:1 notes a marriage alliance Solomon had
made with Egypt by marrying Pharaoh's daughter. She is the first foreign
wife to be noted and so prepares for the effects of the foreign wives
recounted in 1 Kings 11. Wisdom is the motif which bookends
Solomon's reign, but within that we see various ways that Solomon
abuses his power, and references to foreign wives are an important
aspect of this. Mention is also made of the high places where people
were still sacrificing, but there is an immediate note that points out that
this was because the temple had not yet been built. This note shows
that the high places should not be considered problematic at this point.
Yet, although Kings presents the temple's construction positively, not
commenting on Pharaoh's daughter as his wife may be a mechanism by
which the narrator prepares readers for later events in Solomon's reign
where foreign wives are explicitly noted as a problem.

The rest of the chapter divides neatly into two parts. In 1 Kgs 3:3-15,
we read of Solomon's dream at the high place at Gibeon where Yahweh
appeared to him, offering whatever he wanted as a gift. Solomon
responded by affirming Yahweh's steadfast love towards David and
giving thanks for his own accession (1 Kgs 3:4-6). But, casting himself
as a 'little child', he indicated that he did not know how to lead the
nation. In particular, Solomon asked for an understanding mind so that
he could judge the nation. The language of Solomon 'going out' and
'coming in' can refer to military activity (likewise the language of
'judging' if 1 Samuel 8 is in the background),[11] though it can also refer
to the routines of life. Such discernment is consistent with the goals of
wisdom set out in Proverbs 1:5, and once 'judging' is located in the
sphere of legal decision-making it is an obvious goal for good governance. In response, Yahweh declares that because Solomon had asked for

---

[10] With Cook, *Solomon Narratives*, 30.
[11] See Anton van der Lingen, '*bw'-Yṣ'* ("To Go Out and To Come in") as a Military
      Term', *VT* 42 (1992): 59–66.

understanding and not wealth, he would give him a 'wise and discerning mind' (1 Kgs 3:12). Yahweh's response clarifies the link with the wisdom tradition hinted at in Solomon's request, though that wisdom is only now granted to Solomon might also be a mild rebuke in light of David's earlier affirmation of Solomon's wisdom. That is, Solomon had shown the craftiness needed in political manoeuvring, but he had not shown the wisdom needed to function as Israel's king should. This point might be developed further by noting that Yahweh promised to give Solomon long life if he walked in his statutes (1 Kgs 3:14), a possible hint that Solomon's actions to date did not follow this pattern as fully as they should.

The latter part of the chapter (1 Kgs 3:15–28) recounts an encounter between Solomon and two prostitutes who came before him for judgement. In this case, for which there were no external witnesses, each had given birth, but one child had died, and each insisted the living child was theirs. Solomon famously offered to divide the living child and give each half, leading the actual mother to offer him to the other woman so he might live. From this, Solomon recognised the real mother and gave the child to the correct woman. Although the language of wisdom is conspicuously absent from this report, the concluding note (1 Kgs 3:28) indicates that this judgement put the nation in awe of the king because they saw that 'the wisdom of God was in him, to execute justice'. Although the motif of Solomon's wisdom is stressed here, it should be noted that this is specifically judicial wisdom – the wisdom required to be a just leader. Although wisdom can have wider reference than this, the narrative in which this comment is embedded makes clear that this is the particular focus. Such wisdom is commended elsewhere (e.g., Prov 16:10; 20:8), and it is presented positively here.

Wisdom is also a prominent motif in 1 Kings 4.[12] This chapter recounts Solomon's administrative arrangements (1 Kgs 4:1–20) before commenting on the quality of life enjoyed by both people and king under this rule (1 Kgs 4:20–28). Some of these elements might imply some criticism of Solomon (e.g., his increased wealth and expanding military, 1 Kgs 4:26), but it is probably better to read them only as potential problems. This is because 1 Kgs 4:29–34 provides an additional encomium to Solomon's wisdom, effectively closing this part of his presentation, just as the note at 1 Kgs 3:28 had done for 1 Kings 3. Rather than offering criticism, at this point the narrative lays

---

[12] Hebrew 1 Kgs 5:1 = English 1 Kgs 4:21, with the chapter divisions coming together again at 1 Kgs 6:1. All references in this chapter follow the English referencing.

foundations for the explicitly critical comments found in 1 Kings 11. The focus here is on the vastness of Solomon's wisdom, something which exceeded other (apparently) well-known wise men (1 Kgs. 4:31). The extent of this wisdom was such that people came from the courts of other kings because they had heard of his wisdom. But where the wisdom of 1 Kings 3 is judicial, that which was necessary for good governance, the wisdom mentioned here is notably different, as it is focused on the composition of proverbs and songs along with observations on what might now be called the natural world. Such wisdom no longer addresses issues of governance and is instead concerned with learning as a general category.

Such wisdom is received positively elsewhere – we need only consider the 'sluggard' comments in Proverbs which frequently reference learning from other parts of creation (e.g., Prov 6:6–11). This model is also present in the Solomonic material in Proverbs.[13] For instance, in Prov 26:11–17, various observations about dogs or a lion are used to show the failings of the lazy. Yet in such wisdom the things learned from studying flora and fauna are applied to human actions and their outcomes, something that is conspicuously lacking in this report. Moreover, another important shift is introduced here in comparison to 1 Kings 3. There, Solomon had (more literally) asked for a 'listening heart' (1 Kgs 3:9). The focus there was that Solomon should listen to others and thus know how to act justly. Yet now, it is to Solomon's wisdom that others listen (in both cases, using the verb *šmʿ*). This is a subtle shift in focus, one that is not necessarily problematic but which points to more potential problems.[14] But at this point, Solomon's wisdom still contributes to Israel's well-being and so can be assessed positively.[15]

Wisdom is again prominent in 1 Kings 5 as Solomon prepared to construct the temple. The motif is introduced by the Tyrian king, Hiram, when he responded to Solomon's contact by blessing Yahweh for having given David a 'wise son' to succeed him as king (1 Kgs 5:7). But how are we to read Hiram's words? The association with David could be understood in light of David's comment to Solomon about his wisdom (1 Kgs 2:9), in which case Hiram could be praising Solomon for

---

[13] Solomon need not have been the author of these proverbs for them to be considered 'Solomonic' – they could, for instance, be part of a tradition that is tied to him.

[14] See Lissa M. Wray Beal, *1 and 2 Kings*, AOTC (Nottingham, 2014), 98.

[15] With Gary N. Knoppers, *Two Nations under God: The Deuteronomistic History of Solomon and the Dual Monarchies. Volume 1. The Reign of Solomon and the Rise of Jeroboam*, HSM 52 (Atlanta, 1993), 86.

the astute way he began negotiations to obtain the labour and materials required for the temple's construction. But Hiram also seems to be ensuring that he obtains a good payment for his work since Solomon is to provide 20,000 cors of wheat for the royal household. By contrast, Solomon's daily provision was 30 cors of flour and 60 cors of meal (1 Kgs 4:20). This indicates that Solomon was providing Hiram with roughly the same amount as his court received, a significant demand on Israel. Since this is presented as a long-term arrangement, the drain on Israel's coffers would last, a factor that may lie behind the issue of the towns rejected by Hiram in 1 Kgs 9:10–14, though there we are also told that Hiram had provided Solomon with considerable gold. But lest we read this account about Solomon's wisdom too suspiciously, the narrator provides an additional statement about Solomon's wisdom as a gift from Yahweh which also resulted in peace between Hiram and Solomon, recorded in a treaty. We might therefore regard the wisdom shown here as an example of mercantile awareness on Solomon's part, not so much the Realpolitik shown in 1 Kings 2 but its more positive cousin which does occasionally emerge in the wisdom tradition (e.g., Prov 21:5–6).

Although construction of the temple (along with his palace) is clearly presented as a high point in Solomon's reign, there is a notable lack of wisdom vocabulary after his discussion with Hiram. Indeed, the only hint of wisdom occurs in 1 Kings 7:14, though there it refers to the skill with which the artisan Hiram (not the Tyrian king) was endowed for the work of construction, phrasing that intentionally echoes the presentation of Bezalel in his role in making the Tabernacle (Exod 31:3–4). Hiram's wisdom ('skill' in NRSV) is clearly distinct from any of the forms of wisdom shown by Solomon (since he is never shown engaging in any form of manual labour), but it too is likely understood as something God-given. However, wisdom is clearly a minor motif within this section of Kings, and it does not emerge again in Solomon's dedicatory prayer. Perhaps more surprisingly, wisdom does not emerge in the account of Yahweh's second appearance to Solomon in a dream. Rather, submission to God's Torah, expressed through integrity, is stressed (1 Kgs 9:1–9). This submission is important if the temple, now the political and religious centre for the young kingdom,[16] was to be meaningful. Yet issues of submission to Torah are not especially prominent in 1 Kings 9, and the listing of Solomon's other acts (1 Kgs 9:15–28) is full of matters that are potentially problematic when

---

[16] See Hartmut Schmid, *Das erste Buch der Könige* (Wuppertal, 2000), 269.

read in light of Torah.[17] The temple was finished when Solomon established a regular practice of sacrifice there (1 Kgs 9:25), but whether or not he had been wise in this is not stated.

After the relative absence of wisdom language, the Queen of Sheba's visit (1 Kgs 10:1–10) represents a key return to this motif. The visit is said to have come about because the queen had heard of Solomon's fame (1 Kgs 10:1), an observation that again picks up on the language of 'hearing' (Heb. *šamaʿ*) in the Solomon narrative. Where in 1 Kings 3, Solomon had asked for a listening heart, in 1 Kings 4 people came to hear Solomon. But now, it is Solomon's fame (*šēm*) itself a word built on the verb for hearing) that is heard. There is a subtle shift from Solomon listening to others as Yahweh's servant to others listening to Solomon's fame that has been woven through the account. The queen does not come because of his wisdom but because of his fame. This fame clearly includes elements of his wisdom; but in this account, wisdom is part of a range of features typically associated with royalty as the queen is also impressed with the various markers of power, wealth and piety that Solomon demonstrated. But wisdom is still a central motif here as the queen arrived to 'test him with hard questions' (1 Kgs 10:1). The content of these questions is not outlined, though Solomon could answer them all (1 Kgs 10:3). It may be that, by including the report of the visit within material which is focused on Solomon's commercial activities (note that 1 Kgs 9:26–28 and 10:22, with their reference to Solomon's trading fleet, provide a literary envelope for this section), the focus here is on Solomon's ability to generate great wealth. This is potentially problematic, particularly when read in light of Deuteronomy's warning against kings becoming wealthy (Deut 17:17). But Kings withholds a specifically negative judgement here, preferring to focus on the queen's awestruck observations (1 Kgs 10:8–9). Even so, her closing observation, that Yahweh had appointed Solomon to 'execute justice and righteousness' (1 Kgs 10:9) creates an important echo of the basis for wisdom that Solomon had raised in 1 Kgs 3:7–9. Justice was central to the wisdom Solomon was intended to demonstrate; but as we move through Kings' account of his reign, this element falls further into the background.

This shift in focus becomes particularly notable in the summary of Solomon's reign to this point in 1 Kgs 10:23–25. As with the encomium to his wisdom in 1 Kgs 4:29–34, we see how Solomon's wisdom exceeded that of others, except that this time the comparison is with

---

[17]   See Iain W. Provan, *1 and 2 Kings* (Peabody, 1995), 86.

other kings rather than the wise. Solomon, we are assured, exceeded all of them in wisdom and wealth (1 Kgs 10:23). The wisdom discussed here is mercantile, particularly how kings could enrich themselves. For Solomon, his wisdom was itself a source of wealth as everyone (following the pattern of the Queen of Sheba) asked their questions and apparently paid quite handsomely for their answers. As in 1 Kgs 4:20–28, this summary stresses how much Solomon brought to the nation. But where the point there was that everyone lived a secure and prosperous life (1 Kgs 4:26), the concern here is with the king's own wealth (1 Kgs 10:26–29), wealth that at key points seems to go against Torah.

Where various elements in the account to this point were only presented as potentially problematic, 1 Kings 11 then makes explicit the various ways in which Solomon had not remained consistent with Torah. That faithfulness to Torah was central is stressed by the note that Solomon had not done what Yahweh had commanded (1 Kgs 11:10–11). All this prepared for the division of the kingdom under Rehoboam (1 Kgs 12:1–19). Solomon's wisdom can be noted in the final summary of his reign (1 Kgs 11:41), but it is wisdom that was finally tarnished by not being submitted to Torah. Solomon's heart, the very organ that had needed wisdom (1 Kgs 3:9 – NRSV 'mind') had turned aside from Yahweh and his Torah (1 Kgs 11:9). Although Solomon's wisdom had shown great potential, according to the book of Kings he was finally a failure.[18] His wisdom, where it was consistent with Torah, could still be praised, but once it became more about what he could accumulate rather than the fear of Yahweh (Prov 1:7), then it could not be judged positively. The account in Kings still shows Solomon as foundational for wisdom within Israel, but it is also a sobering warning that wisdom on its own is not enough.

SOLOMON IN CHRONICLES

Where Kings uses Torah faithfulness as the means by which Solomon's wisdom is assessed, for Chronicles the interface of wisdom, temple building and faithfulness to Torah is crucial. As with Kings, there is value in noting places where Solomon appears before his accession since these provide key background to the Chronicler's presentation of him and the motif of wisdom. In doing so, our first task is to read Chronicles

[18]   Walter Brueggemann, *1 & 2 Kings* (SHBC, Macon, 2000), 148.

on its own terms and not simply as a variant to the account in Kings, even though it is most likely that Chronicles' account is based on that of Kings.[19] Thus, although 2 Chronicles 1–9 represents the principal text, we need first to consider points where Solomon appears in 1 Chronicles.

Solomon initially appears in 1 Chron 22:2–19. Here, in contrast to 2 Samuel, David began to make arrangements for the temple's construction, even if he knew that he was not the one to build it (1 Chron 22:2–5). He particularly noted that Solomon was young and inexperienced and so would need assistance to ensure the temple was sufficiently magnificent. The balance of the chapter is given to David's charge to Solomon (1 Chron 22:6–16) and then his directive to other leaders to support him (1 Chron 22:17–19). It is in David's charge that the motif of wisdom becomes important.

David's charge to Solomon recalls the promise of 1 Chronicles 17 before expressing the wish that Yahweh might be with Solomon so that he might succeed in building the temple (1 Chron 22:11). He then expresses the further wish that Yahweh might grant Solomon discretion and understanding (*śēkel ûbînâ*, 1 Chron 22:12).[20] Since David had earlier noted Solomon's youthful inexperience, this wish is entirely appropriate to the context, but both these terms are also at home in the wisdom traditions (e.g., *śēkel* in Prov 3:4, *bînâ* in Prov 1:2). The implication is that at this point Solomon lacks the wisdom needed to govern Israel, but (consistent with the pattern in Kings) the heart of discovering this is found in the Torah. Although Torah language is not common in the wisdom tradition, there is no inconsistency with seeing it as foundational to wisdom (see, e.g., Deut 4:6). As Chronicles introduces Solomon, we see that the combination of wisdom, temple-building and Torah are central to his reign.

Solomon appears again in 1 Chronicles 28–29, all in sections associated with the transition from David to Solomon. Specifically wisdom-focused language is not evident here. Instead, the primary concern is with Solomon's role in constructing the temple. Alluding once again to 1 Chronicles 17, David told the various officials gathered in Jerusalem that Solomon's kingdom would be established if he continued in

---

[19] On this approach, see John Jarick, *1 Chronicles* (London, 2002), 1–3. With Yong Ho Jeon (*Impeccable Solomon? A Study of Solomon's Faults in Chronicles* [Eugene, 2013], 99–103), it is a reasonable working hypothesis that Chronicles presumes knowledge of Kings, but we must first read it on its own terms.

[20] The rest of the verse poses some syntactical difficulties but need not detain us here. See Sara Japhet, *I & II Chronicles: A Commentary* (Louisville, 1993), 399.

Yahweh's commandments and ordinances (1 Chron 28:7), something to which the community was also to commit itself (1 Chron 28:8). In light of this, David's specific charge to Solomon was that he should know and serve Yahweh with a willing heart and that this in turn would be the basis for his building the temple (1 Chron 28:9–10). David's own willingness was expressed in the materials and plans that he had put together so Solomon could build the temple. This included the provision of skilled workers, terminology that links this account to Bezalel in the tabernacle's construction (Exod 31:3–4). That Solomon was insufficiently mature to lead this project is again stressed in David's speech to the assembly. Here, he stresses both that God had chosen Solomon to build the temple and that he was young and inexperienced (1 Chron 29:1), echoing his earlier comments about him and the temple (1 Chron 22:2–5). This is why David had provided so much for the temple, resourcing Solomon to build it. As with the earlier passage, the focus is on Solomon as temple-builder, with the motifs of wisdom and Torah faithfulness not given prominence. In spite of this, the brief report of Solomon's accession to the throne does note that he prospered in this role, echoing the statement in 1 Chron 22:13. This passage also prepares for Solomon gaining great wealth by observing that Yahweh granted him royal majesty in a way which exceeded other kings in Israel before him (1 Chron 29:25). Although this language does not have to be rooted in any wisdom tradition, it may provide background to the statement in Eccl 1:16 where Qoheleth, in the guise of Solomon, reflects on how his wisdom exceeded all those who reigned in Jerusalem before him.

The references to Solomon in 1 Chronicles provide important background, but it is in 2 Chronicles 1–9 that he becomes the central figure. Here, the temple's construction is central; and where wisdom becomes prominent, it is particularly associated with the temple. However, although the temple's construction is central, it is notable that Chronicles uses the motif of wisdom to define the boundaries of Solomon's reign since wisdom is particularly stressed in 2 Chronicles 1 and 9.

Second Chronicles 1 reports Solomon's request for wisdom at Gibeon, explaining that the tent of meeting from the wilderness was there, even though David's act in bringing the ark to Jerusalem is noted (2 Chron 1:3–4). Solomon's offerings there could thus take place at the altar that Bezalel had constructed for the tabernacle (2 Chron 1:5). Allusion to Bezalel's skill has already been made as he was known for the artisanal wisdom (i.e., 'skill') he possessed. At Gibeon, God appeared to Solomon in a dream and offered him what he desired. Solomon's response was to acknowledge that he was the recipient of Yahweh's steadfast love in succeeding his father as king. Accordingly, he asked for 'wisdom and knowledge' (ḥokmâ ûmaddāʿ) so he could 'go out and come in' before the people. The word pair 'wisdom and knowledge' recurs in both verses 11 and 12, showing their importance for God's response to the request. 'Wisdom' (ḥokmâ) is, perhaps, self-evidently associated with the wisdom tradition. The late word maddāʿ is less clearly associated with it, but it does appear in Dan 1:4, 17, describing an aspect of the wisdom of Daniel and his friends. Otherwise, it appears in Eccl 10:20, though there it refers to dangerous thoughts someone might have about the king.

Although there are obvious similarities to the parallel account in 1 Kgs 3:7–9, Solomon's request in 1 Chronicles 1 is still distinctive. Solomon's desire to rule (špṭ) well could be taken in a forensic sense, but it is more likely that the verb refers to good governance, perhaps drawing on the background of 1 Samuel 8 to allude to military success. This would make sense of the link the Chronicler makes between Solomon's request and the note that he gathered numerous horses and chariots (2 Chron 1:14). That this is likely can also be seen in that Yahweh promised wealth as well (2 Chron 1:11–12), and the balance of the chapter focuses on the accumulation of this (2 Chron 1:15–17). As such, although some aspects of judicial practice may lie behind Solomon's request for wisdom and knowledge, it is focused more generally on what was needed to be an effective king. Where Kings therefore introduces wisdom through some of its sub-species, Chronicles provides a more general overview. Although Jeon argues that the background in Kings already raises some questions about the validity of Solomon's actions,[21] it is perhaps more probable that the Chronicler presents this positively in that the successes reported here for Solomon are those that emerge from Yahweh's promise to him. More importantly, the issue of Solomon's youth and inexperience that David had highlighted has been addressed.[22]

Unlike Kings, nothing in Chronicles overtly shows Solomon demonstrating the wisdom that Yahweh has given. He had asked for wisdom to rule the people (2 Chron 1:10); but unlike Kings, where the story of the two prostitutes showed Solomon's wisdom, Chronicles instead moves immediately to the construction of the temple, along with his palace (2 Chron 2:1). Yet it is clear that, for Chronicles, the temple is

---

[21] Jeon, *Impeccable Solomon*, 218–220.
[22] Cook, *Solomon Narratives*, 108.

indeed the point where Solomon's wisdom is demonstrated. This is evident in the observation of the Tyrian King Huram who comments on the importance of Solomon being a 'wise son' of David. In context, this relates specifically to the negotiations Solomon has made with him in arranging for skilled workers (2 Chron 2:7), another allusion to Bezalel (Exod 31:3–4). Huram's observation also draws on the commercial terms that Solomon has offered him, terms which partly replicate those in Kings, but with additional payments of wine and barley (2 Chron 2:10). Unlike Kings, Chronicles has already reported the wealth Solomon was generating (2 Chron 1:14–17), making these terms seem perhaps more reasonable here than in Kings. Moreover, in Kings, Hiram was initially asked to set his own terms, but here Solomon is presented as initiating them.[23] This is indicative of the fact that mercantile wisdom is the species in focus here.

The language in Huram's comment about Solomon in 2 Chron 2:12 is noteworthy. This is the most concentrated example of wisdom language in Chronicles. 'Understanding' (bînâ) picks up on David's prayer from 1 Chron 22:12, whilst 'discretion' renders another term David had used there (śēkel), though at that point it is rendered as 'wisdom'. The key point for Chronicles is that in his preparations for the construction of the temple, Solomon was demonstrating the wisdom he had requested and for which David had prayed. This wisdom was focused on providing a context for Israel's worship and in astute commercial arrangements to enable this. It is this that allows Chronicles to focus on the temple as Solomon's principal contribution. There is relatively little wisdom language in the rest of Chronicles' Solomon story. But given that the temple is central to 2 Chronicles 3–8, we can still see this as a demonstration of his wisdom, even if there is no specific language to show this.

However, this changes with the visit of the Queen of Sheba (2 Chron 9:1–12) and the summary statement of how Solomon excelled all the kings in terms of wealth and wisdom (9:22–23). The queen's visit is, like Kings, because of Solomon's fame, except that this time Yahweh's renown is not mentioned as an additional factor. Wisdom is not mentioned as a factor, though since she came to 'test him with hard questions' his wisdom was clearly an important feature. But there is an important shift here which could suggest a slightly more critical attitude towards Solomon in that the focus is on his ability to answer her

---

[23] See William Johnstone, *1 and 2 Chronicles: Volume 1. 1 Chronicles 1–2 Chronicles 9. Israel's Place among the Nations*, LHBOTS 253 (Sheffield, 1997), 311.

questions. Although her breath is taken away by Solomon's answers, we do not know what those questions and answers were. But since the wisdom she observes (2 Chron 9:3–4) follows on from this, we can assume that the matters highlighted here constitute their heart in some way. If so, then, although temple worship features, it comes after her observations on his palace, the quality of the food served there and the various arrangements for his servants. Only after these elements, which focus on Solomon's own grandeur, is possible mention of 'burnt offerings' (NRSV) at the temple made. Yet this reading is drawn from 1 Kgs 10:5, emending a difficult phrase in Hebrew. Although Dillard prefers this emendation, he also notes that the Hebrew can be interpreted as it stands as referring to a processional stairway (cf. ASV, 'and his ascent') from the palace to the temple.[24] In that the other items which had impressed the queen were associated with Solomon's own grandeur, there are strong intrinsic grounds for preferring this sense. If so, the elements which impressed the queen were associated with Solomon's wealth, not with worship at the temple. Indeed, by relegating even mention of the stairway (if that is correct) then Chronicles may also be showing Solomon making important mistakes. This matter cannot be resolved here, but however we understand this text, it seems that it is primarily Solomon's wealth that impressed the queen, linking wealth to wisdom. Temple worship, so central otherwise for Chronicles, is at most a marginal element here.

That the queen equated wisdom and wealth (at least to some extent) is confirmed by her statement about Solomon's achievements and wisdom (2 Chron 9:5–6). There is some ambiguity in her observation since *dābār* (2 Chron 9:5) could refer either to speech or to achievements more generally. If we take this in a more limited sense, then it could refer more specifically to the things Solomon said, and we would perhaps translate the phrase as 'your words and your wisdom'. Contextually, this could make sense of the fact that Solomon has answered her questions, while the linkage between knowledge, speech and wisdom is something recognised elsewhere in the wisdom tradition (e.g., Prov 10:13–14). However, the broader translation of NRSV is probably to be preferred because of the way she develops her speech to focus on how his wisdom worked itself out in the splendour of his kingdom and especially the wealth he accumulated. This understanding would offer a slightly more critical presentation of Solomon in that she

---

[24] Raymond B. Dillard, *2 Chronicles*, WBC 15 (Waco, 1987), 69.

attributes the wisdom only to Solomon, even if Yahweh is praised, and is then shown, along with Huram, as contributing to his wealth. If this interpretation is correct, there may be a reflex of it in Qoheleth's use of Solomon in reflecting on how wealth did not bring any final satisfaction (Eccl 2:1-11).

The queen's visit is presented as an example of other visits as 'all the kings of the earth' sought out Solomon to hear his wisdom (2 Chron 9:22-23). In that his reign's beginning was marked by his request for wisdom (2 Chron 1:7-11), this closing note provides an appropriate conclusion to Solomon's reign. Wisdom is noted at the beginning and the end of the account. But there is an important shift. In Solomon's request, the concern was with the governance of the people, but here Solomon's wisdom is associated with his wealth. Indeed, he 'excelled all the kings of the earth in riches and wisdom' (2 Chron 9:22). Attention to his wealth is particularly evidenced by the references to 'gold' in 2 Chronicles 9. It is mentioned thirty times in the whole Solomon story, but sixteen of them occur in this chapter.[25] That Solomon's wealth was a gift from Yahweh was noted in 2 Chron 1:12, so there is no necessary problem in Chronicles with Solomon becoming wealthy. Likewise, that the kings came to hear the wisdom God had given Solomon shows that his wisdom was not something only to his own glory. One could therefore read this closing note as evidence that God was indeed fulfilling the promise of wealth that had been made. The wider wisdom tradition is certainly open to the possibility that wisdom can lead to wealth (e.g., Prov 14:23-24). But perhaps there is some ambivalence here, along the lines of the preference for the fear of Yahweh found elsewhere in the wisdom tradition (e.g., Prov 15:16). Such a reading would be consistent with Jeon's argument that Chronicles expects readers to draw on their knowledge of Kings.[26] Supporting this approach from within Chronicles, we can note that Solomon's wisdom was meant to be evaluated through the temple, but the temple plays only a very minor role in 2 Chronicles 9. Solomon is not the apostate presented in 1 Kings 11. Yet Chronicles is aware that his wisdom may lead him astray once worship is no longer its focus.

---

[25] Cook, *Solomon Narratives*, 138-139.
[26] Jeon, *Impeccable Solomon*, 99-104.

CONCLUSION

For both Kings and Chronicles, wisdom is central to their presentation
of Solomon. For Kings, 'wisdom' describes a range of intellectual and
artisanal pursuits. As Solomon's story progresses, it gradually demonstrates at least some of the possible varieties of this. Wisdom might be
an insidious expression of Realpolitik, or it could be a sincere desire to
ensure justice is done. Wisdom can describe knowledge of what might
today be described as the natural world, or it might be mercantile and
commercial *nous*. Wisdom might lead to the well-being of the one
possessing it, or it might lead to the well-being of the whole community. In its presentation of Solomon, Kings shows all these species of
wisdom. But it is also careful to show that (unlike Proverbs) even the
wise can be led astray. This is because for Kings, the measure of the
effectiveness of wisdom is always submission to Torah. Where Solomon
walks in its ways, his wisdom can be judged positively; but once his
wisdom is no longer submitted to Torah, then he can be judged as
an apostate.

There are obvious similarities in Chronicles' presentation of
Solomon, probably because it draws on Kings' account. But Chronicles
shapes its own story, and Solomon's wisdom is not simply transplanted
into this new account. Rather, Chronicles recasts the story so that
wisdom is seen in a different light. For Chronicles, the value of wisdom
is seen in the approach to the temple. In David's preparations for the
temple's construction, he had Solomon's need for wisdom; in its construction, Chronicles shows Solomon demonstrating that wisdom. The
focus on the temple in 2 Chronicles 3–7 expresses that wisdom, even if
explicit wisdom language is missing. Yet when wisdom re-emerges as a
motif in 2 Chronicles 9, the temple plays at most a negligible part.
Instead, Solomon's wealth and grandeur are now central. Though less
explicitly problematic than in 1 Kings 11, there are hints here that
Solomon's wisdom was not as well applied as before.

What is then striking is that the various themes presented in both
Kings and Chronicles emerge elsewhere in the wisdom tradition. These
themes need not, of course, emerge through a direct contact with either
of these accounts, though for neither can this absolutely be excluded.[27]
But the extent of these connections shows both that Solomon is
regarded as the primary human source for the wisdom tradition and

---

[27] See Katharine Dell and Will Kynes, eds., *Reading Proverbs Intertextually*, LHBOTS
629 (London, 2018).

also that these traditions draw on themes associated with wisdom in both Kings and Chronicles. The connection with Solomon thus moves from the traditions about him to the wisdom traditions, while the wisdom traditions then also become a critical tool with which to read Solomon's story.

Further Reading

Brueggemann, Walter. *1 & 2 Kings*. SHBC. Macon: 2000.

Cook, Sean E. *The Solomon Narratives in the Context of the Hebrew Bible: Told and Retold*. LHBOTS 638. London: 2017.

Firth, David G., and L. Wilson, eds. *Exploring Old Testament Wisdom: Literature and Themes*. London: 2016.

'Worrying about the Wise: Wisdom in Old Testament Narrative'. Pages 155–173 in *Exploring Old Testament Wisdom*. Edited by David G. Firth and Lindsay Wilson. London: 2016.

Japhet, Sara. *I & II Chronicles: A Commentary*. Louisville: 1993.

Jarick, John. *1 Chronicles*. London: 2002.

Jeon, Yong Ho. *Impeccable Solomon? A Study of Solomon's Faults in Chronicles*. Eugene: 2013.

Johnstone, William. *1 and 2 Chronicles: Volume 1. 1 Chronicles 1 – 2 Chronicles 9. Israel's Place among the Nations*. LHBOTS 253. Sheffield: 1997.

Knoppers, Gary N. *Two Nations under God: The Deuteronomistic History of Solomon and the Dual Monarchies. Volume 1. The Reign of Solomon and the Rise of Jeroboam*. HSM 52. Atlanta: 1993.

Kynes, Will. *An Obituary for 'Wisdom Literature': The Birth, Death, and Intertextual Reintegration of a Biblical Corpus*. Oxford: 2019.

Longman, Tremper III. *The Fear of the Lord Is Wisdom: A Theological Introduction to Wisdom in Israel*. Grand Rapids: 2017.

Provan, Iain W. *1 and 2 Kings*. Peabody: 1995.

Schmid, Hartmut. *Das erste Buch der Könige*. Wuppertal: 2000.

Wray Beal, Lissa M. *1 & 2 Kings*. AOTC. Nottingham: 2014.

Part II

Wisdom Literature in the Hebrew Bible

8 Proverbs

CHRISTOPHER B. ANSBERRY

Appearances can be deceiving. This is the case with the book of Proverbs. For many, the book traffics in basic truths; it projects a simplistic vision of life, mediating the uncritical experience of a 'first naïveté'. Job and Ecclesiastes, by contrast, engender a 'second naïveté' – a nuanced, critical understanding of the complexities of being-in-the-world. This characterisation of Proverbs captures something of the truth. After all, sayings such as 'A slack palm produces poverty; but the hand of the diligent brings riches' (Prov 10:4) and 'No calamity will befall the righteous; but the wicked are filled with evil' (Prov 12:21) seem banal, even non-realistic.[1] But this characterisation of Proverbs does not account for the whole truth. On the surface, the materials within the book are simple. But the scenarios in which the aphorisms may be applied are manifold. The diverse literary forms in the document form the reader in various ways. And the anthology's vision of life intermingles predictable patterns with the inevitable contingencies and inexplicable mysteries of human existence. The meaning-potential of Proverbs is deep. Layers of its depth dimension may be uncovered through an exploration of the history of Proverbs' reception, the nature of the anthology, its structure and its prominent themes, each of which will serve as the focus of attention in this chapter.

THE RECEPTION HISTORY OF THE BOOK OF PROVERBS

The reception history of Proverbs bears witness to the reality that different historical and cultural contexts nurture different approaches that actualise different aspects of a text's potential meaning. While approaches to Proverbs wax and wane throughout its history of interpretation, certain readings of the anthology tend to dominate particular

---

[1] All Hebrew translations are my own.

periods. More than revealing the questions and concerns that influenced interpretation during discrete historical moments, these readings identify specific contours of the text. Among the dominant readings of Proverbs throughout the history of its reception, five typify the major patterns of its interpretation.

The first pattern remains the prevailing reading of Proverbs: from its early reception to the present, Proverbs' concern with the (trans)formation of character has provided a pedagogical paradigm and a resource for the development of didactic traditions. The educational goal of the book (Prov 1:1–7), combined with its aphorisms, images and idioms, were reiterated and recast in Second Temple and early Jewish literature to serve varying didactic ends. Ben Sira, for example, not only described the purpose of his work in terms highly reminiscent of Proverbs (Sir 50:27–29); he also integrated material from Proverbs with narrative and legal traditions to align wisdom with ancient Israel's history in general and to equate wisdom with the Torah in particular (Sir 24:1–34; 44:1–50:21). Similar signs of Proverbs' adaptation are evident in Wisdom of Solomon and certain fragmentary texts from Qumran. The Wisdom of Solomon draws on key themes from Proverbs and filters them through a Platonic lens to extend the anthology's conception of the righteous and the wicked, its portrait of Lady Wisdom and its temporal understanding of life, all of which project a fresh vision of faith and piety in a Hellenistic context. Among the texts from Qumran, *4QWiles of the Wicked Woman* (4Q184) and *4QBeatitudes* (4Q525) rework features of Proverbs 1–9 for particular pedagogical purposes. The former transforms the seductive rhetoric of the 'strange woman' in Proverbs 7 into a sharp description of a calamitous creature who hunts the pious at all costs, threatening to overpower the mature and lead the righteous down into eternal flames. The latter text opens with a virtual quotation of Proverbs 1:2, which links the goal of the work with the pedagogical purpose of Proverbs. And the variety of textual correspondences between 4Q525 and Proverbs 1–9 suggest that Proverbs provided *4QBeatitudes* with motifs that funded its goal of motivating a wise life, marked by Torah piety.[2]

Proverbs' pedagogical vision and didactic techniques were received and reworked in Second Temple and early Jewish literature (cf. *Avot*). The same is true of Christian reception of the anthology. While the New Testament alludes to Proverbs on many occasions, five direct

---

[2] Elisa Uusimäki, *Turning Proverbs towards Torah: An Analysis of 4Q525*, STJD 117 (Leiden, 2016).

quotations from the book indicate that individual aphorisms were redeployed to concretise specific theological or ethical matters (Heb 12:5–6; Jas 4:6; 1 Pet 4:18; 5:5; 2 Pet 2:22). The didactic use of individual aphorisms in the New Testament, in the *catenae* and among the early fathers was accompanied by Proverbs' placement in a broader educational curriculum. Following the Greek fields of human learning, Origen developed a course in 'divine philosophy', associating Proverbs with Ethics, Ecclesiastes with Physics, and Song of Songs with Enoptics. According to Origen, Proverbs taught both 'moral science' and 'logical science'. The book formed one's character through the inculcation of virtue and sharpened one's perception by enabling one to 'discriminate between the meanings of words' and to discover multiple layers of meaning in scripture.[3] Evagrius of Pontus adopted Origen's educational programme, devoting specific attention to Proverbs' pedagogy in his *Scholia on Proverbs*. For Evagrius, Proverbs initiated one into an ascending pedagogy, whereby one's intellectual and spiritual faculties were restored and attuned to creation. These ethical and catechetical forms of Proverbs' reception are also reflected in Basil of Caesarea's *Homilies on the Beginning of Proverbs* and John Chrysostom's commentary on Proverbs. Basil explores Proverbs' multifaceted pedagogy through the ways in which the book banishes vice, cultivates virtue, disciplines desire and develops an appetite for the good. And Chrysostom attends to Proverbs' formation of one's moral and intellectual faculties.

This brief sketch of Proverbs' early reception indicates that the anthology funded discrete didactic traditions concerned with the (trans)formation of one's character or worldview. While the pedagogy of the book may have been pushed to the periphery during subsequent periods of reception, it has never escaped the interpretive horizon of the document. If recent works devoted to Proverbs provide any indication of the future direction of research, its pedagogy appears to represent the most prominent contour of the text.[4]

The second pattern that characterises Proverbs' reception is related to the first; it concerns the nature of proverbial wisdom. The rise of

---

[3] *Comm. Cant.* Prol. 3, R. P. Lawson, trans., Origen: The Song of Songs: Commentary and Homilies, Ancient Christian Writers 26 (Westminster: The Newman Press, 1957), 39–46.

[4] William P. Brown, *Wisdom's Wonder: Character, Creation, and Crisis in the Bible's Wisdom Literature* (Grand Rapids, 2014); Anne W. Stewart, *Poetic Ethics in Proverbs: Wisdom Literature and the Shaping of the Moral Self* (New York, 2016). Cf. Jacqueline Vayntrub, 'The Book of Proverbs and the Idea of Ancient Israelite Education', *ZAW* 128 (2016): 96–114.

idealism and historicism in the eighteenth and nineteenth centuries engendered a reconceptualisation of proverbial wisdom. Whereas Origen considered Proverbs as a piece of 'divine philosophy', eighteenth- and nineteenth-century interpreters considered the book as 'philosophy'. And whereas earlier interpreters construed Proverbs as a document concerned with the formation of virtuous character, eighteenth- and nineteenth-century interpreters construed the book as eudaemonistic. These category shifts reframed the nature and ethos of Proverbs. For some, the wise men were the modern equivalent of the 'humanists'.[5] For others, the sages were 'moralists'.[6] And for most, Proverbs was the fruit of the sages' reflection on the Torah and the Prophets; it stood in continuity with ancient Israel's legal, priestly and prophetic traditions. This characterisation of the sages and Proverbs' relationship with other corpora in the Old Testament canon created strange bedfellows. Proverbs' universalistic, humanistic and individualistic ethos distinguished the sages as independent thinkers, unconstrained by established traditions. At the same time, the book's interrelationship with the Torah and the Prophets intimated some homogeneity in thought. These strange bedfellows could not coexist; so, they parted ways. Proverbs' philosophical character and distinctive ethos prevailed. In fact, by the late twentieth century, Proverbs was considered a document that projected *'a different thought world'*.[7] The conceptual seeds planted in the eighteenth and nineteenth centuries germinated in the twentieth, producing a foreign document in the Old Testament canon.

   Discussions concerning Proverbs' nature and relation to the Torah and the Prophets in the nineteenth century created the conditions for the third pattern of interpretation that marks the book's reception, viz., an interest in matters of date and authorship. Channelling the spirit of historicism, nineteenth-century interpreters linked the value of Proverbs to the date(s) of its composition and its place within the sweep of ancient Israelite religion.[8] The long-standing tradition that the majority of Proverbs was the product of the pre-exilic period was rejected. The titles of many of the collections were deemed unreliable for ascertaining the date and origin of the materials. And Solomon's association with

   [5] T. K. Cheyne, *Job and Solomon: Or, the Wisdom of the Old Testament* (London, 1887), 119.
   [6] C. H. Toy, *A Critical and Exegetical Commentary on the Book of Proverbs*, ICC (Edinburgh, 1899), xiv.
   [7] James Crenshaw, *Old Testament Wisdom: An Introduction* (Atlanta, 1981), 29.
   [8] C. G. Montefiore, 'Notes upon the Date and Religious Value of Proverbs', *JQR* 2(4) (1890): 430–453.

certain collections moved from composer, to collector, to figurehead. The date of the collections was determined by other means. In the light of the purported relationship between Proverbs and other legal or prophetic texts, some used the date of these texts to identify the composition of certain collections in the anthology. Others focused on linguistic and stylistic features. And still others attended to matters of content, reflecting on Proverbs' lack of attention to idolatry, religious institutions and formative events in Israel's history. When the dust settled on the discussion, a variety of dates were attributed to the collections within Proverbs. Little unanimity was reached, with the exception that the collections in general and Proverbs 1–9 and 30–31 in particular were the product of the post-exilic period.

The separation of Proverbs from the Torah and the Prophets was supported by the fourth pattern of interpretation indicative of Proverbs' reception, namely, the discovery of ancient Near Eastern didactic texts and proverb collections. While the publication of the *Instruction of Ptahhotep* (1847) contributed to the international character of Proverbs in the nineteenth century, E. W. Budge's publication of the *Instruction of Amenemope* (1923) spawned a flurry of works pertaining to its relationship to Prov 22:17–24:22 in the early twentieth century. The relationship between these texts fostered the sentiment that Proverbs was influenced by ancient Near Eastern literature. This reinforced the sense of Proverbs' distinctiveness. Proverbs may be a foreigner in the Old Testament canon; but it was a native of foreign literature. The anthology could no longer be studied in isolation from comparable Egyptian and Mesopotamian texts. Comparative analysis of Proverbs produced a wealth of fresh questions concerning the social setting of proverbial wisdom, the concept of world order and the foreign background that inspired the creation of Lady Wisdom, just to name a few. Many of these questions persist today. While they continue to be answered in nuanced ways, a consensus is not forthcoming.

The fifth and final pattern of interpretation concerns the contemporary state of play, which is varied and manifold due to the growing interdisciplinary nature of research on Proverbs. Several forms of interdisciplinary reading deserve a brief comment. Intertextual studies have pushed back against Proverbs' purported distinctiveness, demonstrating that the anthology sits comfortably alongside its canonical bedfellows.[9] Attention to poetry and paremiology have provided fresh insights into

---

[9] Katharine J. Dell, *The Book of Proverbs in Social and Theological Context* (Cambridge, 2006).

the performance context of Proverbs and the function of its aphorisms.[10] Speech act theory has furnished a framework for considering the purposeful application of individual proverbs.[11] Drawing on different streams of philosophy, several studies have explored the heuristic value of certain theories for conceptualising the ethics and epistemology of Proverbs.[12] Together, cognitive linguistics, cognitive psychology and metaphor theory have enriched aesthetic approaches to the discourse in Proverbs, illuminating its poetic texture and pedagogical techniques, on the one hand, and dispelling presumptions of its simplicity, on the other.[13] Sociological theories have complemented aesthetic approaches to Proverbs by clarifying the ways in which morality played a role in protecting and negotiating class distinctions.[14] Feminist approaches to Proverbs have perceived the nature of the anthology's authority structures, its varied use of female imagery and the relationship of this imagery to the social roles of real women.[15] And deconstruction has detected certain cracks in the textual presentation of the female figures in Proverbs 1–9, fissures that suggest the neat distinction between Wisdom and Folly is fragile and far from clear.[16]

This outline of the interpretive patterns that mark the history of Proverbs' reception does not do justice to the variety of ways in which the anthology has been read. More could be mentioned. These interpretive patterns, however, reveal different aspects of Proverbs' textual contours. If nothing else, they intimate that, far from constituting a compilation of banal materials, the meaning-potential of Proverbs is deep. Layers of its meaning have been actualised through the changing

---

[10] Jacqueline Vayntrub, *Beyond Orality: Biblical Poetry on Its Own Terms* (London, 2019), 183–216.

[11] Suzanna R. Millar, *Genre and Openness in Proverbs 10:1–22:16*, AIL 39 (Atlanta, 2020).

[12] Christopher B. Ansberry, 'What Does Jerusalem Have to Do with Athens? The Moral Vision of the Book of Proverbs and Aristotle's *Nicomachean Ethics*', HS 51 (2010): 157–173; Michael V. Fox, 'The Epistemology of the Book of Proverbs', *JBL* 126 (2007): 669–684.

[13] Stewart, *Poetic Ethics*.

[14] Mark Sneed, 'A Taste for Wisdom: Aesthetics, Moral Discernment, and Social Class in Proverbs', in *Imagined Worlds and Constructed Differences in the Hebrew Bible*, ed. Jeremiah W. Cataldo, LHBOTS 677 (London, 2019), 111–126.

[15] Claudia V. Camp, *Wisdom and the Feminine in the Book of Proverbs* (Sheffield, 1985); Carol R. Fontaine, *Smooth Words: Women, Proverbs and Performance in Biblical Wisdom*, JSOTSup 356 (Sheffield, 2002).

[16] Mark Sneed, '"White Trash" Wisdom: Proverbs 9 Deconstructed', *JHS* 7 (2007): 2–10.

historical process of understanding.[17] And the depth dimension of the anthology's varied materials is evinced through the multifaceted nature of the book of Proverbs.

THE NATURE OF THE BOOK OF PROVERBS

The manifold diversity of Proverbs corresponds to the manifold diversity of the created world that it explores. Creation furnishes the curves and the boundaries, the field and the horizon within which God's wisdom is revealed, acquired and embodied. And the interconnectedness of cosmic order and moral character illumines the panorama of Proverbs. This panorama may focus on the shape of creation and character at the expense of covenant relationship and the mighty acts of God. But these concepts are not mutually exclusive. Creation is the context for covenant relationship; and the ethos of covenant relationship corresponds to character attuned to the rhythms of creation.

In the light of its cosmic framework, it is not surprising that Proverbs mirrors creation in its accommodation of distinct collections and diverse poetic forms. As an anthology, the book is a collection of collections. These collections are attributed to various individuals (Prov 1:1; 10:1; 22:17; 24:23a; 25:1; 30:1a; 31:1a). And these collections contain a variety of forms. The title of the book may create the impression that the anthology is a collection of proverbs (Prov 1:1); but a general perusal of its materials indicates that the book of Proverbs is not, in actual fact, a book of proverbs. On the whole, the anthology includes a pastiche of poetic forms that participate in the dynamic genre of Hebrew poetry. This capacious genre welcomes familiar, yet formally distinct materials: instructions (Prov 1:8–19), aphorisms (Prov 10:1–22:16), admonitions (Prov 22:22–29), encomiums (Prov 8:1–36), numerical sayings (Prov 30:18–19) and hymns (Prov 31:10–31), just to name a few.

The identification of multiple forms in Proverbs is the product of the form-critical approach (1901–). This approach's investigation of shared characteristics and structural features (Form) endemic in discrete genres (*Gattungen*) and indicative of their settings in life (Sitz im Leben) promised to uncover the original, oral forms and social contexts that lie behind the literary forms of the biblical materials. Its application to Proverbs revealed a number of forms and their respective social contexts. Folk proverbs that circulated orally among the populace were

---

[17] Hans-Georg Gadamer, *Truth and Method*, 2nd rev. ed., trans. Joel Weinsheimer and Donald G. Marshall (London, 2004), 366.

distinguished from 'artistic sayings' crafted by the literati.[18] Some collections were situated in schools or the royal court; other materials were deemed the literary descendants of an oral, agrarian context. And the genealogy of the various forms in the anthology were traced along common lines. Single-lined oral proverbs begat poetic distiches, which begat extended instructions;[19] and secular sayings begat communal sayings, which begat religious sayings.[20]

Form criticism excavated fresh layers of the formal and social potential of the materials in Proverbs. These interpretive gains, however, came at a cost. Attention to formal structures trumped explorations of poetic features. Hypothetical social settings took precedence over the literary function of the materials. And the assumption that genres are pure ontological categories imposed illegitimate boundaries on the materials in Proverbs. Recent studies on Proverbs have remedied these shortcomings. Poetic features have been foregrounded, such as parallelism, parataxis, polysemy, figurative language and sound play. The variegated didactic and proverbial functions of the materials have been appreciated within an 'oral-written continuum' and with an openness to different social contexts.[21] What's more, genres have been perceived as more fluid, integrating features characteristic of other forms. These welcome advances, however, should not obscure the fact that the context of the materials in Proverbs remains central to its interpretive horizon. While the forms in the anthology do not provide a clear window into their social context, literary context has been called upon to deliver on the failed promise of form criticism.

For many, different forms of literary context in Proverbs compensate for the loss of a live, social context. Put differently, some form of literary context administers the hermeneutical vaccine against Wolfgang Mieder's well-worn expression: 'the proverb in a collection is dead'.[22] To fight the potential death of the materials in Proverbs, interpreters have drawn upon paremiology and the literary architecture of the book. Paremiological studies stress the importance of performance context for determining a proverb's use. A proverb's performance

[18]   Otto Eissfeldt, *Der Maschal im Alten Testament*, BZAW 24 (Giessen, 1913).
[19]   W. O. E. Oesterley, *The Book of Proverbs* (London, 1929).
[20]   William McKane, *Proverbs: A New Approach*, OTL (London, 1970); Bernd U. Schipper, *Sprüche (Proverbia). Teilband 1: Proverbien 1,1–15,33*, BKAT 17.1 (Göttingen, 2018).
[21]   Susan Niditch, *Oral World and Written Word: Ancient Israelite Literature* (Louisville, 1996).
[22]   Wolfgang Mieder, 'The Essence of Literary Proverb Study', *Proverbium* 23 (1974): 892.

context clarifies the components of the communicative situation (i.e., speaker, addressee and social situation), creating a framework through which to understand the illocutionary act performed by a saying. While the materials in Proverbs 10–29 have been removed from their perform-ance settings, their recontextualisation in the anthology generates a new performance context. The *Sitz im Buch* replaces the Sitz im Leben of the materials.

On this account, the literary contexts of the materials in Proverbs provide the components of the communicative situation, reviving their performance. Yet these contexts and their accompanying communication situations vary. For some, intimate connections between the language and imagery of Proverbs 1–9 and 31 indicate that these discourses furnish an interpretive framework through which to read the materials in Proverbs 10–30. Together, they unify the anthol-ogy, identifying comparable speakers and addressees within a particular social context; and they chart the maturation of moral character, cul-minating in the union between the wise student and the incarnation of wisdom.[23] Others disagree. In contrast to ancient Near Eastern instruc-tions, the titles within Proverbs do not stage a particular performance. At best, the poetic framework of Proverbs situates the material in a general performance context; it projects any father or mother instruct-ing any son(s).[24]

In addition to the poetic frame of Proverbs, still others find a literary performance context within Proverbs 10–29. This contention is linked to the assumption that the editors of the central collections produced literary contexts for individual aphorisms that would compensate for their loss of a live, performance context.[25] These literary contexts re-contextualise individual sayings into larger groups, providing hermeneutical guidance to discern their meaning. The search for these literary contexts has uncovered a variety of elements that may link groups of aphorisms together, such as paronomasia, word play, catch-words and verbal repetition. The validity and intentionality of these groupings, however, is challenged by many. And attempts to demon-strate literary and contextual coherence across the central collections

---

[23] Brown, *Wisdom's Wonder*, 64–66.

[24] Vayntrub, *Beyond Orality*, 191–206.

[25] Raymond Van Leeuwen, *Context and Meaning in Proverbs 25–27*, SBLDS 96 (Atlanta, 1988), 30–31; Knut M. Heim, *Like Grapes of Gold Set in Silver: An Interpretation of Proverbial Clusters in Proverbs 10:1–22:16*, BZAW 273 (Berlin, 2001), 24.

has not swayed the general impression that the arrangement of the materials in Proverbs 10–29 is rather haphazard.

But haphazard arrangement does not necessarily entail that the materials in the central collections have become ossified dogma. The polyvalent depth and intratextual harmony among the materials in Proverbs 10–29 is manifested through the dynamic dialogue among the aphorisms. When the sayings are read together, contradictions, ambiguities and variant repetitions emerge, sharpening the worldview, discernment and imagination of the reader. More than revealing the partial and contextual nature of a proverb's meaning, contradictory sayings capture the incongruities of life.[26] These incongruities are preserved through many sayings, especially those devoted to wealth and poverty. Whereas certain aphorisms describe wealth as an indisputable good that accompanies virtuous character and poverty as a deplorable state engendered by immoral character (Prov 10:4; 14:24; 28:19), other sayings indicate that reality is not so simple:

> Treasures of wickedness will not profit;
>> but righteousness delivers from death.
>>> (10:2)

> The wealth of the rich, his fortified city;
>> and like a high wall, in his imagination.
>>> (18:11)

> Better the poor who walks in his integrity,
>> than a person of perverted ways who is rich.
>>> (28:6)

> There is this: one who pretends to be rich and has nothing;
>> one who pretends to be poor and has great wealth.
>>> (13:7)

> An abundance of food – the fallow ground of the poor;
>> but the reality is this: it is swept away without justice.
>>> (13:23)[27]

---

[26] Christine Roy Yoder, 'Forming "Fearers of Yahweh": Repetition and Contradiction as Pedagogy in Proverbs', in *Seeking Out the Wisdom of the Ancients: Essays Offered in Honor of Michael V. Fox, on the Occasion of His Sixty-Fifth Birthday*, ed. R. L. Troxel, K. G. Friebel, and D. R. Magary (Winona Lake, 2005), 167–183.

[27] For the translation of Proverbs 13:7a and 13:23b, see Agustinus Gianto, 'On שׂ of Reflection in the Book of Proverbs', in *'When the Morning Stars Sang': Essays in*

According to these sayings, wealth may be possessed by the perverted or procured by wicked practices (Prov 28:6; 10:2); and riches provide security (Prov 18:11). Unlike virtuous character, however, wealth cannot secure the stable dividend of deliverance (Prov 10:2; 11:4). Poverty may be the product of laziness or haste (Prov 10:4; 13:11; 20:13); in the same way, it could be the result of injustice (Prov 13:23). Despite their poverty, the poor may be virtuous (Prov 28:6). And pretence may obscure economic realities (Prov 13:7). These divergent angles on wealth and poverty are not unique within the anthology. Competing perspectives on friendship, speech and spouses could also be mentioned.[28] These competing perspectives indicate that the collections within Proverbs create a dialogue of disparate discourses. As an invaluable didactic device, contradiction not only reveals the complexities of life; it also relativises Proverbs' presumed dogmatism.

The complexities of life expressed through contradictory aphorisms correspond with the interpretive ambiguities that characterise many sayings in Proverbs. On the surface, the materials within the book are straightforward; but some of the aphorisms are riddled with structural, conceptual or semantic ambiguity as well as pregnant imagery. From a structural perspective, the parallel couplets of many proverbs elude precise, symmetrical relationship. This is surprising, since the majority of sayings in Proverbs 10–29 exhibit balance between parallel lines. The imbalance within a poetic line or between parallel lines creates 'disjointed proverbs' – sayings that require the reader to exercise imagination by filling in particular gaps.[29] Among the asymmetrical sayings in the book, Proverbs 10:13 evinces a gap between parallel lines.

> On the lips of the discerning wisdom is found;
> and a rod for the back of the senseless.

(10:13)

The relationship between the parallel lines in Proverbs 10:13 is unclear. If the body and the concept of place govern the relationship between the parallel statements, then the lines identify the locale of particular things: wisdom is found on the lips of the discerning, whereas a physical rod or verbal chastisement is found on the back of the

---

Honor of Choon Leong Seow on the Occasion of His Sixty-Fifth Birthday, ed. Scott C. Jones and Christine Roy Yoder, BZAW 500 (Berlin, 2018), 158–162.

[28] Peter T. H. Hatton, *Contradiction in the Book of Proverbs: The Deep Waters of Counsel*, SOTSMS (Aldershot, 2008).

[29] Michael V. Fox, *Proverbs 10–31: A New Translation with Introduction and Commentary*, AB 18B (New Haven, 2009), 494–498.

senseless. But if the saying is a disjointed proverb, then it forces the reader to fill in the gaps and form two antithetical sayings. These antithetical sayings may be formulated as follows:[30]

(a)   On the lips of the discerning wisdom is found,
(a*)   on the lips of the fool folly is found.
(b*)   There is no rod for the back of the discerning,
(b)   but a rod for the back of the senseless.

Together with structural ambiguities, some proverbs traffic in conceptual and semantic ambiguity. These forms of ambiguity are manifested in Proverbs 14:33–34:

Wisdom rests in the heart of the discerning;
    while in the midst of fools she makes herself known.
Righteousness exalts a nation;
    and the lovingkindness of people, sin.
    (but a disgrace to people, sin.)

Proverbs 14:33 employs vivid imagery to identify wisdom's residence: she dwells in the heart of the discerning but manifests herself in the middle of fools. The way in which wisdom makes herself known in the midst of fools is ambiguous. The conceptual ambiguity of the second line has engendered two particular readings, each of which seek to clarify the nature of wisdom's presence. Following the LXX, the first inserts a negative particle to read 'among fools wisdom is unknown', rather than 'known'. Despite the absence of an appropriate marker, the second reads the line as a rhetorical question, with the sense 'will wisdom come to be known?' Both proposals provide possible readings. If the MT is retained, however, the nature of wisdom's presence among fools remains open. While the character of the discerning creates a home for wisdom to rest, the moral ontology of fools ensures that wisdom remains one who may enter their midst but not their heart.

The conceptual openness of Proverbs 14:33 provides a backdrop for the semantic ambiguity expressed in Proverbs 14:34. According to the initial line, righteousness cultivates a communal environment of mutual flourishing (v. 34a). The opening phrase of the second line appears to unpack aspects of this environment, for, with the exception of one other instance in the Old Testament (Lev 20:17), the term *ḥesed*

---

[30] Knut M. Heim, *Poetic Imagination in Proverbs: Variant Repetitions and the Nature of Poetry*, BBRSup 4 (Winona Lake, 2013), 232.

means 'lovingkindness'.[31] When one reaches the evaluation 'sin' (v. 34b) at the end of the second line, however, one recognises the 'false lead'.[32] This evaluation uncovers the semantic ambiguity of *ḥesed*. The 'loving-kindness' of people is not sin; rather, sin is a 'disgrace to people'. The ambiguity hones the reader's moral reason, forcing one to double back and reinterpret the rare homonym to produce a clear antithesis.

A final form of ambiguity characteristic of the materials in Proverbs is their pregnant imagery. Images ignite the imagination, inviting readers to inhabit the world they project. The capacious nature of these imagined worlds is condensed by Proverbs 18:20:

> From the fruit of his mouth one's belly is satisfied;
> he is satisfied by the produce of his lips.

The initial line is a variant repetition of Proverbs 12:14a and 13:2a (v. 20a). Similar to these aphorisms, Proverbs 18:20 explores one's moral essence through the conceptual metaphors PEOPLE ARE TREES and WORDS ARE FOOD. These metaphors not only structure the proverb: following Nicole Tilford, the pregnant imagery also encapsulates a compressed sequence.[33] The branches of the mouth produce fruit through speech. This fruit fills others. Others then produce discursive fruit and this fruit fills the speaker. The aphorism compresses this act-consequence connection into a single event: the mouth that produces the fruit of edible speech is the mouth that consumes the fruit.[34] But in contrast to Prov 12:14a and 13:2a, Prov 18:20a does not associate the fruit of one's mouth with 'good things'. The quality of the fruit is unclear. The aphorism cultivates one's moral imagination, inviting one to inhabit its pregnant imagery to determine whether words bring satisfaction or merely a full stomach.

This reading of Prov 18:20 in conversation with Prov 12:14 and 13:2 reveals another dimension of the dialogical nature of the materials in Proverbs. The dialogical unity of Proverbs is evinced through the phenomenon of 'variant repetition'. The anthology is replete with the repetition of whole proverbs, poetic lines or partial lines in modified form. And these twice-told proverbs occur in both the same collection as well as separate collections. The former is exemplified by Prov 14:12

---

[31] Fox, *Proverbs 10–31*, 587.

[32] See Suzanna R. Millar, 'When a Straight Road Becomes a Garden Path: The "False Lead" as a Pedagogical Strategy in the Book of Proverbs', *JSOT* 43 (2018): 72–73.

[33] Nicole L. Tilford, *Sensing World, Sensing Wisdom: The Cognitive Foundation of Biblical Metaphors*, AIL 31 (Atlanta, 2017), 190.

[34] Tilford, *Sensing World*, 190.

and 16:25, while the latter is manifested through Prov 6:10–11 and 24:33–34.

> There is this: a way that is straight before a person;
>> but its end, ways to death.
>
>> (14:12)

> There is this: a way that is straight before a person;
>> but its end, ways to death.
>
>> (16:25)

> A little sleep, a little slumber,
>> a little folding of the hands to rest,
> and poverty will come upon you like a vagabond,
>> and need like an armed warrior.
>
>> (6:10–11)

> A little sleep, a little slumber,
>> a little folding of the hands to rest,
> and poverty will come upon you like a vagabond,
>> and need like an armed warrior.
>
>> (24:33–34)

The repetition of aphorisms in the same collection as well as in collections produced by different scribes at different times is striking. Whether these repetitions represent 'memory variants', permutations of proverbial templates or the deliberate editorial work of scribes,[35] they generate a dialogue among the materials in the anthology, where subtleties, tensions and the depth dimension of topics are explored. Far from merely recycling proverbs or parts of poetic lines, variant repetitions reinforce and reconfigure particular motifs to shape the character and moral reasoning of the reader.

Taken together, the cosmic scope, formal diversity, varying contexts and dialogical quality of the materials in Proverbs produce a general sense of the anthology's multifaceted nature. Each facet, in different ways, contributes to the nature of Proverbs. And each facet reveals a layer of Proverbs' meaning-potential.

---

[35] See David M. Carr, *The Formation of the Hebrew Bible: A New Reconstruction* (New York, 2011), 13–36; Fox, *Proverbs 10–31*, 487–493; and Heim, *Poetic Imagination*, *passim*, respectively.

THE STRUCTURE OF THE BOOK OF PROVERBS

If the multidimensional nature of the book of Proverbs reveals the depth dimension of its parts, the structure of the anthology reflects the degree of continuity and discontinuity across the whole. Proverbs contains several collections, each of which are marked off by titles (Prov 1:1; 10:1a; 22:17; 24:23a; 25:1; 30:1a; 31:1a). While the date(s), setting(s) and compositional development(s) of these collections are contested, the titles orient one to the architecture of the book. In fact, certain titles intimate an awareness of other collections. The use of the adverb 'also' in Prov 24:23 and 25:1 suggests that those responsible for the inclusion of Prov 24:23–34 and 25:1–29:27 in the anthology associated these compendia with existing collections attributed to the wise and Solomon, respectively (Prov 22:17; 10:1a; 1:1). More than serving as structural beams within Proverbs, these titles may bear witness to a deliberate attempt to link the parts of the anthology to the whole.

Signs of deliberate design are also apparent at the frame of the anthology. To extend the discussion of literary and performance contexts above, the shared setting, imagery and language between Proverbs 1–9 and 30–31 indicate that these materials have been placed at the boundaries of the anthology to frame the materials within the whole. The maternal voice mentioned in Proverbs 1–9 (Prov 1:8; 6:20) is given expression in the instruction of Lemuel's mother (Prov 30:1–9). Just as the lectures in Proverbs 1–9 are cast in the confines of the home, so also the words of Lemuel are situated in a domestic setting (Prov 31:1–9). The female imagery that pervades Proverbs 1–9 permeates Proverbs 31. The portrait of the 'valiant woman' (Prov 31:10–31) is painted with terms and expressions used elsewhere only to describe Lady Wisdom.[36] The 'motto' of the anthology – 'the fear of Yahweh' – occurs at the climax of the preamble (Prov 1:7), the conclusion of the prologue (Prov 9:10) and the end of the book (Prov 31:30). And the phrase 'knowledge of the Holy One' is found only in Prov 9:10 and 30:3. Irrespective of whether this link places chapter 30 within the frame of the anthology, few would deny that Proverbs 1–9 and 31 serve as a formal framework for the book. They bracket its diverse materials, creating a unified whole.

In addition to the compositional significance of Proverbs 1–9 and 31, many argue that this framework provides an interpretive lens through which to understand the parts of the anthology. The magnification of

---

[36] A. Barucq, *Le livre des Proverbes*, SB (Paris, 1964), 231.

this interpretive lens, however, differs among interpreters. For some, the frame of the anthology projects a worldview through its network of images and interrelated metaphors. These images and metaphors out-line the conventional structures of the world and the patterns of human life that are filled out through the characters and detailed scenarios within Proverbs 10–29.[37] For others, this framework charts the matur-ation of moral character; it sketches the journey of the addressee from a young adult instructed in the home (Prov 1–9), to one nourished on the fare of Lady Wisdom's table (Prov 10–30), to one seated at the city gate, married to the incarnation of wisdom (Prov 31:10–31).[38] These inter-pretive lenses are helpful, for they bring a measure of clarity to the compositional shape of the diverse materials in Proverbs. But these lenses do not suit many readers. When applied, their magnification is either too weak or too strong. They either fail to clarify the specific nature and function of the materials in Proverbs 10–30 or they distort the particular contributions of these collections.[39]

In the light of the lack of agreement concerning the interpretive significance of the frame of the anthology and the compositional contri-butions of the titles within the book, many have directed their attention to the shape of the individual collections. Whether Proverbs 1–9 is considered a formal introduction to the document or a self-contained unit, the structural contours of the collection are clear. It consists of a preamble (Prov 1:1–7), lectures (Prov 1:8–19; 2:1–22; 3:1–12, 21–35; 4:1–9, 10–19, 20–27; 5:1–23; 6:20–35; 7:1–27) and interludes (Prov 1:20–33; 3:13–20; 6:1–19; 8:1–36; 9:1–18). The preamble delineates the purpose, addressees, pedagogical programme and intended results of the materials in the book, as well as the fundamental posture for achieving the document's goal. The lectures actualise the educational vision of the preamble through various poetic techniques, each of which are designed to form the character of the reader through competing didactic discourses.[40] The interludes complement the lectures. They introduce fresh themes (Prov 6:1–19), extend the concept of wisdom and associate the domestic instruction of the lectures with the ethos of communal life. Taken together, the arrangement of the discourses within Proverbs

---

[37] Raymond Van Leeuwen, 'The Book of Proverbs', *NIB* 5:24.
[38] Brown, *Wisdom's Wonder*, 64–66.
[39] See Arthur Jan Keefer, *Proverbs 1–9 as an Introduction to the Book of Proverbs*, LHBOTS 701 (London, 2020).
[40] J. N. Aletti, 'Seduction et parole en Proverbes I–IX', *VT* 27 (1977): 129–144.

1–9 may not exhibit a logical progression of instruction. This does not mean, however, that the collection lacks coherence.

Irrespective of differing opinions regarding the classification of certain lectures and interludes, most agree that Proverbs 1–9 exhibits considerable cohesiveness.[41] Beyond the use of 'the fear of Yahweh' at the frame of the collection (Prov 1:7; 9:10), however, the nature of this cohesion differs. For some, the unity of the material is due to the work of a single author or editor.[42] For others, it is the product of organic growth: the lectures provided ideas that were cultivated by later authors to produce the interludes and other secondary materials.[43] For still others, the unity of the collection is attributable to the stages of its redaction.[44] Explanations for the cohesiveness of Proverbs 1–9 vary; but the unity and structural contours of the materials are relatively clear.

The same is true of the other collections within Proverbs. As noted above, little unanimity exists regarding the existence and boundaries of larger clusters across Prov 10:1–29:27. But the structural contours of the remaining collections and the interrelationship among the seams of certain compendia are widely acknowledged. The title and aphorism in Prov 10:1 serve as a hinge within the anthology. The title reiterates the expression that opens the book ('proverbs of Solomon', Prov 1:1), linking the collection to the preamble. And the mention of father, mother, as well the wise/foolish son in the initial aphorism (Prov 10:1b–c), mirrors the setting of the lectures in general (Prov 1:8; 6:20) and the antithesis between Lady Wisdom and Woman Folly in particular (Prov 9:1–6, 13–18). The entryway into the central collections looks back to Proverbs 1–9. Together with the title in Proverbs 22:17, it also marks off Prov 10:1–22:16 as a discrete collection. Since the turn of the twentieth century, most interpreters have divided this collection into two sub-units. Whereas antithetical sayings dominate Prov 10:1–15:33, they recede in Prov 16:1–22:16, which includes various forms of poetic parallelism. The precise boundary between these sub-units varies; but the mention of 'the fear of Yahweh' in Prov 15:33 suggests that it provides an appropriate introduction to the second sub-collection.

Similar to Prov 10:1, Prov 22:17a, 24:23a and 25:1 serve as hinges in the anthology. These titles reiterate expressions from the preamble

[41] See Stuart Weeks, *Instruction and Imagery in Proverbs 1–9* (Oxford, 2007).

[42] Arndt Meinhold, *Die Sprüche. Teil 1: Sprüche Kapitel 1–15*, ZBK 16.1 (Zürich, 1991), 43–46.

[43] Michael V. Fox, *Proverbs 1–9: A New Translation with Introduction and Commentary*, AB 18A (New York, 2000), 322–324.

[44] Schipper, *Sprüche*, 94–116.

('words of the wise', Prov 1:6; 22:17a; 'proverbs of Solomon', Prov 1:1; 10:1a; 25:1a), connecting the collections to the opening verses of the book. In addition, these titles also delineate the boundaries of distinct collections (Prov 22:17–24:22; 24:23–24; 25:1–29:27). With the exception of Prov 24:23–34, these collections tend to be divided into sub-units. In the light of the reading 'thirty' in Prov 22:20 and the purported influence of the *Instruction of Amenemope* on the shape and content of Prov 22:17–24:22, many divide the collection into at least two parts: Prov 22:17–23:11 and 23:12–24:22.[45] The former exhibits exclusive dependence on *Amenemope*, while the latter evinces the adaptation of materials from a range of ancient Near Eastern didactic texts. And like Prov 10:1–22:16, most distinguish Proverbs 25–27 and 28–29 on formal and stylistic grounds. Whereas Proverbs 25–27 traffics in vivid images and comparisons, Proverbs 28–29 contains a preponderance of antithetical sayings and a dearth of similes. The titles and formal features of the central collections reveal the structural contours of the anthology's parts. Yet these parts, in different ways, also manifest some relationship to the whole.

The final collections within the anthology open with a pair of comparable titles, each of which share general connections with previous materials. The 'words' in Prov 30:1a and 31:1a recall Prov 22:17a; and the designation 'king' in 31:1a is reminiscent of Prov 1:1 and 25:1. Whether or not these connections intimate that the editors of the anthology attempted to relate the concluding collections to other compendia, the titles in 30:1a and 31:1a introduce materials attributed to foreigners. While the diverse materials in these collections share several lexical and thematic similarities, many discern two sections in these respective units. The extent of Agur's words have proven to be a riddle. On logical grounds or in view of the LXX, however, Agur's discourse may encompass 30:1–9 or 30:1–14. The aphorisms and epigrams in the remainder of chapter 30 constitute the second half of the collection. The words of Lemuel, in the same way, contain two sub-units. The first is a royal instruction (Prov 31:1–9); the second is an alphabetic acrostic that paints a heroic portrait of a 'valiant woman' (Prov 31:10–31). Taken together, these concluding collections are often characterised as 'appendices'. But when they are viewed within the design of the anthology as a whole, they are not subsidiary additions. They play an integral role in the literary and thematic configuration of the book.

---

[45] Franz Delitzsch, *Biblical Commentary on the Proverbs of Solomon*, trans. M. G. Easton, 2 vols. (Edinburgh, 1874), 2:111; Fox, *Proverbs 10–31*, 705–707.

THE MAIN THEMES IN THE BOOK OF PROVERBS

The main themes woven throughout Proverbs play a similar role. They provide focal points that illuminate interrelated motifs within the anthology. Many could be mentioned. Four themes, however, seem to capture the dominant ideas within Proverbs and clarify their interrelationship with subordinate motifs.

The first is 'the fear of Yahweh', which frames the document and orients one to the theological nature of the whole (Prov 1:7; 31:30). For many, 'the fear of Yahweh' is the temporal beginning of wisdom. When one attends to the recurrence of this motto throughout the anthology, however, its temporal precedence is difficult to maintain. According to Prov 1:7a, 'The fear of Yahweh is the rē'šît of knowledge'. As many commentators note, the term rē'šît is polysemous: the fear of Yahweh may be the 'beginning' (temporal), the 'first principle' (logical) or the 'first-fruit' (consequential product) of wisdom. The consequential connotation of the term seems to suit the description of wisdom's acquisition in Prov 2:1–5, where one's active pursuit of wisdom culminates in understanding the fear of Yahweh. But this construal of the fear of Yahweh is called into question by Prov 9:10:

> The tĕḥillat of wisdom is the fear of Yahweh,
> and knowledge of the Holy One is understanding.

While many render tĕḥillat as 'beginning', others contend that it connotes 'first part'.[46] In the light of the openness of the genitive construction in Prov 15:33a, both senses remain possible. Do these intertextual reverberations suggest that the precise relationship between wisdom and the fear of Yahweh is undecidable?

If nothing else, these texts intimate that the temporal precedence of the fear of Yahweh over wisdom is questionable. Following Stuart Weeks and Zoltán Schwáb, the fear of Yahweh is not distinct from wisdom; it is the first-fruits or the initial manifestation of wisdom.[47] This connection between the fear of Yahweh and wisdom mirrors the connection between ontology and epistemology. According to Job Jindo, there is a certain kind of knowledge that accompanies fear and creates a mode of being. That knowledge is perspectival rather than propositional; it is the perception of one's status in the cosmos in relation to

---

[46] Weeks, *Instruction*, 118.
[47] Weeks, *Instruction*, 117–118; Zoltán Schwáb, 'Is Fear of the Lord the Source of Wisdom or Vice Versa?', *VT* 63 (2013): 652–662.

Yahweh.[48] This epistemological insight is inseparable from the fear of Yahweh. Perspectival knowledge (wisdom) is bound up with a mode of being (fear of Yahweh).

Jindo's description of the interrelationship between wisdom and the fear of Yahweh entails that the fear of Yahweh is a mode of being, not a virtue. It is a consciousness of one's place in the cosmos in relation to Yahweh that directs one's inner faculties and external actions. This conception of wisdom and the fear of Yahweh explains why one may grow in one's understanding of the fear of Yahweh (Prov 2:5). The magnitude of one's fear is proportional to the quality of one's knowledge of God.[49] This conception of wisdom and the fear of Yahweh accounts for the severe limits of human wisdom and power (Prov 16:1–9; 21:2, 30–31). And this conception of wisdom and the fear of Yahweh may explain the problem with certain character types in Proverbs, such as the fool, the wicked, the scoffer and the lazy. If the fear of Yahweh refers to a mode of being that is inseparable from a certain type of perspectival knowledge, then the problem with these aberrant character types is not their lack of propositional knowledge; it is their lack of perspectival knowledge, which would allow them to see themselves and the world through a particular mode of cognition. No wonder these sorts of characters cannot learn. They know neither their place in the cosmos nor themselves in relation to Yahweh.

The second prominent theme in Proverbs is related to the first; it concerns the nature of wisdom. For Proverbs, wisdom is not mastery of a body of knowledge; it is not an impersonal 'knowing that' or 'knowing about'. Rather, wisdom is an embodied skill, acquired and developed through interpersonal instruction and correction. And as an embodied skill, wisdom includes the totality of one's being (Prov 1:2–7); it is 'cognitive *and* emotional *and* aesthetic'.[50] On this account, wisdom is a holistic form of embodied knowledge that seeks understanding, conceptualises interactions in the moral world, discerns potential outcomes, loves what is good, hates what is evil, delights in the beautiful, winces at the ethically grotesque and actualises the moral life by living within the limits appropriate to creaturehood, all despite uncertainty.

---

[48] Job Y. Jindo, 'On the Biblical Notion of the 'Fear of God' as a Condition for Human Existence', *BibInt* 19 (2012): 433–453.

[49] Jindo, 'Fear of God', 448.

[50] Fox, 'Epistemology', 684. Also see Tremper Longman III, *The Fear of the Lord Is Wisdom: A Theological Introduction to Wisdom in Israel* (Grand Rapids, 2017), 5–25.

This multifaceted vision of wisdom is refracted through the diverse materials in Proverbs. The lectures and interludes in Proverbs 1–9, for example, inculcate wisdom through competing discourses, designed to cultivate discernment, sharpen perception, direct desire, nurture virtuous dispositions and construct a moral worldview attuned to the cosmic and communal orders of creation. The central collections of Proverbs extend this (trans)formational programme in wisdom through poetic snapshots of particular characters or actions, devised to awaken the imagination, hone one's reasoning, exemplify what is desirable, shape one's behaviour and produce a paradigmatic vision for living in relation within the moral world.[51] Wisdom, for Proverbs, is a holistic, interpersonal, embodied skill; and the diverse materials in the book contribute to the formation of this skill in distinctive ways.

The holistic, interpersonal, embodied nature of wisdom in Proverbs is also explored through a network of interrelated images within the anthology. As a concrete phenomenon, wisdom exists in an intratextual relationship with paths, characters, women, houses, life, and death. The conceptual metaphor LIFE IS A PATH pervades Proverbs; it serves as a window into a larger metaphoric system that includes the concepts of wisdom and folly, life and death.[52] For Proverbs, the way of wisdom and life is straight, clear and open (Prov 3:23; 4:11–12; 11:5). The way of folly and death, by contrast, is crooked, dark and dangerous (Prov 2:12–15; 4:19; 22:5). The intimate relationship between the metaphor and these concepts suggests that the way or path is much more than a course of life; it also concerns one's character, conduct and the consequences of one's behaviour. This means that the wise and the fool may travel on several 'paths' (Prov 1:19; 2:19; 4:26; 5:6), each of which manifest forms of behaviour or choices that may be characterised as wise or foolish, that lead to life or death.

The metaphor of the way also exists in interrelationship with the women and their respective houses within Proverbs. Similar to the path metaphor, these women traverse ways that lead to distinct homes: Wisdom leads to life (Prov 8:35; 9:6), the 'foreign woman' and Folly lead to death (Prov 2:18; 7:27; 9:13–18). And similar to the path metaphor, these women are distinguished by particular virtues or vices: one is marked by wisdom, righteousness and justice (Prov 8:8, 14, 20), the

---

[51] Stewart, *Poetic Ethics.*

[52] N. C. Habel, 'The Symbolism of Wisdom in Proverbs 1–9', *Interp* 26 (1972): 131–157; Raymond Van Leeuwen, 'Liminality and Worldview in Proverbs 1–9', *Semeia* 50 (1990): 111–144.

others by seduction, deception and folly (Prov 2:16; 5:3; 7:5, 21; 9:13). The virtues and vices that characterise these women indicate that they incarnate certain 'ways' of life.[53] When taken together, the interrelated images of paths, characters, women, houses, life and death create a framework through which to perceive the holistic nature of wisdom in Proverbs and its implications for the whole of life.

The third prominent theme in Proverbs is a natural corollary of the fear of Yahweh and wisdom, viz., the moral order and its relation to the created order. While the search for a created order that aligns with the moral order assumed in Proverbs may be more of a modern imposition than a description of the sages' quest, the links between these orders emerge in certain texts. Among these texts, Prov 8, 3:19–20 and 24:3–4 may be the most significant. The encomium in Proverbs 8 indicates that Lady Wisdom possesses the tools necessary for the establishment of social order (Prov 8:14).[54] Wisdom dispenses these tools to those in communal positions of power (Prov 8:15–16). And Wisdom's possession of these tools as well as her instrumental role in the establishment of an ordered society are tethered to her presence at the creation of the cosmos. Lady Wisdom's ability to empower rulers to order society (Prov 8:15) derives from her observance of the order Yahweh established at creation (Prov 8:27, 29). This interrelationship among Yahweh, wisdom, the created order and the socio-moral order is also reflected in Prov 3:19–20 and 24:3–4. The former describes the tools that Yahweh employed to found and fill the cosmos through a sequence of prepositional phrases: 'by wisdom ... by understanding ... by knowledge' (Prov 3:19–20). And this unique sequence of prepositional phrases is reiterated in Prov 24:3–4 to sketch the way in which humans found and fill domestic and social spheres (cf. Exod 31:3; 35:31). If nothing else, these intertextual links suggest that humans imitate the divine architect's ordering of the cosmos through their ordering of society.[55] The formation and filling of the created order is paradigmatic for the formation and filling of the socio-moral order.

Beyond these particular texts, the correspondence between the moral order and the created order may not be pronounced in Proverbs. This does not mean, however, that it is absent. The link is implied in a

---

[53]   Weeks, *Instruction*, 78–79

[54]   See Gerhard Von Rad, *Wisdom in Israel*, trans. J. D. Martin (London, 1972), 144–176.

[55]   Raymond Van Leeuwen, 'Cosmos, Temple, House: Building and Wisdom in Mesopotamia and Israel', in *Wisdom Literature in Mesopotamia and Israel*, ed. R. J. Clifford, SBLSymS 36 (Atlanta, 2007), 77–87.

variety of sayings. The wisdom of the wise son, for example, is manifested through his sensitivity to created time and work in accord with
the rhythm of creation (Prov 10:5). This sensitivity to the calendrical
pattern of creation is also instantiated in the ant (Prov 6:6–11). And a
comparable sensitivity is exemplified by the righteous, who know the
appetite of their livestock (Prov 12:10). Sensitivity to the rhythmical
patterns of creation and the uniqueness of its creatures informs wise
behaviour (cf. Prov 26:1; 27:18). More than this, sensitivity to certain
patterns and the uniqueness of particular creatures may also attune one
to other patterns and creatures, such as when to speak or how to speak
to certain people, when to act and what to do in particular circumstances. These judgements permeate the book of Proverbs. And, to some
extent, these patterned judgements are informed by the patterns of the
created order.

These moral and created patterns, however, are not necessarily
transparent. On the surface, Proverbs may project predictable patterns.
But when one considers the grooves within the anthology, it appears
these patterns are neither mechanistic nor inviolable. This dialectic
provides a backdrop for the fourth and final prominent theme within
Proverbs: retribution and reward. Since the dawn of Klaus Koch's influential essay, many have identified ambiguities and exceptions in particular aphorisms that attenuate Koch's conception of a deterministic
yet synthetic 'sphere of action', where acts are organically connected to
consequences.[56] This inbuilt, 'act-consequence connection' is intimated by many sayings.

> Evil pursues sinners,
>> but the righteous will be rewarded with good.
>>> (13:21)

> Whoever digs a pit will fall into it;
>> and whoever rolls a stone – it will come back on him.
>>> (26:27)

In accord with Koch's proposal, these sayings are patient with an intrinsic connection between act and consequence in which divine, human or
social agency is unnecessary to actualise the fate that accompanies
particular deeds.

---

[56] Klaus Koch, 'Gibt es ein Vergeltungsdogma im Alten Testament', *ZTK* 52 (1955):
1–42.

Other sayings, however, demonstrate that Proverbs is aware of violable patterns, agents who enforce retribution and reward, as well as the contingencies that characterise human existence. The wicked and the violent gain wealth (Prov 10:2; 11:16, 18); and the righteous require deliverance (Prov 11:6, 8, 9; 12:13). The righteous fall (Prov 24:15–16), while the wicked rise to rule over people (Prov 28:12, 28; 29:2, 16). The poor are poor, but they are not necessarily culpable for their poverty (Prov 13:23). These observations not only undermine a strict connection between acts and consequences; they also suggest that 'character-consequence' is a more appropriate designation for retribution and reward in Proverbs.[57] One's character, rather than specific acts, serves as a wide-angle lens with which to consider retribution and reward. What's more, this wide-angle lens creates space to consider the agents involved in retribution and reward. These agents vary among the materials in Proverbs. Some attribute the connection between character and consequence to individuals or society in general (Prov 11:10, 26; 27:18). Others identify Yahweh's active role in the administration of retribution and reward (Prov 12:2; 15:25; 22:12). And still others traffic in passive constructions, leaving the timing and agency behind the connection open to different formulations (Prov 11:25; 13:13; 21:9). Proverbs acknowledges the exceptions to the predictable patterns of life as well as the ambiguities of retribution and reward. And the anthology relates these realities to the contingencies of human existence. In the light of the limits of creaturehood and the incalculable activity of God, 'there always lies a great unknown' between character, act and consequence (Prov 16:1, 9; 27:1).[58] This great unknown may be the 'minority report' in Proverbs. Nonetheless, the minority report qualifies the predictable patterns and orders of life, forcing one to exercise their moral reasoning and develop a nuanced perspective of being-in-the-world.[59]

CONCLUSION

The book of Proverbs is many things. In the light of its reception history, nature, structure and main themes, it appears that labels like banal, dogmatic and abstract are unfortunate caricatures. These pejorative

---

[57] Lennart Boström, *The God of the Sages: The Portrayal of God in the Book of Proverbs*, ConBOT 29 (Stockholm, 1990).

[58] Von Rad, *Wisdom in Israel*, 101.

[59] Hatton, *Contradiction*, 115–116.

characterisations may capture certain aspects Proverbs. But they fail to perceive the poetic richness, pedagogical dynamics, ambiguities and nuances of the anthology. When one takes a closer look at Proverbs, its depth dimension becomes apparent; and the proverb proves to be true: appearances can be deceiving.

Further Reading

Brown, William P. *Wisdom's Wonder: Character, Creation, and Crisis in the Bible's Wisdom Literature*. Grand Rapids: 2014.

Dell, Katharine J. *The Book of Proverbs in Social and Theological Context*. Cambridge: 2006.

Fox, Michael V. *Proverbs 1–9: A New Translation with Introduction and Commentary*. AB 18A. New York: 2000.

Proverbs 10–31: A New Translation with Introduction and Commentary. AB 18B. New Haven: 2009.

Heim, Knut M. *Poetic Imagination in Proverbs: Variant Repetitions and the Nature of Poetry*. BBRSup 4. Winona Lake: 2013.

Origen. Comm. Cant. Prol. 3, R. P. Lawson, trans., *Origen: The Song of Songs: Commentary and Homilies*. Ancient Christian Writers 26. Westminster: The Newman Press, 1957.

Stewart, Anne W. *Poetic Ethics in Proverbs: Wisdom Literature and the Shaping of the Moral Self*. New York: 2016.

Von Rad, Gerhard. *Wisdom in Israel*. Translated by J. D. Martin. London: 1972.

Weeks, Stuart. *Instruction and Imagery in Proverbs 1–9*. Oxford: 2007.

9 Job

WILL KYNES

David Clines once famously asked, 'Why is there a book of Job, and what does it do to you if you read it?'[1] This chapter will ask a different yet related question: What is the book of Job, and how does that affect how you read it? For the last century and a half, the answer to this question was fairly simple and relatively uncontroversial: Job is Wisdom Literature, along with Proverbs and Ecclesiastes. Therefore, it should be read as a product of the same Wisdom tradition that produced those texts, which aimed to provide universal answers to universal questions on the basis, not of Israel's particular history, law or covenant but of the analysis of the world by human reason. However, an undercurrent of discomfort with that classification of the book has coursed beneath this consensus for several decades, slowly wearing away scholarly confidence, such that alternative theories are beginning to bubble up into mainstream interpretation. This difficulty in categorising Job actually accords with early interpreters' struggles to find a consistent place for it in canon lists and the wide range of texts with which they associated it in their exegetical efforts. Each of these readings, both ancient and modern, involve a different conception of what the book is, and therefore how it should be read.

These attempts to identify what Job is inevitably involve comparing it with other texts and grouping it with those with which readers in various times and places perceive it to share one or more significant affinities. In other words, readers have attempted throughout history to understand the book through reading it in various *genres*, which act as formalised shorthand for such intertextual comparisons.[2] Genres are

---

[1] David J. A. Clines, 'Why Is There a Book of Job, and What Does It Do to You If You Read It?', in *Interested Parties: The Ideology of Writers and Readers of the Hebrew Bible*, JSOTSup 225 (Sheffield, 1995), 122–144.

[2] For this definition of genre, see Will Kynes, *An Obituary for 'Wisdom Literature': The Birth, Death, and Intertextual Reintegration of a Biblical Corpus* (Oxford, 2019), 145.

vital for interpretation because they provide a horizon of expectations that make interpretation possible, though still inescapably provisional. However, because this intertextual analysis is performed by readers (even authors can only write in a genre by comparing their work to earlier texts), it is culturally contingent, shaped by the cultural location of those readers, including their knowledge and interests. This means that it is inappropriate to speak of *the* genre to which a text belongs, as the essentialist approach long dominant in biblical studies would have it. Rather than static and absolute categories determined by a text's essential characteristics, the nominalist approach, which has only recently filtered into biblical studies from literary studies, considers genres to be dynamic and contingent groupings that illuminate particular features of a text in relation to others. Texts participate in multiple genres as readers recognise different affinities they share with various other groups of texts, and thus, genres enable readers to comprehend the meaning of texts, but a single genre can never comprehend a text's meaning.

THE BASIC CONTOURS OF THE BOOK

The various genre groupings in which Job is read each tell the book's story differently, emphasising various aspects of its plot and explaining their relationship to one another distinctly. However, the basic contours of the book are as follows. Job is introduced as a paragon of wisdom and righteousness, 'blameless and upright, one who feared God and turned away from evil' (Job 1:1). The narrator's positive evaluation of Job will be repeated twice by God (1:8; 2:3), which reinforces its fundamental importance for understanding both Job, the character and his eponymous book. The former pair of traits, blameless and upright, appear together in descriptions of God (Deut 32:4) and of David, linked to his complete obedience to God's commands (1 Kgs 9:4), as the ground of the psalmist's confidence before God (Ps 25:21; cf. 37:37), and repeatedly in Proverbs, where they are associated with protection (2:7; 2:21), guidance (11:3, 5), and the target of the wicked (28:10; 29:10). The poem about wisdom later in Job will proclaim the other pair of traits, fearing God and turning from evil, the very definition of wisdom (Job 28:28).

The genuineness of Job's piety, however, is questioned by a celestial figure called *haśśāṭān*. Though this is often translated 'Satan' (e.g., NRSV, NIV), the definite article (*ha*) indicates that the term refers to a role, such as 'adversary' or 'accuser' based on the meaning of the Hebrew verb *śāṭan*, rather than being a proper noun. Fulfilling his accusatory role, 'the Adversary' (JPS) questions the genuineness of Job's piety (1:9-11) by suggesting that it is motivated purely by self-interest. He claims that if Job were to lose the blessings God has bestowed on him, Job would 'curse' God (the euphemism *bārak* ['bless'] is used repeatedly in chs. 1-2 to avoid mention of cursing God). God agrees to this challenge, and Job loses his ten children, his wealth and subsequently his health, and yet he maintains his piety and refuses to curse God (1:21; 2:10).

However, Job's response to his suffering changes in ch. 3, and the literary form of the book changes with it, moving from sparse prose to complex poetry. Job curses the day of his birth with a vehemence that expands into a wish for the unmaking of creation itself. Job's three friends, Eliphaz, Bildad and Zophar, who had come to comfort him (2:11), respond to Job's laments in three cycles of speeches, in which Job alternates with each friend in turn. Though they initially treat Job with sympathy and respect (e.g., 4:2-6), his persistent declaration of his innocence (e.g., 10:7) and accusations of divine injustice (e.g., 16:11-17) lead them eventually to turn on him (e.g., 22:5).[3] The third cycle may be dislocated, since Bildad's speech is uncharacteristically short, Zophar's is missing, and Job says things (27:13-23) that seem to fit the friends' position better than his own. An extended poem on wisdom (ch. 28), which declares it beyond human grasp, follows. The speaker of this poem is not clearly indicated. It fits somewhat uncomfortably with the tone and content of Job's speeches, so some have attributed it to the narrator or one of the friends.[4] Job then delivers a final monologue, which concludes with an extensive self-curse (ch. 31) through which Job declares his absolute confidence in his innocence and thereby demands a response from God, declaring 'Here is my signature! Let the Almighty answer me!' (31:35).

Instead of a divine answer, a young man named Elihu, previously unmentioned, steps into the debate. Having deferred to his elders throughout the dialogue, he can no longer resist and intervenes to correct Job for justifying himself at God's expense and the friends for failing to answer Job adequately (32:2-5). The derivative nature of Elihu's arguments, which repeat much from both Job and the friends,

---

[3]   Job's complaints have earned him a similar treatment throughout the history of Christian interpretation. See Will Kynes, 'The Trials of Job: Relitigating Job's "Good Case" in Christian Interpretation', *SJT* 66 (2013): 174-191.

[4]   See Michael V. Fox, 'The Speaker in Job 28', in *'When the Morning Stars Sang': Essays in Honor of Choon Leong Seow on the Occasion of His Sixty-Fifth Birthday*, ed. Scott C. Jones and Christine Roy Yoder, BZAW 500 (Berlin, 2018), 21-38.

combined with his absence from both prologue and epilogue, lead many to conclude that his speeches are a later addition to the book. The debate over the originality of these chapters (32–37) is dwarfed, however, by that over their meaning, which is thoroughly ambiguous. While some, including medieval Jewish interpreters and John Calvin, see Elihu's speeches providing the answer to Job's conundrum, others consider him an 'irascible, presumptuous blowhard', whose main contribution is to anticipate the divine speeches by demonstrating the complete failure of human wisdom.[5]

The storm brewing in the imagery Elihu uses in his final speech (37:2–13) does indeed foreshadow the appearance of God, now referred to as YHWH, in a whirlwind to answer Job. How and whether these divine speeches (chs. 38–41) actually respond to Job's accusations or even address his situation is another area of significant interpretive debate. God unleashes a barrage of rhetorical questions at Job intended to convey to him God's complete and intimate engagement with creation, from the origin of the cosmos (38:4–11) to the care of baby ravens (38:41), birthing mountain goats (39:1) and control of the mighty Behemoth (40:15–24) and Leviathan (40:25–41:26; ET 41:1–34). God's words are understood variously as an evasive change of subject, an attempt to bully Job into submission and an indirect attempt at comfort and consolation.[6] This interpretive decision is related to how one understands Job's response to the divine speeches (42:2–6), particularly its final verse, which is also fraught with interpretive difficulty. The meaning of nearly every word in this verse is disputed, as are the various possible relationships between them. Traditionally, the verse has been understood as Job's repentance (see, e.g., Vul, KJV, NRSV, NIV), though the verb *niḥamtî*, which inspires that translation, could also be translated 'recant' (e.g., JPS), or even to 'find comfort' or 'accept consolation', which is the meaning words from the same root have throughout the book.[7]

---

[5] Robert Alter, *The Art of Biblical Poetry* (New York, 1985), 91.

[6] See, respectively, Johnny E. Miles, *God: A Biography* (New York, 1995), 315–316; Edward L. Greenstein, 'The Problem of Evil in the Book of Job', in *Mishneh Todah: Studies in Deuteronomy and Its Cultural Environment in Honor of Jeffrey H. Tigay*, ed. Nili S. Fox, David A. Glatt-Gilad and Michael J. Williams (Winona Lake, 2009), 353; J. Gerald Janzen, *At the Scent of Water: The Ground of Hope in the Book of Job* (Grand Rapids, 2009).

[7] See Job 2:11; 6:10; 7:13; 15:11; 16:2; 21:2; 21:34; 29:25; 42:11. See David A. Lambert, 'The Book of Job in Ritual Perspective', *JBL* 134 (2015): 557–575.

After Job's response, the book returns to simple prose similar to that in the prologue to describe Job's restored relationship with God and his community. God delivers a judgement on the friends for not speaking of the deity what is right, while approving Job's speech (42:7), though a substantial sacrifice and Job's prayer delivers the friends from divine punishment (42:8–9). God blesses Job with twice as much as he lost, as well as with ten new children, including three daughters of incomparable beauty. Job also receives fellowship, comfort and gifts from his friends and family. The book ends with Job dying 'old and full of days' (42:17).

DATE

Though the apparent patriarchal setting of the book traditionally led it to be considered one of the oldest in the canon, its date of composition has become yet another disputed aspect of the book. Since the text lacks any explicit reference to historical events, efforts to identify a plausible period for Job's composition rely primarily on inner-biblical parallels, linguistic evidence and theories about the development of Israel's religion. However, conclusions based on evidence in each of these categories are tenuous. Inner-biblical parallels can often be interpreted in either direction.[8] Arguments built on linguistic evidence and the development of Israel's religion both rely on the assumption that Israel's language and theology developed in a linear chronological fashion, but distinctions between texts can also be explained sociologically, geographically or even stylistically. Discussions of the inconclusive nature of the evidence for Job's date are, therefore, standard fare in commentaries. As Clines writes, 'Of [Job's] author or date of composition I frankly know nothing, and my speculations are not likely to be worth more than the many guesses that already exist.'[9] Throughout history, suggestions have ranged from the Mosaic age to the Maccabean period,[10] but, in recent scholarship, the book's date is generally placed between the sixth and fourth centuries BCE based primarily on its language, mention of a Satan

---

[8] For example, drawing on apparent allusions between the two texts, Robert Gordis argues Job came after Isaiah 40–55, while Marvin Pope thinks Job is more likely earlier (Marvin H. Pope, *Job*, AB 15, 3rd ed. [Garden City, 1973], xxxix–xl; Robert Gordis, *The Book of God and Man: A Study of Job* [Chicago, 1978], 216).

[9] David J. A. Clines, *Job*, 3 vols., WBC 17–18B (Nashville, 1989), 1:xxix.

[10] Brevard Childs, *Introduction to the Old Testament as Scripture* (Philadelphia, 1979), 530.

figure and challenge of a developed view of retribution,[11] though the occasional argument for a seventh-century date also appears.[12] Within this larger uncertainty about the date at which the book reached its final form are disputes over which sections of the book (prologue, dialogue, ch. 28, Elihu speeches, divine speeches, epilogue) are secondary and the relative dating of each.[13]

WHAT IS THE BOOK OF JOB?

As this brief overview makes clear, Job is a remarkably open text, which leaves ample room for interpretive conjecture and debate. The book's meaning is so underdetermined, even down to the crucial word *niḥamtî* in 42:6, that it is difficult not to see this as the result of authorial intent.[14] This openness inspires the search for a genre classification that might solve the book's mysteries and yet, simultaneously, invites it to be placed in a wide range of genre groupings.

Job as Wisdom Literature

As the essentialist approach to genre has been applied for more than a century in biblical scholarship, the defining genre for Job (as for Proverbs and Ecclesiastes) has been considered Wisdom Literature. John Barton, for example, uses the development of the Wisdom Literature genre as an example of the way 'modern critical study has made it possible to read with understanding texts which previously had to a greater or lesser extent been misread, because they were seen *as something they were not*'.[15] Barton points to a combination of formal characteristics, such as parallel proverbs in metrical form and shared subject matter, primarily related to human social life, as distinguishing Wisdom Literature as a genre. Job does indeed include a small number of proverbs (e.g., 18:5; cf. Prov 13:9) among other similarities in form with Proverbs and

---

[11] E.g., Georg Fohrer, *Das Buch Hiob*, KAT 16 (Gütersloh, 1963), 42; Gordis, *Book of God and Man*, 216; Katharine J. Dell, *The Book of Job as Sceptical Literature*, BZAW 197 (Berlin, 1991), 162; John Gray, *The Book of Job*, The Text of the Hebrew Bible 1 (Sheffield, 2010), 35.

[12] E.g., Pope, *Job*, xl; John E. Hartley, *The Book of Job*, NICOT (Grand Rapids, 1988), 20.

[13] See Choon-Leong Seow, *Job 1–21: Interpretation and Commentary*, Illuminations (Grand Rapids, 2013), 26–39.

[14] William Morrow, 'Consolation, Rejection, and Repentance in Job 42:6', *JBL* 105 (1986): 223, 225.

[15] John Barton, *Reading the Old Testament: Method in Biblical Study*, rev. and enl. ed. (Louisville, 1996), 16–17, emphasis added.

Ecclesiastes, though its thematic connections with them are stronger.[16]
Most notably, the three books share a distinctive emphasis on wisdom,
using the Hebrew word for 'wisdom' (ḥokmâ) more often than any other
texts in the Hebrew Bible (with the exception of 1 Kings 1–11, in which
the word appears at a slightly higher rate than in Job). Their reflections
on wisdom are tied into universal questions of humanistic relevance,
while explicit references to Israel's law, history, covenant or cult are
vanishingly rare. In Ecclesiastes and the dialogue section of Job, even
the divine name of Israel's God, YHWH, is studiously avoided (with the
exception of Job 12:9), and more general terminology, such as Elohim
('God') or Shadday ('Almighty'), is preferred. Further, grouping Job with
the Wisdom Literature has highlighted tensions between it and other
books in regard to wisdom, such as the challenge Job, like Ecclesiastes,
poses to the general confidence Proverbs displays in the blessings of
wise living.

The primary appeal of an essentialist approach to genre in biblical
studies is the way it facilitates extraction of historical information from
a text's literary form. Identifying a text's genre (which is used inter-
changeably with its form)[17] is a means to discern its Sitz im Leben, a
conception of its original 'setting in life'. For Wisdom Literature, this
involves a distinct class of 'wise men', who composed the texts and used
them for instruction. Job, therefore, is considered a product of a purported 'crisis of wisdom', as these sages reflected on the failure of
wisdom to guarantee success.[18] Job's three friends represent the older
traditional wisdom, with its confidence in the doctrine of retribution
that consistently rewards the righteous and punishes the wicked, while
Job raises questions for this doctrine's reliability in both his speeches
and his experience.

Problems with Wisdom Literature

The affinities between the three so-called Wisdom books cannot be
denied. The gains it has provided for understanding Job are also worth
acknowledging. However, genre designations ('Gattungszuweisungen')
are also reading instructions ('Leseanweisungen') that restrict a reader's

---

[16]   See Dell, Book of Job, 63–83.
[17]   Stuart Weeks, 'The Limits of Form Criticism in the Study of Literature, with
       Reflections on Psalm 34', in Biblical Interpretation and Method: Essays in Honour
       of John Barton, ed. Katharine J. Dell and Paul M. Joyce (Oxford, 2013), 17, 19.
[18]   Dell, Book of Job, 168.

interpretive horizon.[19] The texts that various genre designations draw into comparison with Job depict its essence and cultural profile differently; a drama reads differently than a philosophical dialogue, a lament differently than a sapiential disputation. Therefore, Markus Witte argues, interpreters must take into account, not merely questions of Sitz im Leben ('setting in life') and Sitz im Buch ('setting in the book') when evaluating Job's genre, but Sitz in der Welt des Lesers ('setting in the world of the reader') as well.[20] In this regard, classifying Job as Wisdom Literature is not without its problems, in terms of both the category itself and its application to Job.

Job is not grouped in a separate collection with Proverbs and Ecclesiastes as Wisdom Literature until the mid-nineteenth century. Johann Friedrich Bruch is the first to draw together earlier suggestions along these lines in preceding decades into a comprehensive and systematic presentation of a distinct group of texts affiliated with 'the wise' in Israel and to describe the distinct ideas which characterise these texts and the tradition behind them.[21] The date of this 'discovery' would not in itself be problematic (many of the axiomatic principles of biblical scholarship were developed during this time) if it were not for the suspicious correspondence between Bruch's characterisation of 'the wise' and their literature and the philosophical ideas prominent at his time. He speaks, for example, of the 'non-theocratic spirit' of the wise, which 'found no satisfaction in the religious institutions of their nation' and thus sought 'the way of free thinking' to answer life's questions.[22] Though Bruch was eventually all but forgotten in biblical scholarship, his work's widespread influence in the latter nineteenth century created a trajectory for the interpretation of the concept of wisdom in the Hebrew Bible and the three texts primarily associated with it that, over time, has acted both as a 'mirror' reflecting the 'image of the scholar painting her portrait'[23] and an echo chamber, magnifying the type of post-Enlightenment concerns, such as humanism, individualism, universalism, secularism and

---

[19] Markus Witte, 'Die literarische Gattung des Buches Hiob: Robert Lowth und seine Erben', in Sacred Conjectures: The Context and Legacy of Robert Lowth and Jean Astruc, ed. John Jarick, LHBOTS 457 (London, 2007), 123, emphasis original.

[20] Witte, 'Gattung des Buches Hiob', 122.

[21] Johann Friedrich Bruch, Weisheits-Lehre der Hebräer: Ein Beitrag zur Geschichte der Philosophie (Strasbourg, 1851). For the origins of the 'Wisdom Literature' category, see Kynes, Obituary for 'Wisdom Literature', 82–104.

[22] Bruch, Weisheits-Lehre, ix–x.

[23] James L. Crenshaw, 'Popular Questioning of the Justice of God in Ancient Israel', ZAW 82 (1970): 395.

empiricism, that led Bruch initially to associate them, while muffling their connections with the rest of the Hebrew Bible.[24] Thus, the 'most striking characteristic' uniting the Wisdom Literature still remains 'the absence of what one normally considers as typically Israelite and Jewish', notably reference to Israelite history and covenant.[25]

Problems Wisdom Literature Creates for Reading Job
Though comparing Job to Proverbs and Ecclesiastes within the genre category Wisdom Literature has illuminated various features of the book, exclusively classifying Job this way has also distorted its interpretation. Providing the answer 'Wisdom Literature' to the question of what the book of Job is necessarily affects how the book is read. The horizon of expectation the genre provides also limits a reader's field of vision. First, focusing attention on similarities between Job and other Wisdom Literature has led recent interpreters to overlook its connections with other texts across the canon. For example, before links between Proverbs and Amenemope popularised the Wisdom category in the 1920s, Job's airing of the doctrine of retribution drew it into scholarly conversation with texts across the Hebrew Bible that emphasised that doctrine, rather than primarily Proverbs' act-consequence relationship. While discussing Job, nineteenth-century scholar W. T. Davison associates the doctrine with the Deuteronomic covenant, which became 'the traditional teaching of law-givers, wise men, and prophets', and Edouard Dhorme claims that retribution is 'everywhere characteristic of Israelite theology'.[26] However, as Wisdom Literature became established as a category, Proverbs became Job's main dialogue partner and the book's links with retribution across the canon were limited. Clines, for example, acknowledges Deuteronomy as the pre-eminent exponent of retribution but takes Job's questioning of the doctrine as a confrontation of 'the ideology of Proverbs'.[27]

---

[24] For these traits as continuing to distinguish Wisdom Literature, see Douglas B. Miller, 'Wisdom in the Canon: Discerning the Early Intuition', in *Was There a Wisdom Tradition? New Prospects in Israelite Wisdom Studies*, ed. Mark Sneed, AIL 23 (Atlanta, 2015), 91–93.

[25] Roland E. Murphy, *The Tree of Life: An Exploration of Biblical Wisdom Literature*, 3rd ed. (Grand Rapids, 2002), 1.

[26] W. T. Davison, *The Wisdom-Literature of the Old Testament* (London, 1894), 79; Edouard Dhorme, *A Commentary on the Book of Job*, trans. Harold Knight (London, 1967 [1926]), cxxxvii, cxxxix. See also Samuel Davidson, *An Introduction to the Old Testament: Critical, Historical, Theological*, 2 vols. (London, 1862), 2: 217.

[27] Clines, *Job*, 1:lxi–lxii.

Second, this canonical separation has contributed to theological abstraction, which is required to justify a category that can include Job with the other so-called Wisdom books with which it differs substantially. Alistair Hunter provides a straightforward example of how this process works. Though he acknowledges that his efforts to identify the Wisdom Literature on formal linguistic grounds have left Job as a 'glaring omission', he attempts to satisfy the 'effective unanimity among scholars that it belongs in this category' by considering 'the underlying perspectives which emerge from a consideration in broader terms of what these books are concerned with'.[28] These, he claims, are the books' common universalism, humanism, naturalism and intellectualism. This list fairly well summarises the post-Enlightenment approach to reality in which Job was first associated with Wisdom Literature and, when applied to the book, directs attention to an abstract philosophical plane. Thus, according to Claus Westermann, Job's classification as Wisdom 'has clearly exerted a pervasive, perhaps even controlling, influence upon nineteenth- and twentieth-century exegesis', such that Job has been increasingly read as the philosophical treatment of a 'problem'.[29] Reading the book as a philosophical reflection on a question, such as 'How is the suffering of a just man to be reconciled with the existence of a just God?'[30] obscures its contribution to existential questions, such as 'Why must I suffer?' as Westermann argues, or even, 'How should one speak of God in the face of chaos?'[31]

Third, theological abstraction combined with canonical separation has led to hermeneutical limitation in the book's interpretation. As Wisdom Literature, the book's interpretation has been 'hedged in' and 'unduly restricted'.[32] David Wolfers complains of the way the 'relatively modern imposition' of the Wisdom classification 'imposes an estoppal on particular lines of thought'.[33] This 'arbitrary' classification, which relies on 'perfectly circular' reasoning and reflects only 'our own

[28] Alastair Hunter, *Wisdom Literature* (London, 2006), 23.
[29] Claus Westermann, *The Structure of the Book of Job: A Form-Critical Analysis* of *1956*, trans. Charles A. Muenchow (Philadelphia, 1981 [1956]), 1–2.
[30] As Westermann cites Ernst Sellin and Leonard Rost (Westermann, *Structure of the Book of Job*, 1).
[31] Paraphrasing Seow, who also questions 'Wisdom Literature' as the book's genre classification (*Job 1–21*, 108, 61).
[32] Quotations from Timothy Jay Johnson, *Now My Eye Sees You: Unveiling an Apocalyptic Job*, HBM 24 (Sheffield, 2009), 77; and James Edward Harding, 'The Book of Job as Metaprophecy', *SR* 39 (2010): 525, respectively.
[33] David Wolfers, *Deep Things out of Darkness: The Book of Job, Essays and a New Translation* (Kampen, 1995), 48–49. See also Dell, *Book of Job*, 64–83.

decisions as to which works to place into which categories', is, he argues, 'invalid for imposing restrictions on content or form'. Job, he claims, bursts the bounds of the category in content and form, including 'too much beside' to be assigned to Wisdom Literature. Representing a 'whole new intellectual universe' in its content, it borrows broadly from Hebrew literary tradition, combining 'wisdom, prophecy, psalm, drama, contest, lament, theodicy, history, and allegory'.[34] The Wisdom classification obscures the contribution of the book's 'bewildering diversity of literary genres' to its meaning.[35]

Other Genres for Job

Bewildered by this diversity, many conclude that the book is best categorised as sui generis, in a class of its own.[36] Already in the eighteenth century, Robert Lowth argued that the book's 'single and unparalleled' status in the canon indicated that it had 'little connexion with the other writings of the Hebrews, and no relation whatever to the affairs of the Israelites'.[37] Harold Rowley similarly claims, 'It is wiser to recognise the uniqueness of this book and to consider it without relation to any of these literary categories.'[38] However, though the sui generis classification is right to recognise that we cannot cram the complexity of Job into a single genre, it offers no guidance for interpretation, leaving the book 'unreadable'.[39] In fact, if Job is sui generis, this results not from the book's isolation from other texts but its connections with so many of them, and, therefore, its uniqueness is better recognised in its relations with so many other genres rather than its exclusion from them all. As James Crenshaw says, 'Like all great literary works, this one rewards readers who come to it from vastly different starting points.'[40] Therefore, Brevard Childs is on the right track when he argues that the book's 'proper interpretation depends on seeing Job in the perspective, not only of wisdom traditions, but also of Israel's liturgy and historical traditions', though, we need not stop there.[41] Drawing

---

[34] Wolfers, *Job*, 50–51.

[35] Samuel L. Terrien, *The Elusive Presence: Toward a New Biblical Theology*, Religious Perspectives 26 (San Francisco, 1978), 361.

[36] E.g., Pope, *Job*, xxx; Seow, *Job 1–21*, 61.

[37] Robert Lowth, *Lectures on the Sacred Poetry of the Hebrews*, trans. G. Gregory (Boston, 1829 [1753]), 264.

[38] Harold Henry Rowley, *Job*, NCB, rev. ed. (Grand Rapids, 1976), 5.

[39] Tremper Longman III, *Job*, BCOTWP (Grand Rapids, 2012), 30.

[40] James L. Crenshaw, *Old Testament Wisdom: An Introduction*, 3rd ed. (Louisville, 2010), 115.

[41] Childs, *Introduction to the Old Testament*, 544.

together the 'vastly different starting points' readers have brought to Job throughout its history of interpretation will illuminate various features of the book without forcing it to conform to the standards of a particular culturally contingent perspective of what wisdom should be.

Sifrei Emet, Lament and Exemplary-Sufferer Texts

Early Jewish and Christian interpretation offers evidence of several different conceptions of what Job is. It may be the most variably placed book in both Jewish and Christian canon lists, ranging from the beginning of the histories (e.g., Bryennios Manuscript) to the end of the prophets (Josephus, Rufinus). In Jewish lists, Job generally appears in the larger Writings collection, which is unified only by the idiosyncrasy of its contents, which do not fit into the Law or Prophets or form a clearly identifiable category on their own. Job's inclusion therefore highlights its distinctiveness within the canon. However, within the Writings, Job is grouped in a subcollection with Psalms and Proverbs known as the *Sifrei Emet*. Though the logic behind this grouping is unclear, it does underscore how Job in many ways stands between Psalms and Proverbs (as the book does in the lists in b. Baba Batra 14b and the Leningrad and Aleppo codices) and how it, like the other two books, emphasises the contrast between the righteous and the wicked, referring to both at a disproportionately high rate compared to the rest of the canon.[42]

By encouraging Job to be read with the Psalms, the *Sifrei Emet* collection reflects the close connections interpreters have long noticed between the two books.[43] In addition to a range of significant allusions to the Psalms in Job (e.g., Ps 8:5; ET 4 in Job 7:17; Ps 107:40 in Job 12:21, 24), interpreters have noted that Job appears to 'dramatize' the lament genre so prominent in the Psalter.[44] Even those who are wary of using these similarities to determine the book's genre acknowledge that recognising this connection is 'helpful' for highlighting the complaint motifs in Job and the 'numerous formal, thematic, and lexical affinities between parts of the book of Job and the laments of the Psalter and

---

[42] Claus Westermann, *Roots of Wisdom: The Oldest Proverbs of Israel and Other Peoples*, trans. J. Daryl Charles (Louisville, 1995 [1990]), 81; Kynes, *Obituary for 'Wisdom Literature'*, 223.

[43] See Will Kynes, *My Psalm Has Turned into Weeping: Job's Dialogue with the Psalms*, BZAW 437 (Berlin, 2012).

[44] Aage Bentzen, *Introduction to the Old Testament*, 2 vols. (Copenhagen, 1948–1949 [1941]), 1:182; Westermann, *Structure of the Book of Job*, 8.

Lamentations'.[45] Thus, this intertextual comparison provides new exegetical insight into the book, such as the way the lament is 'subverted'
to make God, not the deliverer from enemies but the enemy himself
(e.g., 13:24; 16:9; 19:11).[46] It also invites Job to be read in other groups of
texts that share similar traits, such as the lament psalms and
Ecclesiastes, which are characterised by *Unglück* or 'misfortune',[47] or
Lamentations, the Confessions of Jeremiah and Psalms 73 and 88,
which all wrestle with the failure of divine justice.[48]

This type of comparison need not be limited to the biblical canon.
The dramatised lament interpretation was inspired by affinities
between Job and a Babylonian text, Ludlul Bēl Nēmeqi ('I Will Praise
the Lord of Wisdom'), in which a man similarly laments to his god about
his suffering. With Job, Ludlul fits into a broader group of ancient Near
Eastern texts in which individuals wrestle with unexplained suffering
(e.g., Ludlul, II.33–38), which includes the Babylonian Theodicy, and
two texts, one Babylonian and one Sumerian, both labelled Man and His
God (the latter sometimes referred to as 'the Sumerian Job').[49] All of
these 'exemplary-sufferer texts'[50] share more features with biblical
laments or perhaps, in Ludlul's case, hymns of thanksgiving,[51] than
with Proverbs and Ecclesiastes and therefore discourage the exclusive
classification of Job with those so-called Wisdom books.

*Poetry, Drama and Controversy Dialogue (*Streitgespräch*)*
In the Greek canon lists adopted by the Christian tradition, Job is
predominantly associated with the Poetry collection, which directs
attention to its poetic form. As Robert Lowth concluded, 'It is of little
consequence whether it be esteemed a didactic or an ethic, a pathetic or

---

45 Quotations from Roland E. Murphy, *Wisdom Literature: Job, Proverbs, Ruth,
    Canticles, Ecclesiastes, and Esther*, FOTL 13 (Grand Rapids: 1981), 17; and Seow,
    Job 1–21, 57, respectively.
46 Seow, *Job 1–21*, 58.
47 W. M. L. de Wette, 'Beytrag zur Charakteristik des Hebraismus', in *Studien*, ed. Carl
    Daub and Friedrich Creuzer (Heidelberg, 1807).
48 James L. Crenshaw, *Reading Job: A Literary and Theological Commentary* (Macon,
    2011), 22–23.
49 See R. G. Albertson, 'Job and Ancient Near Eastern Wisdom Literature', in *Scripture in
    Context II: More Essays on the Comparative Method*, ed. William W. Hallo, James
    C. Moyer and Leo G. Perdue (Winona Lake, 1983); Moshe Weinfeld, 'Job and Its
    Mesopotamian Parallels: A Typological Analysis', in *Text and Context: Old
    Testament and Semitic Studies for F. C. Fensham*, ed. W. Claasen, JSOTSup 48
    (Sheffield, 1988).
50 See Seow, *Job 1–21*, 51.
51 Weinfeld, 'Job and Its Mesopotamian Parallels', 217.

dramatic poem; only let it be assigned a distinct and conspicuous station in the highest rank of the Hebrew poetry.'[52]

In addition to supporting the connections with the Psalms discussed above, the Poetry collection also invited comparisons with Song of Songs, which, like Job, was at times interpreted as a drama.[53] This view apparently dates back to Theodore of Mopsuestia (d. 428 CE), since the Fifth General Council (553) condemned his view that Job was composed in imitation of Greek tragedy. Nevertheless, it found a number of prominent supporters in the sixteenth century, such as Johannes Brenz, Johannes Oecolampadius and Theodore Beza, and was widespread from the seventeenth into the nineteenth century.[54] Recently, the book's association with drama has been resurrected,[55] with interpreters noting similarities with both tragedy[56] and comedy.[57] Whether or not the book's limited character development and action merit a dramatic classification, comparison with other dramatic texts serves heuristically to draw the audience into the impassioned 'intellectual action' of the book[58] and accounts well for its dialogic character.[59]

The strongest dramatic element of Job is its use of dialogue, a feature it shares with several other ancient Near Eastern texts, which consist of a debate between two friends on a single specific issue. Some of the texts in this *Streitgespräch* or 'controversy dialogue' form, such as the Babylonian Theodicy, the Akkadian Dialogue of Pessimism and an Egyptian text known as 'A Man and His Ba' or 'The Man Who Grew Tired of Life', engage similar questions as Job.[60] Though this genre comparison fails to encapsulate the book, these texts do offer an apt

[52] Lowth, *Sacred Poetry*, 281.

[53] E.g., Lowth, *Sacred Poetry*, 249; Franz Delitzsch, *Das Buch Iob* (Leipzig, 1864), 11–13.

[54] Seow, *Job 1–21*, 48.

[55] Pauline Shelton, 'Making a Drama out of a Crisis? A Consideration of the Book of Job as a Drama', *JSOT* 83 (1999): 69–82; Françoise Mies, 'Le genre littéraire du livre de Job', *RB* 110 (2003): 336–369.

[56] E.g., George Steiner, 'Tragedy: Remorse and Justice', *The Listener* 18 (1979): 508; Katharine J. Dell, 'Job: Sceptics, Philosophers and Tragedians', in *Das Buch Hiob und seine Interpretationen: Beiträge zum Hiob-Symposium auf dem Monte Verità vom 14.–19. August 2005*, ed. T. Krüger et al., ATANT 88 (Zurich, 2007), 18.

[57] J. William Whedbee, 'The Comedy of Job', *Semeia* 7 (1977): 1–39; Abigail Pelham, 'Job as Comedy, Revisited', *JSOT* 35 (2010): 89–112.

[58] Luis Alonso Schökel, 'Toward a Dramatic Reading of the Book of Job', *Semeia* 7 (1977): 45–61.

[59] Seow, *Job 1–21*, 48.

[60] See Karel van der Toorn, 'The Ancient Near Eastern Literary Dialogue as a Vehicle of Critical Reflection', in *Dispute Poems and Dialogues in the Ancient and Mediaeval Near East: Forms and Types of Literary Debates in Semitic and Related Literatures*, ed. G. J. Reinink and H. L. J. Vanstiphout, OLA 42 (Leuven, 1991), 59–75.

parallel for the form of a major section of Job and its impassioned struggle with issues of justice.

History, Epic, Didactic Narrative and Torah

Though the Poetry and *Sifrei Emet* collections primarily illuminate features of the poetic section of the book, in some ancient canon lists Job appears with the histories, which draws attention to the narrative features of its prose frame. Many Christian Peshitta manuscripts and the four canon lists recorded by Epiphanius place Job directly after either the Pentateuch or Judges, potentially following an addition to the book in Greek (Job 42:17 LXX), which identifies Job and his friends with figures in the genealogy of Esau's descendants (Genesis 36).[61] Origen, on the other hand, puts Job with Esther in a historical subgroup at the end of his canon list, and two of the three canon lists recorded in *Codex Amiatinus* and Cassiodorus' *Institutiones*, Augustine's and 'the Septuagint' also include Job on the later end of the histories. In fact, Job was widely considered historical in the West into the medieval period,[62] and even in the eighteenth century, a definition of 'sapiential' from Chambers' *Cyclopedia* acknowledges 'Historical Books' as a potential classification for Job.[63] However, Job does not have to be considered historical to be connected with Israel's history. Wolfers proposes that the book be read as a politico-historical allegory of the nation's trials similar to Jonah, Esther and Dryden's *Absalom and Achitophel*, which attempts to justify God's involvement in the eighth-century Assyrian invasions.[64] Others consider it a potential allegorical reflection on the exile.[65]

Nahum Sarna sees in the prose tale an 'epic substratum' with close parallels in Ugaritic epics.[66] The epic interpretation of Job, which may go back to Jerome's (mistaken) characterisation of the book's poetry as dactylic hexameter commonly employed by Greek epics, was prominent in Christian interpretation from Gregory the Great, Isidore of

---

[61] Roger T. Beckwith, *The Old Testament Canon of the New Testament Church and Its Background in Early Judaism* (Grand Rapids, 1986), 189–190.

[62] Beckwith, *Old Testament Canon*, 224, n.13.

[63] Ephraim Chambers, 'Sapiential', in vol. 2 of *Cyclopædia: Or, an Universal Dictionary of Arts and Sciences* (London, 1728).

[64] Wolfers, *Job*, 67–70.

[65] E.g., E. E. Kellett, '"Job": An Allegory?', *ExpTim* 51 (1940): 250–251; Konrad Schmid, 'Innerbiblische Schriftdiskussion im Hiobbuch', in *Das Buch Hiob und seine Interpretationen: Beiträge zum Hiob-Symposium auf dem Monte Verità vom 14.–19. August 2005*, ed. Thomas Krüger et al., ATANT 88 (Zurich, 2007), 250.

[66] Nahum M. Sarna, 'Epic Substratum in the Prose of Job', *JBL* 76 (1957): 13–25.

Seville, Bede and Rabanus Maurus to no less than Milton himself.[67] However, in this reading, which understood Job as a heroic paragon of virtue in the face of crushing adversity, the book was compared, not to Ugaritic parallels but Homer's epics or, more often, Boethius' *Consolation of Philosophy*, which similarly wrestles with theodicy, while depicting, not military exploits or adventures but an 'epic of inner life' full of 'struggles and adventures unknown to sense but real to faith'.[68]

Others associate the prose tale with other 'didactic narratives', such as the Joseph story, Esther, Daniel, Aḥiqar and Tobit, which attempt to inculcate virtue by depicting a virtuous individual earning a reward for conquering a test of his character and any who oppose him.[69] However, following the rabbinic suggestion in b. Baba Batra 16b that Job is a *mashal*, others argue that the prose narrative evokes a 'prophetic example story', such as Nathan's parable in 2 Sam 12:1–14,[70] or a 'philosophic fable' like Jonah.[71] The latter suggestion introduces further extra-biblical parallels with philosophical novels such as *Zadig*, *Candide* or *Robinson Crusoe*.[72] All these proposals focus interpretive attention on how the book conveys its message through story.

Beyond associating Job with Israel's history, the book's connections with patriarchal figures in Genesis 36 made explicit by the addition in the Greek version, combined with the rabbinic traditions that Job was a contemporary of Moses and that Moses wrote the book (b. B. Bat. 15a–16b) encourage interpreters to explore parallels between Job and the Torah. Indeed, some canon lists place Job immediately after the Torah. Further, at Qumran, a Job manuscript (4QpaleoJob^c = 4Q101) employs a paleo-Hebrew script only otherwise used for the Pentateuch and Joshua, and Targumim were only found for Job and one of the books of the Torah, Leviticus.[73] Despite the 'paradigmatic assumptions' about

---

[67] Ann W. Astell, *Job, Boethius, and Epic Truth* (Ithaca, 1994), 1–20.

[68] John F. Genung, *The Epic of the Inner Life Being the Book of Job* (Boston, 1891), 23.

[69] Donald E. Gowan, 'Reading Job as a "Wisdom Script"', *JSOT* 17 (1992): 85–95; Hans-Peter Müller, 'Die Hiobrahmenerzählung und ihre altorientalischen Parallelen als Paradigmen einer weisheitlichen Wirklichkeitswahrnahme', in *The Book of Job*, ed. W. A. M. Beuken, BETL 114 (Leuven, 1994), 21–39; Seow, *Job 1–21*, 50.

[70] Carol A. Newsom, *The Book of Job: A Contest of Moral Imaginations* (Oxford, 2003), 41.

[71] Alter, *The Art of Biblical Narrative*, 33.

[72] Mies, 'Le genre littéraire', 339.

[73] Emanuel Tov, 'The Biblical Texts from the Judean Desert: An Overview and Analysis', in *Hebrew Bible, Greek Bible and Qumran: Collected Essays*, ed. Emanuel Tov, Texts and Studies in Ancient Judaism 121 (Tübingen, 2008), 142.

the separation of Wisdom Literature from history and Torah which have discouraged study on this question, Witte argues the rabbinic association of Job with the Torah, followed by several church fathers, is reinforced by the 'almost self-evident' literary and theological relationship between Job and Deuteronomy.[74] Not only does the book wrestle with the Deuteronomic understanding of retribution, Witte argues it alludes to Deuteronomy itself. The influence of the Torah on Job also includes the 'conscious adaptation' of Genesis 1–3 in the prologue,[75] Job's self-curse in ch. 3 as a 'counter-cosmic incantation' reversing Gen 1:1–2:4a[76] and aspects of Exodus,[77] the divine speeches (Job 38–41) as a rival description of the creation in Genesis[78] and connections with the broader Priestly tradition in all of the book's major sections.[79] Torah is itself a rather ungainly genre designation, but to the degree that it describes a common constellation of traits related to creation, covenant, patriarchal history and priestly order, the Joban star is not as distant in the canonical sky as readers commonly assume.

Prophecy, Lawsuit and Apocalyptic

Early interpreters similarly highlight connections between Job and the Prophets, with Job grouped together with them in Ben Sira's Praise of the Fathers (49:8–10), James' praise of their shared 'endurance' (Jas 5:10–11), Josephus' canon list (*Contra Apionis* I, 8) and the rabbinic debate over Job's prophetic status (b. Baba Batra 15b–16a). This underscores common traits extending from the heavenly council in the book's prologue to the divine speeches at its end.[80] Thus, in light of the stylistic and theological influence of prophecy on the book, 'the continuity

---

[74] Markus Witte, 'Job in Conversation with the Torah', in *Wisdom and Torah: The Reception of 'Torah' in the Wisdom Literature of the Second Temple Period*, ed. Bernd Schipper and D. Andrew Teeter, JSJSup 163 (Leiden, 2013), 82–83.

[75] Sam Meier, 'Job I–II: A Reflection of Genesis I–III', *VT* 39 (1989): 183.

[76] Michael Fishbane, 'Jeremiah IV 23–26 and Job III 3–13: A Recovered Use of the Creation Pattern', *VT* 21 (1971): 153.

[77] John Walton Burnight, 'The "Reversal" of *Heilsgeschichte* in Job 3', in *Reading Job Intertextually*, ed. Katharine Dell and Will Kynes, LHBOTS 574 (New York: 2013), 30–41.

[78] Fred Gottlieb, 'The Creation Theme in Genesis 1, Psalm 104 and Job 38–42', *JBQ* 44 (2016): 26–39.

[79] Schmid, 'Schriftdiskussion', 244–248; Samuel E. Balentine, 'Job and the Priests: "He Leads Priests Away Stripped" (Job 12:19)', in *Reading Job Intertextually*, ed. Katharine Dell and Will Kynes, LHBOTS 574 (New York: 2013), 42–53.

[80] Hans Bardtke, 'Profetische Zuge im Buche Hiob', in *Das Ferne und Nahe Wort: Festschrift Leonhard Rost*, ed. Fritz Maass, BZAW 105 (Berlin, 1967), 1–10; J. Gerald Janzen, *Job* (Atlanta, 1985), 217–225.

between Job and prophecy cannot be denied'.[81] Susannah Ticciati, for example, notices several indications of the book's 'indebtedness' to the prophets, including Job's legal dispute (rîb) with God, his desire for a prophetic *môkîaḥ* to intercede between God and humanity (9:33) and the foundational role of the Deuteronomic Covenant in his arguments.[82] James Harding, however, argues that, like Jonah, Job is a 'metaprophecy', which 'draws on themes and ideas present in the prophetical books, in order to wrestle with the assumptions underlying them', such as the 'nexus between divine revelation and theodicy' that grounds the prophetic confidence in entering the divine council and hearing the word of God.[83] Others have joined in drawing prophetic parallels into their interpretation of Job, such as those with Isaiah 40–55, Jeremiah, Ezekiel, Joel, Amos and Habakkuk.[84]

The prophetic *rîb* takes the form of a lawsuit. The lawsuit form plays such a prominent role in Job that some have used it to categorise the entire book. Legal features are evident in vocabulary, metaphors and the judicial complaint in Job 31; legal language appears in 444 verses, outweighing the 346 that deal with wisdom.[85] As with lament, some argue the book dramatises this genre to create a 'lawsuit drama'[86] or 'trial narrative'.[87] Though the 'mere occurrence' of the legal genre, like the lament genre, is insufficient to determine the book's genre as a whole, it similarly has interpretive value in directing attention to the legal features in the book, which 'make the reader aware of the strong claims made by Job'.[88] Grouping Job with lawsuits and laments (like other genres) illuminates certain features of the texts and

---

[81] James L. Crenshaw, *Prophetic Conflict: Its Effect upon Israelite Religion*, BZAW 124 (Berlin, 1971), 108; cf. Crenshaw, 'Popular Questioning', 389.

[82] Susannah Ticciati, *Job and the Disruption of Identity: Reading beyond Barth* (London, 2005), 58–59, 120–137, 156–157.

[83] Harding, 'Metaprophecy', 528. See also Schmid, 'Schriftdiskussion', 253–258.

[84] See the chapters on Isaiah (Kynes), Jeremiah (Dell), Ezekiel (Joyce), Joel (Nogalski) and Amos (Marlow) in Katharine Dell and Will Kynes, eds. *Reading Job Intertextually*, LHBOTS 574 (New York, 2013). For Habakkuk, see Donald E. Gowan, 'God's Answer to Job: How Is It an Answer?' *HBT* 8 (1986): 85–102.

[85] Heinz Richter, *Studien zu Hiob: Der Aufbau des Hiobbuches, dargestellt an den Gattungen des Rechtslebens*, Theologische Arbeiten 11 (Berlin: 1959), 13, 16.

[86] S. H. Scholnick, 'Lawsuit Drama in the Book of Job' (PhD diss., Brandeis University, 1975); cf. Richter, *Studien zu Hiob*, 131–132.

[87] F. Rachel Magdalene, *On the Scales of Righteousness: Neo-Babylonian Trial Law and the Book of Job*, BJS 348 (Providence, 2007), 263, 50.

[88] Murphy, *Wisdom Literature*, 17.

obscures others, just as reading it with other texts concerned with wisdom does.[89]

Finally, Timothy Johnson has proposed that Job be read according to another genre associated with prophecy: apocalyptic. He argues that the book 'is marked by such core apocalyptic features as revelation, plot, heavenly conflict, perseverance in the midst of persecution, and other-worldly mediator and reward due to faithfulness'.[90] Johnson argues that Job is 'an early, undeveloped form of apocalypse', which lacks some features, such as belief in immortality, in later apocalyptic texts.[91] Even without agreeing with all of Johnson's conclusions, his apocalyptic comparison still offers a valuable new perspective on Job's perseverance and the role of revelation in the book, which illuminates the promin-ence of these themes in the later *Testament of Job*.

Parody, Citation and Polyphony

Finally, several genre groupings focus on a prominent meta-generic literary technique that explains the book's incorporation of so many features of other genres. First, Katharine Dell claims that the consistent intentional 'misuse' and parody of these smaller genres or 'forms' throughout Job indicates that the book as a whole is a parody and therefore 'sceptical literature'.[92] Exchanging form criticism for inter-textuality, another approach focuses on the book's allusion to and critical reflection on so many texts from across the Hebrew Bible.[93] Due to the prevalence of this technique, Job could be considered a 'citational text', in which the author expects readers to recognise his widespread use of allusion as relevant to the work's interpretation.[94] Second Isaiah[95] and Revelation[96] would be other biblical examples of this technique, while the poetry of T. S. Eliot and the novels of James Joyce are modern parallels. Third, Carol Newsom combines redaction

---

[89] See Dell, *Book of Job*, 89–93.

[90] Johnson, *Job*, 11.

[91] Johnson, *Job*, 71.

[92] Dell, *Book of Job*.

[93] E.g., Melanie Köhlmoos, *Das Auge Gottes: Textstrategie im Hiobbuch*, FAT 25 (Tübingen, 1999); Schmid, 'Schriftdiskussion'; Dell and Kynes, *Reading Job Intertextually*.

[94] Kynes, *Obituary for 'Wisdom Literature'*, 174.

[95] See Patricia Tull Willey, *Remember the Former Things: The Recollection of Previous Texts in Second Isaiah*, SBLDS 161 (Atlanta, 1997); Benjamin D. Sommer, *A Prophet Reads Scripture: Allusion in Isaiah 40–66* (Stanford, 1998).

[96] See Steve Moyise, *The Old Testament in the Book of Revelation*, JSNTSup 115 (Sheffield, 1995).

criticism and Bakhtinian dialogism to argue that the author intentionally creates a polyphonic dialogue between the various genres incorporated into the book. Each genre provides a different 'perspective on the
world', and they together demonstrate that the idea of piety transcends
'the bounds of a single consciousness' and 'can only be grasped at the
point of intersection of unmerged perspectives'.[97] These meta-generic
proposals recognise Job's connections with texts from a broad range of
other genres, but, unlike the sui generis classification, they draw those
other texts into the interpretation of Job, whether through shared forms,
allusions or genre affinities.

HOW DOES GENRE AFFECT HOW YOU READ JOB?

Each of these meta-generic approaches reinforces what the various
genre groupings in which readers have explicitly or implicitly placed
Job throughout history demonstrate: there is no simple or single answer
to the question, what is the book of Job? As Marvin Pope observes, '[Job]
shares something of the characteristics of all the literary forms that
have been ascribed to it, but it is impossible to classify it exclusively
as didactic, dramatic, epic, or anything else.'[98] Or as Crenshaw puts it,
'No single genre can explain all the facets of the book, and several have
certainly contributed to it.'[99] Properly interpreting the book, therefore,
involves incorporating the insight each comparison between Job and
other texts contributes to its meaning, as each highlights different
significant features of its meaning, from the various themes it addresses
to the range of literary forms through which it presents them.

Like the Wisdom Literature category, each of these intertextual
comparisons was also influenced by culturally contingent presuppositions. Newsom, for example, acknowledges that her interpretation is
motivated by 'the desire to read Job as a book of our own age', in accord
with the inescapable postmodern, multicultural reality of diverse, situated perspectives on meaning.[100] The book's internal dialogue between
genres, she argues, draws in the various reading communities that
encounter it, including her own, as its 'complex and elusive nature
allows interpreters to see mirrored in it perspectives congenial to the

[97] Newsom, Book of Job, 15, 30.
[98] Pope, Job, xxxi.
[99] James L. Crenshaw, 'Wisdom', in Old Testament Form Criticism, ed. J. Hayes (San
Antonio, 1974), 253.
[100] Newsom, Book of Job, 261.

tenor of their own age'.[101] Job's radical hermeneutical openness draws readers into its roiling dialogue over the proper wise response to suffering; what readers believe about God, justice, humanity – even, I would add, hermeneutics – is what they are likely to find it teaching.[102]

However, as long as interpreters acknowledge, like Newsom, the contingent, subjective and partial nature of their proposals, those readings can together provide a fuller and more objective understanding of the book, which multiplies perspectives on its meaning to transcend the limited viewpoint of any one of them.[103] When Wisdom Literature is treated as a taxonomic category that defines what the book of Job is, it prevents this. This is why the category should be discarded, even as the value of a more limited comparison of Job, Proverbs and Ecclesiastes (along with other texts) regarding their shared interest in wisdom as a concept is acknowledged. Job is far more than a Wisdom book. It defies attempts to restrict it to this or any other single genre. And yet the partial insight of each illuminates some shadow cast by the book's craggy inscrutability.

Read in this multi-perspectival way, Job appears as a text which raises important philosophical questions of universal significance, yes, but also one that tackles those questions with the language of worship, living out lament, expressing its message with poetic power, dramatic passion and acrimonious debate, drawing history within itself even as it explodes out of it, teaching through a story of epic conquest over unexplained and unjust suffering, wrestling with divine covenant and law, meeting the deity in the prophetic realm to accuse him for his absence, initiating a trial between humanity and God, persevering with the help of divine revelation, which is cited and parodied, and placing this all in polyphonic dialogue.

Further Reading

Clines, David J. A. *Job*. 3 vols. WBC 17–18B. Nashville: 1989–2011.
    'Why Is There a Book of Job, and What Does It Do to You If You Read It?' Pages 122–144 in *Interested Parties: The Ideology of Writers and Readers of the Hebrew Bible*. JSOTSup 225. Sheffield: 1995.
Dell, Katharine J. *The Book of Job as Sceptical Literature*. BZAW 197. Berlin: 1991.

---

[101] Newsom, *Book of Job*, 3.
[102] Gowan, 'God's Answer', 86.
[103] See Kynes, *Obituary for 'Wisdom Literature'*, 139–141.

Dell, Katharine, and Will Kynes, eds. *Reading Job Intertextually*. LHBOTS 574. New York: 2013.

Harding, James Edward. 'The Book of Job as Metaprophecy'. *SR* 39 (2010): 523–547.

Jones, Scott C. 'Job'. In *The Oxford Handbook of Wisdom and the Bible* 533–550. Edited by Will Kynes. New York: 2021.

Kynes, Will. *My Psalm Has Turned into Weeping: Job's Dialogue with the Psalms*. BZAW 437. Berlin: 2012.

An *Obituary for 'Wisdom Literature': The Birth, Death, and Intertextual Reintegration of a Biblical Corpus*. Oxford: 2019.

Lambert, David A. 'The Book of Job in Ritual Perspective'. *JBL* 134 (2015): 557–575.

Morrow, William. 'Consolation, Rejection, and Repentance in Job 42:6'. *JBL* 105 (1986): 211–225.

Newsom, Carol A. *The Book of Job: A Contest of Moral Imaginations*. Oxford: 2003.

Seow, C. L. *Job 1–21: Interpretation and Commentary*. Illuminations. Grand Rapids: 2013.

Westermann, Claus. *The Structure of the Book of Job: A Form-Critical Analysis*. Translated by Charles A. Muenchow. Philadelphia: 1981. Translation of *Der Aufbau des Buches Hiob*. Tübingen: 1956.

10 Ecclesiastes

METTE BUNDVAD

The book of Ecclesiastes (also known as Qoheleth) meditates on the possibility that human life may be without any real or lasting significance – while also calling its reader urgently to joy. It tolerates contradiction to an almost infuriating degree. Making no attempt to address its God, Ecclesiastes invokes instead a world created in such a way that human beings find it difficult and painful to navigate. It is no wonder that this book has so captivated its readers – artists, philosophers, religious readers and academics alike.

Researchers grappling with the problem of how best to engage this intriguing, yet complicated book have taken a variety of approaches. This chapter explores how three of the most popular angles of approach may facilitate our reading of the book. First, I turn to the contradictions in Ecclesiastes, a feature that has preoccupied researchers enormously. The interpretive choices scholars have made when faced with the book's ambiguities and tensions reveal much about their expectations towards the book and its genre. Second, I take a closer look at the narrator of the book, Qohelet, whose elusive identity continues to pique scholarly interest. Who might Qohelet be and how does his presence in Ecclesiastes shape the book? Finally, I turn to a thematic reading of the book. Qohelet returns to a small collection of themes over and over in order to consider how each of them shapes human life. I suggest that the theme of time, a primary concern of Qohelet's, is a particularly attractive entry point to the book.

ENDLESS CONTRADICTION: A FEATURE OR A PROBLEM?

Most researchers date the book of Ecclesiastes to the third century BCE, primarily for linguistic reasons. The book's language contains features of syntax known mainly from late biblical Hebrew, as well as forms from both late biblical Hebrew and Mishnaic Hebrew.[1] Additionally, fragments of Ecclesiastes have been found at Qumran and the book is quoted by Ben Sira, making it extremely unlikely that it was written much later than the third century BCE. A few scholars, however, have argued in favour of an earlier date than the one generally favoured. Fredericks, for example, dates the book to the exilic period or earlier, arguing that what looks like late biblical Hebrew might instead be features of dialect from an earlier date.[2] To Fredericks, the relatively unique genre of Ecclesiastes should also lead us to expect a 'degree of singularity' in the book's use of language.[3] Seow, too, proposes an earlier date for the book. Turning to its content, he points out a 'curious preoccupation with economic matters', which to him suggests that the book's narrator 'was addressing a particular environment'. This, as well as linguistic features, leads Seow to date the book to the late Achaemenid period.[4]

Ecclesiastes is a difficult text to read.[5] Insofar as the book presents an argument at all, it is not a linearly unfolding one that, after surveying a number of issues, moves neatly to a conclusion. Instead, it retraces its steps endlessly and allows the presence of multiple, contradictory viewpoints throughout. Scholars have made valiant attempts to identify a structural scheme in the book, but none of the proposed models have convinced widely.[6] As Newsom suggests, the drive to identify an overall structure in Ecclesiastes could perhaps be seen as 'attempts to control the meaning of the book by establishing a sort of thematic hierarchy' that may not actually be present.[7]

Unresolved contradictions dominate the book of Ecclesiastes. How scholars have approached this compositional feature has depended to a

---

[1] A useful overview can be found in Shannon Burkes, *Death in Qoheleth and Egyptian Biographies of the Late Period*, SBLDS 170 (Atlanta, 1999), 36.

[2] Daniel C. Fredericks, *Qoheleth's Language: Re-Evaluating Its Nature and Date* (Lampeter, 1988), 32–35.

[3] Fredericks, *Qoheleth's Language*, 28.

[4] Choon-Leong Seow, 'Theology When Everything Is Out of Control', *Int* 55.3 (2001): 239.

[5] For a more extended discussion on different strategies for reading Ecclesiastes, see Mette Bundvad, *Time in the Book of Ecclesiastes*, Oxford Theological Monographs (Oxford, 2015), 9–23.

[6] See for example: Francois Rousseau, 'Structure de Qohelet 1:4–11 et plan de livre', *VT* 31 (1981): 200–217; Addison G. Wright, 'Riddle of the Sphinx: The Structure of the Book of Qoheleth', *CBQ* 30 (1968): 313–334.

[7] Carol A. Newsom, 'Job and Ecclesiastes', in *Old Testament Interpretation: Past, Present, and Future (Essays in Honor of Gene M. Tucker)*, ed. James Luther Mays, David L. Petersen and Kent Harold Richards (Nashville, 1995), 187.

great extent on their expectations of the book and its genre.[8] The
majority view of scholars in the late nineteenth and early twentieth
centuries was that one author would not have created such an inconsistent book and that Ecclesiastes must have gone through a reasonably
lengthy process of redaction. For instance, Siegfried argued that the
book as we now have it contains six layers of redaction.[9] Building upon
his scheme and simplifying it somewhat, McNeile suggested that at
least three redactors added their own material to the original author's
text. The first redactor added traditional wisdom material in the form of
proverbs, as well as the epilogue in 12:11ff. The second sought to temper
the rampant scepticism of the book. Through the insertion of material
about the duty of fearing God and the judgement of God, he brought the
book more in line with mainstream religious thinking. Finally, a third
redactor added the introduction in 1:1–2 and possibly 12:9–10.[10]

One might question, however, how successful these assumed
redactors have been. It is immediately clear that the book of
Ecclesiastes has not been transformed into a harmonious, orthodox
whole. Instead, as Fox notes, the sceptical reflections of the assumed
original author are frequently given the final word.[11] It is also worth
pointing out that the contradictions are often so deeply embedded in the
text that they cannot easily be excised by attributing discrete sections of
the book to different redactors. In fact, Ecclesiastes seems to delight in
establishing tension and ambiguity. It makes a mystery of the identity
of its primary narrator even on the level of his name. And it abounds in
internally inconsistent passages (e.g., 8:10–14), as well as passages that
are consistent when read on their own but incompatible with the
argument in other sections of the book (e.g., 2:1 and 2:10 and 8:5–6
and 9:1–2).[12]

Newer scholarship often takes a different approach to the compositional history of Ecclesiastes: instead of assuming an extensive process
of redaction, scholars now frequently argue that most of the book may
well have been written by one author, though the majority still consider

[8] As noted by John Barton, *Reading the Old Testament: Method in Biblical Study.
    Revised and Enlarged* (Louisville, 1996), 64–65.
[9] Carl Siegfried, *Prediger und Hoheslied übersetzt und erklärt*, HKAT
    (Göttingen, 1898).
[10] Alan Hugh McNeile, *An Introduction to Ecclesiastes* (Cambridge, 1904), 22–23.
[11] Michael. V. Fox, *Qohelet and His Contradictions* (Sheffield, 1989), 34–35.
[12] Bundvad, *Time*, 12.

the third-person framework in 1:1–2 and 12:8–14 secondary.[13] Verse 7:27, which interrupts the flow of the first-person narration – referring to the primary narrator, Qohelet, in the third person, as do 1:1–2 and 12:8–14 – is frequently considered a later addition too. Some researchers also suggest that a poem in 1:4–11, which establishes a cosmic frame-work for Qohelet's philosophical reflections, is secondary,[14] while a few exclude the final poem about human ageing and death in 12:1–7 too.[15]

If one wishes to approach the book as the work of one author, however, then another explanation for its contradictions is needed. They can no longer be a symptom of multiple authors with different theologies working on the same text. Instead, they must have been worked into the text on purpose and the reader should consider *why*. Many scholars now understand the contradictions in Ecclesiastes an integral feature of the book, whilst interpreting them in differing ways.

Some researchers argue that the contradictions in Ecclesiastes only *appear* contradictory. Read carefully, they reveal themselves to be rhet-orical techniques through which the narrator explores complex, philo-sophical issues. For example, Loader argues that the book is structured so as to examine a series of polar opposites.[16] According to Herzberg, Ecclesiastes makes use of so-called *Zwar-Aber Aussagen* (indeed-but statements) to present viewpoints that appear true (indeed it is so that . . .) but are then modified into what many readers have mistaken for contradictory statements (but it is also true that . . .).[17]

I am sceptical of systematising efforts like these. As an example of why, let us take a look at Greenstein's attempt to bring order to the statements about wisdom and the wisdom tradition in Ecclesiastes by suggesting that they are not as contradictory as they initially seem. Greenstein argues that even though the narrator of Ecclesiastes attacks

---

[13] For dissenting views, see Fox, 'Frame-Narrative and Composition in the Book of Qohelet', *HUCA* 48 (1977): 83–106; Carolyn Sharp, 'Ironic Representation, Authorial Voice, and Meaning in Qohelet', *BibInt* 12 (2004): 37–68.

[14] For example, Tremper Longman III, *The Book of Ecclesiastes* (Grand Rapids, 1998); Oswald Loretz, *Qohelet und der alte Orient: Untersuchen zu Stil und theologischer Thematik des Buches Qohelet* (Freiburg, 1964). Differently, Naoto Kamano, *Cosmology and Character: Qoheleth's Pedagogy from a Rhetorical-Critical Perspective*, BZAW 312 (Berlin, 2002); Tomás Frydrych, *Living under the Sun: Examination of Proverbs and Qoheleth*, VTSupp (Leiden, 2002); and Bundvad (*Time* [New York, 2015]) considers the poem an integral part of the book proper.

[15] E.g., Yee-Von Koh, *Royal Autobiography in the Book of Qohelet*, BZAW 369 (Berlin, 2006).

[16] James Alfred Loader, *Polar Structures in the Book of Qohelet*, BZAW 152 (Berlin, 1979).

[17] Hans Wilhelm Hertzberg, *Der Prediger (Qohelet)* (Leipzig, 1932), 7.

the teachings of wisdom, he still assigns wisdom practical value.[18] However, the narrator in Ecclesiastes never actually indicates which of the divergent views of wisdom in the book is the 'right' one. He presents wisdom both as somewhat valid (9:18), universally valid (2:13; 8:12b–13) and as entirely without value (2:14b–15; 6:8). To me, an unresolved presentation like this highlights the discrepancy between the different views offered by the author rather than advocating a *via media* of sorts.[19]

Another way to approach the ambiguous presentation in Ecclesiastes is to consider contradiction itself central to the message of the book. For example, Ingram sees ambiguity as a primary feature of the book on a thematic as well as linguistic level, and he argues that Ecclesiastes' exploration of ambiguity assists the reader in engaging with the ambiguity of human life.[20] Salyer notes similarly that 'incongruities, ironies, paradoxes and opacities abound throughout the discourse'.[21] This feature of the book's form *and* content should guide our reading of it, he suggests: 'Ambiguous texts beg for a both-and, rather than an either-or paradigm when dealing with their meaning and interpretation ... Closure is not part of the reading experience.'[22] Finally, Koosed suggests a somewhat related connection between the book's presentation and its message: the problem of mortality, she argues, is explored in Ecclesiastes both on the content level and through the structure of the book which – through its breaks and discontinuities – mimics the structure of death. To Koosed, the structure of Ecclesiastes 'decays and disintegrates like the dying body', moving towards 'coherency only to pull away again'.[23]

Approaches that understand the contradictions of Ecclesiastes as a key feature of the book rather than a problem are appealing. Frequently, they offer compelling reading strategies precisely because they are able to accept the presence of tensions and ambiguities in the text without

---

[18] Edward L. Greenstein, 'Sages with a Sense of Humour: The Babylonian Dialogue between a Man and His Servant and the Book of Qoheleth', in *Wisdom Literature in Mesopotamia and Israel*, ed. Richard J Clifford, SBL Symposium Series 36 (Atlanta, 2007), 64.

[19] Bundvad, *Time*, 12–13.

[20] Doug Ingram. *Ambiguity in Ecclesiastes*, LHBOTS 431 (New York; London, 2006), 54–55. He sets out his approach in detail on pages 44–74.

[21] Gary D. Salyer, *Vain Rhetoric: Private Insight and Public Debate in Ecclesiastes*, JSOTSupp 327 (Sheffield, 2001), 166.

[22] Salyer, *Vain Rhetoric*, 1.

[23] Jennifer L. Koosed, *(Per)Mutations of Qohelet: Reading the Body in the Book*, LHBOT 429 (London, 2006), 94.

needing to resolve them. Still, when evaluating any reading that claims to uncover hidden meaning in the broken structure and thematic set-up of Ecclesiastes, it is important to ask: to what extent are these readings actually engaging the book and to what extent are they the result of readers themselves creating the very coherence that they hope to discover in the book? What if Ecclesiastes has no overall strategy and no coherent perspective? In our eagerness to make sense of the book, we might be failing to do justice to the text in front of us. Some scholars have argued that there is almost no overall coherence in Ecclesiastes, a radical example being Galling's suggestion that the book is entirely fragmented, ordered neither in terms of thematic concerns nor through a logical organisation of its material.[24] Galling's view that the book consists of thirty-seven fairly unconnected sayings has not convinced widely, and it does not convince me either. Still, I find myself returning again and again to the question of the expectations we bring with us as readers. Are we asking the right questions of the book when we try to work out how its contradictions are *really* meant to be read or are we in fact mistaking its character whenever we go hunting for coherence?

Bartholomew sensibly points out that the book of Ecclesiastes allows its readers an unusual amount of interpretative leeway.[25] The book's contradictions and structural ambiguities require us to participate actively in assembling its argument and message. Some ideas must be foregrounded, others relegated to the background. It is hardly surprising, then, that good, critical readings of Ecclesiastes can disagree fundamentally about the book's message – and about whether there even is one. While there may not be a single, coherent proposal at the heart of Ecclesiastes – ready to be revealed if only we solve the mystery of the book's contradictory presentation – my sympathy is with readings that engage the book imaginatively to illuminate the myriad of ways that Ecclesiastes *can* be read.

THE ROYAL DISGUISE: WHO IS QOHELET?

Despite the lack of a structural plan or a clearly progressing argument, readers often experience a sense of cohesion in Ecclesiastes. One reason for this is the book's relative thematic coherence, to which I will return below. Another is the narrative voice of the book's main character,

---

[24] Kurt Galling, 'Koheleth-Studien', *ZAW* 50 (1932): 276–299.
[25] Craig G. Bartholomew, *Reading Ecclesiastes: Old Testament Exegesis and Hermeneutical Theory*, AnBib 139 (Rome, 1998), 268.

Qohelet, which is present throughout most of the work. Crenshaw admits his fascination with a narrator who makes his 'own scepticism appear solidly biblical'.[26] Fox talks about encountering Qohelet's 'brooding consciousness' in the book, while Stone meets 'old man Qoheleth'.[27] The prominence of the narrator is also what encourages Christianson to read the book as a character-driven narrative.[28]

Ecclesiastes 1:12 explicitly introduces the first-person narrator of the book, Qohelet, and his account of his struggle to understand human life and its value. Qohelet initially presents himself as a king who uses his royal position, wisdom and riches to carry out an extended investigation of sorts: 'to search out by wisdom all that is done under heaven' (1:13). He explores both wisdom and folly and samples every pleasure available to him, seeking to understand what is 'good for mortals to do under heaven during the few days of their life' (2:3). After concluding initially that the reward for his toil is the pleasure he has taken in the work itself (2:10), Qohelet reconsiders, introducing one of the book's central contradictions. There is nothing to be gained under the sun, he now states, nothing new to be achieved, and while wisdom does surpass folly, both the wise man and the fool must die – and both will be forgotten (2:11–16). 'So I hated life', Qohelet laments, 'because what is done under the sun was grievous to me; for all is vanity and a chasing after wind. I hated all my toil in which I had toiled under the sun, seeing that I must leave it to those who come after me' (2:17–18).

After the failure of his royal investigation, Qohelet never again refers directly to himself as a king. In a sense, the royal fiction breaks down. The 'I' of the first-person narration persists, but Qohelet the King never explicitly takes the stage again. In the rest of the book, Qohelet's reflections are presented in the form of philosophical-theological contemplation, poems, didactic tales and proverbs. They are supplemented by a slender, interpretive framework in 1:1–2 and 12:8–14 in which a third-person narrator introduces and concludes upon Qohelet's undertaking.

The identity of the first-person narrator in Ecclesiastes has proved elusive and continues to attract scholarly interest. Even the name Qohelet is ambiguous. Qohelet is a *qal* participle of *qāhal*, to gather or

---

[26]   James L. Crenshaw, *Ecclesiastes*, OTL (Philadelphia, 1987), 53.

[27]   Fox, *Qohelet and His Contradictions*, 159; Elizabeth Stone, 'Old Man Qoheleth', *JBR* 10 (1942): 98–102. See also Rachel Z. Dulin, '"How Sweet Is the Light": Qoheleth's Age-Centered Teachings', *Int* 55 (2001): 260–270.

[28]   Eric A. Christianson, *A Time to Tell: Narrative Strategies in Ecclesiastes*, JSOTSup 280 (Sheffield, 1998).

collect, a verb that is nowhere else attested in *qal*. It is used as a name in some verses, for instance, 1:1–2. At the same time, the definite article in 12:8 (*the* Qohelet) seems to suggest a title of sorts. Once, in 7:27, Qohelet takes a feminine verb. Salyer has argued that ambiguities like these are meant to draw the attention of the reader towards the identity of the narrator.[29] If, indeed, the difficulties surrounding the name Qohelet have been inserted in the text on purpose, Ingram's observation that they may be a 'literary ploy to draw a veil of mystery over the main character of Ecclesiastes' seems persuasive.[30]

In traditional Jewish and Christian receptions of Ecclesiastes, the presentation of Qohelet in 1:1 as the son of David and in 1:16 as the wisest of the kings in Jerusalem was taken at face value. Qohelet was king Solomon. The narrator and the author of the book were collapsed into one: not only was King Solomon the narrator of the book; he had written it too.[31] As noted by Bolin, intriguing interpretive issues arise once one accepts that Solomon did not author Ecclesiastes: 'To read Qohelet as adopting a Solomonic guise raises questions about ancient authors and their use of irony and pseudonymity'.[32] The author of Ecclesiastes, whoever they may have been, chose to employ a royal persona, but why?

When scholars today talk about the royal guise in Ecclesiastes, they tend to argue that this narrative ploy is used deliberately by the author to evoke certain expectations towards kingship and its responsibilities. Koh, for example, suggests that the author has Qohelet present himself as a great king to 'affirm an essential continuity with a past tradition where wisdom was once associated with the king'.[33] Crenshaw argues similarly that the royal guise allows Qohelet to speak authoritatively.[34]

The view that the royal fiction imbues the narrator of Ecclesiastes with authority is not unproblematic, however. First, as already mentioned, the royal fiction might not extend beyond chapter two when king Qohelet appears to give up on his quest. Second, the book contains a number of potentially anti-royal passages (4:1–3, 13–15; 5:7; 9:13–17) that appear to deconstruct the very royal authority that Qohelet bases his quest on in the beginning of the book. Might the language of royal

[29] Salyer, *Vain Rhetoric*, 244.
[30] Ingram, *Ambiguity*, 84–85.
[31] See, for example Thomas M. Bolin, *Ecclesiastes and the Riddle of Authorship* (New York; London, 2017), 20–33.
[32] Bolin, *Ecclesiastes*, 51.
[33] Koh, *Royal Autobiography*, 18.
[34] Crenshaw, *Ecclesiastes*, 70.

autobiography be used, then, not to imbue Qohelet's philosophical statements with authority but to show that 'even kings can have no real control over matters that are beyond human grasp'?[35] Perdue goes further still, arguing that Qohelet's aim is to offer a harsh critique of both earthly monarchy and the divine power, which he exposes as oppressive and tyrannical.[36]

The royal identity of Ecclesiastes' narrator connects him to the kings of the biblical tradition, as well as to the wider ancient Near Eastern world. The book's audience would, as Barbour argues, 'have had a complex and multi-layered idea of what a king is'.[37] Their expectations towards kingship provided the author with a rich fabric from which to fashion their narrator figure. Part of the audience's expectations towards kingship would come from biblical traditions about the roles played by kings in the national, historic drama. Barbour suggests that the author uses the royal guise purposefully to address the nation's shared past, including the trauma of the exile.[38] To her, Qohelet does not simply pretend to be any one king from the past. Instead, he is 'a pastiche figure of a king . . . a layering of one king on top of another in individual iterations of a standard pattern'.[39]

This suggestion is intriguing, especially given frequent scholarly assertions that the book of Ecclesiastes is uninterested in the history of the nation and that it barely engages the rest of the Hebrew Bible.[40] Barbour is not alone, however, in re-examining the intertextual links between Ecclesiastes and other biblical texts.[41] The greater awareness of such possible connections is an important addition to interpretations that read King Qohelet's quest in the light of material from the wider ancient Near East, such as ancient Near Eastern royal inscriptions[42] and fictional royal autobiographies.[43] The growing scholarly curiosity about

---

[35] Choon-Leong Seow, *Ecclesiastes: A New Translation with Introduction and Commentary*, AB 18 (New Haven, 2008), 98.

[36] Leo G. Perdue, *Wisdom and Creation: The Theology of Wisdom Literature* (Nashville, 1994), 220–224.

[37] Jennifer Barbour, *The Story of Israel in the Book of Qohelet: Ecclesiastes as Cultural Memory*, Oxford Theological Monographs (New York, 2012), 11.

[38] Barbour, *The Story of Israel*, 36.

[39] Barbour, *The Story of Israel*, 17.

[40] An exception is the *Urgeschichte* in Genesis 1–11, with which Qohelet's dialogue has long been associated. See Forman, 'Koheleth's Use of Genesis', *JSS* 5 (1960): 256–263; Verheij, 'Paradise Retried: On Qohelet 2:4–6', *JSOT* 50 (1991): 113–115.

[41] See, for example, *Reading Ecclesiastes Intertextually*, ed. Katharine Dell and Will Kynes, LHBOTS 587 (London, 2014).

[42] Loretz, *Qohelet*; Koh, *Royal Autobiography*; and Seow, *Ecclesiastes*.

[43] Longman, *The Book of Ecclesiastes*.

the intertextuality of Ecclesiastes helps us understand the figure of Qohelet because it increases our awareness of the influence that a variety of texts, cultural expectations and religious traditions had upon the author of Ecclesiastes and the book's first readers. Whether or not the author refers to any of this material directly, it will have shaped their views on kingship, the endeavours of wisdom and royal achievements.

In the epilogue of Ecclesiastes (12:1–9), the third-person narrator who made his first appearance in the book's introduction (1:1–2) returns. He now offers an evaluation of Qohelet's quest – and one which reinterprets it radically. While Qohelet's search was largely self-reliant, with him reaching his own conclusions after observing the world and reflecting upon it, the epilogist appeals directly to the 'words of the wise' (12:11). He inserts Qohelet into their company, incidentally describing him as a teacher of wisdom rather than a king. Whereas Qohelet the narrator allowed the presence of unresolved contradictions, the epilogist knows exactly what should be concluded on the basis of Qohelet's investigation: 'Fear God, and keep his commandments; for that is the whole duty of everyone. For God will bring every deed into judgment, including every secret thing, whether good or evil' (12:13–14). This affirmation of divine justice runs counter to much of Qohelet's depiction of the relationship between God and humankind.[44]

The two narrative voices cannot easily be reconciled and I do not think we should try. Whatever one's view of the compositional history of Ecclesiastes, the book as we now have it offers several portrayals of Qohelet: narrator, king, wise man. Bolin has argued persuasively that, despite many readers' experience of encountering the consciousness of Qohelet throughout the book, there is in fact 'no one "spirit" of any one "persona," or any singular "presence," brooding or otherwise, in Ecclesiastes'. Instead, Ecclesiastes offers a variety of 'fragmentary authorial voices that often frustrate more than they clarify our attempts to read the text as a coherent unit'. The book of Ecclesiastes manages to instill a strong sense of authorial presence in its reader, while also offering conflicting perspectives of multiple narrators. This may be, as Bolin notes, one of the genuinely distinctive aspects of the book in the context of the Hebrew Bible.[45]

---

[44] With a particularly stark example in 9:1–2.
[45] Bolin, *Ecclesiastes*, 6.

READING ECCLESIASTES THROUGH ITS DISCUSSION
OF TIME

Throughout the book of Ecclesiastes, a small group of themes forms the
centre of Qohelet's exploration of life. He revisits them over and over.
They include mortality and ageing, the human experience of time,
humanity's place within the created world, the relationship between
God and humanity, the power structures within human society and the
value of enjoyment and wealth. Mostly, Qohelet discusses these themes
as they shape the lives of individuals and of humankind as a whole.

As I have argued elsewhere, the theme of time provides an excellent
entry point into the book of Ecclesiastes.[46] Time is a central concern
throughout the book.[47] Qohelet's reflections on this theme are unusually
coherent, although – unsurprisingly – some ambiguities persist. Instead of
describing time as a neutral reality, Qohelet explores how the temporal
order of the world obstructs human attempts to build meaningful lives.
The rest of this chapter offers a brief exploration of the book of Ecclesiastes
through its discussion of time. Qohelet does not develop any of his themes
in isolation. Exploring the theme of time in the book, then, will also entail
touching upon the important, related themes of morality and joy.

Before the self-presentation of the book's primary narrator in 1:12,
Ecclesiastes offers a poem on the natural world and its temporal structures (1:4–11).[48] As well as describing this overall set-up, the poem
explores the temporal situation of humankind within the world. The
poem also functions as a first response to the question in 1:3 that
introduces the philosophical endeavour of the whole book: 'What do
people gain from all the toil at which they toil under the sun?' It is
worth looking at this poem in some detail, then.

The first four verses of the poem describe the temporal structure of
the world as one of constant repetition: the sun sets and rises, only to set
again. The rivers continue to run to the sea, which never fills. While
some researchers maintain that humankind fits seamlessly into this
structure of cyclicality and renewal,[49] I would argue that the picture is

---

[46] Bundvad, *Time*.

[47] See also Peter Machinist, 'Fate, miqreh, and Reason: Some Reflections on Qohelet and
     Biblical Thought', in *Solving Riddles and Untying Knots: Biblical, Epigraphic, and
     Semitic Studies in Honor of Jonas C. Greenfield*, eds. Ziony Zevit, Seymour Gitin and
     Michael Sokoloff (Winona Lake, 2005), 259–275.

[48] For a detailed study of this poem, see Bundvad, *Time*, 46–61.

[49] For example, Daniel C. Fredericks, *Coping with Transience: Ecclesiastes on Brevity in
     Life*, Biblical Seminar 18, 25–26, 56. Also to some extent Fox, *A Time to Tear Down
     and a Time to Build Up: A Re-reading of Ecclesiastes* (Grand Rapids, 1999), 166.

more complicated than that. Thus, already in verse 1:4, the poem seems to suggest two types of temporal existence: while the world remains forever, individual people die and are replaced.

The final four verses of the poem explore the human situation within the temporal structures of the world in more detail. The temporal order is judged explicitly in these verses, which speak of weariness (1:8). Since the world consists of endless repetition, nothing is ever really new (1:9). People mistake this state of affairs, believing themselves able to point out genuinely new things. However, everything they might experience as new has existed long before they did, Qohelet argues (1:10). It is our lacking memory of the past that causes us to believe that change does take place. Verse 1:11 makes this cognitive problem explicit: 'The people of long ago are not remembered, nor will there be any remembrance of people yet to come by those who come after them'. The Hebrew text here talks of the 'former' (ri'šōnîm) and the 'later' ('aḥărōnîm) without making it clear whether these are the people from long ago or long-ago times and events. Both possible meanings are probably in view.

In 1:10–11, the process of forgetting is shown to be built into the fabric of time. As Berger convincingly argues, 'lack of memory is, for Qohelet, the erasure of history, toil, and gain. Time is engaged in a process by which it continually washes itself out'.[50] Qohelet's problem here is twofold. First, our inability to remember what has been severs our connection to the past. Second, if the same type of event continually recurs, there will always be a new present to replace the current one – and there will never be space to remember the time passed and those who die away with it.[51] Thus, the individual human being is cut off from the future too, destined to be forgotten, just as they themselves have forgotten the past. We are utterly isolated in the present, unable to establish real connections with either past or future and thus unable to build a continuity that can match that of nature. When King Qohelet concludes his wisdom quest in chapter two, he returns to this problem, even reusing language from 1:10–11.[52] He restates the universality of oblivion (2:16) and the inaccessibility of the future (2:18–19). Qohelet

---

[50]   Benjamin Lyle Berger, 'Qohelet and the Exigencies of the Absurd', BibInt 9 (2001): 148.
[51]   Bundvad, Time, 58.
[52]   Verse 2:16 reuses the phrase 'ēn zikārôn (there is/will be no remembrance) from 1:11, as well as kəbār (already) and 'ôlām (eternity) from 1:10. See also Bundvad, 'At Play in Potential Space', in Perspectives on Israelite Wisdom: Proceedings of the Oxford Old Testament Seminar, ed. John Jarick (London; 2016), 260–261.

too must die and be forgotten and he is prevented from knowing anything about those who will succeed him. Even wisdom offers no protection against this reality.

At this point, the theme of time ties in closely with that of death. In
her monograph on death in Ecclesiastes, Burkes argues that it is in this
book that 'death makes its entrance into the Hebrew traditions as a
phenomenon to be reckoned with .... The symbolic immortalities
offered elsewhere in the Bible, the memory and endurance of a good
name, survival through one's children and people ... fail utterly in
Qoheleth's opinion'.[53] Certainly, the spectre of mortality is present in
many of Qohelet's reflections on human life (such as 2:14–16; 3:1–21;
5:14–16; 7:15–17; 8:10; 9:3–5; 12:1–7). Death negates every human distinction, nullifying our every achievement, and it threatens to empty
even the good, joyful life of meaning. To Burkes, Qohelet's attitude to
human mortality is a response to an 'atmosphere of distress, confusion,
and chaos' set off initially through the national exilic experience.[54]

Other researchers have offered cheerier readings of Ecclesiastes,
even when focusing on the theme of mortality. For example,
Fredericks argues that while Qohelet does contemplate the condition
of mortality, he does not see it as an all-consuming threat. Focusing on
the transience of human life, Fredericks suggests that Qohelet balances
death with the enjoyment of life, arguing that the value of life is to be
found not in its length but its joy.[55] He seeks support for his reading in
one of Qohelet's favourite metaphors, *hebel* (literally meaning breath or
wind), which is used as a kind of refrain throughout the book. Most
interpreters argue differently from Fredericks that *hebel* connotes something unsatisfactory or severely frustrating. For example, Miller has
argued that the *hebel*-metaphor evokes something insubstantial, transitory and foul.[56] Fredericks prefers the translation 'transitory' but cautions his readers to keep this idea separate from notions of futility,
emptiness and meaninglessness.[57]

Many passages in Ecclesiastes support Fredericks' claim that
Qohelet describes human life as transitory but not meaningless. In
seven striking passages, Qohelet calls his reader to enjoy life here and
now (2:24–26; 3:12–13, 22; 5:17–19; 8:15; 9:7–9; 11:8). These are also key

---

[53] Burkes, *Death*, 75.
[54] Burkes, *Death*, 118.
[55] Fredericks, *Coping with Transience*, 37–41.
[56] Douglas Miller, 'Qoheleth's Symbolic Use of הבל', *JBL* 117 (1998): 437–454.
[57] Fredericks, *Coping with Transience*, 15, 47.

passages for researchers such as Whybray and Lee who argue that Qohelet is, essentially, a preacher of joy.[58] Yet other passages, such as 2:16–23 and 6:9–12 describe death as a condition so destructive that it makes even joy in the present moment seem impossible.

Even aside from the threat of mortality, however, human beings struggle to make sense of their day-to-day existence. In the famous poem on time in Ecclesiastes 3:2–8 and the interpretation of it in 3:9–11, Qohelet resumes his exploration of the world's temporal structures, this time in order to argue that we are also unable to understand how they govern our present. After having stated in 3:1 that there is a season or a moment for everything, the poem in 3:2–8 lists fourteen pairs of activities: a time to be born and a time to die, a time to tear and a time to sew, a time to be silent and a time to speak and so on. Read on its own, the poem is comforting. Stylistically well-structured, it seems to set out a coherent, framework for our daily lives: while nothing is permanent, every event is fitting for its particular moment.[59] Even death loses some of its sting if there really is a right time to die.[60] Then, however, Qohelet turns to an appraisal of the poem's temporal framework. 'What gain have the workers from their toil?' he asks in 3:9. While God has made everything beautiful in its time and – as the Hebrew text in verse 3:11 has it – placed eternity in the heart of humankind, he has also made it so that 'they cannot find out what God has done from the beginning to the end'. Qohelet clearly takes issue with the harmonious temporal set-up described in the poem, but why?

I suggest that in 3:11 Qohelet once again takes aim at our inability to understand the temporal set-up. As argued by Barr, this verse draws attention to the discrepancy between our longing to understand the world we live in and our inability to figure out anything about it at all.[61] Qohelet has already argued in chapters one and two that the horizons of past and future are inaccessible to the individual human being. In chapter three, he suggests that we do not understand the temporal framework as it governs our lives in the present either. Although the temporal set-up in 3:2–8 may appear harmonious, it does

---

[58] R. Norman Whybray, 'Qoheleth, Preacher of Joy', *JSOT* 23 (1982): 87–98; Eunny P. Lee, *The Vitality of Enjoyment in Qohelet's Theological Rhetoric* (Berlin, 2005).

[59] Jarick offers a beautiful structural reading of the poem, focusing on the notion of perpetual change: John Jarick, 'The Hebrew Book of Changes: Reflections on *hakkol hebel* and *lakkol zeman* in Ecclesiastes', *JSOT* 90 (2008): 465–483.

[60] Bundvad, *Time*, 100.

[61] So also James Barr, *Biblical Words for Time*, SBT 33 (London, 1962), 117–118. See also Bundvad, *Time*, 103.

not help us make sense of our day-to-day lives because we have no way
of knowing if it is accurate and, if so, how to make appropriate use of it.
As Perdue states, 'humanity is trapped in an opaque, mysterious, and
ambiguous present .... It is impossible even for sages to know the
appropriate time for episodic events'.[62]

Qohelet returns repeatedly to humankind's inability to grasp the
temporal realities of the world, both when it comes to the larger horizons of past and future and in terms of our daily life in the present. He
consistently assigns the responsibility for this state of affairs to God: 'In
the day of prosperity be joyful, and in the day of adversity consider; God
has made the one as well as the other, so that mortals may not find out
anything that will come after them', he advises in 7:14. He also continues to describe humankind's divinely enforced ignorance as an obstacle that cannot be overcome: 'When I applied my mind to know
wisdom ... I saw all the work of God, that no one can find out what is
happening under the sun. However much they may toil in seeking, they
will not find it out; even though those who are wise claim to know, they
cannot find it out' (8:16–17).

No one thematic reading can foreground all parts of Qohelet's
reflections or eliminate the contradictions in the book. Still, approaching Ecclesiastes through its depiction of time encourages us to ask new
questions about the broken structure of the book, as well as its mysterious narrator. Qohelet argues that human beings are unable to understand the temporal structures of the world. Yet those structures and
their impact on our attempts to build meaningful lives are exactly what
he tries to describe when engaging with the theme of time. As a result,
the book is full of tensions between statements of ignorance and statements of knowledge, between Qohelet professing himself unable to
investigate the temporal dimension of human life and trying to do so
anyway. Might these ongoing tensions on the content level of the book
have contributed to its author's compositional choice to introduce
breaks, incongruities and stark contradictions into the text? May the
form of the text, at least in part, reflect Qohelet's attempt to describe
something he considers it impossible to understand?

Qohelet's discussion of time also encourages us to take yet another
look at the narrator of the book. In the beginning of the book, Qohelet
introduces himself as a king from the distant past. He also claims,
however, that the past is entirely inaccessible and that everybody and

---

[62] Perdue, *Wisdom and Creation*, 217.

everything past will be forgotten. Given this tension, what are we as readers supposed to do with the wise reflections of a past king? May Qohelet's view that the past is a lost country lend a new dimension to the elusiveness of his own identity?

Further Reading

Bolin, Thomas M. *Ecclesiastes and the Riddle of Authorship*. New York: 2017.

Bundvad, Mette. *Time in the Book of Ecclesiastes*. Oxford Theology and Religion Monographs. Oxford: 2015.

Burkes, Shannon. *Death in Qoheleth and Egyptian Biographies of the Late Period*. SBLDS 170. Atlanta: 1999.

Christianson, Eric A. *A Time to Tell: Narrative Strategies in Ecclesiastes*. JSOTSup 280. Sheffield: 1998.

Crenshaw, James L. *Ecclesiastes*. OTL. Grand Rapids: 1987.

Fox, Michael V. *A Time to Tear Down and a Time to Build Up: A Re-reading of Ecclesiastes*. Grand Rapids: 1999.

Ingram, Doug. *Ambiguity in Ecclesiastes*. LHBOTS 431. New York; London: 2006.

Machinist, Peter. 'Fate, miqreh, and Reason: Some Reflections on Qohelet and Biblical Thought'. Pages 259–275 in *Solving Riddles and Untying Knots: Biblical, Epigraphic, and Semitic Studies in Honor of Jonas C. Greenfield*. Edited by Ziony Zevit, Seymour Gitin and Michael Sokoloff. Winona Lake: 2005.

Miller, Douglas. 'Qoheleth's symbolic use of הבל'. *JBL* 117 (1998): 437–454.

Newsom, Carol A. 'Job and Ecclesiastes'. Pages 177–194 in *Old Testament Interpretation: Past, Present, and Future (Essays in Honor of Gene M. Tucker)*. Edited by James Luther Mays, David L. Petersen and Kent Harold Richards. Nashville: 1995.

Seow, Choon-Leong. *Ecclesiastes: A New Translation with Introduction and Commentary*. AB 18. New Haven; London: 2008.

11 The Song of Songs

JENNIFER L. ANDRUSKA

Including the Song of Songs in a companion to the biblical wisdom literature is controversial, as the Song has not always been considered a wisdom text. Yet I would argue for its consideration, though as discussed below, this depends largely on how one defines wisdom.

There are hints in the Song's reception history that it has been understood as a type of wisdom or associated with other biblical wisdom texts at various times. Yet it is more recently that the Song's relationship to wisdom, as currently understood, has come under investigation. The current state of wisdom research has seen a number of recent shifts and a lack of consensus concerning the definition and scope of wisdom makes it particularly difficult to compare the Song of Songs to it. I will attempt to identify where wisdom scholars seem to be agreeing in the discussion before presenting my own arguments for understanding the Song as wisdom. As we will see, regardless of whether the Song is seen as a wisdom book or simply displaying strong wisdom influence, it is doing something very different from other ancient Near Eastern love song texts.

A BRIEF HISTORY OF RECEPTION[1]

In both Judaism and Christianity, the allegorical interpretation of the Song dominated until the nineteenth century. The Song was interpreted as an allegory depicting the relationship between either God and Israel in the Jewish tradition or Christ and the Church or individual soul in

---

[1] For more extensive surveys of the Song's history of interpretation, see H. H. Rowley, 'The Interpretation of the Song of Songs', in *The Servant of the Lord and Other Essays on the Old Testament*, 2nd ed. (London, 1954), 187–234; Marvin H. Pope, *Song of Songs: A New Translation with Introduction and Commentary*, AB 7C (New York, 1977), 89–229; Roland E. Murphy, *Song of Songs: A Commentary on The Book of Canticles or The Song of Songs*, Hermeneia (Minneapolis, 1990), 11–41; Duane Garrett and Paul R. House, *Song of Songs/Lamentations*, WBC 23B (Nashville, 2004), 59–91.

the Christian tradition. Our earliest indication of a debate between allegorical and literal understandings of the Song is found in Rabbi Akiva's (ca. 100 CE) comments against those who sang the Song as a ditty or common love song at banquets,[2] which indicates that some at the time understood it as an erotic song. Theodore of Mopsuestia (ca. 350–428 CE) read the Song literally as Solomon's love song to Pharaoh's daughter, thought that it should be expelled from the canon and was condemned for these views among others after his death. Sebastian Catellio, a Protestant Reformer and colleague of John Calvin, understood the Song similarly, was opposed by Calvin and was sent away from Geneva.[3] Further mention should be made of the recently published twelfth-century anonymous Jewish commentary on the Song from northern France, which attests to an early literal reading of the book as a dialogue between lovers without any reference to the allegorical interpretation.[4]

In the nineteenth century, the allegorical interpretation gave way to literal approaches, particularly the interpretation of the Song as a drama involving either two or three characters. The three-character approach, promoted by J. F. Jacobi, S. Löwisohn, H. Ewald and Christian D. Ginsberg,[5] understood the Song as a love triangle drama between Solomon, a woman and her shepherd lover, to whom she remains loyal. The two-character approach, popularised by Franz Delitzsch,[6] saw Solomon alone as the male lover. In the mid-nineteenth century, J. G. Wetzstein also popularised the view of the Song as a collection of wedding songs.[7]

In the twentieth-century, cultic interpretations, like those proposed by Theophile J. Meek and Samuel N. Kramer, saw the Song as a sanitised work with origins in the fertility cult or sacred marriage practices

[2] t. Sanh. 12.10.

[3] J. Cheryl Exum, Song of Songs, OTL (Louisville, 2005), 73–74.

[4] See Sara Japhet and Barry Dov Walfish, The Way of Lovers: The Oxford Anonymous Commentary on the Song of Songs (Bodleian Library, MS Opp. 625): An Edition of the Hebrew Text, with English Translation and Introduction (Leiden, 2017).

[5] Discussed in Rowley, 'Interpretation', 203–204; Christian D. Ginsburg, The Song of Songs: Translated from the Original Hebrew, with a Commentary Historical and Critical (London, 1857).

[6] Franz Delitzsch, Commentary on the Song of Songs and Ecclesiastes, trans. M. G. Easton (Edinburgh, 1877).

[7] See J. G. Wetzstein, 'Appendix: Remarks on the Song', in Delitzsch, Song, 162–178.

of Mesopotamia.[8] However, Michael V. Fox's extensive comparison of the Song of Songs with ancient Egyptian love songs demonstrated strong parallels and established a general consensus that, like the ancient Egyptian love songs, the Song of Songs depicts unmarried lovers.[9] The end of the twentieth century also gave rise to a number of feminist interpretations of the Song that still carry weight today,[10] including their focus on potential female authorship of the book, female voice, agency and desire, the centrality of female figures, the egalitarian nature of the lover's relationship and its subversion of patriarchal models found in other biblical books, though there were some dissenting voices.[11] Scholars also began discussing the Song's relationship to the wisdom genre at this time.

The idea that the Song of Songs conveys wisdom can be traced back to the early church father Origen, though he seems to have understood wisdom as a type of divine philosophy, a pursuit of things 'unseen and eternal' and 'communion with God' that culminated in the Song of Songs, which 'instills into the soul the love of things divine and heavenly'.[12] This is quite different from contemporary understandings of wisdom as practical knowledge and skill for living a successful life. The *Synopsis Scripturae sacrae* (PG 56:316) attributed to John Chrysostom refers to Proverbs, Ecclesiastes, the Song of Songs and Ben Sira as 'advice' (*to symbulutikon*).[13] The sixteenth century medieval Jewish exegete Don Isaac Abravanel read the Song as an allegory of Solomon's love for Wisdom, interpreting the female lover as an allegorical representation of Wisdom.[14]

---

[8]   Theophile J. Meek, *The Song of Songs: Introduction and Exegesis*, IB V (New York, 1956); Samuel N. Kramer, *The Sacred Marriage Rite* (Bloomington, 1969); cf. Pope (*Songs*), who saw the Song's origin in cultic mortuary feasts.

[9]   Michael V. Fox, *The Song of Songs and the Ancient Egyptian Love Songs* (Madison, 1985).

[10] E.g., Phyllis Trible, 'Depatriarchalizing in Biblical Interpretation', *JAAR* XLI/1 (1973): 30–48, here 45; Marcia Falk, *The Song of Songs: A New Translation and Interpretation* (San Francisco, 1990); Carol Meyers, 'Gender Imagery in the Song of Songs', in *The Song of Songs*, ed. Athalya Brenner, FCB 1 (Sheffield, 1993), 197–212; Exum, *Songs*.

[11] E.g., J. Cheryl Exum, 'Ten Things Every Feminist Should Know about the Song of Songs', in Brenner and Fontaine, *Song of Songs*, 24–35; Fiona C. Black, *The Artifice of Love: Grotesque Bodies and the Song of Songs*, LHBOTS 392 (London, 2009).

[12] Will Kynes, *An Obituary for 'Wisdom Literature': The Birth, Death, and Intertextual Reintegration of a Biblical Corpus* (Oxford, 2019), 73; Origen, *Comm. Cant.* prologue, trans. by R. P. Lawson, *Origen: The Song of Songs Commentary and Homilies* (Westminster, 1957), 44, 41.

[13] Kynes, *Obituary*, 74.

[14] Rowley, 'Interpretation', 199.

More recently, a number of biblical scholars have begun discussing the Song's relationship to the biblical wisdom genre. In 1979, B. S. Childs argued that the Song of Songs is wisdom literature and may reasonably be read as a wisdom book, which rules out other contexts for understanding it.[15] He has been followed by Michael Sadgove, George M. Schwab, Kenton L. Sparks and Rosalind Clark, who all understand the Song as a wisdom book.[16] Katharine Dell takes a middle approach, maintaining that the Song's genre is love poetry, yet noting a number of wisdom features and thinking that it displays wisdom influence.[17] Sadgrove, Roland E. Murphy and Dell have all argued that the Song went through an editorial stage of redaction by wisdom authors who endowed it with sapiential characteristics, so that as edited, it can be read or interpreted as wisdom.[18] Murphy thinks that the Song was likely included in the canon because it was seen as belonging to the wisdom corpus.[19] It is grouped with other wisdom books in the Septuagint, as well as in early canonical lists.[20] The Vulgate lists it with Proverbs, Ecclesiastes, Job, Psalms, Wisdom and Ben Sira in its *libri didactici* or 'pedagogical literature' division, and Josephus lists it with Proverbs, Ecclesiastes and the Psalms as those which 'contain hymns to God and precepts for the conduct of human life'.[21]

Those who have suggested such connections to wisdom have been criticised for not demonstrating that they are extensive enough to be meaningful and for being vague as to what precisely the book's wisdom

---

[15]   Brevard Childs, *Introduction to the Old Testament as Scripture* (Philadelphia, 1979), 574.

[16]   Michael Sadgrove, 'The Song of Songs as Wisdom Literature', in Papers on the Old Testament and Related Themes. Vol. 1 of *Studia Biblica 1978: Sixth International Congress on Biblical Studies, Oxford, 3–7 April 1978*, ed. E. A. Livingstone, JSOTSupp 11 (Sheffield, 1979), 245–248; George M. Schwab, *The Song of Songs' Cautionary Message concerning Human Love*, StBibLit 41 (New York, 2002), 150–158; Kenton L. Sparks, 'The Song of Songs: Wisdom for Young Jewish Women', CBQ 70.2 (2008): 277–299, here 278; Rosalind Clark, 'Seeking Wisdom in the Song of Songs', in *Exploring Old Testament Wisdom: Literature and Themes*, ed. David G. Firth and Lindsay Wilson (London, 2016), 100–112, esp. 104.

[17]   Katharine Dell, 'Does the Song of Songs Have Any Connections to Wisdom?', in *Perspectives on the Song of Songs*, ed. Anselm C. Hagedorn, BZAW 346 (Berlin, 2005), 9, 16.

[18]   Sadgrove, 'Song', 246; Roland E. Murphy, *The Tree of Life: An Exploration of Biblical Wisdom Literature* (Grand Rapids, 1990), 106; Dell, 'Connections', 16.

[19]   Murphy, *Tree of Life*, 106–110.

[20]   Clark, 'Seeking Wisdom', 100–101, n.3.

[21]   Will Kynes, 'The Nineteenth-Century Beginning of "Wisdom Literature"', in *Perspectives on Israelite Wisdom: Proceedings of the Oxford Old Testament Seminar*, ed. John Jarick (London, 2016), 89; Josephus, *Ag. Ap.* 1.8.

message might be,[22] criticisms which I hope to dispel. Many who currently understand the Song as wisdom think that its message is to wait for a sexual relationship until marriage[23] or avoid love entirely.[24] I have proposed something entirely different, arguing that the Song's wisdom message is to pursue a particular type of love relationship modelled by the unmarried lovers throughout the Song.[25]

DEFINITION OF WISDOM

In order to assess the Song's relationship to biblical wisdom, one must first arrive at a working definition of wisdom. Some have attempted to define wisdom based on vocabulary, yet as Norman Whybray's study demonstrated, wisdom vocabulary occurs across a significant portion of the Hebrew Bible.[26] Others have used a lack of wisdom vocabulary as a criterion; for example, Annette Schellenberg notes a lack of specific wisdom terminology in the Song of Songs and sees this as excluding it from the wisdom genre.[27] Yet, whilst the Song does not contain explicit references to wisdom, as Paul-Alain Beaulieu notes, in ancient Mesopotamia, the Sumerian word for wisdom *nam-kù-zu* and its Akkadian equivalent *nēmequ* rarely occur in what are considered wisdom writings and there are no explicit statements that its purpose is to teach, address or opine on the topic of wisdom directly.[28]

Simon Chi-Chung Cheung and Katharine Dell have proposed the idea of family resemblances as a way of understanding the relationship

[22] J. Cheryl Exum, 'Unity, Date, Authorship and the "Wisdom" of the Song of Songs', in *Goochem in Mokum/Wisdom in Amsterdam*, ed. George J. Brooke and Pierre van Hecke, *OtSt* 68 (Leiden, 2016), 64–65, 67–68; Annette Schellenberg, 'Questioning the Trend of Classifying the Song of Songs as Sapiential', in *Nächstenliebe und Gottesfurcht: Beiträge aus alttestamentlicher, semitistischer und altorientalistischer Wissenschaft für Hans-Peter Mathys zum 65. Geburtstag*, ed. Hanna Jenni and Markus Saur, AOAT (Münster, 2016), 396–402.

[23] Sparks, 'Wisdom', 283, 278; Clark, 'Seeking Wisdom', 106, 111–112; Ian Duguid, *The Song of Songs*, TOTC 19 (Downers Grove, 2015), 150–151, 155–156, 42–43, 40.

[24] Schwab, *Cautionary*, 69, 45, 47, 49; cf. Kathryn Imray, 'Love Is [Strong as] Death: Reading the Song of Songs through Proverbs 1–9', *CBQ* 75 (2013): 651–652, here 663.

[25] Jennifer L. Andruska, *Wise and Foolish Love in the Song of Songs* (Leiden, 2019).

[26] R. Norman Whybray, *The Intellectual Tradition in the Old Testament* (Berlin, 1974).

[27] Schellenberg, 'Questioning', 396–397.

[28] Paul-Alain Beaulieu, 'The Social and Intellectual Setting of Babylonian Wisdom Literature', in *Wisdom Literature in Mesopotamia and Israel*, ed. Richard J. Clifford (Atlanta, 2007), 3–4, 18. Egyptian wisdom does display distinctive vocabulary; see Nili Shupak, 'The Contribution of Egyptian Wisdom to the Study of Biblical Wisdom Literature', in *Was There a Wisdom Tradition? New Prospects in Israelite Wisdom Studies*, ed. Mark R. Sneed (Atlanta, 2015), 269, 286–287.

between wisdom writings and wisdom influence.[29] Cheung uses the criteria of a ruling wisdom thrust or interest in wisdom, an intellectual tone and didactic intention to assess the wisdom psalms, and Dell applies this to the relationship between the wisdom books and beyond. Books where all three are found in large measure are considered at the centre of the wisdom family, whilst those with a ruling thrust in other genres are considered more distant relatives.[30] There must be a family resemblance to the mother and father or 'core' of biblical wisdom, that is, Proverbs and Qohelet, to which other texts are either more closely or distantly related.[31] Job might be considered a cousin, as it has strong wisdom elements but incorporates a number of other generic forms and has its ruling thrust in other genres: psalmic, legal and lament. The idea of family resemblances is a helpful way to understand the relationship between wisdom texts. Yet problems arise when these core wisdom books are used to evaluate wisdom influence in a text that likely influenced them. As I have discussed elsewhere, the direction of influence seems to indicate that the biblical wisdom books, especially Proverbs, used language and motifs from the Song of Songs.[32] To try to use Proverbs, then, to show that the Song shares affinities with wisdom would be a circular inner-biblical argument. As J. Cheryl Exum notes, 'the use of motifs from love poetry in "wisdom" contexts, either consciously or unconsciously, and either from the Song of Songs or a work like it, cannot be used to argue that the Song of Songs is wisdom literature'.[33] I will not argue that the Song's wisdom features are the result of specific parallels with the biblical wisdom books. Instead, I will look outside the biblical evidence at the antecedent ANE didactic or advice literature genre and what characterised it, as well as biblical wisdom's unique approach to it. Dell makes an important point about a historical aspect to the family link in her discussion of family resemblances: within family lineage, one may refer to ancestors and successors, just as a genre's context also has an ancestry and succession of

---

[29] Simon Chi-Chung Cheung, *Wisdom Intoned: A Reappraisal of Classifying Wisdom Psalms*, LHBOTS 613 (London, 2015), 19, 32, 36–37; Katharine J. Dell, 'Deciding the Boundaries of "Wisdom": Applying the Concept of Family Resemblance', in Sneed, *Was There a Wisdom Tradition?*, 155–156.

[30] Cheung, *Wisdom Intoned*.

[31] Dell, 'Boundaries', 156.

[32] Andruska, *Wise and Foolish*, 12–13, 35–42. Cf. Dell, 'Connections', 24; Claudia Camp, *Wisdom and the Feminine in the Book of Proverbs* (Sheffield, 1985), 98; Pope, *Song*, 675; Gerhard von Rad, *Wisdom in Israel*, translated from the German (1970) by James D. Martin (London, 1972), 166–168.

[33] Exum, 'Unity', 67.

readers and interpreters.[34] In literary terms, the biblical wisdom books also have a generic ancestry stretching thousands of years before them into the ANE and a generic succession in other works after.

Most wisdom scholars agree that what underlies the various wisdom books is a shared interest in wisdom.[35] Weeks notes that this interest shapes how the books present themselves and the generic forms and conventions they use. The biblical wisdom writers drew upon a long-established generic tradition in the region, a type of didactic or advice literature that had existed in the ANE for over a thousand years, so that what shaped it – its generic self-presentations and the particular forms and conventions that it used – also shaped the biblical wisdom texts.[36] Like ANE advice literature, the purpose of biblical wisdom was to impart advice about living a successful life or wisdom,[37] so that it drew upon this genre and the forms and conventions that it used, yet exercised considerable freedom in its use. Wisdom scholars generally agree that there were two primary forms of advice literature in the ANE grounded in different types of authority: proverbs and instructions passed on by an authoritative individual to the next generation, typically to their sons.[38] Proverbs expressed common truths and derived their authority from common experience and their generally accepted currency, whilst instructions were passed on by authoritative individuals, who were considered authoritative precisely because they had lived a successful life in a particular area and this gave authority to their advice. The 'father-son setting' is a literary convention that utilises the concept of parental advice to children and immediately associates the work with others that use the same convention, so that it is a mark of genre rather than social setting.[39] Biblical wisdom drew upon these familiar sources of authority to substantiate its content but also subsequent literary forms and conventions. Both Job and Qohelet draw on other traditions of composition besides advice literature,

---

[34] Dell, 'Boundaries', 156.

[35] E.g., Michael V. Fox, 'Three Theses on Wisdom', in Sneed, *Was There a Wisdom Tradition?*, 79–82; Dell, 'Boundaries', 151, 149; Stuart Weeks, *An Introduction to the Study of Wisdom Literature* (London, 2010), 1; Schellenberg, 'Questioning', 394–395; Murphy, *Tree*, 102; Kynes, *Obituary*, 248.

[36] Weeks, *Introduction*, 2–3. Cf. Michael V. Fox, *Proverbs 1–9: A New Translation with Introduction and Commentary*, AB 19A (New York, 2000), 11, 17; Beaulieu, 'Babylonian', 7; Yoram Cohen, *Wisdom from the Late Bronze Age*, ed. Andrew R. George (Atlanta, 2013), 14–15.

[37] Beaulieu, 'Babylonian', 3, Cohen, *Wisdom*, 14–15; Weeks, *Introduction*, 126.

[38] Katharine Dell, *Get Wisdom Get Insight: An Introduction to Israel's Wisdom Literature* (London, 2000), 15–16; 'Boundaries', 145–149; Weeks, *Introduction*, 3–4; Fox, 'Theses', 79; Murphy, *Tree*, 154, 160; Shupak, 'Egyptian', 268, 285–286.

[39] See the discussions in Fox, *Proverbs*, 8–9, 18; Weeks, *Introduction*, 4.

so that 'if there are certain literary genres that play an important role in wisdom writing, it is also true that the writers did not confine themselves to those genres'.[40] The biblical wisdom books combine the advice literature genre with other genres, forms and content. Scholars have noted a number of other subsequent literary forms typical of ANE didactic or advice literature: didactic poems, fable/allegory, hymns/prayers, lists, *Streitgespräch* or dialogue and autobiographical narrative/confession, which are found in the biblical wisdom books to varying degrees.[41] Some of these forms, like dialogue, occur in other biblical literature, yet all the wisdom books display the primary forms of proverbs and instructions as a mark of their interest in advice or wisdom. Scholars agree that the primary content of wisdom literature is an interest in wisdom, and this interest extended beyond the simple conveyal of information to character formation – the transformation of the reader into a person who is wise and able to implement such wisdom into their life and actions. The content of wisdom also often includes a number of other themes or emphases: creation, a search for order, two ways, wisdom learned/observed and given by God, peace and life as the supreme good, Lady Wisdom and the fear of the Lord. Some of these themes, like creation, are found in other biblical literature as well, but all the wisdom books are concerned with conveying wisdom and character transformation into a person who is wise. Since some of these forms and themes occur in other biblical literature, we can expect to see points of contact with other texts. Yet wisdom is defined primarily by the forms found in ANE advice literature and its interest in wisdom and transformation into a wise person, and these serve as the main criteria for determining what is 'wisdom'.

THE SONG OF SONGS AS WISDOM LITERATURE

There is quite a large debate ensuing over wisdom as a biblical category or genre,[42] and this certainly complicates an endeavour to compare the Song to it. In my book, I identified where wisdom scholars seem to be agreeing in the discussion, concerning primary forms and content, as well as other forms and themes seen as typical of ANE didactic writing and commonly cited in wisdom discussions, in order to develop a model

---

[40] Weeks, *Introduction*, 5. Cf. Fox, 'Theses', 78; Murphy, *Tree*, 10.

[41] James Crenshaw, 'Wisdom (1974)', in *Urgent Advice and Probing Questions: Collected Writings on Old Testament Wisdom*, ed. James L. Crenshaw (Macon, 1995), 47; von Rad, *Wisdom*, 35–50; Beaulieu, 'Babylonian', 3, 4, 8, 17; Dell, 'Boundaries', 155.

[42] Will Kynes, 'The Modern Scholarly Wisdom Tradition and the Threat of Pan-Sapientialism: A Case Report', in Sneed, *Was There a Wisdom Tradition?*, 23, 32; Kynes 'Nineteenth', 99–102.

for comparing the Song to it.[43] What I will demonstrate is that the Song utilises a number of forms and conventions found in ANE didactic or advice literature, which are also found in the biblical wisdom books themselves. Space will not permit a full treatment of every wisdom form and theme found in the Song, but I will highlight a number and present arguments in favour of this position.

As noted above, there were two primary forms in ANE advice literature: the proverb and instructions passed on by an authoritative individual to the next generation. Both of these forms appear in the Song of Songs. The *mashal* or proverb appears in 8:6–7 to teach a general truth about love that the entire book is dedicated to displaying through its characters and their actions. It expresses a common experience with memorable words. Those who have been in love truly know that love is as strong as death, jealousy as unyielding as the grave and that it burns like an unquenchable mighty flame. It exhibits characteristics that many argue define the proverb: metrical form and rhythmic structure, parallelism (here, synonymous), consonantal and vocalic assonance, a terse (condensed) and vivid style, observational tone, a similitude eluci- dating the likeness between two situations or phenomena, a structure giving a topic + comment/description and a general truth made clear with images and examples.[44] It illustrates one of the most common but import- ant experiences in human relationships, drawing analogies between nature and the experience of being in love, in order to help readers further understand and therefore master love by noting a regular pattern: those who awaken love encounter powerful forces of emotion. As Exum notes, 'one aphorism does not a wisdom book make',[45] but as we will see, the presence of other forms will push this impression further.

In the Song, advice is also passed on to future generations in the 'do not awaken' instructions given to the daughters of Jerusalem in 2:7, 3:5 and 8:4. Just as instruction was often passed down to the next gener- ation in advice literature by using the 'father-son' literary convention, provocatively in the Song, it is passed down from the woman to daugh- ters, for she is the foremost authority on love in the text. This has been established by the superlative nature of her love relationship

---

[43] Andruska, *Wise and Foolish*, ch. 4.

[44] Otto Eissfeldt, *Der Maschal im Alten Testament*, BZAW 24 (Giessen, 1913), 48–52; Suzanna R. Millar, *Genre and Openness in Proverbs 10:1–22:16*, AIL 39 (Atlanta, 2020), 7, 20, 31–32, 36–37. Cf. James Crenshaw, *Old Testament Wisdom: An Introduction*, 3rd ed. (Atlanta, 2010), 62–63; Dell, *Get Wisdom*, 15, Weeks, *Introduction*, 4; Murphy, *Tree*, 7–8.

[45] Exum, 'Unity', 67.

throughout the book; the title of the book itself is a superlative: *šîr haššîrîm* ('the song above all songs').[46] She has lived her love life successfully and found love, accrediting her the authority to impart advice to the next generation, so that they might also find the same type of love in their own lives. Instructions from a previous generation were a recognisable feature of the advice literature genre.[47] This type of instruction would immediately signal to the reader that they were encountering a didactic genre.

I have argued that these refrains are instructing the audience, the daughters of Jerusalem, and by extension the reader, not to awaken love until the type of love displayed throughout the Song is present.[48]

'im tā'îrû wə'im tə'ôrərû 'et-hā'ahăbâ 'ad šettehpāṣ

Do not arouse or awaken love until it desires[49]

The *he* in *hā'ahăbâ* is anaphoric, pointing to the love being described and displayed throughout the Song, *'wr* is best translated as 'arouse/awaken' and *'ad šettehpāṣ* is elliptical, so that one is not to arouse 'that love' within themselves until 'that love', *the type of love described throughout the Song*, desires to awaken or is present. The refrain also indicates how one is to know that love is present, that it has 'desired to awaken'. For if *hā'ahăbâ* refers to the love displayed throughout the Song and *'ad šettehpāṣ* is elliptical, then it is also the presence of 'that love', the type of love displayed throughout the Song, that shows that love is actually present. Love's presence is defined by *its similarity to the type of love depicted throughout the Song between the lovers.*

'Awakening' occurs throughout the Song. The poem opens in *medias res* with their love awakened and him kissing her. Spring awakens and blossoms with the awakening of their love in 2:12–13, 6:11 and 7:13–14. The day awakens or 'breathes' as the shadows flee in 2:17 and 4:6. In 4:16, she calls on the north wind to *'wr* ('awaken') and the south wind to come blow upon her garden as he comes into it to eat of its luscious fruits. She awakens to search for her lover in chapters three and five, and in 5:2 she uses the same verb *'wr* to explain that her heart was 'awake' whilst she slept. If the MT of 7:10 [ET 7:9] is correct that her

---

[46] A singular noun in the construct state before the same noun in the plural is used to express the superlative in Hebrew, see GKC §133i.

[47] Stuart Weeks, 'Wisdom, Form and Genre' in Sneed, *Was There a Wisdom Tradition?*, 166.

[48] Andruska, *Wise and Foolish*, 45–61, esp. 59–60.

[49] My translation.

mouth is like the best wine *dôbēb śiptê yəšēnîm* ('gliding over sleeping lips'), then she awakens him with kisses, and in 8:5 she has *'wr* ('aroused/awakened') him under the apple tree.[50] The love of the couple is clearly already awakened or present. So the female lover must mean that the audience, the daughters of Jerusalem and by extension the reader, is not to cause (*tā'îrû* is a *hifil* imperfect, causative active, and *tə'ōrərû* is a *polel* imperfect, intensive causative active) that type of love to awaken where it is not yet present, within themselves, before that love, the love being described throughout the Song, is actually present.

Even apart from the *he*'s anaphoric function, the Song has been defining what 'love' is and looks like when it awakens throughout its discourse, so that the elliptical nature of *'ad šettehpāṣ* ('when love desires to awaken/be present') is still defined by its similarity to the love in the Song. The poet didactically shows us, through the lovers' speeches and actions, what love looks like when it is present, when it has desired to awaken. As many Songs commentators observe,[51] the love displayed between the unmarried lovers in the Song is mutual, peaceful, equal, proactive, devoted, desirous, erotic, exclusive, committed and timeless or abiding – a love that seems to go on forever. This list is not meant to be exhaustive or to provide a checklist of character traits but rather to describe what typifies the type of relationship depicted in the Song. It is 'that love's' presence or absence that shows whether a love like the Song *is* present. This is what it looks like when love has desired to awaken. The refrains advise one not to awaken this love within themselves until this type of love is actually present, for as the *mashal* or proverb in 8:6–7 shows, love is extremely powerful. It is then wise to be careful whom, or what type of relationship, one awakens this powerful emotion for.

The Song of Songs stands out from other ANE love songs in a few important ways that indicate that it is attempting to do something different with the love song genre and has a didactic aim. First is its

---

[50] Contra some commentators (e.g., Fox, *Songs*, 109–110) who understand *'wr* as 'disturb' in the refrains, *'wr* would not be properly translated as 'disturb' in 4:16, 5:2 or 8:5.

[51] Exum, *Songs*; Fox, *Songs*; F. W. Dobbs-Allsopp, 'The Delight of Beauty and the Song of Songs 4:1–7', *Int* 59.3 (2005): 270–271; Murphy, *Songs*; Tremper Longman III, *Song of Songs*, NICOT (Grand Rapids, 2001); Dianne Bergant, 'My Beloved Is Mine and I Am His (Song 2:16): The Song of Songs and Honor and Shame', *Semeia* 68 (1994): 23–40; Daniel Grossberg, 'Two Kinds of Sexual Relationships in the Hebrew Bible', *HS* 35 (1994): 1–25; Carol Meyers, 'Gender Imagery in the Song of Songs', *HAR* 10 (1986): 209–223.

inclusion of wisdom forms. There are no other examples of ANE love song texts that are instructional or attempt to give advice that one *should* pursue a certain type of love.[52] Even if we set aside the content of the instruction in the refrains and the *mashal* in 8:6–7, it is the very occurrence of the forms themselves that is unusual. There are no other ANE love songs, or at least none that are currently extant, that stop or cut in to give instruction to the audience or make any type of general or objective statement about love. The fact that the Song of Songs stops to instruct the audience to do anything concerning love or gives a general reflection on love is really very different from anything we see in the antecedent love literature. These forms themselves, regardless of their content, are wisdom forms – instruction and proverb.

The Song of Songs also stands out from other ANE love songs in the specific type of relationship that it displays. Love songs throughout the ANE depict a variety of lovers in different types of love relationships, attempting to show what it feels like to be in love in various types of situations. The Song of Songs, by contrast, presents one consistent picture of its lovers, their personalities and the type of relationship they share throughout. Unlike other ANE love songs, the Song of Songs does not include depictions of unrequited love, abandonment, rejection, pouting resentment, passive sexual fantasising, suspicion, infidelity, disappointed hopes or the separation of lovers by fate. Yearning after a faded romance, the agony of unrequited love or the betrayal of unfaithfulness are common motifs in love poetry, yet these topics are noticeably absent from the Song of Songs. Love is never presented as unrequited or non-exclusive. These are not pictures of love that the Song wishes to demonstrate. This is because, as Fox notes,[53] the Song of Songs is concerned to present a *particular vision of love* displayed in a

---

[52]   As an examination of the following shows: *ANET*; *COS*; Nathan Wasserman, *Akkadian Love Literature of the Third and Second Millennium BCE*, Leipziger Altorientalistische Studien 4 (Wiesbaden, 2016); Fox, *Songs*; Martti Nissinen, 'Love Lyrics of Nabû and Tašmetu: An Assyrian Song of Songs?' in *'Und Moses schrieb diese Lied auf' Studien zum Alten Testament und zum alten Orient. Festschrift für Oswald Loretz zur Vollendung seines 70. Lebensjahres*, ed. von Manfried Dietrich and Ingo Kottsieper, AOAT 250 (Münster, 1998), 585–634; Wilfred G. E. Watson, 'Some Ancient Near Eastern Parallels to the Song of Songs', in *Words Remembered Texts Renewed: Essays in Honour of John F. A. Sawyer*, ed. John Davies, Graham Harvey and Wilfred G. E. Watson, JSOTSup 195 (Sheffield, 1995), 253–271; Joan Goodnick Westenholz, 'Love Lyrics from the Ancient Near East', *CANE* IV (New York, 1995), 2471–2486.

[53]   Fox, *Songs*, 220–225, 259–262, 264, 296–297, 305, 316, 324–326, 330; cf. Exum, *Songs*, 9; Exum, 'The Poetic Genius of the Song of Songs' in Hagedorn, *Perspectives on the Song of Songs*, 79.

particular type of love relationship between particular types of lovers as the *highest knowledge of love,* and I would add, its *superlative display.* Again, the title of the book itself is a superlative: *šîr haššîrîm.* I have proposed that this is because it has a didactic aim: it has one clear vision of what love *should* look like.[54] It is not presenting different forms of love or types of lovers but one specific type of love relationship that is to be aimed at and striven for. The Song of Songs stands out from other ANE love songs, not only in its presentation of a specific type of love relationship but also *in its instruction to awaken love for this type of love relationship, and not others.* The adjurations are strong appeals asking the audience to swear by oath not to do something, not to arouse love within themselves when the love of the Song is not present, for relationships that do not reflect the love of the Song, for example, relationships that are unrequited, one-sided, unfaithful, non-exclusive, lacking commitment, transitory, full of conflict, lacking desire or the resolve and devotion to pursue the other whole-heartedly. This is wisdom. For as many other ANE love songs and love songs throughout history show, these relationships often result in pain and heartbreak. Those who expose themselves to these powerful emotions when they do not share the type of love displayed in the Song often get hurt. The Song advises wisdom in the *type of relationship* one awakens love for.

The Song is not pure instruction. It is a love poem that incorporates instruction to communicate its wisdom message. Job and Qohelet are also not pure instruction, and they do not contain instruction prologues. Jacqueline Vayntrub has recently argued that Proverbs is not pure instruction, as it has the wrong type of prologue: it does not name the protagonist who gives the spoken instruction on a particular occasion.[55] Whether these biblical books are 'instruction' in the ANE sense of the word can be debated, yet they all incorporate instruction within their discourse. The Song is not pure instruction or a collection of proverbs, but it incorporates these wisdom forms, and their presence really is something very different from what we see in other ANE love songs. None of these forms alone show that the Song is wisdom, but their accumulation indicates that the Song is doing something very different from other ANE love songs by using forms commonly associated with wisdom.

---

[54] Andruska, *Wise and Foolish,* 148–153, esp. 153.
[55] Jacqueline Vayntrub, 'The Book of Proverbs and the Idea of Ancient Israelite Education', *ZAW* 128.1 (2016): 96–114.

The primary forms used in ANE advice literature appear in the Song. Scholars have noted a number of other forms typical of ANE didactic or advice literature and found in the biblical material to varying degrees: long didactic poems, fable/allegory, hymns/prayers, lists, *Streitgespräch* or dialogue and autobiographical narrative/confession.[56] With the exception of hymns/prayers all are found in the Song.[57] It can be debated whether these secondary forms should be included as criteria for defining 'wisdom', but what I am attempting to show is that the primary forms in ANE advice literature occur in the Song, as well as a number of these secondary features that have been discussed for many years now. Whilst space does not permit a full treatment,[58] I will briefly look at autobiographical narrative/confession.

In the ANE, wisdom's emphasis on experience gave rise to a confessional style in which the writer instructed through autobiographical narrative, recounting their own experience. This is similar to the instructions given by an authoritative individual except that in autobiographical narrative it is related as the sage's personal experience and discovery. The book of Proverbs contains small autobiographical narratives where the reader is taught by the experience of the author.[59] These didactic narrative poems often preserved a stereotyped didactic allusion, such as the 'fate of the wicked', and aimed to instruct through a specific context of events.[60] The entire Song employs a similar method, autobiographically describing the love of the couple in order to guide the reader in their own pursuit of love. The lovers recount their own experience, which is presented entirely as personal discovery, in order to instruct the reader and show them what type of relationship to awaken love for. The stereotyped didactic allusion is to 'when love has awakened' or is present, and the fulfilment that comes from waiting to awaken, and therefore finding, this type of love. It teaches, through a specific context of events, important lessons about how love is meant to look and what it looks like when it has awakened, allowing the

---

[56] See n. 54.

[57] Didactic poems: 3:1–4; 5:2–7; 2:10–14; 7:11–13; 4:1–7, 9–15; 5:10–16; 6:4–10; 7:1–9a; 8:6–7. Fable/allegory: 4:12–5:1; 2:15–16, etc. Lists: 6:8, 2:11–17, 4:1–5:1, 5:11–16, 6:5–11, 7:2–14. *Streitgespräch* or dialogue: throughout and 5:9–16 (contest discussion). Autobiographical narrative/confession: 1:5–6; 2:1–7; 2:8–14; 3:1–5; 4:9–5:1; 5:2–8; 6:5; 6:10; 8:1–5; 8:6–7; 8:12, etc.

[58] See the full treatment of these forms in Andruska, *Wise and Foolish*, 115–123.

[59] E.g., Prov 7:6–23; see Crenshaw, 'Wisdom', 75, 70; Dell, *Get Wisdom*, 16; Robert Alter, *The Art of Biblical Poetry* (New York, 1985), 57.

[60] Von Rad, *Wisdom*, 38, 46.

characters to show that it is mutual, peaceful, equal, devoted, exclusive, committed and timeless. The lovers' experience in finding this type of love accredits them the authority to communicate this instruction. Just as Robert Alter notes that Proverbs 7 takes a common metaphor in Proverbs – going on a way or path – and assigns it a 'strong narrative realization' in Proverbs 7,[61] the Song takes its own metaphor for wise love – when to awaken love – which is a sort of didactic allusion to a straight path in love and gives it a strong narrative realisation and concretisation throughout the Song. The lovers are the narrative realisation of when to awaken love, giving a concretisation to the path that the 'do not awaken' refrains instruct others to follow.

The Song also displays content typical of ANE advice literature. The main content of wisdom literature was an interest in wisdom, and this interest extended beyond the conveyal of information to character formation – the transformation of the reader into a person who is wise and able to implement such wisdom into their life and actions.[62] All the wisdom books are interested in wisdom and seek to impart wisdom concerning various topics. The Song of Songs shares this interest in wisdom, that is, wisdom concerning love. The Song is certainly about 'love' rather than the topic of wisdom in general, yet a number of wisdom books convey wisdom concerning particular topics. Job could be seen as wisdom concerning innocent suffering just as Qohelet could be seen as wisdom concerning the transience of human existence. The Song of Songs is wisdom concerning love. The Song is love poetry, but the structuring of the refrains and the *mashal* and its numerous wisdom features reveal the purpose of the book: to impart wisdom concerning love.

The Song's interest in wisdom goes beyond the conveyal of knowledge or information as it seeks to transform the reader through character formation into a lover who is wise.[63] As Exum has noted, the Song invites the audience, and by extension the reader, to participate in and partake of their relationship. Songs 5:1 explicitly invites us to participate in their love and, as Exum says, 'become lovers as well: "Eat, friends, drink yourselves drunk on embraces!"'[64] As she notes, the Song also invites its readers to identify with the lovers themselves.[65] The anonymity of the lovers, their non-specific identities and physical

---

[61] Alter, *Poetry*, 61.
[62] Weeks, *Introduction*, 123.
[63] See the extensive discussion in Andruska, *Wise and Foolish*, ch. 6, esp. 153–176.
[64] Exum, *Songs*, 158, 110, 7.
[65] Exum, *Songs*, 8–9.

features, is a literary device that allows them to be universally relatable to all readers who can, therefore, identify with them. It allows the woman to represent all women and the man to represent all men. That is, their anonymity serves to *enable reader identification*. It allows readers, as Temper Longman says, to 'place themselves in the position of the woman and the man'.[66] Yet, whilst their identities are non-specific, they are specific types of lovers with discernible and consistent character traits. The lovers are not specific individuals or identifiable historical people but rather literary characters constructed to represent lovers who display a specific type of character, again, in a particular type of love relationship.[67] That is, the lovers that we identify with are not just any lovers but specific types of lovers in a particular type of relationship, who represent the highest knowledge of love: *wise lovers*. The experience of love that we are invited to participate in is not just any experience of love but a specific type of love experience that is distinct from the various types of love experiences depicted in other ANE love songs. The Song aims to inspire us, not only to become lovers ourselves but *the particular type of lovers they are*. Its invitation to participate in their love is an invitation to participate in *the particular type of love relationship they display*. We are meant to identify with these lovers because we are meant to emulate them by participating in a similar type of love relationship, so that we find the same type of love they enjoy.[68]

Like all biblical wisdom literature, the Song's approach to character has its roots in ANE forms, particularly Egyptian instruction, in which a certain character, who embodies prudence, wisdom and success in life, is profiled to lend coherence to instruction.[69] In the Song, the lovers embody these wise characteristics in love and are profiled to lend coherence to the instruction in the refrains, because like Egyptian instruction, emulation is, as William Brown describes it, 'the central feature of the intended relationship between the reader, who is to appropriate the wise teachings, and the character profiled in the literature'.[70] The Song encourages readers to identify with the lovers, invites them to participate in their experience of love and directs them towards pursuing a similar type of love because it aims to transform its readers, through character formation, into wise lovers themselves.

---

[66] Longman, *Songs*, 91.
[67] Exum, *Songs*, 96–97; Exum, 'Poetic', 83 n.14.
[68] See Andruska, *Wise and Foolish*, 153–160.
[69] William P. Brown, *Character in Crisis: A Fresh Approach to the Wisdom Literature of the Old Testament* (Grand Rapids, 1996), 19–20.
[70] Brown, *Character*, 20.

The Song displays the primary content typical of ANE advice literature. Biblical wisdom is also thought to have included a number of other
themes or emphases commonly associated with wisdom writing: creation, a search for order, two ways or choices, wisdom learned/observed
and given by God, peace and life as the supreme good, Lady Wisdom and
the fear of the Lord. With the exception of the fear of the Lord theme, all
of these are found in the Song,[71] though the idea of reverent fear is not
totally absent. The Song has particularly strong parallels with Lady
Wisdom, as a significant portion of the language and motifs used to
describe Lady Wisdom in Proverbs, Sirach and Wisdom of Solomon
derive from the Song of Songs.[72] This list of themes is of course debated,
and different scholars would see some of these emphases as more
important than others, but what I am attempting to show is that the
Song evidences the primary content of wisdom literature and a number
of these other themes and emphases as well. The pervasiveness of these
secondary forms and themes in the Song has been treated extensively
elsewhere.[73]

Crenshaw suggested that, 'when a marriage between form and content exists, there is Wisdom literature. Lacking such oneness, a given
text participates in biblical wisdom to a greater or lesser extent'.[74]
Stuart Weeks suggests the idea of a graph with formal and thematic
axes, so that any text 'can be assigned coordinates which place it in
relation to the area where our wisdom books cluster'.[75] If one were to
construct such a graph with formal and thematic axes, assigning a point
for each form and theme that occurs, then the Song would sit quite
comfortably among the other wisdom books.[76] Such a model would not
account for the number of occurrences of various forms and themes in
the different books, which would also need to be looked at in relation to
the length of the book as a whole to determine pervasiveness. Perhaps
the primary forms and content should have more points than the secondary forms and themes. Some scholars would want to debate some of
these forms or rank certain themes or emphases as being more important or having more points on the graph than others. Such a model could
be adjusted in a number of ways and would be a complicated endeavour,

---

[71] See the full treatment of these themes in Andruska, *Wise and Foolish*, 123–138,
      172–173.
[72] See the extensive discussion of this in Andruska, *Wise and Foolish*, 131–136, cf. 42.
[73] Andruska, *Wise and Foolish*, 112–138.
[74] Crenshaw, *OT Wisdom*, 12.
[75] Weeks, *Introduction*, 143.
[76] See this graph constructed in Andruska, *Wise and Foolish*, 138–141.

as it would require wisdom scholars to agree on which forms and themes should be included, how heavily they should be weighed (number of points) and how extensively they are displayed in the various books, within a given number of verses, depending on how narrowly or broadly they are defined. There is no consensus within wisdom discussions about such things.

What I have attempted to demonstrate is that a number of the features that have been observed in wisdom writing for many years now – forms and conventions, themes and emphases – appear in the Song of Songs. The Song evidences a pervasiveness of wisdom forms and themes throughout, which are determinate for the structure, focus and overall purpose of the book, and this is why Solomon's name appears in the superscription. It links the book with the wisdom tradition.

CONCLUSION

The Song of Songs has combined elements of the ANE love song and advice literature genres to produce a wisdom literature about romantic love. This conclusion is based on a broader understanding of what was typical of ANE didactic or advice literature, as well as biblical wisdom, rather than on specific parallels between the Song and the biblical wisdom books alone. I have focused on the wisdom forms and conventions used in the Song and shown how strange it is that these are occurring in a love song at all. The number of these forms, themes and conventions, and the fact that they are woven so intricately throughout the work, makes it unlikely that these didactic elements are mere editorial glosses giving it a sapiential flavour. The *mashal*, superscription and 'do not awaken' instructions supply an overall structure and purpose to the book, showing that the entire work is devoted to depicting the truth of what they teach, through autobiographical narrative and characterisation. The depiction of the lovers' relationship throughout is the concretisation and didactic narrative realisation of when love has awakened, or when 'that love' is present, and this means that its wisdom message is intricately woven through the entire book. The Song evidences a pervasiveness of forms, conventions and content typical of ANE didactic or advice literature, that is, what we call 'wisdom'.

The purpose of this exploration into the Song's use of these conventions is not to label the Song as 'wisdom' proper, or to have it categorised as such, but rather to understand what the presence of these features means for the interpretation of the Song itself. The Song of

Songs is clearly a love song, yet it also does something quite different from other ancient Near Eastern love song texts by combining the love song genre with the ancient Near Eastern advice literature genre to produce a wisdom literature about romantic love and how to pursue love wisely. These connections to wisdom in the Song are extensive enough to change the way that we understand the book. The Song is not just a celebration of love or entertainment but is providing wisdom concerning romantic love.

Further Reading

Andruska, J. L. *Wise and Foolish Love in the Song of Songs*. Leiden: 2019.

Clark, Rosalind 'Seeking Wisdom in the Song of Songs'. Pages 100–112 in *Exploring Old Testament Wisdom: Literature and Themes*. Edited by David G. Firth and Lindsay Wilson. London: 2016.

Dell, Katharine. 'Does the Song of Songs Have Any Connections to Wisdom?'. Pages 8–26 in *Perspectives on the Song of Songs/*. Edited by Anselm C. Hagedorn. BZAW 346. Berlin: 2005.

Exum, J. Cheryl. 'Unity, Date, Authorship and the "Wisdom" of the Song of Songs'. Pages 53–68 in *Goochem in Mokum/ Wisdom in Amsterdam*. Edited by George J. Brooke and Pierre van Hecke. OtSt 68. Leiden: 2016.

Murphy, Roland E. *The Tree of Life: An Exploration of Biblical Wisdom Literature*. Grand Rapids: 1990.

Sadgrove, Michael. 'The Song of Songs as Wisdom Literature'. Pages 245–248 in Papers on the Old Testament and Related Themes, vol. 1 of Studia Biblica 1978: Sixth International Congress on Biblical Studies, Oxford, 3–7. April 1978, Edited by E. A. Livingstone. JSOTSup 11. Sheffield: 1979.

Schellenberg, Annette. 'Questioning the Trend of Classifying the Song of Songs as Sapiential'. Pages 393–407 in *Nächstenliebe und Gottesfurcht: Beiträge aus alttestamentlicher, semitistischer und altorientalistischer Wissenschaft für Hans-Peter Mathys zum 65. Geburtstag*. Edited by Hanna Jenni and Markus Saur. AOAT. Münster: 2016.

Schwab, George M. *The Song of Songs' Cautionary Message concerning Human Love*. StBibLit 41. New York: 2002.

Sparks, Kenton L. 'The Song of Songs: Wisdom for Young Jewish Women'. *CBQ* 70.2 (2008): 277–299.

12 Wisdom Psalms

SIMON CHI-CHUNG CHEUNG

A quick survey of recent works on wisdom psalms will show that research on this group of psalms has been described as 'a difficult, and contestable, endeavor',[1] a topic of 'great debate',[2] characterised by 'great divergence and shifting opinions',[3] so that their many aspects 'have largely remained an unresolved riddle',[4] and our understanding of them 'is as elusive as ever'.[5] The task to nominate which psalms to be sapiential suffers the most severe criticism. James Crenshaw likens the return of such an enterprise to 'gold dust' of little worth,[6] and William Brown declares, noting the minimal consensus on the candidacy for these psalms, that 'the project fails'.[7] Brown therefore reiterates an earlier suggestion that future work on wisdom psalms should turn away from the purely taxonomic concern to expend more effort to examine the 'interaction' between the psalmic tradition and wisdom.[8] Granted that this new line of research is of considerable value, it still has to begin with a sample of psalms which are believably influenced by

[1] Catherine Petrany, *Pedagogy, Prayer and Praise: The Wisdom of the Psalms and the Psalter*, FAT 2 83 (Tübingen, 2015), 21.

[2] William H. Bellinger Jr., 'Psalms and the Question of Genre', in *The Oxford Handbook of the Psalms*, ed. William P. Brown (Oxford, 2014), 321.

[3] John L. McLaughlin, *An Introduction to Israel's Wisdom Traditions* (Grand Rapids, 2018), 153.

[4] Erhard S. Gerstenberger, 'Non-Temple Psalms: The Cultic Setting Revisited', in *The Oxford Handbook of the Psalms*, 343.

[5] Diane Jacobson, 'Wisdom Language in the Psalms', in *The Oxford Handbook of the Psalms*, 155.

[6] James L. Crenshaw, 'Gold Dust or Nuggets? A Brief Response to J. Kenneth Kuntz', *CurR* 1.2 (2003): 157.

[7] William P. Brown, 'Psalms', in *The Wiley Blackwell Companion to Wisdom Literature*, ed. Samuel L. Adams and Matthew Goff (Hoboken; Chichester, 2020), 71.

[8] William P. Brown, '"Come, O Children … I Will Teach You the Fear of the Lord" (Psalm 34:12): Comparing Psalms and Proverbs', in *Seeking Out the Wisdom of the Ancients: Essays Offered to Honor Michael V. Fox on the Occasion of His Sixty-Fifth Birthday*, ed. Ronald L. Troxel, Kelvin G. Friebel and Dennis R. Magary (Winona Lake, 2005), 85–120; Brown, 'Psalms', 81.

wisdom, and that makes the question of identification inevitable. Besides, numerous studies on the editorial shape and shaping of the Psalter also draw heavily on the wisdom psalm research. Various scholars allege that the final form of the Psalter has been heavily 'sapientialized' so as to turn this collection of prayers and hymns into a book to be studied and meditated upon.[9] Markus Saur, for instance, claims that it is more productive to study wisdom psalms in association with the 'sapiential impregnation' that takes place in the Psalter through placing these psalms at critical points in the book.[10] Nevertheless, the success of that claim depends partly, if not entirely, on how he discerns the presence of wisdom influence in the book of Psalms. Further discussions on this type of psalm should not be limited to those of its recognition, nor can they evade it.

This chapter seeks to study the 'wisdom psalm' problem afresh by drawing insights from genre theories. In her instructive essay on genre criticism, Jeannie Brown helpfully sketches the history of development of genre studies by specialists outside the guild of biblical studies. The dispute over the value and practice of genre classification has long existed since the age of Aristotle until now. Contemporary studies of genre attempt to illuminate the pragmatic side of a genre, portraying the deployment of a certain genre as an authorial decision to accomplish the author's specific communicative goal. With these theoretical developments in mind, Brown asserts that well-informed 'genre awareness and analysis' may offer considerable inputs for the discipline of biblical studies.[11] This, I think, is particularly the case of the 'wisdom psalms'. Adducing the insights from the genre theorists, I want to delineate this category of psalms as a family that includes psalms of graded degrees of membership and is identifiable by a wisdom-oriented constellation of its generic elements, made manifest in several salient features which

---

[9] See the incisive summary in Susan E. Gillingham, '"I Will Incline My Ear to a Proverb; I Will Solve My Riddle to the Music of the Harp" (Psalm 49.4): The Wisdom Tradition and the Psalms', in *Perspectives on Israelite Wisdom: Proceedings of the Oxford Old Testament Seminar*, ed. John Jarick, LHBOTS 618 (London; 2016), 279–282.

[10] Markus Saur, 'Where Can Wisdom Be Found? New Perspectives on the Wisdom Psalms', in *Was There a Wisdom Tradition: New Prospects in Israelite Wisdom Studies*, ed. Mark R. Sneed, AIL 23 (Atlanta, 2015), 181–204.

[11] Jeannine K. Brown, 'Genre Criticism and the Bible', in *Words and the Word: Explorations in Biblical Interpretation and Literary Theory*, ed. David G. Firth and Jamie Grant (Nottingham, 2008), 111–150.

are appropriate to its communication goal.[12] Psalm 34 will be adduced as a test case for illustrating the issues in question.

A CATEGORY TO BE WIPED OFF THE MAP

Disagreement over the definition and configuration of a specific genre is common in the discussion of genres within any medium. 'Maps' are drawn to represent the system of genres and are invariably disputed.[13] For the psalmic literature, Hermann Gunkel charted the most well-known 'map' of its kind, and 'wisdom poem' is one landscape found on his map,[14] although this term was already in use in the nineteenth-century German scholarship.[15] Gunkel does not include the 'wisdom poems' within other mainstream psalm genres, recognising that they arose late in the history of ancient Israel from a setting that was distinct from those of the other genres.[16] To him, the form of 'addresses' (*Anreden*), occasionally designated explicitly as 'wisdom', 'teaching', a 'riddle' or a 'proverb', dominates this category of psalms, which are composed to admonish or teach. Other content-related indicators, which some later interpreters may regard as formal elements, of the presence of instructions include the expression *hinnēh*, 'better than' sayings, the use of similes, rhetorical questions, numerical sayings, the beatific formula and the autobiographic style. The doctrines on the contrastive profiles and consequent fates of the righteous and the wicked, as well as the question of theodicy, in Gunkel's depiction of wisdom poems, are the most prominent topics of instructions. As for their provenance, Gunkel firmly believes that they had their origin outside the cult but, thanks to their popularity, were later introduced into the worship service by the cultic functionaries.[17]

---

[12]   Simon Chi-chung Cheung, *Wisdom Intoned: A Reappraisal of the Genre 'Wisdom Psalms'*, LHBOTS 613 (New York; London, 2015).

[13]   Daniel Chandler, 'An Introduction to Genre Theory', 1997, 1, www.aber.ac.uk/media/ Documents/intgenre/chandler_genre_theory.pdf. Accessed on 19 May 2020.

[14]   Hermann Gunkel and Joachim Begrich, *Introduction to Psalms: The Genres of Religious Lyrics of Israel*, trans. James D. Nogalski, Mercer Library of Biblical Studies (Macon, 1998). Translated from the German original *Einleitung in die Psalmen: Die Gattungen der religiösen Lyrik Israels*. HKAT (Göttingen, 1933)

[15]   Johann Friedrich Bruch, *Weisheit-Lehre der Hebräer: Ein Beitrag zur Geschichte der Philosophie* (Strassburg, 1851), 150–151; Otto Zöckler, *Die Sprüche Salomonis: Theologisch-Homiletisch Bearbeitet* (Bielefeld; Leipzig, 1867), 14.

[16]   Gunkel and Begrich, *Introduction to Psalms*, 21 (German original, 30).

[17]   Gunkel and Begrich, *Introduction to Psalms*, 293–305 (German original, 381–397).

Gunkel's scheme of configuring wisdom psalms suffers from a lack of clarity. He does not make a very clear distinction between the formal and thematic markers of wisdom. In enumerating what constitutes 'teaching', Gunkel seems to have interlaced a list of both formal and thematic markers, leaving a lot of clarifications to be made. Besides, Gunkel insists that there should be no problem to include wisdom sayings in the Psalter (like Psalms 127 and 133) in the same literary group with other psalms that assert or question the divine retributive justice (like 1, 37, 49, 73, 91, 112 and 128). He argues that all these psalms share the same subject matter and are unified in form. However, not all of the so-called sapiential forms are found across the board in all these psalms, so commentators look askance at the degree of cohesion alleged to exist among these psalms. Moreover, as Gunkel readily admits, wisdom expressions or ideas have intruded the other lyrical *Gattungen*, such as the thanksgiving songs, hymns, individual laments and the mixed type of poetry. In reverse, some of what he calls 'wisdom poems' are influenced by these other psalm types. In Psalm 73, classed as a 'wisdom poem' by him, there is a clear section of lament. The motif of expressing trust in Yahweh, which is unusual in wisdom psalms, was interpolated by a 'late hand' into Psalm 49, another of Gunkel's 'wisdom poems'.[18] While he acknowledges mutual infiltration of wisdom psalms and other psalm types, Gunkel does not quite clearly explain how he decides if a certain psalm is wisdom influenced by lament, so to speak, or a lament exhibiting some wisdom features.

Not a few subsequent works avoid the term 'wisdom psalms' or disavow its usefulness as a genre label. For one, Sigmund Mowinckel prefers the title 'learned psalmography', accentuating both the compositional role of the educated class as well as the nature of such poetry as 'prayers'.[19] Scribes and temple officials were in constant contact in ancient Israel and exchanged knowledge on cultic conventions and the so-called wisdom mode of writing and thinking. As traditionalists, these learned men made their own attempts to compose psalms, both as a pious art and to preserve the long-standing conventions and rules guiding human-divine interactions. The latter purpose, hence, marks

---

[18] Gunkel and Begrich, *Introduction to Psalms*, 298–299 (German original, 387–389).

[19] Sigmund Mowinckel, 'Psalms and Wisdom', in *Wisdom in Israel and in the Ancient Near East: Presented to H. H. Rowley by the Society for Old Testament Study in Association with the Editorial Board of Vetus Testamentum, in Celebration of His Sixty-Fifth Birthday, 24 March 1955*, ed. Martin Noth and D. Winton Thomas, VTSup 3 (Leiden, 1955), 205–224; Sigmund Mowinckel, *Praise in Israel's Worship* (Grand Rapids, 1962), 2:104–125.

such a group of psalms with strong didacticism. Besides, patent resonances with poetry attested in the wisdom books can be recognised in them. Alongside Gunkel, Mowinckel places the origin of these psalms outside the temple. Without the binding power of the cult, these 'learned psalms' slowly showed signs of degeneration, an evolvement which is poorly esteemed by Mowinckel as 'a disintegration of style'.[20]

That 'wisdom psalms' are alleged to be non-cultic has sparked off the categorical rejection of their existence by Ivan Engnell.[21] Engnell maintains that all psalms can and must be interpreted as cultic poetry.[22] It is interesting to note that he does not oppose the idea that the nature of the Psalter was made didactic by its collectors and editors,[23] a proposition frequently shared in recent decades by editorial critics of the Psalter. However, to Engnell, it is not necessary to have a category of wisdom psalms to transform the book's nature. More persistently, Crenshaw argues that the genre label 'wisdom psalms' should be left in disuse. He avers that the search for wisdom-specific criteria is futile, noting first that the so-called wisdom themes suggested for identifying wisdom psalms can just be easily found in non-wisdom literature. Amos, for instance, airs in his social critique (5:5–15) a sharp distinction between the righteous and the wicked, and the two-path imagery and the doctrine of divine retribution are clearly evident in Amos' prophetic tirade.[24] Second, the criterial formal features are also not qualified as wisdom markers, to Crenshaw, because they 'do not constitute unique stylistic features of the sages'.[25] He therefore prefers to speak of psalms which 'resemble wisdom literature'[26] or 'psalms with affinities to wisdom'.[27] Such a proposed change in title reflects Crenshaw's caution over the laxity of assigning sapiential authorship and of attributing to

---

[20] Mowinckel, *Praise in Israel's Worship*, 2:111. In an earlier work, he rather disdainfully commented that the didactic poems (*Lehrgedichte*) of Psalms 1 and 112 are standing at a rather low standard in terms of psalmic style. See Sigmund Mowinckel, *Psalmenstudien V: Segen und Fluchen in Israels Kult und Psalmdichtung* (Amsterdam, 1923), 123–126.

[21] Ivan Engnell, *Critical Essays on the Old Testament*, trans. John T. Willis (London, 1970), 68–122, esp. 99–103. Translated from Swedish original *Svenskt Bibliskt Uppslagsverk* (Stockholm, 1962).

[22] Psalm 137 may be a possible exception. See Engnell, *Critical Essays on the Old Testament*, 103.

[23] Engnell, *Critical Essays on the Old Testament*, 99.

[24] James L. Crenshaw, 'Wisdom Psalms?', *CurBS* 8 (2000): 10–11.

[25] Crenshaw, 'Wisdom Psalms?', 11.

[26] Crenshaw, 'Wisdom Psalms?', 15.

[27] James L. Crenshaw, *Old Testament Wisdom: An Introduction*, 3rd ed. (Louisville, 2010), 187–194.

the sages interests or involvement in the cultic sphere.[28] Moreover, in
his brief response to his critic, Kenneth Kuntz, who favours the stance
that the sages have sapientialised the Psalter by placing wisdom psalms
at critical junctures of the book,[29] Crenshaw takes this view to task.[30]
Apart from the unsettled disputes over their cultic/non-cultic origin,
the definitional task of what constitutes 'wisdom psalms' seems further
compounded by concerns over the editorial agenda of the Psalter.

In her recent essay on wisdom psalms, Susan Gillingham gives a
panoramic review of the questions at stake.[31] She first introduces the
diverse and sometimes diametrically opposite views on the degree of
wisdom influence on individual psalms and the Psalter on the whole.
Then she shows how elusive it is to talk of 'wisdom' with respect to its
literary, intellectual or social dimensions by sampling some of the thirty
so-called 'psalms under wisdom influence'. When it comes to her selection of wisdom psalms, Gillingham nominates with reservation nine
psalms[32] in which she sees 'a confluence of [wisdom] characteristics'.[33]
Two points may be worthy of comment here. In using the word 'confluence', Gillingham has rightly asserted that the status of a 'wisdom
psalm' cannot be judged primarily on one single criterion. However,
I want to stress that by 'confluence', one should not envisage a sheer
mechanical adding-up of all the so-called qualified wisdom features. As
it will be shown later, to make a generic decision, one should consider,
in our case, how the wisdom and non-wisdom elements are dynamically
arranged to evince an overall wisdom orientation. Second, Gillingham
further remarks that with the mere number of nine psalms that can be
called close kin to the wisdom writings, 'it is difficult to speak of
"wisdom psalms" as a separate category'.[34] This brief verdict comes as
a bit of a surprise. Earlier on, when writing on Hebrew poetry,
Gillingham has introduced several psalm groups of even smaller sizes.[35]
It prima facie appears to reflect a sentiment similarly aired by Crenshaw

[28] Crenshaw, *Old Testament Wisdom*, 194.
[29] J. Kenneth Kuntz, 'Wisdom Psalms and the Shaping of the Hebrew Psalter', in *For a
      Later Generation: The Transformation of Tradition in Israel, Early Judaism and Early
      Christianity*, ed. R. A. Argall, B. A. Bow and R. A. Werline (Harrisburg, 2000).
[30] Crenshaw, 'Gold Dust or Nuggets?', 157.
[31] Gillingham, 'I Will Incline My Ear to a Proverb'.
[32] Psalms 34, 37, 49, 73, 90, 111, 112, 127 and 128.
[33] Gillingham, 'I Will Incline My Ear to a Proverb', 303.
[34] Gillingham, 'I Will Incline My Ear to a Proverb', 303.
[35] For these groups, I refer to those of 'Zion psalms' (five psalms), 'kingship psalms' (six
      psalms), 'communal thanksgiving' (six psalms), 'communal psalms of confidence'
      (four psalms), 'liturgies' (three psalms), and 'prophetic exhortations' (eight psalms).

who compares the result of such a classificatory endeavour to 'gold dust'.[36] Nevertheless, a broader concern with the overall editing of the Psalter, I surmise, may have been factored in. To her previous quote in that wisdom psalm essay, Gillingham immediately adds, 'and it is more difficult to speak of the Psalter as a Wisdom Book'. This comment is in line with her interest in arguing that the final form of the Psalter shows an unswerving emphasis on the temple and the people's singing and worship, and hence it is not turned a meditative text, as proffered by the advocates of a sapientialised Psalter.[37] I wish to point out here the implicit relation between the taxonomic decision of an individual psalm and the perceived-to-be theological arrangement of the Psalter. This shift of focus from a psalm's Sitz im Leben to its *Sitz im Buch*, so to speak, is a change which, in all probability, Gunkel could have never foreseen.

THE IDENTITY OF THE 'WISDOM PSALMS' FAMILY

I have so far reviewed the works of those scholars who hold a rather negative view of the worth of identifying wisdom psalms, trying to illustrate some of the issues involved in solving the crux of this problem. Despite these intricacies, I still believe that some psalms stand apart as a separate group on account of their close resemblances with other wisdom texts in the Old Testament. Their authors may find it necessary to evoke wisdom resonances in order to create anew a type of psalm that may serve communication goals that other existing psalm types do not. Such goals may be to teach or edify, to arouse deeper deliberation on an issue, to organise his experience and thoughts or to elicit a certain response from its reader that only a wisdom mode of writing may achieve. A genre, after all, is 'an important component in the production of meaning'.[38] It shapes how writers produce, and readers respond to, literary works,[39] and it sounds unwise to write off lightly the existence of any one of them. In varying ways, the

---

See Susan E. Gillingham, *The Poems and Psalms of the Hebrew Bible*, Oxford Bible Series (Oxford, 1994), 206–231.

[36] Crenshaw, 'Gold Dust or Nuggets?'.

[37] See more recently, Susan E. Gillingham, 'The Levites and the Editorial Composition of the Psalms', in *The Oxford Handbook of the Psalms*, 201–213.

[38] Mark R. Sneed, *The Social World of the Sages: An Introduction to Israelite and Jewish Wisdom Literature* (Minneapolis, 2015), 380.

[39] David Fishelov, *Metaphors of Genre: The Role of Analogies in Genre Theory* (University Park, 1993), 8–10.

aforementioned scholars fall under the spell of what we call 'genre realism'. Genre realists perceive the task of genre analysis to be to locate where to erect partitions between genres and to pigeonhole the right texts into each.[40] The failure to do so correctly becomes a source of perpetual vexations. However, as Alastair Fowler writes, 'genres have to do with identifying and communicating rather than with defining and classifying. We identify the genre to interpret the exemplar'.[41] This attempt to discover what makes up the group of 'wisdom psalms' is carried out in the hope of furnishing a better understanding of each individual text within it. In what follows, I wish to elaborate on my description of wisdom psalms as a family of psalms, with varying degrees of membership, that exhibit a wisdom-oriented constellation of its generic elements.

(a) *A family of psalms.* A classificatory endeavour easily falls prey to a binary logic. A particular text is assessed against an inventory of necessary and sufficient conditions to decide its status in a 'class', which can only be either in or out.[42] However, it is rare to find all members in the same class to have uniformly embodied all these traits. Rather, some are linked by a certain trait (like subject matter) whilst others by another feature (like language), and they are linked together to form a web of interconnections. These traits are better envisaged as marks of 'family resemblance', which, to go along with the familial metaphor, may include 'build, features, colour of eyes, gait, tempera-ment' and so on.[43] Though the list of such marks may go on, member-ship of a family cannot be infinitely multiplied.[44] Some core traits, like familial bloodline or DNA, exist to mark off one family from another.[45] These core traits can be observed from the so-called prototypes of a

---

[40]   Kenton L. Sparks, 'Genre Criticism', in *Methods for Exodus*, ed. Thomas B. Dozeman (Cambridge, 2010), 60.

[41]   Alastair Fowler, *Kinds of Literature: An Introduction to the Theory of Genres and Modes* (Oxford, 1982), 38.

[42]   Carol A. Newsom, 'Spying out the Land: A Report from Genology', in *Seeking Out the Wisdom of the Ancients: Essays Offered to Honor Michael V. Fox on the Occasion of His Sixty-Fifth Birthday*, ed. Ronald L. Troxel, Kelvin G. Friebel and Dennis R. Magary (Winona Lake, 2005), 445.

[43]   Fowler, *Kinds of Literature*, 41–42.

[44]   David Fishelov complains that some genre theorists misuse this family analogy to demonstrate the futility of locating the essential characteristics of genre. He rather thinks that this analogy asserts the presence of certain hard core characteristics within a genre. See Fishelov, *Metaphors of Genre*, 61–63.

[45]   K. S. Whetter, *Understanding Genre and Medieval Romance* (Aldershot, 2008), 20.

family.[46] To use an example from the cinema, the *Avengers* series is definitely more prototypical of superhero movies than either *Deadpool* or *Captain Underpants*. In other words, to speak of a genre as a family is to acknowledge that its boundary is fluid and flexible and to make it possible to identify members with various shades and degrees of affinities as a next of kin or a distant relative.

(b) *Constellation of generic elements*. A popular impression of grouping texts according to genres may run like this: an analyst holds a bunch of checklists at hand, each listing an array of criteria characterising a genre. A text gaining many 'ticks' on one list will be assigned to the genre represented by that list. This may be the same impression we gather while reading some of the most referenced works on identifying wisdom psalms.[47] 'Wisdom psalm' is portrayed as a two- or three-dimensional grid, each axis representing one of its characteristic aspects (style, diction or content).[48] A candidate that is awarded the right score on each axis will have reached the threshold of being classed sapiential. While the present work may also convey a similar impression, it tries to distinguish itself from those previous attempts by the way the scores are calculated. Following Jeannie Brown, I do not consider a genre as a container that merely holds all the necessary generic elements together. Instead, all these generic moments are dynamically interrelated and aptly constellated in the service of the author's communicative objective, so as to ensure a felicitous uptake by the hearers/readers.[49] In other words, the mere presence of disparate sapiential markers does not necessarily imply that a psalm is a wisdom psalm prototype. It needs to be taken into account whether such markers are 'contagious' enough to colour the other non-wisdom elements with a sapiential flavour or whether the predominance of other types of elements determines the use of these markers in ways other than that of wisdom.[50] It follows that each psalm has to be studied as an integral whole and focus should not be placed only on those items that are reminiscent of wisdom writings.

---

[46] A concept developed by the cognitive psychologist Eleanor Rosch in her 'Cognitive Representations of Semantic Categories', *J. Exp. Psychol. Gen.* 104.3 (1975): 192–233.

[47] For example, Roland E. Murphy, 'A Consideration of the Classification "Wisdom Psalms"', in *Congress Volume Bonn 1962*, ed. G. W. Anderson, VTSup 9 (Leiden, 1962), 156–167; J. Kenneth Kuntz, 'Canonical Wisdom Psalms of Ancient Israel', in *Rhetorical Criticism: Essays in Honour of James Muilenburg*, ed. J. J. Jackson and M. Kessler (Pittsburgh, 1974), 186–222.

[48] I recognise that these scholars are aware of the interdependence of content and form.

[49] Brown, 'Genre Criticism and the Bible', 122–123.

[50] Cf. Christopher Corwin, 'Classifying Wisdom Psalms' (Unpublished PhD diss., Graduate Theological Union, 1998).

A second ramification of emphasising the wholesome constellation of
the generic elements relates to the quest for wisdom-specific features.
To react against a tendency of 'over-sapientializing' the Old Testament,
so to speak, some scholars determine that wisdom influence outside the
wisdom literature can only be firmly established by the presence of
some wisdom-specific elements. In the case of the Psalter, these elements of high wisdom specificity may include particular vocabulary,[51]
forms of writing (e.g., 'discussion literature')[52] or themes.[53] However, it
sounds unnatural that an author's main concern in composing a psalm
is to leave in it 'signature marks' that may help the hearers/readers to
decipher the author's background. More conceivably, an author
intending to create a lyrical work that can communicate in ways that
works other than wisdom cannot will deploy features that can be
arranged in the most effective ways for accomplishing his purpose.
Pragmatic concerns, for a writer, should always take precedence over
taxonomic ones.

(c) *Wisdom-oriented*. I have mentioned that there are some core
traits, like DNA, that set a family apart from another. So how is the
'DNA' of wisdom psalms made identifiable? There may be three facets
to it: a thematic focus that is predominantly wisdom, an intellectual
tone and a pedagogical intention.

Theme has always been taken as the most crucial indicator of
psalmic wisdom.[54] Claus Westermann primarily considers 'wisdom
psalm' as a thematic category. In his analysis, sapiential psalms are
those which have as their subject matter concerns over questions
related to earthly practical instructions, the opposition between the
pious and the wicked, the teaching or questioning of the doctrine of

---

[51] The most notable examples are those written by Avi Hurvitz: 'Wisdom Vocabulary in
the Hebrew Psalter: A Contribution to the Study of "Wisdom Psalms"', VT 38.1
(1988): 41–51; *Wisdom Language in Biblical Psalmody (Hebrew)* (Jerusalem, 1991);
'"Tsadîq" = "Wise" in Biblical Hebrew and the Wisdom Connections of Psalm 37
(Hebrew)', in *'Sha'arei Talmon': Studies in the Bible, Qumran and the ANE presented
to Shemaryahu Talmon*, ed. Michael Fishbane and Emmanuel Tov (Winona Lake,
1992), *131–*135.

[52] James L. Crenshaw, *Old Testament Wisdom: An Introduction*, rev. and enl. ed.
(Louisville, 1998), 171–175.

[53] For instance, Stuart Weeks argues that the unique interest of wisdom literature is in
the fate of individuals, how they may shape their future and how likely they can do it.
See Stuart Weeks, 'Wisdom Psalms', in *Temple and Worship in Biblical Israel*, ed.
John Day (London, 2005), esp. 297.

[54] Katharine J. Dell, 'Deciding the Boundaries of "Wisdom": Applying the Concept of
Family Resemblance', in *Was There a Wisdom Tradition: New Prospects in Israelite
Wisdom Studies*, ed. Mark R. Sneed, AIL 253 (Atlanta, 2015), 151.

just retribution and the brevity of human existence.[55] Taking psalmic literature that develops further down the line as evidence, Matthew Goff concludes that the post-canonical wisdom psalms in 11QPs^a are mostly recognisable by their 'specific sapiential motifs'.[56] Goff's study of two of the hymns there provides a good example of how to decide that a psalm exhibits (or does not) a chief wisdom thematic focus.[57] 'Hymn to the Creator' (11QPs^a 26: 9–15) extols God as a creator, soliciting the help of wisdom in creation. When taken separately, these two themes may be regarded as thematic echoes with the Old Testament wisdom books. On closer look, this psalm does not personify wisdom as an aide to God in the primordial creation, a theme which is clearly found in Prov 8:22–31. Goff, hence, rightly rejects this hymn as having a clear thematic focus on wisdom. Psalm 154 (11QPs^a) is a hymnic praise of Yahweh's majesty. It is, however, through an implicitly personified wisdom that one may appreciate the divine mightiness. Goff judges that this psalm can be regarded as wisdom, noting that the blend of wisdom and praise is a later development outside the canonical wisdom corpus. I contest Goff's conclusion, however, that the role of the personified wisdom here is subservient to the aim of promoting the exaltation of Yahweh, and this demonstrates instead that the main theme of Psalm 154 is one of praise but is not sapiential. These two cases serve to illustrate my point that, by a wisdom thematic focus, or as what I will call 'a ruling wisdom thrust', I mean that the poetic work on the whole should be centring round a clear wisdom-related theme(s). All the wisdom- or non-wisdom-associated themes are thus organised in such a conceptual schema that the wisdom theme predominates.

The wisdom orientation of a psalm can also be sensed in its general tone. The 'tone' of a piece of literature is more an abstract quality which can only be subjectively assessed and imprecisely defined as its 'spirit', 'atmosphere' or 'aura'.[58] Citing as evidence Qoheleth's stubborn probing of wisdom, the heated debate between Job and his three companions, and the advisory materials in Proverbs, Alistair Hunter asserts that these features converge in a quality of what he dubs as 'an intellectual

---

[55] Claus Westermann, *Der Psalter*, 4th ed. (Stuttgart, 1980), 93–97.

[56] Matthew J. Goff, *Discerning Wisdom: The Sapiential Literature of the Dead Sea Scrolls*, VTSup 116 (Leiden; Boston, 2007), 230–263.

[57] Goff, *Discerning Wisdom: The Sapiential Literature of the Dead Sea Scrolls*, 240–247, 257–260.

[58] T. V. F. Brogan and Fabian Gudas, 'Tone', *The New Princeton Encyclopedia of Poetry and Poetics*, eds. A. Preminger and T. V. F. Brogan (Princeton, 1993), 1293–1294.

approach to the problems and challenges of life'.[59] The acquisition and
validation of knowledge, here, is not made by an appeal to divine
revelation, and a noetic quality pervades the text. Knowledge is accrued
via observing the created world, drawing inferences from what is seen
and conventional wisdom, meditative reflection or a process of
reasoning and deliberating with others. By this, I am not saying that
wisdom literature promotes a kind of autonomous human rationality
that may operate at its maximum capacity without divine aid. The
central axiom of Proverbs in 1:7 and 9:10, after all, pitches the fundamental step of pursuing wisdom at revering Yahweh.[60] This 'intellectual approach' is about a generic quality, the literary convention, so to
speak, to which the author of sapiential literature subscribes in order to
prepare the hearer/reader to engage with the intellect the questions
posed or the values imparted by the author. Hence, we may also notice
a frequent use of knowledge-related lexemes or causal clauses.
Apparently unrelated or contradictory sayings may simply be juxtaposed to induce the hearer/reader to ponder their interrelations. Even
the use of acrostics can be a way of creating this kind of intellectual
spirit, if one concedes Elie Assis' cogent argument that an acrostic
structure is composed with particularly careful, premeditated rumin-
ation so as to draw its readers into deeper reflection.[61] The use of these
stylistic devices on their own by no means become indicative of an
intellectual tone. They have to be considered in the context of the
whole psalm before it can be decided whether their use contributes to
the intellectual tone of the work.

To genre theorists, 'purpose' or 'intention' is a significant generic
component.[62] Therefore, to evince a wisdom orientation, a psalm
should also display a concomitant purpose. 'Wisdom literature is explicitly didactic and pedagogical.'[63] Various forms of wisdom literature
may be applied in a number of settings, all of which, as Roland

---

[59] Alastair G. Hunter, *Wisdom Literature* (London, 2006), 24.

[60] For the limits of human knowledge as expressed in Proverbs, Ecclesiastes and Job, see
    Gerhard von Rad, *Wisdom in Israel*, trans. James D. Martin (London, 1972), 97–110;
    Ryan P. O'Dowd, *The Wisdom of Torah: Epistemology in Deuteronomy and the
    Wisdom Literature*, FRLANT 225 (Göttingen, 2009), 111–161.

[61] Elie Assis, 'The Alphabetic Acrostics in the Book of Lamentations', *CBQ* 69.4 (2007):
    710–724.

[62] E. D. Hirsch Jr., *Validity in Interpretation* (New Haven, 1967), 100–101.

[63] Matthew J. Goff, 'Scribes and Pedagogy in Ancient Israel and Second Temple Judaism',
    in *The Wiley Companion to Wisdom Literature*, 195.

Murphy claims, are didactically related.[64] Its main subject matter of teaching, according to William Brown, is about the formation of moral character in light of the order of creation.[65] Psalmic wisdom may have slightly different foci of formation, but its interest in teaching is similar. There are some who are sceptical of using didacticism to isolate wisdom psalms. David Firth, among others, argues that, once canonised, all psalms assume a teaching role. In other words, psalms of all form-critical categories are teaching-related.[66] While I agree that such a change in use may take place even when a piece of classical literature is preserved and used by later generations, one also needs to note the critical difference between a psalm composed for instructions and one used for instructions, that is, between the question about authorial intention and that of the psalm's reception history. Matthew Gordley's instructive study helps to elucidate the disparity here. In ancient times, there are hymns as hymns per se and hymns written more for teaching than for exalting the deity. In the former case, they may be used by later generations for edification, an application which they are not at first intended for. As for the didactic hymns, their instructional intention is also reflected in its generic elements. For instance, those unconventional hymns usually include direct addresses to the human audience or make claims about the object of praise or the community in laudation.[67] Similarly, any genre of psalms found in the Old Testament can become teaching materials, but this is not the same as saying that all are written at first for such a purpose. In the latter case, its teaching purpose can be reflected in the composed poem itself.

A GENETIC TEST FOR PSALM 34

Psalm 34 may serve as an illustration for such an understanding of 'wisdom psalms'. To decide on the genre of this psalm is not so straightforward; and to some commentators, any 'firm judgment' regarding its

---

[64] Roland E. Murphy, 'Form Criticism and Wisdom Literature', *CBQ* 31.4 (1969): 475–483.

[65] William P. Brown, *Wisdom's Wonder: Character, Creation, and Crisis in the Bible's Wisdom Literature* (Grand Rapids; Cambridge, 2014).

[66] David G. Firth, 'The Teaching of the Psalms', in *Interpreting the Psalms: Issues and Approaches*, ed. Philip S. Johnston and David G. Firth (Leicester, 2005), 159–174.

[67] Matthew E. Gordley, *Teaching through Song in Antiquity: Didactic Hymnody among Greeks, Romans, Jews, and Christians*, WUNT II/302 (Tübingen, 2011), 10.

literary type is difficult to make.[68] While some categorise it with other thanksgiving psalms,[69] some are disposed to align it with the sapiential poems.[70] There are still others who go for a *via media* and judge the psalm to be hybrid.[71] In what follows, I will subject Psalm 34 to an analysis under the above suggested understanding of 'wisdom psalms'.

A red thread that runs through this psalm is found in the second versets of vv. 4, 6, 17 and 19: 'and [the LORD] delivered me from all my fears', 'and [this poor soul] was saved from every trouble', 'and [the LORD] rescues them from all their troubles' and, finally, 'but the LORD rescues them from them [afflictions] all'. These four versets are constructed similarly, each begins in Hebrew the word *ûmikkol* ('and from all/every'), contains an active verb that denotes a succouring action and, in three of them, a noun that pertains to an unnamed plight faced by the protagonist(s) in that verset. Structurally speaking, these claims are found in the fourth and sixth lines from the beginning and the sixth and fourth lines from the end of the psalm, forming a balanced framework that surrounds the central panel of instructions (vv. 7–16). The core thrust of the psalm is, therefore, to testify to a deity who rescues those who seek his help from all their straits. Twice, this act of deliverance is depicted as Yahweh's response after hearing the suppliant's plea (vv. 6, 17). The psalmist's testimony also serves to encourage the 'lowly' (*'ănāvîm*, *'ānî*, vv. 2, 6) to take joy in Yahweh who responds to the prayer of a lowly person like the psalmist. The psalmist then exhorts his audience to revert to Yahweh for assistance in times of distress (vv. 7–8), substantiating his claim with a cluster of instructions. I offer below my translation of this middle portion of the psalm.

---

[68] Peter C. Craigie, *Psalms 1–50*, 2nd ed., WBC 19 (Nashville, 2004), 278. *Pace* Hans-Joachim Kraus, *Psalms 1–59*, trans. Hilton C. Oswald (Minneapolis, 1988), 382.

[69] Hermann Gunkel, *Die Psalmen: Übersetzt und erklärt*, HKAT (Göttingen, 1926), 142–143; Frank Crüsemann, *Studien zur Formgeschichte von Hymnus und Danklied in Israel*, WMANT 32 (Neukirchen-Vluyn, 1969), 251–252; Kraus, *Psalms 1–59*, 382.

[70] Alfons Deissler, *Die Psalmen*, 7th ed. (Düsseldorf, 1993), 140; Murphy, 'A Consideration of the Classification "Wisdom Psalms"', 162–163; Kuntz, 'Canonical Wisdom Psalms of Ancient Israel', 191–220; Hurvitz, *Wisdom Language in Biblical Psalmody (Hebrew)*, 62–75; Weeks, 'Wisdom Psalms', 301; Walter A. Brueggemann and W. H. Bellinger Jr., *Psalms*, NCB (Cambridge, 2014), 168.

[71] Artur Weiser, *The Psalms: A Commentary*, OTL (London, 1962), 296–297; LarsOlov Eriksson, *'Come, Children, Listen to Me!' Psalm 34 in the Hebrew Bible and in Early Christian Writings*, ConBOTS 32 (Uppsala, 1991), 63–79; Craigie, *Psalms 1–50*, 278; Frank-Lothar Hossfeld and Erich Zenger, *Die Psalmen I*, NEchtB 29 (Würzburg, 1993), 210–211.

PSALM 34:7–16 (MT VV. 8–17)

7 The messenger of Yahweh encamps, surrounding his fearers, and delivers them.

8 Taste so as to see that Yahweh is good! Blessed is the person who seeks refuge in him.

9 Fear Yahweh, his holy ones, since for those who fear him lack nothing!

10 Young lions suffer want and are famished, but those who seek Yahweh lack no good thing.

11 Come, children, listen to me! I shall teach you the fear of Yahweh.

12 Who is the man who desires life, loves many days in order to see good?[72]

13 Guard your tongue from evil, and your lips from speaking deceit.

14 Turn from evil and do good. Pursue peace and chase after it.

15 The eyes of Yahweh are turned towards the righteous, and his ears towards their cry.

16 The face of Yahweh is against those who do evil in order to cut their remembrance from the land.

After making the assertion about Yahweh's protective care for those who revere him, the psalmist invites his audience to experience the goodness of Yahweh and to pitch their revering faith in him (vv. 7–9). The leonine metaphor in v. 10 helps to underscore this assuring claim that Yahweh is a secure source of help. It is significant to note that here a fearer of Yahweh is virtually synonymous with one who seeks him (vv. 9–10).

Rather abruptly, the psalmist next takes up the guise of a paternal instructor and lashes out with a series of ethical guidelines for attaining a flourishing life (vv. 11–14). The content of his paraenesis squarely resonates with the characteristic teachings in the proverbial literature in the Old Testament, lending the psalm the strongest thematic presence of wisdom. Avi Hurvitz also spots in these five verses the highest density of what he defines as uniquely wisdom phraseology.[73] To some, the thematic elements here warrant typifying this psalm as wisdom.

However, if the place of these teachings is examined in context with other thematic elements in this psalm, it may be argued that the main thrust of the psalm is not entirely constellated towards a wisdom orientation. A closer look at vv. 7–16 reveals that they are configured in a concentric pattern:

---

[72] The NRSV renders *lir'ôt tôb* into 'to enjoy good'.

[73] These include: *sûr mēra'* (MT v. 15), *ləkû bānîm šim'û lî* (MT v. 12), *nəṣor ləšôn* (MT v. 14), *hāpēṣ ḥayyîm* (MT v. 13), *'ohēb yāmîm* (MT v. 13) and *rə'ôt tôb* (MT v. 13). To Hurvitz, there are nine such occurrences in this psalm. See Hurvitz, *Wisdom Language in Biblical Psalmody* (Hebrew), 62–75.

A Yahweh favours his fearers (v.7 MT v. 8)

    B Advice to see good: seek refuge in Yahweh (vv. 8–10 MT vv. 9–11)

        X Invite the 'children' to learn the fear of God (v. 11 MT v. 12)

    B' Advice to see good: seek peace in words and deeds (vv. 12–14 MT vv. 13–15)

A' Yahweh treats differently the righteous and the evildoers (vv. 15–16 MT vv.1 6–17)

Figure 12.1 Ps. 34:7–16 (MT 8–17) arranged in a concentric pattern

Two lists of advice are set in foil in these verses, one on how to see Yahweh's goodness (vv. 8–10) and the other on how to see goodness in life (vv. 12–14). Those who live by these counsels have demonstrated their reverence for Yahweh (vv. 7, 9, 11), to whom v. 15 refers indirectly as the righteous. It is perhaps right to say that a righteous God-fearer is one who both invariably takes refuge in Yahweh and exhibits all the interpersonal traits enshrined by the wise. Without the latter, the faithful reliance on Yahweh is only an incomplete demonstration of a fearful heart for the deity.[74] Yet the psalm does not end in commending the worthy deeds of the righteous. It further associates them with those 'broken-hearted' and 'crushed in spirit' (v. 17), victims of an, perhaps, oppressive, exploitative situation or system. The special characteristic of these people is that they may benefit from God's saving presence while they cry out in danger. In fact, the final word of the psalm is about those who seek Yahweh as their shelter. Brown has astutely summed up the different pedagogical points between this psalm and Proverbs in general: 'In the psalm, reverence establishes "refuge" from evildoers; in Proverbs, the "fear of YHWH" provides enlightenment and fosters integrity …. For the psalm, salvation – rather than formation – is paramount.'[75] I am more inclined to say that the psalm portrays that a person who practises daily the counsels of the wise as a way to form a revering attitude to Yahweh is more attuned to turn to Yahweh for help in desperate plights.[76] In other words, the principal melodic theme of

---

74   *Pace* Walter Brueggemann and William Bellinger, who write, 'The implication of this portrayal of the righteous is that they are not those who earn their way by doing morally correct deeds. Rather, the righteous are those who live out of fidelity to their relationship with YHWH with just human relationships.' See Brueggemann and Bellinger, *Psalms*, 170.

75   Brown, '"Come, O Children … I Will Teach You the Fear of the Lord" (Psalm 34:12)', 91–92.

76   Contra Hermann Spieckermann who argues that the 'lesson' beginning in v. 12 is 'adapted as catalysts for the praise of God'. See Hermann Spieckermann, 'What Is the Place of Wisdom and Torah in the Psalter?', in *'When the Morning Stars Sang': Essays*

Psalm 34 remains within a salvific scope, and so a ruling wisdom thrust is not so evident.

As for its tonal quality, Psalm 34 displays some measures of intellectualism. To drive his instructional message home, the psalmist does not make inference to any divine revelation. An intellectual approach is evidenced by the use of three teaching tactics in the psalm. Personal testimony, at the outset, sets the psalmist as an exemplar. As one of the 'lowly', the psalmist showcases what it means to be reliant on Yahweh and, by narrating one's experience, invites all other 'lowly' ones to learn from it and to emulate the psalmist when facing their own troubles. Second, the psalmist invites the hearers/readers to 'taste and see' the goodness of Yahweh (v. 8). The intent of this gustatory experiment is to encourage the hearers/readers to draw conclusions on their own regarding the benefits of seeking refuge in Yahweh. A similar approach is found in Proverbs (Prov 24:30–34) and Ecclesiastes. The use of the alphabetising scheme in composing this psalm is a sign not only that this psalm is probably originated 'at the desk'[77] but also that it is thoughtfully crafted on behalf of a community with a well-meditated message to say.

The didactic purpose of this psalm is embedded in its alphabetic structure as an 'inscribed code', as Anthony Ceresko has shown.[78] In Hebrew, the first line of the psalm proper is made up of twenty-five letters (excluding the vowel letters), while the first, thirteenth and last of them are the alphabets *aleph-lamed-pe*, which spell the verb 'to learn' (*'lp*). Vertically speaking, as one might say, the acrostic scheme of this psalm departs at points from the normal alphabetical order. Most pertinent to our case, the original sixth letter *waw* is missing, thus making a *lamed*-beginning line (v. 11 MT v. 12) stand at the mid-point of the entire poem. Besides, an extra line beginning with the letter *pe* (v. 22 MT v. 23) is added after the *taw*-line (v. 21 MT v. 22). Hence, the letters that begin the first, middle and last lines of the poem are again the combination of *aleph-lamed-pe*. The psalmist makes most explicit his intention to teach in v. 11 and calls the hearers/readers 'children' in the same breath. The Hebrew word *ben* in its unmarked plural form is used

in Honor of Choon Leong Seow on the Occasion of His Sixty-Fifth Birthday, ed. Scott C. Jones and Christine Roy Yoder, BZAW 500 (Berlin, 2018), 302.

[77] Hans Schmidt, *Die Psalmen*, HAT 15 (Tübingen, 1934), 46.

[78] Anthony R. Ceresko, 'The ABCs of Wisdom in Psalm Xxxiv', *VT* 35.1 (1985): 99–104.

eight times as a vocative in the MT, in seven out of these occurrences, in contexts where the addressees are invited to heed the ensuing advice or follow an impassioned call to repent.[79] Although the psalmist at the outset registers an intention to praise Yahweh and to invoke jubilant exaltation from the lowly (vv. 1–3), the hearer/reader's expectation to engage in a hymnic thanksgiving song is soon defied. For one, never in this psalm does the psalmist address Yahweh, who is referred to only in the third person. The psalmist only directly speaks to the community of hearers/readers. The section of testimony common to all thanksgiving songs is also atypically condensed. The elaborate form of narrating the psalmist's dire situation, invocation of divine help and experience of rescue is compressed into a one-liner (v. 4), which is patently shorter than the didactic section that begins as early as v. 7. In his classical form-critical study on thanksgiving psalms, Frank Crüsemann argues that both the dominant impetus to teach and the acrostic style make this psalm an 'exception' to his thanksgiving psalm category. While it is dubious whether the requirement to comply with an alphabetising scheme is to be blamed, Crüsemann has rightly observed this psalm's didactic emphasis.[80] Alfons Deissler aptly shows that the generic elements of a 'thanksgiving song' are used here as a 'container' to serve the psalmist's teaching purpose.[81] Cumulatively, these generic elements point out that this psalm is demonstrably didactic.

Psalm 34 is clearly set for a pedagogic end, composed in a tone that fairly reflects an intellectual approach. These generic moments share the most affinities with those of the principal wisdom writings in the Old Testament. Some wisdom themes invoked notwithstanding, they are subsumed under the main message of seeking refuge in Yahweh, a lesson more commonly found in psalmic than sapiential corpus. This serves to account for the misgivings of many who cannot recognise this psalm as a wisdom psalm prototype.

CONCLUSION

The voices that call for re-charting the trail of studying wisdom psalms are well-warranted, but have, contrary to their original intention, made

---

[79] The addressees ('children') are asked to listen to a 'teacher-figure' speaking in Prov 4:1, 5:7, 7:24, 8:32 and Ps 34:11 and to repent in Jer 3:14, 22.
[80] Crüsemann, *Studien zur Formgeschichte von Hymnus und Danklied in Israel*, 251–252 n.2.
[81] Deissler, *Die Psalmen*, 140.

the task of better delineating this group of psalms more poignantly needed. Those who advocate for entirely abandoning this psalm group have not succeeded to convince. To some measures, they have highlighted the need to investigate the overall editing of the Psalter in association with a better understanding of this crucial psalm genre. Research in genre theories helps move forward our conceptualising of wisdom psalms as a genre, in allowing it to have members with graded degrees of affinities in the family and in leading us to reformulate our method of weighing their generic qualities. Arguably, the bloodline of this genre family lies in a combination of its predominant thematic thrust related to wisdom, a literary tone characterised by intellectualism and a purpose to teach. In this light, Psalm 34 is not prototypically wisdom, contrary to the judgement of many commentators. Such an analysis enables us to speak more accurately about the substance of the influence of wisdom on a psalm or the Psalter.

Further Reading

Brown, Jeannine K. 'Genre Criticism and the Bible'. Pages 111–150 in *Words and the Word: Explorations in Biblical Interpretation and Literary Theory*. Edited by David G. Firth and Jamie Grant. Nottingham: 2008.

Brown, William P. 'Psalms'. Pages 67–86 in *The Wiley Blackwell Companion to Wisdom Literature*. Edited by Samuel L. Adams and Matthew Goff. Hoboken; Chichester: 2020.

Cheung, Simon Chi-chung. *Wisdom Intoned: A Reappraisal of the Genre 'Wisdom Psalms'*. LHBOTS 613. New York; London: 2015.

Crenshaw, James L. 'Wisdom Psalms?'. *CurBS* 8 (2000): 9–17.

Fishelov, David. *Metaphors of Genre: The Role of Analogies in Genre Theory*. University Park: 1993.

Gillingham, Susan E. '"I Will Incline My Ear to a Proverb; I Will Solve My Riddle to the Music of the Harp" (Psalm 49.4): The Wisdom Tradition and the Psalms'. Pages 277–309 in *Perspectives on Israelite Wisdom: Proceedings of the Oxford Old Testament Seminar*. Edited by John Jarick. LHBOTS 618. London; 2016.

Gunkel, Hermann, and Joachim Begrich. *Introduction to Psalms: The Genres of Religious Lyrics of Israel*. Translated by James D. Nogalski. Mercer Library of Biblical Studies. Macon: 1998.

Kuntz, J. Kenneth. 'Canonical Wisdom Psalms of Ancient Israel'. Pages 186–222 in *Rhetorical Criticism: Essays in Honour of James Muilenburg*. Edited by J. J. Jackson and M. Kessler. Pittsburgh: 1974.

Mowinckel, Sigmund. 'Psalms and Wisdom'. Pages 205–224 in *Wisdom in Israel and in the Ancient Near East: Presented to H. H. Rowley by the Society for Old Testament Study in Association with the Editorial Board of Vetus Testamentum, in Celebration of His Sixty-Fifth Birthday, 24 March 1955*. Edited by Martin Noth and D. Winton Thomas. VTSup 3. Leiden: 1955.

Murphy, Roland E. 'A Consideration of the Classification "Wisdom Psalms"'. Pages 156–167 in *Congress Volume Bonn 1962*. Edited by G. W. Anderson. VTSup 9. Leiden: 1962.

Sneed, Mark R. *The Social World of the Sages: An Introduction to Israelite and Jewish Wisdom Literature*. Minneapolis: 2015.

13 Wisdom's Wider Resonance

MICHAEL C. LEGASPI

Wisdom research is predicated on the idea that the scholar who is attuned to the literary reflexes of wisdom, however defined, is prepared to understand aspects of the biblical writings that others who are not so attuned are likely to neglect or misunderstand. By directing attention to wisdom, the wisdom researcher seeks to shed light on various dimensions of biblical literature: its origins in scribal practice, its ancient internationalism, the pedagogical aims of its authors, the philosophical understandings implicit in its claims, intertextual relations linking disparate and discrete compositions and so on. In the case of certain biblical compositions like the so-called wisdom books of the Hebrew Bible (Proverbs, Job, Ecclesiastes), the rationale for a specialised, wisdom-oriented approach is obvious. The purpose of this chapter, however, is to assess the profitability of 'wisdom-seeking' in connection with parts of the Hebrew Bible that may be related to wisdom in subtler ways. The goal is to see whether certain understandings of wisdom may have had a 'wider resonance', one that extended beyond texts commonly associated with wisdom and that shaped compositions seemingly remote from sapiential contexts and concerns.

Anxieties about 'pan-sapientialism' reflect scholarly worries about arbitrary or undisciplined efforts to sniff out the influence of wisdom or wisdom-thinking in all types of biblical literature.[1] Those opposed to pan-sapientialism rightly question the usefulness of finding 'wisdom influence' in all corners of the canon. If wisdom stands behind everything, then wisdom, as a category of analysis, no longer means anything. Thus, in order for an inquiry into wisdom's wider resonance to be useful, it must be subject to certain controls. In what follows, I will

---

[1] See, for example, Will Kynes, *An Obituary for 'Wisdom Literature': The Birth, Death, and Intertextual Reintegration of a Biblical Corpus* (Oxford, 2019), 1–2, 27, 31; James Crenshaw, *Old Testament Wisdom: An Introduction*, rev. ed. (Louisville, 1998), 29–30.

examine select biblical passages in which words related to the *ḥ-k-m*
root are prominent and which, nevertheless, do not register widely in
common scholarly treatments of wisdom. The present study, however,
is not lexicographic; it is not a programmatic attempt to restrict the
study of wisdom to a specific word or vocabulary. The aim, instead, is to
see whether references to wisdom that do not typically figure into
treatments of wisdom as genre, tradition, category or school nevertheless open onto overlooked dimensions of wisdom more broadly construed. How might closer study of passages normally considered
marginal to wisdom inquiry enrich understandings of biblical wisdom
as a whole? This chapter turns to two sets of passages in order to bring
out features of wisdom that do not align readily with intellectualistic
construals of wisdom as the bailiwick of secular, cosmopolitan, scribal
elites. One cluster of passages has to do with the construction of the
Tabernacle and the Temple; a second, related set of passages includes
references to wisdom in the prophetic books, namely, Jeremiah 8–9 and
Ezekiel 28. One aim of the study, then, is to detect the resonance of
wisdom in two parts of the canon (Torah, Prophets) where it is sometimes underappreciated. Stuart Weeks rightly cites instances of *ḥokmâ*
in Exodus, Jeremiah and Ezekiel as evidence that uses of *ḥokmâ* are not
confined to the so-called biblical wisdom books; yet he mentions these
references in order to caution against attempts to detect the apparent
influence of wisdom by connecting a given passage (for example, Exod
28:3 or Ezek 27:8) to 'some distinctive feature' that is supposedly
'common to all biblical wisdom books'.[2] Such a connection would
indeed be tenuous if predicated solely on occurrences of *ḥokmâ* or other
wisdom words; it might also be circular if based on an assumed understanding of what is common to wisdom literature. But if 'minor' attestations of words like *ḥokmâ* are taken as clues to neglected aspects of
what biblical writers understood by 'wisdom', then there may be exegetical benefits to taking them seriously.

KNOWLEDGE OF DIVINE AND HUMAN THINGS

One obstacle to procuring these benefits has been the standard division
between a putatively earlier and more basic understanding of wisdom as
'cleverness' or practical 'skill' and a later, secondary use of the word to

---

[2] Stuart Weeks, 'Is "Wisdom Literature" a Useful Category?', in *Tracing Sapiential
Traditions in Ancient Judaism*, ed. Hindy Najman, Jean-Sébastien Rey, and Eibert
J. C. Tigchelaar, JSJSup 174 (Leiden, 2016), 17.

denote certain concepts or abstractions that are accessible only through higher-order thinking. In Greek thought, wisdom (*sophia*) is often said to have undergone just such a transformation of meaning.[3] In line with understandings of wisdom as cleverness, Xenophon, for example, could use the word to refer to musical skill.[4] Characters in Plato's dialogues used *sophia* to speak of skill in such things as persuasion (*Rep.* 365d), poetic performance (*Rep.* 398a) or medicine (*Rep.* 406b), even though Plato himself identified true *sophia* with an intellectual grasp of divine, cosmic and social order.[5] A generation later, it fell to Aristotle in works like *Metaphysics* and *Nicomachean Ethics* to systematise higher and lower understandings of wisdom inherited not only from Plato but from Pythagoras, Heraclitus and popular opinion as well.[6] For him, *sophia* proper involves an intellectual understanding of higher causes; by contrast, *sophia*-as-skill, which involves production and performance, is lower and less prestigious. The Aristotelian *sophos* theorises, contemplates and orders; he does not manufacture things or produce effects in the world. Biblical scholars have at times drawn a similar distinction between higher and lower senses of *ḥokmâ*, dividing between contemplative and productive aspects of words derived from the *ḥ-k-m* root. In the work of James Crenshaw, for example, the tendency to identify wisdom with a class of sages prompts a sharp division between wisdom-as-skill and wisdom conceived as an intellectual pursuit: natural ability and expertise in particular crafts, he asserts, 'have nothing whatever to do with a professional class of "the wise"'.[7] Noting this tendency to treat instances of 'skill' dismissively, Raymond van Leeuwen traces the hyper-intellectualisation of *ḥokmâ* to the influence of Norman Whybray's 1974 work, *The Intellectual Tradition in the Old Testament*, in which the latter described passages identifying *ḥokmâ* with craftsmanship as 'nonsignificant'.[8] Van Leeuwen, however, argues

---

[3] Joseph Owen, 'Aristotle's Notion of Wisdom', *Apeiron* 20 (1987): 1–16.

[4] Owen, 'Aristotle's Notion of Wisdom', 1.

[5] Michael C. Legaspi, *Wisdom in Classical and Biblical Tradition* (Oxford, 2018), 146–153.

[6] Thus Owen summarises: by the mid-fourth century, the meaning of *sophia* 'had been transferred from the humble proficiencies of the carpenter and the flute-player to a knowledge to a knowledge of reality as a whole, a knowledge that bore upon truth itself instead of upon a particular kind of object' ('Aristotle's Notion of Wisdom', 3).

[7] Crenshaw, *Old Testament Wisdom*, 20.

[8] Raymond C. van Leeuwen, 'Cosmos, Temple, House: Building and Wisdom in Ancient Mesopotamia and Israel', in *From the Foundations to the Crenellations: Essays on Temple Building in the Ancient Near East and Hebrew Bible*, ed. Mark J. Boda and Jamie Novotny, Alter Orient und Altes Testament 366 (Münster, 2010),

for a more expansive, integrated understanding of wisdom, rightly asking how *ḥokmâ* encompasses both the practical and the theoretical.[9] Weeks relates the two through an analogical process of semantic development. Acknowledging a simple, underlying meaning of *ḥokmâ* as 'skill' or 'know-how', Weeks suggests that wisdom acquired a more general, philosophical attitude when skill in particular things like sewing or metal-working was extended to the conduct of one's whole life, the 'know-how' involved in living one's life well.[10]

There may indeed have been a shift from the particular to the general, as Weeks argues, or from the practical to the theoretical as one observes in Greek philosophy of the fourth century BCE. The issue here, however, is not *Begriffsgeschichte* (a history of ideas) but the interpretive consequences of making skill irrelevant to wisdom. The subordination of craft or skill to generalised, philosophical understanding in discussions of *ḥokmâ* is not problematic primarily because it devalues skill and divides practical knowledge from theoretical knowledge (though this division certainly merits scrutiny in the context of biblical wisdom).[11] Rather, it poses difficulties because it obscures a different set of opposing terms that framed ancient conceptions of wisdom: the human and the divine. To the extent that *ḥokmâ* figures importantly in the construction of *sacred* buildings (sanctuaries and temples) and *cultic* objects (e.g., priestly vestments), it bears a significant relation to the religious sphere of life in which the human and the divine are at once distinguished from another and brought into harmonious coexistence. Scholars often distinguish 'wisdom' from other strains of biblical literature by pointing to wisdom's supposed indifference to cultic matters, but such a distinction may be unwarranted or at least overstated. Many of the so-called lesser, 'nonsignificant' attestations of *ḥokmâ* that pertain to the cult (and cultic backgrounds in the

---

418. Roland Murphy ('Wisdom, in the OT' *ABD* VI: 920–931) identifies Gerhard von Rad's 1972 *Wisdom in Israel* as the first work in recent scholarship to see biblical wisdom philosophically, in terms of its larger 'understanding of reality' (921–922).

9   Van Leeuwen, 'Cosmos, Temple, House', 418.

10 Stuart Weeks, *An Introduction to the Study of Wisdom Literature* (London, 2010), 2.

11 On understandings of wisdom as 'construction' or 'building' that mirrors God's wisdom in creating the cosmos, see Van Leeuwen, 'Cosmos, Temple, House', 399–421; Zoltán Schwáb, *Toward an Interpretation of the Book of Proverbs: Selfishness and Secularity Revisited*, JTISup 7 (Winona Lake, 2013), 190–212; Stéphanie Anthonioz, 'A Reflection on the Nature of Wisdom: From Psalm 1 to Mesopotamian Traditions', in *Tracing Sapiential Traditions in Ancient Judaism*, ed. Hindy Najman, Jean-Sébastien Rey and Eibert J. C. Tigchelaar, JSJSupp 174 (Leiden, 2016), 43–56.

prophetic books) attest an understanding of wisdom by which certain kinds of practical skill are dignified not by their contribution to theoretical understanding but, instead, by their role in joining the sacred and non-sacred realms, sanctifying components of human life and bringing them into alignment with divine order.[12] The fact that ḥokmâ in these cases appears to operate outside the sphere of sagely theorising and literary production – rather than discredit them as instances of wisdom – suggests instead that the world of the scribe and the theatre of wisdom, as it were, were not one and the same.

It may be helpful in this connection to recall the old definition, well-attested in classical sources, of wisdom (sophia) as knowledge (epistēmē) of human and divine matters (theiōn te kai anthrōpinōn).[13] This deceptively simple definition, which originated with the Stoics but was adopted and referenced more widely, identifies wisdom with a form of knowledge that coordinates the 'human' and the 'divine' as two separate realms of concern. Wisdom does not collapse all into a single category of being but rather recognises two distinct categories of things; wisdom understands how the two are coordinated. To paraphrase slightly, wisdom is a knowledge of *both* human *and* divine things as well as the principles and causes particular to each. Cicero accepted the definition as a commonplace (*Tusc. Disp.* 4.25.57). Jewish thinkers found the two-sided understanding of wisdom useful as well. Commenting on Gen 2:8, Philo explained that paradise, planted by God, represents wisdom, an 'intelligence both human and divine', by which man might be moved 'by the sight of the world and the things that are contained in it' to discern the supreme cause of the universe and attain thereby 'a correct notion of the praise due to the Father' (*Questions on Genesis* 1.6).[14] In commending Torah obedience as a path to rational self-mastery, the author of 4 Maccabees quotes the Stoic definition of wisdom before explaining that Jews who carefully follow the Mosaic law gain not only virtue and knowledge of human affairs but

---

[12] On the importance of 'order' as a point of contact between sages and cultic functionaries, see Leo Perdue, *Wisdom and Cult: A Critical Analysis of the Views of Cult in the Wisdom Literature of Israel and the Ancient Near East*, SBLDS 30 (Missoula, 1977), 9, 362.

[13] Plutarch *SVF* 2.35. Quoted in René Brouwer, *The Stoic Sage: The Early Stoics on Wisdom, Sagehood, and Socrates* (Cambridge, 2014), 8.

[14] Philo, *The Works of Philo: Complete and Unabridged*, trans. C. D. Yonge (Peabody, 1993), 792; cf. also *Questions on Genesis* 3.43, where Philo explains the extension of the name Abram to Abraham as a reflection of the fact that the patriarch's wisdom was enlarged to include the human and the divine, the visible and the invisible.

also a reverent understanding of divine matters (4 Macc 1:16–17). With its concern for life lived in conscious deference to divine authority and to rational norms of human morality, Torah ought to be regarded by all would-be sages as an effective and legitimate source of wisdom. For the author of 4 Maccabees, the conventional, two-sided understanding of wisdom was a matter of religious performance as well as knowledge. Returning to the Stoics, one sees that they too connected knowledge to action; in addition to being an *epistēmē*, wisdom was also, for them, something identifiable with skill or expertise (*technē*).[15] They held that an indispensable reflex of 'knowledge of things human and divine' was an ability to act fittingly or appropriately in the world on the basis of that knowledge. One (Stoical) possibility for acting expertly to coordinate the human and the divine in one's life is the rational cultivation of *virtue* in the ethical sphere.

Nevertheless, another possibility is *virtuosic* activity in the cultic sphere, for nowhere are human and divine things more concretely related than in sacred space. Notable in this regard is Pheidias, the renowned Greek sculptor who flourished in the middle of the fifth century BCE. As the artist responsible for the creative aspects of Pericles' ambitious building program, Pheidias played a key role in the construction and renovation of temples in the city. Credited with oversight of the building of the Parthenon, Pheidias was also remembered for his great skill (*sophia*) as sculptor.[16] By all accounts, the most impressive achievement of Pheidias was the massive ivory statue of Zeus in his temple in Olympia (Pisatis). Counted as one of the seven wonders of the world, it was hailed as the greatest and most successful attempt to represent divinity in all of Greek civilisation. Pheidias departed from tradition when, instead of depicting Zeus as a striding figure with thunderbolt in hand, he portrayed Zeus sitting serenely on his throne with his head so close to the ceiling that he would break through the roof were he to stand erect.[17] When asked how it occurred to him to depict Zeus in this way, Pheidias reported that he took inspiration from

---

[15] Brouwer, *The Stoic Sage*, 8, 41–49.
[16] In Plato's *Meno*, Socrates compares the *sophia* of Pheidias to that of the sophist Protagoras (91c). Aristotle contrasts the *sophia* of Pheidias with intellectual *sophia* (*Nicomachean Ethics* 1141a). In other sources, authors attribute *sophia* to Pheidias straightforwardly, without distinguishing it from other types of wisdom (e.g., Pausanius, *Description of Greece*, 6.4.5).
[17] Walter Burkert, *Greek Religion*, trans. John Raffan (Cambridge, MA, 1985), 124-125.

a scene in *Iliad* (1.528–530).[18] The first-century CE Greek orator Dio Chrysostom praised the *sophia* of Pheidias. In his 'Olympic Discourse', Dio explains that Pheidias produced a visual representation of Zeus that accords with Zeus' character as the just, peaceable and benevolent ruler of all. Dio commended artists and workmen like Pheidias whose *sophia* aided apprehension of the divine by expressing and strengthening an innate human reverence for the gods (*Discourses* 12.45–46). The *sophia* of a craftsman, far from being a simple or lowly form of mechanical proficiency, aligned with wisdom in its most philosophically articulate form.

Hellenistic writings open a holistic perspective on wisdom that forms an instructive contrast with scholarly understandings of wisdom oriented more narrowly toward theoretical understanding, scribal activity and the conventions of literary production. By beginning with a basic understanding of wisdom as a knowledge of the human and the divine that is enacted expertly in the world, it is possible to see the reflexes of wisdom in sacred art and architecture as well as in the more familiar wisdom domains of rulership and philosophy. On this view, divine knowledge figures into a wide variety of intellectual, cultural and political enterprises that aspire to excellence and higher being, and 'wisdom' names the way in which ontology, ethics and various types of human skill cohere within the context of that pursuit. It was and is possible to see a manifestation of wisdom in the ability to render dedicated spaces and objects fit for proper worship and, in this distinctive way, demonstrate knowledge both of the human and the divine.

WISDOM AND THE TABERNACLE

In the Hebrew Bible, artisans who produced structures or furnishings for the Tabernacle and Temple are described as wise (Exod 31:3, 6; 1 Kgs 7:14; 2 Chr 2:12). Whatever this wisdom involves, there can be no question of its consisting in a specific ability to produce a fitting image of God or the gods. Other skillful applications of human and divine knowledge, which accord with biblical prohibitions against divine images, must be sought out. How, then, should the *ḥokmâ* of certain craftsmen in Exodus, 1 Kings and 2 Chronicles be understood? One possible point of contact between cultic construction projects and wisdom is the cosmos, more specifically divine creation of the cosmos.

---

[18] Strabo, *Geography*, 8.353–354.

Jon Levenson, for example, has argued persuasively that a 'homology' between the world and the Temple (and Tabernacle) informed biblical thought.[19] According to Levenson, influence ran in both directions such that the world and the Temple were understood to conform to one another. As he puts it, the Temple is a microcosm, and the world is a macro-Temple.[20] If the cosmos is inserted as a third term alongside cult and wisdom, then it may be possible to connect the latter two via a shared concern for cosmic order or cosmic principles. Philo and Josephus, for example, explained the particularities of the Jewish cult as symbols of cosmic realities. Philo affirmed that the world itself was the true temple (*Spec. Leg.* 1.66), and he interpreted the attire of the high priest as a marvellous representation of the entire cosmos (*Spec. Leg.* 1.93–97). Josephus saw the structure of the Tabernacle in cosmic terms and, like Philo, understood the priestly vestments to correspond to things in the natural world: sky, lightning, thunder, the navel of the world, the four elements and the twelve zones of the zodiac (*Ant.* 3.179–187). Seen from this perspective, the cult may share in wisdom by symbolising a rational piety attuned to God's role as creator of an ordered cosmos. In this way, Jewish worship is seen as an aid to and expression of true philosophy.

The limitations of a philosophical construal, however, come into view when one considers the instructions for the building of the Tabernacle (Exodus 25–31), the description of the workers (Exod 31:1–11) and the carrying out of these instructions (Exodus 35–40). The Tabernacle is not described as a mirror of the cosmos but rather as a sanctuary (*miqdāš*) by which 'I [God] will dwell in their midst (*wəšākantî bətôkām*; 25:8)'. Its purpose is not contemplation but cohabitation. The aim of the Tabernacle project, so stated, creates a tense atmosphere of preparation and expectation in all that follows. The project is an intricate and demanding 'work' (*məlā'kâ*) to which the people contribute (Exod 35:29) and which Moses and those under him carefully execute. The narrative records highly specific instructions, reports of fastidious attention to detail and a disastrous attempt on the part of the people to create their own cultic apparatus (Exod 32). With the exception of sabbaths and events surrounding the Golden Calf episode, the 'work' occupies the entire Israelite camp until it is brought to a momentous close by Moses himself (Exod 40:33), who personally

---

[19] Jon D. Levenson, *Creation and the Persistence of Evil: The Jewish Drama of Divine Omnipotence* (Princeton, 1988), 82.

[20] Levenson, *Creation*, 86.

arranges the completed altars and vessels in advance of the promised theophany (Exod 40:34). The people, led by Moses, produce a portable shrine, a large and impressive artifact within which the God of Israel takes residence at the centre of the camp. With the divine presence comes a clear and present danger to the people, who can ill afford to make mistakes (Lev 10:1–11). The prospect of dwelling with God is fraught with fear and foreboding. Walter Burkert observes that 'religion bears an intimate relation to anxiety' such that, in various cultures, expressions for dealing with the divine are taken from words having to do with fear.[21] So, too, in ancient Israel.

The reality of divine danger lends urgency to the entire Tabernacle project. An impression of unease is reinforced by the minuteness of God's instructions to Moses and God's insistence that Moses do precisely what is commanded. In addition to verbal commands, Moses is also shown a 'pattern' (tabnît; Exod 25:9, 40) to guide the work on the Tabernacle and its furnishings.[22] Moses is thus permitted to see the finished product before the work is undertaken. He alone is granted a vision of the Tabernacle in its completed form. By contrast, the people have no recourse to sight or the seeing faculty. They merely experience the divine voice (Deut 4:33, 36); it is theirs 'to do and to hearken' (na 'ăśeh wənišmā'; Exod 24:7). The distinction between the two modes of perception suggests that, as overseer of the work, Moses has been placed in a superior epistemic position. There was a clear, specific and predetermined telos for the Tabernacle project, toward which Moses, as overseer, was obligated by God to direct the people's efforts. Everything involved with the work, then, was patterned and prescribed, and nothing was left to chance. It is against the backdrop of Israel's precarious life with God – not a leisured contemplation of cosmic first principles – that wisdom becomes intelligible and necessary in Exodus. Oddly, however, it is not the wisdom of Moses that plays a role in the narrative. He is nowhere described as wise or as possessing wisdom. The ability of Moses to follow the tabnît might plausibly have been regarded as an indication of wisdom; yet, the biblical text makes no such attribution.

Wisdom is attributed, instead, to the workers under Moses' supervision. After Moses has seen the pattern and heard detailed descriptions of

---

[21] Burkert, Greek Religion, 272–273.

[22] The tabnît is first mentioned in connection with Moses' personal audience with God on Mt. Sinai (Exod 25:9), where, presumably, he first sees the pattern. Subsequent references to this event reinforce the importance of sight. Even when the word tabnît is lacking (Exod 27:8) or replaced by another word (mišpaṭ; Exod 26:30), Moses is directed to remember what was shown to him 'on the mountain'.

what must be made, God makes Moses aware of specific individuals
who will implement the various designs: first, Bezalel son of Uri son of
Hur of the tribe of Judah and, second, Oholiab son of Ahisamach of the
tribe of Dan (Exod 31:1, 6). Few figures in the Bible are praised as
lavishly for their wisdom and spiritual endowments as Bezalel. The
introduction of Bezalel into the Tabernacle narrative at the beginning
of Exod 31 emphasises his chosenness and, in a manner of speaking, his
individuality. As if to avoid possible misidentification, God refers both
to the father and grandfather of Bezalel and states that he called this
Bezalel 'by name'. He is not merely an example of a skilled artisan; he is
a rather a specific person whom God filled with 'the spirit of God,
wisdom, understanding, knowledge, and the capacity for every kind of
work' (wā'ămallē' 'ōtô rûaḥ 'ĕlōhîm bəḥokmâ ūbitbūnâ ūbəda'at
ūbəkol-məlā'kâ; Exod 31:3). The profusion of wisdom words in this
short description and the explicit mention of 'the spirit of God' suggest
that Bezalel is an unusually inspired and elevated figure. To say that he
falls short of wisdom would require an ad hoc devaluation of other
sapiential attributes: understanding, knowledge and the divine spirit.
Indeed, to call him wise, even in the fullest sense of that term, would
appear to be an understatement. Given the high stakes involved in the
Tabernacle project and the intense pressure to implement prescriptions
for the divine dwelling with precision, it makes sense that the workers
should be equal to the task. Much depends on Moses' ability to carry out
instructions in accordance with the pattern, but so too does success
depend upon the quality of the physical work itself. Pattern and process
are inextricably linked.

Just as God called Bezalel by name and filled him with wisdom, he
'appointed' (nātattî) Oholiab to the work and 'endowed' the hearts of
skilful workers with additional wisdom (ūbəlēb kol-ḥakam-lēb nātattî
ḥokmâ; Exod 31:6). The verses that introduce the workers (Exod 31:1, 6)
employ the active voice, emphasising that God 'calls', 'fills', 'appoints'
and 'endows' them. The point of the passage is not to report that there
happened to be some skilled workers among the Israelites. It is rather to
affirm that God made certain individuals fit for a very specific task. The
wisdom of Bezalel, Oholiab and the workmen is carefully circumscribed. For them, wisdom is not a matter of enjoying the status or
position of a sage; nor is it a matter of possessing a general understanding of things in the manner of a philosopher.[23] Their wisdom is rather a

---

[23] When Moses repeats God's description of Bezalel and Oholiab in Exodus 35, he adds
    the tantalising detail that the two were also inspired to teach others (ūləhôrōt nātan

divine endowment that fits them for particular tasks. The text delimits their capabilities with reference to certain materials (gold, silver, bronze, precious stones, wood, fabric, oil, incense) and objects (the tent of meeting, the ark of the covenant, the mercy seat, lampstand, altars and vestments). As if to prevent the reader from generalising their wisdom, it makes clear just what their remit is. Just as the text clearly specifies the materials to be used in the Tabernacle (Exod 25:1–7), the description of the workers in Exod 31 identifies needed expertise as a divine endowment. The entire project is sourced fully by the divine realm. No less than in sapiential texts, God is understood here to be the giver of wisdom (cf. Job 12:13; Prov 2:6; Eccl 2:26). What is distinctive about the Tabernacle narrative, however, is that the 'givenness' of wisdom is addressed to the problem of how the Israelites may create a habitation for the divine and dwell safely with their God.

WISDOM AND THE TEMPLE

Not surprisingly, wisdom also features in the account of the building of the Temple in 1 Kings and 2 Chronicles. As with the Tabernacle, wisdom was needed for the Temple's construction. What is at least mildly surprising, however, is that *this* wisdom was not connected to Solomon himself. Despite the strong emphasis placed in these books on Solomon's celebrated wisdom, the connection between Solomonic wisdom and the Temple project is not straightforward. As is clear from the story of the dream at Gibeon, Solomon's wisdom is a divine grant (1 Kgs 3:4–15; 2 Chr 1:7–13). Yet Solomon's initial request is to be able to govern the people with 'wisdom and knowledge' (ḥokmâ ūmaddāʿ; 2 Chr 1:10). In granting this request, God likewise makes it clear that Solomon's wisdom is concerned with rulership (2 Chr 1:11–12).[24] Solomon's wisdom does not appear to concern cultic matters in general nor the Temple project in particular. Given the great importance of the Temple in accounts of Solomon's reign and the emphasis they place on divine knowledge, this seems odd – especially since God appeared to Solomon in a dream at a cultic site before Solomon began work on the

bəlibbô hûʾ wəʾoholîʾāb; v. 34). This suggests that their wisdom was in some sense transmittable, perhaps a skill or set of skills that could be taught, but to say more than this would be unhelpfully speculative.

[24] In the DH, the inclusion of the story of Solomon's ingenious resolution of the dispute concerning the two women and the infant immediately following the Gibeon episode (1 Kgs 3:16–28) supports the notion that Solomon's wisdom is concerned with rulership.

Temple. Noting the connection between personal divine revelation and the founding of sanctuaries in a number of biblical and ancient Near Eastern texts, Moshe Weinfeld has argued that 'the original dream of Solomon at Gibeon ... was a prophetic vision whose purpose was to grant divine approval for the sanctuary'.[25] If Weinfeld is correct, then an earlier tradition identifying Solomon with the wisdom or revelation needed to build the Temple was superseded by alternative understandings. Other perspectives, evident in 1 Kings and 1 and 2 Chronicles, suggest that although Solomon may have been the builder of the Temple, he was not its founder. Solomon's wisdom, peerless and prodigious though it was, was not the basis of the Temple project. For this, a different wisdom was needed.

The craftsman Hiram, called Huram-abi by the Chronicler and not to be confused with king Hiram of Tyre, functions in the role of the inspired Tabernacle workers in Exodus. The account of the Temple in 1 and 2 Chronicles resembles the Tabernacle narrative in many ways. For the Chronicler, initiative for the Temple project lies principally with David, who thought Solomon too young and inexperienced to handle so great a task (1 Chr 22:5). As in Exodus, work on the sanctuary is guided by a *tabnît*, which David receives from God in written form and shares with Solomon (1 Chr 28:11, 19). David enumerates all the gold and silver vessels and furnishings required for the Temple service (1 Chr 28:11–18), thus indicating that everything has already been designed and configured. Nothing will be left to chance, whim or foreign influence. He also assures Solomon that most of the raw materials and skilled personnel are already available (1 Chr 22:14–16; 28:21). Solomon, however, will need additional timber (1 Chr 22: 14). Obediently, Solomon waits for the appropriate time and then contacts king Hiram of Tyre to secure what is needed (2 Chr 2:3–10). A long-time ally of David, king Hiram agrees to supply wood from Lebanon and, importantly, a wise man capable of carrying out the work: the skilled worker Huram-abi, son of a Tyrian man and an Israelite woman from the tribe of Dan. Not only does he have an Israelite mother, he is also descended from the same tribe as Oholiab.[26] Described in Bezalel-like terms, Huram-abi is a 'wise man, one who knows insight' (*'îš-ḥākām yôdēa' bînâ*; 2 Chr 2:12), whose areas of expertise include metals, fabrics and engravings. King Hiram stipulates further that Huram-abi will work

---

[25] Moshe Weinfeld, *Deuteronomy and the Deuteronomic School* (Oxford, 1972), 248.
[26] In 1 Kings, Hiram's mother is said to come from the tribe of Naphtali (7:14).

collaboratively with the skilled craftsmen whom David already provided (2 Chr 2:14).

David plays a less active role in the Temple project in the Deuteronomistic History (DH). Though he makes the original proposal to build the Temple, God instructs the prophet Nathan to tell David that Solomon will do it after David has died (2 Samuel 7). There is no mention of a *tabnît* and no description of David preparing for Temple construction. Moreover, David's last words to Solomon (1 Kgs 2:1–9) make no reference to the Temple project. When Solomon begins to reign, he demonstrates judicial wisdom and administrative expertise, but it is unclear how (or whether) he has the knowledge of cultic matters necessary to build the Temple. Whereas Solomon initiates contact with king Hiram in 2 Chronicles, it is Hiram who reaches out to Solomon in 1 Kings (5:15; ET 5:1). In responding to Hiram, Solomon refers to the dormant Temple project and requests Hiram's help in carrying it out. Evidently pleased that Solomon means to maintain David's alliance with him and to draw on Tyrian expertise, King Hiram 'rejoices greatly' and praises Solomon as a 'wise son' of David (1 Kgs 5:21; ET 5:7). The note of congratulation here seems to recognise Solomon's wisdom in cultic matters insofar as Solomon has turned to the king of Tyre for assistance in building the Temple.[27] The impression that Solomon lacks the capacity to build the Temple apart from Hiram's help is reinforced by a brief but significant note that follows the successful conclusion of a treaty between Solomon and Hiram, according to which the latter will provide wood and workers and the former large amounts of wheat and oil. In summarising the proceedings, the text notes that 'YHWH gave wisdom to Solomon as he promised him. There was peace between Hiram and Solomon; the two of them made a treaty' (1 Kgs 5:26; ET 5:12). The prudence of turning to Hiram for help in building the Temple must be counted among the numerous reflexes of Solomon's wisdom in 1 Kings. The sagacity of this decision is confirmed when Solomon invites and receives the craftsman Hiram (Huram-abi) at a critical stage in Temple construction. When he arrives, he is described with virtually the same words applied earlier to Bezalel, as one who is 'filled with the wisdom, the understanding, and the knowledge to do every kind of bronzework' (*wayyimmālē' 'et-haḥokmâ wə'et-hattəbūnâ*

---

[27] Second Chronicles also records the note of congratulation and the mention of Solomon as a 'wise son', but it contains a fuller statement, in which Hiram minimises the Tyrian contribution and emphasises that Solomon is the true builder of the Temple (2:12).

wə'et-hadda'at la'ăśôt kol-məlā'kâ bannəḥōšet; 1 Kgs 7:14).[28] The grandeur of the Temple is enhanced greatly by the two huge bronze pillars, the molten sea, the wheeled bronze stands and the large basins produced by Hiram. The skill to create them was beyond what Solomon or his workers possessed, but it was, in the view of 1 Kings, undoubtedly a wise decision for Solomon to seek help from Tyre and employ a man who did.

UNWISE LEADERS

Certain prophetic condemnations of rulers and people in positions of authority take aim, specifically, at the putative 'wisdom' of those leaders. Turning to select passages in Ezekiel and Jeremiah, this section explores the possibility that some of these condemnations reflect an understanding of wisdom that is related to expertise in cultic matters. The first set of passages concerns the portrayal of Tyre in the book of Ezekiel. In descriptions of the building of the Temple, the kingdom of Tyre, as we have seen, provides valuable expertise and needed materials. First Kings contains a fuller recognition of Tyrian help than Chronicles allows, but, given similarities with the Tabernacle project and the Bezalel-like characterisation of the worker Hiram (Huram-abi) in the texts, it seems that both the DH and the Chronicler saw Solomon as the beneficiary of Tyrian wisdom in his capacity as builder of the Temple. The question here is whether a similar perspective on Tyre is discernible in the book of Ezekiel. With its unusual depiction of the king of Tyre as a one-time denizen of the heavenly realm, Ezekiel 28 stands out among Ezekiel's oracles against the nations. At issue here is the role that this depiction plays in explaining why Tyre stands under divine judgement. Given the reputation of Tyre as a source of the specialised skills and fine materials needed to construct, adorn and furnish temples, it stands to reason that the close association of the king of Tyre with the divine dwelling in this chapter bears some relation to Tyre's reputation for cultic expertise. Indeed, if wisdom is understood as expert knowledge of cultic matters, then the remarkable profusion of references to 'wisdom' (*ḥokmâ*) in chapter 28 (vv. 3, 4, 5, 7, 12, 17) fits quite well with the prophet's extraordinary portrayal of the king of Tyre as

---

[28] English translations (e.g., RSV, NRSV, Tanakh, NASB) do not typically translate the definite articles in this verse, making Hiram's skill somewhat more generalised. However, the inclusion of the definite article in this verse serves to emphasise the special fitness of Hiram to build important features of the Temple.

one who lived at one time in the divine sanctuary. References to wisdom in Ezekiel 28 suggest that proximity to the divine, skill in sacred architecture and the specialised knowledge of human and divine things that this skill entails have all somehow degraded, turning into a specific form of wickedness expressed by the prophet's statement that 'you [i.e., the king of Tyre] have corrupted your wisdom' (šiḥattâ ḥokmātəkā; 28:17).

The context for this statement bears consideration. Ezekiel 28 is part of a larger section of the book devoted especially to Tyre (Ezekiel 26–28).[29] The oracle against the city in Ezekiel 26 blames the Tyrians for seeing the fall of Jerusalem as an opportunity to enrich themselves (v. 2). What they do not see, however, is that their city is also vulnerable. Despite the city's reputation for being a mighty island fortress (v. 17), it will fall to its enemies and be utterly destroyed. The subsequent lamentation over Tyre in the chapter that follows takes up a different theme. In Ezekiel 27, Tyre is not an impregnable city protected by the sea; it is a great ship laden with rich cargo, out on the open waters (v. 25). A catalogue of international trading partners and the various commodities and luxury items that they exchanged with Tyre (vv. 12–25) sets up the description of a spectacular maritime disaster in which the ship of Tyre, battered by the waves, sinks into the depths with all its crew and precious cargo (v. 34). Tyre's vast commercial wealth, far from saving it, merely hastens and dramatises its demise. The final parts of this section (Ezek 28:1–10, 11–19) turn to a third theme: the vaunted wisdom of the king of Tyre. The fact that the king, a mortal man, thinks of himself in God-like terms (vv. 2, 6, 9) and has grown haughty on account of his power (v. 5) and beauty (v. 17) has led many commentators to see pride, arrogance or hubris as the characteristic sin of the king of Tyre.[30] The point here is not to dispute the thematic importance of pride but rather to suggest that the oracle of judgement only makes sense if the king has

---

[29] On the fourfold structure of this section, see Greg Goering, 'Proleptic Fulfillment of the Prophetic Word: Ezekiel's Dirges over Tyre and Its Ruler', *JSOT* 36 (2012): 483–505. Goering marks (1) a judgement oracle against the city of Tyre (26:1–21) followed by (2) a dirge over the city of Tyre (27:1–36) and then (3) a judgement oracle against the ruler of Tyre (28:1–10) followed by (4) a dirge over the ruler of Tyre (28:11–19).

[30] The interpretation of 'wisdom' as related to Tyre's commercial success, wealth and arrogance is common. See, for example, Goering, 'Proleptic Fulfillment', 490–491; William R. Osborne, 'Wisdom Gets "Tyred" in the Book of Ezekiel', in *Riddles and Revelations: Explorations into the Relation between Wisdom and Prophecy in the Hebrew Bible*, ed. Mark J. Boda, Russell L. Meek, and William R. Osborne (London, 2018), 118.

a reason to be proud in the first place. Just as the Tyrians took pride in their city's defences (Ezekiel 26) and in their wealth (Ezekiel 27), so the king of Tyre takes pride in a distinctive proximity to the divine and the advantages that this affords. In other words, he takes pride in his wisdom.

This wisdom, though good in itself, has two blameworthy reflexes. The first is an intemperate ambition to profit from cultic expertise, to amass gold and silver in the city treasuries (28:4) using religious knowledge. Ezekiel connects the acquisition of wealth, specifically, to commercial activity undertaken in connection with wisdom: 'in your great wisdom, in your trade, you have increased your wealth' (*bərōb ḥokmātəkā bīrkūllātəkā hirbîtā ḥêlekā*; 28:5). That this wisdom is not simply skill in making money but rather a certain skill in understanding divine matters is evident from the following verse in which the prophet notes that the ruler has compared himself to God (*tittəkā 'et-ləbābəkā kəlēb 'ĕlōhîm*; 28:6). The wisdom of the Tyrian ruler, then, was not a commercial skill only but rather the lucrative knowledge of a consultant who is able to profit by providing the nations with materials and advice for the construction of sacred buildings. The promised punishment, then, does not have to do merely with a loss of wealth as in Ezekiel 27; instead, the punishment is an assault on Tyre's own temples, a violent destruction of the 'beauty of [its] wisdom' and a 'defiling of [its] splendor' (*wəhērîqû ḥarbôtām 'al-yəpî ḥokmāteka wəhilləlû yip'āteka*; 28:7). The second blameworthy reflex is the isolation of cultic expertise from other moral and ontological dimensions of wisdom. In elaborating the religious psychology of the king, the prophet, remarkably, does not accuse the Tyrian ruler of idolatry. Instead, he affirms the real and legitimate proximity of the king to the divine dwelling, referred to both as 'Eden, the garden of God' (v. 13) and as 'the mountain of God' (v. 16).[31] How the king of Tyre came to enjoy this exalted position is mysterious; what is clear, though, is that he was intimate with Eden's precious stones, fine details and sacred precincts

---

[31]   The historical and mythological background of Ezekiel's depiction of the king of Tyre as a 'cherub' (v. 14) or the companion of a cherub (LXX) has been the subject of much scholarly discussion. Whether Ezekiel draws here on Ugaritic El traditions (Marvin Pope, *El in the Ugaritic Texts* [Leiden, 1955], 97–103), the book of Genesis (Norman Habel, 'Ezekiel 28 and the Fall of the First Man' *Concordia Theological Monthly* 38 [1967]: 516–524) or a different story about primeval man (John Van Seters, 'The Creation of Man and the Creation of the King', *ZAW* 101 [1989]: 333–342), it is clear that he identifies the king with intimate knowledge of the divine.

as one would expect a cultic expert to be.[32] For this reason, the king is identified not only with the beauty of the divine dwelling (*ūkəlîl yōpî*); he is also described as one who is 'full of wisdom' (*mālē' ḥokmâ; 28:12*). This wisdom, when oriented properly, includes a fitting understanding of divine authority and human limitation. The king's fall, which is attributed to 'iniquity' and 'violence' related to trade, occurs when the king transgresses moral and ontological boundaries inherent in wisdom (v. 16). The king grew haughty, valuing the 'splendour' (v. 17) arising from his commercial empire and cultic virtuosity. In this way, he incurred God's fiery wrath (v. 18). An important distinction, then, must be observed: the king's fall resulted not from his lack of wisdom but rather from the 'corruption' of a wisdom that he already possessed (v. 17).

Certain references to wisdom in the book of Jeremiah, though connected with Jerusalem rather than Tyre, may reflect a similar understanding. Just as Ezekiel criticised the Tyrians for trusting in their wisdom, wealth and unassailability, Jeremiah tells the Judahites not to glory in precisely these things: 'Let not the wise man glory in his wisdom, let not the mighty man glory in his might, let not the rich man glory in his riches' (RSV; Jer 9:23). Ezekiel asserted that it was foolish for the king of Tyre to trust in the city's defences and commercial success and to take pride in his intimate knowledge of the divine sanctuary. Similarly, Jeremiah, standing at the gate of the Temple, instructs the people not to trust that its sacredness will somehow save them from divine judgement (Jer 7:1–15; 26:4–6). Judah's cultic excellence will not avail the people of Jerusalem when God calls them to account for murder, adultery, dishonesty and idolatry. Neither will wisdom derived from the law, which has been falsified by the 'lying pen of the scribes' (RSV; Jer 8:8). The burden of the prophet is to explain how Judah, despite having the Temple and its revered priesthood, the Law and its learned interpreters, yet stands on the brink of unimaginable disaster. Jeremiah characterises resistance to the prophetic message as a systematic understanding – a wrong-headed 'wisdom' – that prevents the people and their leaders from accepting the prophet's message of doom. For this reason, the commitment of religious leaders to a

---

[32] Robert Wilson accounts for the mysterious position of the king of Tyre in 'Eden' by arguing that the oracle against Tyre alludes to the Jerusalem temple and its priests and functions as an oblique oracle against them. See Robert R. Wilson, 'The Death of the King of Tyre: The Editorial History of Ezekiel 28', in *Love and Death in the Ancient Near East*, ed. John H. Marks and Robert M. Good (Guildford, 1987), 211–218.

notion of Judahite exceptionalism has become a wisdom that will be confounded. To make the point, Jeremiah draws a gendered contrast between available wisdoms. On the one hand, 'the wise man' of Judah (hā'îš heḥākām; 9:11; ET 9:12), whether scribe or priest, has failed to reckon with the imminence and justice of a divine judgement that will bring ruin upon the land. The wise man will thus be proven disastrously wrong. On the other hand, the women of Judah possess a wisdom that answers perfectly to the moment. Instead of heeding the wise man, the people ought to call for the 'mourners' (məqônənôt), the 'wise women' (haḥākāmôt), to raise a lament for Judah (9:16; ET 9:17). It is the skilful work of the women who mourn, not the ruling wisdom of Judah's elites, that in this case reflects an accurate knowledge of human and divine things.

CONCLUSION

In studies of biblical wisdom, much scholarly effort has gone into the identification of wisdom as a more or less discrete thing: a literary corpus, an intellectual enterprise, a scribal class, a body of tradition, a theological outlook, a social movement. In essentialising wisdom in this way, such studies have raised important questions about the poetics, social dynamics and literary forms of many biblical compositions. Scholars have discerned important commonalities among texts within the biblical canon and the wider body of ancient Near Eastern literature. In doing so, they have made it possible to isolate wisdom and to analyse its influence on a variety of non-wisdom texts.[33] This chapter, however, suggests that it may be useful to revisit understandings of wisdom in a more capacious way than has sometimes been undertaken – not merely as a literary or sociological phenomenon but rather as a flexible concept useful in a wide array of rhetorical contexts. Put differently, this chapter begins with the idea that 'wisdom' (sophia; ḥokmâ) is a word that carries an assortment of meanings and connotations. It has focused attention on one ancient, time-honoured strand of meanings – wisdom as

---

[33] For criticisms of scholarly attempts to trace the 'influence' of wisdom on other types of biblical literature, see essays by Mark Sneed ('Methods, Muddles, and Modes of Literature: The Question of Influence between Wisdom and Prophecy', 30–44), Will Kynes ('"Wisdom" as Mask and Mirror: Methodological Questions for "Wisdom's" Dialogue with the Canon', 19–29) and Stuart Weeks ('Overlap? Influence? Allusion? The Importance of Asking the Right Questions', 45–54) in *Riddles and Revelations: Explorations into the Relation between Wisdom and Prophecy in the Hebrew Bible*, ed. Mark J. Boda, Russell L. Meek and William R. Osborne (London, 2018).

'knowledge of things human and divine' – in order to explore the wider resonance of wisdom in texts that are not always given their due in scholarly discussions of wisdom as a social or literary phenomenon. By correlating knowledge of human and divine things specifically to cultic activity, the chapter argues that wisdom as word or concept was useful to biblical authors concerned to address an assortment of political, social and theological issues. As we have seen, 'wisdom' captures the special giftedness by which workers in Exodus, 1 Kings and 2 Chronicles were able to complete the difficult, delicate and dangerous task of rendering sacred space fit for the divine presence.[34] Thus, wisdom resonates in the cult. For Ezekiel and Jeremiah, 'wisdom' was useful in expressing how religious knowledge, moral attitudes and cultic expertise coalesce into systematic understandings of the relation between God and humanity – and useful, too, in describing how these understandings go awry when they become presumptuous and self-serving and so turn into false or bad wisdoms. In this way, 'wisdom' resonates in the prophetic literature. It would, of course, be possible to identify other resonances of wisdom throughout the biblical canon or, indeed, to dispute those put forward in this chapter. However the wider meanings of wisdom are explored, though, it may be helpful to remember that detecting the resonance of a sound depends as much on what one tunes out as on what one tunes in.

Further Reading

Boda, Mark J., Russell L. Meek and William R. Osborne, eds. *Riddles and Revelations: Explorations into the Relation between Wisdom and Prophecy in the Hebrew Bible.* London: 2018.

Brouwer, René. *The Stoic Sage: The Early Stoics on Wisdom, Sagehood, and Socrates.* Cambridge: 2014.

Burkert, Walter. *Greek Religion.* Translated by John Raffan. Cambridge, MA: 1985.

Kynes, Will. *An Obituary for 'Wisdom Literature': The Birth, Death, and Intertextual Reintegration of a Biblical Corpus.* Oxford: 2019.

Legaspi, Michael C. *Wisdom in Classical and Biblical Tradition.* New York: 2018.

---

[34] In the New Testament, Paul portrays himself in Bezalel-like terms when he describes his role as the builder of the Corinthian church. After criticising human pretensions to wisdom in terms of ruling knowledge, he nevertheless refers to himself as a 'wise master-builder' (*sophos architektōn*; 1 Cor. 3:10) in order to affirm this 'architectural' aspect of wisdom. See Legaspi, *Wisdom in Classical and Biblical Tradition*, 234–236.

Levenson, Jon D. *Creation and the Persistence of Evil: The Jewish Drama of Divine Omnipotence*. Princeton: 1988.

Najman, Hindy, Jean-Sébastien Rey and Eibert J. C. Tigchelaar, eds. *Tracing Sapiential Traditions in Ancient Judaism*. JSJSup 174. Leiden: 2016.

Perdue, Leo. *Wisdom and Cult: A Critical Analysis of the Views of Cult in the Wisdom Literature of Israel and the Ancient Near East*. SBLDS 30. Missoula: 1977.

Schwáb, Zoltán. *Toward an Interpretation of the Book of Proverbs: Selfishness and Secularity Revisited*. JTISup 7. Winona Lake: 2013.

Van Leeuwen, Raymond C. 'Cosmos, Temple, House: Building and Wisdom in Ancient Mesopotamia and Israel'. Pages 399–421 in *From the Foundations to the Crenellations: Essays on Temple Building in the Ancient Near East and Hebrew Bible*. Edited by Mark J. Boda and Jamie Novotny. AOAT 366. Münster: 2010.

Part III

Wisdom Literature beyond the Hebrew Bible

14 Ben Sira

SETH A. BLEDSOE

INTRODUCTION

The book of Ben Sira is named for its author, Yeshua ben Eleazar ben Sira (50:27), who is the *ben* (= '(grand)son') of one Sira. In Greek, the grandfather's name is rendered Sirach, which became a common alternative title. In the Latin tradition, it carried the designation *Liber Ecclesiasticus* ('the church book') or, simply, Ecclesiasticus.

Composed originally in Hebrew during the first quarter of the second century BCE, the book of Ben Sira is a wisdom text comprising a diverse collection of proverbial instructions, lengthy musings and poems and hymns. As in many wisdom texts, Ben Sira adopts a pedagogic voice, offering readers guidance and instruction on ethics, society and the cosmos with the aim of inculcating in its 'students' the highest values so they may attain wisdom and thus live a successful and happy life. The work most closely resembles Proverbs, a text on which Ben Sira undoubtedly depended. Yet much of Ben Sira is distinctive from Proverbs and other early instructional literature. The poetic and hymnic passages strongly echo Psalms and the book of Job. Specific images and sayings also evoke the book's Hellenistic literary milieu. Most notably, Ben Sira *expands upon the inherited wisdom tradition* of Proverbs by explicitly connecting it with the broader Jewish themes of Torah and covenantal history.

CANON, COMPOSITION AND TEXTUAL TRADITION

The book of Ben Sira occupies an important position in the history of Jewish literature and, notably, in the history of canon development. While Ben Sira did not come to be included in the Hebrew Bible (i.e., the Tanakh), the inclusion of the Greek translation of Ben Sira in the manuscript tradition of the Septuagint (LXX) afforded it an eventual canonical status among early Christians and, subsequently, the

Roman Catholic and Eastern Orthodox traditions. Most Protestants do
not consider it to be canonical, relegating it to the status of 'Apocrypha'.
Still, the work is seen by many as a sort of 'Archimedean Point for
Israelite-Jewish literature',[1] given its relatively secure dating and its
palpable awareness of and reflection on literary traditions that came to
be recognised as canonical. The grandson's Prologue contains the earliest references to the threefold division of what would become the
Hebrew Bible. Three times in his short homage to 'Jesus son of Sirach'
the grandson mentions 'the Law, the Prophets and the other books of
our ancestors' (Sirach Prologue). It is generally agreed that this threefold
reference is not attesting to a canon per se but rather to discrete groupings of texts that were held in high esteem, even as they were still
in flux.

The composition of the original Hebrew work can be dated to
sometime in the first quarter of the second century BCE, with suggested
dates between 198 and 175 BCE. The solidity with which the text can be
dated depends largely on the reference to the high priest Simon
(50:1–24), generally taken to be Simon II (d. 195 BCE), who served as
high priest in Jerusalem (219–195 BCE) after his father Onias II
(cf. Josephus, *Ant.* 12.224). Most scholars understand the work's praise
of this figure as a sort of eulogy (cf. 50:1). Thus, scholars date this text to
the end of Simon II's life or the years just after his death. Notably, the
work seems to betray no hint of the tumultuous Maccabean era beginning in the mid-170s – although some have pointed to the hymn of
deliverance and mercy (35:20–36:22), and its specific focus on Jerusalem
(cf. 36:18–19), as a possible allusion to the crisis.

The early second century BCE dating is further supported by evidence in the Prologue to the Greek translation. The translator claims to
be the grandson of Jesus (= Yeshua) and that he undertook the translation of his grandfather's work after arriving in Egypt in the thirty-eighth
year of Euergetes, typically understood to be Ptolemy VIII Euergetes II
(r. 170–163, 145–116), thus supposing the year 132 BCE. Since he claims
to have produced the translation 'some time' after arriving in Egypt, a
general suggestion is around 120 BCE. This dating of the translation,
presumably two generations after the original, fits reasonably well with
an early second century date of the Hebrew composition.

---

[1] Markus Witte, 'Key Aspects and Themes in Recent Scholarship on the Book of Ben
    Sira', in *Texts and Contexts of the Book of Ben Sira/Texte und Kontexte des
    Sirachbuches*, ed. Gerhard Karner, Frank Ueberschaer and Burkard M. Zapff
    (Atlanta, 2017), 1.

Ben Sira presents a tremendously complex picture in terms of textual witnesses and transmission history, with the work attested in Hebrew, Greek, Latin and Syriac (among others). The Hebrew witnesses from the Cairo Genizah, Masada and Qumran are important as they attest the original language of composition; however, the evidence is incomplete (equalling only about two-thirds of the total text) and each witness contains variant readings in comparison with both the other Hebrew manuscripts and the Greek versions, including divergences in the text's arrangement. Therefore, most modern editions and translations of Ben Sira are based on the Greek witnesses, though these also present a complicated picture, not only because they 'differ not a little' (Sirach Prologue) when compared with the Hebrew manuscripts but given that both a short and long version are extant.[2]

The available ancient manuscripts demonstrate clearly that the transmission history of Ben Sira was multivalent and remained fluid for centuries after its composition.[3] Thus, when it comes to understanding both the composition and significance of Ben Sira for early Jewish and Christian communities, each individual witness should be treated as a particular 'instance' of the text with its own socio-historical, material, literary and interpretive history.[4]

THE SAGE, THE SCRIBE AND THE SOURCES OF HIS WISDOM

Ben Sira is somewhat exceptional in that its author is named (50:27), though it preserves few other biographical details. Ben Sira was a sage and scribe operating among the upper echelons of Judean society during the late third and early second century BCE, perhaps in Jerusalem itself as suggested by his prominent attention to and familiarity with the priesthood (7:29–31) and sacrificial system (34:21–35:13; a few scholars have consequently argued that Ben Sira was himself a priest).[5]

---

[2] Pancratius C. Beentjes, *The Book of Ben Sira in Hebrew: A Text Edition of All Extant Hebrew Manuscripts and a Synopsis of All Parallel Hebrew Ben Sira Texts*, VTSup 68 (Leiden, 1997 [repr. and rev. ed. Atlanta, 2006]), 1–10; and Witte, 'Key Aspects', esp. 4–9.

[3] Jean-Sébastien Rey, 'Scribal Practices in the Ben Sira Hebrew Manuscript A and Codicological Remarks', in *Texts and Contexts of the Book of Ben Sira/Texte und Kontexte des Sirachbuches*, ed. Gerhard Karner, Frank Ueberschaer and Burkard M. Zapff (Atlanta, 2017), 99–112.

[4] Rey, 'Scribal Practices', 99–100.

[5] Cf. Samuel L. Adams, *Wisdom in Transition: Act and Consequence in Second Temple Instructions*, JSJSup 125 (Leiden, 2008), 161–162.

As a sage, Ben Sira was a well-educated and wise figure, trained in and conversant with 'the wisdom of the ancient ones' (39:1), likely meaning an inherited tradition of wise sayings and instructions, such as those found in Proverbs.[6] The sage was both a *model for* as well as *purveyor of* wisdom or wise behaviour,[7] hinting at Ben Sira's professional role as an educator committed to 'instruction' (Heb. *musar;* Grk. *paideia*). As a teacher, Ben Sira ostensibly wrote for his students, and the authorial voice he adopted, therefore, is one of pedagogy, a rhetorical position evident in his dramatic occupation of the role of teacher – often metaphorically configured as father/parent to '(my) child' (e.g., 3:12; 6:18, 32; 31:22). Ben Sira encouraged his students to learn from the 'discourse of the sages' and their 'maxims', a probable allusion to Proverbs and other materials (8:8–9). The sage also invited students to come and learn at his 'house of instruction' (51:23, Heb. *bet midrash*), though it is unclear whether this may refer to a formal institution (i.e., a 'school') or simply the practice of well-to-do youths being sent to the home of a revered sage to be trained in an apprentice-like fashion.[8] Some have seen this pedagogic perspective as an emulation of the Greek concept of 'paideia' or disciplined instruction (cf. 16:24–25). In any case, Ben Sira's work reflects the attitudes and worldview of an esteemed *literatus* who proffers a body of knowledge and wisdom that has been carefully curated for elite, (ostensibly) male youths in preparation for life in general and for service in the upper echelons of society in particular.

The specific professional function of Ben Sira and his students-in-training is that of a scribe. While scribes operated among the social elite, they were not *of* them per se. Several passages make this distinction clear, with references to proper behaviour *before* a ruler or noble (e.g., 4:27, 41:17) especially at a banquet (e.g., 13:9–11) and a few even admonishing against the student's potential desire to become rich and powerful (e.g., 7:6, 13:2). In one of the more exceptional passages (38:24–39:11), Ben Sira outlines the advantages of scribes over farmers, artisans and other types of workers 'who rely on their hands' (38:31), a passage reminiscent of the Egyptian Instruction of Dua-Khety, also known as

---

[6] Jeremy Corley, 'An Intertextual Study of Proverbs and Ben Sira', in *Intertextual Studies in Ben Sira and Tobit: Essays in Honor of Alexander A. Di Lella, O.F.M.*, ed. Jeremy Corley and Vincent Skemp, CBQMS 38 (Washington, 2005), 155–182.

[7] Benjamin Wright, 'Ben Sira on the Sage as Exemplar', in *Praise Israel for Wisdom and Instruction: Essays on Ben Sira and Wisdom, the Letter of Aristeas and the Septuagint*, ed. Benjamin Wright, JSJSup 131 (Leiden, 2008), 165–182.

[8] John J. Collins, *Jewish Wisdom in the Hellenistic Age* (Louisville, 1997), 35–39.

the 'Satire of Trades'.[9] While the Egyptian text is generally understood to have a more denigrating tone toward the other professions – 'each of which is more wretched than the other'[10] – Ben Sira offers a gentler evaluation, noting that 'without them no city can be inhabited, and wherever they live, they will not go hungry' (38:32–34). Nevertheless, Ben Sira promulgates the skill and prestige of the scribe, who does not depend on fulfilling mundane tasks simply to avoid hunger but rather has 'the opportunity of leisure' (38:24) and serves 'among the great and appears before rulers' (39:4).

Ben Sira frequently alludes to the sources of a sage's wisdom. He calls for his students and would-be scribes to 'seek out the wisdom of the ancients' (39:1), but he also suggests the scribe should busy himself with 'prophecies' and 'meditate on mysteries' (39:7). In contrast to Proverbs, Ben Sira highlights that the source of one's wisdom lies not only in study and reflection but also in piety:

> [The scribe] sets his heart to rise early to seek the Lord who made him and to petition the Most High; he opens his mouth in prayer . . . . If the great Lord is willing, he will be filled with the spirit of understanding and will pour forth words of wisdom of his own . . . . The Lord will direct his counsel and knowledge. (39:5–7)

The image of the sage as a passive vessel through which the revelation from God could flow like water (cf. 24:30–34) mimics the prophetic tradition more than the studious sage of the proverbial model. Indeed, Ben Sira's description of the pious scribe dependent on divine revelation blurs the boundary between sage and seer.[11]

A prominent source of Ben Sira's wisdom, perhaps even more than Proverbs, is the Torah. According to the grandson's prologue, Ben Sira was a devoted student of the inherited literary traditions of Israel, arguing he had gained 'considerable proficiency in them' (Sir Prologue). The Praise of Ancestors (chs. 44–50) clearly draws on the written traditions of the Torah and Prophets in highlighting prominent figures from Israel's past. Several other passages throughout the work may be understood as exegesis of Torah, especially Genesis. For example, Ben Sira 17:1–24 is an elaboration upon the creation of

---

[9] Patrick W. Skehan and Alexander A. Di Lella. *The Wisdom of Ben Sira*, AB 39 (New York, 1987), 449–453.

[10] Translation from Miriam Lichtheim, *Ancient Egyptian Literature*, 3 vols, 2nd ed. (Berkeley, 2006), 1:189.

[11] Benjamin G. Wright III, 'Conflicted Boundaries: Ben Sira, Sage and Seer', in *Congress Volume Helsinki 2010*, ed. Martti Nissinen, VTSup 148 (Leiden, 2012), 229–253.

humankind and clearly evokes the creation stories – for example, humans created from the earth and return to it (17:1), the granting of authority over beasts (vv. 2–4), created 'in his own image' (v. 3).

Ben Sira has further carefully crafted his pedagogic instruction by using a variety of sources beyond the inherited traditions of Israel. Ben Sira's maxims have especially strong parallels with Egyptian instructions, including the Satire of Trade noted above, the Demotic Papyrus Insinger (also referred to as the Instruction of Phibis) and, to a lesser extent, Ankhsheshonqe.[12]

Ben Sira also demonstrates awareness of Greek literature and thought. While the extent of his familiarity is debated,[13] several passages suggest at least a passing knowledge, if not direct influence. For instance, Ben Sira's comparison of humanity's generations to falling leaves (14:18) is generally understood to have been inspired by the *Iliad* 6.146–149. There is also general agreement that Ben Sira utilised, to some extent, the Greek poet Theognis. This is particularly evident in his discussion of friendship, where he employs specific language and imagery linked to the poet but, importantly, not found in Proverbs' treatment of the topic (e.g., friends 'who sit at your table', cf. Theognis 115–116).[14] Some scholars have further seen the praise of Wisdom in ch. 24 as inspired not only by Proverbs but also by the contemporaneous Isis aretalogies.[15] Additionally, Ben Sira's general theological outlook as it relates to God, creation and theodicy has been connected with Stoic philosophy.[16] The hymn to God the creator in 42:15–43:33 contains several images that suggest Stoic influence, especially the notion of things created in opposing pairs (42:24; cf. 33:14–15) and the seemingly pantheistic statement in 43:27 ('We could say more but could never say enough; let the final word be *"He is the all"'*).[17]

In his praise of scribes, Ben Sira seems to confirm this outward-looking stance for acquiring wisdom by promoting travel as a useful

---

[12] Adams, *Wisdom in Transition*, 170–177.

[13] Collins, *Jewish Wisdom*, 39–41.

[14] Samuel L. Adams, 'Reassessing the Exclusivism of Ben Sira's Jewish Paideia', in *Second Temple Jewish 'Paideia' in Context*, ed. Jason M. Zurawski and Gabriele Boccaccini, BZNW 228 (Berlin, 2017), 51; Collins, *Jewish Wisdom*, 40.

[15] Judith H. Newman, 'Hybridity, Hydrology, and Hidden Transcript: Sirach 24 and the Judean Encounter with Ptolemaic Isis Worship', in *Jewish Cultural Encounters in the Ancient Mediterranean and Near Eastern World*, ed. Mladen Popović, Myles Schoonover and Marijn Vandenberghe, JSJSup 178 (Leiden, 2017), 157–176.

[16] D. Winston, 'Theodicy in Ben Sira and Stoic Philosophy', in *Of Scholars, Savants, and Their Texts*, ed. R. Link Salinger (New York, 1989), 239–249.

[17] Adams, 'Reassessing the Exclusivism', 53; Collins *Jewish Wisdom*, 84–89.

endeavor: the scribe is one who 'travels in foreign lands, and learns what is good and evil in the human lot' (39:4). The sage himself, in one of several personal reflections, speaks about his own travels and the tangible benefits they afforded him, such that he was even able to 'escape death because of these experiences' (34:12–13; cf. 51:13).

All in all, Ben Sira represents himself as a highly educated sage who has incorporated not only the Israelite/Jewish literary tradition but also the literary and intellectual traditions of the broader Hellenistic world, having gained some of his wisdom through personal experience among the elite or in travel to foreign lands. Previously, it was thought that Ben Sira represented a 'traditional Jewish' perspective that actively resisted and even castigated the inroads of Hellenism. Yet the sage's dependence on sapiential and philosophical traditions external to the Jewish context and his frequent allusions to Hellenistic cultural themes – for example, physicians (38:1–15), banquets (31:12–32:13), travel (34:9–13), honour/shame (41:17–42:8)[18] – mitigate against such an exclusivist interpretation.[19]

STRUCTURE, GENRES AND CONTENT

The book of Ben Sira exhibits a wide variety of content and genres. As a text reasonably situated under the scholarly category of 'wisdom literature', Ben Sira includes numerous examples of proverbial sayings, admonitions and aphorisms typical to this designation. Ben Sira is notable, however, for its extensive use of other (sub-)genres, such as hymns, poems and prayers. Some of these feature in earlier chapters – especially poems in praise of wisdom (e.g., 1:1–10; 4:11–19) and the works of God (e.g., 16:24–17:20; 18:1–14) – but, beginning with the hymn to Woman Wisdom in ch. 24, the rest of the work largely comprises lengthy poetic sections, such as encomia for the physician (38:1–15) and the scribe (38:16–39:11), petitionary prayers for individual (22:27–23:6) and communal deliverance (36:1–22), hymns in praise of God's creative actions (39:12–35; 42:15–43:33), theological reflections on death (41:1–15) and the 'Praise of Fathers' (chs. 44–50).

---

[18] Otto Kaiser, 'Jesus Sirach: Ein jüdischer Weisheitslehrer in hellenistischer Zeit', in *Texts and Contexts of the Book of Ben Sira/Texte und Kontexte des Sirachbuches*, ed. Gerhard Karner, Frank Ueberschaer and Burkard M. Zapff (Atlanta, 2017), 53–69, esp. 66.

[19] Cf. Adams, 'Reassessing the Exclusivism', *passim*.

Ben Sira's thematic concerns, especially among the proverbial instructions, cover a variety of typical 'wisdom' topics, many of which are arranged in a lengthy series of sayings unified by theme and/or form. Some prominent examples of the practical and ethical instruction include almsgiving and treatment of the poor (3:30–4:10); friendship (6:5–17); honouring parents (e.g., 3:1–16) and, conversely, disciplining children (e.g., 30:1–13); discretion in speech (20:1–8); sexual deviance (23:16–27); loans and going surety (29:1–20). Contrasts between the righteous and the sinner (e.g., 32:16–17) and the wise and the foolish are also regularly present (e.g., 21:13–22). Such clusters among wisdom collections are not novel to Ben Sira – in fact, they are typical of Egyptian instructions like *Amenemope* or *Ptahhotep* that are arranged according to 'chapters' – but they are demonstrably more frequent and more extensive than the types of clusters one finds in the biblical Proverbs.

WISDOM, TORAH AND TRADITION

Ben Sira offers advice and reflection on ethical and practical matters, yet it is Wisdom herself who takes center stage. From the very first lines and throughout the work, one finds lengthy praises of Wisdom's attributes, rewards and lofty associations (1:1–10, 14–20; 4:11–19; 6:18–37; 14:20–15:10; 24:1–34; 33:7–15). In many of these poetic excerpts, Ben Sira connects wisdom directly with creation – a theme inspired at least in part by Proverbs 8. Ben Sira also takes up another issue connected to wisdom in Proverbs: the fear of the Lord. Yet unlike Proverbs, Ben Sira elaborates upon wisdom's associations with creation and piety by articulating these themes with respect to particularly Israelite/Jewish literary traditions and mythology. Wisdom, declares Ben Sira boldly and innovatively, is to be identified with the Torah (24:23).

Wisdom, Creation and the Fear of the Lord
From its first lines, the book of Ben Sira points to Wisdom's divine origin and function in creation: 'All Wisdom is from the Lord ... and Wisdom was created before all other things' (1:1, 4). Wisdom was not only created first by God but was integral to God's creation of the world (1:9). Elsewhere, the sage clarifies that by means of 'wisdom' and 'knowledge' the Lord imposed organisation upon the world, including its temporal rhythms and movements (33:7–9; 16:26–27; cf. Job 38).

In extoling Wisdom's divine origins and purposes, Ben Sira sets her among the unfathomable secrets of the cosmos, known only to God, and thus also highlights the limitations of humanity's ability to fully grasp her mysteries (1:2–8), much like the famous passage in Job 28 (esp. vv. 20–23). In contrast to Job (esp. 28:12–22), Ben Sira does not linger on the hiddenness or mysteriousness of Wisdom. Rather, God has 'poured her out upon all his works, upon all the living according to his gift' (Sir 1:9b–10a). Wisdom reveals the order of God's creation, for those that are attentive and know where to look (16:24–25; cf. 33:8–15). To be sure, Ben Sira acknowledges that only God knows the fullness of Wisdom and creation (16:19–20) and that humans have no business searching 'for what is hidden' (3:22), yet the sage directly counters the logic of Job 28 by asserting that wisdom is apparent in creation. What value is there, asks the sage, in 'hidden wisdom and unseen treasure?' (41:14; cf. 20:30). By the end of Ben Sira's reflections on wisdom and creation, the attention has shifted to the mysteries of God and the fullness of God's knowledge, only a part of which has God divulged to humankind via Wisdom (42:32–33).

For Ben Sira, creation is not only an occasion for reflecting on Wisdom but also an opportunity to acknowledge and praise the wonder of the divine. On several occasions, Ben Sira pauses to reflect in laudatory fashion on the 'works of the Lord' in creation. In this respect, Ben Sira's hymnic quality bares traces of Genesis, Job and the Psalms. The Lord created the world in an orderly fashion, with clear boundaries and roles for its inhabitants (16:26–30; cf. Job 38:10; Ps 74:17). In a lengthy poem (42:15–43:33), echoing the imagery and language of Genesis 1 and several Psalms (e.g., 33, 74, 104), Ben Sira affirms that the Lord created the world with 'the word' (42:15) and that it is God's command which sustains the cosmos (43:5, 10, 13, 17). Several poems on wisdom and creation focus specifically on the creation, or rather *createdness*, of humanity (17:1–24; 18:1–10; 24:28–29; 33:10–13). The final poem in praise of God as creator (42:15–43:33) closes with an intriguing summation – 'we could say more (about the works of the Lord) but could never say enough; let the final word be: "He is the all"' (43:27) – that hints at a pantheistic intimacy of the divine with the created cosmos.[20]

In response to the exultation of Wisdom, the sage calls on his students to actively pursue and seek her out in all her cosmically divine facets (6:18–27). Though the way may be difficult (e.g., 6:19–22), Wisdom is attainable, for she 'teaches her children and gives help to those who seek her' (4:11) and calls to those willing to listen: 'Come to

---

[20] Cf. Collins, *Jewish Wisdom*, 88–89.

me, you who desire me, and eat your fill of fruits' (24:19). The sage advocates study, discipline and discipleship as a sure path to acquiring wisdom (e.g., 6:18–36). She can be found among the wise teachings of the ancients (39:1–3) or through personal experience, including travel (39:4). Above all, wisdom comes from the Lord and, therefore, the best student of wisdom is one who exhibits piety.

Ben Sira's association between wisdom and piety is not entirely novel. Proverbs regularly extols the pious or righteous alongside the 'wise' and likewise juxtaposes wickedness with foolishness (e.g., 10:18–27). Ben Sira, though, adopts the latent piety in Proverbs and elaborates on it dramatically (1:11–29). For example, the sage takes Proverbs' pious refrain about 'fear of the Lord' but argues that not only is it 'the beginning of wisdom' (Sir 1:14; cf. Prov 1:7), but it is Wisdom's 'fullness' (Sir 1:16), 'crown' (1:18) and 'root' (1:20). The 'fear of the Lord' permeates the sage's work – compare the seventeen occurrences of this phrase in Proverbs with 48 in Ben Sira – and has been adapted to become one of the central aspects of what it means to be wise. This is poetically emblemised in the numerical saying of the $x/x + 1$ type in Sir 25:7–11, where the speaker claims 'I can think of nine whom I would call blessed, and a tenth my tongue proclaims'. As is typical with this type of saying, the '$x + 1$' aspect takes pride of place. In this case the tenth, and thus most outstanding, category of a 'happy' person is the one who 'fears the Lord' (25:10). Notably, the ninth is 'the one who finds wisdom'; thus 'fear of the Lord' is intimately related to but ultimately 'surpasses' the acquisition of wisdom (25:10–11).

Piety, then, is a crucial aspect of Wisdom such that the sage has even linked piety with the *attainment* of Wisdom: 'If you desire wisdom, keep the commandments, and the Lord will lavish her upon you, for the fear of the Lord is wisdom and discipline' (1:26–27a). In short, the sage's exalted elaboration on piety, as exemplified in the phrase 'the fear of the Lord', epitomises the inherited wisdom tradition in Proverbs, yet it also points to the Ben Sira's most telling innovation: piety and wisdom are directly connected to Torah.

Wisdom and Torah: Wisdom's Self-Praise (Ben Sira 24)

In chapter 24, we find the words of Woman Wisdom herself, a poem regarded by scholars as 'the centrepiece' of the entire work,[21] for in it one finds a crystallisation of the text's major themes and innovations.

---

[21] Collins, *Jewish Wisdom*, 49.

Here, like Proverbs 8, a personified Wisdom offers her own self-praise, championing herself as one whose origins are divine and heavenly (24:2–4; cf. Prov 8:22). Yet while in Proverbs Wisdom's role in creation is secondary to God's and passive (or, if active, only implicitly; cf. 8:30), for Ben Sira Wisdom directly and loudly proclaims her divine and actively creative qualities. Indeed, in Ben Sira Woman Wisdom makes a number of bold claims which align her with traditional images of the divine. In 24:4, she claims a throne that sits 'in a pillar of cloud', which bears a conspicuous similarity to the image of the divine presence from the Exodus traditions (e.g., Ex 13:21–22; Ps 99:7). Wisdom again appropriates imagery typically reserved for the Lord when she claims: 'Alone I compassed the vault of heaven and traversed the depths of the abyss. Over waves of the sea, over all the earth, and over every people and nation I have held sway' (24:5–6). These images bear striking resemblance to traditional depictions of the Lord (e.g., Prov 8:27 *of God*; Job 38:16–20), but here they have been assigned to Wisdom herself.

The poem continues by revealing itself to be a mythic narrative that describes not only her divine origins but also her descent into and inhabitation of the world. Here we find Ben Sira's most innovative addition: Wisdom, by divine decree, took root in a specific place, among a specific people: 'The Creator of all things gave me a command .... "Make your dwelling in Jacob, and in Israel receive your inheritance"' (24:8). Ben Sira reinterprets the otherwise universal implications of Proverbs' association between wisdom and creation and situates wisdom's reception in a specifically Israelite/Jewish context. The subsequent lines (vv. 9–17) elaborate on this process of indwelling or 'taking root' (v. 12) and are replete with biblical imagery – for example, 'the holy tent' (i.e., tabernacle; cf. Ex 25:8–9), 'Zion' and 'Jerusalem', 'cedar of Lebanon'. She concludes her speech with a cornucopia of fruitful imagery which evokes Eden and the tree of life (cf. Prov 3:18; Ps 1:3). Here, the sage adds an uncharacteristically *nationalistic* aspect to Wisdom when compared with Proverbs, Job and Qoheleth, placing the central figure of the proverbial tradition specifically within Israel.

Immediately after Woman Wisdom concludes her self-praise comes the sage's most outstanding statement in the entire work: '*All this* is the book of the covenant of the Most High God, the Law that Moses commanded us as an inheritance for the congregations of Jacob' (24:23). The apparent identification of Wisdom with Torah (or vice versa) has, unsurprisingly, garnered much scholarly debate. Notably, this passage is only extant in Greek, leaving some degree of speculation when it comes to understanding the mind of the sage himself. While opinions are divided, it is unlikely that what Ben Sira means here is that Wisdom (i.e., the summation of all transmitted knowledge about the universe) can be encapsulated in the Torah (i.e., the five books of Moses; cf. Baruch 4:1) – though the reverse may be the case: the Torah, when interpreted correctly, reveals to its reader or, rather, imbues her/him with wisdom.

The subsequent verses (24:25–29) are poignantly and ironically emblematic of this particularising move of the universalistic. The sage continues by likening 'it' (i.e., the book of the covenant/wisdom) to the overflowing waters of six rivers. Four of these – the Pishon, Tigris, Euphrates and Gihon – directly evoke the creation myth in Genesis 2. Normally this would strike one as universalistic given the narrative setting. However, the sage's interpretative agenda is revealed through the mention of two extra rivers, the Jordan and the Nile, both of which hold a particular place in the nationalistic history of Israel. Just as Ben Sira has seemingly cast the otherwise universalistic wisdom tradition in a particularistic Jewish garb by associating Wisdom with Torah, so too has he particularised his interpretation of Wisdom *a la* creation by associating the cosmogonic sources of water with those exclusively tied to Israelite tradition. Nevertheless, the passage concludes with an assertion that Wisdom cannot be encapsulated in the Torah/rivers, 'for her thoughts are more abundant than the sea, and her counsel deeper than the great abyss' (24:29). Wisdom, therefore, subsumes Torah, not the other way around.

Wisdom and Tradition: The Praise of Ancestors (Ben Sira 44–50)

Beyond the enthralling association of Wisdom and Torah in ch. 24, Ben Sira regularly integrates Israelite/Jewish traditions with his pedagogical enterprise, for example, as epistemological exemplars for wise behaviour. In other words, wisdom can be acquired by looking to the past, by *exegeting* the Torah.[22] Nowhere is this more evident than in his extended review of 'biblical' history in chs. 44–49, culminating in the praise of the high priest Simon II in ch. 50. While absent from Proverbs and other early wisdom literature, this review of history has a striking parallel in Wisdom of Solomon 10–19 – though the two differ in style

---

[22] Benjamin G. Wright III, 'Biblical Interpretation in the Book of Ben Sira', in *A Companion to Biblical Interpretation in Early Judaism*, ed. Matthias Henze (Grand Rapids, 2012), 363–388, esp. 373–375.

and details.[23] For example, Wisdom of Solomon never mentions the figures by name, only through subtle allusions. In fact, the point of the review of history in Wisdom of Solomon is, above all, to praise 'Wisdom's' work in history. For Ben Sira, however, the attention is almost entirely on the figures themselves, while God and Wisdom function largely as the interpretive backdrop.

The Praise of Ancestors, as this section is called, also speaks to Ben Sira's greater themes and pedagogical objectives. The passage begins, for example, with reference to creation, implying that these figures and their great deeds are, like the cosmos itself, part of the divine plane (44:2). Ben Sira calls to mind the famous figures of Israelite's past as *models* of wisdom. The first named figure is Enoch. Famous for being 'taken up' rather than dying, Ben Sira adds – enigmatically from the modern interpreter's perspective – that Enoch is an 'example of repentance to all generations' (44:16). The figures are especially revered for their Torah-observance. Abraham, for example, has received his blessings because 'he kept the law of the Most High' (44:20).

In general, the passage moves in order through the Torah and then the Prophetic (or Historical) books. Moses (45:1–5) and Aaron (45:6–26) figure prominently, though it is the latter that receives greater attention. As expected, Samuel (46:13–20) and David (47:11) are looked on favourably. Interestingly, Solomon (47:12–22), despite his otherwise glowing reputation in the wisdom tradition, receives a somewhat sobering assessment, praiseworthy for his 'youthful wisdom' (47:14) but lamentable for the promiscuity of his later years (47:19–21). Hezekiah (48:17–22) and Josiah (49:1–3) are predictably treated approvingly. Prophets, including Nathan, Elijah, Isaiah, Ezekiel and collectively 'the Twelve', are all mentioned (47–49). Notably absent is Ezra, especially given the mention of Nehemiah and the author's otherwise devoted attention to priestly figures. No women are named, highlighting the androcentric tenor of Ben Sira's work in general.[24] Oddly, the last lines return to figures from Genesis, repeating the refrain of Enoch being 'taken up' and including the previously overlooked figures of

[23] Maurice Gilbert, 'The Review of History in Ben Sira 44–50 and Wisdom 10–19', in *Rewriting Biblical History: Essays on Chronicles and Ben Sira in Honor of Pancratius C. Beentjes*, ed. Jeremy Corley and Harm van Grol, DCLS 7 (Berlin, 2011), 319–334.

[24] Núria Calduch-Benages, 'The Absence of Named Women from Ben Sira's Praise of the Ancestors', in *Rewriting Biblical History: Essays on Chronicles and Ben Sira in Honor of Pancratius C. Beentjes*, ed. Jeremy Corley and Harm van Grol, DCLS 7 (Berlin, 2011), 301–317.

Joseph, Shem, Seth, Enosh and, finally, Adam, who is honoured 'above every other created living being' (49:14–16).

Overall, the implication one gets is that 'one grows toward wisdom through *emulation*', a sentiment echoed in the sage's earlier appeal for his students to cling to wise figures whose wisdom is indicated by their encouragement to reflect and meditate upon the commandments/statutes of the Lord (6:34–37).[25] That one can, and should, look to contemporary, wise leaders for a similar model is emphatically conveyed by the section's culmination in a lengthy encomium to Simon II (50:1–21). The praise of Simon is founded, in part, on his own emulation of the previous 'famous fathers' of Israel. Like Nehemiah, Simon 'laid the foundations' for the walls of Jerusalem (50:1–2; cf. 49:13); Simon also dug a cistern to 'save his people from ruin' just as Hezekiah had done (50:3–4; cf. 48:17). Most of all, though, Simon's exultation depended on his priestly association as the greatest among the 'sons of Aaron' (50:13, 16), with much of the praise devoted to lavish descriptions of the high priest's attire, which is likened to the celestial bodies in their splendour (esp. 50:6–11).

WEALTH, POVERTY AND CHARITY

Much of the financial advice in Ben Sira recalls that of Proverbs; however, it is much more prominent. The sage returns to issues of riches, loans and almsgiving throughout his instructions, making matters of wealth perhaps the most prominent pragmatically oriented theme in the entire work outside of wisdom. The sage's advice on these matters speaks to an overall social ethic that demonstrates a respect for wealth but also emphasises that a truly wise person is content and, above all, willing to be charitable with their riches.[26] Ben Sira ultimately exalts piety ('fear of the Lord') and wisdom above material success.[27]

As noted above, Ben Sira has its social location in the professional scribal class, most likely of the royal court. Ben Sira imagines an audience that is wealthy or, at the very least, has access to wealth (e.g., Sir

---

[25] Elisa Uusimäki, 'The Formation of a Sage according to Ben Sira', in *Second Temple Jewish 'Paideia' in Context*, ed. Jason M. Zurawski and Gabriele Boccaccini, BZNW 228 (Berlin, 2017), 64, emphasis added.

[26] Cf. Bradley Gregory, *Like an Everlasting Signet Ring: Generosity in the Book of Sirach*, DCLS 2 (Berlin, 2010).

[27] Benjamin G. Wright and Claudia V. Camp, '"Who Has Been Tested by Gold and Found Perfect?": Ben Sira's Discourse of Riches and Poverty', in *Praise Israel for Wisdom and Instruction: Essays on Ben Sira and Wisdom, the Letter of Aristeas and the Septuagint*, JSJSup 131 (Leiden, 2008), 71–96.

3:17: 'My son, in *your* wealth go about with humility'). This view accords well with the idealised scribe from chs. 38–39 who occupies an elevated position in the social hierarchy. Wealth, one may presume, is what affords the scribe 'the opportunity of leisure' (38:24). Though the scribe may not be at the top of the social-economic ladder, Ben Sira operates under the assumption that the scribe, more often than not, sits comfortably above most of his peers.

Wealth itself has a mixed presentation in Ben Sira. On the one hand, there are advantages to being wealthy (e.g., 10:30–31; 31:3–4). Unlike the poor, the rich usually have a reliable support system in the event of a mishap, financial or otherwise (13:21–22). Similarly, the rich are given the benefit of the doubt in public matters, whereas the poor are all but ignored (13:23). In a somewhat vicious illustration, the sage points to an analogy in nature to express the truth about the unequal balance between the rich and the poor: 'Wild asses in the wilderness are the prey of lions; likewise, the poor are the feeding grounds for the rich' (13:19).

On the other hand, riches, or more pointedly the *pursuit* thereof, can be a cause for concern. Obsession with the attainment of riches, warns the sage, 'has ruined many' and even 'perverted the minds of kings' (8:2). Revelling in the excesses of luxury can lead to financial ruin (18:32). Thus, acquiring wealth is a dangerous pursuit since one may be tempted to gain it through deceit or some other malicious manner (13:24; 27:1). While wealth gained honourably is to be lauded, more attention is given to the pitfalls (31:5–8). A handful of sayings suggest that wealth is not the surest indicator of happiness (e.g., 30:14; cf. 26:4) and that, when it comes to being righteous before the Lord, there is no distinction based on wealth (10:22 LXX).

References to the poor, the needy or the hungry in Ben Sira are largely in the context of the sage's exhortation to charitable giving. The sage encourages his students not to neglect the cries of the hungry and needy (4:4–10; 7:32–36); in fact, this is tantamount to murder (34:24–27). At times, the sage must even admonish his students against the temptation to actively abuse the poor (4:1). In a similar manner to Tobit (e.g., 14:8–11), Ben Sira encourages almsgiving for its added benefits. The Lord blesses those who 'stretch out their hands to the poor' (7:32; cf. 4:10). Giving charitably can 'atone for sin' (4:30) and, moreover, it is a cautiously wise thing to do as a pre-emptive act of reciprocity (4:31; 22:23).

Ben Sira's discussions about wealth and poverty include specific advice about loans and going surety. At times, this mirrors Proverbs.

Both works acknowledge the common wisdom that advises against lending or going surety because they frequently end in loss, even financial ruin (8:12–13; 29:18; cf. Prov 6:1–11; 20:16; 22:26–27). Yet, in contrast to Proverbs' absolute prohibition against giving loans, Ben Sira advocates doing so, at least in certain circumstances. In a lengthy passage on loans and other financial matters (29:1–20), Ben Sira repeatedly encourages the addressee to 'lose your silver for the sake of a brother or friend' (v. 10). The prevailing notion is that one ought to lend to their neighbours as an act of mercy that fulfils the commandments of Torah.

WOMEN AND SEXUALITY

Like Proverbs and most instructional literature before him, Ben Sira writes from a decidedly male perspective, offering instruction for an imagined male audience. While a few sayings offer some positive images of female figures – for example, Ben Sira admonishes his attentive youth to respect both father *and mother* (3:1–4; 7:28–29; cf. Prov 23:22) – most verses which feature women are decidedly negative. Ben Sira is not unique in this regard – as several sayings in Proverbs (e.g., 19:13; 21:9, 19) have a downright sexist (if not misogynistic) ring to a modern reader's ear – but he certainly appears more emphatic than his predecessor. One can hardly find an adequate parallel to the famous praise of the 'capable wife' from Proverbs 31. Of course, one should not neglect the positive implications of the exalted Woman Wisdom. In several of the poetic praises of Wisdom, though, one can discern a prominent sexual overtone that suggests the work's strong male gaze, even if it complicates the work's general ethic on sexuality.

Aside from Wisdom herself, women, in Ben Sira, have no agency. They are spoken of only with regard to how they affect the presumed male audience. This androcentric perspective is evident throughout the work, particularly among those sayings which comprise advice on social and familial relationships. Often in proverbial form, the sage reflects on the advantages of a 'good wife' and the pitfalls of a 'bad wife'. The positive reflections are framed in terms of how they might make a man 'happy' (26:1–4), adding that the 'good' wife is one who is 'silent', 'modest' and 'beautiful' (26:13–18). Regarding the 'bad' wife, however, the sage professes, 'I would rather live with a lion and a dragon than with an evil woman' (25:16). Such a woman is further likened to a venomous snake (25:15), a stinging scorpion (26:7) and a stubborn dog (26:25).

The sage also includes several passages about the struggles of parenthood, with many specifically indicating daughters – a social category completely ignored in Proverbs – as a potential source of trouble. Much of the sage's deliberation on daughters, like that on wives, conveys a decidedly misogynistic tone. Daughters are a lamentable result of pregnancy, according to the sage, and might as well be counted as a loss (22:3b). At best, they can be married off to a proper suitor (22:4a); at worst, they are a source of shame and disgrace (22:4b).

The advice about wives and daughters also speaks to the sage's views on sexuality. While not encompassing all of his attention, the sage is primarily worried about their potential for promiscuity, which would bring shame and dishonour on *him*. A daughter, the sage admits, is a 'secret anxiety' to a father, who worries not only about her potential future (i.e., marriage) but that she will be 'seduced' (42:9–10). The sage implores his male audience to 'keep strict watch over a headstrong daughter ... [for] as a thirsty traveler opens his mouth and drinks from any water near him, so she will sit in front of every tent peg and open her quiver to the arrow' (26:10–12). What's at stake, ultimately, is not the daughter's well-being but that by her indiscriminate actions the father would become a laughing stock and suffer public disgrace (42:11).

To be sure, Ben Sira also includes advice that at least indirectly places the blame on men for illicit sexual activity. Indeed, the sage warns his charges about the dangers of sexual deviancy. They are to avoid promiscuity, for it will lead to their (financial/public) downfall (9:1–9). Succumbing to one's passions can lead to public shame (6:1–4; cf. 19:2).

Yet Ben Sira's view on sexuality is more nuanced than these passages might suggest. The sage's encouragement for his students to pursue wisdom intentionally and quite fervently employs sexualised imagery.[28] The passages about Woman Wisdom are often sexual in tone and content, both directly and in literarily clever ways. The addressee is invited to 'come to her like one who plows and sows' (6:19), drawing on the familiar erotic double-entendres of agricultural metaphors (cf. Judg 14:18). Also, in an ironic reversal, the sage utilises similar imagery in warnings against the potential promiscuity of the daughter to, instead, encourage the pursuer of wisdom to 'fasten his tent peg' within wisdom (14:24–25; cf. 26:1–12). Ben Sira concludes with his 'most erotically-charged wisdom poem' (51:13–30), though the sexual innuendo is apparently more evident in the Hebrew than the Greek.[29]

Despite the honoured status of Woman Wisdom as heavenly and divine, the overt sexual objectification of the figure as something *to be*

---

[28] Balla, *Ben Sira on Family*, 169–217; Ellis, *Gender in the Book of Ben Sira*, 172–178.

[29] Balla, *Ben Sira on Family*, 227–228.

pursued by the (presumably) male audience seems to mitigate any profound elevation of the female in Ben Sira. Such a potential positive view on womanhood in general is also countered by the two most misogynistic statements in the text. In a startling declaration, Ben Sira apparently offers the earliest interpretation of the creation story in Genesis 2–3 that places the blame squarely on Eve's shoulders: 'From a woman sin had its beginning, and because of her we all die' (25:24). It is unclear how seriously one should take Ben Sira here, given that else-where he emphasises both God's preordained limitations on human life (17:1–2) as well as humanity's free choice to do good or evil (15:14; see discussion below). Even if this is a passing hyperbolic statement, the degrading presentation of women is difficult to overlook. The second passage likewise gestures toward the inherent wickedness of woman (42:12), with the result that the sage opines, 'Better is the wickedness of a man than a woman who does good; it is woman who brings shame and disgrace' (42:14).

THEODICY, DEATH AND THE LEGACY OF A NAME

In most cases, the sage's advice about mundane, day-to-day topics feeds into a broader outlook or perspective on the world that is informed by the assumption that one's deeds (including, if not especially, one's words) come with certain consequences and that one becomes wise by acquiring the correct knowledge of *what to do* and *when to do it* to achieve the best possible outcome. In some examples, one could con-clude that Ben Sira, like Proverbs before him, understood the world to operate according to a so-called *Tun-Ergehen Zusammenhang*, or acts-consequences nexus,[30] whereby each action is followed by a correspond-ing reaction, whether good or bad. 'Whoever digs a pit will fall into it' (Sir 27:26) begins a common proverbial expression of this sort (cf. Prov 26:27). Yet Ben Sira offers a more complicated reflection on human behaviour, free will and the negative aspects of life (and death; 41:1–13). In this regard, several passages of Ben Sira appear to be in dialogue with the pessimism and fatalism of Qoheleth and Job, even if he ultimately works to repudiate their conclusions.[31]

Ben Sira wavers in his discussion of humanity's free will to choose evil and good. On the one hand, the sage appears to explicitly deny those who would claim that God is ultimately responsible for humanity's

---

[30] Adams, *Wisdom in Transition*, esp. 154, 210–212.
[31] Adams, *Wisdom in Transition*, 153–154.

downfall and sinful nature (15:11–12). To the contrary, God created humanity with 'the power of their own free choice' (15:14), being free to choose evil or good (vv. 15–17; cf. 17:7), adding fervently that God 'has not commanded anyone to be wicked' (15:20a). However, in a later poem (33:7–13), Ben Sira offers a strikingly different picture. Here, the sage emphasises the (potentially) Stoic notion of the cosmos arranged by the Creator in a set of opposites. This also applies to humanity, some of whom God 'made holy' while others 'he cursed and brought low' (v. 12). The abject passivity of humanity is further illustrated by the image of God as a potter, moulding humanity the clay, with the result being either good or evil (vv. 13–14). The implication would be that God is the source of evil by way of the necessity of a balanced creation. Yet later, Ben Sira reverses this by emphasising that God created according to a pattern and an order, but that order is unequivocally 'good' (39:16). In what may feel like a direct response to the appeals of Job, Ben Sira twice repeats 'No one can say "What is this?" or "Why is that?"' (39:17a, 21a). The somewhat unsatisfying solution is the resolute affirmation that God's justice will, *in the end* (i.e., 'at the appointed time' 39:17), prevail.

Despite some appearances and the lingering perplexity of life's toils and death (40:1–5), the justice of the Lord, Ben Sira promises, will ultimately prove true. 'You who fear the Lord' will eventually receive the mercy and benevolence of God (2:7–11). At times the sage seems to acknowledge the complexities of life (11:10–13, 21), but he assures his addressees that the system of divine justice is beyond repute (11:22). In the end, Ben Sira suggests that all will be made right by the day of one's death (11:26). Importantly, though, Ben Sira denies the existence of an afterlife by asserting the finality of death and the restful silence of Hades (41:1–4; cf. 38:23; 44:14). Some have taken the sage's disavowal of such as a direct response to the increasing popularity of this view – perhaps due to Greek philosophical influence – among several Jewish communities, especially the budding apocalyptic movements as represented by the Danielic and Enochic traditions. Death awaits everyone, righteous and sinner, rich and poor, kings and beggars (40:3–5; cf. 11:14). There are gentle allusions to the complaints of Qoheleth as it relates to death: both in its unexpectedness, which suggests a futility to the exhausting efforts of life (Sir 11:10–19; cf. Qoh 2), as well as in his reflection on the perplexity of death in the face of good and evil, which likewise suggests a certain futility to the pursuit of wisdom. Yet Ben Sira attempts to affirm the justness of God, adding that for sinners the fear of death is 'seven times more' (40:8), while 'those who fear the Lord will have a happy end; on the day of their death they will be blessed' (1:13; cf. 2:3).

On the one hand, Ben Sira reflects the conventional wisdom of Proverbs in its underlying motivations: namely, that the wise listener who adheres to the proffered wisdom will be successful. Usually this success is conceived of in material and/or moralistic terms. The wise person will have material gains – or, at least, the avoidance of loss/ disaster – commensurate with their righteousness. However, Ben Sira does not disregard the real concerns that arise when confronted with the seeming inequalities of life, especially at the end. How can one explain justice in the face of death? In addition to the assurances that God's reward will be evident 'at the end' and the gentle admonishments against questioning the system in the first place, Ben Sira is notable in his frequent attention to one's social standing. Status, it seems, is the prize for which one should strive and/or for which one's wisdom offers a buttress against external threats. In other words, Ben Sira inherits a variety of traditional wisdom tropes and truisms, yet many of these are refracted through the ancient Mediterranean discourse of honour and shame.

The sage's answer for the problems of theodicy and death is to extol the glories of establishing and protecting one's name. Ben Sira champions the power of an honourable name to outlive death. In the praise of the scribe, for example, he exults in the idea that a scribe can gain 'a name greater than a thousand' and whose 'memory will not disappear' (39:9–11). Ben Sira elsewhere exclaims: 'Have regard for your name, since it will outlive you' (41:12). This exhortation fronts a lengthy passage that ruminates on those things for which one should feel shame – for example, sexual immorality, lies and breaking oaths, gossip and divulging of secrets (41:17–22). This is followed by a list (42:1–5) of things for which one should *not* feel shame – above all, 'the law of the Most High and his covenant' (42:2). As indicated above, one of the primary sources of potential shame is an individual's wife and daughter (42:6–14).

Death is lamentable, but it can be overshadowed by building a lasting legacy. This is epitomised by one of his numerous numerical sayings: 'Of three things my heart is frightened, and of a fourth I am in great fear: slander in the city, the gathering of a mob, and false accusation – all these are worse than death' (26:5). The fourth fear of the sage is the public shame of a wife with a loose tongue (26:6). The passage illustrates that the sage holds his public esteem in higher regard than death itself (cf. 28:15–21). In answer to one who might question the finality of death in light of the supposed beneficence of God, the sage responds that, while God has proclaimed death for all, God's justice is evident in his defence of the pious one's *honour*. His advice for his students, then, is to do whatever they can to protect themselves against public shame and, on the more positive side, to seek to *establish* their name. Conventional wisdom – which the sage himself frequently speaks to – holds that one's name can be established by one's children (i.e., one's literal/biological legacy) and by one's building activities (cf. Simon II in 50:1–2), yet Ben Sira emphasises that the acquisition of wisdom trumps each of these (40:19). Like the famous ancestors of Israel (chs. 44–49), whose immortal memory is echoed by the sage himself, the good standing of the righteous and wise will not suffer the 'flame' of public shame (28:22), but 'those who forsake the Lord will fall into [shame's] power; it will burn among them and will not be put out' (28:23). Ben Sira has creatively drawn on the prevalent notions of the afterlife and the immortality of the soul and reconfigured them into an illustration of God's justice. People die and that death is final, but their *names* (not souls!) live on. Here is where one can discern the proper justice of God.

CONCLUSION

The book of Ben Sira is a testament to the creativity and erudition of a prominent sage living in or around Jerusalem in the late third/early second century BCE. Ben Sira has produced a tremendous work of collected wisdom that relies on but also *seriously reimagines* the sapiential tradition as exemplified in the book of Proverbs. The most innovative and impactful adaptation is the sage's reinterpretation of wisdom in light of the concept of Torah, a body of written traditions and general attitudes towards those traditions that was becoming increasingly central to Jewish identity during Ben Sira's day. His work depends in significant measure on the inherited tradition of Israel's past, its stories, its themes and its legacy of exemplary figures. Yet Ben Sira is far from the myopically focused repeater of Jewish tradition. Several of his themes and reflections reveal a familiarity with a broader range of literature and issues current in the eastern Mediterranean, which he has carefully and uniquely interwoven to create a product that is more than a sum of its parts. The end result is an amalgamation of poetry, paraenesis and pedagogic flourish that calls on his listeners (i.e., students) to reflect profoundly on the world around them, to emulate and adhere to the wisdom of the ancients and to pursue knowledge and understanding by looking to the Wisdom evident in creation.

Further Reading

Adams, Samuel L. 'Reassessing the Exclusivism of Ben Sira's Jewish *Paideia'*. Pages 47–58 in *Second Temple Jewish 'Paideia' in Context*. Edited by Jason M. Zurawski and Gabriele Boccaccini. BZNW 228. Berlin: 2017.

Askin, Lindsey. *Scribal Culture in Ben Sira*. JSJSup 184. Leiden: 2019.

Beentjes, Pancratius C. *The Book of Ben Sira in Hebrew: A Text Edition of All Extant Hebrew Manuscripts and a Synopsis of All Parallel Hebrew Ben Sira Texts*. VTSup 68. Leiden: 1997. Repr. and rev. ed. Atlanta: 2006.

Balla, Ibolya. *Ben Sira on Family, Gender, and Sexuality*. DCLS 8. Berlin: 2011.

Camp, Claudia V. *Ben Sira and the Men Who Handle Books: Gender and the Rise of Canon-Consciousness*. HBM 50. Sheffield: 2013.

Ellis, Teresa Ann. *Gender in the Book of Ben Sira: Divine Wisdom, Erotic Poetry, and the Garden of Eden*. BZAW 453. Berlin: 2013.

Goering, Greg Schmidt. *Wisdom's Root Revealed: Ben Sira and the Election of Israel*. JSJSup 139. Leiden: 2009.

Gregory, Bradley. *Like an Everlasting Signet Ring: Generosity in the Book of Sirach*. DCLS 2. Berlin: 2010.

Skehan, Patrick W., and Alexander A. Di Lella. *The Wisdom of Ben Sira*. AB 39. New York: 1987.

Wright, Benjamin G. III. 'Biblical Interpretation in the Book of Ben Sira'. Pages 363–388 in *A Companion to Biblical Interpretation in Early Judaism*. Edited by Matthias Henze. Grand Rapids: 2012.

15 The Book of Wisdom

JOACHIM SCHAPER

The Book of Wisdom (also known as The Wisdom of Solomon) is a deutero-canonical or 'apocryphal' book that went out of fashion a long time ago. While it has received, in recent decades, a considerable amount of attention in academic biblical exegesis, it remains on the margins of Christian theology and devotional practice and plays no role in Judaism. There are many reasons for its widespread neglect, none of them compelling. In this chapter, I should therefore like to provide insights into some of the book's enduringly important theological concepts and some other important features that characterise it.

To deny canonical status to the Book of Wisdom has rightly been questioned by recent Protestant exegetes, not least because of its key position in the biblical and early Jewish history of tradition. Pauline theology offers a good example: 'For if Paul's use of Adamic imagery is to be canonical, as it is to most traditional Christians and communities, surely it makes better sense if Wisdom is canonical too?'[1] As Barr rightly emphasises, some key concepts found in the book of Genesis, particularly that of Adam's fall, are given a significant interpretation in *Sapientia Salomonis*, which in turn had an impact on the New Testament.[2] At the same time, the interpretation of Genesis found in the book of Wisdom represents a bridge towards the 'natural theology' of the Hellenistic-Roman world.[3] And however one perceives the problem of the demarcation of the canon, it should be noted that Wisdom, as a monumental expression of the history of tradition, connects the Old and New Testaments: 'Wisdom, and other books from the same period and tendency, are important, whether or not they are canonical, just

---

[1] Cf. J. Barr, 'The Authority of Scripture: The Book of Genesis and the Origin of Evil in Jewish and Christian Tradition', in *Bible and Interpretation: The Collected Essays of James Barr*, vol. 1: *Interpretation and Theology*, ed. J. Barton (Oxford, 2013), 387.

[2] Cf. Barr, 'The Authority of Scripture', 387.

[3] Cf. J. Barr, 'Mowinckel, the Old Testament, and the Question of Natural Theology', in Barton, *Bible and Interpretation*, 432.

because they witness to the history of interpretation that links Genesis with St Paul.'[4] Both the natural theology of the book of Wisdom and its understanding of Adam's fall link up the Old Testament with the Pauline epistles.[5]

I should now like to provide an overview of some of the most salient philosophical and theological features of the Book of Wisdom, in order to give a 'flavour' of its wide intellectual range and its place in the history of Hellenistic Jewish as well as early Christian thought.

One of its most prominent traits is the book's virulent anti-'idol' polemic, which is much more than just a polemic. It is connected with its theology of creation. Thus, the Book of Wisdom forms part of the tradition of the anti-'idol' polemic found in Israelite and Judahite prophecy and especially in the books of Isaiah and Ezekiel.[6] The author of Wisdom continued the prophetic polemic, transformed it and placed it in the context of his own wisdom theology and practice. This opened up new possibilities for both Hellenistic-Jewish sapiential speculation and Jewish theologies of creation,[7] possibilities which can only be fully understood in the context of the coming together of the great theological streams of tradition in the history of Israelite and Judahite religion and were of key importance for the formation of the New Testament and early Christian Christologies. At a time when two originally separate streams of tradition, 'Torah' and 'Wisdom', came together, Wisdom combined the two but left them their distinct identities.[8]

However, the theological significance of the book of Wisdom is still greater than this. It is not only a milestone in the history of the reception of Genesis and Exodus and an important 'transmission belt' from Israelite prophecy and wisdom to the theological melting pot of the first Christian centuries. The book of Wisdom is also a milestone in the

---

[4] Barr, 'The Authority of Scripture', 387.

[5] Barr, 'Mowinckel', 432.

[6] Cf. J. Schaper, '"... denn er ist besser als das, was er anbetet" (Sapientia Salomonis 15,17): Bilderpolemik und theologische Anthropologie in der Sapientia Salomonis', in *Was ist der Mensch, dass du seiner gedenkst? (Psalm 8,5): Aspekte einer theologischen Anthropologie. Festschrift für Bernd Janowski zum 65. Geburtstag*, ed. M. Bauks et al. (Neukirchen-Vluyn, 2008), 455–464.

[7] Cf. Schaper, '... denn er ist besser als das, was er anbetet'.

[8] On wisdom and Torah and their amalgamation in the course of tradition history, cf. H. Gese, *Alttestamentliche Studien* (Tübingen, 1991), 139–148. Also cf. J. Schaper, 'Νόμος and Νόμοι in the Wisdom of Solomon', in *Wisdom and Torah: The Reception of 'Torah' in the Wisdom Literature of the Second Temple Period*, ed. B. U. Schipper and D. A. Teeter, JSJS 163 (Leiden; Boston, 2013), 293–306.

interpretation of the Pentateuch's exodus narrative,[9] characterised as it is by an unusual, individualising conceptualisation of the exodus event devised to guide and educate the book's readers (of which more later).

And yet another important question regarding the development of ancient Jewish theology finds an answer in the book of Wisdom: namely, the question of the relationship between 'Judaism' and 'Hellenism' at a crucial point in their common history.[10] How far do characteristic 'Jewish' *theologoumena* and 'Hellenistic' *philosophoumena* penetrate each other in Wisdom? Does the question make any sense in the first place? As a rule, it is rightly perceived as quite a reasonable question,[11] although one is tempted to ask whether it is not a bit anachronistic to assume that one can neatly distinguish between 'Jewish' and 'Hellenistic' features in a piece of religious literature that was written almost three centuries after Alexander's conquest in the city of Alexandria. We shall see whether it makes sense to draw demarcation lines such as the one between 'biblical' thought and its supposed ornamentation with philosophical terminology.[12]

From the abundance of features and themes of the book of Wisdom, I shall have to choose just a few. I shall concentrate on some of those that make Wisdom such an unusual and rewarding book which deserves the Bible reader's and the scholar's attention: it is intricately structured and well written, in good (and at times beautiful) Greek, it is the result of a complete amalgamation of 'Hellenistic' thought (more precisely, of

---

[9] On the reception of Exodus in Wisdom, cf., for example, P. Enns, *Exodus Retold: Ancient Exegesis of the Departure from Egypt in Wis [10:]15–21 and 19:1–9*, HSM 57 (Atlanta, 1997); and F. V. Reiterer, 'Beobachtungen zum äußeren und inneren Exodus im Buch der Weisheit', in *Die Rezeption des Exodusmotivs in deuterokanonischer und frühjüdischer Literatur*, ed. J. Gärtner and B. Schmitz, DCLS 32 (Berlin; Boston, 2016), 187–208.

[10] Cf. the 'classic' exploration of their correlation in M. Hengel, *Judentum und Hellenismus: Studien zu ihrer Begegnung unter besonderer Berücksichtigung Palästinas bis zur Mitte des 2. Jh.s v. Chr.*, WUNT 10 (Tübingen, 1988).

[11] Cf. J. M. Reese, *Hellenistic Influence on the Book of Wisdom and Its Consequences*, AnBib 41 (Rome, 1970). In his words, a 'systematic attempt' to assess that 'influence' (p. 1).

[12] J. Fichtner (*Weisheit Salomos*, HAT II/6 [Tübingen, 1938], 8–9) provides a typical example: 'Die Aufnahme philosophischer Termini hat die Vorstellungswelt der Sap keineswegs grundlegend beeinflußt .... Ein Teil von ihnen benennt Vorstellungen, die der Welt des AT nicht fremd sind ... andere Termini werden für biblische Vorstellungen verwendet, deren Gehalt ihnen an sich nicht innewohnt ... und öfters werden rein philosophisch klingende Wendungen ... oder Ausführungen ... so durch echt biblische Worte und Gedanken fortgeführt ... daß sie ihre selbständige Bedeutung verlieren, zumal im folgenden dann nicht auf die philosophischen Begriffe und Vorstellungen, sondern auf die biblischen aufgebaut wird.'

a form of middle-Platonic philosophy) and early Jewish Wisdom theology and it had an enormous effect on the development of Jewish and
Christian spirituality.

Accordingly, this chapter will provide (1) an overview of the
structure and content of the book, as well as an overview of its versions,
and will then discuss the Book of Wisdom (2) in its contemporary
intellectual context, (3) as an example of philosophical theology paving
the way towards a universalistic understanding of God and the human
self in history and (4) as a spiritual exercise.

THE BOOK'S STRUCTURE AND THEMES: THE ANCIENT VERSIONS

Understanding the *structure* of the book is fundamental to understanding the book. This insight is particularly important in relation to literary
works of the ancient world because the ancient authors did not have at
their disposal some of the aids and techniques[13] which today's authors
can make use of. Many commentators agree in distinguishing between
three parts in our book, a 'Book of Eschatology', a 'Book of Wisdom' and
a 'Book of History'.[14] After Grimm, in the nineteenth century, over-
came the view that these three 'books' were attributable to three different authors,[15] his thesis of uniform authorship prevailed (after a
temporary revival of theories to the contrary).[16] However, the exact
division of the book remains controversial.

---

[13] Maurice Gilbert, *La Sagesse de Salomon/The Wisdom of Solomon: Recueil d'études/
Selected Essays*, AnBib 189 (Rome, 2011), 9–10: 'Ancient authors did not have the
typographical aids which we make use of to organize a discourse and to indicate its
several parts. They did not have headings, subheadings, etc., paragraphs, chapters, etc.,
with the result that for them the only way to indicate the organization of a text was
the use of words which are part of the text itself. Repetition of certain words at certain
points in a discussion served to indicate a linking between two phases of the
argument, or an inclusion which opened and concluded a topic, or the
announcement of a theme before it is developed with use of repetition of the key
words found in the announcement. By noting the patterns of such repetitions one can
see how the ancient author structured his presentation.'

[14] See John J. Collins, *Jewish Wisdom in the Hellenistic Age* (Edinburgh, 1998), 179: 'The
book is usually divided into three main parts: the "book of eschatology" in 1:1–6:21,
the "book of wisdom" in 6:22–10:21, and the "book of history" in chapters 11–19, but
there are numerous variations in the exact definition of these units. Some scholars
define the "book of eschatology" as chapters 1–5, or 1–6, or associate chapter 10 with
the final section of the book.'

[15] C. L. W. Grimm, *Das Buch der Weisheit*, Kurzgefaßtes exegetisches Handbuch zu den
Apokryphen des Alten Testamentes, 6. Lieferung (Leipzig, 1860).

[16] See the discussion in Collins, *Jewish Wisdom*, 180.

We propose the following structure: 1:1–6:25; 7:1–9:18; 10:1–19:18. As headings for the three parts we choose 'Wisdom, the Wise and the Godless', 'The History the Wise have with Wisdom' and 'The History of Wisdom with the World' (this third part re-narrates the exodus events found in the Pentateuch to great effect, of which more later). This serves to clarify that and how the three parts of the book are related. All three are concerned with cosmic Wisdom as the mediator between God and humanity, with Wisdom being viewed from three different perspectives: as the Wisdom that gives freedom to the wise and whose neglect seals the fate of the godless; as a cosmic divine force which enters into a personal relationship with the wise, whose life it liberates; as a cosmic force that has been active in the history of creation and continues to be historically effective. In this way, it becomes apparent how Wisdom as the (material!) *pneuma* of God holds the cosmos together and educates the wise to understand their royal humanity, thus liberating them to enjoy the freedom that God has in store for them. The discovery of concentric structures, particularly by Reese[17] and Gilbert,[18] ties in with the division I have suggested, although the precise details remain to be determined.[19]

As far as the beginning of the book's third part is concerned, Collins' analysis seems convincing: 'The definition of the third section as chapters 10–19 has much to commend it, since chapter 10 initiates the biblical paraphrase that is continued in chapters 11–19, but it is also true that Wisdom is the primary subject in chapter 10 (and in 11:1), as it was in 6,22–9,18.'[20] In view of the last observation made by Collins, it should be noted that chapter 10 is to be understood as a joint between 7:1–9:18 and 11–19, but clearly belongs to 11–19, inasmuch as the content is concerned.

The book of Wisdom exercised considerable influence amongst its Jewish and Christian audiences in antiquity. This is witnessed by the remarkable number of translations that were produced, in the following languages: Latin Coptic, Syriac (the Peshitta and the Syro-Palestinian and Syrohexaplaric translations), Ethiopic (Ge'ez), Arabic and Armenian.

The standard critical edition of the Greek text of Wisdom was produced by J. Ziegler and published as part of the Göttingen Septuagint project (published in 1962, second edition in 1980). Today

---

[17] J. M. Reese, 'Plan and Structure in the Book of Wisdom', *CBQ* 27 (1965): 391–399.
[18] Cf. M. Gilbert, *La Sagesse*, especially the discussion on pp. 10–14.
[19] Cf. Joachim Schaper, *Das Buch Weisheit*, HThKAT (Freiburg, 2021).
[20] Collins, *Jewish Wisdom*, 180.

it is the main basis of exegetical work on the book of Wisdom. According to the guidelines defining the Göttingen project, it is an eclectic edition based on all relevant textual documents: the Greek uncial and minuscule manuscripts, papyrus fragments, Greek commentaries, the ancient versions – see above – as well as indirect ancient and medieval Christian witnesses (quotations) and modern print editions.

The most important ancient translation of Wisdom is the old Latin version. Its textual witnesses were presented in the critical edition of the Vetus Latina published by the Archabbey of Beuron (1977 to 1985). The Vetus Latina translation was taken over into the Latin version produced by Jerome, the Vulgate, which constitutes the standard biblical text for the Church of the Latin Rite.

THE BOOK OF WISDOM IN THE INTELLECTUAL CONTEXT OF ITS TIME

In the tradition history that spans the Old Testament, 'intertestamental' literature and the New Testament, wisdom literature holds the key position. Canonical and extra-canonical wisdom literature are of paramount importance when it comes to understanding the connection between Old Testament, 'intertestamental' and New Testament literatures and *theologoumena*. The contemporary exegesis of the book of Wisdom is in danger of neglecting this connection – and the larger connection in which the Israelite-Jewish wisdom traditions stand with other biblical traditions. There are two main reasons for this; they do not require discussion here.[21]

---

[21] H. Gese, *Alttestamentliche Studien* (Tübingen, 1991), 219: 'Für eine äußerliche Betrachtung scheint die weisheitliche Tradition im A.T. mehr ein Randgebiet zu sein, das eben nur spät und sekundär eine gewisse Frömmigkeitsbedeutung erlangt, aber nicht die Grundlage des A.T. mitbestimmt.' ('From an external point of view, the wisdom tradition in the O[ld] T[estament] seems to be more of a marginal area that only attains a certain significance for piety late in time and in a secondary manner, but does not contribute to the basis of the O[ld] T[estament].') Also cf. p. 218: 'Vielleicht ist eine Schwierigkeit, den inneren Zusammenhang von Altem und Neuem Testament zu beschreiben, darin begründet, daß das späte Alte Testament von vornherein nicht richtig eingeschätzt wird. Die Fülle und bunte Vielfalt der späten alttestamentlichen Texte läßt nur schwer einen geschlossenen Eindruck entstehen, und die bei einem traditionsgeschichtlich entstandenen Werk typische Aufnahme und Verarbeitung, Zitierung und Abwandlung des älteren Materials erscheint einer modernen Beurteilung nur allzuleicht als epigonenhafter Mangel an Originalität, als bloße Abschattung des klassischen Vorbilds und nur als letzter Ausläufer ursprünglicher literarischer Höhe.' 'Perhaps one of the difficulties in describing the inner connection between the Old and New Testament is that the late Old Testament

Suffice it to say that a clear understanding of the stream of tradition that runs through Old Testament, early Jewish and early Christian Wisdom theology enables a deeper understanding of the book of Wisdom to arise. In Wisdom literature, an international, cross-cultural and inter-religious orientation was present from the outset. It is therefore not surprising that the author of Wisdom was open to 'foreign' – in this case, 'pagan'-Hellenistic – influence. Thus, the wisdom tradition of Israel, in a form even more internationalised than before (i.e., as a 'Hellenised' tradition), became something of an organising principle of the development of a 'biblical theology' spanning the Hebrew Bible, 'intertestamental' literature and the New Testament: a development in the history of tradition which eventually also integrated and transformed messianic concepts and amalgamated them with saptiential ones.[22] The book of Wisdom plays a special role in this, because – unlike other Jewish wisdom literature, such as Jesus Sirach – it effectively became *the* interface between biblical wisdom traditions and Hellenistic philosophy.

This can perhaps best be demonstrated using the following example. In Wisdom, the term πνευμα (*pneuma*) has a special significance and function, and it may seem strange to modern readers how πνευμα is not thought of as being immaterial but as being *material*. The same idea can be found in Stoic philosophy. A conceptualisation very similar to that of the book of Wisdom's πνευμα (which is identified with personified Wisdom in Wis 1:6–7) is present in Sir 24:3, where Wisdom, which is described as coming 'from the mouth of the Most High', envelops and penetrates the earth like 'fog': What is expressed at the beginning of Sir 24 is the penetration of the entire creation by Wisdom, proceeding from God (cf. especially in vv. 4–6), and the 'fog' offers a particularly suitable image to illustrate this concept: fog is not really tangible, but it is undoubtedly present. The work of creation is the work of Wisdom, and the book of Wisdom fully unfolds this conceptualisation of Wisdom.[23]

---

is, from the outset, not correctly assessed. The abundance and colourful diversity of the late Old Testament texts hardly gives a coherent impression, and the typical inclusion and processing, citation and modification of the older material in a work that has arisen from the process of the history of tradition appears all too easily, in the context of modern assessment, as an epigone-like lack of originality, as a mere shadow of the classical model and only as the last offshoot of the original literary height.'

[22] Gese, 'Weisheit', 218–248.

[23] Gese, *Alttestamentliche Studien*, 226–227: 'wird zuerst das Schöpfungswirken nach der jetzt verbindlichen Tradition von Gen 1 als Werk der Weisheit dargestellt .... Die Weisheit ist der göttliche Logos selbst, das Schöpfungswort, und die lange Tradition der Erschaffung durch das Wort mündet ein in diese Konzeption der Weisheit .... (Die konsequente und völlig durchgeführte Darstellung der Weisheit als πνευμα finden wir

The book of Wisdom is the high point and a turning point in the conceptualisation of Wisdom; here we actually have the interface between the Old and the New Testaments, to the extent that here, in the book of Wisdom, the biblical wisdom tradition reaches the point in its development where, on the one hand, it becomes fully compatible with the philosophy of Middle Platonism in its Stoic form and, on the other hand, becomes a focus for other biblical traditions, with which it can amalgamate. That amalgamation in turn enabled New Testament authors to interpret the divine act of creation in the light of the figure of Christ. The book of Wisdom thus has a key position in the history of biblical tradition, leading up to the Christology of the prologue of the Gospel of John.

The 'connectivity' of the Old Testament and early Jewish wisdom tradition is also evident in its compatibility with ideas that are not only not of Jewish-monotheistic origin but originate from Egyptian-Hellenistic polytheism, namely, from the veneration of Isis. Again and again, comparisons have been made between the conceptualisation of Wisdom in the *Sapientia Salomonis* and in the Isis Aretalogies and, in particular, comparisons between the Book of Wisdom and Plutarch's *De Iside et Osiride*. For chronological reasons, it is clear that Plutarch's work cannot have influenced the author of the book of Wisdom. But the philosophical vocabulary they have in common indicates that they originated from the same intellectual milieu. Peter Schäfer speaks of a 'peculiar mixture of Platonic, Stoic and Egyptian elements',[24] which in his view gives Wisdom book its very special 'colour'.

WISDOM AS AN EXAMPLE OF PHILOSOPHICAL THEOLOGY IN THE BIBLICAL CANON[25]

As we have already seen, the exodus motif plays a great role in the Book of Wisdom, namely, in its third part, where the events of the exodus

---

dann im 1. Jh. v. Chr. in der Sapientia Salomonis.)' ('the work of creation is first presented as the work of Wisdom, according to the now binding tradition of Gen 1 .... Wisdom is the divine Logos itself, the word of creation, and the long tradition of creation through the word flows into this conception of wisdom .... The consistent and fully implemented representation of wisdom as πνευμα we find in the 1st century BC in the Sapientia Salomonis.').

[24] P. Schäfer, *Mirror of His Beauty: Feminine Images of God from the Bible to the Early Kabbalah*, Jews, Christians, and Muslims from the Ancient to the Modern World (Princeton; Oxford, 2002), 38.

[25] This section contains, in significantly modified form, some material also found in Joachim Schaper, '"Out of the Iron Furnace": Exodus, Death, and the Reception History of Freedom', *Aegyptiaca* 4 (2019): 179–187.

described in the biblical book of the same name are re-narrated. However, the actual Greek term – that is, εξοδος – occurs *earlier* in the book, and it is only used on those two occasions in the whole book, viz., in 3:2 and 7:6. In these passages, it signifies the *way out of physical life*, of the earthly existence.[26] The *result* of that εξοδος is painted in glorious colours in chapter 3:

> ¹ Δικαίων δὲ ψυχαὶ ἐν χειρὶ θεοῦ,
> καὶ οὐ μὴ ἅψηται αὐτῶν βάσανος.
> ² ἔδοξαν ἐν ὀφθαλμοῖς ἀφρόνων τεθνάναι,
> καὶ ἐλογίσθη κάκωσις ἡ ἔξοδος αὐτῶν
> ³ καὶ ἡ ἀφ' ἡμῶν πορεία σύντριμμα,
> οἱ δέ εἰσιν ἐν εἰρήνῃ.

1 But the souls of the righteous are in the hand of God,
and no torment will ever touch them.
2 In the eyes of the foolish they seemed to have died,
and their exodus was thought to be an affliction,
3 and their going from us to be their destruction;
but they are at peace.

(RSV, modified)

And in chapter 7:5–6:

> ⁵ οὐδεὶς γὰρ βασιλέων ἑτέραν ἔσχεν γενέσεως ἀρχήν,
> ⁶ μία δὲ πάντων εἴσοδος εἰς τὸν βίον ἔξοδός τε ἴση.

5 For no king has had a different beginning of existence;
6 there is for all mankind one entrance into life, and a common
departure

(RSV)

This exodus, then, was an exodus very different from the one described in the book of that name. Nevertheless, as we have seen, the biblical account of the exodus was hugely important to the author of the book of Wisdom. In the new type of wisdom discourse he was creating, he used it to provide the historical background to the Hellenistic Jewish experience of individual liberation through the practice of Wisdom in his own day: an experience that focused on individualising concepts of liberation

---

[26] See F. V. Reiterer, 'Beobachtungen zum äußeren und inneren Exodus im Buch der Weisheit', in *Die Rezeption des Exodusmotivs in deuterokanonischer und frühjüdischer Literatur*, ed. J. Gärtner and B. Schmitz, DCLS 32 (Berlin; Boston, 2016), 198–200.

and reconceptualised its social and political dimensions.[27] The re-narration of the Exodus story is given much space in the third part of the book of Wisdom: the Exodus motif is used to great effect in Wis 10:15–11:16, and that use is continued in chapters 16:1–19:21. The motif thus receives much attention, and that includes copious references to Egypt, the Egyptians and the religion of Egypt. In 10:15–16, Sophia is said to have established herself in the soul of Moses, the servant of the Lord, thus having enabled him to confront Pharaoh and to liberate the Israelites from a 'people of oppressors' (vv. 15–16):

> 15 A holy people and blameless race
> wisdom delivered from a nation of oppressors.
> 16 She entered the soul of a servant of the Lord,
> and withstood dread kings with wonders and signs.
>   (RSV)

Wisdom is thus credited with the actions that are ascribed directly to the God of Israel in the original account in the book of Exodus. Wisdom (σοφία) is conceptualised as 'spirit' (πνευμα) – a spirit which is essentially identical with God himself. It is his hypostasis and is active *ad extra*: see, for example, the parallel between 'spirit' and 'God' in Wis 1:6. By means of his hypostasis, God can permeate the cosmos because Wisdom, as πνευμα, is composed of the finest matter (!) and can thus, in a manner of speaking, extend God's presence throughout his creation. There is no systematically conceptualised teaching of the omnipresence and omniscience of God in the book of Wisdom, but the idea of the inescapability of the divine presence is vividly expressed by means of biblical and Stoic imagery.

The book of Wisdom engages with the Exodus motif across six chapters out of nineteen altogether. Neither the Exodus itself nor Egypt, the Pharaoh or Moses are ever referred to by name. Indeed, *not a single biblical figure* is ever mentioned by name. Nevertheless, for a Jewish reader, the references to biblical figures were of course easy to understand.

Let us now turn to a few central concerns of the chapters which the Wisdom of Solomon devotes to its re-narration of the Exodus story. Pieter Willem van der Horst writes:

> In a series of seven antitheses, the author compares the Egyptians and the Israelites. For instance, the Egyptians were being slain by locusts and flies, while the Israelites survived a serpent attack

---

[27] On the social and political situation of the Jews of Alexandria, cf. P. M. Fraser, *Ptolemaic Alexandria*, vol. 1 (Oxford, 1972), 54–58.

through the agency of the bronze serpent; the Egyptians were unable to eat because of the hideousness of the beasts sent against them, while Israel, after briefly suffering want, enjoyed exotic quail food; on the same night that the Egyptian firstborn were destroyed, Israel was summoned to God and glorified.[28]

So far, so good. But something surprising happens in the book's last chapter:

> the Egyptians are accused of *misoxenia*, 'hatred of foreigners' or 'hostility toward strangers' (19.13), exactly the same accusation that was leveled against the Jews by Alexandrian Jew-haters from the very beginning. This cannot be sheer coincidence. 'In styling the conduct of the Egyptians as *misoxenia*, the author is reversing the very charge made against the Jews by pagan contemporaries.' And the reversal of the charge is here made in the context of the exodus story.[29]

Van der Horst concludes that '[a]pparently, this story in its anti-Jewish form was still in the air in the time of this author, as writers such as Chaeremon and Apion prove'.[30] Accusing the unnamed 'people of oppressors' of *misoxenia* serves the purpose both of exonerating the Jews – who had been subject to the abuse of non-Jews – and of making a general point about the *misoxenia* they and others encountered in their lives. This could be a direct reflection of the oppression experienced by Alexandrian Jews in the first century BCE.[31]

Wisdom 11:9–14 thus seems to be not just a re-narration of Exodus events but a reflexion of the actual experience of co-existence with Gentiles in Alexandria (with a focus on the Gentiles) and of the hope for justice:

> 9 For when they were tried, though they were being disciplined in mercy,
> they learned how the ungodly were tormented when judged in wrath.

---

[28] P. W. van der Horst, 'From Liberation to Expulsion: The Exodus in the Earliest Jewish-Pagan Polemics', in *Israel's Exodus in Transdisciplinary Perspective: Text, Archaeology, Culture and Geoscience*, ed. T. E. Levy, T. Schneider and W. H. C. Propp (Cham, 2015), 395.

[29] Van der Horst, 'From Liberation to Expulsion', 395.

[30] Van der Horst, 'From Liberation to Expulsion', 395.

[31] While there was a large Jewish community in Alexandria, relations with the non-Jewish majority population were at times tense, cf. Fraser, *Ptolemaic Alexandria*, vol. I, 805–806.

10 For thou didst test them as a father does in warning,
but thou didst examine the ungodly as a stern king does in
    condemnation.
11 Whether absent or present, they were equally distressed,
12 for a twofold grief possessed them,
and a groaning at the memory of what had occurred.
13 For when they heard that through their own punishments
the righteous had received benefit, they perceived it was the Lord's
    doing.
14 For though they had mockingly rejected him who long before had
    been cast out and exposed,
at the end of the events they marveled at him,
for their thirst was not like that of the righteous.

(RSV)

We must remember that these texts were probably intended to be
read by Jews and non-Jews alike: their Jewish readers knew what biblical
groups and figures they referred to, and non-Jewish readers could read
the texts as stories that make points about the power and significance of
God as well as Sophia and her righteous adherents, points applicable to
Jews and non-Jews alike.

Why did the author use the exodus motif in such a sustained
manner, across several chapters of a fairly slim book devoted to a topic
that seems far removed from the concerns of the book of Exodus?
Anathea Portier-Young sees 'the historical review, cast in the form of
prophetic prediction', which 'asserts the transience and finitude of
temporal powers, affirms God's governance of time and the outworking
of God's plan in history, and gives hope for a transformed future', as '[a]
key discursive strategy of resistance shared by Daniel, the Apocalypse of
Weeks, and the Book of Dreams'[32] – and, I should like to add, the book of
Wisdom. While it does not 'cast' its transformed exodus narrative in 'the
form of prophetic prediction', that narrative shares all the other aspects
of the 'discursive strategy of resistance' with Daniel and the other books
mentioned by Portier-Young.

While the Book of Wisdom is not a typical exponent of 'resistance
literature', it nevertheless shares some key characteristics with such
literature. But we also find, in Jewish Hellenistic literature, examples
of – so to speak – a *permutation* of that kind of apocalyptic hope, and

---

[32] A. E. Portier-Young, *Apocalypse against Empire: Theologies of Resistance in Early Judaism* (Grand Rapids; Cambridge, 2011), 27.

that permutation is the hope for *individual* liberation, an expression of the individual's quest for freedom and the individual's desire for the liberation of what one may call the 'inner self'.[33]

A powerful narrative of collective liberation was thus transformed into an exemplar of the formation of individuals in the service of Wisdom and thus, ultimately, of God. Crucial in that process was the enhanced significance of the figure of Wisdom in Hellenistic Judaism. As we saw, the term εξοδος was not used to designate the liberation from Egypt but another liberation: the liberation from the body, from earthly existence. And that way out, that εξοδος, is indeed seen as the individual's liberation: the liberation of his or her soul from the body that used to imprison it. The difference between the εξοδος from the 'iron furnace', Egypt, and the εξοδος from the body could scarcely be greater, but both are conceptualised as *the gateway to a better existence*.

In the book of Wisdom, Sophia is described as a divine hypostasis that brings about the individualisation and internalisation of Israel's Exodus from Egypt: the original Exodus is seen as the unique event of *communal* liberation which serves as the background to the experience of *personal and individual* liberation, of a transition *from life through death to a new life* under the guidance of Sophia. Yet, at the same time, the social and political exodus becomes a focus of a *new communal eschatology*. Between the writing of the original exodus story in its classic form in the Pentateuch and the writing of the book of Wisdom, roughly half a millennium had elapsed, and the social and cultural circumstances had, of course, undergone a dramatic transformation. The situation in which the Jews of Alexandria, one of whom was the author of the book of Wisdom,[34] found themselves in the first century BCE was not conducive to the development of apocalyptic literature along the usual lines, that is, driven by a desire for a universal, cathartic transformation of the cosmos and the beginning of the immediate and eternal reign of God.[35] Rather, in the Wisdom of Solomon we have a dialogue between wisdom traditions and apocalyptic thought in which the *wisdom element in apocalypticism* comes much more to the fore

---

[33] Cf. J. Assmann and G. G. Stroumsa, eds., *Transformations of the Inner Self in Ancient Religions*, Studies in the History of Religions 83 (Leiden; Boston; Cologne, 1999); see also A. I. Baumgarten, J. Assmann and G. G. Stroumsa, eds., *Self, Soul and Body in Religious Experience*, Studies in the History of Religions 78 (Leiden; Boston; Cologne, 1998).

[34] See L. Mazzinghi, *Weisheit*, IEKAT (Stuttgart, 2018), 30–34.

[35] On the book of Wisdom and key characteristics of apocalypticism, cf. M. Gilbert, *La Sagesse de Salomon*, 89–107; and Mazzinghi, *Weisheit*, 237.

than its eschatological component. But the eschatological component is not absent. In the book of Wisdom, the exodus is an eschatological event in the sense that every *individual wise person* will experience it as the crowning moment of his or her own eschatological progress, that is, their progress from their earthly existence through death and on to the communion of their souls with the deity. One might call this a quietistic transformation of apocalyptic beliefs. In any case, what we have here is one of the roots of Jewish mysticism, as described by P. Schäfer.[36]

Quietistic or not, Wisdom's transformation of the exodus motif fulfils a desire which Michael Walzer identified in his *Exodus and Revolution*. 'The Exodus', Walzer writes, 'may or may not be what many of its commentators thought it to be, the first revolution. But the Book of Exodus (together with the Book of Numbers) is certainly the first description of revolutionary politics'.[37] But revolutionary politics is not everything. As Walzer rightly puts it: 'Why be content with the difficult and perhaps interminable struggle for holiness and justice when there is another promised land where liberation is final, fulfillment complete? History itself is a burden from which we long to escape, and messianism guarantees that escape: a deliverance not only from Egypt but from Sinai and Canaan, too.'[38] But, one might add, messianism is not the ultimate answer to the desire for the escape from history either: that escape is fulfilled by the escape from the body. It is the body that involves us in history, that defines and to a great degree determines us as physical, social and political beings.[39]

It now becomes clearer why the author of the book of Wisdom applies the term εξοδος only to death, *indeed only to the death of the just*. This is 'where liberation is final, fulfillment complete'. It is the state in which is realised, eschatologically transformed, the innerworldly promise of liberation held up by the original Exodus narrative.

The personalisation and internalisation of liberation through *the ultimate* εξοδος that is physical death could be conceptualised, by the Alexandrian Jews among whom the author of Wisdom grew up, as the final escape from the oppression exercised by the real and the metaphorical Egypt which they experienced. At the same time, non-Jewish readers of *Sapientia* could learn from the book how to escape what they

---

[36] Schäfer, *Mirror of His Beauty*, 33–38.
[37] M. Walzer, *Exodus and Revolution* (New York, 1985), 134.
[38] Walzer, *Exodus and Revolution*, 135–136.
[39] On the significance of the body, cf. M. Merleau-Ponty, *Phénoménologie de la Perception*, Bibliothèque des Idées (Paris, 1945).

experienced as *their* metaphorical Egypt: the lack of philosophical and ethical orientation in the 'globalised' world of Eastern Mediterranean Hellenism and the absence of an eschatological hope for their lives.

The book of Wisdom shares at least one centrally important tenet with the examples of resistance literature discussed by Portier-Young, viz., 'an eschatology which saw human and divine affairs moving inexorably towards the predetermined divine and universal victory'.[40] It is precisely *this* view of eschatology that drives the book of Wisdom: the progress towards the ultimate goal of liberation is inexorable. The book's hope is for an individualised *eschaton* for which the individual sets out in his or her own earthly life with the assistance of Wisdom, an *eschaton* in which they will arrive after having undergone the exodus that is their physical death. That transition is the fulfilment of their personalised and internalised eschatological hope. The entry of death into the world (Wis 2:24: *eiserchesthai*) is contrasted with the *exodos* of the Just from the world. The latter *exodos* is seen as something entirely positive: it ensures the reunification of the soul, conceived of as *pneuma*, with the *pneuma* of divine Wisdom – and thus with God himself.[41] But it takes place within the framework of a wider communal eschatology. However, that expectation of communal liberation is no longer restricted to Israel but is extended to all those who serve Wisdom and follow her instructions, irrespective of the disciples' origins.

THE BOOK OF WISDOM AS A SPIRITUAL EXERCISE

How was the book of Wisdom intended to spread the belief in the guidance of Wisdom on the soul's path towards God through unification

[40] S. K. Eddy, *The King Is Dead: Studies in the Near Eastern Resistance to Hellenism, 334–31 B.C.* (Lincoln, 1961), 42.

[41] Philo later developed the same concept in a different manner. As J. S. Allen ('The Despoliation of Egypt: Origen and Augustine – From Stolen Treasures to Saved Texts', in Levy et al., *Israel's Exodus*, 348, n.1), rightly states with regard to the treatment of Gen 15:14 (τὸ δὲ ἔθνος ᾧ ἐὰν δουλεύσωσιν κρινῶ ἐγώ μετὰ δὲ ταῦτα ἐξελεύσονται ὧδε μετὰ ἀποσκευῆς πολλῆς) in Philo's *Quis rerum divinarum heres sit*: 'The ὧδε (or "here") refers to the promised land which for Philo represents the soul's true destination in God. Rene Bloch (in "Leaving Home: Jewish-Hellenistic Authors on the Exodus") has pointed out that in Philo's *Life of Moses*, the destination point for the exodus is always left uncertain. Bloch suggests that Philo wants us to view Moses as a cosmopolitan citizen of the world and thus he sought to de-emphasize his status as founder of the land of the Jews. I add that Philo's de-emphasis on the destination point also helps the biblical story to function as allegory. The real destination of Moses and his people who have escaped Egyptian bodily passions is the ultimate "here" of heaven; the soul's true home.'

with Lady Wisdom's *pneuma*? In order to arrive at an answer, one has to understand the book's genre. As far as *Sapientia*'s classification according to literary genres is concerned, the situation is more complex than it appears at first glance. For example, Fichtner refers to the genres that Sapientia has in common with the wisdom books in the proto-canonical Scriptures. However, he adds the following proviso: '[Sapientia] shows a stronger preference for theoretical explanations and uses a larger number of literary genres'[42] than earlier Wisdom literature. This tendency towards the 'theoretical' and the broader range of genres used are explained by the paedagogical-pastoral impetus of the book, which is not unlike that of traditional wisdom instruction. But the former is not simply identical with the latter.

The question of the book's genre is crucial with regard to under-standing the book's intended function. In some of the more recent commentaries, Wisdom is classified by some as an example of the genre of *logos protreptikos*, a genre of didactic exhortation. Reese holds this view but draws attention to the fact that other genres are also repre-sented in Wisdom.[43] This is a reasonable assessment of the evidence. But what was the didactic exhortation intended to accomplish? It is important to see that the author of Wisdom did not just intend to impart religious *knowledge*. He also wanted to provide the basis for spiritual practices – practices that Foucault called 'technologies of the self'[44] (using an expression which he apparently borrowed from the work of P. Rabbow,[45] of whose work he had become aware of through the writings of P. Hadot).[46] We shall see that the book of Wisdom is

---

[42] Fichtner, *Weisheit Salomos*, 6. For convenience, quotations from Fichtner's commentary are given in English translation.

[43] Reese, *Hellenistic Influence*, 90–121, esp. 117–121.

[44] M. Foucault, *Technologies of the Self: A Seminar with Michel Foucault*, ed. L. H. Martin, H. Gutman and P. H. Hutton (Amherst, 1988).

[45] P. Rabbow (*Seelenführung: Methodik der Exerzitien in der Antike* [Munich, 1954], 16) discusses 'die Technologie der sittlichen Lebensbehandlung und -bemeisterung'. Foucault calls them 'technologies of the self' (Foucault seems to have first coined the term in English; in any case, he first used it in print in English, not in French, in his *Technologies of the Self*). Foucault does not mention Rabbow in *Technologies of the Self* but it is clear that he knew his work; cf. M. Foucault, *L'herméneutique du sujet: cours au Collège de France (1981–1982)* (Paris, 2001) (in the German translation – *Hermeneutik des Selbst: Vorlesungen am Collège de France (1981/82)*, trans. U. Bokelmann (Frankfurt am Main, 2009) – Rabbow is mentioned on p. 456).

[46] P. Hadot, *Exercices spirituels et philosophie antique* (Paris, 1981), 198. His *Philosophie als Lebensform: Antike und moderne Exerzitien der Weisheit*, trans. I. Hadot and C. Marsch (Frankfurt am Main, 2002) contains translations of six chapters from the second French edition (chapters 1, 3, 4, 7, 8 and 9 in the German

eminently practice-orientated and that it encourages a form of spiritual exercise, an exercise that can be seen as a forerunner of similar ('pagan' and Christian) practices in late antiquity. They have been known as *exercitia spiritualia* from the times of the early Church onwards[47] but have even deeper roots. As Rabbow and Hadot have shown, such exercises already existed among Hellenistic philosophers,[48] maybe even in classical Greece.[49]

With regard to the type of exercise that shaped the book of Wisdom, we have to differentiate, with Rabbow,[50] between moral and spiritual exercises:[51]

> As a moral exercise ['sittliche Übung'] we designate a single act, a definite act of self-influencing ['Selbstbeeinflussung'], which is carried out with the conscious intention of bringing about a certain moral effect; it always points beyond itself in that it is either itself repeated or is combined with other, equally directed acts to form a planned whole.

The 'spiritual' exercise is, according to Rabbow, the 'twin' of the moral exercise, different from it only in its focus on the strengthening of the person's spiritual life along the lines of religious beliefs.[52]

As far as moral exercises are concerned, Stoic philosophy offers a particularly rich treasure of ethical literature that is very practically orientated, and here the work of Chrysippus is of the highest importance, not least because Chrysippus devoted an entire book to mastering

---

edition) as well as three chapters (2, 5 and 6) that are not part of that edition. The references in this essay are to the German edition.

[47] Rufinus, *Historia Monachorum*, PL vol. 21, 410 D ('quadraginta annis fuisset in exercitiis spiritualibus conversatus').

[48] Rabbow, *Seelenführung*, 23–150.

[49] Hadot, *Philosophie*, 13–47.

[50] Cf. Hadot's view, as expressed in the quotation referenced in n. 49.

[51] Cf. Rabbow (*Seelenführung*, 18) for the full passage: 'Als "sittliches Exerzitium" [sittliche Übung] bezeichnen wir eine einzelne Vornahme, einen bestimmten Akt der Selbstbeeinflussung, der mit der bewußten Absicht eines bestimmten sittlichen Effekts ausgeübt wird; er weist insofern stets über sich hinaus, als er entweder selbst wiederholt oder mit anderen, gleichgerichteten Akten zu einem planvollen Ganzen verbunden wird. Als sittlich charakterisiert das Exerzitium sich im Unterschied von geistiger Übung, etwa die Einübung eines Lehrstoffs, und gymnastischer Übung; die bewußte Absicht unmittelbaren sittlichen Effekts scheidet es von gewöhnlichem Durchdenken sittlicher Probleme. Daß solche Übung [Exerzitium] entweder selbst wiederholt, Regel, Selbstgewöhnung wird [wie es meistens der Fall ist] oder im Ganzen eines Planes, eines Systems mit anderen, gleichgerichteten zusammenwirkt, ist mit dem Sinn des Übens gegeben.'

[52] See quotation in n. 51.

affects.[53] The book of Wisdom is also about mastering disordered affects: it opens up access to a practice which is intended to guide its readers in their spiritual life, in finding their bearings in a complex, disorientating world. The book of Wisdom, theologically anchored in the Israelite and early Jewish tradition of wisdom literature and practice, thus adopted an educational approach that had been developed and brought to fruition in the Hellenistic philosophical tradition: an approach that was dedicated to transforming the personality of the individual to ensure its temporal and eternal well-being. 'The philosophical activity extends not only to knowledge, but to one's own person and existence: it is a progression that lets our being grow and makes us better; it is conversion that changes all of life and changes the nature of whoever performs it.'[54]

The author of *Sapientia* took up and adjusted ideas and practices that ultimately had their roots in classical Greek philosophy and were firmly anchored in Hellenistic Judaism, as can be seen from the example of the practices of the therapists described by Philon (for example, in his *De vita contemplativa*). In *Quis rerum divinarum heres sit* § 253 and *Legum allegoriae* III § 18, Philo gives us an overview of the structure of spiritual exercises.[55] The book of Wisdom was, according to the intriguing reconstruction of D. Georgi, held in special esteem by a community of believers who placed great store by its teachings and received their guidance and formation from the appropriation of those teachings. In what seems to have been a 'Wisdom movement' in Hellenistic Judaism, they were close to the Apocalyptic Wisdom 'branch' of that movement.[56] Practices such as those described in Philo's texts may have been used by the members of that community.

Wisdom must be perceived and understood as part of the tradition history of biblical wisdom literature, as intrinsic to the dialogue between Judaism and Hellenistic Egyptian religion and as a guide to the spiritual life. Because it was all that, it also acquired a crucial place

---

53 J. Gould, *The Philosophy of Chrysippus* (Albany, 1970), 186.

54 Hadot, *Philosophie*, 15. Cf. his comment: 'Conversion leads him from the state of a fake life, obscured by unconsciousness and consumed with worry, to the state of a real life in which human beings attain consciousness of themselves, the true view of the world, peace and inner freedom.'

55 While Philo's text was authored in the first decades CE, it reflects much earlier practices.

56 D. Georgi, 'Das Wesen der Weisheit nach der "Weisheit Salomos"', in *Gnosis und Politik*, ed. J. Taubes, Religionstheorie und Politische Theologie 2 (Munich, 1984), 66–81.

in the history of Jewish and Christian mysticism. As W. Horbury rightly observes, this becomes clear as soon as early Jewish literature is not perceived in isolation but in connection with the New Testament as well as rabbinic and patristic texts:[57] 'an emotional and intellectual mysticism was focused before and during the time of Christian origins on the figure of wisdom as presented within the Solomonic corpus in the Wisdom of Solomon and Ecclesiasticus, both of them being viewed together with Proverbs'.[58]

As we have seen, the Wisdom of Solomon is not just a book of significant philosophical and theological substance that stands out as a literary monument to Hellenistic Judaism. It also is a milestone in the history of Jewish mysticism and religious and philosophical paedagogics. For all these reasons – and more! – it deserves the attention both of the devotional reader and the scholar, both in Judaism and in Christianity.

Further Reading

Collins, John J. *Jewish Wisdom in the Hellenistic Age*. Edinburgh: 1998.
Enns, Peter. *Exodus Retold: Ancient Exegesis of the Departure from Egypt in Wis [10:]15–21 and 19:1–9*. HSM 57. Atlanta: 1997.
Fichtner, Johannes. *Weisheit Salomos*. HAT II/6. Tübingen: 1938.
Georgi, Dieter. 'Das Wesen der Weisheit nach der "Weisheit Salomos"'. Pages 66–81 in *Gnosis und Politik*. Religionstheorie und Politische Theologie 2. Edited by J. Taubes. Munich: 1984.
Gese, Hartmut. *Alttestamentliche Studien*. Tübingen: 1991.
Gilbert, Maurice. *La Sagesse de Salomon/The Wisdom of Solomon: Recueil d'études/Selected Essays*. AnBib 189. Rome: 2011.
Horbury, William. 'The Books of Solomon in Ancient Mysticism'. Pages 185–201 in *Reading Texts, Seeking Wisdom: Scripture and Theology*. Edited by D. F. Ford and G. Stanton. London: 2003.

---

[57] W. Horbury, 'The Books of Solomon in Ancient Mysticism', in *Reading Texts, Seeking Wisdom: Scripture and Theology*, ed. D. F. Ford and G. Stanton (London, 2003), 48: 'In antiquity texts of importance for mysticism were supplied by the Wisdom of Solomon and Ecclesiasticus, themselves developing Proverbs, on the one hand, and by the Song of Solomon, on the other; but mystical attention was not evenly shared between the wisdom books and the Canticle.' Cf. his comment: 'After the Second-Temple period the principal mystical focus then seems to shift within the Solomonic books from Wisdom and Ecclesiasticus towards Solomon's Song. A related and partly comparable variation, between Christian use of all three of these books and Jewish concentration on the Song of Solomon and Proverbs, appears when the Solomonic biblical foci of mediaeval Jewish and Christian mysticism are compared with one another.'
[58] Horbury, 'Books of Solomon', 48.

Portier-Young, Anathea E. *Apocalypse against Empire: Theologies of Resistance in Early Judaism*. Grand Rapids; Cambridge: 2011.

Reese, James M. 'Plan and Structure in the Book of Wisdom'. *CBQ* 27 (1965): 391–399.

Hellenistic Influence on the Book of Wisdom and Its Consequences. AnBib 41. Rome: 1970.

Reiterer, Friedrich Vinzenz. 'Beobachtungen zum äußeren und inneren Exodus im Buch der Weisheit'. Pages 187–208 in *Die Rezeption des Exodusmotivs in deuterokanonischer und frühjüdischer Literatur*. DCLS 32. Edited by J. Gärtner and B. Schmitz. Berlin; Boston, 2016.

Schäfer, Peter. *Mirror of His Beauty: Feminine Images of God from the Bible to the Early Kabbalah*. Jews, Christians, and Muslims from the Ancient to the Modern World. Princeton; Oxford, 2002.

Schaper, Joachim. '"... denn er ist besser als das, was er anbetet" (Sapientia Salomonis 15,17): Bilderpolemik und theologische Anthropologie in der Sapientia Salomonis'. Pages 455–464 in *Was ist der Mensch, dass du seiner gedenkst? (Psalm 8,5): Aspekte einer theologischen Anthropologie. Festschrift für Bernd Janowski zum 65. Geburtstag*. Edited by M. Bauks et al. Neukirchen-Vluyn: 2008.

'Νόμος and Νόμοι in the Wisdom of Solomon'. Pages 293–306 in *Wisdom and Torah: The Reception of 'Torah' in the Wisdom Literature of the Second Temple Period*. JSJS 163. Edited by B. U. Schipper and D. A. Teeter. Leiden; Boston: 2013.

16 Wisdom at Qumran

DAVID A. SKELTON

In the last thirty years, wisdom studies at Qumran has branched away from the Hebrew Bible and carved out its own position in the field. During this time, a general consensus has emerged regarding which texts belong in this category and what they demonstrate in terms of the development of the wisdom tradition in the Second Temple period. These texts are the following: 4QInstruction (1Q26, 4Q415–418, 423); The Book of Mysteries (1Q27, 4Q299–301); 4QWiles of the Wicked Woman (4Q184); 4QSapiential Work (4Q185); 4QWords of the Maśkîl (4Q298); 4QWays of Righteousness (4Q420–421); 4QInstruction-like Composition B (4Q424); 4QBeatitudes (4Q525).[1] One could add to this the Treatise of the Two Spirits from the Community Rule (1QS 3:13–4:26) and several psalms from the Cave 11 Psalms Scroll (Ps 154 in 11Q5 18; Sir 51:13–30 in 11Q5 21:11–17 and 22:1; and the Hymn to the Creator in 11Q5 26:9–15).[2] Recently, this consensus has come under fire. There has been a wide range of criticism regarding which texts belong in the wisdom category as well as attempts to dispense with the category altogether. Before analysing this criticism, I will first give an overview of how biblical scholarship has typically understood wisdom literature and how interpretation and analysis of the wisdom texts from the Dead Sea Scrolls have both upheld and challenged this consensus in recent decades. Second, I will conclude with an examination of wisdom as a concept and suggest that tabling the genre discussion will open up the texts typically labelled as wisdom literature to new comparisons with a broader range of Jewish and Hellenistic literature.

---

[1] This list comes from John Kampen, *Wisdom Literature* (Grand Rapids, 2011).

[2] See Matthew J. Goff, *Discerning Wisdom: The Sapiential Literature of the Dead Sea Scrolls*, VTSup 116 (Leiden, 2007); and Daniel J. Harrington, *Wisdom Texts From Qumran* (New York, 1996).

THE WISDOM LITERATURE CONSENSUS

Before discussing the main contributions the Dead Sea Scrolls have made to our understanding of wisdom, it is important to clarify how the concept has generally been understood in biblical scholarship. Biblical scholarship tends to label Proverbs, Job and Qohelet as wisdom literature along with a handful of psalms (e.g., Psalms 1, 36, 73, 119) and three texts from the Greek Septuagint (Ben Sira, Wisdom of Solomon and Baruch 3:9–4:4). It does so because of the predominance of the term *ḥokmah/sophia* and their semantic field in these books and the relationship of these 'wisdom' terms with each other.[3] Particularly predominant is the virtue of attaining wisdom, which contains with it the assumption that doing so will lead to a blessed life, whereas pursuing foolishness will ultimately bring about destruction. Along with the need to gain wisdom and avoid folly, 'fear of YHWH' is a common refrain. Nonetheless, conclusions regarding right or correct living are drawn more from observing the consequences of one's actions rather than divine revelation. Because of this, wisdom literature is often seen as being more universal than priestly or prophetic literature, which seems to be confirmed by the parallels many proverbial texts share with Egyptian and Mesopotamian proverbial collections. Finally, wisdom literature is often associated with scribal education, particularly for those who participated in life at the royal court.

A sampling of recent textbooks on the Hebrew Bible demonstrate how pervasive this understanding of wisdom literature still is. In his *Old Testament: A Very Short Introduction*, Michael Coogan states that wisdom literature 'focuses on the human condition and is often universal' making it 'international, with remarkable cross-fertilization among various cultures'.[4] John Collins' textbook notes that 'this kind of literature is called "wisdom literature" because of the frequency with which the words for wisdom and folly occur',[5] and it is 'associated especially with scribes at the royal court'.[6] Douglas Knight and Amy Jill-Levine state that wisdom literature contains 'the most concentrated form of inquiry and reflection on the nature of human existence in the world'

---

[3] A similar argument could be made for the *mashal* form, which is typically translated as 'proverb' and thought of as unique to wisdom literature but also attested outside of it. See Jacqueline Vayntrub, *Beyond Orality: Biblical Poetry On Its Own Terms* (New York, 2019), 70–102.

[4] Michael Coogan, *The Old Testament: A Very Short Introduction* (Oxford, 2008), 102.

[5] John J. Collins, *Introduction to the Hebrew Bible*, 3rd ed. (Minneapolis, 2018), 521.

[6] Collins, *Introduction*, 268.

and emphasises 'the notion of order, the relationship between cause and effect, the realistic confrontation with the world, and the place of the divine in human affairs'.[7] Their definition is similar to Leo Perdue's description of wisdom in the *Sword and the Stylus* where he notes 'acquiring knowledge through empirical experience', a 'quest for "order"' and 'service of institutions of wealth and powers' as key components of the Hebrew Bible's concept of wisdom.[8] While none of these examples are exhaustive, their general agreement demonstrates a consensus in terms of how to define wisdom literature that has been the predominant lens through which Dead Sea Scrolls scholarship reads and classifies the Qumran wisdom texts.

QUMRAN'S CHALLENGE TO THE CONSENSUS

Although there are several points of continuity with the wisdom literature of the Hebrew Bible (such as advice regarding deliberation in one's speech in 4Q420–421, 4Q424 and 4Q525) there are also notable absences along with several themes present in the wisdom literature from Qumran not in the wisdom literature of the Hebrew Bible.[9] Some of these themes correspond with what was already known from other late Second Temple wisdom texts, such as the Wisdom of Ben Sira (180 BCE) and the Wisdom of Solomon (first century CE) but others are quite distinctive to the Dead Sea Scrolls.

No Solomon

One surprise for those more familiar with the biblical wisdom literature is the lack of references to Solomon among the Qumran wisdom texts as well as the scrolls in general.[10] Solomon as the founder of Israelite wisdom is a common motif in biblical literature (1 Kgs 5:11–12; Prov 1:1; 10:1; Qoh 1:1), which is a status he also maintains in several Second

---

[7] Douglas Knight and Amy Jill-Levine, *The Meaning of the Bible: What the Jewish Scriptures and Christian Old Testament Can Teach Us* (New York, 2011), 427–428.

[8] Leo G. Perdue, *The Sword and the Stylus: An Introduction to Wisdom in the Age of Empires* (Grand Rapids, 2008), 11–13.

[9] Matthew Goff notes 'neither the theodicy of Job nor the epistemological despair of Qoheleth resonates with this corpus' (*Discerning Wisdom*, 289), *contra* Armin Lange, *Weisheit und Prädestination: Weisheitliche Urordnung und Prädestination in den Textfunden von Qumran*, STDJ 18 (Leiden, 1995).

[10] Cf. Armin Lange, 'Solomon', in *Encyclopedia of the Dead Sea Scrolls*, ed. Lawrence H. Schiffman and James C. VanderKam (Oxford, 2000), 2:886; and Blake Jurgens, 'The Figure of Solomon', in *The Wiley Blackwell Companion to Wisdom Literature*, ed. Samuel L. Adams and Matthew Goff (Hoboken; Chichester, 2020), 159–176.

Temple texts contemporaneous to the scrolls (Wis 7–9; Sir 47:12; Josephus, *Ant.* 8.23). One possible exception is the authorial voice in 4Q525, which Uusimäki attributes to Solomon due to the influence of Proverbs on the text,[11] but the beginning of the text is too fragmentary to know for sure.

Personified Wisdom Toned Down

The personification of wisdom, where she speaks as a woman, is a major sapiential trope, which is especially evident in Proverbs 1–9 but also present in some ways in Job 28 and Sirach 24. Wisdom is also a character in its own right in several places in the scrolls. So 11Q5 18:3–4 states, 'For wisdom has been granted to make YHWH's glory known, in order to recount his many deeds she has been taught to man.'[12] In 4Q525, the reader is directed to 'rejoice in her', 'search for her' and 'think of her'. The same can be said of Lady Folly in 4Q184 who dwells in the 'midst of eternal fire' (v. 7) at the entrance to Sheol (vv. 10–11). She has eyes and eyebrows (v. 13) along with a mouth and feet. Here, 4Q184 utilises many of the positive images of wisdom from Proverbs for the Wicked Woman (cf. ll. 8–9 and Prov 3:17–18) along with the negative images of the Strange Woman (cf. ll. 2–3 and Prov 5:5). While the personification of both wisdom and folly has been heavily influenced by Proverbs 1–9, wisdom is also much more passive in the scrolls.[13] Most notably, in the largest wisdom text, 4QInstruction, she is not present at all in the fragments as we have them. When she is present in other texts she only speaks a few times (4Q525 11–12 2; 4Q525 24 ii 2), and it is unclear in many of these places if the person speaking is Wisdom or Torah (4Q185 1–2 i 13–14). The former seems more likely, but even if that is the case, Lady Wisdom is not as central of a motif in the scrolls as she is in Proverbs 1–9, Job 28 or Sirach 24. Her form as a woman is also quite toned down as well, which may have something to do with an even stronger disconnect between the metaphor of Lady Wisdom with real

[11] Elisa Uusimäki, *Turning Proverbs towards Torah: An Analysis of 4Q525*, STDJ 117 (Leiden, 2015), 63, 226.

[12] All translations follow Florentino García Martínez and Eibert J. C. Tigchelaar, *The Dead Sea Scrolls: Study Edition* (Leiden, 1997).

[13] Sidnie White Crawford, 'Lady Wisdom and Dame Folly at Qumran', *DSD* 5 (1998): 355–366; Benjamin G. III, 'Wisdom and Women at Qumran', *DSD* 11 (2004): 240–261; and Goff, *Discerning Wisdom*, 105–106, 136, 215. *Contra* Laura Quick, 'The Hidden Body as Literary Strategy in *4QWiles of the Wicked Woman* (4Q184)', *DSD* 27 (2020): 234–256.

women in the late Second Temple Period.[14] Nevertheless, Proverbs 1–9 is much more influential overall in Qumran wisdom literature than the collection of short sayings one finds in Proverbs 10–22 and other wisdom texts in the ancient Near East.[15]

Torah-Wisdom Pairing

The equation of wisdom with Torah and its descent from heaven as a divine gift to Israel is notable in several Second Temple texts, especially Bar 3:9–4:4 and Sir 24:1–34. In both texts, God makes wisdom dwell among Israel alone (Bar 3:36; 24:8) specifically in written form (Bar 4:1; Sir 24:23), with the latter even more explicitly connecting her to 'the book of the covenant' and the 'law that Moses commanded'. Similarly, 4Q525 states, 'Blessed is the man who attains wisdom and walks in the law of the Most High' (4Q525 2 ii + 3 3–4). Likewise, 11Q5 18:12–14 connects the pious who listen to wisdom's voice to those whose 'meditation is on the Law of the Most High'. The implication here, as Uusimäki notes, is 'that wisdom is equivalent to torah obedience'.[16] Sapiential Admonitions B (4Q185) may also have the wisdom-Torah connection in mind when it states, 'blessed is the one to whom she has been given', and 'blessed is the one who does her' (4Q185 1–2 ii 8, 13). It makes this statement in conjunction with God bestowing wisdom to Israel as an inheritance (also, cf. ll. 8–10). While it is unclear when this moment took place, the reference to the Exodus in fragment 1 and the ancestors may suggest the writer had Sinai in mind. At the least, the reference to doing the 'words of the covenant' in column 3 suggests a connection between God's gift earlier in 4Q185 and Moses. If this reading is correct, then 4Q185 demonstrates the merging of Torah and wisdom was not simply a rhetorical device but was seen as a specific moment in the larger trajectory of Israel's history (4Q185 1–2 i 13–ii 2). Wisdom as the guiding principle leading from creation at large to Israel occurs even more predominately in both the Wisdom of Solomon (chs. 10–19) and the book of Ben Sira (chs. 44–50) and is a trajectory that also appears in several other places in the scrolls (see 1Q34;

---

[14] Wright, 'Wisdom and Women', 257–258. For this argument that the metaphor of Lady Wisdom had a nuanced connection with actual women in the Persian Period that it loses in the Hellenistic, see Claudia Camp, *Wisdom and the Feminine in the Book of Proverbs* (Sheffield, 1985); *Ben Sira and the Men Who Handle Books: Gender and the Rise of Canon-Consciousness*, HBM 50 (Sheffield, 2013).

[15] Harrington, *Wisdom Texts*, 89.

[16] Uusimäki, *Turning Proverbs towards Torah*, 179.

4Q370; 4Q381).[17] Finally, the placement of Sabbath halakhic material (4Q421 11 and 13) alongside short proverbs, the 'yoke of wisd[om]', and a call to 'study righteous' (4Q420 1a ii–b 3–4; 4Q421 1a ii–b 10, 14–15) in 4QWays of Righteousness may also be another representation of the conflation of Torah and wisdom in the scrolls.[18]

Apocalypticism and Creation

What has received the most attention among the wisdom texts found at Qumran are the 'conflicted boundaries'[19] between the wisdom and apocalyptic genres. The strongest example in this regard is the largest wisdom text from the scrolls: 4QInstruction (1Q26; 4Q415–18; 4Q423). While the text has 'several traditional wisdom themes',[20] the main motif throughout the work is studying the *raz nihyeh* ('the mystery of existence' or 'mystery that is to be') and living according to it. It is unclear what this may be, but the term *raz* occurs in apocalyptic texts in the Second Temple period in conjunction with higher revelation, often in the form of dreams and visions (Dan 2:18; 4:6; Enoch in 4Q201–204). In 4QMysteries, the term *raz nihyeh* occurs in the context of eschatological judgement (1Q27 1 i 13 = 4Q300 3 3), but while the *niphal* participle, *nihyeh*, can refer to future events, several places in 4QInstruction make clear it has the totality of time in view (4Q418 123 ii 3–4; 4Q417 2 I 3–4). The text of 4QInstruction also emphasises the elect status of its readers (called the *mebin* or 'understanding ones'), who have been separated from the 'fleshy spirit' and placed alongside the angels (4Q418 81 + 81a 1–2) as 'spiritual people'. God has given them the 'inheritance of the sons of Adam', special knowledge and placed them in the garden of Eden (4Q423 1–2). Concern for humanity's relationship with angels and the Genesis creation account is pervasive throughout Second Temple literature, but 4QInstructions shares with Ben Sira (Sir 16:26–17:10) an overall positive view of the knowledge received in the Garden rather than viewing it as the means through which sin entered the world.[21]

---

[17] Mika Pajunen, *The Land to the Elect and Justice for All: Reading Psalms in the Dead Sea Scrolls in Light of 4Q381*, JAJSup 14 (Göttingen, 2013), 158, 341–345, 358.

[18] Goff, *Discerning Wisdom*, 172–173.

[19] Benjamin G. Wright III and Lawrence M. Wills, eds., *Conflicted Boundaries in Wisdom and Apocalypticism*, SBLSymS 35 (Atlanta, 2005).

[20] John J. Collins, 'Wisdom Reconsidered In Light of the Scrolls', *DSD* 4 (1997): 269–271.

[21] Ben Sira and 4QInstruction here are part of a larger trope of connecting creation, election and praise in the Second Temple period; see Mika S. Pajunen, 'The Praise of

Several other deterministic features alongside esoteric knowledge can be found in 4QInstruction: 4Q417 1 i 10–12 refers to the 'birth-times of salvation' the 'eras of wickedness and truth', and 4Q417 2 i 14 depicts God engraving rewards and punishments, presumably on heavenly tablets. Divine election and determinism through 4QInstruction suggests that the *raz nihyeh* may be 'an overarching divine plan that endows history and creation with a rational structure' (4Q 417 1 i 10–12).[22] What is clear is that the *mebin* must study the *raz nihyeh* and meditate on it (4Q416 2 iii 13 = 4Q418 9+9a 13), but it is not clear how the *mebin* does study it or what form the 'mystery' is in. Studying and meditating are often used for written texts, and allusions to the Pentateuch throughout suggest that the community knew and utilised it.[23] Nonetheless, it is clear that, while the *raz nihyeh* may contain parts of the Mosaic Torah, it is not coterminous with it.[24] The text of 4QInstruction also directs the *mebin* to a heavenly 'book of remembrance', which contained a 'vision of meditation' or 'Vision of Hagu'. These allowed the spiritual people to distinguish between good and evil (4Q417 1 i 15–16), which likely referred to 'broad insights into the nature of reality' rather than moral decision-making.[25] It is unclear if this vision of a heavenly book is the same as *raz nihyeh* or different, but they both function as a signifier of the *mebin's* elect status. As 'spiritual people', the *mebin* has received them; the 'fleshy spirit' has not. Overall Goff's label for 4QInstruction, 'wisdom with an apocalyptic worldview',[26] is a moniker one could place on several wisdom texts from Qumran (Mysteries and the Treatise on the Two Spirits) and is one of the leading factors for reconsidering the fluidity of the wisdom category in the Second Temple period.[27]

Poverty

While there is a concern for taking care of the poor in biblical wisdom literature (Job 31:16, 19; Prov 14:21, 31; 19:17; 22:9, 22), the connection

---

God and His Name as the Core of the Second Temple Liturgy', *ZAW* 127 (2015): 475–488.

[22] Goff, *Discerning Wisdom*, 33.

[23] One example is the connection between the fifth commandment and the *raz nihyeh* in 4Q416 2 iii 15–19.

[24] Benjamin Wold, *4QInstruction: Divisions and Hierarchies* (Leiden, 2018), 146–195.

[25] Matthew J. Goff, *4QInstruction: A Commentary*, WLAW 2 (Atlanta, 2013), 164.

[26] Goff, *Discerning Wisdom*, 9.

[27] One can also point to the influence of wisdom on apocalyptic texts. See Cornelis Bennema, 'The Strands of Wisdom Tradition in Intertestamental Judaism: Origins, Developments and Characteristics', *TynBul* 52 (2001): 74–77.

between almsgiving and righteousness becomes even more predominant in Second Temple literature. For example, the book of Tobit points
to his almsgiving as a demonstration of his righteousness (Tob 1:6; 2:14)
and suggests it will deliver one from death and stand in for a Temple
offering (4:10–11). Likewise, almsgiving is a pervasive theme throughout the book of Ben Sira (Sir 3:14, 30; 7:10; 12:3; 17:22; 18:15; 29:8, 12;
35:4; 40:17, 24). For the latter, almsgiving can even 'atone for sins' (3:30)
and substitute for a grain offering (35:3). Like Ben Sira and Tobit, 4Q424
(4QInstruction-like Composition B) uses the term 'righteousness' in
conjunction with giving alms to the poor (4Q424 3 9–10) and addresses
surety (4Q424 2 3).[28] Even more striking is the implication that the
intended audience of 4QInstruction is quite poor and must deal precar-
iously with loan-borrowing and debt collection. For example, 4Q416 2 3
1 states, 'remember that you are poor' and 4Q416 2 1 18 warns that they
should not hide from their lender. Because much of the wisdom literature in the Hebrew Bible and larger ancient Near East gives advice
regarding proper behaviour before rulers, many scholars have assumed
that wisdom literature was produced by a retainer class of scribes as a
means of education for a position in court.[29] While poverty and charity
is not a defining characteristic across the wisdom literature corpus, the
production of writing by impoverished and oppressed communities in
4QInstruction places it much more in line with apocalyptic literature.[30]

Hymnody

Along with the fluidity between wisdom and apocalypticism, one also
finds a similar blurring of boundaries between wisdom and liturgical
texts. The Great Psalms Scroll from Cave 11 contains several 'extra'
hymns that have wisdom components. One such psalm mirrors the
hymn at the end of the book of Ben Sira (11Q5 21:11–22:1 = Sir
51:13–30), which is a book that contains several hymns and prayers
alongside proverbial adages and macarisms. I have already mentioned
the personification of wisdom from Psalm 154 in 11Q5 18:1–16, but the
Hymn to the Creator (11Q5 26:9–15) also has some parallels with Ben
Sira (cf. Sir 42:16–17; 47:10) and its coupling with 'David's
Compositions' suggests that one can read this hymn pedagogically to

---

[28] 4QWays of Righteousness (4Q420–421) may allude to this as well. Goff, *Discerning Wisdom*, 164–165.

[29] Even Proverbs is not stereotypical in this regard. Jacqueline Vayntrub, 'The Book of Proverbs and the Idea of Ancient Israelite Education', *ZAW* 128 (2016): 96–114.

[30] Anathea E. Portier-Young, *Apocalypse against Empire: Theologies of Resistance in Early Judaism* (Grand Rapids, 2011).

encourage the acquisition of wisdom. It is also interesting to note that 'David's Composition' (11Q5 27:2–11) depicts David as both a singer and a sage, which dovetails with both the Levitical singers in Chronicles (1 Chron 25), who are also teachers (2 Chron 17:7–8; 34:12–13), and the depiction of the *maskil* in several *yaḥad*-oriented texts.[31]

One could connect the idea of a singing sage to Pajunen's suggestions that psalms had become primarily valued in the Second Temple period for their historical and ethical value and had lost their liturgical connection.[32] In other words, the texts were not interested in actual musical performance but more with songs as an object of study and spiritual formation. Another possibility is that the creation and performance of songs played a larger role in Jewish education in the Second Temple period than previously thought.[33] Ben Sira assumes that his audience will compose and perform songs (Sir 32:5; 39:15) and provides them models of how to do so. The *maskil* is likewise depicted as both a teacher (1QS 3:13; 9:18) and a singer (1QS 9:12–11:22) whose songs are often represented as a means of conveying knowledge to the *yaḥad* (1QS 10:8; 1QHᵃ 5:13; 4Q511 18 ii 8). It is also worth noting the famous depiction of Solomon's Wisdom in 1 Kings 5:12 (MT) depicts him composing Proverbs *and* songs and the names of the sages he is supposedly wiser than are known in other places in the Hebrew Bible for composing *maskil* psalms (Pss 88–89) or singing at the temple (1 Chron 15:17–19; 25:1–6). While the construction of the sage as a singer could simply be a literary metaphor, there is evidence that it has some basis in reality. 'Scholar-singers' existed in Mesopotamia until Seleucid times where training in music was both a form of knowledge acquisition and a helpful mnemonic device for pedagogical purpose.[34] Instruction in music was also paramount in early Greek education, and Plato often

---

[31] See Ming Kim Ho's chapter on education and Levitical singers in *The Levite Singers in Chronicles and Their Stabilizing Role* (Bloomsbury, 2017), 151–182.

[32] Pajunen, *The Land to the Elect*, 340. Also, cf. Mark S. Smith, 'The Levitical Compilation of the Psalter', *ZAW* 103 (1991): 258–263; and more recently, Susan E. Gillingham, 'The Levites and the Editorial Composition of the Psalms', in *The Oxford Handbook of the Psalms*, ed. William P. Brown (Oxford, 2014), 201–213.

[33] Katharine Dell has made a similar point regarding wisdom and the cult in ancient Israelite religion where she affirms Mowinckel's point that 'praise often incorporates the didactic'. See her 'I Will Solve My Riddle to the Music of the Lyre' (Psalm XLIX 4 [5]): A Cultic Setting for Wisdom Psalms?', *VT* 54 (2004): 452.

[34] For musical pedagogy in Mesopotamia, see Kim (*Levite Singers*, 29–61) and my chapter on musical pedagogy in the ancient world in my forthcoming book *Singers of Wisdom: Music and Pedagogy in Ben Sira and the Second Temple Period*, JSJSup (forthcoming).

depicts the sophists (*Prot.* 316e) as teachers who used songs to attract students. Overall, there is fruitful grounds for not only studying the content of wisdom themes in psalms from the scrolls but also the role songs played in early Jewish pedagogy.[35]

Wisdom and the *Yaḥad*

The only unanimous wisdom text connected to the *yaḥad* is 4Q298, which is a text for the *maskil* in order to give understanding to 'children of dawn'. Most of it is in cryptic script, so it is difficult to know who all could read it. Because its implied audience is the community, the *maskil* could have read it orally.[36] It does seem to have some sort of eschatological focus and its emphasis on the divine plan, appointed time and examining ancient things is typical of other *maskil* works. The Treatise of the Two Spirits is another *maskil* text with a pedagogical focus. Its deterministic language and division of humanity into two groups with two spirits is often compared to 4QInstruction and classified a wisdom text accordingly.[37] Similarly, the *yaḥad*'s song-collection, the Hodayot, often utilises language from 4QInstruction (e.g., 'fleshy spirit') and while most Qumran wisdom texts are not from the *yaḥad*, they do demonstrate what the *yaḥad* valued and there is some fruitfulness in examining how the *yaḥad* could have interpreted them. The connection between the 'smooth words' of the Wicked Woman (4Q184 1:17) and the 'Seekers After Smooth Things' (CD 1:18; 1QH^a 10:17, 34; 4Q163 23 ii 10; 4Q169 3–4 i 6–8) is well known, but another good example is the phrase 'the dawn with knowledge' in the *Hymn to the Creator* (11Q5 26:11). This phrase could have served as support of the practice of daily liturgy known from other scroll texts (e.g., 1Q34–34bis; 4Q503–509; 5Q504) that was an important aspect of the *yaḥad*'s theology (1QS 9:26–10:4; and 1QM 14:12–14).[38]

---

[35] See David A. Skelton, 'Sages as Singers in Sirach and the Second Temple Period', in *Sirach and Its Contexts: The Pursuit of Wisdom and Human Flourishing: Proceedings of the Virginia Conference on the Book of Sirach and Its Contexts*, eds. Samuel L. Adams, Greg Schmidt Goering and Matthew J. Goff, JSJSup 196 (Leiden 2021), 167–182.

[36] Shem Miller, *Dead Sea Media Orality, Textuality, and Memory in the Scrolls from the Judean Desert*, STDJ 129 (Leiden, 2019), 184–185. Here Miller is building off of observations by Hempel and Pfann.

[37] But also see the 'two spirit' language in the *Vision of Amram*.

[38] A non-*yaḥad* paraphrase of the Flood (4Q370) dated to the late first century BCE may also draw influence from *Hymn to the Creator* in (cf. 11Q5 26:23–14 and 4Q370 I 1–2) and 4Q185 (cf. 4Q185 and 4Q370 2 7).

Wisdom MSS

Finally, I should briefly mention a handful of wisdom books from the Hebrew Bible that are attested in the scrolls in general. Most notably Prov 1:27–2:1 (4Q102); Proverbs 13–15 (4Q103); parts of Job 8–14 (2Q15) and 31–37 (4Q99–101) as well as the targums of Job (4Q157; 11Q10); parts of Qoheleth, chs. 1 and 5–7 (4Q109–110); a small fragment of Sir 6:13–31 (2Q18); the acrostic version of Sir 51:13–30 from 11QPs[a] mentioned above and a stichometric version of Sir 39:27–44:17 from Masada.[39]

WHY IS THERE A CONSENSUS?

Because many of the texts mentioned above were not fully published until the last few decades, it is not unreasonable that much of the discussion has centred on classifying exactly what type of literature it is and rethinking what these texts mean for reconceptualising the wisdom category.[40] In his early overview of wisdom at Qumran, Collins states, 'There is universal agreement that wisdom does not constitute a literary genre, and that it can find expression in various literary forms.'[41] Sarah Tanzer also notes, 'wisdom literature as a literary genre has eluded definition' and goes on to 'remind us that genre definitions are scholarly constructs and limited'.[42] Mark Sneed has lobbied for 'genre nominalism' over 'genre realism' in order to accentuate the arbitrariness of genres while still allowing for their necessity in producing and organising meaning.[43] Even more bold is the death knell sounded by Will Kynes who provides a genealogy of the creation of the wisdom literature category in order to call for its removal from biblical scholarship. Kynes still believes there is value in analysing wisdom as a concept or placing other books in conversation with Proverbs but contends that the category as it has been constructed is

---

[39] Eugene Ulrich, ed., *The Biblical Qumran Scrolls: Transcriptions and Textual Variants*, VTSup 134 (Leiden, 2010), 694–725, 727–733, 746–747.

[40] Much of the conversation was concerned initially with establishing the text itself, which concentrates on fragment reconstruction and materiality. With texts reasonably established and published fully, other methods are coming to the fore.

[41] Collins, 'Wisdom Reconsidered', 265. Also, cf. the collection of essays in Mark R. Sneed, ed., *Was There a Wisdom Tradition? New Prospects in Israelite Wisdom Studies* (Atlanta, 2005).

[42] Sarah Tanzer, 'Response to George Nickelsburg "Wisdom and Apocalypticism in Early Judaism"', in *Conflicted Boundaries*, 39–50. Also, Kampen, *Wisdom Literature*, 13.

[43] Mark R. Sneed, 'Is the "Wisdom Tradition" a "Tradition"?', *CBQ* 73 (2011): 66–67.

too arbitrary and limiting to be helpful. For Kynes, 'wisdom literature' has a stranglehold on how to read these texts and should be abandoned altogether in favor of a more variegated 'intertextual network' that subsumes genre under intertextuality.[44] Like the problem with defining religion in religious studies in general, one's classification of wisdom as a category often says more about the one making the classification (in this case Western, Enlightenment ideals) than how ancient Israel read and understood these books.[45] Thus Kynes' approach attempts to help scholars of wisdom break free from the 'definitional circle'.[46]

The adjective 'wisdom' in wisdom tradition and wisdom literature is a second-order, etic category but it can be utilised if one is precise in how it is being used as a term of comparison. While it may not correspond to reality, it can still serve as a useful heuristic for 'selecting data to compare'[47] whether one is examining terms for wisdom, its personification or variations in the father-son dialectic that often serves to perpetuate wisdom to future generations.[48] Regarding Proverbs, reading Ben Sira and 4QInstruction in light of it is not completely arbitrary, as they participate in many of Proverb's themes and modes of discourse, and their differences from Proverbs help elucidate some of their areas of distinctiveness such as the equation of Wisdom with the Torah of Moses in Ben Sira and with the *raz nihyeh* in 4QInstruction. Nonetheless, Ben Sira (and to a lesser extent 4QInstruction) engages with a slew of other texts from the Hebrew Bible as well as other ancient traditions, which makes comparing them only to Proverbs and a select group of wisdom texts limiting. In this chapter, I have been utilising wisdom and wisdom literature as a means of overviewing the texts that

44 Most recently, see Will Kynes, *An Obituary for 'Wisdom Literature': The Birth, Death, and Intertextual Reintegration of a Biblical Corpus* (Oxford, 2019), 82–106. For his critique of Wisdom at Qumran more specifically, see pp. 47–49. Also, cf. Stuart Weeks 'Is "Wisdom Literature" a Useful Category?', in *Tracing Sapiential Traditions in Ancient Judaism*, ed. H. Najman, J.-S. Rey and E. Tigchelaar, JSJSup 174 (Leiden, 2016), 3–23.

45 Jonathan Z. Smith, *Drudgery Divine: On the Comparison of Early Christianities and the Religions of Late Antiquity* (Chicago, 1994); Pierre Bourdieu, *Distinction: A Social Critique of the Judgment of Taste* (Cambridge, 1984), 479, 481.

46 This quote comes from Michael L. Satlow, 'Disappearing Categories: Using Categories in the Study of Religion', *MTSR* 17 (2005): 287–298.

47 Satlow, 'Disappearing Categories', 293.

48 For pushback against Kynes, see Matthew Goff, 'The Pursuit of Wisdom at Qumran: Assessing the Classification "Wisdom Literature" and Its Application to the Dead Sea Scrolls', in *The Oxford Handbook of Wisdom and the Bible*, ed. Will Kynes (New York, 2021), 617–634.

Qumran scholarship has defined as such, a definition due, in part, to their relationship with texts from the Hebrew Bible, and the ancient Near East more broadly, that scholarship has placed in the wisdom literature category. Nonetheless, the assumptions behind the texts classified as such and their comparison with each other are not without problems.

Kynes' overall critique is helpful for illustrating the problem of categorising wisdom texts in Qumran scholarship. To illustrate, among the published editions of the scrolls, the lists of wisdom texts are quite divergent. The two Sapiential editions of *DJD*, vols. 20 and 34 list 4QWords of the Maskil; 4QMysteries; 4QpapAdmonitory Parable (4Q302); 4QMeditation on Creation (4Q303–305); 4QSapiential Hymn (4Q411); 4QSapiential-Didactic Work A (4Q412); 4QComposition concerning Divine Providence (4Q413); 4QWays of Righteousness (4Q420–421); 4QSapiential-Didactic Work B (4Q425); 4QSapiential-Hymnic Work A (4Q426); and 4QInstruction (1Q26, 4Q415–418, 423). In addition, 4QWiles of the Wicked Woman (4Q184) and 4QSapiential Work B (4Q185) were already published with Cave 1 in *DJD* 5 and 4QBeatitudes (4Q525) with a collection of miscellaneous Hebrew texts, though its editor, Émille Puech, refers to it as a 'wisdom writing' (écrit de sagesse) and notes its connection to the other wisdom writings of Cave 4.

The volume on Sapiential Texts in Parry and Tov's *Dead Sea Scrolls Reader* reproduces the catalogue of texts in *DJD* 39, which agrees with most of the classification above but also includes 4Q424; 1QS 3:13–4:26; and 4QThe Two Ways (4Q473). In his latest edition of *The Complete Dead Sea Scrolls in English*, Geza Vermes includes most of what is listed above but omits 4Q303–305; 4Q411; and 4QInstruction-Like Composition A (4Q419) while including 4Q424; 4Q473; 4QBarki Nafshi (434–438); 4QLament By a Leader (4Q439); 4QIncantation (4Q444); and 4QSongs of the Sage (4Q510–511). Martínez's translation is much more paired down, only including 4Q184; 4Q185; 4Q298; 4Q413; 4QInstruction; 4Q419–420; and 4Q525, along with the strange edition of 4QMessianic Apocalypse (4Q521) to the category of 'wisdom poems'. Even more sparse is Armin Lange's contribution to vol. 3 of *Outside the Bible*, which only includes 4Q184; 4Q298; The Book of Mysteries; 4Q525; 4Q424; and 4QInstruction. Matthew Goff agrees with the list of wisdom texts represented by Kampen's commentary, though in his monograph Goff also treats as wisdom literature some of the hymns in the cave 11 Psalms Scroll as does Daniel Harrington. While placing any of these texts in conversation with each other for the sake of comparison will lead to interesting results, it is difficult to say from these lists alone what texts count as definitive wisdom texts and what texts do not.

BEYOND THE CONSENSUS

Perhaps, then, Kynes is right to call for a move beyond the wisdom literature consensus or, at the least, it may be time for Qumran scholarship to move beyond over-reliance on comparisons with the Hebrew Bible's wisdom corpus. Questions of defining wisdom literature based on form and genre have been pervasive, but if one chooses to no longer prioritise classification and form criticism then different questions can be asked of these texts and new insights can be gained. In this way, I am not necessarily denying 'wisdom literature' as a hermeneutical tool for scholars who want to use it. I am choosing to table it in order to utilise different analytical lenses. Overall, I will group Qumran wisdom beyond classification into four categories: (1) Wisdom as a Concept Outside of Wisdom Literature, (2) Wisdom in a Hellenistic Context, (3) Scribal Practice and Early Jewish Pedagogy and (4) Orality and Embodiment.

Wisdom as a Concept Outside of Wisdom Literature

I have already mentioned connections between the wisdom scrolls and hymnic literature such as 11QPs[a] and the Hodayot, with the latter directly borrowing language from 4QInstruction. Pajunen has also examined 4Q381 (4QNon-Canonical Psalms B) alongside 4Q184 and 4Q525 and there have been several fruitful studies on the temple/Eden/Jerusalem matrix in Second Temple literature that include wisdom texts but cuts across genres.[49] One area that has been overlooked has been the relationship between wisdom and law.[50] In a case study comparing Proverbs 1–9 with the Community Rule (1QS), Charlotte Hempel demonstrates a complex interplay between the concepts of wisdom and law in the Dead Sea Scrolls as well. Among the comparisons are the following: cumulative growth of smaller collections of often diverse material (cf. 1QS with 4Q255, 4Q256, and 4Q257),[51] the importance of the root *śkl*, a shared concern for counsel and reproof, an emphasis on polarity (i.e., 'two ways') and retribution

---

[49] For a recent study of this theme in relation to 4QInstruction, the Treatise on Two Spirits, the Hodayot, the Songs of the Sabbath Sacrifice and the Songs of the Sage, see Eric R. Montgomery, 'A Stream from Eden: The Nature and Development of a Revelatory Tradition in the Dead Sea Scrolls' (PhD diss., McMaster University, 2013). Also cf., Ezek 28:12–19; *Jub.* 3:8–14; 8:19; 1QS 4:23; 4Q174 3:6; 4Q265 7:11–17.

[50] This has not been the case with the Hebrew Bible where many scholars have examined their close relationship. See Hempel's article for references.

[51] Besides the different redactional layers, 1QS and other cave 4 versions end with a Maskil Hymn, whereas 4QS[e] (4Q259) ends with a calendar (4QOtot = 4Q319).

and the rhetoric of 'walking in perfection'. Their different uses of the same terms also illuminate some key aspects of the *yaḥad*. On the one hand, Proverbs 1–9 has a more hierarchal or top-down approach to knowledge transmission (father-son), rather than the idealised reciprocity of 1QS, and has more concern for women or domestic settings. On the other hand, Proverbs 1–9 lacks the cultic language of 1QS and limits divine revelation to a select few. Overall, Hempel suggests 'a meta-social compass behind the tradents of wisdom and law' and is surely correct to contend that Qumran scholars often miss these shared connections by focusing too much on specialisation.

Wisdom in a Hellenistic Context

While scholars have made considerable comparisons between wisdom literature and the Hebrew Bible (along with their Near Eastern counterparts), not much attention has been given to reading them in their Hellenistic context. As Hindy Najman notes, 'scholars have generally applied to these new texts the old categories and classifications' of genre distinctions such as wisdom and apocalypticism before the Dead Sea Scrolls and the Cairo Genizah were discovered.[52] These categories and classifications have, in turn, been used to 'prohibit or downplay the significance of comparisons that cross lines introduced by scholars'.[53] She goes on to examine 4QInstruction as one such Hebrew text that nonetheless exhibits strong Hellenistic influence by introducing concepts that originate in Greek philosophical traditions (a case which one could also make about Ben Sira as well). Najman uses the angelic *tabnit* in 4Q417 1 i 17–18 and the heavenly *paradigma* in Philo (*QE* 2.52; *Moses* 2.74) to demonstrate that 4QInstruction should be read 'in the larger context of Philonic traditions'.[54] Both are concerned with human beings using wisdom to pattern themselves after divine archetypes. There is also close conceptual parallel between Philo's concept of 'Two Adams' and 4QInstruction's bifurcation of two types of people at creation: one fleshly and the other spiritual.[55] The equation of Mosaic

---

[52] Hindy Najman, 'Jewish Wisdom in the Hellenistic Period: Towards the Study of a Semantic Constellation', in *Is There a Text in This Cave? Studies in the Textuality of the Dead Sea Scrolls in Honour of George J. Brooke*, ed. Ariel Feldman et al (Leiden, 2017), 461.

[53] Najman, 'Jewish Wisdom', 460.

[54] Najman, 'Jewish Wisdom', 462.

[55] Matthew Goff, 'Genesis 1–3 and Conceptions of Humankind in 4QInstruction, Philo and Paul', in *Early Christian Literature and Intertextuality*, ed. C. Evans and H. D. Zacharias (London, 2009), 2:114–125.

Torah with natural law and its following of cosmic order is also similar to the role the *raz nihyeh* plays in 4QInstruction.[56] While one does not necessarily have to set aside the category of wisdom altogether to make comparisons with other Hellenistic literature, it does help facilitate comparisons that cut across genre boundaries as is the case between Philo and 4QInstruction.

Elisa Uusimäki points to Philonic and other conceptual parallels in the construction of the sage across multiple scrolls. Building on Hadot's concept of philosophy as a way of life, Uusimäki examines the depiction of the sage in the scrolls in the character of the *maskil*, which she then relates to other such depictions in Hellenistic Jewish literature (Qohelet, Ben Sira, Wisdom of Solomon, Philo).[57] Her comparison helpfully notes that wisdom was not simply an abstract concept but a lived practice with both pedagogical and practical implications. For Philo, one performed wisdom through ascetic or mental practices such as reading, listening, meditation and self-mastery (*Leg.* 3.18–19; *Her.* 252–253), which would bring about the ascent of one's soul and form one into a 'sage who displays emotional and ethical perfection'.[58] The *maskil* performed wisdom through instruction, song, apotropaic rituals and prayer, serving as both an exemplar and a guide for the *yaḥad*'s desire to receive the 'glory of Adam'. Moreover, 'the lived and exemplary aspect of the Maskil's persona creates a conceptual link to Graeco-Roman philosophers' by creating a way of life and lived practices for the community to emulate.[59] The practice of 'spiritual exercise' brought about character formation, and more attention should be given to how and what type of

---

[56] Najman, 'Jewish Wisdom', 469. Also, C. Andrew Ballard, 'The Mysteries of Paideia: "Mystery" and Education in Plato's *Symposium*, 4QInstruction, and 1 Corinthians', in *Pedagogy in Early Judaism and Early Christianity*, eds. K. Hogan, M. Goff and E. Wasserman (Atlanta, 2017), 243–282. For Philo's combination of Stoicism with Jewish law, see Maren Niehoff, *Philo of Alexandria: An Intellectual Biography* (New Haven, 2018): 149–170.

[57] Elisa Uusimäki, 'Maskil among the Hellenistic Jewish Sages', *Journal of Ancient Judaism* 8 (2018): 42–68; 'Spiritual Formation in Hellenistic Jewish Wisdom Teaching', in *Tracing Sapiential Tradition in Ancient Judaism*, ed. Hindy Najman et al., JSJSup 174 (Leiden, 2016), 59–69.

[58] Uusimäki, 'Maskil among the Hellenistic', 45. For similar analysis regarding the maskil, see Newman below and Carol A. Newsom, *The Self as Symbolic Space: Constructing Identity and Community at Qumran*, STDJ 52 (Leiden, 2004), 91–190.

[59] Uusimäki, 'Maskil among the Hellenistic', 45. I would add to this analysis that the depiction of the sage as a singer in the figure of the *maskil*, Ben Sira and David in 11Q5 has parallels with the Graeco-Roman depictions of sages as well, especially the combination of musical instruments (the lyre and double-pipe in 1QS 10:8 and Sir 40:21). Songs also served as helpful manifestations of wisdom, and music could serve as a helpful *askesis* into the way of life in the *yaḥad* movement.

character traits Qumran wisdom literature desired to inculcate among its ideal audience.

Pedagogy and Scribal Practice

Another area that has gained considerable interest in the last few years has been scribal practice and early Jewish pedagogy. Three collections of essays were published on this topic in 2017 alone.[60] Many of these essays also cross genres while asking questions concerning instruction, knowledge transfer, scribal practice, literacy, authority and identity formation. There seems to be broad agreement that the teacher gained predominance as an authoritative interpreter of tradition or revelation. While there also seems to be increased emphasis in training in writing among many Second Temple archives (Elephantine Bar Kokhba letters and Babatha and Salome Komaise and archives),[61] there is little evidence for school and writing exercises at Qumran, which presumes that either most of its members were already literate or rudimentary education in writing was not a concern for the *yaḥad*.[62] As for the scribe, one could classify Qumran itself as a scribal library[63] with several texts that reflect on the agency of the scribe and the writing process itself.[64] A fruitful comparison could focus on questions regarding the orality/literacy divide in antiquity by placing texts that prioritise writing as means of reliable teaching and memory alongside texts that prioritise oral methods of intergenerational knowledge transmission.

[60] George J. Brooke and Renate Smithuis, ed., *Jewish Education from Antiquity to the Middle Ages: Studies in Honour of Philip S. Alexander* (Leiden, 2017); Jason M. Zurawski and Gabriele Boccaccini, eds., *Second Temple Jewish 'Paideia' in Context*, BZNW 200 (Berlin, 2017); Hogan, Goff and Wasserman, eds., *Pedagogy in Early Judaism and Early Christianity* (Atlanta, 2017).

[61] Christine Schams, *Jewish Scribes in the Second-Temple Period*, JSOTSup 291 (Sheffield, 1998), 209–216.

[62] Matthew Goff, 'Students of God in the House of Torah: Education in the Dead Sea Scrolls', in *Second Temple Jewish 'Paideia' in Context*, 89; 'Scribes and Pedagogy in Ancient Israel and Second Temple Judaism', in *Wiley Blackwell Companion to Wisdom Literature*, ed. Samuel L. Adams and Matthew Goff (Hoboken; Chichester, 2020), 195–212.

[63] For a recent argument, see Sidnie White Crawford, *Scribes and Scrolls at Qumran* (Grand Rapids, 2019), 238–260.

[64] Cf. *Book of Watchers, Aramaic Levi Document, Admonitions of Qahat, New Jerusalem*, and *Visions of Amram*. Cf. Annette Y. Reed, *Demons, Angels, and Writing in Ancient Judaism* (Cambridge, 2020), 114–115. For the role of Aramaic in the transmission of knowledge in scribal circles, see Seth L. Sanders, *From Adapa to Enoch: Scribal Culture and Religious Vision in Judea and Babylonia* (Tübingen, 2017), 153–196.

Orality and Embodiment

Of course, an emphasis on writing does not mean one should pit orality and textuality against each other. David Carr has already demonstrated their interplay, but more studies have shifted away from the scribal hand to focus on orality and embodiment.[65] In one recent study, Judith Newman emphasises the role of the liturgical body in creating, shaping and reinforcing texts by examining the prayer posture of the *maskil* in the Hodayot. Full prostration (see 1QH[a] 5:12 and 20:7) served as a counter-cultural prayer posture, which reenacted the supplication of Moses and embodied the anthropological *Niedrigkeitsdoxologie* that is so well-known throughout the Hodayot.[66] If one imagines this public act occurring in song then one could make a similar case for the role of music in enculturation and embodiment. Music not only affects one's somatic and neurological processes, but the act of singing a community's own set of songs, likely in unison (*yḥd* occurs twenty-two times in 1QH[a]), creates a sense of solidarity as well as separation from those who do not belong to the in-group. Shem Miller has also examined the oral-textual interplay among the scrolls by utilising the material evidence itself as a well as reference to orality throughout various scrolls (e.g., 'smooth words' in 4Q184 and 4Q185). For Miller, the *vacats*, marks in the margins (e.g., 1QpHab 6:11–13), stichography and other spacing patterns (4Q424; 4Q525) verify the use of these scrolls in oral performance by an oral community who utilised them in a complex interface of writing, orality and memory.[67] For our purposes, Miller's suggestion that one understand the 'mystery of existence', the 'wonderful mysteries' and the 'ruling' in 1QS 6:9 as part of the development of 'oral-traditional texts' provides another means of analysis that cuts across the genre divide.[68]

CONCLUSION

While wisdom as a category may not be as dead as some have claimed, the Dead Sea Scrolls have demonstrated notable problems with its

[65] David M. Carr, *Writing on the Tablet of the Heart: Origins of Scripture and Literature* (Oxford, 2005), 215–240.

[66] Judith Newman, *Before the Bible: The Liturgical Body and the Formation of Scriptures in Early Judaism* (New York, 2018), 107–140. Also, Angela K. Harkins, *Reading with an 'I' to the Heavens: Looking at the Qumran Hodayot through the Lens of Visionary Traditions*, Ekstasis 3 (Berlin, 2012), 114–205.

[67] Miller, *Dead Sea Media*, 11. For another work on performance and textuality in the scrolls, see Marvin Lloyd Miller, *Performances of Ancient Jewish Letters: From Elephantine to MMT*, JAJSup 20 (Göttingen, 2015), 221–266.

[68] Miller, *Dead Sea Media*, 94–106, 111–114.

traditional formulation. First, there are several factors distinctive among the traditional Qumran wisdom corpus not present in its Hebrew Bible counterparts, such as lack of reference to Solomon, a toning down of wisdom's personification as a woman, the equation of Wisdom with Torah, an emphasis on esoteric knowledge and eschatology, a grounding of revelation in creation (particularly the Genesis creation accounts) and an overt concern for charity and poverty. These factors along with significant blends between apocalyptic, legal and liturgical themes make it difficult to read the Qumran wisdom corpus solely as wisdom literature as it is traditionally defined. Second, in most editions and translations of the Qumran wisdom texts, there are significant divergences over what texts belong in this category. Third, while comparing the wisdom scrolls to the Hebrew Bible and the wisdom category in general has demonstrated the elasticity of the wisdom category, prioritising definitions of wisdom literature as a genre category prevented Qumran scholarship from focusing on other means of analysis and comparison, such as the relationship of these scrolls to Hellenistic philosophy, their role in ancient Jewish pedagogy, their depiction of the sage and their contribution to debates over orality, textuality and knowledge in the Second Temple period. While the wisdom category remains on life support, when the scrolls classified as such are read more synchronically with a wider range of texts from the Hellenistic world, they are freed up for other lenses of analysis and more avenues for comparison.[69] Rather than truncating their analysis, a move away from wisdom as a category may, in fact, lead to a renaissance in their study.

Further Reading

Bennema, Cornelis. 'The Strands of Wisdom Tradition in Intertestamental Judaism: Origins, Developments and Characteristics'. *TynBul* 52 (2001): 61–82.

Collins, John J. 'Wisdom Reconsidered In Light of the Scrolls'. *DSD* 4 (1997): 269–271.

Gregory Sterling and Ruth A. Clements, eds. *Sapiential Perspectives: Wisdom Literature in Light of Proceedings of the Sixth International Symposium of The Orion Center for the Study of the Dead Sea Scrolls and Associated Literature, 20–22 May, 2001.* STDOJ 51. Leiden: 2004.

---

[69] Also, it should be noted that outside of Lady Folly in 4Q184 and questions of poverty in 4QInstruction, not much work has been done on reading wisdom scrolls through the lens of race, gender, class and sexuality. Qumran studies is woefully behind in this regard overall.

Falk, Daniel K., Florentino García Martinez and Eileen Schuller, eds. *Sapiential, Liturgical and Poetical Texts from Qumran: Proceedings of the Third Meeting of the International Organization for Qumran Studies, Oslo 1998*. Leiden: 2000.

Goff, Matthew. *Discerning Wisdom: The Sapiential Literature of the Dead Sea Scrolls*. VTSup 116. Leiden: 2007.

——— *4QInstruction: A Commentary*. WLAW 2. Atlanta: 2013.

Harrington, Daniel J. *Wisdom Texts from Qumran*. New York: 1996.

Hempel, Charlotte, Armin Lange and Hermann Lichtenberger, eds. *The Wisdom Texts from Qumran and the Development of Sapiential Thought*. Leuven: 2002.

Hogan, Karina M., Matthew Goff and Emma Wasserman, eds. *Pedagogy in Early Judaism and Early Christianity*. Early Judaism and Its Literature 41. Atlanta: 2017.

Lange, Armin. *Weisheit und Prädestination: Weisheitliche Urodnung und Prädestination in den Textfunden von Qumran*. STDJ 18. Leiden: 1995.

Miller, Shem. *Dead Sea Media Orality, Textuality, and Memory in the Scrolls from the Judean Desert*. STDJ 129. Leiden: 2019.

Newsom, Carol A. *The Self as Symbolic Space: Constructing Identity and Community at Qumran*. STDJ 52. Leiden: 2004.

Uusimäki, Elisa. 'Maskil among the Hellenistic Jewish Sages'. *Journal of Ancient Judaism* 8 (2018): 42–68.

Woude, A. van der. 'Wisdom at Qumran'. Pages 244–256 in *Wisdom in Ancient Israel: Essays in Honour of J. A. Emerton*. Edited by J. Day, R. P. Gordon and H. G. M. Williamson. Cambridge: 1995.

Wright, Benjamin G. III, and Lawrence M. Wills, eds. *Conflicted Boundaries in Wisdom and Apocalypticism*. SBLSymS 35. Atlanta: 2005.

17 Egyptian Wisdom

MICHAEL V. FOX AND SUZANNA
R. MILLAR

Egypt left a rich legacy of wisdom. The designation 'Wisdom Literature', though, was created by biblical scholars to describe biblical texts and is applied to Egyptian works somewhat artificially. It is not a native Egyptian category. Terms for 'knowledge' and 'skill' do occur in Egyptian texts (e.g., *rḫ*, *sꜣꜣ*, *sꜣr*, *siꜣ*, *šsꜣ*, *ḥmw*, *ꜥrk*)[1] but none of these is such a developed or central a concept as biblical *ḥokmâ*.

That said, though, there is a genre of texts which teach skills and values for successful living. They call themselves 'instructions' (*sbꜣy.t*; Demotic *mtr[t]*) and usually depict a father advising his son. They form a significant and long-lasting literary tradition, with multiple examples extant from the Old Kingdom to the Late Period. As cultural classics, they were used in the context of scribal training.[2] We have evidence of New Kingdom scribal students diligently copying out instructions from earlier periods, not only training them in technical scribal skills but also enculturating them into the values and socio-moral world of the pharaonic state.

This chapter will consider the wisdom offered by such Egyptian instructions. It will begin with an overview of extant examples and then consider some important themes and issues, namely, Ma'at, character development, pedagogy, and transmission. Finally, it will turn to the possible influence of Egyptian instructions on biblical texts.

---

[1] See Nili Shupak, *Where Can Wisdom Be Found? The Sage's Language in the Bible and in Ancient Egyptian Literature*, OBO 131 (Göttingen, 1993), 217–229.
[2] Though they were not composed expressly for the purpose as 'school textbooks'. See Stuart Weeks, *Instruction and Imagery in Proverbs 1–9* (Oxford, 2007), 16–25.

OVERVIEW OF EXTANT EXAMPLES

The following Egyptian instructions have been preserved well enough to be readable. There exist also numerous fragments of unidentified, largely lost wisdom books.[3]

Old Kingdom (Dynasties 3–8; ca. 2650–2621 BCE)

Djedefhar (or *Hordjedef*)[4]: This fragmentary text is ascribed to a Fifth Dynasty prince, but the extant documents are later. A sentence is even quoted in a first-century CE text. In the extant portions, Djedefhar addresses his infant son, recommending mortuary preparations.

Kagemeni:[5] This instruction is actually *to* Kagemeni, spoken by his father the vizier, whose name is lost. Only the final portion of the text is extant, which advocates a quiet demeanour and moderation in eating. An epilogue reports that the vizier gave this instruction in written form to his children, including Kagemeni, who later became vizier himself.

First Intermediate Period (Dynasties 9–11 [First Half]; ca. 2135–2040 BCE)

Ptaḥḥotep[6]: This is the earliest fully preserved instruction. The book is set in the reign of Isesi in the Fifth Dynasty (2388–2356 BCE), but the language and the extant manuscripts belong to the early Middle Kingdom and the book was probably composed then. (The earliest manuscripts are from the mid-Twelfth Dynasty.) In the prologue, the vizier Ptaḥḥotep, approaching death, describes the miseries of old age and asks of Pharaoh permission to appoint his son as his successor, called a 'staff of old age'. He receives permission to do so and to instruct him in 'the words of the ancestors'. Then follow thirty-seven maxims (varying from four to eighteen lines in length), each on its own topic. Ptaḥḥotep prescribes proper behaviour for various levels of officialdom and good relations with other people, including superiors, inferiors,

---

[3] The following discussion is adapted from Michael V. Fox, *Proverbs 1–9*, AYB 18A (New Haven, 2000), 19–23. For an extensive translation of Egyptian literature, including Wisdom Literature, see Miriam Lichtheim, *Ancient Egyptian Literature*, 3 vols. (Berkeley, 1973–1980); and Lichtheim, *Late Egyptian Wisdom Literature*, OBO 120 (Freiburg, 1983), 70–92. For a complete translation, with many supplementary documents, see Helmut Brunner, *Altägyptische Weisheit* (Zürich, 1988).

[4] Emma Brunner-Traut, 'Die Weisheitslehre des Djedef-Hor', *ZÄS* 76 (1940): 3–9.

[5] Pap. Prisse 1–2. A. E. Gardiner, 'The Instruction Addressed to Kagemeni and his Brethren', *JEA* 32 (1946): 71–74.

[6] Pap. Prisse. Edited with a translation and commentary by Z. Žába, *Les Maximes de Ptaḥḥotep* (Prague, 1955).

one's wife, friends and friends' wives. He cultivates the virtues of moderation, generosity, honesty and modesty. In an epilogue, he compares two kinds of sons, those who 'listen' (i.e., understand and obey the teachings) and those who refuse to do so.

Merikare[7]: This instruction is spoken to King Merikare by his father, a monarch apparently named Cheti. It has the form of royal testament, offering a treatise on kingship perhaps intended to legitimise the ruling monarch at a period of political instability. Much of the advice is relevant only to the royal office and concerns topics such as urging repression of political incitement and rebellion, mustering troops and performance of religious duties. The king speaks of his own accomplishments but also, extraordinarily, confesses his guilt in failing to prevent the desecration of certain mortuary monuments. He describes the judgement of the dead and advocates truth and justice. He concludes with a meditation on divine retribution and a hymn to the creator.

Middle Kingdom (Dynasties 11 [Second Half]–14; ca. 2040–1650 BCE)

Amenemḥet[8]: This is a political apologia in the guise of a wisdom instruction delivered by King Amenemhet I to his son, Sesostris I. The New Kingdom Papyrus identifies the actual author as the scribe Chety, who is the same as the Duachety mentioned below. Amenemhet describes in vivid terms a successful palace coup that apparently left him dead. Hence, Amenemhet is speaking from the realm of the dead, as in a tomb autobiography. Made bitter by experience, he teaches, in short, to trust nobody.

Duachety son of Duauf (or *Satire on the Trades*)[9]: This entertaining work seems to have been very popular, with more than 250 whole or partial copies remaining. In it, Duachety offers advice to his son, who is beginning scribal school. The first part offers encouragement to love the scribal arts, along with a satirical mockery of all other professions. The second part gives miscellaneous advice about social behaviour.

Loyalist Teaching[10]: The main witness to this is the stele of Seḥetibre. The middle section is designated as an 'instruction' preaching

[7] Pap. Leningrad 116A. A. Volten, *Zwei altägyptische politische Schriften*, AAeg II (Copenhagen, 1945).

[8] Volten, *Zwei altägyptische politische Schriften*.

[9] W. Helck, *Die Lehre des Dw3-Htjj* (Wiesbaden, 1970).

[10] Georges Posener, *L'Enseignment loyalist* (Geneva, 1976).

loyalty to the king. It extols the divinity of the king and promises loyal sages the reward of eternal life.

A Man to His Son (or *The Instruction Which a Man Made for His Son*)[11]: This anonymous teaching praises skills of rhetoric and interpretation, urges quiet, reserved speech and warns against 'hot talk'. It promotes virtues of loyalty and obedience, especially towards the king, whose power it praises. The king can aid the unfortunate and make 'the last be first'; blessings will come to those who serve him.

Ramesseum Papyri I and II[12]: These fragmentary papyri contain various observations and sayings. Ramesseum I has a frame narrative about a scribe, Sisobek, who was imprisoned and placed in danger. After his release, he declaims on the unpredictability of human fortunes and the futility of indulgence in passion and loquacity. He offers various counsels, particularly on proper demeanour in speech. (A very similar device introduces the later books of Anchsheshonq and the Aramaic Ahiqar.) The ideal of the silent man characterised by inner calm and soft speech is prominent.

From this period, we also have related texts such as the *The Dispute of a Man with His Ba*, the *Prophecies of Neferti* and the *Admonitions of Ipuwer.*[13]

New Kingdom (Dynasties 18–20; ca. 1550–1080 BCE)

Amenemope (or *Amenemophis*)[14]: In thirty numbered chapters, each with its own message, the scribe Amenemope teaches his son 'the way of life' and advocates the ideal of the 'truly silent man', who accepts God's will in serenity and trusts in his justice. One must show respect for the manifold varieties of God's creation, including the defenceless and weak, who are under God's special protection. The great vices are dishonesty, lack of self-control and greed, which is evidenced in straining too hard for success. As discussed below, Proverbs 22:17–23:11 is based on Amenemope.[15]

---

[11] Hans Goedicke, 'Die Lehre eines Mannes für seinen Sohn', *ZÄS* 94 (1967): 62–71.

[12] John W. B. Barns, *Five Ramesseum Papyri* (Oxford, 1956). Ramesseum I: plates 1–6, pp. 1–10; Ramesseum II: plates 7–9, pp. 11–14. Translation Brunner, *Altägyptische Weisheit*, 193–195.

[13] For all of these, see Lichtheim, *Ancient Egyptian Literature*, vol. 1.

[14] Pap. BM 10474. Text, translation, commentary: H. O. Lange, *Das Weisheitsbuch des Amenemope* (Copenhagen, 1925); Glendon E. Bryce, *A Legacy of Wisdom* (Lewisburg, 1979).

[15] For a detailed comparison and further bibliography, see Michael V. Fox, *Proverbs 10–31*, AB 18B (New Haven, 2009), 707–733.

Anii[16]: This text defines itself as an 'educational instruction' by a scribe of the (mortuary) temple of Queen Nefertari. Anii addresses behaviour in the personal sphere: good speech, proper demeanour toward superiors and conformity to rank and custom. He tells how to treat one's wife, family, friends and family spirits. He insists on proper deportment in the temple and at festivals. Throughout, he underscores the importance of remaining calm and composed. He also urges his son to study the ancient writings. In a remarkable exploration of pedagogy in an epilogue, Anii and his son debate the ways and limits of education.

Amennakhte[17]: In this text, the scribe Amennakhte addresses his apprentice Horimin, the son of his friend Hori. He urges dedication to study, emphasising personal cultivation of the virtues befitting a wise man. This text might be read alongside another, *Hori*: In an 'educational instruction', Hori addresses the son of Amennakhte (now deceased), telling him to become a scribe like his father.

Other relevant texts from this period include *Amenemhet Priest of Amon* (a tomb autobiography that includes a brief moral instruction); *Instruction According to Old Writings* (a brief list of 'don'ts'; two other ostraca are extant, both fragmentary); and *Papyrus Chester Beatty IV* (a miscellany of wisdom texts directed to the young scribe).

Late Period Egypt

Starting in the sixth or fifth century BCE, a new form of wisdom book developed. The hieratic Brooklyn Wisdom Papyrus, the earliest of this genre, is more discursive and prosaic than the others, which are probably of Hellenistic, perhaps late Hellenistic, origin, and are written in a later script, Demotic. These teachings are composed of long strings of self-contained sentences, usually in the form of one-line sayings arranged in topical groupings. They give practical advice but also emphasise the paradoxical nature of life and humanity's inability to understand it or to secure success. In form and content, these differ radically from the older Egyptian wisdom books, especially in their emphasis on life's uncertainties and the inscrutability of the god's will.

The Brooklyn Wisdom Papyrus[18]: This papyrus begins with a description of the pharaoh's campaign to Nubia, then offers a series of

---

[16] Joachim Friedrich Quack, *Die Lehren des Ani*, OBO 141 (Göttingen, 1994).
[17] Various ostraca. Georges Posener, 'L'exorde de l'Instruction éducative d'Amennakhte (Recherches littéraires, V)', *Revue d'Egypte* 10 (1955): 61–72.
[18] Richard Jasnow, *A Late Period Hieratic Wisdom Text (p. Brooklyn 47.218.135)*, SAOC 52 (Chicago, 1992).

instructions lacking in thematic arrangement. In general, the instructions address the proper relationship between superiors and inferiors.

Anchsheshonq[19]: This text begins with a narrative describing how Anchsheshonq, a priest of Re, is wrongfully put in prison for colluding in a plot to kill the pharaoh. While there, he instructs his son, writing on potsherds for lack of papyrus. His instructions consist of single-lined maxims, some cast as imperatives and others as general observations.

Phibis (or *The Demotic Wisdom Book*)[20]: This text contains twenty-five chapters, each numbered and given the title 'teachings'. Each chapter groups together single-lined sayings in a loose thematic arrangement. Binary contrasts are prevalent, particularly between the wise man and the fool, the silent man and the hothead. The text emphasises the inscrutability and free will of the deity, and revels in paradoxical formulations.

Other relevant texts include the *Louvre Demotic Papyrus 2414*,[21] *Louvre Demotic Papyrus 2377*, *Ashmolean Papyrus 1984.77* and the *Demotic Book of Thoth*.[22]

THEMES AND ISSUES IN EGYPTIAN INSTRUCTIONS

Ma'at

Many important themes and issues might be studied in relation to the Egyptian instructions. This chapter will focus on four: Ma'at, character development, pedagogy and transmission. A central concept in Egyptian instructions is Ma'at. The scholarly understanding of Ma'at has developed in recent decades, but a certain idea remains pervasive: that Ma'at represents 'world order'.[23] This idea has had a profound impact on biblical scholarship, with several scholars of the 1950s and 1960s arguing that Ma'at/world order underlies not only Egyptian wisdom but Israelite wisdom too.[24] H. H. Schmid, for example, argued that this all-

---

[19] Pap. BM 10508. Lichtheim, *Late Egyptian Wisdom Literature*, 70–92.
[20] Pap. Insinger, Pap. Carlsberg. Lichtheim, *Late Egyptian Wisdom Literature*, 197–234.
[21] Lichtheim, *Late Egyptian Wisdom Literature*, 94–95.
[22] Richard Jasnow and Karl-Theodor Zauzich, *The Ancient Egyptian Book of Thoth: A Demotic Discourse on Knowledge and Pendant to the Classical Hermetica*, 2 vols. (Wiesbaden, 2005).
[23] E.g., R. Anthes, 'Die Maat des Echnaton von Amarna', *JAOS* 14 (1952): 1; Henri Frankfort, *Ancient Egyptian Religion* (New York, 1948; 1961), 63.
[24] E. Gese, *Lehre und Wirklichkeit in der alten* Weisheit (Tübingen, 1958); E. Würthwein, *Die Weisheit Ägypyens und das Alte* Testament (Marburg, 1960). For a more extended critique of this view, see Michael V. Fox, 'World Order and Ma'at: A Crooked Parallel', *JANESCU* 23 (1995): 37–48.

embracing, cosmic *Weltordnung* was central to wisdom literature across the ancient Near East, undergoing the same historical developments in Egypt, Mesopotamia and Israel.[25] For such scholars, this world order was not the mere predictable causality of events. Rather, it was a mechanistic nexus, a universal, independent force constraining events and ensuring justice.

However, more recent studies demonstrate that this view of Ma'at is erroneous (not to mention the hypothesised influence of Ma'at on Israel). Ma'at is not 'order' as such but the force which creates and maintains order, namely, truth/justice. Truth and justice here are not separable but together constitute a primary ethical principle. As the maintainer of order, Ma'at is not some impersonal nexus meting out rewards and punishment; rather, Ma'at is realised through interpersonal solidarity and reciprocity.[26] This explains the common Egyptian expressions which describe 'enjoying', 'speaking' and 'doing' Ma'at (and so on). These make little sense if Ma'at is an impersonal nexus but are fully comprehensible if Ma'at is truth/justice.

Character Development

Ma'at undergirds the moral outlook of Egyptian wisdom, ensuring justice and right order through interpersonal acts of social solidarity. Accordingly, the principal virtues, repeated throughout the instructions, are those which strengthen social bonds conducive to community flourishing. Egyptologist Miriam Lichtheim delineates these as 'honesty and truthfulness; justice, kindness, and generosity; temperance and patience; thoughtfulness, diligence, and competence; loyalty and reliability'.[27] By contrast, vices which threaten social relations (such as lying, greed and aggression) are condemned. The instructions intend to inculcate socio-moral values for the character development of their students. Their focus is on everyday practical ethics rather than abstract moral concepts or extreme ethical cases, and they are holistic in their advice, aiming to develop their student's goodness, temperament and intellect.

Particularly important in some instructions are specific character types, sketched in polar opposition.[28] A notable pair is the silent man

---

[25] Hans-Heinrich Schmid, *Wesen und Geschichte der Weisheit*, BZAW 101 (Tübingen, 1966).

[26] Jan Assmann, *Ma'at: Gerechtigkeit und Unsterblichkeit im Alten Ägypten* (München, 1990).

[27] Miriam Lichtheim, 'Didactic Literature', in *Ancient Egyptian Literature: History and Forms*, ed. A. Lopriendo, Probleme der Ägyptologie (Leiden, 1996), 261.

[28] Nili Shupak, 'Positive and Negative Human Types in the Egyptian Wisdom Literature', in *Homeland and Exile: Biblical and Ancient Near Eastern Studies in*

(grw) and the heated man (šmm/hmm or t'[w]), who are especially prominent in Amenemope. Through vivid arboreal imagery, Amenemope sets their fates in direct contrast: 'As for the heated man in the temple, he is like a tree growing indoors; A moment lasts its growth of shoots, Its end comes about in the woodshed .... The truly silent, who keeps apart, He is like a tree grown in a meadow. It greens, it doubles its yield' (Amenemope VI. 1–3, 7–9).[29] The silent man is (unsurprisingly) restrained in speech, but his qualities go beyond this – he is self-controlled, calm, modest, slow to anger and obedient to authority. He has a pacifying effect on potential quarrels. From the New Kingdom, his character has a religious aspect: he has piety, humility before the god and trust in divine intervention. In contrast is the heated man, who is quarrelsome, aggressive, violent, impatient and impulsive. He is known for his inability to hold his tongue in angry outbursts, gossip and slander. He disrupts the fabric of the community.

Another binary pair is the wise man and the fool, who appear particularly in the Demotic Instructions (especially Phibis).[30] The wise man (rmt-rḫ) is a 'fully drawn moral person',[31] manifesting the central virtues of Egyptian morality and piety. By contrast, the fool (lḫ, ḥnn, rmt swg) is characterised by the full range of moral, religious and intellectual vices.

Pedagogy

There is some dispute within Egyptian wisdom literature about who is capable of learning, who might be able to fulfil these ideals of character development. Three competing opinions are advocated.[32] The first opinion asserts that some people are incapable of learning. This view is sometimes born out of the teacher's frustration at the student's obtuseness. Thus, the teacher in Pap. Lansing laments 'even if I beat you with a stick of whatever kind, you do not listen!' (2.4–3.3). Elsewhere, the matter is considered in quasi-deterministic manner. For Ptahhotep, the capacity to 'listen' (a precondition for learning) is instilled before

Honour of Bustenay Oded, ed. G. Galil, M. Geller and A. Millard, VTSup 130 (Leiden, 2009), 245–260.

[29] Lichtheim, *Ancient Egyptian Literature*, 150–151.

[30] Miriam Lichtheim, 'Observations on Papyrus Insinger', in *Studien zu Altägyptischen Lebenslehren*, ed. E. Hornung and O. Keel, OBO 28 (Göttingen, 1979), 283–306.

[31] Lichtheim, *Moral Value in Ancient Egypt*, 91.

[32] See Michael V. Fox, 'Who Can Learn? A Dispute in Ancient Pedagogy', in *Wisdom, You Are My Sister: Studies in Honor of Roland E. Murphy, O. Carm, on the Occasion of His Eightieth Birthday*, ed. Michael L. Barré (Washington, 1997), 62–77.

birth, and the obtuse man is 'one for whom an impediment was assigned (already) in the womb' (l. 207). Similarly, in O. Petrie 11, 'Every man is compelled [lit., "dragged"] by his character just as by his limbs' (recto 4),[33] and in Pap. Insinger, 'It is the god who gives the heart, gives the son, and gives the good character. The fate and the fortune that come, it is the god who determines them' (9.19f).[34]

This contrasts with a second opinion, namely, that everyone can be taught, though this might require harsh methods. Images of forcing and bending are common here, and some texts compare students to animals in need of training. Thus in Pap. Anastasi III, we read 'Pay attention and listen to what I have said, that it may be of use to you. Apes can be taught to dance; horses can be tamed; a kite can be put in a nest; a falcon can be pinioned. Persevere in seeking advice and do not weary of it' (4.1–4). Similarly, Anii asserts that education 'conquers' character, for wild animals can be tamed and dogs and geese trained (22.17–23.7).

However, Anii's opinion comes into direct conflict with that of his son Khonsuhotep, who represents a third pedagogical perspective. Khonsuhotep responds that students are not in fact cattle in need of forceful handling (23.9). He asks his father instead to take gentler methods: 'Do not make your strength overbearing .... Has there never arisen a man who relaxed his arm, so as to hear an appropriate response?' (23.7–8). Kinder methods are more suited to the students' nature, because they are the likeness [snw] of God (23.8–10). Throughout the debate with his father, Khonsuhotep advocates pleasantness and moderation in teaching, such that the student himself wants to learn.

Assuming that the students are able to learn, what does learning entail? We might reduce the answer to two pairs of imperatives: *Hear and do* and *study and understand*.[35] The former pair is self-explanatory. Students should practice obedience and enact their teachers' directions in their own lives. But this is not the entirety of the wisdom enterprise; the latter is important too. Some texts invite readers to study them in depth, developing their erudition, intellect and interpretive competence. Thus, the introduction to Amenemope commends: 'Give your ears to hear the things that are said. Set your heart to interpret them'

---

[33] J. Černy and A. H. Gardiner, *Hieratic Ostraca* (Oxford, 1957), plate 1, recto.

[34] Lichtheim, *Late Egyptian Wisdom Literature*, 206.

[35] See Michael V. Fox, 'Wisdom and the Self-Presentation of Wisdom Literature', in *Reading from Right to Left: Essays on the Hebrew Bible in Honour of David J. A. Clines*, ed. J. Cheryl Exum and H. G. M. Williamson (Sheffield, 2003), 153–172.

(§1), and its conclusion exhorts the reader to 'become one who interprets them, who interprets them as a teacher' (§30). The word 'interpret' here is wḥ ', literally 'untie' or 'loosen', which figures the instructions as 'knots' (ṯsw) to be untied.[36] Similarly, Papyrus Chester Beatty IV (§3, 4.6) and the Instruction of Anii (20.4–5; cf. 15.4) suggest that when their readers have become experts [sšs '], they should 'penetrate' ['ḳ] the teachings.

Transmission

The pedagogy of the instructions extends beyond the student directly taught within the narrative.[37] Egyptian instructions are sometimes self-conscious about their own transmission to future generations. Their advice is placed within a narrative framework which depicts it being spoken at an idealised moment of transmission. Almost all of the known Egyptian examples are given a familial context, in which a father gives his instructions to his son. This is usually framed as a moment of succession: the father – usually an eminent official within the pharaonic institution – prepares to pass on his position to his son and gives him advice for the job. This narrative setting is one of the few features shared between most instructions and is one of the key markers of the genre.[38]

The transmission does not stop with the son, however. Indeed, the son might pass on the advice to his own children. So Ptahhotep says, 'When [the obedient son] grows old and reaches veneration, he will speak likewise to his children, renewing the teaching of his father . . . . He speaks to (his) children; then they may speak (to) their children' (11. 590–596). Likewise, the father in the 'Loyalist Instruction' says to his children: 'Practice the rules which I have made. Then you can speak to your children' (§7.6–§8.1).

The advice might be disseminated more broadly, outside of the single generational life. The epilogue of Amenemope, for example, commends itself to all readers and reflects on when its instructions 'are read before an ignorant person'. This imagines a written text spoken before an audience, an interplay of written and spoken characteristic of textual transmission in the ancient world (where reading would rarely be in silence). Oral and literary belong together in a complex matrix, warning us against trying to separate them out. Many Egyptian Instructions seem to have intended both hearers and readers.

---

[36] Cf. Shupak, *Where Can Wisdom Be Found?*, 63–64.
[37] See Fox, 'Wisdom and the Self-Presentation'.
[38] Weeks, *Instruction and Imagery*, 12, 30.

Amenemope, for example, assumes both a spoken context ('Give your ears to hear the things that are spoken'; §1) and also a written one ('Look to these thirty chapters'; §30). Merikare's father orally advises him to imitate the ancestors, whose words 'remain in their books' (l. 35).

EGYPTIAN INFLUENCE ON BIBLICAL WISDOM

Egypt is imagined in the Bible as a place of wisdom (which makes the apparently superior wisdom of Israel shine all the more brightly; Isa 19:11–13, 3:2–3; Ps 105:21–22; cf. Acts 7:22). The 'discerning and wise' Joseph is situated amongst the other 'wise men' of Pharaoh's court (Gen 41:8, 33),[39] and Solomon's wisdom 'surpassed ... all the wisdom of Egypt' (1 Kgs 5:10 [ET 4:30]). Egypt's reputation for wisdom was clearly known to some biblical authors, then. Some scholars go further, suggesting that Egypt's instructional texts might have directly influenced such authors too.

Some have suggested significant cultural contact between the nations, particularly during the reign of Solomon (the so-called Solomonic Enlightenment). Tryggve Mettinger argued that Solomon's bureaucracy imitated Egyptian administrative institutions,[40] and Albrecht Alt alleged that Solomon's 'nature wisdom' (1 Kgs 5:13 [ET 4:33]) was modelled after Egyptian texts (see further below).[41] An 'international wisdom tradition' has been suggested, resulting in cross-fertilisation. We must exercise caution here, however. The alleged Egyptian connections of Solomon's reign are probably baseless,[42] and the 'wisdom tradition' idea needs significant revision.[43] It is debatable whether Judahite scribes could have had access to Egyptian instructions, and if they did have access, whether they would be able to read them.[44]

That said, however, there are some undeniable connections. The biblical Book of Proverbs contains at least one clear case of borrowing from an Egyptian text (viz., Amenemope), and there are other plausible connections too. From at least the late monarchy period, there is wider

---

[39] See especially Gerhard von Rad, 'The Joseph Narrative and Ancient Wisdom', in *The Problem of the Hexateuch and Other Essays* (Edinburgh, 1966), 292–300.

[40] Tryggve N. D. Mettinger, *Solomonic State Officials* (Lund, 1971).

[41] Albrecht Alt, 'Die Weisheit Salomos', *TLZ* 76 (1951), cols. 139–144.

[42] See Stuart Weeks, *Early Israelite Wisdom* (Oxford, 2000), 110–131.

[43] Mark Sneed, 'Is the "Wisdom Tradition" a Tradition?' *CBQ* 73.1 (2011): 50–71.

[44] Weeks, *Instruction and Imagery*, 33–38.

evidence of cultural contact between the nations.[45] Accordingly, this section will assess some commonly proposed connections between Egyptian and Israelite wisdom literature. It will focus mainly on Proverbs (where most of the connections have been found), but it will also consider Job and Ben Sira.

Proverbs

The Book of Proverbs is sometimes described as an instruction, modelled after Egyptian prototypes. There are some notable similarities. A basic structure is common to both: title, prologue, advice.[46] Like several Egyptian instructions, Proverbs begins with a title giving the nature of the work, the name of the speaker and the speaker's official role ('The proverbs of Solomon, son of David, king of Israel' cf., e.g., 'Beginning of the Instruction made by the Hereditary Prince, Count, King's Son, Hardjedef.')[47] There follows a prologue, depicting a situation of educational transmission from a father to a son. Subsequently comes the content of the advice, which consists of ethical reflection of successful living.

However, we must exercise caution here. This straightforward analysis glosses over the significant differences that exist between Egyptian instructions themselves and the distinctive features of Proverbs. Regarding the prologue, Stuart Weeks points out that Proverbs 1–9 is different from Egyptian examples, offering multiple voices (rather than the singular voice of the father), general exhortations (rather than specific advice) and extended reflections on types of women (rather than passing comments). He concludes that 'the foreign instructions offer, at most, a very shallow basis for understanding Proverbs 1–9'.[48] The body of the advice too is distinctive (Proverbs 10–29). In Proverbs, the sayings are not obviously connected with each other in literary sequence, differentiating them from the majority of Egyptian instructions, in which the advice is cohesively linked together into sections. Some late Egyptian works do share Proverbs' atomism (especially Anchsheshonq), but these works differ from Proverbs in offering single-lined sayings, rather than two-lined sayings with a stylised parallel structure. These cautions notwithstanding, there are some specific

---

[45] Bernd Schipper, *Israel und Ägypten in der Königszeit: Die kulturellen Kontakte von Salomo bis zum Fall Jerusalems*, OBO 170 (Göttingen, 1999).

[46] This is the case for many Egyptian instructions but not all; some do not have prologues.

[47] Lichtheim, *Ancient Egyptian Literature*, 1:58.

[48] Weeks, *Instruction and Imagery*, 176.

examples of influence worthy of consideration. As we will see, connections with the Instruction of Amenemope are particularly strong.

The Influence of Amenemope in Proverbs 22:17–23:11

The first assertion of direct influence was proposed, and in our opinion proved, by Adolf Erman.[49] In 1924, one year after the publication of the Instruction of Amenemope, he argued that Prov 22:17–24:10 was in part translated from this text. The word 'translation' is imprecise because the verbal affinity is often loose and the parallels are actually confined to the first half of this section (22:17–23:11). But Erman's basic thesis of the derivation of this unit still stands. It has been strengthened over the decades and can be strengthened further.

The similarities between Amenemope and Prov 22:17–23:11 have been explained in various ways. One explanation is that there is no particular relationship. Proverbs 22:17–23:11 is just a loose collection of older maxims known from various sources, including other Egyptian wisdom books. They might just be similar responses to similar situations. Another view is that Prov 22:17–23:11 is dependent on Amenemope but only as a loose borrowing of motifs, themes and concepts. It arose by a process of 'rereading' of tradition, such as we see throughout the Egyptian wisdom tradition generally.

We support a stronger theory, namely, that Prov 22:17–23:11 is derived directly from, and only from, Amenemope, which was known to the Hebrew composer in a form very close to the one we have now in the primary source manuscript of Amenemope (Pap. British Museum 10474) and further that the entire scope of the book, if not demonstrably every line, was known in Israel and had a wide impact on the formation of the book of Proverbs. We can see with some precision how selections from Amenemope were shaped into Prov 22:17–23:11 by lining up the well-recognised Amenemope parallels in the order they have in the MT.[50]

The composer of Prov 22:17–23:11 was not just trolling at random for interesting material. He had a sense of the new composition he wished to create and a procedure that would serve those ends. He created a new instruction from old materials. This was a highly literate, learned activity, not folk wisdom and not proverb collecting, and it is

---

[49] Adolf Erman, 'Eine ägyptische Quelle der "Sprüche Salomos"', SPAW, 15 (1924): 86–93.

[50] See the charts in Michael V. Fox, 'From Amenemope to Proverbs', ZAW 126.1 (2014): 76–91.

suggestive of what other compilers and editors of Proverbs could do. Since the composer used materials from the entire scope of his scroll, from beginning to end and many places in the middle, he must have had the whole book of Amenemope before him, though the possibility of local omissions cannot be disproved.

The Influence of Amenemope Elsewhere in Proverbs

The imprint of Amenemope is not restricted to Prov 22:16–23:11 but is visible in all sections of Proverbs, except the appendices in chapters 30–31. For example, there are two templates in Proverbs which were based on Amenemope. A template is a recurrent pattern of syntax or wording that serves as a mould for constructing new texts.

First is the form of the prologue (Prov 1:1–7 and Amenemope I, 1–12). The key feature shared by the two prologues is a nominal title with a series of dependent infinitival clauses which express the book's goals. The infinitives of purpose are *r* + infinitive in Egyptian, which is the exact equivalent of *lamed* + infinitive in Hebrew. Amenemope's begins with a long nominal clause, 'The beginning of the teaching for life, the instruction for well-being, all the rules for relations with elders, the customs for (dealing with) courtiers' and continues with lines beginning 'to know', 'to bring back', 'to bring back', 'to guide', 'to make descend', 'steering', 'to save' and 'that he be'. There are seven lines beginning with *r* + infinitive as well as two lines that are dependent on the infinitive clauses. Proverbs' prologue, 1:1–7, begins with a nominal clause, 'The proverbs of Solomon the son of David, king of Israel' and continues with lines beginning, 'to know', 'to take', 'to give', 'to understand', 'let hear' (jussive), 'to understand' and 'fear' (noun). There is nothing like this series of infinitives dependent on a nominal clause elsewhere in Egyptian wisdom literature or in the Bible. The prologue to Proverbs must have had a foreign sound.

Another template learned from Amenemope is the quadripartite 'better-than' template ('Better A with B than A' with B''). This is not found in other Egyptian instructions and is apparently Amenemope's invention. It turns a simple comparison into a subtle ratio. The point is that B is so good that it outweighs something everyone desires (the A') *even when* combined with something less desirable (the A). There are two examples in Proverbs 15:16–17: 'Better a little with the fear of the Lord than a great storehouse with turmoil in it. Better are provisions of greens where there is love than a fattened ox where there is hatred.' The double saying is based on the double saying in Amenemope 9.5–8:

'Better is poverty in the hand of the god, than wealth in the storehouse. Better are (mere) loaves of bread when the heart is pleasant than wealth with vexation.' This template is used twelve times in Proverbs (15:16, 17; 16:8, 19, 32a, 32b; 17:1; 19:1; 21:9, 19; 25:24; 28:6), of which four instances (15:16, 17; 16:8; and 17:1) are directly dependent on Amenemope. Subsequently, Qohelet (4:13) and Ben Sira (10:27; 20:31 = 41:15) used the template. Whilst originating in Amenemope, this template has taken on a life of its own. The varied applications of these templates show that Amenemope was not only cited; it was assimilated into Israelite wisdom and became a creative force there.

Another example of influence from Amenemope is found in Prov 25:21–22:

> 21 If your enemy hungers,
> feed him bread,
> and if he is thirsty,
> give him water to drink.
> 22 For you will heap coals on his head,
> and the Lord will reward you.

This is based on Amenemope 4.10–5.6:

> (4.10)   Do not make an outcry against him who transgresses against you,
> (11)   nor reply to him yourself ...

A little later Amenemope urges:

> (5.3)   Raise him up; give him your hand;
> (4)   leave him in the hands of God.
> (5)   Fill his belly with your own bread,
> (6)   that he may be sated and ashamed.

Mercy is the best revenge. If you treat your enemy humanely, you will put him to shame, either pricking his conscience or scorching his pride, and God will reward you. (Note how the parallel solves an exegetical crux, the meaning of hot coals. They are a metaphor of shame.) And consider Amenemope's motivation for helping one's enemies: 'that we not act like him' (5.2). Even justified vindictiveness corrupts the avenger. The Babylonian Counsels of Wisdom too warns against revenge in a passage that concludes with the admonition, 'Requite with good the one who does evil to you.'[51] It is important to note that Proverbs' foreign

---

[51] Benjamin R. Foster, *Before the Muses: An Anthology of Akkadian Literature* (Bethesda, 1993), 329.

connections are not with Egypt alone. Wisdom could travel in all directions together with the scribes who were essential to commerce and diplomacy. But in this case, the affiliation of the Hebrew maxim is primarily with Amenemope, which shares with Proverbs the advice to give one's enemy bread and also the utilitarian motivation for showing mercy – to humble one's enemies – together with the expectation that God will bring the matter to a just conclusion. Moreover, Proverbs and Amenemope alone advise actually helping one's enemy and not only to refrain from vengeance.

Egyptian Parallels in Proverbs 8

Beyond these connections with Amenemope, there is evidence that Proverbs has been influenced by other Egyptian texts. One intriguing but uncertain case is Prov 8:1–36, in which wisdom is personified as a human (or divine) woman speaking to humans. She praises herself, then teaches them wisdom and ethics. Christa Bauer-Kayatz proposed that Lady Wisdom is based on the Egyptian goddess Ma'at.[52] Bauer-Kayatz identified various features as signs of Egyptian origin (though these were not specifically linked to wisdom texts). Examples are the mutual love formula ('I love him who loves me' and variants), the self-predication (or 'self-revelation') formula ('I am X ...'), Wisdom's existence before creation, Wisdom as beloved child of God playing before him, Wisdom as lover and beloved, her service as dispenser of life and protection and her status as the effective power in the royal regime.[53] All these features are characteristically Egyptian. However, they are not associated exclusively with Ma'at. Overall, Lady Wisdom seems like an Egyptian divinity, but Ma'at is not the deity portrayed. Ma'at nowhere gives a speech like Lady Wisdom's; in fact, she never seems to speak at all. Ma'at is what Thorkild Jacobsen called an 'intransitive' deity, meaning that she achieves her effects not by action but by her existence.[54] And unlike some other Egyptian deities, Ma'at never developed an international persona of her own but only in syncretism with others. It is doubtful that ancient sages, Egyptian or Israelite, could have extracted the concept of Ma'at from scattered uses in wisdom, cultic and mortuary texts and grafted it on to an Israelite figure of wisdom.

The strongest parallel is not Ma'at but the Egyptian goddess Isis, particularly as developed in the Hellenistic world as a universal divinity

52   Christa Bauer-Kayatz, *Studien zu Proverbien 1–9,* : Eine form- und motivgeschichtliche Untersuchung unter Einbeziehung Ägyptischen Vergleichmaterials. WMANT 22 (Neukirchen-Vluyn, 1966).

53   Bauer-Kayatz, *Studien zu Proverbien 1–9,* 119 and *passim.*

54   Thorkild Jacobsen, *Treasures of Darkness: A History of Mesopotamian Religion* (New Haven; London, 1976), 9–11.

who was widely worshipped in aretalogies. In these hymns, Isis praises herself in much the same way as Lady Wisdom does in Proverbs 8. And Isis is the wise goddess.

> I am Isis, ruler of all lands,
> and I was educated by Hermes ...
> I set down laws for men and legislated that which no one can alter.
> I am the eldest daughter of Kronos.[55]

In the Metternich magical stele, Isis says:

> My father (Re') educated me to knowledge.
> I am his daughter, the beloved one (born) of his body ...
> I am Isis, the divine,
> mistress of magic, who does magic,
> effective in pronouncing spells.
>   (Translated from the Greek)

Isis would have made an excellent model for Proverbs 8. The Isis identification does not exclude connection with Ma'at, because the two goddesses were often identified syncretistically, and many of the Ma'at symbols as were adopted by Isis as well.

Egyptian Parallels in Prov 23:12–24:22

Finally, there are also to Egyptian parallels to Prov 23:12–24:22. The (very funny) mocking of the drunkard in Anii 17.6–11 may lie behind (the likewise funny) Prov 23:31–35, though possibly the similarities may result from the universal facts of what happens to drunks. Anii himself is picking up a topos from school letters, in which a father castigates his son for dissolute behaviour.

Proverbs 24:10–12 may have an Egyptian source. It reads:

> 10   If you are lax in the day of distress,
>   your strength will be constrained.
> 11   Save those who are being taken away to death,
>   and those who are tottering on (the brink of) slaughter, do
>   not stint (in helping).
> 12   For if you say, 'We did not know this',
>   will not he who examines hearts perceive,

---

[55] The Cyme Aretalogy. See Gail Corrington Streete, 'An Isis Aretalogy from Kyme in Asia Minor, First Century B.C.E.', in *Religions of Late Antiquity in Practice*, ed. R. Valantasis, Princeton Readings in Religions (Princeton, 2018), 369–384.

> will not the guardian of your soul know,
> and repay a man according to his deed?

This passage may derive from Papyrus Chester Beatty IV, 1.13–2.2:

> (1.13b) If you are rich (2.1) and power has come to you,
> your god having built you up,
> do not ignore a man you know [*lacuna*].
> Save everyone.
> Release a man whom you find (2) bound.
> Be a protector for the sufferer.
> He is called 'good' who does not act unknowing. (Literally, 'act very
> dumb'.)

The Egyptian teaching, like Proverbs, demands helping one who is afflicted and in danger. This is not a person slated for judicial execution in Proverbs, or one who is bound in judicial punishment in Beatty IV, because one should not interfere in the working of justice. The person who is bound may have been the victim of cruel overseers, like the wretched peasant man and woman described in Papyrus Lansing. When you see someone unjustly bound and in danger, both maxims say, it is wrong to play dumb, to say 'I did not know this'.

To help establish a connection between parallels, it is necessary to find *unpredictable* similarities or shared features that would not arise simply because of shared topic. In this case, the unpredictable similarity is the identity of the God who will punish your failure to help a sufferer. In Proverbs, it is intriguing that it is *this* God who demands that you help the helpless. The second link is the excuse one may give for refusing involvement, namely, pretending ignorance of what was happening or, as the Egyptian maxim puts it, playing dumb. It cannot be determined if the text we have was the immediate source of the maxim in Proverbs, but the relationship is not coincidental.

Job

Most of the evidence of Egyptian influence on Israelite wisdom texts relates to the Book of Proverbs. There have, however, been some suggestions of influence on Job and Ben Sira too. Some scholars have tried to connect Job 38–39 to alleged quasi-scientific texts from Egypt.[56] Albrecht Alt popularised the view that a 'science of lists'

---

[56] See a more extended discussion of this issue in Michael V. Fox, 'Egyptian Onomastica and Biblical Wisdom', *VT* 36.3 (1986): 302–310.

(*Listenwissenschaft*) existed in Egypt, represented textually through onomastica.[57] Especially important was the Onomasticon of Amenope (On Am), which constituted for Alt an 'attempt at an encyclopedia of all knowledge'.[58] This grandiose claim might be rooted in the title of the onomasticon, which begins 'Beginning of the teaching for clearing the mind, for instruction of the ignorant and for learning all things that exist.'[59] On Am's alleged purpose was to organise and systematise natural phenomena, revealing orders and hierarchies, such that the sequence of items represented the structures of reality. Building on Alt's foundation, Gerhard von Rad argued that this 'science of lists' forms the background to God's first speech to Job, in which God enumerates phenomena from the natural world.[60] Though von Rad granted that we cannot assume direct literary dependence, he nonetheless observed multiple similarities between Job 38–39 and On Am, leading him to conclude that a common 'scientific schema' underlies both.

However, this argument can be challenged from two perspectives. First, Egyptian onomastica are not, in fact, attempts to organise the natural world into systematic encyclopedias. Though they do categorise phenomena, the rationale for the categorisation is often lacking, most categories do not show internal structuring and the relationship between categories is not elucidated. The grand title of On Am is a literary exaggeration, not a genuine statement of purpose, and the actual purpose is likely to have been the teaching of writing. Second, the relationship between Job and On Am is tenuous at best. Von Rad lists thirty-nine items in Job 38:12–39:26, but only nine of these might be said to have a correspondent in the onomasticon, and the order of the items is quite different. There is no single schema common to these texts (or indeed to the other extant Egyptian onomastica). Furthermore, Job 38–39 is not (as this hypothesis would suggest) an attempt to empirically discover quasi-scientific truths about the world. Rather, the emphasis is on the mystery and wonder of God's creation.

---

[57] Alt, 'Die Weisheit Salomos'.

[58] 'Versuch einer Enzyklopädie alles Wissens'. Alt, 'Die Weisheit Salomos', 141. For an edition of the onomastica, see A. H. Gardiner, *Ancient Egyptian Onomastica* (London, 1947).

[59] Gardiner's translation, *Ancient Egyptian Onomastica*, 2

[60] Gerhard von Rad, 'Hiob xxxviii und die altagyptische Weisheit', SVT 3 (1955): 293–301.

Ben Sira

More plausibly, Egyptian texts may have influenced the writings of Ben Sira, who self-professedly learns from the wisdom of other nations (39:1–4). The popular Middle Kingdom text *Satire on the Trades* may have inspired the excursus on different professions in Sir 38:24–39:11, and the Demotic Instruction *Phibis* may have exerted an influence throughout the book. Indeed, Jack T. Sanders argues that Ben Sira was directly dependent on Phibis.[61] He finds structural parallels between the two, noting sections on filial piety towards the beginning of both and hymns to the creator God towards the end. Both are concerned that the reader become wise, pious, generous, disciplined and self-controlled. Sanders gives numerous examples of specific sayings reflected in both: 'The bee is small among flying creatures, but what it produces is the best of sweet things' avers Ben Sira (11:3); 'The little bee brings the honey' agrees Phibis (25,2). Sometimes, the sayings occur in the same order, and overall, he claims that over 15 per cent of Phibis is reflected in Ben Sira.[62]

There has, however, been some scepticism about this suggestion. Matthew J. Goff argues that many of the posited connections are in fact independent reflections of common sapiential tropes.[63] Ben Sira did not need Phibis to learn about wisdom and moderation – he could get that from Proverbs. Those themes which cannot be explained this way (e.g., the reflections on human plight and the cosmos) might instead be explained as being influenced by the broader Hellenistic milieu. Goff also points out potential problems around dating, for Phibis may in fact have been written after Ben Sira. Equally, there are problems around language, as Sanders' theory requires either the writer of Ben Sira to know Demotic or the existence of an otherwise unattested translation of Phibis into, for example, Aramaic.

Conclusion

Ancient Egypt provides us with a wealth of wisdom, from the Old Kingdom through to the Late Period. Narrated as advice from a father to a son, the 'instruction' texts present an ethics grounded in Ma'at and conducive to character development. At times they reflect on their own

---

[61] Jack T. Sanders, *Ben Sira and Demotic Wisdom*, SBLMS 28 (Chico, 1983).

[62] Sanders, *Ben Sira and Demotic Wisdom*, 97.

[63] Matthew J. Goff, 'Hellenistic Instruction in Palestine and Egypt: Ben Sira and Papyrus Insinger', *JSJ* 36.2 (2005): 147–172.

pedagogy and their own transmission in oral and written forms. We must be cautious when discerning connections between these and biblical texts, but in at least one case (Amenemope and Proverbs), Egyptian influence seems almost certain.

Further Reading

Assmann, Jan. *Ma'at: Gerechtigkeit und Unsterblichkeit im Alten Ägypten.* München: 1990.

Fox, Michael V. 'World Order and Ma'at: A Crooked Parallel'. *JANESCU* 23 (1995): 37–48.

'From Amenemope to Proverbs'. *ZAW* 126.1 (2014): 76–91.

Lichtheim, Miriam. *Ancient Egyptian Literature.* 3 vols. Berkeley: 1973–1980.

'Didactic Literature'. *Ancient Egyptian Literature: History and Forms.* Edited by A. Loprieno. Probleme der Ägyptologie. Leiden: 1996.

Moral Value in Ancient Egypt. OBO 155. Göttingen: 1997.

Shupak, Nili. *Where Can Wisdom Be Found? The Sage's Language in the Bible and in Ancient Egyptian Literature.* OBO 131. Göttingen: 1993.

18 The Syro-Palestinian Wisdom of the Late Bronze Age

NOGA AYALI-DARSHAN[*]

INTRODUCTION

The literary works unearthed in the archives of Anatolia, Syria-Palestine and Egypt of the Late Bronze Age (LBA) can be divided into two groups: works in Akkadian (including bilingual works), whose origins are in Mesopotamia, and works in the local languages. The use of Akkadian as the *lingua franca* of the Near East for a millennium required the local scribes to develop expertise in that language, expertise that was attained at scribal schools by reading and copying imported Akkadian texts of various genres, including the wisdom literature. In addition, cultures whose scribes were skilled in writing their local language committed their vernacular works to writing too.[1] However, unlike the finds in Akkadian, no genuine Syro-Palestinian wisdom works have been found so far but rather only a few sayings embodied in the local literary texts.

The present chapter thus seeks to survey both the Akkadian wisdom works and the vernacular wisdom sayings of the LBA Syro-Palestinian region. To date, while the former were found in the cities of Emar and Ugarit (Tell Meskene and Ras Shamra in modern Syria), the latter were unearthed only in Ugarit. This finding does not necessarily indicate the absence of vernacular works in additional Syro-Palestinian cities yet to be unearthed, as Akkadian and vernacular works in various

[*] I am grateful to Yoram Cohen, Nili Samet and Ronit Neudorf for their constructive comments on the manuscript.

[1] For the Mesopotamian curricula of the scribal schools at Ugarit and Emar (and Hattusa), see Yoram Cohen, *Wisdom from the Late Bronze Age*, WAW 34 (Atlanta, 2013); Matthew T. Rutz, *Bodies of Knowledge in Ancient Mesopotamia: The Diviners of Late Bronze Age Emar and Their Tablet Collection*, AMD 9 (Leiden, 2013). For discussion of a putative local curriculum at Ugarit, see Robert Hawley, 'On the Alphabetic Scribal Curriculum at Ugarit', in *Proceedings of the 51st Rencontre Assyriologique Internationale held at the Oriental Institute of the University of Chicago, July 18–22, 2005*, ed. Robert D. Biggs, Jennie Myers and Martha T. Roth, SAOC 62 (Chicago, 2008), 57–67.

Table 18.1

Imported works from Mesopotamia	Manuscripts at Ugarit	Manuscripts at Emar	The language of the work at Emar and Ugarit
Practical Wisdom			
A Precepts Collection	1		Akkadian-Hurrian
The Fowler		2	Sumerian-Akkadian
Instructions of Shuruppak		1?	Akkadian-Hurrian
Critical Wisdom			
The Ballad of Early Rulers	3	1	Sumerian-Akkadian
Enlil and Namzitarra	1	1	Sumerian-Akkadian
Hear the Advice	3	1	Akkadian
Disputation Poems and Fables			
The Date-Palm and the Tamarisk		1	Akkadian
Series of the Fox	1		Akkadian
The Fox, the Wolf and the Hyena	1		Sumerian (-Akkadian)
Righteous Sufferer Compositions			
A Hymn to Marduk	1		Akkadian

genres were unearthed northward in Hattusa (Boghazköy in modern Turkey), the capital of the Hittite kingdom, and southward in Akhetaten (Amarna), the capital of Akhenaten's Egyptian kingdom. Rather, the Ugaritic finding may serve as a representative of the vernacular compositions of the Syro-Palestinian culture as a whole.

Below, the Akkadian wisdom works from Mesopotamia that were found in the Syro-Palestinian region will be discussed according to the rubrics presented in table 1. Following each rubric, the associated vernacular wisdom sayings will also be examined

The existence of many bilingual texts, as noted in Table 18.1, is due to two different circumstances: Sumero-Akkadian texts (including a third column of phonetic Sumerian) are related to the Mesopotamian heritage of the works, while Akkado-Hurrian texts are associated with the activity of local scribes.

Before we survey the compositions, we must offer three important remarks. The first relates to the definition of the wisdom genre. Certain Mesopotamian works that today would be considered as belonging to this genre – some of which are listed in Table 18.1 – were copied together on compilation tablets (*Sammeltafeln*), listed as a homogenous group in an Old Babylonian catalogue of literary works (ETCSL 0.2.11) and/or were attributed to a wise old man named Sidu (in the Neo-Assyrian text K 1870).[2] While scholars disagree as to whether or not this evidence suggests a distinct emic Mesopotamian genre, modern scholarship counts such works, *ab initio*, as wisdom literature, because of their resemblance to certain biblical compositions considered often as wisdom literature, such as Job, Proverbs and Ecclesiastes. The following survey and the cataloguing of the works under various modern rubrics, as in Table 18.1, continue that common convention.[3]

The second remark relates to the origin of the Akkadian wisdom texts found at Emar and Ugarit. Apart from the first and last works listed in Table 18.1, versions of all the compositions were unearthed also in their homeland, Mesopotamia. Some of them are dated to the Old Babylonian period, prior to the finds from Emar and Ugarit, while others – due to present circumstances – have only a later copy. Despite the occasional differences between those versions and the significant adaptations some of them have undergone, there is no justification to argue for a Syro-Palestinian reworking, unless the grammar or the lexicography so indicate.[4] As we shall see below, from all the works examined here, only the last one may reveal signs of local adaptation, manifested by unique lexicography uncommon in Akkadian.

The third remark emphasises the significance of the distinction between the Akkadian works and the vernacular ones. This distinction is not related only to their different origins (works imported from Mesopotamia vs. local works) and their languages (works in the lingua franca Akkadian vs. works in the local language) but also to the chain of transmission associated with them. Since Akkadian was not the spoken language in Syro-Palestinian cities, the transmission, if at all, of themes and motifs from Akkadian works to the vernacular ones were limited to the guild of scribes. In contrast, the chain of transmission of vernacular works may have been both oral and textual, and their audience is likely to have been much broader. We will come back to this issue following our survey.

---

[2] See Yoram Cohen, 'Why "Wisdom"? Copying, Studying, and Collecting Wisdom Literature in the Cuneiform World', in *Teaching Morality in Antiquity*, ed. Takayoshi M. Oshima, ORA 29 (Tübingen, 2018), 41–59.

[3] See, e.g., Wilfred G. Lambert, *Babylonian Wisdom Literature* (Oxford, 1960) (hereafter BWL).

[4] This issue is much discussed among scholars. For the opposing views, see Maurizio Viano, *The Reception of Sumerian Literature in the Western Periphery*, Antichistica 9/Studi Orientali 4 (Venezia, 2016), 299–313.

PRACTICAL WISDOM

Aphorisms and advice, anecdotes and instructions are all commonly catalogued under the rubric of practical wisdom, as all of them deal with human behaviour in daily life and seek to guide the individual toward success. Since daily life includes a range of activities in a variety of areas, such as economics, religion, ethics, society and the like, practical wisdom refers to all of these. The most basic unit – the independent advice or aphorism – could have been set in any genre, literary or non-literary, while only a collection of advices, for example, the book of Proverbs, is in fact categorised as a practical wisdom work. Nevertheless, in order to survey the practical wisdom disseminated in the Syro-Palestinian region as a whole, we will examine both collections of sayings and isolated sayings set in other genres.

Akkadian Compositions
A Precepts Collection

A small tablet from Ugarit (RS 15.10) comprises two instructions in Akkadian, each followed by a Hurrian translation. The small dimensions of the tablet suggest that it was a student's exercise, extracted from a larger collection. The instructions deal with the requirement to make payment of a vowed amount and the requirement to be conscious of sin when addressing one's god:

> [1-4]Place the silver for (the payment of) the oath ceremony! You will receive it back from the god .... He who swears by the river(-god), (but) holds on to the payment – his wife will not bear him a son forever and ever.

> [10-11]Ignorant of (his) sin, he rushes to his god, he does not consider (his deeds), in haste he lifts his hands (in prayer) to his god.[5]

Although no version or copy of these instructions has yet been found in Mesopotamia, their Mesopotamian background is clearly manifest by the identity of the god in whose name one swears: the river god, who is also known as the Mesopotamian god of oath. In the Hurrian translation, both the river god of the first instruction and the personal god – before whom one should not pray in haste – of the following instruction

---

[5] The translation from Akkadian follows Cohen, *Wisdom from the Late Bronze Age*, 208–209.

were replaced by a single divinity, the Hurrian moon god (cf. Eccl 5:1–6).[6]

The Fowler

These fragmentary pieces of an anecdote, found at Emar (E 768–770), tell of an incident that occurred to a fowler. While the content of this anecdote is not clear – a Late Babylonian version of this is also fragmentary – its significance and categorisation as wisdom literature are indicated by its attribution in the Neo-Assyrian text to Sidu the wise (K 1870:11). A short aphorism set in a Neo-Assyrian collection, telling about a fowler who claimed to be able to catch fish with his net, may constitute a sort of synopsis of that anecdote.[7]

Instructions of Shuruppak

The Instructions of Shuruppak is considered the earliest example of a collection of Sumerian instructions – its earliest manuscripts are dated to the twenty-fifth century BCE – and one of the most widely disseminated in Mesopotamia, both geographically and across time. It includes various instructions given by a father, the man of Shuruppak, to his son. Over time, the son came to be identified with the flood hero Ziusudra, thus giving the text a status of antediluvian wisdom. During the second millennium, this piece was translated into Akkadian in various places independently. One of these Akkadian copies – only a fragment of it being preserved – was translated in turn into Hurrian (Private coll. in Alster 2005: 48ff.). Its paleography and Hurrian language ascribe it to the LBA Syro-Anatolian region. According to Bendt Alster, it belongs to the scribal school of Emar.[8]

---

[6] For the Hurrian translation, see Meindert Dijkstra, 'The Akkado-Hurrian Bilingual Wisdom-Text RS 15.010 Reconsidered', *UF* 25 (1993): 157–162; Gernot Wilhelm, 'Bemerkungen zu der akkadisch-hurritischen Bilingue aus Ugarit', in *Literatur, Politik und Recht in Mesopotamien: Festschrift für Claus Wilcke*, ed. Walther Sallaberger, Konrad Volk, and Annette Zgoll, OBC 14 (Wiesbaden, 2003), 341–345.

[7] For the Emarite text, see Daniel Arnaud, *Recherches au pays d'Aštata, Emar VI.4: Textes de la bibliothèque, transcriptions et traductions*, Synthese 28 (Paris, 1987), 365–367. For the Late Babylonian version, see *BWL* 221. For the Neo-Assyrian aphorism, see *BWL* 217, ll. 42–43. While some (like Viano, *The Reception*, 313–314) link this anecdote also with a Sumerian text entitled The Fowler and His Wife, others (such as Rutz, *Knowledge*, 272) negate this connection.

[8] For an extensive discussion of the various versions of the Instructions of Shuruppak, including the present version, see Bendt Alster, *Wisdom of Ancient Sumer* (Bethesda, 2005), 31–220, and Wilhelm's comments there (204–208) on the Hurrian translation. Cf. also Manfred Krebernick, 'Fragment einer Bilingue', *ZA* 86 (1996): 170–176.

This Akkado-Hurrian fragment preserves the end of the exposition, presenting the father who offers advice to his son (cf. Prov. 1:8 *et passim*). Then, it continues with various kinds of advice and proverbs (paralleling entries 11–16; 60–67 of the Sumerian edition), such as:

> Don't buy [a braving ass]; it will split [your yoke!]
> Don't place [a well in your own field; people will do ha]rm to you.
> [The slanderer] rolls [his eyes] like a spindle.[9]

Apart from a few differences between this fragment and the versions unearthed in Mesopotamia, the order of the proverbs as well as their wording are very close. We may thus surmise that this is true also for the rest of approximately 200 sayings that the composition originally contained.

Significantly, three additional compositions written in the Instructions model were unearthed at Emar and Ugarit, making it a well-disseminated category in the Syro-Palestinian region. However, because these three compositions have been integrated into a framework of critical wisdom, they will be discussed in the next section.

Vernacular Texts

The extant Ugaritic literature has no collections of proverbs and advice, anecdotes and instructions. Nevertheless, the content of a few expressions embodied in epic literature may attest to the existence of an oral Ugaritic wisdom tradition. The best example of this is set in Baal's speech during a divine banquet (The Baal Cycle; *KTU* 1.4 III 17–21). The exceptional nature of the expression, regarding its content, language, and style, attests to its independent origin:

> There are two feasts that Baal hates, three – that the Rider of the
>   Clouds (hates):
> A feast of shame, and a feast of contention, and a feast of the
>   lewdness of maids.[10]

Although the exact meaning of this aphorism is vague – due to its linguistic register and lack of context – it appears to warn against inappropriate celebrations. Its close similarity to Prov 6:16 ('There are

---

9   The translation follows Alster (*Wisdom*) with modification.

10 The translation follows Edward L. Greenstein ('Wisdom in Ugaritic', in *Language and Nature: Papers Presented to John Huehnergard on the Occasion of His 60th Birthday*, ed. Rebecca Hasselbach and Na'ama Pat-El, SAOC 67 [Chicago, 2012], 73) with modification. For further discussion and bibliography, see Greenstein.

six things that YHWH hates, and seven that are an abomination to him') and, inversely, to Aramaic Ahiqar, ll. 187 ('There are two things that are beautiful, and three that are beloved by the sun god.') strengthen its classification as a wisdom saying.[11]

An additional text, set in the Legend of Kirta, suggests a unique use of the Instructions model, that is, advice delivered from father to son, in a reversal of roles: instead of the king, Kirta, instructing his son Yaṣṣib, the son rebukes his father for neglecting of his moral and legal obligations (*KTU* 1.16, VI 41–50):

> Hear now, O noble Kirta, Hearken, alert your ear:
> You've let your hand fall to vice; You don't pursue the widow's case,
> You don't take up the wretched's claim; You don't expel the poor's oppressor.
> You don't feed the orphan who faces you; Nor the widow who stands at your back.[12]

Interestingly, Kirta's illness, which compelled him to cease performing his royal tasks, broke out after he was late in paying off his pledge to the goddess Athirat. Since offspring were born to him despite his sin, it appears that the Ugaritic author did not regard infertility as a punishment for non-payment of a pledged amount – as inscribed in the Akkado-Hurrian precepts above – but rather a major illness would be that punishment.

Akkadian Proverbs in Letters
The letters that were sent by the Syro-Palestinian vassal rulers to the kings of Egypt, found at Akhenaten's capital, were replete with metaphors, sayings and proverbs.[13] As these letters were written in

---

[11] The translation for Proverbs follows the NRSV, with modification. The translation for Ahiqar follows CAL: http://cal.huc.edu/, with modification.

[12] The translation follows Greenstein 'Wisdom', 74–75. For Kirta as a wisdom text, see Herbert Niehr, 'Weisheit in den Königsepen aus Ugarit', in *Teaching Morality in Antiquity*, ed. Takayoshi M. Oshima, ORA 29 (Tübingen, 2018), 71–78. Note that the son's words here particularly resemble the instructions works from Egypt (such as The Instructions for King Merikare, ll. 46–49). For fulfilling these 'neglected' obligations by Aqhat in another Ugaritic composition, see *KTU* 1.17 V 7–8.

[13] In fact, most of the Amarna expressions collected by scholars (see, e.g., Cohen, *Wisdom*, 226–228; Greenstein, *Wisdom*, 71) are mainly similes, such as 'I am situated like a boat in the midst of the sea', 'I have become like a copper cauldron in pledge because of the Suteans' and 'Like a bird which is caught in a trap, thus I am in Byblos', and do not necessarily belong to wisdom literature. The two examples presented below are exceptional.

Akkadian, it is difficult to ascertain whether these expressions are of Mesopotamian heritage or whether these are rendering of local wisdom traditions. Here are two examples:

The saying 'My field is like a wife without a husband for lack of cultivator' appears in four letters of Rib-Hadda, the ruler of Byblos, as a complaint about his city's difficult situation (EA 74; 75; 81; 90).[14] The saying's original meaning is revealed in a Mesopotamian bilingual collection, which cites together several proverbs whose purpose is to prove the necessity of leadership:

> A people without a king (is like) sheep without a shepherd.
> A people without a foreman (is like) water without a canal inspector.
> Laborers without a supervisor (are like) a field without a plowman.
> A house without an owner (is like) a woman without a husband.[15]

At first glance, it seems that the Rib-Hadda's saying is another version of these, composed of the second half of each of the last two proverbs. However, the context in which the saying is set in Rib-Hadda's letters suggests that the scribe/ruler did not use the proverb in its original meanings; rather, he simply compared Byblos' abandoned fields to a woman without a husband (cf. Judg 14:18).[16]

An additional proverb, 'When ants are smitten, they do not just curl up, but they bite the hand of the person who smote them', is set in the letter of Labaya, the vassal ruler of Shekhem (EA 252). Labaya uses this proverb in order to emphasise the absurdity of the Pharaoh's demand to protect the hostile conquerors of his cities. Since no other versions or copies of this proverb – or of the unique motif embodied in it – have been recognised in other Near Eastern texts, its provenance remains obscure.[17]

---

[14] The translation of this proverbs and the following follows Anson F. Rainey, *The El-Amarna Correspondence: A New Edition of the Cuneiform Letters from the Site of El-Amarna Based on Collations of All Extant Tablets*, ed. William M. Schniedewind and Zipora Cochavi-Rainey (Leiden; Boston, 2015), 455 and elsewhere, 1023, respectively.

[15] *BWL* 228, 232.

[16] And cf. also The Instructions of Ptahhotep ll. 325–330, among others. For claiming of local Levantine elements in this saying, see David Marcus, 'A Famous Analogy of Rib-Haddi', *JANESCU* 5 (1973): 281–286.

[17] While the sagacity of the ant is mentioned in biblical proverbs (Prov 6:6; 30:25) as well, these proverbs focus on the ant's hard work in anticipation of winter, rather than on how it protects itself.

CRITICAL WISDOM

The Mesopotamian compositions counted in this category criticise the positive worldview reflected in the practical wisdom, according to which if a person would only act as advised, he would succeed in all his endeavours. The most nihilist compositions state that since human life is so short, and death is infinite, there is no value to any advice. Significantly, while this pessimistic view is dominant in three Akkadian compositions found at Emar and Ugarit, two of them reverse it, toward the end of the composition, into a motivation for enjoying the short life as long as possible, à la carpe diem, or into a motivation for moral behaviour. Sayings that emerge from a pessimistic point of view can be found, sparingly, in the Ugaritic epic literature as well. In the biblical literature, Ecclesiastes is a sole representative of this category.[18]

Akkadian Compositions
The Ballad of Early Rulers
Of this work, of about twenty lines, one fairly complete version was preserved at Emar (E 767+) with two fragmentary duplicates from Ugarit (RS 25.130; RS 23.34 (+) 23.484 + 23.363), and an additional version was preserved fragmentarily at Ugarit (RS 25.424). The Ballad begins with a few statements on the futility of the short life in contrast to one's eternal stay in the netherworld. As an example of those statements, the work lists several Mesopotamian legendary kings and heroes – such as Etana, Gilgamesh and Enkidu – who lived thousands of years and did mighty deeds but eventually died in spite of their fame. It concludes with the question: 'Life without light – how can it be better than death?' Three different answers to this question are given in the various versions of the work; one in the Sumerian version from Mesopotamia of the Old Babylonian period, and two in the bilingual versions from the LBA Emar and Ugarit.

The Old Babylonian version regards the question as a rhetorical one, to which the answer is negative – this short life is indeed no better than the long death – and thus it remains true to the original essence of the work. The two LBA versions, on the other hand, respond to the question affirmatively by interpolating additional lines at the end of the work.

---

[18] Cf. Nili Samet, 'Religious Redaction in Qohelet in Light of Mesopotamian Vanity Literature', *VT* 66 (2016): 133–148; Victor Avigdor Hurowitz, 'The Wisdom of Šūpê-Amēlī: A Deathbed Debate between a Father and Son', in *Wisdom Literature in Mesopotamia and Israel*, ed. Richard J. Clifford, SymS 36 (Atlanta, 2007), 44–45.

One of them, of which three manuscripts have been found, states that because a life without light is indeed no better than death, a young person should rejoice, and thus the burden of his life will be lightened. A comparison of the closing lines shows how the later version was developed from the earlier one[19]:

Old Babylonian version (from Sippar)
[19]Life without light – how can it be
  better than death?

[20]Instead of one day of joy, a time of
  silence lasting 36,000 years will
  surely come.
[21][Lasting life] was given to the gods.
  [Where is the man] who seeks life?
[22]This is the fate of humanity, [*those*]
  *who live in the house of the young
  man.*

LBA version (from Emar)
[19]Life without light – how can it be
  better than death?
[20]Young man let me [teach you] truly
  what is (the nature of) your god.
[21]Repel, drive away sorrow, scorn
  silence!
[22]Instead of one [day of j]oy, let pass a
  time [of silence] lasting 36,000
  (years).
[23]May [Siraš (the Wine Goddess)]
  rejoice over you as if over (her) son!
[24]This is the fate of humanity.

The development marked in the conclusion of this LBA version (which differs in other matters from the Old Babylonian version), in comparison to the older one, is significant for understanding the entire work; beginning as a nihilistic text that regards the short human life-span as purposeless, it transforms – by adding three more sentences – an optimistic work that encourages joy in human life. While no Mesopotamian equivalents exist for this interpolation, the carpe diem approach by itself is reflected in other Old Babylonian compositions, such as Nothing is of Value, named for its first line – 'Nothing is of value, but life is good' – and in Siduri's speech in the Epic of Gilgamesh. Since these compositions share further ideas and expressions with The Ballad of Early Rulers (Nothing is of Value was also inscribed on a compilation tablet together with The Ballad), they appear to have originated in a closely related literary school.

The second LBA version of The Ballad updates the negative ending of the older version in a different way. Following the original conclusion

---

[19] The translation follows Jacob Klein, 'The Ballad about Early Rulers: Eastern and Western Traditions', in *Languages and Cultures in Contact: At the Crossroads of Civilizations in the Syro-Mesopotamian Realm: Proceedings of the 42th RAI*, ed. Karel van Lerberghe and Gabriela Voet, OLA 96 (Leuven, 1999), 203–216. For further discussion see Klein.

of the old Babylonian version, which, as mentioned, replies in a pessimistic manner to the fateful question, 'Life without light – how can it be
better than death', this LBA version repeats the three opening lines of
the work, which deal with the fate of human beings, then cites a series
of moral instructions – whose main point is that a person does not know
the length of his life or his fate, therefore he should not behave with
hostility toward others – and concludes with the same three opening
lines, as a sort of framework. According to this addition, so it appears,
the moral behaviour is the reply to the original pessimist composition.

Two Mesopotamian equivalents may have implications for the
origin of the latter interpolation. A Sumerian fragment from the Old
Babylonian period, which cites identical instructions, suggests that this
section was part of an independent Mesopotamian composition before
being joined to this version of The Ballad of Early Rulers. A bilingual
fragment from the library of Assurbanipal, quoting a similar framework
with different instructions in between, reveals another variant of the
same literary development.[20]

Enlil and Namzitarra

A well-preserved copy of this work, of about thirty lines, was found at
Emar (E 771 [+] E 772 [+] E 773 [+] E 774 [+] E 592) and another very
fragmentary copy – at Ugarit (RS 22.341 + RS 28.053A). Most of the
work is a dialogue between the god Enlil, the head of the Sumerian
pantheon and a man named Namzitarra. While only a few words of the
exposition are extant, the missing lines are reconstructed according to
the Sumerian version of the Old Babylonian period. It indicates that the
two protagonists met when Namzitarra was leaving Enlil's temple for
home. Upon their encounter, after Namzitarra revealed Enlil's identity,
the god offered him gifts of silver and precious stones, cattle and flocks.
Namzitarra, however, spurned those gifts, saying, 'The day of mankind
is approaching, so where does your wealth lead?'[21] From that point, the
two versions – the Sumerian from the Old Babylonian period and the
bilingual from the LBA Emar and Ugarit – diverge.

In the Old Babylonian version, Enlil answers that in place of a one-
time gift, Namzitarra's sons will be endowed with a priestly gift forever.
Namzitarra is apparently appeased, as the work ends there. It thus
appears that although the work is replete with wordplay and sapiential

---

[20] For the Sumerian (CBS 13777) and the bilingual (K 6917 + K 13679) fragments, see
    Alster, *Wisdom*, 323–326, 320–322, respectively.
[21] Some scholars posit that this question is in fact asked by Enlil.

sayings and was copied on a compilation tablet together with another wisdom work – all these indicating scribal reworking – it originally served as an etiological story, telling how the descendants of Namzitarra were given priestly gift.

The LBA version ends completely differently. Rather than justifying the privileges afforded to Namzitarra's family, the later scribe developed Namzitarra's answer into a statement about the brevity of life that makes material gifts valueless (Sec. B: 18′–26′):

> To where will I take your silver, your lapis-lazuli gems, your cattle, your sheep? The days of mankind are near, day after day – so it will diminish; month after month – so it will diminish; year after year – so it will diminish. 120 years – such is the limit of mankind's life . . . from that day until now as long as mankind lived.[22]

In this version, Enlil does not grant anything to Namzitarra or his offspring; rather, the narrative ends with the same first three lines with which it had opened, telling about Namzitarra going home. The protagonist's sceptical speech indicates that the wisdom adaptation of this etiological story – the first signs of which are already discernable in the Old Babylonian version – has been intensified over the years. Like the Old Babylonian author of The Ballad of Early Rulers, here too the later scribe was frustrated by the worthless short human lifespan.

It may be, however, that an additional scribe updated the negative ending of the LBA version into an affirmative one, in a manner reminiscent of the second LBA version of The Ballad from Ugarit. Following the end of Enlil and Namzitarra, which – as mentioned – repeated exactly the three opening lines of the text, a series of instructions, such as '(You should not speak) disgracefully against whoever', ordered by a dead father to his sons on his way to the netherworld, is inscribed. Most scholars held it as a kind of appendix with a slight, if any, connection to the preceding composition. However, the LBA version of Enlil and Namzitarra may in fact have originally ended with the sceptical speech of Namzitarra, while the first three lines of the work that follow this speech were added only in a later stage – together with the series of

---

[22] The translation follows Cohen, *Wisdom*, 154–155. Regarding 120 years as the human lifespan, similarly to Gen 6:3, see Jacob Klein, 'The "Bane" of Humanity: A Lifespan of One Hundred Twenty Years', *ASJ* 12 (1990): 57–70. While the latter suggested that it is a Syro-Palestinian motif, it in fact fits well the sexagesimal system common in Mesopotamia. For discussion, see further Viano, *The Reception*, 312.

independent didactic advice – as its framework.[23] By its interpolation
after the speech of Namzitarra, the later scribe thus appears to identify
the protagonist, who passed up the material gifts and went home, with
the dead father who goes to the netherworld – his eternal home – and
offers affirmative advice to his sons in their brief lives.

Hear the Advice

This long composition, of about 150 lines, is the sole example of a
wisdom work that was found not only in Ugarit (RS 22.439; RS
94.2544+; RS 94.5028) and Emar (E 778–780) but also in Hattusa (KUB
4.3+KBo 12.70). Unlike the compositions above, it was composed initially in Akkadian (at Hattusa it was also translated into Hittite), as is
attested by its Akkadian title in an Old Babylonian literary catalogue
(ETCSL 0.2.11). The composition is divided into two parts: practical
advice given by the father Shūpê-Amēli to his son and the son's
response. As in the Instructions of Shuruppak, here too, it begins with
a short introduction, followed by the father's instructions, such as:

> [60]As much as your strength is of a king, do not grapple with a strong
> (er) man.
> [61–61]Do not jump over a wide canal; you will hurt yourself and you
> will have a wound.
> [65–66]Do not open your heart to your beloved woman; 'submit!' (she
> will say).[24]

In the last thirty lines of the work, the son unexpectedly answers the
father, presenting his own nihilistic view. According to him, since one's
lifespan is so short, compared to the everlasting death, there is no point
in all that advice (ll. 140'–42'):

---

[23] The independent nature of the instructions is concluded by its exposition ('Let me
praise your old father, for the advice he gave to his sons') and its monolingual
Akkadian, in contrast to the bilingual work. While Thomas R. Kämmerer, *Šimâ
milka. Induktion und Reception der Mittelbabylonischen Dichtung von Ugarit,
Emār und Tell el-ʿAmarna*, AOAT 251 (Münster, 1998), 116–117, posits that it was
added by a local scribe, Viano, *The Reception*, 312–313, assumes that it is all a work by
a Mesopotamian scribe.

[24] The translation follows Cohen, *Wisdom*, 98–99. For the development of these sayings
in later Syro-Palestinian collections of instructions, see Noga Ayali-Darshan, 'The
Sequence of Sir 4:26–27 in Light of Akkadian and Aramaic Texts from the Levant and
Later Writings', *ZAW* 130 (2018): 436–449; Noga Ayali-Darshan, '"Do Not Open Your
Heart to Your Wife or Servant" (Onch. 13:17): A West-Asiatic Antecedent and Its
Relation to Later Wisdom Instructions', in *Teaching Morality in Antiquity*, ed.
Takayoshi M. Oshima, ORA 29 (Tübingen, 2018), 95–103.

Few are the days in which we eat (our) bread, but many will be the days in which our teeth will be idle. Few are the days in which we look at the sun, but many will be the days in which we will sit in the shadows. The netherworld is teeming, but its inhabitants lie sleeping.

The son's response does not seem to relate the advice given in the first part of the composition but to the very existence of practical wisdom. It appears, therefore, that in composing the son's reply, the author was criticising instruction as a category.

Unlike The Ballad of Early Rulers and Enlil and Namzitarra, the available Mesopotamian version of Hear the Advice cannot be of assistance regarding the question of reworking.[25] However, in light of the essential difference between the father's advice and the son's reply, it is assumed that the present composition comprises an original work and a concluding interpolation as well. In this case, the interpolation wishes to update the affirmative instructions into a nihilistic and sceptical conclusion, which upends the initial meaning of the original work.[26] It is reminiscent of Namzitarra's observations about the vanity of possessions in a person's short life, and of the speaker in the early version of The Ballad, but unlike the adaptation of The Ballad, which ends with a call to rejoice or to behave ethically, and unlike the adaptation of Enlil and Namzittara, whose very end apparently also suggests behaving with integrity, Hear the Advice could not be adapted in such an affirmative manner, since these are precisely the principles rejected in the son's words. This composition is, therefore, the most extreme of the three compositions counted among the critical wisdom category that served Syro-Palestinian scribes.

Vernacular Texts

Some vernacular sayings embodied in the Ugaritic epic literature are close in their view to the Mesopotamian critical wisdom texts mentioned above, although no discernable genetic connection between

---

[25] The Neo-Assyrian copy was identified and provided with a preliminary partial edition a few years ago by Rim Nurullin, 'An Attempt at Šima Milka (Ugaritica V, 163 and Duplicates): Part I: Prologue, Instructions II, III, IV', *Babel & Bibel* 7 (2014): 175–229.

[26] Note that among the contemporaneous Egyptian instructions literature, at least one composition concludes as well with a son's negative answer to his father the instructor (The Instructions of Ani 22:13 ff, whose earlier manuscripts are dated to the nineteenth dynasty). Here, however, the father in turn replies in anger to his son and thus uproots the sceptics to the very end.

them exists.[27] One of them, which contrasts the eternal life of the gods with the short lives of human beings, is set in the speech of Aqhat, who mocks the goddess Anat for offering him eternal life in exchange for his mighty bow (the Legend of Aqhat; *KTU* 1.17, VI 34–38):

> Don't lie to me, girl, your lies are despicable to a real man;
> A mortal – what future can he attain? What hereafter can a mortal attain?
> (In my death) glaze will be poured on (my) head; Plaster on my crown.
> [I] will die the death of everyman; I will die like any mortal.[28]

Although Aqhat's speech does not refer to the vanity of life, but simply ridicules the possibility of granting an eternal life to a mortal being, it appears to emerge from the same frustration revealed in the Mesopotamian works over the brevity of human life and the inevitability of death.

DISPUTATION POEMS AND FABLES

To this category belong two types of compositions that tell about non-human entities who behave like human beings.

The Disputation Poems focus on dialogue between a pair of entities, such as animals, plants or metals, each of which argues for its superiority over the other. Since the rivals stand in as prototypes, the prologue of the earlier Disputation Poems sets the action in the time of Creation. Following the disputation section, a judge – a god or a king – determines the victor of the disputation. Composing the Disputation Poems required familiarity with the characteristics of each rival and expertise in the rhetoric of disputation. Such skills were apparently valued among Mesopotamian scribes, as the genre of Disputation Poems existed from the Old Babylonian period to the end of the cuneiform culture. While no vernacular texts of that sort have been found at Ugarit, the influence of

---

[27] In contrast, for the possible influence of the Mesopotamian critical wisdom literature upon contemporaneous Egyptian literature through Syro-Palestinian mediators, see Noga Ayali-Darshan, 'II. Literature: Egyptian and Levantine Belles-Lettres – Links and Influences during the Bronze Age', in *Pharaoh's Land and Beyond: Ancient Egypt and Its Neighbors*, ed. Pearce P. Creasman and Richard H. Wilkinson (Oxford, 2017), 203–205.

[28] The translation follows Greenstein, *Wisdom*, 73, with modification. For the question of a mortal death in the Ugaritic Legend of Kirta, lacking, however, sapiential features, see *KTU* 1.16 I 2–23 *et passim*.

the Mesopotamian Disputation Poems may appear in contemporaneous Egyptian literature, as well as in first millennium works, such as Aramaic Ahiqar (ll. 101–102) and Hellenistic texts.[29]

The term 'Fables' refers to compositions in which there are more than two – usually animal – figures, and whose plot is much more complex than the dialogical structure of the Disputations. Given that the extant Mesopotamian compositions of this category are all in very fragmentary form, and only a few of them are known to date, it is difficult to ascertain whether this type of work seeks to teach something about human nature by using animals, as is common, for example, in contemporaneous Hurrian (KBo 32.12; 14) and later biblical (such as Judg 9:7–20) fables, or whether it serves another purpose. In the Ugaritic literature, no closely related texts have been found.[30]

Akkadian Compositions
The Date-Palm and the Tamarisk

This composition was found at Emar on thirteen fragments forming one tablet (E783–84). Composed in Akkadian, it opens with a prologue describing how the gods at the beginning of time decided, in their love for humans, to give them a king. This generic king planted in his garden the Date-Palm and the Tamarisk. During a feast, the trees began to debate which one of them is more beneficial to gods and humans. While the Palm argued, for example, that it bears fruit for consumption, the Tamarisk argued that it provides wood for construction. Each tree added arguments for its superiority over six rounds, until finally – in the third section of the composition, which was not preserved in the Emarite or in any of the other Mesopotamian extant manuscripts – the judge (probably the king), decided in favour of one of the trees.[31]

---

[29] For the Disputation Poems in Mesopotamia and their contemporaneous and later parallels, see Enrique Jiménez, *The Babylonian Disputation Poems with Editions of The Series of the Poplar, Palm and Vine, The Series of the Spider, and The Story of the Poor, Forlorn Wren*, CHANE 87 (Leiden, 2017), 128–132, and further bibliography in that work.

[30] For the suggestion that the talmudic expressions in bSukkah 28a: The Speech of Palm Trees and the Fox Fables refer to two of the compositions unearthed in the Syro-Palestinian region: The Date Palm and the Tamarisk and Series of the Fox, respectively, see Erica Reiner, 'At the Fuller's', in *Vom Alten Orient zum Alten Testament. Festschrift für Wolfram Freiherrn von Soden zum 85. Geburtstag am 19. Juni 1993*, ed. Manfred Dietrich and Oswald Loretz, AOAT 240 (Neukirchen-Vluyn, 1995), 407.

[31] For the text, see Cohen, *Wisdom*, 180–190. For a recent discussion of the various versions, see Jiménez, *Disputation Poems*, 29–39.

Since this part is broken off, it is unknown which of the trees won the debate. Nevertheless, it should be emphasised that, like the other (Sumerian) Disputation Poems of the Old Babylonian period, this one too does not compare the material superiority of the tree to moral superiority, nor does it draw a parallel between the trees and famous kings, as do the biblical fables of Jotham (Judg 9:7–20) and Jehoash (2 Kgs 14:9–10). It rather simply lists the advantages of each tree, choosing the most accomplished in the conclusion.

Series of the Fox

This Akkadian composition, whose (Series of the) Fox title is recorded on Mesopotamian catalogue tablets, was very popular in Mesopotamia and was distributed widely over more than a thousand years, until the last quarter of the first millennium BCE. Among the many manuscripts of this composition, the fragment discovered at Ugarit (RS 25.526A) is the earliest, but it is plausible that like the other works that made their way to the Syro-Palestinian realm, this composition was also composed in the Old Babylonian period.

The content of Series of the Fox is not clear, since all the tablets known to date are very fragmentary and only about 300 non-consecutive lines of the original 1500–1800 lines have come to light. Nevertheless, based on the composition's title and in light of its opening and closing telling of Fox's deeds, it appears that Fox is its main protagonist. Alongside him are mentioned Wolf, Fox's rival, who occasionally cooperates with him; Dog, a rival by himself of the two opponents; Lion, who apparently accuses Fox and Wolf of stealing his flock; and other mute animals. In the fragment found at Ugarit, whose place in the plot sequence is unclear, one character – apparently Fox – runs to a particular destination, perhaps fleeing from Dog, and a second figure – perhaps Fox's wife – greets him. The story continues by telling of Fox entering his den and arguing against Dog, who guards outside.[32]

The large number of participants and the rich plot reflected in the various Mesopotamian fragments suggest that this was a kind of folkloristic work, its features quite similar to later animal fables. Thus, Fox is called 'wise', 'crafty' and 'thief'; Dog is the guardian, who protects the city, the flock and finally also the dens of the fleeing Wolf and Fox; and Lion is the privileged character. Nevertheless, the work's Sitz im Leben,

---

[32] For the text from Ugarit, see Daniel Arnaud, *Corpus des textes de bibliothèque de Ras Shamra-Ougarit (1936–2000): En sumérien, babylonien et assyrien*, AuOr Sup 23 (Barcelona, 2007), 186–189.

its messages and the question of its relationship with characteristics modern scholars associate with the wisdom genre still need further clarification.

The Fox, the Wolf and the Hyena

This composition (RS 86.2210) was preserved in Ugarit only in Sumerian, but in light of the other compositions found in the Syro-Palestinian region, it had almost certainly had an additional Akkadian column, which had been the main reason for its presence in the Ugaritic scribal school.[33] The text from Ugarit, as well as the two additional Sumerian copies from the Old Babylonian period, are all very fragmentary and apparently are of three different versions.[34] The story tells of Enlil, disguised as a merchant, who sails on the Euphrates from Nippur to Larsa. On his way he meets Fox, who later meets Dog, and both run away. Later, Fox goes into the den of Hyena, who mocks him; his words are quoted in the Ugaritic fragment. The rest of the plot is unknown.

RIGHTEOUS SUFFERER COMPOSITIONS

Compositions assigned to this category enquire into the reason of human suffering: whether caused by a sin the individual has committed or perhaps by a god's arbitrary whim. Scholars have often related Mesopotamian prayers and confessions to that category too, despite their occasional lack of sapiential features, apparently due to their supposed similarity to the biblical book of Job.[35] Nonetheless, given the priority of Mesopotamian Righteous Sufferer compositions in the form of a prayer or a confession, they might be considered as the initial stage in the formation of this genre, and thus they bear significance.

---

[33] Cf. Viano, *The Reception*, 332; Jiménez, *Disputation Poems*, 54–56.

[34] For the text from Ugarit, see Daniel Arnaud, '6. Textes de bibliothèque', in *Études Ougaritiques 1. Travaux 1985–1995*, ed. Marguerite Yon and Daniel Arnaud, Ras Shamra-Ougarit 14 (Paris, 2001), 333–334; Arnaud, *Corpus*, 189. For corrections and a comparison with the two Old Babylonian texts, see Viano, *The Reception*; Jiménez, *Disputation Poems*. For the supposed relation of this text to the Series of the Fox, see there also.

[35] Cf. Moshe Weinfeld, 'Job and Its Mesopotamian Parallels: A Typological Analysis', in *Text and Context: Old Testament and Semitic Studies for F. C. Fensham*, ed. Walter Claassen (Sheffield, 1988), 217–226.

Akkadian Composition

A Hymn to Marduk

A fragmentary tablet from Ugarit (RS 25.460) inscribed with a thanks-giving prayer to Marduk, the main god of the city of Babylon, represents this genre in the Syro-Palestinian realm. Neither theological questions nor theodicy occur in this prayer, either because those were recorded in the broken opening or closing of the prayer, or because they never appeared in it. It was in fact only its striking similarity to the later Babylonian composition *Ludlul bēl nēmeqi*, which in turn is reminis-cent of the biblical Job, that led scholars to assign this prayer to the present category. From the extant lines, it appears to be a prayer of a dying person – his relatives had even begun to bewail his demise – whom Marduk eventually healed, and ever since he is grateful to the god of Babylon. At the end of the prayer, the erstwhile sufferer expresses Marduk's control over life and death:

> [28'-29']I praise, I praise the deeds of my lord, [the deeds of] Marduk
>   I praise ...
> [38']He cast me aside but picked me up again.
> [39']He threw me down but raised me up.
> [40']He saved me from death's/Mūtu's mouth;
> [41']He raised me from the netherworld.[36]

Although no copy of this prayer has been found in Mesopotamia, it is difficult to cast doubt on its Babylonian provenance, given its dedication to Marduk, the god of Babylon, and its close ties with the later Babylonian composition *Ludlul bēl nēmeqi* (some have even argued that this is a forerunner of *Ludlul*), as stated above.

Nevertheless, unlike the works surveyed above, the footprints of a local adapter appear to be reflected in the vocabulary of the prayer. As has already been argued, West-Semitic roots such as *r-z-y* and *b-d-q* were apparently integrated into the Akkadian text, thus indicating the identity of a local scribe.[37] In addition, the image of Marduk rescuing the sufferer from death (l. 40' above) seems to be based on a local phraseology. At first glance, the 'death's mouth' (*pī mūti*), from which the sufferer was rescued, sounds like a mere figurative expression; however, this expression does not occur in any other Akkadian texts.

---

[36] The translation follows Cohen, *Wisdom*, 168–169, with modification.

[37] Cf. Takayoshi Oshima, *Babylonian Prayers to Marduk*, ORA 7 (Tübingen, 2011), 205–215; Cohen, *Wisdom*, 174. According to the latter, these verbs can, with some difficulty, be understood as Akkadian roots as well.

In West-Semitic literary texts, on the other hand, it was common to figure the god of the netherworld, Môt, as a hungry god who devours human beings in his huge mouth, thus bringing about their death. As described in the Ugaritic Baal Cycle (*KTU* 1.5 I 4–8; 14–22; II 2–6; 1.6 II 15–23), echoes of that occurring in the biblical literature as well (Isa 5:14; Hab 2:5), the descent into Môt's throat was compared to the way into the netherworld. In light of this, the word *mūtu* in l. 40' should not be analysed as the Akkadian common noun for death, but rather as the Ugaritic name of the Levantine god of the netherworld, Môt, into whose mouth people, animals and gods enter on their way to the world of the dead. The sufferer then gives thanks to Marduk for having taken him out of Môt's mouth and thus raising him up from the netherworld.

CONCLUSION AND RELATION TO BIBLICAL AND EXTRA-BIBLICAL LITERATURE

This chapter seeks to gather all the wisdom compositions that have been found in the LBA Syro-Palestinian region and to provide information regarding the sort of adaptations they have undergone. Among all the archives of the western reaches of the cuneiform world unearthed so far (including Hattusa and Akhetaten), those of Emar and Ugarit were the richest in Akkadian wisdom compositions. It is thus surprising to find out that, to date, no independent vernacular compositions of wisdom literature have been discovered in the LBA Syro-Palestinian region. One may suggest that Ugaritic wisdom works have yet to be discovered, but in light of the fact that at Hatti as well, no such vernacular works were unearthed, it might be cautiously posited that the local scribes, who produced various compositions of other genres, refrained for some reason from composing wisdom works, despite their close familiarity with the genre.

Since the Akkadian language was used in the LBA Syro-Palestinian region only by scribes, acquaintance with the Mesopotamian compositions was limited to this group who learned Akkadian by reading and copying them. Therefore, when Akkadian ceased to serve as the lingua franca of the Near East, toward the end of the second millennium BCE, schooling in Akkadian outside Mesopotamia discontinued. In light of this, one can presume that the essential affinity between the LBA Akkadian compositions presented in this chapter and the Syro-Palestinian compositions of the first millennium BCE – such as the books of Proverbs and Ecclesiastes, Ahiqar and Sirach – does not reflect the reception of the former by the LBA local population.[38] Rather, this affinity originated through a renewed encounter of the Hebrew and Aramaean scribes with the Mesopotamian literature in the first millennium BCE. Then, perhaps for the first time in the history of the Syro-Palestinian realm, genuine vernacular compositions of the wisdom genre began to be written down, drawing from the ancient local-oral traditions and from their current neighbouring ancient Near Eastern written literature.

Further Reading

Alster, Bendt. *Wisdom of Ancient Sumer*. Bethesda: 2005.

Arnaud, Daniel. *Corpus des textes de bibliothèque de Ras Shamra-Ougarit (1936–2000): en sumérien, babylonien et assyrien*. AuOr Sup 23. Barcelona: 2007.

Ayali-Darshan, Noga. 'The Sequence of Sir 4:26–27 in Light of Akkadian and Aramaic Texts from the Levant and Later Writings'. *ZAW* 130 (2018): 436–449.

Cohen, Yoram. *Wisdom from the Late Bronze Age*. Edited by Andrew R. George. WAW 34. Atlanta: 2013.

'Why "Wisdom"? Copying, Studying, and Collecting Wisdom Literature in the Cuneiform World'. Pages 41–59 in *Teaching Morality in Antiquity*. Edited by Takayoshi M. Oshima. ORA 29. Tübingen: 2018.

Greenstein, Edward L. 'Wisdom in Ugaritic'. Pages 69–89 in *Language and Nature: Papers Presented to John Huehnergard on the Occasion of His 60th Birthday*. Edited by Rebecca Hasselbach and Naama Pat-El. SAOC 67. Chicago: 2012.

Hurowitz, Victor Avigdor. 'The Wisdom of Šūpê-Amēlī: A Deathbed Debate between a Father and Son'. Pages 37–45 in *Wisdom Literature in Mesopotamia and Israel*. Edited by Richard J. Clifford. SymS 36. Atlanta: 2007.

Jiménez, Enrique. *The Babylonian Disputation Poems with Editions of The Series of the Poplar, Palm and Vine, The Series of the Spider, and The Story of the Poor, Forlorn Wren*. CHANE 87. Leiden: 2017.

Kämmerer, Thomas R. *Šimâ milka. Induktion und Reception der mittelbabylonischen Dichtung von Ugarit, Emār und Tell el-'Amarna*. AOAT 251. Münster: 1998.

Klein, Jacob. 'The "Bane" of Humanity: A Lifespan of One Hundred Twenty Years'. *ASJ* 12 (1990): 57–70.

---

[38] For comparative studies of the LBA Syro-Palestinian wisdom literature and the biblical and extra-biblical texts of the first millennium BCE, see, e.g., nn. 10, 18, 19, 24, 27, 30, 35. In most of these studies, the transmission from earlier to later works is not discussed but rather their shared empirical model and the usage of closely resembling similes.

The Ballad about Early Rulers: Eastern and Western Traditions'. Pages 203–216 in *Languages and Cultures in Contact: At the Crossroads of Civilizations in the Syro-Mesopotamian Realm. Proceedings of the 42th RAI*. Edited by Karel van Lerberghe and Gabriela Voet. OLA 96. Leuven: 1999.

Lambert, Wilfred G. *Babylonian Wisdom Literature*. Oxford: 1960.

Niehr, Herbert. 'Weisheit in den Königsepen aus Ugarit'. Pages 70–91 in *Teaching Morality in Antiquity*. Edited by Takayoshi M. Oshima. ORA 29. Tübingen: 2018.

Rutz, Matthew T. *Bodies of Knowledge in Ancient Mesopotamia: The Diviners of Late Bronze Age Emar and Their Tablet Collection*. AMD 9. Leiden: 2013.

Viano, Maurizio. *The Reception of Sumerian Literature in the Western Periphery*. Antichistica 9/Studi Orientali 4. Venice: 2016.

19 Mesopotamian Wisdom

PAUL-ALAIN BEAULIEU

Wisdom is not a native category in Mesopotamian literature. The Akkadian word for wisdom is *nēmequ* (Sumerian, nam-kù-zu), which also means 'skill, knowledge, intelligence', and the adjective for 'wise' is *emqu*. Wisdom was above all considered a skill. Akkadian has several words describing qualities related to *nēmequ*, most importantly *ḫasīsu* 'intelligence, wisdom, sagacity' (*ḫassu, ḫāsisu* 'intelligent, learned, wise'), *itpešu* ('expert, competent'), *mūdû* ('knowledgeable').[1] The word *nēmequ* occurs infrequently in wisdom texts. However, the god Marduk, the supreme god of Babylon, is called 'lord of wisdom' in one of the most important works of Mesopotamian literature, *Ludlul bēl nēmeqi* ('Let me praise the lord of wisdom'). Along with the gods, Mesopotamia had a tradition of sages and wise men called *apkallu* and *ummânu*. The term *apkallu* applied mostly to antediluvian sages who taught humans the arts of civilisation, raising them from their primitive state. They lived in the transcendental realm. The god Marduk was *apkal ilī* ('the sage of the gods'). The term *ummânu* ('skilled expert') referred mostly to craftsmen. Eventually it acquired the meaning of 'scholar' because scholars mastered the scribal craft. A tradition of historical scholars and royal advisors called *ummânu* emerged in the late second millennium, among them Saggil-kīna-ubbib, who wrote the Babylonian Theodicy, a major piece of wisdom literature and one of the few Mesopotamian literary compositions with a named author.

The fact that there is no emic category of wisdom literature in Mesopotamia means that the definition of that corpus rests on our own perceptions and that its boundaries are therefore fluid. While a core of texts, such as *Ludlul* and the Babylonian Theodicy, is by common accord readily ascribed to wisdom, others remain open to discussion. In fact, several compositions that we do not habitually think

---

[1] List of words and discussion in Sara Denning-Bolle, *Wisdom in Akkadian Literature: Expression, Instruction, Dialogue* (Leiden, 1992), 32–38.

of as wisdom literature could be included in that group. Gilgameš illustrates this ambiguity. The opening verses of the Standard Babylonian version hail Gilgameš as 'he who grasped all wisdom' (I, 6. [napḫ]ar nēmeqi ša kalāmi i[ḫuz]). There is no doubt that Gilgameš offers a deep reflection on the human condition. Nevertheless, we usually classify Gilgameš as an epic, although there is no such word in Akkadian or Sumerian and no indication that a literary category akin to 'epic' existed in Mesopotamia. Therefore, the definition of Mesopotamian wisdom literature still depends largely, but not solely, on parallels with biblical literature, where wisdom, ḥokmāh, defines a specific corpus.[2] Yet, ḥokmāh is not a close synonym of nēmequ or of Egyptian ma'at, reflecting the fact that the concept of wisdom in these neighbouring and interdependent civilisations rested on different foundations. At the same time, it is obvious that many of the same themes run through the wisdom literatures of Mesopotamia, Egypt and ancient Israel. In Mesopotamia, these themes are addressed mainly in texts that reflect on the human predicament (theodicy, 'pious sufferer' compositions, the futility of life) or in distinctive literary genres with didactic aim such as proverbs, precepts and admonitions, instructions, disputations and debates.

Although the existence of wisdom compositions was already recognised in the early days of Assyriology, the first comprehensive study devoted to the subject, J. J. A. van Dijk's *La sagesse suméro-akkadienne*, did not appear until 1953. Van Dijk focused on the early wisdom literature, preserved in the Sumerian language. He defined ancient wisdom as an 'aesthetic' position, the fostering of good and proper conduct, stressing the importance of gods and antediluvian culture bringers in the transmission of such notions to humanity. Wisdom literature was taught in schools, the *edubba*, where apprentices received their training from master scribes who made them fully civilised, reiterating the upbringing of primal humans at the beginning of time. Van Dijk also established the categories of Sumerian wisdom, paying specific attention to disputations, a genre he was the first to describe in detail. W. G. Lambert's *Babylonian Wisdom Literature* appeared in 1960. Somewhat paradoxically, Lambert started his book with the disclaimer that 'wisdom is strictly a misnomer as applied to Babylonian literature'. However, he retained the label as a convenient category to discuss texts which correspond in subject matter to the Hebrew wisdom books. Like Van Dijk, he considered that wisdom covered the same domain that we,

---

[2] However, this traditional view is now being challenged, including in several contributions to this volume.

in the footsteps of the Greeks, call philosophy. With his monumental study, which includes meticulous editions of all wisdom texts in the Akkadian language known at that time, Lambert set high standards of excellence in philological inquiry that have remained a model to this day.

Since the publications of van Dijk and Lambert, the corpus of Sumerian literature has grown almost exponentially. We now have modern editions of almost all Sumerian compositions studied in Old Babylonian schools (eighteenth century BCE).[3] On the Akkadian side, the progress has been less spectacular, yet the discovery of new manuscripts has filled important gaps in such works as *Ludlul*. Previously unknown texts have also been identified. At the same time, the question as to how to define wisdom literature has remained open, even as the term continues to be used frequently, if defensively. In his *Wisdom of Ancient Sumer* (published 2005), which includes editions of several important texts, B. Alster defines wisdom as 'an existential attitude rather than a genre description', while he nevertheless also states that 'wisdom is retained as a useful label'. For him 'cleverness and insight into human life' should be considered decisive features of wisdom texts (p. 24). A more confident positivist approach is adopted by Y. Cohen in his *Wisdom from the Late Bronze Age* (published 2013). He recommends 'an intuitive understanding of wisdom literature based on common humanistic traditions; this will suffice to allow readers to recognize elements current in ancient Near Eastern literature that mark out certain compositions as wisdom literature, even if on a provisional basis' (p. 16). Cohen also insists on the need to contextualise wisdom texts to understand their place in the literary traditions of the ancient Near East. This seems preferable to the minimalist approach. The fact that Sumerian and Akkadian lack a specific designation for 'wisdom literature' does not invalidate the use of the category as analytical tool. Indeed, they also do not have a word for 'literature', but nobody would seriously claim on that basis that the category 'literature' does not apply to Mesopotamian writings. Therefore, I include here under the label 'wisdom' most compositions which are traditionally or by common agreement subsumed under this category, either for reason of their didactic content or because their main purpose is to address philosophical and existential issues common to all humanity.

---

[3] Preliminary editions are available on the ETCSL Web Site (Electronic Text Corpus of Sumerian literature).

Before reviewing the various genres, it may be useful to say a few words on the geographic and chronological range of Mesopotamian wisdom. The earliest known manuscripts come from Abu Ṣalābikh near Nippur and date to ca. 2600; the latest ones from the libraries of the Seleucid and Parthian periods (third–first centuries). The geographic spread is wide since we find them not only in Mesopotamia proper but also in the Levant (Ugarit, Emar), Anatolia (Hattuša) and southwestern Iran (Susa). Thus, the temporal and geographic range of Mesopotamian wisdom texts is roughly the same as that of cuneiform writing itself. Their distribution, however, is uneven. Most of the Sumerian literature is known from manuscripts found in the scribal schools (*edubba*) of Nippur and Ur and dates to the latter part of the eighteenth century, at a time when Sumerian had ceased to be spoken but still retained prestige as language of schooling. In most cases, we can only make guesses at the actual time of composition of these texts. The transition to the Middle Babylonian period witnessed the loss of the larger part of the Sumerian corpus. The compositions which survived were often provided with intra-linear Akkadian translations. Wisdom literature in Akkadian emerged slowly, with few examples from the eighteenth century. The libraries of Emar and Ugarit (thirteenth–twelfth centuries) preserve compositions which still show a strong dependence on Sumerian models, most of them being translations and adaptations. The great creative period of Babylonian wisdom literature in Akkadian must be placed during the late Kassite and Isin II Dynasties (fourteenth–eleventh centuries), possibly extending into the early part of the first millennium. However, except for a few examples from Assur (thirteenth–twelfth centuries), that literature is preserved primarily in first millennium libraries from Assyria (Nineveh, Sultantepe, Assur) and Babylonia (Babylon, Sippar, Uruk). All these texts were written in Standard Babylonian, a literary form of Akkadian which emerged during the Middle Babylonian period and remained in use until the later part of the first millennium. Aramaic eventually replaced Akkadian as the everyday language of Mesopotamia and by the Hellenistic period Akkadian had probably become, like Sumerian, a strictly written language. With it died the cuneiform writing system, whose very last examples come from the first century of our era.

We must also briefly consider the style and format of wisdom compositions. Most are written in verse and display typical features of poetry such as metre, caesura, alliteration, parallelism and repetition. Others, like proverbs and instructions, are organised in short sentences or statements espousing a rhythmic structure that would have aided memorisation. Many wisdom compositions adopt the form of dialogues (disputations, debates) or monologues (instructions, admonitions). Thus, although these texts were scribal creations, their structure reflects the predominantly oral nature of that society, one in which knowledge, and thereby wisdom, were transmitted mainly by word of mouth. In Greece, a similar phenomenon is evident in the writings of Plato, which are also mostly in the form of dialogues and mirror the belief that truth emerges more clearly from debate than from reading or individual reflection. Mesopotamian debates and disputations, however, do not exhibit the dialectical method of Socratic dialogues. They differ completely from the latter, both in the manner of argumentation and the topics treated.

DISPUTATIONS

Disputations rank as one of the most original literary creations of Mesopotamia. All manuscripts of Sumerian disputations date to the late eighteenth century and come from the finds at Nippur and Ur. Six such compositions have come to light, and the large number of extant manuscripts allows us to reconstruct them almost completely. Disputations oppose two non-human contestants boasting about their merits and value for society. We have disputations opposing Hoe and Plow, Ewe and Grain, Summer and Winter, Tree and Reed, Bird and Fish, Silver and Copper. They range in length between ca. 200 to 300 verses each and display a rigid tripartite structure. All except one begin with a mythological introduction which explains how the two contestants came into being when the gods created the world. This is followed by the disputation proper. The concluding part consists of the declaration of the winner by a god, although in Bird and Fish and Tree and Reed the adjudicator is Šulgi, the second ruler of the Third Dynasty of Ur (r. ca. 2094–2047). Adjudication by a king seems natural since early Mesopotamian rulers, Šulgi included, were often deified. This might also indicate that the disputations were composed or at least edited in their final form during the rule of that dynasty; two more of its rulers, Ur-Namma and Ibbi-Sîn, are mentioned in them. Sumerian disputations are the only wisdom genre with a native name. They are designated in their subscriptions as *adamin* 'contest'. However, the rubric *adamin* also describes two poems (often described as 'epics') narrating conflicts between Enmerkar, the lord of Uruk, and his opponent the lord of Aratta, yet they lack the tripartite structure of disputations. The word *adamin* also refers to the composition Dumuzi and

Enkimdu, which opposes these gods (a shepherd and a farmer) as prospective grooms for the goddess Inanna. However, this text has a different structure and purpose and is further qualified as *balbale* (unclear meaning) in its subscription. Some evidence suggests that *adamin*s were performed as plays in the context of rituals or court entertainment.

Disputations are not dialectical, they are eristic. There is no attempt to reason each contestant's claims, no apparent logical progression towards a conclusion, and the adjudication rests solely on arguments of authority. For example, Bird and Fish begins with a mythological introduction describing how the god Enki created the land and endowed it with pastures and animals, founded cities, allowed humans to multiply and provided them with the institution of kingship.[4] Then he created the marshland of southern Iraq and brought Bird and Fish into being to populate them. The conflict erupts as they both nest among the reed beds. There follow heated exchanges where each extols its own attributes (e.g., Bird sings, has beautiful plumage; Fish provides food for people and gods) while hurling insults at the other (Fish stinks; Bird scatters its droppings). Things finally get out of hand when, in a passage reminiscent of animal fables, Fish destroys Bird's nest and smashes its eggs, while Bird retaliates, snatching Fish's spawn from the water. King Šulgi resolves the debate: 'I shall instruct you in the divine rules and just ordinances of our dwelling-place. Like the god Enki, I am successful in finding solutions, and am wise in words.' Bird is declared the winner because it takes precedence in the temple of the god Enlil and provides rejoicing in the king's palace. The ontological basis of disputations is clear. They revolve around the order of things willed by the gods at the beginning of time, and after the debate has run through all the qualities and defects of the contestants, the text comes full circle to a god or god-like king who declares the winner. Therefore, the contestants argue about the nature bestowed on them at creation, their 'fate' in the Mesopotamian terminology (Sumerian nam-tar, Akkadian *šīmtu*), and the texts demonstrate how divine wisdom manifests itself in the world.[5]

Sumerian disputations vanished after the Old Babylonian period, but the genre itself lived on in Akkadian literature. Unfortunately,

---

[4] The disputation Bird and Fish is available in translation in Jeremy Black et al., *The Literature of Ancient Sumer* (Oxford, 2004), 230–235.

[5] For a penetrating analysis of disputations along the lines proposed here, see Jean Bottéro, 'La "tenson" et la réflexion sur les choses en Mésopotamie', in *Dispute Poems and Dialogues in the Ancient and Mediaeval Near East*, ed. G. J. Reinink and Herman L. J. Vanstiphout, OLA 41 (Leuven, 1991), 7–22.

while Sumerian disputations are well preserved thanks to large numbers of manuscripts, Akkadian ones have come down to us in a highly fragmentary state. Eight Akkadian disputations have been identified thus far: Tamarisk and Date Palm, the Series of the Fox, the Series of Ox and Horse, the Series of the Poplar, the Series of the Spider, Palm and Vine, the Donkey Disputation, Nissaba and Wheat and the Story of the Poor Forlorn Wren.[6] The term 'Series' reflects a native designation (iškāru) for compositions or compilations with standardised editions. Thus, the Epic of Gilgameš was known as the Series of Gilgameš (iškār Gilgameš) but also by its first words ša nagba īmuru ('He who saw the depth') (this was the customary way to refer to works of literature and scholarship). Of these eight disputations, only Tamarisk and Date Palm is attested by Old Babylonian manuscripts (two in Akkadian from Tell Harmal, ancient Šaduppûm, near Baghdad, and one of them in Sumerian from Susa, probably a translation from the original Akkadian). It also made it into the Syro-Mesopotamian corpus of the late Bronze Age, being attested at Emar; other manuscripts come from Assur and date to the late second millennium. Other Akkadian disputations are known mainly from first millennium copies, some datable as late as the Seleuco-Parthian period. However, they may well have been composed earlier. No fewer than three of them came with attributions of authorship in a late catalogue: the Series of the Fox to Ibni-Marduk, son of Ludumununna, a scholar (ummânu) from Nippur; the Series of the Poplar to Ur-Nanna, the exorcist (āšipu), a scholar from Babylon; and the Series of the Spider to a son of Šumu-libši, a lamentation priest (kalû) and scholar from Eridu. Ludumununna, Ur-Nanna and Šumu-libši are attested as family names in the second and first millennium, but these specific individuals cannot be traced in the extant documentation. As always with ancient claims of authorship, these attributions might be spurious.

Some Akkadian disputations adhere closely to the agonistic model of Sumerian adamins. This is clear for Tamarisk and Date Palm, as well as Palm and Vine. Others display a more complex structure. The Series of the Fox, for instance, is a hybrid of disputation and animal fable with a mixture of narrative sections and debates. It also involves at least three contestants: a fox, a dog and a wolf. The Series of the Fox was the most popular Akkadian disputation, with over thirty manuscripts

---

[6] The most recent discussion is by Enrique Jiménez, *The Babylonian Disputation Poems: With Editions of the Series of the Poplar, Palm and Vine, the Series of the Spider, and the Story of the Poor, Forlorn Wren*, CHANE 87 (Leiden; Boston, 2017).

from Assyria and Babylonia and one late Bronze Age manuscript from Ugarit. It is also the longest one, with ca. 300 lines preserved and a possible original length of over 1,500 verses, which, if these calculations prove right, would make it one of the longest compositions in the Akkadian language (Gilgameš, the longest one by far, totalled ca. 3,000 verses). The social and scribal context of Akkadian disputations appears to have been different from the Sumerian *adamins*, which clearly served for rhetorical training in the Old Babylonian schools. By contrast, the Series of the Fox is the only Akkadian disputation known to have been copied on elementary school tablets in the first millennium. In his recent study of the genre, E. Jiménez has stressed their significant level of intertextuality with masterworks of Akkadian literature, including Gilgameš and the Babylonian Theodicy, but also *Ludlul* and the Myth of Etana. He argues that they originated as parodies of high literature, legitimising it by creating critical distance while insisting on its preservation. The genre of Mesopotamian disputations survived the demise of the civilisation that created it and was transmitted to later literatures of the Middle East, with examples in Syriac, Persian and Arabic, and eventually reached Medieval Europe in the form of the *tenson* of Provençal troubadours.

PROVERBS AND FABLES

Proverbs are a trans-cultural phenomenon, and one well attested in Mesopotamia both as literary genre and living rhetorical device. Proverbs are short, elliptical statements which encapsulate a verity about human behaviour, often by means of metaphor, allegory or other allusive imagery. Mesopotamian proverbs share these broad characteristics. They can also make use of stylistic devices such as parallelism, alliteration and assonance. Old Babylonian schools, mostly at Nippur and Ur, have yielded a large number of manuscripts with groups of Sumerian proverbs. No fewer than 28 groups have been identified, ranging from a few entries to nearly 200 for the larger ones (Collections 1 and 3).[7] Like most Sumerian literature, these manuscripts come from a period when Sumerian had ceased to be spoken, and therefore these proverbs no longer existed as living utterances but were still used as educational tools, their school setting often enhanced by

---

[7] The standard edition is Bendt Alster, *Proverbs of Ancient Sumer*, 2 vols. (Bethesda, 1997). The proverbs quoted below refer to this edition (e.g., 1.66 means Collection 1, Entry no. 66).

their organisation according to keywords in imitation of lexical lists. There is no doubt, however, that Sumerian proverbs reflect an inherited traditional wisdom. While the term 'proverb collections' has generally been accepted by scholars, many entries do not fit easily under this label, being closer to adages, aphorisms, maxims and other traditional sayings. Proverbs sometimes remain obscure to us, either due to our deficient knowledge of Sumerian grammar and rhetoric, or simply because we just don't grasp their social or cultural context. However, some can be unambiguously understood, and a few even find modern parallels. Thus, 'In the city of the lame, the halt are couriers' (1.66 and 2.119) corresponds to 'In the land of the blind, the one-eyed man is king'; and 'In the city without a dog, the fox is overseer' (1.65 and 2.118) seems equivalent to 'When the cat's away, the mice will play'. Other examples come closer to instructions and admonitions: 'He who eats too much cannot sleep' (1.103) or 'Never a thought has given birth to hatred, only speech has given birth to hatred' (1.105).

Second and first millennium libraries have also produced bilingual Sumerian-Akkadian proverb collections. Many of them adapt unilingual Sumerian proverbs from the Old Babylonian period with Akkadian translations.[8] Proverbs do not seem to have developed into a widely popular genre in Akkadian literature; few tablets inscribed with unilingual Akkadian proverbs have come down to us. Proverbs may have been confined mostly to oral transmission. At the same time, however, we have examples of Akkadian and bilingual Akkadian-Hittite proverbs from Hattuša and an Akkadian-Hurrian bilingual tablet with proverbs from Ugarit, all dating to the late Bronze Age.[9] Starting with the Old Babylonian period, the epistolary genre underwent considerable development in Akkadian. Thousands of letters have been discovered in various contexts. Some of them quote proverbs and sayings.[10] A well-known example warns the king of Mari (eighteenth century) against the treacherous peace offerings of the king of Ešnunna: 'Beneath the straw, water runs', commonly taken to mean that appearances can be deceptive, but the saying might have the intentional ambiguity of a Delphic oracle since it was uttered by a prophetess in a temple. Akkadian has a

---

[8]   These are edited by Wilfred George Lambert, *Babylonian Wisdom Literature* (Oxford, 1960), 213–282. Select translations by Benjamin R. Foster, *Before the Muses: An Anthology of Akkadian Literature*, 3rd ed. (Bethesda, 2005), 422–433.

[9]   Edition by Yoram Cohen, *Wisdom from the Late Bronze Age*, SBL-WAW 29 (Atlanta, 2013), 199–211.

[10] Edition and discussion of proverbs quoted in letters by Cohen, *Wisdom from the Late Bronze Age*, 213–231.

specific word for 'proverb', *tēltum*, which can introduce a traditional saying in a letter, as another example from Mari illustrates: 'As the proverb goes (*kīma ša tēltim*): 'When fire consumes a reed, do its two companions stay silent?', that is to say, trouble spreads quickly. Similarly, a letter from the Assyrian king Esarhaddon (seventh century) to a group he calls the 'non-Babylonians' begins by quoting a proverb: 'It is said in a popular proverb (*ina tēlti ša pī niši*): "The potter's dog, when it enters the kiln, barks at the potter."' Remarkably, this proverb resurfaces in the Ahiqar tradition in a more explicit form: we learn that the dog entered the kiln to warm himself. The proverb highlights the ingratitude of subordinates and the perils of showing compassion to the wicked.[11]

Animals occur frequently in proverbs and two Sumerian collections are wholly devoted to them (Collections 5 and 8).[12] Among these we also find short fables such as The Lion and the She-Goat (5.55): a lion captures a she-goat and she promises him a ewe if he lets her go, whereupon the lion agrees if the goat tells him her name, which is revealed as I-am-cleverer-than-you, and when the lion comes later to the fold to claim his prize, she tells him 'You released me, how clever you were, but the sheep do not reside here!'. This fable would easily find a home in the Aesopic collections, and the Greek claim of Aesop's Phrygian origin points to the Near East as the initial locus of this literary form. Similar fables include Nine Wolves and a Fox (5.A.71 and 5.B.72) and The Fox who Demanded Horns of Enlil (8.B.20). While proverbs, fables and disputations share certain motifs, one important distinction must be borne in mind: in proverbs and fables, animals stand metaphorically for humans, but this is not really the matter of disputations. However, occasionally the three genres could be mixed in the same composition. Such is the Sumerian fable of The Heron and the Turtle, which exhibits features of folk tales, fables, myths and disputations.[13] Classification is problematic in this case; even though more than 200 lines are preserved, the second half of what we have is fragmentary and difficult to follow and the end of the composition is lost altogether.

---

[11] Edition and discussion of these in Lambert, *Wisdom Literature*, 281.
[12] These fables are also edited separately by Bendt Alster, *Wisdom of Ancient Sumer* (Bethesda, 2005), 342–367.
[13] Translation with brief introduction by Black et al., *Literature*, 235–240.

INSTRUCTIONS AND ADMONITIONS

Instructions and admonitions exemplify the didactic method: a person in a position of authority delivers a speech to instil proper conduct in the recipient of the teaching. The Instructions of Šuruppak are the most important such composition from Mesopotamia, adding up to nearly 300 lines.[14] The text can be reconstructed with minor gaps. These instructions enjoyed great circulation in early scribal schools. Manuscripts from Abu-Ṣalābikh (ca. 2600) and Adab (ca. 2500) attest to the existence of early versions, and many Old Babylonian manuscripts (eighteenth century) turned up at Nippur and Ur with the Standard Version. All these are in Sumerian. We also have fragments of translations into Akkadian from the late second millennium and an Akkado-Hurrian bilingual translation probably from Emar. The text seems to have fallen into oblivion in the first millennium. The Instructions follow the father-to-son pattern. The name of the father is Šuruppak, son of Ubar-Tutu. The latter was known traditionally as the last ruler before the flood; he was king of Šuruppak, one of the antediluvian cities. In the Instructions, the name of the sage Šuruppak is written like the name of the city (with the determinative for geographical names); therefore, one could understand his name as '(the man from) Šuruppak', although this is never made more explicit in any manuscript. In the Standard Version, the name of his son is Ziusudra. The latter is the well-known flood hero who appears under his Akkadian name Utnapištim in the Akkadian Epic of Gilgameš, but his Sumerian name resurfaces in the Hellenistic period in the writings of Berossus, who names the flood hero Xisouthros. The passing of instructions from Šuruppak to Ziusudra exemplifies the survival of antediluvian knowledge essential to the re-establishment of civilisation after humanity had been nearly wiped out. In Berossus, this is accomplished by the burying of tablets at Sippar to be rediscovered by the flood survivors. In the Instructions of Šuruppak, the transmission of knowledge is oral. The text can be divided into three parts, introduced each time by the names of the protagonists. Brevity rules and few counsels reach more than a couple of lines, although many are connected thematically to form larger units. The counsels seem mostly practical, emphasising the importance of cautious social behaviour: 'Don't loiter about where there

---

[14] Edition with extensive discussion and commentary by Alster, *Wisdom of Ancient Sumer*, 31–220.

is a quarrel! (line 22); Don't curse with violent intent; it will turn back on you! (line 50); The slanderer moves his eyes (quickly) like a spindle. (line 65).' Many proverbs and proverbial statements found their way in the Instructions of Šuruppak and the two genres are often difficult to distinguish, except that instructions are sometimes attributed to a sage while proverb collections are always anonymous. One notes in the Instructions of Šuruppak the near complete absence of the gods. Also, the text pays no attention to rulership and state administration, a perplexing omission given the presumed royal status of the main characters, but the mythical-historical framework may just be a pretext to display age-old wisdom for everyman.

Divine and royal focus surface, however, in the Instructions of Ur-Ninurta.[15] Few manuscripts of these instructions are known, all are Old Babylonian except one Middle Babylonian example. The most important copy was discovered at Tell Harmal near Baghdad. The composition is relatively short, seventy-one lines in total. The opening lines set these instructions in primeval times 'after the flood had swept over (the land)' (line 4). The name of the teacher is uncertain, possibly the god Ninurta of Nippur, lord of the Ešumeša temple. The purpose of the instructions is to ascertain the rule of king Ur-Ninurta of Isin (ca. 1923–1896): 'in order to consolidate the foundation of Ur-Ninurta's shepherd[ship]' (line 11). The first half of the text consists of advice on how to lead a pious life and is summed up as 'these are instructions of a god' (line 37). The counsels are often elaborate, running over several lines; for instance, lines 19–29 explain that the man who performs the rituals and respects his god will earn a long life and his descendants will make libations for him after his death. The second half consists mostly of agricultural advice summed up as 'instructions of a farmer' (line 64). This segment recalls another set of Sumerian instructions, the Farmer's Instructions, delivered by a man called Ud-ul-uru ('Old-Man-Farmer') to his son but also claimed at the end to be 'Instructions of the god Ninurta, the son of the god Enlil'.[16] However, these instructions are clearly technical and for that reason are habitually excluded from discussions of wisdom literature. The Instructions of Ur-Ninurta conclude with an injunction to be submissive to royal authority. The text is preserved on two large manuscripts (*Sammeltafel*) together with a series

---

[15] Edition with commentary by Alster, *Wisdom of Ancient Sumer*, 227–240.

[16] Edition by Miguel Civil, *The Farmer's Instructions: A Sumerian Agricultural Manual*, *AuOr* Sup. 5 (Sabadell, 1994); the total line count is 109.

of poorly preserved Counsels of Wisdom whose introduction and historical setting are lost.[17]

This tradition of Sumerian instructions continued in the Akkadian language. Among the rich epigraphic finds of the northern Levantine port city of Ugarit, one notes the Instructions of Šūpê-amēli to his son.[18] The composition was known in Antiquity by its incipit line *šimâ milka* ('Hear the advice'), mentioned in an Old Babylonian literary catalogue. However, extant manuscripts of the composition exist only from the Middle Babylonian period and outside Mesopotamia. In addition to Ugarit, fragments were discovered at Emar and a bilingual Akkadian-Hittite version is known from a tablet found at Hattuša. The text included up to 150 lines originally, but the manuscripts preserve only parts of the composition. First millennium libraries attest to the continuation of the genre of instructions.[19] Some of these counsels adapt or repeat verbatim those found in Sumerian collections and still follow the father-to-son model. Aramaic began to replace Akkadian as the vehicular language during the Neo-Assyrian Empire. The tradition of instructions continued in Aramaic in the story of Ahiqar, a high official at the Assyrian court. The narrative about his fall and reinstatement frames a series of instructions to his ungrateful nephew whom he had adopted as a son. The last instructions composed in Akkadian are known as Advice to a Prince. Couched in the form of omens texts, these admonitions, unlike most previous instructions from Mesopotamia, concern the realm of politics and statecraft exclusively: for example, 'If the king has no regard for due process, his people will be thrown into chaos (and) his land will be devastated'. They are known from eighth- and seventh-century manuscripts discovered at Nippur and Nineveh.[20] In the category of instructions and admonitions, we may add a literary hymn to the god Šamaš which Lambert edited in his *Babylonian Wisdom Literature* under the label 'preceptive hymn'.[21] The text is known in several first millennium manuscripts, mostly from Assyria, but reflects an earlier, possibly late second millennium Babylonian creation. Šamaš, in his quality as sun god, presided over justice, and

---

[17] Edition and discussion by Alster, *Wisdom of Ancient Sumer*, 241–264.

[18] Edition and discussion by Cohen, *Wisdom from the Late Bronze Age*, 81–128; translation by Foster, *Before the Muses*, 416–421.

[19] Edition of the Counsels of Wisdom by Lambert, *Wisdom Literature*, 96–107; translation by Foster, *Before the Muses*, 412–415 ('Words of the Wise').

[20] Translation by Foster, *Before the Muses*, 867–869.

[21] Edition by Lambert, *Wisdom Literature*, 121–138; translation by Foster, *Muses*, 627–635.

accordingly, unlike other hymns to deities, this long composition (200 lines) offers many moral precepts and admonitions commending rightful conduct. Because of this, it seems justified to include it within the category of wisdom, although the hymn ends with poorly preserved directives which seem to imply a cultic setting.

THEODICY AND THE PIOUS SUFFERER

Texts addressing the problem of theodicy have elicited much interest because of their perceived affinities with the Book of Job. It is Leibniz who coined the term theodicy in his 1710 book *Essais de Théodicée sur la bonté de Dieu, la liberté de l'homme et l'origine du mal* ('Essays of Theodicy on the Goodness of God, the Freedom of Man and the Origin of Evil'). Theodicy, in its classical expression, addresses the problem of evil: how can a god who is omnipotent and infinitely good tolerate the existence of evil in his own creation? In the Mesopotamian view, the problem is cast differently. The treatment of theodicy focuses on the relationship between god and worshipper and the predicament of individual divine retribution. The earliest treatment of the Pious Sufferer motif occurs in the Sumerian composition Man and his God, known from a few Old Babylonian manuscripts from Nippur.[22] The first line is also quoted in a contemporary Sumerian literary catalogue. Thus, it was a well-known literary composition, albeit not an excessively popular one. The text includes ca. 143 verses with some gaps. The sufferer and his god are never named, but the drama takes place among the learned classes: 'I, the young man, the learned one, my knowledge is of no avail to me' (line 28). The first half of the text details the symptoms of the suffering: the worshipper finds himself ostracised socially and soon disease and depression afflict him (lines 1–81). He confesses his guilt and begs for divine forgiveness (lines 82–119), and then the god accepts his prayers, erases the disease from his body and provides him with favourable protective spirits to ensure his social reintegration and feeling of joy in life (lines 120–132). The text ends with the worshipper's praise of his god (lines 133–143). The term 'Just Sufferer' has often been applied to such compositions. However, several scholars have pointed out that Mesopotamian sufferers readily admit their guilt, although

[22] Edition by Johannes J. A. van Dijk, *La sagesse suméro-akkadienne* (Leiden, 1953), 119–134; English translation by Jacob Klein in William W. Hallo and Lawson R. Younger, eds., *Context of Scripture: Canonical Compositions from the Biblical World, Volume 1* (Leiden, 2003), 573–575.

they usually confess not knowing the nature of their offence. In fact, a specific fault is never named, only guessed at, and thus the source of divine displeasure, albeit real and justified, cannot be truly articulated. This does not preclude the existence of sin, be it cultic or moral. The purpose of Pious Sufferer compositions is to illustrate the abject dependence of humans on the gods whose will is unfathomable and seemingly capricious. The same view is expressed in countless prayers, penitential psalms and letters to the gods (letter-prayers) and pervades the entire historical and literary record of ancient Mesopotamia. The only answer is blind faith in the gods.

The genre of the Pious Sufferer continued to develop in Akkadian. The Old-Babylonian composition Man and his God, known from a manuscript datable to the seventeenth century, is poorly preserved, very challenging linguistically and runs up to about seventy lines.[23] The structure closely parallels that of its Sumerian counterpart and expounds similar ideas. A late second millennium manuscript from Ugarit preserves only about forty-five lines of a composition sometimes called A Sufferer's Salvation. The god who punishes and forgives the sufferer is no longer an anonymous personal deity but the god Marduk, who is praised in a long passage extolling his power and compassion.[24] A Sufferer's Salvation thus provides a strong parallel to Ludlul bēl nēmeqi and may ultimately derive from it or from a common source. Ludlul, known exclusively from first millennium manuscripts, contains the most elaborate and sophisticated exposition of the Pious Sufferer motif. It was divided into four tablets of 120 lines each, for a total of 480 verses. Only Tablets I and II are nearly complete, with III and IV still marred by important gaps; however, a recent assessment by T. Oshima assumes a longer composition in five tablets with more substantial gaps than previously thought.[25] Contrary to its predecessors, Ludlul gives precise information on its social, personal and historical context. The sufferer is a certain Šubši-mešrê-Šakkan. According to the poem, he is a man of high station, a Babylonian courtier. His name, which means

[23] Translations by Foster in Before the Muses, 148–150 ('Dialogue Between a Man and his God'); and in Hallo and Younger, Context of Scripture, 485.

[24] Edition by Cohen, Wisdom from the Late Bronze Age, 165–175; translations by Foster in Before the Muses, 410–411; and in Hallo and Younger, Context of Scripture, 486.

[25] Recent editions by Amar Annus and Alan Lenzi, Ludlul bēl nēmeqi: The Standard Babylonian Poem of the Righteous Sufferer, SAACT VII (Helsinki, 2010); and by Takayoshi Oshima, Babylonian Poems of Pious Sufferers: Ludlul bēl nēmeqi and the Babylonian Theodicy (Tübingen, 2014); translations by Foster in Before the Muses, 392–409; and in Hallo and Younger, Context of Scripture, 486–492.

'Create wealth, O god Šakkan!', is unusual and belongs to an extremely rare type. This has encouraged his identification with a high official of the same name who appears in two administrative texts dated to the reign of the Kassite king Nazi-Maruttaš (ca. 1307–1282), who is in fact probably mentioned in a damaged line of the poem. While most scholars assume that this official is the protagonist of *Ludlul*, he is not necessarily its author. Its date of composition should be placed in the thirteenth or twelfth centuries. This is further suggested by the overwhelming presence of the god Marduk, who rose to undisputed prominence at that time in Babylonia, becoming the god who created the world and the focus of personal piety and hope for salvation.

The first segment of the poem (I, 1–36) eulogises the paradoxical nature of Marduk, a god who is furious and relenting, punishes and saves, inflicts diseases and heals. The protagonist will experience this dual nature of the god. After the introductory hymn, the poem moves to a description of the sufferer's symptoms: social rejection, feelings of loneliness, depression, frightening dreams and portents, bodily ailments, diseases. However, they receive in *Ludlul* a more elaborate treatment than in previous examples of the genre. In Tablet III, the Sufferer receives successive dreams which herald his healing. In the last dream, he is visited by an exorcist named Ur-Nintinugga, coiffed with a tiara and carrying a writing-board; he is sent by the god Marduk to bring him a cure. The name Ur-Nintinugga is typical of the contrived Sumerian of Babylonian intellectuals and its meaning, 'Servant of the goddess Nintinugga', emblematises his craft. Nintinugga, a form of the medicine goddess Gula, means 'the mistress who revives the moribund', an epithet also applied to Marduk in *Ludlul* (I, 38). The exorcist (*āšipu* or *mašmaššu*) rose to prominence during the late Kassite period to become in the first millennium the leading Mesopotamian intellectual. Although a polymath, the exorcist was first a medical specialist who healed body and soul and stood as intermediary and intercessor between his patient and the gods. Diseases being often seen as divine afflictions, the exorcist sought to redress the balance between the angry gods and his patient in addition to providing actual remedies. This is the most notable contribution of *Ludlul* to the tradition of the Pious Sufferer.[26] Tablet IV (or V according to Oshima) describes Šubši-mešrê-Šakkan

---

[26] This important aspect of the poem is discussed by Paul-Alain Beaulieu, 'The Social and Intellectual Setting of Babylonian Wisdom Literature', in *Wisdom Literature in Mesopotamia and Israel*, ed. R. J. Clifford, Society of Biblical Literature Symposium Series 36 (Atlanta, 2007), 3–19.

progressing through the gates of Esagil, the temple of Marduk in Babylon, singing the praise of the great god who initially punished but then relented and rescued him.

In light of *Ludlul*, it comes as no surprise that an exorcist should have been the author of the other great wisdom text in the Akkadian language, the Babylonian Theodicy. The Theodicy is known from several manuscripts discovered in first millennium Assyrian and Babylonian libraries.[27] It totals 297 lines with some gaps in the middle portion. The text is cast as a dialogue between the sufferer and a friend and thus comes closest to the Book of Job in terms of structure. Each speech makes a strophe, for a total of twenty-seven strophes of equal length (eleven lines each). In each strophe all lines begin with the same cuneiform sign, and these twenty-seven initial signs form an acrostic which reads as follows: *anāku Saggil-kīna-ubbib mašmaššu kāribu ili u šarri* ('I, Saggil-kīna-ubbib, the exorcist, who praises god and king'). Saggil-kīna-ubbib appears in later texts as a scholar (*ummânu*) who allegedly lived during the time of the Babylonian kings Nebuchadnezzar I (ca. 1121–1100) and Adad-apla-iddina (ca. 1063–1043), and the incipit of the Theodicy appears in a very damaged entry of a catalogue of texts and authors. His name, which means 'O Saggil temple, clear the righteous' (Saggil is a form of Esagil, the temple of Marduk in Babylon), seems programmatic in the context of the Pious Sufferer tradition. Although one can always suspect pseudepigraphy, it seems reasonable to assume that the exorcist Saggil-kīna-ubbib was the actual author of the Theodicy. However, nowhere is it stated in the composition that he should be identified as any of the two protagonists. It contains no explicit clue as to its historical, temporal or social setting, and maintains the debate at an abstract level, which is in and of itself an innovation for that genre. While the sufferer voices some personal complaints, mostly of a social nature, the dialogue centres on general considerations on the unfairness of life. Why is it that the gods seem to favour the dishonest, while fate persecutes the righteous and god-fearing? The friend tries to soothe the sceptical sufferer and offers advice that conforms to the traditional Mesopotamian view: the purpose of the gods is unfathomable, but humanity must surrender to their will and accept its fate. In his concluding speech, the friend describes the corrupt nature of humans, such as

---

[27] Recent editions by Takayoshi Oshima, *The Babylonian Theodicy*, SAACT IX (Helsinki, 2013): and by Oshima, *Babylonian Poems*; translations by Foster in *Muses*, 914–922 (the one quoted here); and in Hallo and Younger, *Context of Scripture*, 492–495.

was bestowed on them by the gods at creation: 'Enlil, king of the gods, who created teeming mankind, majestic Ea, who pinched off their clay, the queen who fashioned them, mistress Mami, gave twisted words to the human race, they endowed them in perpetuity with lies and false-hood' (lines 276–280). This is the clearest articulation of the Mesopotamian view of the origin of evil. The corrupt nature of human beings was willed by the gods at the time of creation. Therefore, it must be accepted as part of human destiny, and it explains the permanence of retributive punishment. The Babylonian Theodicy, with its reiteration and justification of the original world order, seems in this respect close to the Sumerian *adamin*s. One cannot rebel against the nature of things, which embodies fate.

THE FUTILITY OF LIFE

Such a bleak view of the human predicament could easily give rise to the notion that life itself might be worthless. Three Sumerian compos-itions address this question: Nothing is of Value, Enlil and Namzitarra and the Ballad of Early Rulers. Nothing is of Value has come down to us in Old Babylonian manuscripts from Nippur and other sites.[28] The composition seems to have been fluid and we know more than one version, yet the longest one barely exceeds twenty lines. It relishes paradox (lines 1–2): 'Nothing if of value, (but) life itself should be sweet-tasting. A man who owns nothing is (still) a man who owns something.' The first line is taken from the Instructions of Šuruppak (line 252) or a source common to both. As recognised by Alster, it enunciates the Carpe diem theme: 'seize the day', 'enjoy life while it lasts', which forms the core advice of the tavern-keeper Siduri whom Gilgameš encounters at the edge of the world in his quest for immortal-ity (X, 79–85): 'When the gods created mankind, they established death for mankind, and withheld eternal life for themselves. As for you Gilgameš, let your stomach be full, always be happy, night and day. Make everyday a delight, night and day play and dance.'[29]

The short Sumerian composition Enlil and Namzitarra is known in several Old Babylonian copies from Nippur.[30] Fragments of a bilingual (Sumerian-Akkadian) version from the Late Bronze Age were discovered

[28] Editions by Alster, *Wisdom of Ancient Sumer*, 266–287.
[29] Benjamin R. Foster, *The Epic of Gilgamesh*, 2nd ed. (New York; London, 2019), 78.
[30] Editions by Alster, *Wisdom of Ancient Sumer*, 327–338; and by Cohen, *Wisdom from the Late Bronze Age*, 151–163; translation by Black et al., *Literature*, 112–113.

at Emar and Ugarit. The text does not exceed thirty lines in its main
version, but at Emar it seems to have been expanded to include proverbial sayings. The tale seems at first amusing. Namzitarra, returning from
the temple of Enlil after his turn of duty, is accosted by the god disguised
as a raven. After a brief exchange, Namzitarra recognises Enlil who
abruptly changes the mood of the narrative and replies to the temple
servant: 'You may acquire precious metals, you may acquire precious
stones, you may acquire cattle, or you may acquire sheep; but the day of
mankind (i.e. death) is always getting closer, so where does your wealth
lead?' Then Enlil grants Namzitarra and his descendants a permanent
office in his temple. The message is clear: worship of the gods is the only
thing of lasting value. It is surprising that this composition did not
survive into the first millennium given the increasing insistence on
the worth of ancient priestly lineage in that era.

The Ballad of Early Rulers is another short composition totalling
twenty-four lines in its longest version.[31] The Old Babylonian manuscripts are few and come from northern Babylonia (Sippar and/or
Babylon). A modified bilingual (Sumerian-Akkadian) version is attested
at Ugarit and Emar (fourteenth–thirteenth centuries) and still occurs in
a single Neo-Assyrian manuscript from Nineveh (eighth–seventh century). The text laments the passing of time, recalling the existence of
former rulers with a tone of nostalgia: 'Where is Gilgameš, who, like
Ziusudra, sought the (eternal) life?' (line 11); 'Where are those kings, the
vanguards of former days?' (line 14); 'All life is an illusion' (line 18). The
bilingual version ends with an invitation to enjoy the present moment,
and the mention of the beer goddess Siraš adds to the impression that
Carpe diem is the main message of the Ballad of Early Rulers, which is
also the earliest known example of the Ubi sunt motif (cf. Baruch
3:16–19).

The Dialogue of Pessimism, an Akkadian composition known
exclusively from first millennium libraries, extends over ca. eighty-five
lines with a small gap in the middle.[32] It opposes two characters
described as master and servant. The master addresses his servant
repeatedly with proposals to engage in a specific activity: driving to
the palace, banqueting, hunting, marriage, loving a woman, leading a

---

[31] Edition by Alster, Wisdom of Ancient Sumer, 288–322; and by Cohen, Wisdom from
the Late Bronze Age, 129–150; translation by Foster, Before the Muses, 769–770 ('The
Ballad of Former Heroes').

[32] Edition by Lambert, Wisdom Literature, 139–149; translations by Foster, Muses,
923–926; and by Alasdair Livingstone in Hallo and Younger, Context of Scripture,
495–496.

rebellion, business, etc. Each time the servant endorses his master, giving a sound reason to support his decision. Then the master changes his mind and proposes the exact opposite course of action, and the servant finds an equally compelling reason to justify his change of plan. The last proposal is a philanthropic benefit for the country (distributing free rations of foods to the people), but when the master, true to himself, changes his mind, the servant approves again with a statement describing the futility of human existence that would easily find a place in the Ballad of Early Rulers: 'Do not perform (the philanthropic benefit), master, do not perform (it)! Go to the ancient mounds and walk about! See the (mixed) skulls of plebeians and nobles: who is the malefactor, and who is the benefactor?' The Dialogue ends in a non sequitur, contemplating a suicide pact and lamenting the limitations of human capabilities: 'Who is so tall as to ascend to heaven, who is so broad as to encompass the entire world?' This curious text has been the subject of conflicting interpretations, a serious philosophical piece for the majority of scholars, while others take it with a grain of salt, perhaps even a humorous composition. The Dialogue is not without evocations of the *dissoi logoi* ('pairs of arguments') of the Greek Sophists: each reasoning implies its exact opposite, reaching an absolute truth is impossible, any course of action can be good or bad depending on the person and even for the same individual, with equally convincing reasons on both sides of the argument. The *dissoi logoi* probably originate with the Sophists of the late fifth century, but the manuscript has reached us as an appendix to the works of the Pyrrhonian philosopher Sextus Empiricus. Therefore, the dialogue between the master and his servant, who acts really as his alter ego, might best be called the Dialogue of Scepticism.

SCHOOL DEBATES

Other texts are occasionally included under the label of 'wisdom': riddles, humorous tales, school debates (*edubba* literature). A text published by A. George in 2009 under the title The Scholars of Uruk makes an intriguing addition to the genre of school debates.[33] It is a bilingual composition from the late Old Babylonian period (seventeenth century) with intra-linear translation. However, it seems clear that the Sumerian version, although it is presented as the original, was translated from the Akkadian. The composition is almost complete, with 63 lines (126

---

[33] Andrew R. George, *Babylonian Literary Texts in the Schøyen Collection*, CUSAS 10 (Bethesda, 2009), 78–112.

counting both versions). The text is a long tirade by a father, who is a learned scribe, to his inept son and pupil. He berates him for neglecting scholarship and extols Nissaba, the patron goddess of writing, as the fount of wisdom: 'Nissaba it is who is a scribe, Nissaba it is who is wise (*emqet*), Nissaba it is who is the mistress of sagacity, Nissaba, the mistress of intelligence' (lines 23–24). He also praises the god Ea (Enki) who bestowed sagacity on his city and 'eternal wisdom' (*nēmequ dariu*) on his country, sending a sage (*apkallu*) with intellect (*ḫassu*) to teach the scribal art and the Sumerian language to his city, the goddess Nissaba providing the rest (lines 44–49). The text reiterates the fundamental Mesopotamian idea about wisdom. It is a skill that resides with the gods exclusively but that they have imparted to humans in primeval time either personally or through the agency of civilising heroes, the scribal art and schools being the privileged means and locus for its transmission. Recently, B. Foster and A. George published another Old Babylonian school debate, entirely in Akkadian, and probably of slightly earlier date (eighteenth century).[34] The text is recorded on a prism and possibly originates from Larsa in southern Iraq. Only part of the original text is preserved, and it originally ran over 500 short lines. The composition belongs to the father-to-son type. The name of the father is Put-Ištar, abbreviated to Putti in the speech of his son, whose name is Mannu-utarrissu, sometimes shortened to Mannu-utar by his father. Although the text begins as straightforward instructions, the father is quickly interrupted by his son who disparages learning and wisdom, and soon the debate degenerates into a series of invectives and curses. In this respect, the text bears some resemblance to The Scholars of Uruk. Interestingly, the father receives the epithet 'the sage Watar-hasis' (*apkallu Watar-ḫāsis*), a direct reference to the name of the flood hero, Atrahasis ('surpassingly intelligent'), in the Akkadian epic associated with his name. Thus, although the text seems to parody the genre of instructions, it still associates wisdom with antediluvian knowledge and sages. It also provides a welcome testimony to the development of a wisdom literature in the Akkadian language already in the eighteenth century.

CONCLUSION

To conclude, this chapter has drawn attention to the variety of Mesopotamian wisdom literature, and its remarkable longevity and

---

[34] Benjamin R. Foster and Andrew R. George, 'An Old Babylonian Dialogue between a Father and his Son', *Zeitschrift für Assyriologie* 110 (2020): 37–61.

spread in the ancient Near Eastern world and beyond. Even if scholars disagree on the definition of wisdom and the delineation of its corpus, the texts included here share certain traits and ideas that are useful to rehearse. Firstly, one notes that, by contrast with the general anonymity of Mesopotamian literature, wisdom texts are often associated with specific individuals, either as author or protagonist. Some belong to the realm of myth (e.g., Šuruppak, Šūpê-amēli), some are historical figures (e.g., Šubši-mešrê-Šakkan), while others are alleged authors (e.g., Saggil-kīna-ubbib, Ibni-Marduk). Authorship attribution became more common during the late second millennium, and it coincided with the rise of new classes of intellectuals, chiefly the *āšipu* ('exorcist') and the *kalû* ('lamentation singer'). They claimed prestigious lineage and considered themselves the successors of antediluvian civilising heroes, the *apkallū*. Regarded as expert scribes (*ummânu*), they replaced the teachers of the *edubba*, an institution which vanished during the poorly documented transition to the Middle Babylonian period (sixteenth–fifteenth century). Linking texts with named figures emphasised their content as the product of individual reflection, even if the ideas and sentiments they express belonged to the common heritage of Mesopotamian culture and were believed to derive ultimately from an unchallengeable divine wisdom. The absolute and mysterious power of the gods is a recurrent motif of wisdom texts and indeed of all Mesopotamian literary production. Wisdom literature communicates an accumulated experience about human nature and society but also reflections on the human predicament, the seemingly arbitrary nature of divine punishment and the inevitability of death. Indeed, Mesopotamian wisdom highlights the limits of human knowledge, and the incomprehensibility of the world is experienced as the result of the unfathomable will and nature of the gods. Finally, even if wisdom as a category defies ancient and contemporary attempts at defining it (after all, neither could Plato define *sophia* satisfactorily in his dialogue Charmide), there are some clues that ancient scribes considered wisdom composition to be somehow related. As we have seen, there are clear examples of intertextuality between wisdom texts of different genres, sometimes borrowing motifs and even entire quotations. We also have evidence that some of these texts were grouped together in the school curriculum, occurring together on the same large tablet (*Sammeltafel*) and listed sometimes after one another in ancient literary catalogues.[35]

---

[35] Discussion by Cohen, *Wisdom*, 60–62.

Thus, it seems that the scribes had an intuitive understanding of what constituted wisdom, even if they demurred from defining an explicit category for it.

Further Reading

Alster, Bendt. *Proverbs of Ancient Sumer*. 2 vols. Bethesda: 1997.
    Wisdom of Ancient Sumer. Bethesda: 2005.
Annus, Amar, and Lenzi, Alan. *Ludlul bēl nēmeqi: The Standard Babylonian Poem of the Righteous Sufferer*. SAACT VII. Helsinki: 2010.
Cohen, Yoram. *Wisdom from the Late Bronze Age*. SBLWAW 29. Atlanta: 2013.
Jiménez, Enrique. *The Babylonian Disputation Poems: With Editions of the Series of the Poplar, Palm and Vine, the Series of the Spider, and the Story of the Poor, Forlorn Wren*. CHANE 87. Leiden; Boston: 2017.
Lambert, Wilfred George. *Babylonian Wisdom Literature*. Oxford: 1960.
Oshima, Takayoshi. *The Babylonian Theodicy*. SAACT IX. Helsinki: 2013.
Van Dijk, Johannes Jacobus Adrianus. *La sagesse suméro-akkadienne. Recherches sur les genres littéraires des textes sapientiaux*. Leiden: 1953.

Part IV

Themes in the Wisdom Literature

20 Creation in the Wisdom Literature

ZOLTÁN SCHWÁB

Some of the most memorable biblical creation texts are in Wisdom Literature, such as God's longest (and in the Hebrew canon last) speech in Job 38–41 or the enigmatic description of Lady Wisdom's role in creation in Proverbs 8, which, in turn, is echoed and developed throughout Sirach and the Wisdom of Solomon (e.g., Sir 16:24–17:14; 39:16–31; 42:15–43:33; Wis 6:12–25; 8–9). Other passages, even if they do not emphasise God's creative activity, provide a powerful description of the created world (e.g., Job 28, Eccl 1:3–11; 3:1–11). The Song of Songs, just like Job, uses an exceptionally high number of images from nature.

Especially in the second half the twentieth century, some concluded that Wisdom Literature contains a special 'creation theology' that contrasts with the historical accounts of the rest of the Bible.[1] However, this might be an oversimplification. Not everything in wisdom is about creation,[2] other biblical books also write about creation[3] and the phrase 'creation theology' can superimpose a false unity on the diverse creation texts of Wisdom Literature.[4]

Nonetheless, even if saying that Wisdom Literature has a 'creation theology' is too simple, the significance of creation[5] in these books has

---

[1] Cf. Gerhard von Rad, *Wisdom in Israel*, trans. James D. Martin (London, 1972), 289–296.

[2] Lennart Boström, *The God of the Sages*, ConBOT 29 (Stockholm, 1990), 80.

[3] Will Kynes, *An Obituary for 'Wisdom Literature': The Birth, Death, and Intertextual Reintegration of a Biblical Corpus* (Oxford, 2019), 102–104.

[4] Stuart Weeks, *An Introduction to the Study of Wisdom Literature*, T&T Clark Approaches to Biblical Studies (London, 2010), 111–112.

[5] 'Creation' is a tricky word. It can refer to the act of creation and to its result. It can be used to contrast human society with creation (non-human nature), or technology with creation (nature, including humans), or God with creation (every being). While I prefer the last of these understandings, the term will inevitably change its connotations in this chapter as I describe diverse scholarly opinions. Hopefully, the context will always reveal its precise meaning.

always been recognised. I will first observe this history of interpretation which, as I will argue, has significantly contributed to the transformation of our theological, scientific and ethical thinking. Then, I will attempt to describe wisdom literature's teaching on creation in a way that grasps its main thrust without neglecting its diversity. Finally, as a specific test case, a more detailed investigation of creation in Ecclesiastes will follow.

HISTORY

Spiritual Theology in Antiquity

> Solomon's wisdom surpassed the wisdom of all the Easterners, and all the wisdom of Egypt. He was wiser than anyone ... He spoke of the trees, from the cedar that is in the Lebanon to the hyssop that grows on the wall. He spoke of the beasts, birds, creeping things, and fish.
>
> (1 Kgs 5:10–13 [ET 4:30–33])[6]

These words suggest a special relationship between wisdom and nature. After mentioning the most magnificent and humble plants respectively, a taxonomy of animals follows. The big animals, birds and fish are the inhabitants of the three biblical life-spheres: land, air and sea. Therefore, 1 Kgs. 4:30–33 describes a *comprehensive* and *exhaustive* knowledge of creation. The Wisdom of Solomon has Solomon elaborate on this even more:

> God gave me unerring knowledge of what exists, to know the structure of the universe and the operations of the elements ...; the varieties of plants and the powers of roots; the hidden, as well as the visible, I knew, for the fashioner of all, wisdom, taught me.
>
> (Wis 7:17–22)

These passages intrigued early biblical interpreters, partly because the so-called Solomonic books (Proverbs, Ecclesiastes, Song of Songs, Wisdom of Solomon) do not seem to live up to their promise. Although these books often speak about creation, they hardly offer *comprehensive* and *exhaustive* teaching about it. One would look for an exposition of 'the powers of roots' in them in vain. As Ambrose of Milan (ca. 340–397 CE) puts it in his book on the six days of creation,

> The reins of my diffuse discourse should ... be checked, lest I may seem to usurp the wisdom divinely conferred on Solomon in the

---

6 Biblical quotations are my own translations, unless otherwise noted.

Scriptures in expounding the 'diversities of plants and the virtues of roots ...'. *Yet, these things were not revealed by him in a clear light.*[7]

It is, of course, easy to account for the seeming deficiency of the Solomonic books by saying that they simply do not contain everything that Solomon knew. Ambrose himself hints at this possibility elsewhere.[8] But here, instead of simply saying 'these things were not revealed by him', Ambrose writes that 'these things were not revealed by him *in a clear light*'. This suggests that Solomon then might actually have revealed quite a bit about creation but only in a hidden way. If this is so, however, then perhaps creation is lurking in the Solomonic works even where it is invisible to uneducated eyes. Ambrose himself offers plenty of examples.

> The fish knows 'the time to be born' [Eccl 3:2a].... Fish are not deceived in this knowledge, because they follow an instinct of nature, the true teacher of loyal devotion .... By man alone are such times undetermined and ill-planned. The other creatures seek out a season of clement weather. It falls to women alone to give birth in seasons of inclemency. An unsettled and arbitrary desire to produce offspring leads to an uncertain time for childbirth.[9]

Most modern readers would probably not think of fish or, indeed, of any animal, when Eccl 3:1–2a writes that 'there is a season for everything, a time for every matter under heaven: a time to be born, and a time to die ...'. Not so Ambrose. He presupposes that, were Solomon asked to explain his words, surely he would use nature imagery, as 1 Kings 4 or Wisdom of Solomon 7 suggest. Thus, Ambrose simply fills in the sketchy account of Ecclesiastes, in the spirit of Solomon. He observes that Solomon's words are only true about animals, such as the fish, but not about human beings, who do not give birth in a set season. This, concludes Ambrose, is the result of our constant, insatiable and unregulated sexual drive. This is how Ecclesiastes 3:1–2, accompanied by fish, becomes a teacher of modesty!

Of course, it was not only the Solomonic books that helped in 'reading creation' but any creation-related text in the Bible. The book

---

[7] Ambrose of Milan, 'Hexaemeron', in *The Fathers of the Church*, trans. John J. Savage, vol. 42 (New York, 1961), day 3, section 64, my emphasis.

[8] For example, in the rest of his discussion of day 3, section 64.

[9] Ambrose of Milan, 'Hexaemeron', 185 (day 5, section 30).

of Job had a prime place among these texts,[10] which is understandable, considering that besides Solomon (cf. Prov 6:6) Job is the other biblical hero who provides an explicit incentive to learn from fellow creatures: 'ask the animals, they will teach you; the birds of heavens will reveal to you; or speak to the earth, it will teach you, the fish of the sea will relate to you' (Job 12:7–8).

Modern Science in Early Modernity

This fascination with creation in Job continued into early modernity. It even played an important role in the famous controversies over the heliocentric worldview. When Copernicus' *On the Revolutions of the Heavenly Spheres* (1543) was put on the Index of the Sacred Congregation in 1616, it was accompanied by another book that was condemned for its heliocentric views. This was *A Commentary on Job* (1584) by Diego de Zuñiga, who, mainly on the basis of Job 9:6a ('Who shakes the earth out of its place'), argued for the movement of the earth.[11]

Solomon also remained a great inspiration. In contrast to earlier times, however, his knowledge of nature was not only an encouragement for meditation but a scriptural legitimation of curiosity. As Edward Topsell (ca. 1572–1625), the author of a popular bestiary wrote,

> Salomon, as it is witnessed in holy Scripture, wrote of Plants, of Birds, of Fishes, and Beasts, and even then when he stood in good favour with God, therefore it is an exercise of the highest Wisdome to trauell in, and the Noblest mindes to study in; for in it as I will shew you ... there is both the knowledge of god and man.[12]

'The writings of Solomon' and Job were seen as supporting modern scientific endeavours. None other than Francis Bacon (1561–1626), 'the father of modern science', explains that the works of Job and Solomon

---

[10]   See, for example, Cyril of Jerusalem, 'Lecture IX. On the Words, Maker of Heaven and Earth, and of All Things Visible and Invisible', in *Cyril of Jerusalem, Gregory Nazianzen*, trans. Edwin Hamilton Gifford, vol. 7 of *Nicene and Post-Nicene Fathers 2* (Edinburgh, 1893), 51–56; Gregory the Great's 'literal interpretation' of Job 12:7–8 in Part Three, Book XI. St. Gregory the Great, *Morals on the Book of Job*, trans. Charles Marriott (London, 1844).

[11]   Kimberly Susan Hedlin, 'The Book of Job in Early Modern England' (PhD diss., University of California, 2018), 259–265. Zuñiga retracted his view about the movement of the earth in his later works.

[12]   Edward Topsell, *The Historie of Foure-Footed Beastes. Describing the True and Liuely Figure of Euery Beast, with a Discourse of Their Seuerall Names, Conditions, Kindes, Vertues (Both Naturall and Medicinall)* ... (London, 1607), Epistle Dedicatory.

are examples of natural history.[13] This shows an interesting shift in how people used this biblical material. Previously, the emphasis was on using Solomon and Job for guiding meditation on nature and for drawing moral and theological teachings from it. In early modernity, however, the little that these writings reveal about creation was often taken to be an encouragement to go beyond biblical knowledge and do scientific research.

Liberal Ethics in (Post)modernity

Fast forward to the second quarter of the twentieth century, when the Nazis wanted to build German identity on the ideals of wildness and beauty in nature.[14] They told Christians that racial hierarchies are just an extension of the divine order that is visible in nature.[15] At that time, those who did not espouse Nazism's ideology were also hampered in promoting anything similar to its focus on nature. Gerhard von Rad (1901–1971), who opposed National Socialism, might have been influenced by this ideological milieu when he claimed that the truly distinctive feature of Israel's faith was the confession of God's historical acts and not its teaching on creation. Therefore, the creation texts in Wisdom Literature were seen at that time as of secondary importance in the theological structure of the Bible.[16]

However, creation and Wisdom Literature were (re)discovered around the 1960s. Biblical scholars started to emphasise the concept of 'order in creation', which, allegedly, is most visible in Wisdom Literature.[17] Even Gerhard von Rad argued in his last book (1970) that wisdom's witness to God's order in creation is on an equal footing with the *Heilsgeschichte* of the other parts of the Bible.[18]

---

[13] Francis Bacon, *The Twoo Bookes of Francis Bacon. Of the Proficience and Aduancement of Learning, Diuine and Humane To the King.* (London, 1605), 29–30.

[14] Richard Smyth, 'Nature Writing's Fascist Roots', *New Statesman*, 2019, www.newstatesman.com/culture/books/2019/04/eco-facism-nature-writing-nazi-far-right-nostalgia-england.

[15] Susannah Heschel, *The Aryan Jesus, Christian Theologians and the Bible in Nazi Germany* (Princeton, 2008), 19.

[16] Gerhard von Rad, 'The Theological Problem of the Old Testament Doctrine of Creation', in *Creation in the Old Testament*, ed. Bernhard W. Anderson (London, 1984), 53–64 [German original: 1936].

[17] E.g., Hartmut Gese, *Lehre Und Wirklichkeit in Der Alten Weisheit* (Tübingen, 1958); Walther Zimmerli, 'The Place and Limit of the Wisdom in the Framework of the Old Testament Theology', *SJT* 17 (1964): 146–158; Hans Heinrich Schmid, *Wesen Und Geschichte Der Weisheit*, Beihefte Zur Zeitschrift Für Die Alttestamentliche Wissenschaft (Berlin, 1966).

[18] Von Rad, *Wisdom in Israel*.

Just as the move away from the theme of creation might have been motivated by the context of a struggle against Nazism, the return to it also went hand in hand with the socio-political developments of the 1960s. The hippie movement, the gradual recognition of environmental pollution and the accompanying sexual revolution provided unanimously positive connotations to 'nature'. At the same time, the protests against the Vietnam war (ca. 1963–1972), the civil rights movements (cf. Martin Luther King's activity or the second wave of feminism in the 1960s) and the 1968 student protests promoted suspicion of political and religious institutions. The turn to nature and criticism of institutions favoured   a   celebration   of   biblical   creation   texts   over   its historical accounts.

This cultural milieu helped biblical interpreters to recognise some new ways in which Wisdom Literature's creation texts can address the modern world. Let me provide five examples. First, secularism: Walter Brueggemann saw in Wisdom Literature a theological resource that puts an emphasis on the mundane regularities of creation. This fits the secular mindset that struggles to recognise God's interventions in history.[19] Second, natural law: many have argued that an emphasis on 'creation order' could provide a biblical precedent for natural law, an approach that does not base ethics on biblical revelation.[20] Third, human rights: some contended that the frequent references to the creator of the individual in Wisdom Literature (Prov 16:4; 17:5; 20:12; 22:2; 29:13; Eccl 12:1; Job 10:8–12; 31:15; 32:22; 33:4, 6; 35:10; 36:3; Wis 6:7; Sir 1:14; 7:30; 39:5) provides a theological basis for ideas of unalienable human dignity and the Human Rights Movement.[21] Fourth, feminism: several authors argued that the female figure of Wisdom as the foremost creature of, or even co-creator with, God (Prov 3:19–20; 8; Wis 6:22; 8:5–6; 9; Sir 1:4; 24) challenges male-dominated life.[22] Finally, fifth, ecology: with the growing concerns over environmental issues,

[19] Walter Brueggemann, *In Man We Trust* (Atlanta, 1972); Walter Brueggemann, *Theology of the Old Testament* (Minneapolis, 1997), 333–358.

[20] John J. Collins, 'The Biblical Precedent for Natural Theology', *JAAR* 45.1.1 (1977): 25–67; James Barr, *Biblical Faith and Natural Theology* (Oxford, 1993).

[21] Peter Doll, *Menschenschöpfung und Weltschöpfung in der alttestamentlichen Weisheit*, SBS 117 (Stuttgart, 1985).

[22] Rosemary Radford Ruether, *New Woman New Earth, Sexist Ideologies & Human Liberation* (Minneapolis, 1975), 43–44; Claudia V. Camp, *Wisdom and the Feminine in the Book of Proverbs* (Sheffield, 1985).

Wisdom Literature gave birth to ecological readings that recognised the intrinsic value of nature.[23]

Some Reflections on the History of Interpretation

A special relationship between creation and Wisdom Literature has always been perceived. However, the understanding of this 'special relationship' kept changing, like a chameleon. When people wanted spiritual lessons, these creation teachings offered that. When people were fascinated by new scientific discoveries, these texts supported experimental scientific methods. More recently, the same texts 'promoted' feminism.

The story could easily be continued. One of the more recent cultural developments is the growing popularity of veganism and the intense debate about a non-anthropocentric ethics and animal rights.[24] Lo and behold, suddenly creation in Wisdom Literature is about these issues! Many recognise that the divine speeches in Job 38–41 focus on animals and hardly mention humans,[25] that Prov 12:10 and similar verses presuppose a moral status of animals[26] and that Wisdom Literature in general is strangely preoccupied with wild animals.[27] Therefore, one is tempted to be sceptical and suspect that the changing interpretations of these creation texts are mainly dictated by the most recent trend of the day.

However, there are good reasons to resist this temptation. Historical and literary approaches might be content with concentrating on the closed world of the text, but theological and other ideological approaches have always emphasised that the key task is to read reality

---

[23] Robert K. Johnston, 'Wisdom Literature and Its Contribution to a Biblical Environmental Ethic', in *Tending the Garden*, ed. W. Granberg-Michaelson (Grand Rapids: 1987), 66–82; Katharine J. Dell, '"Green" Ideas in the Wisdom Tradition', *SJT* 47 (1994): 423–451.

[24] Christine M. Korsgaard, *Fellow Creatures: Our Obligations to the Other Animals* (Oxford, 2018); Shelly Kagan, *How to Count Animals, More or Less* (Oxford, 2019).

[25] Cf. Barry R. Huff, 'From Societal Scorn to Divine Delight: Job's Transformative Portrayal of Wild Animals', *Int* 73.3 (2019): 248–258; Abigail Pelham, *Contested Creations in the Book of Job, The-World-as-It-Ought-and-Ought-Not-to-Be* (Leiden, 2012), 75; Kathryn Schifferdecker, *Out of the Whirlwind, Creation Theology in the Book of Job*, HTS (Cambridge, MA, 2008), 2, 100, 129, etc.; Ronald A. Simkins, 'Anthropocentrism and the Place of Humans in the Biblical Tradition', *Religion & Society, Supplements* 9 (2013): 25–27.

[26] Celia E. Deane-Drummond, *Theological Ethics through a Multispecies Lens: The Evolution of Wisdom* (Oxford, 2019), 65–69.

[27] Carey Walsh, 'The Beasts of Wisdom: Ecological Hermeneutics of the Wild', *BibInt* 25.2 (2017): 135–148.

in the light of the text and vice versa.[28] In the case of creation, this task is especially inviting because of the growing tension between humanity and nature. The 'human animal' moved inside into houses and cities a long time ago and spends increasingly more time there. Somewhere in the second half of the twentieth century, the mass of humanity (anthropomass) surpassed the zoomass of wild terrestrial mammals,[29] and for every kilogram of human body there are fifteen tonnes of infrastructure: roads, houses, power plants, utility grids.[30] This 'strange new world' often generates deep longings for nature, and these feelings inevitably influence one's interpretation of creation-texts. Add to this the harm that anthropogenic climate change and pollution do to the whole biosphere, and it becomes clear that a morally responsible reading of biblical accounts of creation almost demands an interaction with contemporary issues.

However, the concept of ever-changing interpretation can be defended even if one only considers 'the closed world of the text'. That 'closed world' displays a bewildering diversity that can feed equally diverse interpretations. Job 38–41 highlights the marginal role humans play in creation. Ecclesiastes 1:1–11 speaks about the unchangeable world. The Song of Songs uses natural images to speak about sensual love. Sirach emphasises social hierarchy (33:7–15) and God's omniscience (42:15–25). Wisdom of Solomon 13:1–9 teaches that God can be known from his creatures. The list goes on, but this suffices to prove that the theme of creation is used to make many different points. It is not even that these diverse creation teachings always easily complement each other. For example, Proverbs, Ecclesiastes, Song of Songs and Job hardly ever mention the Law or Israelite history and even if they occasionally allude to them they do not explicitly connect them with a discussion of creation. By contrast, the later books of Sirach and Wisdom of Solomon describe how the creator God directs history and how he uses creation to rescue the Jews from Egypt and punish the Egyptian (Wis 12:19–19:21; cf. Sir 39:17–18).[31] Proverbs 8 clearly

[28] Francis Watson, *Text, Church and World, Biblical Interpretation in Theological Perspective* (Edinburgh, 1994), 75.

[29] Vaclav Smil, *Harvesting the Biosphere: What We Have Taken from Nature* (Cambridge, MA, 2013), 618.

[30] Jedediah Britton-Purdy, 'Paleo Politics', *The New Republic*, 1 November 2017, https://newrepublic.com/article/145444/paleo-politics-what-made-prehistoric-hunter-gatherers-give-freedom-civilization.

[31] Darrin W. Snyder Belousek, 'God the Creator in the Wisdom of Solomon: A Theological Commentary', 2015, www.academia.edu/15912414/God_the_Creator_in_the_Wisdom_of_Solomon_A_Theological_Commentary; A. Jordan Schmidt, *Wisdom, Cosmos, and*

associates wisdom with creation. Job 28, however, emphasises that one would mine nature in vain for wisdom. Qohelet[32] teaches that life is short; consequently, one should enjoy it when one can (Eccl 3:12; 5:18; 8:15; 9:1–10). But the Wisdom of Solomon teaches that it is precisely the fools who talk like this as the creator 'created us for incorruption' (2:23) and the righteous will live with the creator eternally (Wis 1:12–15; 2:16–18; 5:15). It is understandable that readers in different contexts resonate with different parts of this wide palette of 'creation-teachings'. Not dismissing the possibility of reading their interests into these biblical texts, new cultural contexts also enable readers to recognise hitherto neglected parts of the many creation teachings.

However, the diversity of these creation texts might promote a more legitimate scepticism about another issue, namely, about the existence of 'the' creation theology of Wisdom Literature. In 1964, Walther Zimmerli summarised the scholarly consensus succinctly: 'Wisdom thinks resolutely within the framework of a theology of creation.'[33] In the following decades, claiming that the theology of Wisdom Literature is 'creation theology' became almost like a truism. But speaking about *the* creation theology of Wisdom Literature[34] might be misleading when the theme of creation serves diverse theological interests.

THEOLOGY

'Creation Theology' vs. 'Creator Theology'

Because of its diversity, it is not easy to grasp Wisdom Literature's teaching about creation in a simple formula. Yet many have offered helpful formulas to grasp at least some aspects of that teaching, for example, that it displays an interplay between human centred (anthropological) and divine centred (cosmological) metaphors (Leo Perdue)[35]; or that it generates wonder and awe (William P. Brown)[36]; or that it

---

Cultus in the Book of Sirach, vol. 42 of *Deuterocanonical and Cognate Literature Studies* (Boston; Berlin: 2019), 104.

[32] I use the word 'Qohelet' to refer to the main protagonist of Ecclesiastes who talks in Eccl 1:2–12:8. Even if Ecclesiastes as a book does not endorse the teachings of Qohelet, it certainly does not envisage an eternal life as Wisdom does.

[33] Zimmerli, 'The Place and Limit', 148.

[34] See how Zimmerli repeatedly writes about 'the sapiential theology of creation' in the above mentioned article. Zimmerli, 'The Place and Limit', 158.

[35] Leo G. Perdue, *Wisdom and Creation: The Theology of Wisdom Literature* (Nashville, 1994).

[36] William P. Brown, *Wisdom's Wonder: Character, Creation, and Crisis in the Bible's Wisdom Literature* (Grand Rapids, 2014); Cf. Craig G. Bartholomew and Ryan

expresses three main principles, namely, the sustaining of life, the flourishing of life and the interrelatedness of nature, human society and God (Katharine Dell).[37]

Regardless of which 'summarising formula' one prefers, the vast majority agrees that one of the focal points of these texts is the teaching about world-order.[38] Yet it might not be immediately obvious why a teaching about world-order is significant; after all, no one would dispute the existence of regular patterns ordering the world. We do not expect lions to be devoured by sheep! But this 'world-order' is supposedly more than that. It includes the following elements:

– Nature and human society obey the *same* order;
– It is an *ethical* order;
– It derives *from God*;
– It is maintained *by God*.

From a modern perspective, this understanding of world-order may seem confused. Many would argue that concepts of justice in human society are human constructs and not God-given, and rocks and badgers certainly do not follow ethical principles, let alone midges. Nonetheless, the argument goes, accepting this world-order enabled biblical sages to connect unrelated natural and social phenomena, such as the biting serpent with the effects of alcohol (Prov 23:32) or 'clouds and wind without rain' with 'one who boasts of a gift never given' (Prov 25:14).[39] It also serves as an incentive for ethical behaviour, as in such an ordered world following righteousness means promoting the main principle of the universe,[40] and reward or punishment will inevitably follow our actions.[41]

However, caution is needed so as not to oversimplify biblical teaching on world-order. Wisdom writings themselves recognise all sorts of

---

P. O'Dowd, *Old Testament Wisdom Literature: A Theological Introduction* (Nottingham, 2011), 263, 298–299.

[37] Katharine J. Dell, 'The Significance of the Wisdom Tradition in the Ecological Debate', in *Ecological Hermeneutics, Biblical, Historical and Theological Perspectives* (London, 2010), 58–59.

[38] Cf. Hans Heinrich Schmid, *Gerechtigkeit Als Weltordnung* (Tübingen, 1968); for some further examples, see Katharine J. Dell, 'God, Creation and the Contribution of Wisdom', in *The God of Israel*, ed. R. P. Gordon (Cambridge, 2007), 60–72.

[39] John Barton, *Ethics in Ancient Israel* (Oxford, 2014), 115; John L. McLaughlin, *An Introduction to Israel's Wisdom Traditions* (Grand Rapids, 2018), 176; Von Rad, *Wisdom in Israel*, 119–120.

[40] Schmid, *Gerechtigkeit Als Weltordnung*; cf. Bartholomew and O'Dowd, *Old Testament Wisdom Literature*, 285.

[41] Klaus Koch, 'Is There a Doctrine of Retribution in the Old Testament?', in *Theodicy in the Old Testament*, ed. James L. Crenshaw, trans. Thomas H. Trapp (London, 1983).

complexities. For example, righteous people can suffer. Job is a case in point, but see also Prov 15:16–17 or Eccl 7:15. One possible reason for this is that delivering God's justice can take a long time (Eccl 8:11). Another is that the same suffering can serve as punishment for the bad person and as a character-forming test for the good, as Sirach seems to presuppose (cf. Sir 2:1; 4:17).[42] A different explanation is simply that we do not see the bigger picture and have no idea why certain things happen (Eccl 7:24). Finally, one could argue that the bigger picture might have some place for what humans would call 'disorder'; after all, as God's speeches in Job inform us, although God cares for herbivorous animals (Job 39:1–25), he also gives them as food to carnivorous ones as he cares for them too (Job 38:39–41). He rejoices in the disruptive powers of Leviathan (Job 41:1–34), and what is more, he tenderly cares even for the Sea (Job 38:8–9), which is typically taken as a symbol of negative powers.[43]

In addition to all these complexities, it is also unclear if the teaching on a 'religious world-order' really pervades everything in Wisdom Literature. That the effects of alcohol are compared to the bite of a serpent is a metaphor that can be appreciated by an atheist biologist without any belief in a divinely instituted ethical world order, so we might read too much into such metaphors.

Therefore, although a world-order is probably presupposed by each of the wisdom writings, it is characterised differently by different texts and it is not always in the forefront of their concerns. Thus, an over-emphasis on a clear world-order as the focus of these texts might miss the point. The point, instead, seems to be that behind the world, includ-ing nature and society, is a ruler: God. The order is not a perfectly understandable mechanistic clockwork. It is a reassuring but some-times mysterious and frustrating effect of God's rule. Consequently, it might be better to speak about 'the creator theology' of Wisdom Literature instead of its 'creation theology'. No matter whether its diverse material depicts a comprehensible or incomprehensible order, one which excludes all injustice or one that allows it, the main point is that there is an 'orderer' behind the world.

Power and Beauty

However, these texts do more than simply point to a creator, and this brings us back to the problem of grasping their main teaching while

---

[42] Schmidt, *Wisdom, Cosmos*, 121–129.
[43] Schifferdecker, *Out of the Whirlwind*, 75–76, 119.

acknowledging their diversity. Let me suggest a pair of concepts that might be able to help in this: power and beauty. These two concepts are explored in virtually all creation texts of Wisdom Literature, thereby creating a certain unity in diversity.

I take my cue from Wis 13:5: 'by analogy, from the greatness and beauty of created things, their creator is seen'. As the previous verses speak about creation's beauty (*kallonē*, v. 3) and power (*dynamis*, v. 4), I take verse 5 as continuing those themes, so when it mentions 'greatness and beauty' (*megethos kai kallonē*), I understand it mainly as 'power and beauty'.[44] That power and beauty form the two sides of the same coin is nicely captured by Wis 19:18 and its context, too. It compares the created world to a harp and God to the harpist. God is in complete control, but using that control he is playing a beautiful melody. Nevertheless, not all biblical passages pay equal attention to both sides of this coin, so it might be worth taking a look at them separately.

Power

It is easy to see that a creator can do anything he wants in a universe which is continuously created and sustained by him. Wisdom Literature discusses this divine power repeatedly in its diverse teachings on creation. God's final speeches in the book of Job (Job 38–41) provide a showcase of his power.[45] 'Were you there when I created this; do you understand how it works; can you control it?' asks God. No, Job was not there, he does not understand, and he cannot control it. God has the knowledge and the power.

The Song of Songs sings about power in a very different key. While human lovemaking takes the central stage instead of a powerful God, yet, as Fontaine reminds us, the 'power that undergirds the cosmos speaks everywhere through the natural images employed by' its poets.[46] Passion and love are strong as death (Song. 8:6), and, as the Song reminds us, we participate in this life-sustaining energy when, 'flooded with

---

44 Cf. commentary in Luca Mazzinghi, *Wisdom*, International Exegetical Commentary on the Old Testament (Stuttgart, 2019).

45 For a bibliography for the centrality of power in the book of Job in general, see Pelham, *Contested*, 80–82.

46 Carole R. Fontaine, '"Go Forth into the Fields": An Earth-Centered Reading of the Song of Songs', in *The Earth Story in Wisdom Traditions*, ed. Norman C. Habel and Shirley Wurst, vol. 3 of *The Earth Bible* (Sheffield, 2001), 137.

perceptions of riotous beauty ... we burn bright with an earthly flame which cannot be doused'.[47]

Proverbs 8 describes Wisdom as privy to God's creation (8:22–31) and also as someone who has strength (8:14) and who empowers the rulers of this world (8:15–21). Interestingly, as God 'marked out' (*ḥqq*) the sea (8:27, 29), so human rulers 'mark out' (*ḥqq*) 'what is just' (8:15).[48] The power of the creatures resembles the power of the creator.

Ecclesiastes expresses the infinite power-imbalance between the creator and creature. *Everything* 'under the sun' is made by God, and human beings are unable to add to the world or take anything from it (cf. 3:14; 8:17; 11:5). Wisdom of Solomon strongly disagrees with Ecclesiastes on a number of things. Unlike Ecclesiastes, it emphasises God's salvation-history and a post mortem reward for the righteous. But it agrees on the point of God's power. It teaches that God's 'all-powerful hand, which created the world' (11:17) could create new beings at any moment, even though God normally uses the existing creatures for his purposes.[49] Sirach also teaches that God's creation includes the physical universe as well as salvific history[50] and that 'everything that is pleasing is by his command' (Sir 39:18). Therefore, although in diverse ways, God's power is intrinsically connected with the theme of creation in these texts. God is absolute ruler over nature and society.

Beauty

Beauty is everywhere. In the Song of Songs, the lovers use natural images to praise the beauty of each other's bodies (e.g., 4:1; 5:10).[51] But the beauty of awakening nature at spring time is also appreciated simply for itself, thereby providing a lyrical description of nature unique in the entire Hebrew Bible (cf. 2:10–14).[52] As Francis Landy puts it, 'Beauty in the Song is an all-pervasive quality that one cannot separate from the love of the lovers, the world they inhabit or the language in which the poem is written.'[53]

---

[47] Fontaine, 'Go Forth', 141.

[48] Bartholomew and O'Dowd, *Old Testament Wisdom Literature*, 302–303.

[49] Cf. Belousek, 'God the Creator', passim.

[50] Schmidt, *Wisdom, Cosmos*, 102.

[51] Fontaine, 'Go Forth', 131–132.

[52] Cf. Michael V. Fox, *The Song of Songs and the Ancient Egyptian Love Songs* (Madison, 1985), 285.

[53] Francis Landy, *Beauty and the Enigma, and Other Essays on the Hebrew Bible* (Sheffield, 2001), 38.

Sirach, in a less heated way, also recognises the relationship between creation and desire ('all his works are desirable', Sir 42:22), but his approach is more educational. He wants to cultivate the aesthetic sensibilities of his students by listing the beauties of creation (42:15–43:33).[54] Even Qohelet sees beauty in creation. He declares that '[God] has made everything beautiful [*yāpeh*] in its time' (3:11), even death (3:2). Although *yāpeh* arguably means something like 'fitting' here, the author of such texts as Eccl 12:1–8 surely also recognised the painful beauty of our mortal lives.

Lady Wisdom in Proverbs finds her delight in creation more enthusiastically ('I was ... having fun in his habitable world, and my delight was in humanity'; 8:31). At the end of Job, God displays a similar delight and enjoyment in his creation. As Ellen Davis puts it, God asks Job (and through him the reader) in those divine speeches (Job 38–41): 'Can you appreciate and love those things and creatures simply because they are wild and beautiful and of great intrinsic value ...?'[55]

Thus, the beauty of creation that invites divine and human desire runs through and through Wisdom Literature. Equally significantly, its *form* also displays beauty. A quick look at Job will help me to explain why this is so important. People usually think that the book of Job is a contest in opinions. Of course, it is that. But it is also a contest in rhetoric, a contest in beauty.[56] The friends, using natural images (4:9–11, 19; 5:10, 22–23, 25; 8:2, 11; etc.), speak about God's lofty power. Job, using even more natural images and longer 'creation texts' (e.g., 9:5–10; 12:13–16; 26:5–14), affirms God's lofty power. Then God, in the most elaborate creation text in the Bible, speaks about his own lofty power. Therefore, on the level of content, it does not make much sense to ask who is more persuasive about God's power. They all say the same! But they are not only competing in who has the best theology but also in who can use natural images more powerfully. This is, arguably, true about all the creation texts in wisdom books. They are simultaneously exercises in theology and poetry. If we miss beauty, we miss half of the equation.

---

[54] Schmidt, *Wisdom, Cosmos*, 26.

[55] Schifferdecker, *Out of the Whirlwind*, 131, quoting Ellen F. Davis, *Getting Involved with God: Rediscovering the Old Testament* (Cambridge, MA, 2001).

[56] Cf. Lance R. Hawley, *Metaphor Competition in the Book of Job*, Journal of Ancient Judaism Supplements (Göttingen, 2018).

A Summary of Wisdom's Teaching about Creation

The diversity within Wisdom Literature's creation texts makes it difficult to speak about its 'creation theology'. However, as these texts univocally point to God as the creator, the phrase 'creator theology' could still work. Gregory of Nyssa argued that the created world is a beautiful hymn to the power of God.[57] This could be a fitting summary of that 'creator theology', as 'beauty' and 'power' grasp its special flavour without losing its diversity.[58] However, such generalities hardly do justice to the richness of individual texts. To offer a glimpse of that richness, I will close this chapter with a closer look at one wisdom book: Ecclesiastes.

ECCLESIASTES

(Lack of) Creation in Ecclesiastes

Ecclesiastes is not the most obvious choice for a discussion of creation in Wisdom Literature. It does not contain such magnificent descriptions of God's creative activity as Proverbs 8 or Job 38–41. Even though the book begins with natural images (sun, wind, streams; Eccl 1:5–7), they only express the perpetual continuity of the world without any reference to their createdness[59] or to the act of creation in general.[60] Although, elsewhere, it is affirmed that God makes ($\check{s}h$) everything (11:5) and he is called 'your creator' once ($b\hat{o}r'\bar{e}k$ Eccl 12:1), these only emphasise that God has been generating and sustaining everything. As Stuart Weeks explains, these statements do not ground God's 'creative activities' in a specific act of creating the world'[61] and 'when we see $\check{s}h$ associated with God, the usage in the book gives us no reason to make an automatic link with some theological notion of creation, except insofar as any activity or achievement can be called "creative"'.[62]

---

[57] In Psalmorum inscriptiones, XLIV, 441B; see Gregory of Nyssa, *On the Inscriptions of the Psalms*, Archbishop Iakovos Library of Ecclesiastical and Historical Sources (Brookline, n.d.), 19, www.lectio-divina.org/images/nyssa/On%20the%20Inscriptions%20of%20the%20Psalms.pdf.

[58] Compare with Genesis 1 where beauty and power are presupposed yet not mentioned explicitly.

[59] Stuart Weeks, *Ecclesiastes 1–5: A Critical and Exegetical Commentary on Ecclesiastes*, The International Critical Commentary (London; New York, 2019), 268.

[60] Stuart Weeks, *An Introduction to the Study of Wisdom Literature*, T&T Clark Approaches to Biblical Studies (London, 2010), 111–112.

[61] Weeks, *An Introduction*, 111.

[62] Weeks, *Ecclesiastes 1–5*, 510.

Yet this is a potentially misleading description of Ecclesiastes. Emphasising that natural images are metaphors that serve (only) to express simple teachings such as the 'perpetual continuity of the world', and that primary creation is not even mentioned, can give the impression that these metaphors and God's sustaining of his creation are not that important. I would like to take issue with this and argue that the theme of creation, broadly understood, is important both for the argument of Ecclesiastes and for our theological appropriation of it.

WIND

Many twenty-first-century western people, I imagine, have positive thoughts when reflecting on wind (and, indeed, on any part of nature). Biblically versed people might even be reminded of God's *rûaḥ*, that is, his spirit/wind, hovering over the waters in Gen 1:2 or God's *rûaḥ*, breath/spirit/wind, enlivening the dry bones in Ezek 37:9–10. Qohelet (the speaker of Eccl 1:1–12:8) is different. Moving air, his 'favourite' part of creation, reminds him of unpleasant things. He famously compares everything with *hebel*, moist air (=breath?),[63] and this is not a cause for rejoicing: 'So I hated life, because whatever is done under the sun seemed bad to me; for all is *hebel*' (2:17).

Soon after mentioning *hebel* the first time (1:2), Qohelet turns to another type of air movement, the great 'atmospheric circulation'. 'Going to south and turning to north, turning and turning, the wind goes and to its surroundings the wind keeps returning' (Eccl 1:6). Again, this is not a source of awe. Together with other never-ending natural processes, it just reminds Qohelet that human beings can never make a real difference and can never be fully satisfied (Eccl 1:3, 8). He finds this image of the never-ending swirling of wind so expressive that, besides *hebel*, he makes it into another overarching metaphor for our frustrating human life. 'I gave my mind to know wisdom ... I saw that this, also, is *rĕ'ût rûaḥ* ('desiring' or 'pursuing' or 'shepherding' wind)' (Eccl 1:17); 'I turned towards all the achievements that my hands achieved ... all was *hebel* and *rĕ'ût rûaḥ*' (Eccl 2:11, see also 2:17, 26; 4:4, 6; 6:9). Thus *rûaḥ*, a word pregnant with positive connotations of life-giving and energising (divine) force in other parts of the Bible, becomes a symbol of human frustration in Ecclesiastes.

---

[63] Weeks, *Ecclesiastes and Scepticism*, 105.

Control

A major source of this frustration is the lack of control. 'There is no one who rules over the wind[64] to restrain the wind, there is no ruling over the day of death' (Eccl 8:8). The wind goes round and round, people are born and then die – the atmospheric circulation and the life-sustaining human spirit are equally outside of our control.

However, this resigned acknowledgement of our lack of control does not encourage inactivity. Even if one cannot control the winds, it is still possible to sail by them. Similarly, Qohelet gives advice about how to live with the uncontrollable winds of life.

> 11:1 Send your bread out upon the water
> for within many days you may/will find it.
> 2 Give a share to seven or even to eight
> for you do not know what disaster will happen on the earth.
> 3 If clouds will be filled [then it is] rain [that] they will pour onto the earth,
> and if a tree falls in the south or the north [wind],
> wherever it will have fallen there it will be.
> 4 He who watches winds will not sow
> and he who observes the clouds will not harvest.
> 5 As you do not know what the way of the wind/spirit is, like the limbs in the womb of a pregnant woman, so you do not know the work of God who brings about everything. 6 In the morning sow your seed and in the evening do not rest your hand, for you do not know which [time] is the right one, this or that or whether both of them are equally good.

This pericope advises that it is better to work hard and be prepared for all eventualities precisely because one cannot predict the future. Be busy with distributing your means (11:1) and with agriculture (11:4), because even if wind, falling trees or other disasters destroy part of your means, other parts will remain (11:2b, 3–4). In other words, do not be paralysed by the unpredictability of the future but work, wait, hope and, as modern game theory teaches, use mixed strategy. Bet on as many things as possible, and, something, eventually, will pay (11:2, 5–6).

Ecclesiastes 11 echoes Ecclesiastes 1 in interesting ways.

> 1:3 What gain is there for a human in any of his labour at which he labours under the sun? 4 A generation goes and a generation comes

---

64 Or 'breath' or 'spirit'.

but the world stays forever. [5] The sun has risen but [then] the sun has gone down and it rushes to its place where it rises [again]. [6] Going to south and turning to north, turning and turning, the wind goes and to its surroundings the wind keeps returning. [7] All rivers go to the sea but the sea is not full; to the place where the rivers go they keep going.

Both chapters are interested in 'economics': what can human beings gain and how can they maximise their profit (1:3, 11:1, 6). Both chapters use natural phenomena to reflect on this question: water (1:7; 11:1), wind (1:6; 11:4), human reproduction (1:4; 11:5) and the daily cycle (1:5; 11:6). However, while in Ecclesiastes 1 the main point is their repetitive,[65] predictable movement, Ecclesiastes 11 is about their unpredictable nature. There is no contradiction though. One can see how the huge body of water on Earth circulates continually (Ecclesiastes 1), but this does not help in predicting if she will have enough water next week (Ecclesiastes 11). What we should do is to count on the unalterable repetitive nature of the world in the big scheme (Ecclesiastes 1) and to use mixed strategy to alleviate the haphazard nature of our individual fortune (Ecclesiastes 11).

Role of Images

To sum up my discussion so far, Qohelet makes wind and breath his driving metaphors for the whole of human experience and he starts and closes his argument with a meditation on the natural cycles of wind, water, sunrise and birth.[66] It is true that the main interest of the book is not the detailed investigation of creation but answering a practical question: how one should live in an uncontrollable and unalterable world? Natural images primarily provide metaphors and similes. However, metaphors and similes are not just insignificant decorations

---

[65] Stuart Weeks argues that the movement of sun, wind and water in Eccl 1:4–7 is not circular (Weeks, *Ecclesiastes and Scepticism*, 46–53). Even if he is right, the point seems to be that the (human and natural) world will repeatedly 'start again', nothing is decisively accomplished. It is a matter of detail whether that 're-start' follows a regular cycle or a random movement. The re-start, predictably, will come.

[66] Strictly speaking, Eccl 11:1–6 is not the end of the book. It is followed by a section on youth, old age, death (11:7–12:8) and by an epilogue (11:9–14). However, 11:7–12:8 just continues 11:1–6 in that it is also a reflection on the predictable grand natural cycles and their unpredictability at the level of the individual (i.e., all human beings will die, but they do not know exactly when). That, towards the end of the book, so many words and motives recur from its beginning, is intriguing and worthy of further investigation.

of the argument. I wonder whether Qohelet would have reached the same conclusions without the use of them. Even if he had, their frequency, their placement at key points of the argument and the fact that they provide the 'thesis statement' (cf. 'everything is a breath and desiring of wind', *hakkōl hebel ûrĕ'ût rûaḥ*) invite the reader to meditate on wind, water, sun, etc. This is a guided meditation, Qohelet tells the reader what their conclusions should be. Nonetheless, it is hard to read through the book without ever stopping to ponder the wind.

God Creates Everything

However, let us allow, for the sake of argument, that wind, streams, regeneration and the sun are 'only' images that help to convey a message that is independent of them. Does the theme of creation have anything to do with that message itself?

It is true that the book only refers to God's continuous creative work, without mentioning primeval creation. But putting it like this is misleading as it emphasises what is missing at the expense of what is there. One could just as well say that Genesis 1 'only' concentrates on primeval creation. The emphasis on God's continuous creative work is no more trivial than an emphasis on God's primeval creation. Using the example of Psalm 104 might clarify what I mean. It has been observed that in that psalm God's creation activity follows a similar order to that of Genesis 1.[67] It seems likely that the writing of the two texts is somehow interrelated.[68] Besides the similarities, however, they display a number of striking differences. The one which concerns me is that the psalm, unlike Genesis 1, emphasises God's 'on-going creation': 'you cause grass to grow for the cattle ...' (Ps 104:14); 'you bring darkness, and it is night, when all the animals of the forest are creeping around' (v. 20); '... you gather their breath (*rûaḥ*), they die and to their dust they return. You send out your spirit (*rûaḥ*), they are created' (vv. 29–30). The pair of Genesis 1 and Psalm 104, their resonances together with their differences, suggests that primeval creation and sustaining creation might not have been that far apart in the heads of ancient authors as in our heads.

---

[67] Creation of heaven and earth (Ps 104:1-4; Gen 1:1-5), waters pushed back (Ps 104:5-9; Gen 1:6-10), waters used beneficially (Ps 104:10-13; Gen 1:6-10), vegetation (Ps 104:14-18; Gen 1:11-12), luminaries (Ps 104:19-23; Gen 1:14-18), sea creatures (Ps 104:24-26; Gen 1:20-22), living creatures (Ps 104:27-30; Gen 1:24-31); see John Day, *Yahweh and the Gods and Goddesses of Canaan*, JSOTSup 265 (Sheffield, 2000), 101.

[68] Leslie C. Allen, *Psalms 101–150*, Word Biblical Commentary 21 (Waco, 1983), 30–31.

That 'creation' is a broader category than 'primeval creation' is not the only lesson one can learn from these writings. They also suggest that 'creation' is not hermetically divided from history and culture. Psalm 104:26–27 speaks about the human and non-human worlds with one breath: 'there ships go about, Leviathan that you formed to play with. All of them await you to provide their food at its time'. The most natural reading would be to take the words 'all of them' (kullām) as referring to Leviathan and the ships. That is, the human world, together with its shipbuilding and commerce, is just as dependent on God as Leviathan.

What is just a faint hint in Psalm 104, is a well-developed teaching in Ecclesiastes. God's creative activity incorporates the whole sphere of human society. The human world, the world 'under the sun', is in the centre of Qohelet's attention. This is a spectacularly active world and this futile human business frustrates Qohelet. He contrasts it with the activity of God: 'I know that whatever God brings about will stay: no adding to it, no taking away from it; God acts so that they would fear before him' (3:14). It is not that humans and God compete in who can create more enduring things and God wins the competition, but rather that human acts themselves are made by God (cf. 3:10–11; 8:17; 11:5). Humans might think that they are adding something to God's work, but in fact God is simply working through them. Somehow everything flows from God's creative activity, including both material objects and immaterial human deeds. Therefore, besides the dividing line between original creation and present maintenance, the divide between creation (divine activity) and history (human activity) is also blurred – or more than that, non-existent. This 'holistic' depiction of God's creative activity is put to the service of expressing an important theological point. To put it briefly, it contrasts the human condition with the 'divine condition': we are limited, God is not.

We Do Not See That God Creates Everything

Furthermore, we are blind. Paradoxically, the 'wonderful human works' are visible, but the really decisive divine activity is not. This is why humans can be deluded and think that they see reality. On the contrary, human acts are part of a bigger scheme that humans cannot comprehend. This is why humans can be deluded and disregard what really matters. As Eccl 7:24 puts it, 'that which is, is far away (rāḥôq), and deep ('āmōq), deep; who can find it?'

Ecclesiastes 7:24 is reminiscent of the beginning of the story of Gilgamesh. There Gilgamesh is described as someone '[who saw the

Deep, the] foundation of the country ... [he was wis]e in everything! ...
The sum of wisdom about everything he [grasped] .... He came a distant
road and was weary but relaxed'.[69] The epic of Gilgamesh, not the most
cheerful work itself, is more optimistic than Ecclesiastes. Gilgamesh
travels far, and although he is not able to obtain the antidote to death, he
can at least see the Deep, and this enables him to achieve marvellous
things and this grants him rest. Not so Qohelet. He has also achieved
some marvellous things, but that is not enough for him. 'That which is,
is far away, and deep, deep; who can find it?'[70]

The case can be made that the deep which Qohelet is unable to find
is the invisible, continuous (creation) work of God and his intention
behind it.[71] As Ps 92:5 [H: 92:6] puts it, 'how great are your works
(ma 'áśêkā – a key word in Ecclesiastes), O Lord! Your thoughts are very
deep ('āmĕqû)!'[72] But again, what appears wonderful to the psalmist
frustrates Qohelet. Creation, including human deeds and artefacts, is
frustrating because we cannot see its 'bottom line'. Its meaning
is locked.

Creation in Ecclesiastes: A Conclusion

Finally, let me return to the themes of beauty and power. For all one
knows, Qohelet is aware of creation's beauty. He claims that life is
beautifully organised (3:11), and he uses nature-images with mesmeris-
ing eloquence. However, while he can help his reader to see creation's
beauty, he himself does not seem to be moved by it. He is interested in
power: God's almightiness and human powerlessness. His emphasis on
God's *continuous* creation, including the creation of human actions,
underlines that everything is in God's hands.

Consequently, Stuart Weeks' statement that 'when we see *'śh*
[to make] associated with God, the usage in the book gives us no
reason to make an automatic link with some theological notion of

---

[69] Standard Babylonian version, I:1–2, 6, 9; my translation.

[70] I am not claiming a direct literary dependence. The different connotations of the
Akkadian *naqbu* (deep, sweet water) and the Hebrew *'mq* (deep) make a direct
dependence unlikely. Nonetheless, the similarities between the two works
are illuminating.

[71] See 7:14, the previous occurrence of *mṣ'*, 'to find', and also 8:17.

[72] The words *'śh* (to do, to make), *n'śh* (deed, work), and *m'śh* (work, deed,
accomplishment, maker, doer) are frequent in Ecclesiastes. They often refer to
human as well as to divine activities as the book compares these two types of
'creation' (Eccl 1:9, 13, 14; 2:2, 3, 4, 5, 6, 8, 11, 12, 17; 3:9, 11, 12, 14, 17, 22; 4:1, 3,
4, 17; 5:5; 6:12; 7:13, 14, 20, 27, 29; 8:3, 4, 9, 10, 11, 12, 14, 16, 17; 9:3, 6, 7, 10; 10:19;
11:5; 12:12, 14).

creation'[73] might require some nuancing. That God makes everything expresses the contrast between creature and creator which I take as a fundamental theological notion. The admonition in 12:1 sums this up neatly: 'Remember your creator'. Remember that you are *not* the creator. Remember that you should enjoy what you have when you have it because, sooner or later, as a creature, you will return to dust.

Therefore, in a sense, 'creation' is at the heart of the book. This does not mean that God is praised for it. On the contrary, the created world frustrates. It invites human beings to control it or at least to discover God's intentions behind it. Sadly, despite the alluring invitation, neither of these is possible. Only an awareness of the all-powerful creator is available.

CONCLUSIONS

My reading of Ecclesiastes is not unlike that of Zimmerli, who argued that Qohelet 'meets with a reality that is determined and cannot be apprehended. Behind all this determination and all this ability not to be apprehended it is God, who cannot be scrutinised, who is free, who never reacts, but always acts in freedom'.[74] This is, actually, the same article in which Zimmerli advocates a description of the theology of Wisdom Literature as 'the sapiential theology of creation'.[75] At this point, however, I suggest to divert from his approach. Sapiential teachings on creation are diverse and they often overlap with the creation-teachings of other biblical books. Therefore, it is difficult to contrast '*the* sapiential theology of creation' with the rest of the Hebrew Bible.

I have also suggested that the common emphasis among interpreters on the importance of 'order' is somewhat misleading. What is more clearly and explicitly emphasised in most wisdom writings is the 'orderer' behind creation. Therefore, 'creator theology' might work better as a description of the theological interests of wisdom books than the usual 'creation theology'. This 'creator theology', through its emphasis on the beauty, power (and weakness) of creatures and their creator invites the reader to look beyond their constrained horizons.

---

[73] Weeks, *Ecclesiastes 1–5*, 510.
[74] Zimmerli, 'The Place and Limit', 146.
[75] Zimmerli, 'The Place and Limit', 158.

Further Reading

Belousek, Darrin W. Snyder. 'God the Creator in the Wisdom of Solomon: A Theological Commentary', 2015. www.academia.edu/15912414/God_the_Creator_in_the_Wisdom_of_Solomon_A_Theological_Commentary.

Brown, William P. *Wisdom's Wonder: Character, Creation, and Crisis in the Bible's Wisdom Literature*. Grand Rapids: 2014.

Dell, Katharine J. 'The Significance of the Wisdom Tradition in the Ecological Debate'. Pages 56–69 in *Ecological Hermeneutics, Biblical, Historical and Theological Perspectives*. London: 2010.

Habel Norman C., and Shirley Wurst, eds. *The Earth Story in Wisdom Traditions*. Vol. 3 of *The Earth Bible*. Sheffield: 2001.

Huff, Barry R. 'From Societal Scorn to Divine Delight: Job's Transformative Portrayal of Wild Animals'. *Int* 73.3 (2019): 248–258.

Johnston, Robert K. 'Wisdom Literature and Its Contribution to a Biblical Environmental Ethic'. Pages 66–82 in *Tending the Garden*. Edited by W. Granberg-Michaelson. Grand Rapids: 1987.

Linafelt, Tod. 'The Wizard of Uz: Job, Dorothy, and the Limits of the Sublime'. *BibInt* 14.1–2 (2006): 94–109.

Schifferdecker, Kathryn. *Out of the Whirlwind, Creation Theology in the Book of Job*. HTS. Cambridge, MA: 2008.

Schmid, Hans Heinrich. *Gerechtigkeit Als Weltordnung*. Tübingen: 1968.

Schmidt, A. Jordan. *Wisdom, Cosmos, and Cultus in the Book of Sirach*. Vol. 42 of *Deuterocanonical and Cognate Literature Studies*. Boston; Berlin: 2019.

Walsh, Carey. 'The Beasts of Wisdom: Ecological Hermeneutics of the Wild'. *BibInt* 25.2 (2017): 135–148.

Zimmerli, Walther. 'The Place and Limit of the Wisdom in the Framework of the Old Testament Theology'. *SJT* 17 (1964): 146–158.

21 Reward and Retribution

PETER T. H. HATTON

Like many binaries, 'reward and retribution' can be reduced to a single phenomenon; in this instance along the lines that something, or some-one, in the cosmos, will ensure that merit is rewarded and vice reproved. In the recent interpretation of the biblical wisdom literature, just such a reduction has been entertained, not least because scholars have thereby hoped to find a way of reducing the sometimes baffling complexities of these texts to something simpler and more easily comprehensible. However, what appeared to offer a helpful interpretative strategy has led much modern scholarship to accept a paradigmatic understanding which has, arguably, led to distorted and misleading views of these books. I shall examine how such a partial, indeed pejorative, view of biblical wisdom developed and then seek to develop a more fruitful approach in which these concepts can be understood in a less all-encompassing way, one that more accurately reflects the thought world of this literature. These concepts may retain a certain validity but not as abstract laws or 'constructs'. Rather, they should be understood in terms of relationship, above all of relationship with the God of Israel.

A word on method; in what follows, it will be assumed that, no matter what the formation history of these texts may have been, they can be interpreted as meaningful in their canonical forms. So, for example, whether or not the final verses of Qohelet are to be regarded as the work of an editor or of the author of the body of the text, such differing voices are intended to be heard within the confines of the final canonical form. These books are not bland and univocal but dialogical; they seek to prompt deep consideration of life's complexities.

WHAT GOES AROUND COMES AROUND?

Proverbs begins its teaching with a warning against joining a violent gang. In a characteristically lively passage, it portrays sinners luring a young man to join them with promises of rich spoil from unfortunate victims (Prov 1:11–14). However, the text contends that the real victims are the robbers themselves:

... they lie in wait – to kill themselves!
and set an ambush – for their own lives!
(Prov 1:18)

Essentially, the same claim is made again at the end of the chapter when Wisdom cries out that those who reject her, will, in their turn, be rejected by her and abandoned to their own self-destructive impulses.

Therefore, they will eat the fruit of their own way
and be sated by their own devices.

(Prov 1:31)

This notion, that, in some undisclosed fashion, the evil intentions of the wicked will rebound on their own head, is often encountered in wisdom literature (e.g., Prov 11:17; 21:3; Job 18:7; and in the 'deutero-canon' Sir 27:27) as well as elsewhere in the Hebrew Bible (e.g., Ps 9:15; Joel 3:7). However, to see the point made twice in these early crucial passages in Proverbs – a book often regarded as the wellspring of traditional Israelite wisdom – emphasises the importance of this claim, particularly in Proverbs but also in wisdom generally.

What are we to make of such a strong doctrine that wickedness provokes a retribution matching the harm that its perpetrators intended? Significantly, it is expressed not as a prayer or a wish but in an indicative mood; not 'may the wicked fall into their own trap!' but 'the wicked will fall into the pit they have dug'. One might think, in certain moods, that such an outcome would be very welcome; although, one might also reflect how rarely this occurs in common experience. Indeed, this is counter-intuitive teaching. How might it have arisen?

The similarities with the 'eye for an eye' punishments in the Pentateuch (Exod 21:23–25; Lev 24:19–21; Deut 19:15–21), the so-called *lex talionis*, are striking, particularly in Deuteronomy's discussion of the 'malicious witness' to be requited with the identical punishment intended for the person he falsely accused. One conclusion we might reach is that, while they shared the Pentateuchal authors' sense that the punishment should fit the crime, some of the wisdom writers, particularly those responsible for Proverbs, appear to have gone further. Could it be that they believed there was some cosmic law, or mechanism, that would lead, sooner or later, to appropriate retribution for evil deeds?

As we read on in Proverbs, such suspicions might be confirmed. Indeed, some might conclude the book teaches that not only evil deeds but virtuous actions are also appropriately and invariably recompensed. The remaining eight chapters of Proverbs 1–9 declare repeatedly that following Wisdom leads to good things but that succumbing to the temptations offered by her dark counterpart, the 'strange woman', leads to death. Furthermore, it is repeatedly asserted in the sayings material, the *měšalîm*, of the later chapters, that the values endorsed in Proverbs – wisdom, righteousness, diligence, humility and the 'fear of the LORD' – lead to flourishing, while their negative counterparts – folly, wickedness, laziness, arrogance and irreligion – end in poverty, ruin and death. There is a particular concentration of such sayings in the first three chapters of the 'Proverbs of Solomon' section (e.g., Prov 10:2–4, 27; 11:28; 12:3, 11, 21, 27; 13:4, 6, 13, 14, 18, 25) but there is no shortage elsewhere (e.g., Prov 16:4–6; 17:20–21; 19:8, 15, 23; 20:4, 13, 17; 21:7, 13; 22:8; 24:15–16, 30–34).

A PEJORATIVE PARADIGM

Once again, it might be thought that such confidence that virtue is rewarded and wickedness punished is, in the light of experience, rather misplaced: counter examples readily occur. Von Rad, in a sensitive discussion of the use of maxims in biblical wisdom, appeals for some understanding of this tendency: 'for the men of old it was precisely the breakthrough to the generally and universally valid that was the most important thing'.[1] However, might not such a breakthrough be at the cost of any claim to truth or realism?

This is precisely the conclusion that many scholars have arrived at. Take, for example, this comment by Clines, author of a magisterial commentary on Job, writing in a volume on the emergence of the Hebrew Bible:

> Proverbs is, next to Deuteronomy, the most stalwart defender in the Hebrew Bible of the doctrine of retribution .... Everywhere it is asserted – or else taken for granted – that righteousness is rewarded and sin is punished (e.g., 11:5–6) .... Job and Ecclesiastes introduce the needed element of sophistication and realism.[2]

---

[1] Gerhard von Rad, *Old Testament Theology: Volume One, the History of Israel's Historical Traditions*, trans. D. M. G. Stalker (Edinburgh, 1962), 420.

[2] David J. A. Clines, 'The Wisdom Books', in *Creating the Old Testament: The Emergence of the Hebrew Bible*, ed. S. Bigger (Oxford, 1989), 272.

We may have some sympathy with his claim that Proverbs links actions and consequences in a particularly strong way but that there are no exceptions to this teaching ('everywhere it is asserted') is more questionable. We should also note his contrast between Proverbs' supposed lack of realism and the more sophisticated Job and Ecclesiastes. In fact, the claims that Proverbs always propounds an unexamined, implausible doctrine of retribution and reward and that the two other canonical wisdom texts take issue with this, are key claims of a dominant interpretative tradition: one endorsed by many eminent Old Testament scholars. They are elements of a paradigm in which Proverbs is compared unfavourably with other wisdom texts whose understanding of reward and retribution is, supposedly, more realistic and 'sophisticated'.

Accordingly, a popular introduction to Old Testament theology, co-authored by several distinguished scholars, comments:

> The *theodic settlement* [italics original] of Proverbs had insisted, in an endless recital of close, didactic observations, that the world works so that deeds have consequences .... Sowing leads to reaping. Righteousness and wisdom lead to life; wickedness and foolishness lead to death.[3]

An impatience with Proverbs is evident in the tone here, particularly in the expression 'endless recital'; a more serious allegation follows. These 'close, didactic observations' are, apparently, self-serving. Proverbs' authors, who were, supposedly, 'established elders in the familial community or ... privileged intelligentsia in the royal entourage', apparently believed that their privileges had been earned by their righteousness. All is not lost, however; there is a 'counter-testimony' in the wisdom tradition. 'The book of Job may be regarded as the principal *theodic protest* [italics original] in the Old Testament that challenges the serene justifications of social reality given in the book of Proverbs.'[4]

Philip Davies affirms essentially the same charges in a particularly critical way. The authors of Proverbs were, he believes, elite scribes who coupled their justification of 'the *status quo*, a system in which the haves deserve their having and the poor are poor because they are not wise but foolish', with the development of a monotheistic theology. Monotheism's 'logical consequence' is, apparently, a notion of a moral

---

[3] Bruce C. Birch et al., *A Theological Introduction to the Old Testament* (Nashville, 1999), 393.

[4] Birch et al., *Introduction*, 393.

order built into the 'fabric of creation' that ensures 'the wicked suffer, the righteous blossom, the indolent starve, the foolish come to grief, the wise prosper'. Not only is such an understanding of how the cosmos works 'half-baked', it also betokens a self-serving lack of integrity: 'That intellectuals believe or are told to believe in this philosophy is not to their credit, but perhaps we can understand that it would be very unwise to publish under the name of King Solomon anything suggesting the contrary (or wait for the writer of Qohelet).'[5] The agreement of such distinguished scholars on the essential outline of the case against Proverbs' teaching on 'retribution and reward' is striking. This teaching, they allege, is not only unrealistic but actively oppressive. It constitutes, apparently, a counter-intuitive but convenient understanding justified in essentially metaphysical terms. The complacent sages who compiled Proverbs supposedly took for granted the existence of a cosmic order guaranteeing that deeds have their appropriate consequences. Furthermore, it is held that Job and Qohelet offered more realistic, liberating challenges to this status-quo-supporting dogma.

THE ACTS-CONSEQUENCE 'CONSTRUCT'

These scholarly opinions are typical of a paradigm still widespread in academic approaches to the Wisdom books particularly at an introductory level. Certainly, teaching biblical hermeneutics at master's level, I have discovered that most of my students bring this understanding with them from previous teaching. Arguably, much in this paradigm's content, the vocabulary in which it continues to be expressed and, indeed, its persuasive power can be traced to a specific source – Klaus Koch's article 'Gibt es ein Vergeltungsdogma im Alten Testament?' ('Is there a Dogma of Retribution in the Old Testament?'). Writing in 1955, Koch took issue with what he regarded as the scholarly assumption that a notion of divine retribution was deeply rooted in the Old Testament.[6] He argued that, in the Old Testament, God does not actively intervene to punish and reward. Rather, these texts teach that humans fashion their own good fortune when they act in ways that are *gemeinschaftstreu* ('faithful to the community'). On the other hand, they invariably

---

[5] Philip Davies, 'The False Pen of the Scribes', in *Sense and Sensitivity: Essays on Reading the Bible in Memory of Robert Carroll*, ed. A. Hunter and Philip Davies, JSOTSup 348 (Sheffield, 2002), 123.

[6] Klaus Koch, 'Gibt es ein Vergeltungsdogma im Alten Testament?', *ZTK* 52 (1955): 1–42.

suffer when they deal 'wickedly' (*frevlerisch*).[7] Indeed, this relationship between deeds and consequences is, Koch thought, understood in much of the Old Testament, particularly the book of Proverbs, to be an inescapable moral mechanism built into the order of the cosmos, one which is, moreover, quite independent of any deity.

Indeed, God, on this account, never acts 'like a judge' (*richterlich*) to punish or reward. The language of 'retribution' (*Vergeltung*) is primarily for Koch a legal term and, as such, is inappropriate in this context. God, Koch argues, is never portrayed in these texts as judicially engaged in these processes for which human beings must take sole responsibility. True, the deity can play a limited auxiliary role, bringing to completion what humans have begun; so in a striking image, Koch suggests that sometimes '*Jahwe*' offers '*Hebedamedienst*' ('midwifery services').[8] However, sometimes even this limited divine agency is impossible and God 'must observe helplessly' while events take their course.[9]

Given that most of the supporting texts Koch cites are from Proverbs (with a particular concentration of citations from Proverbs 11), it appears that he considered this understanding of divine and human agency to be especially prevalent in the book. He held it to be so ingrained there that, even when it was 'shaken to the foundation' by the criticisms of Qohelet and Job, there was 'no fundamental break-through to another way of thinking'.[10]

The striking scholarly assertions noted in the previous section, particularly that Proverbs is 'the most stalwart defender' of a doctrine that deeds invariably have condign consequences; that the book teaches God is complicit in, or simply goes along with, this state of affairs; and that Job and Qohelet protest, in vain, against this unrealistic over-simplification can, thus, all be traced back to Koch's seminal article. There are some perhaps predictable developments, particularly the suggestion (in spite of Koch's denial of any divine involvement in these matters) that this counter-intuitive mechanism was part of a 'monothe-istic' ideology. Nevertheless, in its essentials, the schema can be attributed to Koch's analysis.

Moreover, it was, perhaps, unfortunate that when his article appeared in an English version, Koch's preferred phrase for the relation-ship he had identified – '*eine schicksal-wirkende Tatsphäre*' (literally,

---

[7] Koch, 'Vergeltungsdogma', 2.
[8] Koch, 'Vergeltungsdogma', 3–5.
[9] Koch, 'Vergeltungsdogma', 12.
[10] Koch, 'Vergeltungsdogma', 36.

'a fate-producing deed-sphere') – required, apparently, no less than thirteen words to render it into idiomatic English as 'a sphere of influence in which the built-in consequences of actions takes effect'.[11] It is not, perhaps, surprising that another of Koch's description of the cause-and-effect mechanism in the moral life, the *'Tat–Ergehen Zusammenhang'* ('act-consequence connection') claimed readers' attention more readily, especially when this was rendered 'action–consequence construct'.[12] However, this translation is a problematic one, for *Zusammenhang* does not mean 'construct' but 'connection' or 'relationship'. Nevertheless, it is in this form that the phrase is often, unfortunately, quoted; 'unfortunately' for, of course, such a 'construct' (whether it exists or not!) is a great target for that scholarly sport, 'deconstruction'.

DIFFICULTIES WITH THE ACTS-CONSEQUENCE CONSTRUCT

The notion that Israel's wisdom literature taught that there was an inevitable connection between acts and their consequences may well have first been brought to the attention of English-speaking scholars in 1972 when the English version of Gerhard von Rad's *Wisdom in Israel* (1970) appeared. Discussing Proverbs in this influential work, Von Rad (who had supervised Koch's doctoral thesis on which his article had been based) opined that 'only recently' had it been fully understood that Israel, like much of the rest of the ancient world, 'was convinced that by every evil deed or every good deed a momentum was released which sooner or later also had an effect on the author of the deed'.[13] Von Rad granted the general validity of this conclusion but, careful scholar that he was, noted that there are many 'paradoxical assertions' in Proverbs that complicate matters.

Von Rad did not offer examples of these 'complications', but he may well have been thinking of several sayings in Proverbs that, as it were, constitute a 'minority report' alongside the many others which do indeed seem to support Koch's thesis. These include several verses (Prov 10:2; 11:4; 13:11; 15:16; 16:8) which insist that the unwise and even the wicked can be blessed with wealth, even if it will not save

---

[11] Koch, 'Is there a Doctrine of Retribution in the Old Testament?', in *Theodicy in the Old Testament*, ed. James Crenshaw, trans. Thomas J. Trapp (London, 1983), 78.

[12] Koch, 'Vergeltungsdogma', 62.

[13] Gerhard von Rad, *Wisdom in Israel*, trans. James D. Martin (London, 1972), 126.

them 'in the day of trouble'. Even more strikingly, Prov 11:16 – 'violent [men] gain wealth and attractive women gain honour'[14] – asserts that good things can accrue to those who do not earn them through good behaviour. Moreover, Prov 13:23 bemoans the fact that the poor's fertile land would produce much food but that oppression snatches it away.

Proverbs, then, contains an awareness that, as far as worldly prosperity is concerned, people do not always get their just deserts. Furthermore, against the paradigmatic understanding that, in Proverbs, the virtuous always prosper and the poor are the authors of their own misfortune, we might note those sayings that link riches with injustice but do not even hint that poverty is blameworthy. So we have,

> The poor are disliked even by their neighbours
> but the rich have many friends.
>
> (Prov 14:20)

Lest we think this is simply an observation without any moral evaluation, it is immediately followed by,

> Those who despise their neighbours are sinners
> but happy are those who are kind to the poor.
>
> (Prov 14:21)

Another saying familiar to popular piety is, in similar fashion, followed by a verse that offers a sly commentary on the belief that wealth is a panacea for all ills:

> The name of the LORD is a strong tower
> the righteous run into it and are safe.
> The wealth of the rich is their strong city;
> in their imagination it is like a high wall.
>
> (Prov 18:10–11)

Indeed, there are other difficulties flagged up in Proverbs for accepting a simple equation of wisdom/righteousness with prosperity and folly/wickedness with poverty. They include the difficulty of assessing people's true wealth from their lifestyle, for as Prov 13:7 observes, there are those who are impoverished but put on a show of wealth, while some conceal their riches so as to appear poor. Furthermore, a righteous mind may be of more true value than

---

[14] A literal rendering following the Hebrew text rather than the Greek and one which avoids the various devices through which translators seek to conform the verse to the book's 'majority report'.

abundance of wealth, a truth encapsulated in a class of so-called 'better ... than' sayings, for instance:

> Better is a little with the fear of the LORD
> than great treasure and trouble with it.
>
> (Prov 15:1)

DIVINE INVOLVEMENT IN RETRIBUTION AND REWARD

It seems then that Proverbs sees a rather less predictable 'connection' between virtue and prosperity and vice and disaster than Koch allowed for. However, further objection to his conclusions on what might be called 'theological grounds' should be noted. Koch's claim that the Old Testament, as a whole, contains no doctrine of God as a judge punishing bad conduct and rewarding good is surely questionable. There are, for instance, many instances of God being described as a judge in the Psalms (e.g., 7:8, 11; 50:1, 4, 6; 72:2; 82:8; 94:2; 98:9; 119:84), and examples outside the Psalter are not lacking. The threatened destruction of Sodom and Gomorrah, explicitly described by Abraham in Genesis 18:25 in terms of a judicial action ('Shall not the Judge of all the earth deal justly?') is particularly striking. So too is the prayer of Solomon, the patron of wisdom, in 1 Kgs 8:32, in which he pleads with God to 'judge his servants' and 'reward them in accordance with their righteousness'. Koch might point out that the rendering 'rewarding them' of most of the English versions here is misleading as the original Hebrew speaks simply of 'giving to him [the righteous] according to his righteousness' (lātet lô kəṣidqātô). Even so, there is sufficient judicial language in the prayer, including the use of the root špṭ 'to judge', to make it clear that God is not envisaged as a passive bystander observing an independent process, powerless to intervene.

So it seems hard to sustain Koch's thesis as an assertion about the whole of the Hebrew Bible; might it not, however, have a more restricted validity to the wisdom literature and Proverbs in particular? We may freely grant that God is not explicitly described as a Judge in Proverbs. However, there are sayings that suggest he is, nevertheless, intimately involved in the judicial process. The poor and afflicted are not to be oppressed 'in the gate':

> for the LORD pleads their cause
> and despoils of life those who despoil them.
>
> (Prov 22:23)

The phrase 'at the gate' sets the context unmistakably as a judicial one, for it is 'in the gates' of the pre-exilic Israelite city that justice was conducted. Indeed, the thought here may be that God is, as it were, the supreme judge who will punish those who abuse the legal system to their own wicked ends. Fox cites the parallel passage in *Amenemope* 4.19, in which 'the Moon' declares the crime of the oppressor and, commenting that 'the Moon is Thoth, the god of scribes and the administration of justice', argues that here 'Israel's deity has replaced Thoth'.[15]

Indeed, Prov 29:26 implies that the real source of justice is God when it declares that, while 'many seek to gain the favour of earthly authorities, it is from the LORD that one obtains justice' (*mēyhwh mišpaṭ-'iš*). Certainly, as Fox notes, '*mišpaṭ*' (justice) here may include 'any decision the ruler makes and not only a judicial verdict'.[16] However, this only serves to emphasise that 'judging' in ancient cultures, including Israel, was not limited to a narrow range of criminal and contractual issues. It involved a much broader spectrum of contested matters as, for instance, in Israel, such procedures as those stipulated in Deut 17:2-7 (execution of idolaters) and 25:5-10 ('levirate' marriage) indicate. Arguably, even more striking to those accustomed to viewing judges as impartial arbiters, the judge was not seen as an aloof, uncommitted figure but one whose role was actively to promote human flourishing. Crucially, vindicating the innocent is as important in such a role as condemning the guilty.[17] Given the above, to deny the term 'judicial' (*richterlich*) to how Proverbs understands God to be acting in these sayings seems unwarranted.

Nevertheless, Koch is correct when he notes the relative paucity (though not complete absence) of juridical language in connection with God in Proverbs. Apart from anything else, it highlights an interesting contrast with Job who will plead again and again for God to grant him a day in court and vindicate him. However, Koch's notion of a passive, even helpless God is more difficult to sustain. God is often seen in Proverbs as actively promoting the good and thwarting socially harmful behaviour, whether or not he does so in a judicial capacity.

---

[15] Michael V. Fox, *Proverbs 10-31: A New Translation with Introduction and Commentary*, AB 18B (New Haven; London, 2009), 714-715.

[16] Fox, *Proverbs 10-31*, 847.

[17] For a fuller description of the judicial system in Ancient Israel, see Hans Boecker, *Law and the Administration of Justice in the Old Testament and the Ancient East* (Minneapolis, 1982).

REWARD AND RETRIBUTION IN PROVERBS:
A RELATIONAL UNDERSTANDING

Koch's article merits the attention I have given it. He is to be commended for pointing out that God's actions are not understood in scripture as always involving direct interventions in human affairs but are
sometimes seen as being more subtle. Moreover, even when he overstated his case and thereby introduced powerful distortions into the
interpretative tradition, his very exaggerations may prompt us to arrive
at some more helpful insights.

Accordingly, Koch's confidence that the wisdom texts assume an
inevitable relationship between deeds and their consequences acted as a
spur to those who wanted to offer more nuanced understandings. Such a
stress on individual deeds needed to be corrected by William P. Brown's
insight that the book's prime aim is not to promote wealth and prosperity but rather to encourage the formation of moral, communal virtues in
a person's character.[18] Again, and perhaps paradoxically, Koch's very
insistence on the existence of such a connection might highlight the
small, but not insignificant, number of sayings that, as we have seen,
deny or problematise it.

Moreover, Koch's notion that God in Proverbs is somehow subordinated to *Schicksal* ('fate') – that is, a force generated by human actions
with which he may be able to cooperate but that he cannot counter-
mand – throws a spotlight on the very different picture of the deity
assumed everywhere in Proverbs; namely, that the God attested therein,
as elsewhere in Scripture, is held to be all-powerful, radically free and
without earthly (or for that matter, heavenly) rivals. Such a theological
tendency makes sense of what we might call, somewhat anachronistically, the key 'virtue' of the wisdom texts, namely, the 'fear of the
LORD'. The prominence given to this at the beginning of Proverbs –
the fear of the LORD is the beginning of knowledge; fools despise
wisdom and instruction (Prov 1:7) – is, of course, deeply significant.
This initial prominence and the sixteen other sayings in the book that
mention 'the fear of the LORD' suggest that such fear is not just one
more item in a stock list of virtues but offers a vital key to the interpretation of Proverbs. Indeed, we shall see that it is deeply significant in
the other wisdom books, especially in relationship to reward
and retribution.

---

[18] See William P. Brown, *Character in Crisis: A Fresh Approach to the Wisdom
Literature of the Old Testament* (Grand Rapids, 1996).

We should note that 'the fear of the LORD' is essentially a relational stance in Proverbs. Whenever it is employed, it implies that those who enter into such a relationship will gain benefits. Proverbs 3:8 insists that 'if we fear the LORD and turn away from evil' then 'our flesh will be made whole and our bodies refreshed'. The fear of the LORD is equated with 'wisdom and insight' in Prov 9:10, and we are assured that this will lead to 'length of days'. In Prov 22:4, the point is made even more strongly: humble god-fearers will be rewarded with wealth, respect and (long) life. However, on the other hand, we might recall Wisdom's stern warning in Prov 1:30–31 that those who do not choose to fear the LORD, and 'who despise her reproof', will suffer dire but appropriate consequences; they will 'eat the fruit of their own way'.

Taken together, these 'fear of the LORD' verses suggest that Koch's contention that Proverbs holds there to be a sphere in which deeds bring about their inevitable consequences – consequences, that, humanity being as it is, are often negative ones – may be accepted in part. Proverbs may conceive of such a sphere but it does not hold that it is all-embracing; it is where, perhaps, those who do not fear the LORD end up. However, those who come into a relationship with God are thereby removed from such a sphere and brought into one of generosity in which they may expect favour and blessing. In such a gracious context, even what might be conceived of as punishments normally perform the positive function of discipline (mûsār) in which the pain involved in correction is ultimately a sign of favour, even fatherly love (Prov 3:12).

This conclusion, we should note, is one at odds with that of Joachim Becker in his seminal discussion of the 'fear of the LORD'.[19] Becker argues that most of the occurrences of the phrase in Proverbs are linked with retribution. However, on inspection, the verses he cites in support (Prov 10:27; 14:26–27; 15:16; 16:6; 19:23; 22:4) are all more readily understood in terms of this relational understanding. Take, for example, Prov 10:27 where, yes, the wicked are told that their days will be short, but the same verse also assures those who fear the LORD that their lives will be long. This is typical; indeed, all the sayings cited by Becker are more concerned to assert that fearing God is a source of blessing than they are to speak of retribution upon the wicked.

The evidence then that 'the fear of the LORD' does not have to do solely with retribution is, in my view, compelling. Such 'fear' denotes an attitudinal stance towards Israel's deity that brings those who display

---

[19] Joachim Becker, *Gottesfurcht im Alten Testament* (Rome, 1965), 221–228.

it into a realm of favour in which any harsher elements experienced in the relationship constitute a discipline intended to promote their well-being. The language of retribution does not apply in such a realm. Reward is more acceptable, if it denotes the, as it were, natural consequences of this relationship but not if it points to exceptional benefits conferred on those who do good, perhaps as a prize or an inducement to further good conduct.

However, and this is of the utmost importance, much as the normal expectation might be that those who fear the LORD may enjoy material blessings, Proverbs is perfectly aware, as we have noted, that this is not always the case; the wicked may flourish and the poor be further impoverished by oppression. Nevertheless, even if we do not prosper, fearing the LORD is its own reward:

> Better is a little with the fear of the LORD,
> than great treasure and trouble with it.
>
> (Prov 15:16)

By its very nature, this relationship looks beyond present misery or prosperity in hope and does not see such things as necessarily either punishment or reward (Prov 23:17–18).

REWARD AND RETRIBUTION IN THE OTHER CANONICAL BOOKS

Job

We have examined the thesis that Proverbs' understanding of reward and retribution is controlled by a flawed, counter-factual belief in a mechanism ensuring deeds are appropriately rewarded and found it flawed. We should then be open to the possibility that the three canonical wisdom books share rather more similar approaches to these matters than is commonly understood; and so it transpires.

Indeed, the prose prologue with which Job commences (Job 1–2) seems designed to cast doubt on the notion that Israel's God is subject to an impersonal force generated by human action. While we may be perplexed – indeed, even affronted – by the notion that Job the 'blameless and upright' should be reduced to utter misery in order to resolve a controversy between the LORD and one of his more sinister subordinates, haśāṭān ('the Accuser'),[20] there can be no question here of God

---

[20] Or 'Adversary'; see the discussion in David J. A. Clines, *Job 1–20*, WBC 17 (Nashville, 1989), 19–23.

being forced into taking these actions. Whatever the rights and wrongs of his allowing Job to be so sorely tested, God does so of his own volition unconstrained by 'fate'.

Furthermore, the very question posed by the Accuser which initiates the action of the book involves a form of the same key phrase so significant in Proverbs.

Does Job fear God ['$\bar{e}l\bar{o}h\hat{i}m$] for nothing [$\d{h}inn\bar{a}m$]?

(Job 1:9)

We should note here the use of '$\bar{e}l\bar{o}h\hat{i}m$ as the divine name in the expression 'fear God' rather than, as always in Proverbs, YHWH; '$\bar{e}l\bar{o}h\hat{i}m$ was also employed in Job 1:1 where Job is described as 'one who feared God and turned away from evil'. This variation is, in my view, significant, and we shall return to it later. However, the main issue raised is the one also raised (rather more obliquely) in Proverbs; namely, are those who fear God – that is, those who have entered into a relationship with the deity, one characterised by awe, deep respect and love – motivated purely by the rewards they hope to receive from this relationship? Or are there motives, as we might say, disinterested?[21] That is, do they fear God simply for his own sake?

This is, in my view, the main issue raised by the entire book. The other question often seen as the main focus of the book's interest, 'Why do bad things happen to good people?' is certainly important – it is voiced in the Accuser's question through the ambiguity of the word $\d{h}inn\bar{a}m$ which can mean 'to no purpose', implying that Job's virtue will seem meaningless when it is no longer linked to prosperity – but it is subordinated in the book's exploration of its deeper interest in what we may expect if we fear God.

It is striking that both Job and the friends who become his accusers – Eliphaz, Bildad and Zophar – for all their differences, share similar expectations of that relationship. They agree that it comes with benefits and, if they are not forthcoming, then either something has gone drastically wrong with the relationship or it was never real at all. As the book's dialogues progress, it becomes clear that Job affirms increasingly strongly the former opinion; God has, for reasons he cannot fathom, failed to act justly and is subjecting him to inappropriately harsh punishment. Accordingly, Job appeals as a plaintiff for vindication from a deity conceived in judicial terms as a judge or prosecutor. His friends, on

---

[21] Clines, *Job 1–20*, 22; cf. J. Janzen, *Job* (Louisville, 1990).

the other hand, insist with increasing vehemence that Job's predicament indicates that he never truly feared the LORD but is at home in something very much like Koch's *schicksal-wirkende Tatsphäre*, an arena where the evil deeds, they assume he must have committed, are now coming home to roost.

Accordingly, in Job 22:9–11, Eliphaz ends his denunciation of Job with an accusation that he has oppressed widows and orphans; that is why he is trapped and terrified, in darkness and covered by the floods. Although the Hebrew here does not use the precise wording of the flood narrative in Genesis 6–9 (the poetic *šipaʿat-mayim* ['abundance of waters'] rather than *mabbûl* ['flood']), Eliphaz may be implying that Job, like one of God's human enemies in Genesis, is to be obliterated in a divine reversal of creation. Ironically, this chimes with Job's own desire not to have been created, as he begins his complaints with a wish never to have been born, expressed in language which suggests a return to the darkness of the uncreated cosmos (Job 3:1–18). This is the underlying logic of the commitment Job and his friends share to something very like the 'acts-consequence relationship'. Wickedness, in this view, brings humanity to a place where the consequences of deeds that spring from irrational wilfulness lead to a return to the *tōhû wabōhû*, the 'disordered chaos' before creation. Yet there are signs even in the dialogue sections of the book that Job, in contrast to his friends, is able to move beyond this to something more profound.

Job 28 comes as a surprising interruption in the cycles of accusation and impassioned defence between Job and his friends. From these we turn aside to consider a subject of consuming interest in all these texts,

> Where then does wisdom come from?
> (Job 28:20)

Musing that this wisdom is 'hidden from the eyes of all living' Job concludes that only 'God understands the way to it' and, accordingly, that only in relationship to him can wisdom be obtained:

> Truly, the fear of the LORD, that is wisdom;
> and to depart from evil is understanding.
> (Job 28:28)

We may note here that, for the first time, the name of Israel's God is placed on the lips of Job, who as the text clearly indicates (Job 1:1, 3) is not an Israelite. Until now Job and his friends have employed *ʾĕlōhîm* (or the related forms *ʾēl* and *ʾĕlōah*) and the more enigmatic descriptor *šadday* ('the Almighty'). We may credit the use of these names, and the book's setting in the land of Uz outside Israel, to what we might call its 'universalism' – its laudable interest not just in Israelite piety but in the more general human condition. However, the egregious use of YHWH in Job 28:28 hints at another possibility; the text may be asking us to distinguish between 'fearing God' – a generalised, semi-pagan piety through which we may hope to receive rewards but in which we may also receive dire retribution if we act wickedly – and 'fearing the LORD', a relationship characterised, yes, by favour and blessing, but also one which transcends merely material understandings of these things. Accordingly, 'to fear YHWH' offers a wisdom that is a surpassing good in itself; one that is of inestimable value, whether or not we enjoy material well-being.

Such a relational understanding makes sense of the book's surprising ending in which Job, who, though he is not granted his 'day in court', confesses that he sees the divine nature – and it is significant that here, in Job 42:1, he addresses God again as 'the LORD' (YHWH) – in a new, transformed light:

> I had heard of you by the hearing of the ear,
> but now my eye sees you;
> therefore I despise myself,
> and repent in dust and ashes.
>
> (Job 42:5–6)

Clines' argument that the 'repent' here (Hebrew *niḥamti*) might be better rendered 'I am consoled for' is convincing.[22] That is, the theophany of the preceding chapters, and the new vision of God it offers, means that Job can now accept some consolation for the miseries of his recent existence. Although Job's complaints have not been addressed and his fortunes have not yet been restored, what he has now seen of the glory and majesty of the LORD and the extent of divine responsibility for a creation which is radically wild and untamed offers him a new perspective into what is truly rewarding. With this new perspective comes consolation – an awareness, perhaps, that he is in a new, or renewed and deeper, relationship with God.

Qohelet

In Qohelet, we find the most explicit denial that anything like the 'acts-consequence relationship' can be relied upon as a guide to how we may live flourishing, rewarding lives:

---

[22]   David J. A. Clines, *Job 38–42*, WBC 18B (Nashville, 2009).

There is a vanity that takes place on earth, that there are righteous people who are treated according to the conduct of the wicked and there are wicked people who are treated according to the conduct of the righteous. (Qoh 8:14)

What some verses in the 'minority report' in Proverbs dare to say, and what is implied in the whole narrative of Job, comes here to the fore as part of a radical exploration of what it might mean to be treated well or badly in life.

Qohelet begins with a statement of its central thesis, that all is 'vanity' (hebel); and so, in a world where no human achievements abide and death awaits us all, what profit do we have from wealth and power, and even from wisdom, given all the trouble that comes with them? The next two chapters (Qohelet 1 and 2) can be read as a 'thought experiment' as they envisage someone who has everything that, in common understanding, makes life rewarding – power, wealth, honour and wisdom – yet hates their life because it will close in the oblivion and forgetting that comes with death (Qoh 2:14–23).

However, despair is not where these chapters or, in my judgement, the book as a whole finally settle. If we abandon our futile search for meaning and happiness in 'vanity' (a rather weak rendering of the enigmatic term hebel which holds together notions of impermanence, futility and even, as Fox argues,[23] absurdity) and seek to be accepted by God, then we can find things of true value in a relationship with him. Thus, Qohelet 2:26 asserts that to those who are favoured in his eyes (ləʾādām šeṭṭôb ləpānāyw), God offers wisdom and joy; but to those outside that relationship, God gives over to fruitless toil that will benefit others but not themselves. This saying is, arguably, close to what Proverbs and Job affirm. Those books, as we have seen, also recognise what is implied here: that to have God's favour transforms our understanding of what is truly valuable and meaningful. Such a transformation allows us to see through the emptiness of what are commonly regarded as indications of success or failure – or even as divine retribution and reward – and discern what are the 'solid joys and lasting pleasures' offered to humanity by a good God. To these simple things – eating and drinking, the sense of a job well done, the company of loved ones – explicitly described as gifts 'approved' by God, Qohelet repeatedly returns (Qoh 2:24, 3:12–13, 5:18–20, 9:7–10).

---

[23] Michael V. Fox, A Time to Tear Down and a Time to Build Up: A Re-reading of Ecclesiastes (Grand Rapids, 1999), 30–32.

In this reading of Qohelet, the 'acts-consequence construct' is not so much 'deconstructed' as re-interpreted. Many of the things commonly held to be blessings, the 'rewards' of life, turn out to be harmful, or even absurd, because they can only be gained with such effort that the things that make life truly rewarding are neglected. This, once again, is in fundamental agreement with some of the sayings in Proverbs:

> Better is a little with the fear of the LORD
> than great treasure and trouble with it.
>
> (Prov 15:17)

Qohelet's final exhortation to that same relational attitude to God towards which both Proverbs and Job urge us should come then as no surprise:

> The end of the matter: all has been heard. Fear God and keep his commandments; for that is the whole duty of everyone.
>
> (Qoh 12:13)

The NRSV's rendering of the last phrase (kî-zeh kol-hā' ādām) follows a rather misleading traditional understanding, for there is no mention of 'duty' or obligation in the original; 'all [there is] for a person' would be a more literal rendering. This is undeniably enigmatic but it may, perhaps, be best understood in the light of our argument. In the canonical wisdom books 'to fear God' is already to have all that we may need by way of 'reward'. In the words of Teresa of Avila, *solo Dios basta* ('God alone suffices').

CONCLUSION

Re-visiting Koch's influential thesis for the purposes of this chapter, I felt much less inclined to dismiss his argument *in toto* than previously. It is a polemic, and, in the nature of all such exercises, it obscures as much as it reveals, but it is a brilliant one. Moreover, Koch cannot be blamed for the misleading ways, devoid of nuance, in which his insights were sometimes adopted, especially in English-speaking scholarship. Indeed, Koch's analysis does point us to a feature of Proverbs' teaching that – perhaps out of an understandable anxiety to avoid the extremes of so-called prosperity theology – we may seek to minimise. After all, in many societies, industry, sobriety, truth-telling and piety do tend to be 'rewarded' in lives which are ordered, meaningful and, yes, even prosperous, although, of course, this is not always the case. Nor is Koch's theological position totally without support in these texts. God's agency is depicted in them in some subtle ways which include the aspects of completion and divine withdrawal that Koch focuses on.

However, it is Koch's willingness to generalise from some verses to the whole and to ignore the evidence of a God in scripture who intervenes and, indeed, judges, that cannot be sustained. Moreover, he failed to see that the wisdom books are convinced that a relationship with God changes everything, transferring us from a realm where 'what we sow we must reap' to one in which both human blessing and woe are caught up into purposes which are ultimately beneficial. Plainly, this involves a faith commitment and whether it will console us when grave, egregious suffering comes upon us, we cannot foretell. Perhaps, however, a desire to micro-manage our future is a sure sign that we are looking for the false certainties of the acts-consequence 'construct':

> The human mind plans the way,
> but the LORD directs the steps.
> (Prov 16:9)

Further Reading

Boström, Lennart. *The God of the Sages: The Portrayal of God in the Book of Proverbs*. ConBOT 29. Stockholm: 1990.

Brown William P. *Character in Crisis: A Fresh Approach to the Wisdom Literature of the Old Testament*. Grand Rapids: 1996.

Clines, David J. A. 'The Wisdom Books'. Pages 269–291 in *Creating the Old Testament: The Emergence of the Hebrew Bible*. Edited by S. Bigger. Oxford: 1989.

Forti, Tova. 'The Concept of "Reward" in Proverbs: A Diachronic or Synchronic Approach?' *CurBR* 12 (2014): 129–145.

Fox, Michael V. *A Time to Tear Down and a Time to Build Up: A Re-reading of Ecclesiastes*. Grand Rapids: 1999.

Hatton, Peter T. H. 'A Cautionary Tale: The Acts-Consequence Construct'. *JSOT* 35 (2011): 375–384.

Janzen, J. Gerald. *Job*. IBC. Louisville: 1990.

Koch, Klaus. 'Is There a Doctrine of Retribution in the Old Testament?' Pages 57–87 in *Theodicy in the Old Testament*. Edited by James Crenshaw. Translated by Thomas J. Trapp. London: 1983.

Limburg, James. *Encountering Ecclesiastes: A Book for Our Time*. Grand Rapids: 2006.

Lucas, Ernest. *Proverbs*. THOTC. Grand Rapids: 2015.

Von Rad, Gerhard. *Wisdom in Israel*. Translated by James D. Martin. London: 1972.

22 From Rebuke to Testimony to Proverb: Wisdom's Many Pedagogies

WILLIAM P. BROWN

The so-called wisdom corpus of the Hebrew Bible is as eclectically diverse as it is pedagogically versatile, which is why the notion of biblical wisdom is so hard to pin down, let alone define. One can, to be sure, identify various characteristics or 'salient features' within the wisdom corpus,[1] from concrete guidance for success and moral instruction to contemplative reflection on the vicissitudes of daily life and the inscrutable wonders of God and creation.[2] But there is no one-size-fits-all definition, given the sheer diversity of the literature and the questionable notion that 'wisdom' constitutes its own 'tradition'.[3] Throughout Proverbs, Job and Ecclesiastes, biblical wisdom covers the epistemological spectrum from confident certainty to unsettling uncertainty. If anything, wisdom is fluid.

While defining biblical 'wisdom' in terms of a common outlook is impossible,[4] one can nevertheless say something about wisdom's general features first by enumerating what wisdom is *not*. Hebrew biblical wisdom is non-historiographical, non-prophetic and by and large (though not exclusively) non-cultic in orientation. In place of national history as the subject of theological reflection, the natural world stands front and centre in much of the literature.[5] Instead of Zion's temple, we

---

[1] See, e.g., Simon Chi-chung Cheung, *Wisdom Intoned: A Reappraisal of the Genre 'Wisdom Psalms'*, LHB OTS 613 (London, 2015), 22–52.

[2] William P. Brown, *Wisdom's Wonder: Character, Creation, and Crisis in the Bible's Wisdom Literature* (Grand Rapids, 2014), 24–27.

[3] Mark Sneed, 'Is the "Wisdom Tradition" a Tradition?', *CBQ* 73 (2011): 50–71.

[4] Stuart Weeks, 'Is "Wisdom Literature" a Useful Category?', in *Tracing Sapiential Traditions in Ancient Judaism*, ed. Hindy Najman, Jean-Sébastien Rey and Eibert J. C. Tigchelaar (Leiden, 2016), 12–13.

[5] David Geoffrey Smith sums it up well: 'Wisdom understands the natural world as pedagogical' (*Practice of Wisdom*, Critical Pedagogy Today 5 [London, 2014], 52), a claim comparable to Gerhard von Rad's proposal that biblical wisdom is in part the 'self-revelation of creation' conveyed didactically (*Wisdom in Israel*, trans. James D. Martin [Nashville, 1972], 144–176 [esp. 169–172]).

find the home, the city gates and the marketplace shaping wisdom's landscape. Wisdom's primary orientation, in the broadest possible terms, is human living, specifically the praxis of living with understanding, both individual and communal. Drawing from the complexities and paradoxes of human experience,[6] much of biblical wisdom deals with matters of human character and conduct. Some have suggested that biblical wisdom operates primarily in a 'mode of reflective deliberation'[7] or with an 'intellectual tone'.[8] However, such abstract attempts at definitional containment do not quite account for the broad spectrum that biblical wisdom covers. Such characterisations may work well with Job and Ecclesiastes, but many sayings in Proverbs address the everyday vagaries of human living and can be considered relatively 'banal' by comparison, distinctly lacking in so-called intellectual reflection.[9]

Nevertheless, something can be said positively, not simply negatively, about wisdom's overarching umbrella, and it is this: wisdom *imparts* wisdom. Such a claim, although seemingly banal, if not tautological, highlights two important dimensions: wisdom's dynamic nature and wisdom's telos. First, by its very nature, wisdom is to be shared, whether widely or selectively. It is to be given and received by many or by only a few. Wisdom kept to itself without the prospect of being shared is hardly wisdom; it is simply a secret destined to die with its keeper. Wisdom is wisdom when it is imparted. Thus, from the tiniest proverb to the mightiest rebuke, wisdom never sits still, as it continues to be passed on to those who have ears to hear, eyes to read and hearts to receive. Moreover, the very diversity of the wisdom corpus serves hermeneutically to host an ongoing dialogue for its readers. Second, wisdom is wisdom when it is deemed worthy of imparting, suggesting that there is a worthy goal in view, namely, human edification of some sort, that is, the 'building' of human agency that comes with the gaining of insight and guidance for the challenging task of living beyond merely surviving, of living with understanding. In short, wisdom is worth imparting, and it is worth imparting because of wisdom's edifying goal of informing and shaping human perception and conduct, in short, character.[10]

---

[6] With the major exception of YHWH's revelatory address in Job 38–41. See below.

[7] Markus Sauer, 'Where Can Wisdom Be Found? New Perspectives on the Wisdom Psalms', in *Was There a Wisdom Tradition? New Prospects in Israelite Wisdom Studies*, ed. Mark R. Sneed (Atlanta, 2015), 181.

[8] Cheung, *Wisdom Intoned*, 30–33.

[9] E.g., Prov 12:5, 8, 17; 13:16; 14:33; 19:20.

[10] For a recent defence of the use of character ethics for exploring the coherence and diversity of the wisdom corpus, see William P. Brown, 'Virtue and Its Limits

The generative, conduct-shaping power of wisdom can be demonstrated, for example, by noting how various proverbs cultivate a level of critical discernment needed for moral growth or maturity. An individual proverb can encourage or even mandate an individual course of action, but when it is nested in a collection of proverbs that conflict with it or offer different perspectives, then the reader is left to discern the favourable course of action in a given situation. In so doing, the reader fosters critical discernment. Take, for example, the well-discussed 'duelling' proverbs of Prov 26:4–5, which were singled out by the Rabbis as a point of controversy about the book that required urgent resolution (*b. Shabbath* 30b):

> Do not answer a fool according to his folly,
>> or you yourself will be just like him.
> Answer a fool according to his folly,
>> or he will be wise in his own eyes.

Two unmistakably contradictory proverbs are set side by side, mandating two opposite courses of action, accompanied by different motivating reasons. So what are readers (who are not 'fools') to do? Instead of being paralysed by indecision, readers themselves must figure out which action to take by weighing the pros and cons of responding to 'fools' in a given encounter. Discerning, deciding and acting with informed judgement, as well as suffering the consequences, all make for moral growth. As we shall see, by their sheer volume and diversity, the various collections of proverbs continue this journey of cultivating critical discernment, establishing an overall pedagogical movement.[11]

While attempts at defining wisdom have focused largely on content, overlooked are wisdom's pedagogical dimensions, the various ways in which wisdom imparts itself. Reflecting its generative, 'impartable'

---

in the Wisdom Corpus: Character Formation, Disruption, and Transformation', in *The Oxford Handbook of Wisdom and the Bible*, ed. Will Kynes (New York, 2021), 45–54.

[11] For extended studies on this topic, see William P. Brown, 'The Pedagogy of Proverbs 10:1–31:9', in *Character and Scripture: Moral Formation, Community, and Biblical Interpretation*, ed. William P. Brown (Grand Rapids, 2002), 150–182; Christine Roy Yoder, 'Forming "Fearers of Yahweh": Repetition and Contradiction as Pedagogy in Proverbs', in *Seeking Out the Wisdom of the Ancients: Essays Offered to Honor Michael V. Fox on the Occasion of his Sixty-Fifth Birthday*, ed. Ronald L. Troxel, Kelvin G. Friebel and Dennis R. Magary (Winona Lake, 2005), 167–183; Peter T. H. Hatton, *Contradiction in the Book of Proverbs: The Deep Water of Counsel* (Aldershot, 2008).

nature, wisdom is by nature pedagogical.[12] James Crenshaw, for example, identifies two basic teaching 'modes' in the wisdom corpus: the 'expository', conveyed through aphorisms and instructions, which 'emphasizes the teacher's authority and depends heavily on the power of example', and the 'hypothetical', which 'shifts the focus to students, who are challenged to engage in an exciting quest to discover answers to intriguing questions'.[13] But such a binary schema is far too simplistic and rigid to account for the multiple 'modes' by which wisdom is communicated in the Hebrew corpus. For one thing, the rhetoric of 'rebuke' in Proverbs, as explored below, breaks the kind of binary that Crenshaw proposes. Moreover, wisdom is wedded to its various media, to its plurality of pedagogies, such as repetition and revision, rebuke or correction, disputation, indirection, learning by analogy and metaphorical teasing,[14] all of which are marshalled to address the human subject for the sake of living well, however 'well' is to be defined. Nevertheless, Crenshaw offers an important lens by which to examine the variegated nature of wisdom's pedagogy, namely the relational dynamics configured between 'teacher' and 'student', or more broadly between the imparter of wisdom and the implied receiver of wisdom. Pedagogy not only operates *within* this relational matrix; it defines the matrix. We begin with Proverbs.

PROVERBS

According to the prologue with its cluster of instructional verbs (1:2–6), the book of Proverbs bears the overall aim to *teach* and thus edify the intended reader on a whole range of matters, from righteousness to prudence, from skill in navigating life to understanding riddles.[15] The

---

[12] By 'pedagogy', I aim to extend the discussion beyond scholarly reconstructions of 'educational' settings, ranging from court schools to family and folk settings. See Katharine J. Dell, *The Book of Proverbs in Social and Theological Context* (Cambridge, 2006), 18–89, 190–195. 'Pedagogy', broadly defined, attends to the manner of presentation or delivery designed to meaningfully impact the receiver across social contexts. It can range from the so-called banking model, in which teaching is simply a way of 'depositing' information into the student, to Socratic dialogue and other more interactive models.

[13] James L. Crenshaw, *Education in Ancient Israel: Across the Deadening Silence*, ABRL (New York, 1998), 27.

[14] See Charles F. Melchert, *Wise Teaching: Biblical Wisdom and Educational Ministry* (Harrisburg, 1998), 47–58, 71–72.

[15] For Prov 1:2–6 as the hermeneutical key to the book as a whole, see Timothy J. Sandoval, 'Revisiting the Prologue of Proverbs', *JBL* 126 (2007): 455–473. Sandoval reads vv. 2–4 as introductory to the book's educational 'purpose', whereas vv. 5–6

range of values and virtues profiled in the prologue reflects the range of audience implied in the book of Proverbs, from the 'inexperienced' (*petî*) and 'youth' (*na'ar*) in v. 4 to the 'wise' (*ḥākām*) in v. 5.[16]

Proverbs then gets down to business by imparting wisdom in the form of disciplinary instruction disseminated by various voices ranging from the parental to that of Wisdom. In the first nine chapters, the voice of the 'father' dominates, while the silence of the 'son' is deafening. It is this ethos of patriarchal instruction that compels the reader to take on the position of the silent son, who by definition is on the receiving end of such discourse, compliant figure that he is. Pedagogically, the repeated reference to 'my son', with variation, is a form of commanding address that aims to insert or 'interpellate' the reader into the relational matrix of patriarchal discourse.[17] Such discourse is ascribed not only to the parent but also to YHWH, who is analogously depicted as a 'father' whose 'discipline' (*mûsār*) and 'rebuke' (*tôkaḥat*) are to be gladly borne as a sign of parental favour (3:11–12). Such is the pedagogy of patriarchy, a pedagogy that establishes an unquestionable hierarchy of authority that is sustained, in part, by the rhetoric of 'rebuke'. Nevertheless, pedagogically the rebuke proves to be more relationally versatile within the pedagogical mix in Proverbs and, as we shall see, Job. But we begin with the harshest rebuke in Proverbs, namely, Wisdom's own.

Wisdom's Rebuke

Wisdom's 'rebuke' (*tôkaḥat*, v. 23) in 1:22–33 is consistently 'critical and negative'.[18] She directly addresses the 'simple ones' (*pětāyim*), persons characterised by inexperience and gullibility. She condemns them, along with 'scoffers' and 'fools', for having rejected both her 'counsel' and earlier 'rebuke' (vv. 24–25; cf. 29). Disaster awaits them (vv. 26–28).

---

issues the 'invitation' to engage the purpose. Such a clean distinction does not hold, since the latter verses also highlight important values and skills featured in the book. Conversely, the purpose of Proverbs as outlined in the prologue *is* inherently invitational.

[16] Bernd U. Schipper discerns in the prologue three 'levels' of audience addressed in the prologue (specifically vv. 4–6): the beginner, the advanced and the 'wise scribe' or '*literatus*' (*Proverbs 1–15: A Commentary*, Hermeneia [Minneapolis, 2019], 9–10).

[17] See the repeated references to 'my son', with variation, in Prov 1:10, 15; 2:1; 3:1, 11, 21; 4:1 (plural minus first person possessive), 10, 20; 5:1, 7; 6:1, 3, 20; 7:1, 24 (plural); 8:32 (plural). For discussion of the patriarchal rhetoric and the dynamic of 'interpellation', see Carol A. Newsom, 'Woman and the Discourse of Patriarchal Wisdom: A Study of Proverbs 1–9', in *Gender and Difference in Ancient Israel*, ed. Peggy L. Day (Minneapolis, 1989), 143–144.

[18] Michael V. Fox, *Proverbs 1–9*, AB 18A (New York, 2000), 99.

Such rhetoric of judgement, however, turns pedagogical at the end, for the last two verses summarise the lesson behind the rebuke: folly kills but attending to Wisdom yields security (vv. 32–33). For all its dire warnings and indictments, Wisdom's discourse ends on a (relatively) positive note, balancing the consequences of folly and wisdom. On the one hand, Wisdom resolves *not* to listen when called upon (v. 28). Wisdom claims that when she had spoken earlier, in her previous rebuke, she was met only with resistance, hence her indictments (vv. 24–25, 29–30). On the other hand, she insists that she be heard (v. 33). While her words spell certain doom, they also preserve a modicum of hope to those who would (re)turn to her and 'listen'.

In short, the pedagogical aim of Wisdom's rebuke is to throw her implied audience (including the reader) off guard, casting them into a state of uncertainty as to whether they have knowingly or unknowingly failed to heed Wisdom. Her rebuke inspires a guilty conscience from the start. Coupled with dire warnings, she aims ultimately to move those who teeter on the edge of folly to turn back: a second chance couched in the language of condemnation.[19] Such is the pedagogy of Wisdom's rebuke.

In view of this most dramatic example of rebuke in Proverbs, one must ask more generally about the nature of sapiential 'rebuke' (*tôkaḥat*) and its rhetorical aim. First, a semantic overview: the noun *tôkaḥat* is most widely attested in Proverbs, containing two-thirds of all occurrences in the Hebrew Bible (16x). Outside of Proverbs, the noun denotes punishment or chastisement from God (Ps 39:12; Ezek 5:15; 25:17) or from the wicked (Ps 73:14). In two cases, it designates a complaint or retort that either is a response or expects a response (Ps 38:15; Hab 2:1). In Job, the term is akin to legal argumentation (13:6; 16:4), as we shall see. The participial form of the verb frequently takes on substantive force (*môkîaḥ*): for example, Job 9:33 (heavenly arbiter); 32:12 (an arguer with Job [from Elihu]); 40:2 (one who disputes with God); Ezek 3:26 (the rebuker Ezekiel); Amos 5:10 (rebuker at the city gate). In Proverbs, the wise rebuker is commended (25:12; 28:23). The verb *ykḥ* can have YHWH as its subject ('as a father'; 3:12; cf. 30:6) but more typically the wise. Objects or targets of rebuke include the wicked (24:25), the scoffer (15:12; 9:7), the wise or 'intelligent' (9:8b; 19:25b), as

---

[19] For a more thorough reading of Wisdom's rebuke, see William P. Brown, 'When Wisdom Fails', in *'When the Morning Stars Sang': Essays in Honor of Choon Leong Seow on the Occasion of His Sixty-Fifth Birthday*, ed. Scott C. Jones and Christine Roy Yoder, BZAW 500 (Berlin, 2018), 210–211.

well as the 'listening ear' (25:12) and anyone else who might need a good rebuking (28:23).

Within Wisdom's initial discourse, the term is twice paired with 'counsel' ('ēṣâ). Beyond chapter 1, however, *tôkaḥat* is more often associated with 'discipline' (*mûsār*), as in 3:11.[20] 'Discipline' (*mûsār*) is 'always given by a superior to an inferior'.[21] It can even designate punishment (*piel yṣr*).[22] The close connection between *tôkaḥat* and *mûsār* is illustrated in 6:23, which pairs them together in construct form: the 'rebukes of discipline' (*tôkĕḥôt mûsār*).

Whatever a rebuke is precisely in sapiential rhetoric, it is clearly opposed to flattery (28:23). Rebuke excels in the art of critique for the sake of correction, painful as it may be. In Prov 15:10, 31; 19:25, rebuke is reserved not just for the fool, the simple and the wicked (24:25). The wise, too, are fair game:

> Whoever corrects (*yōsēr*) a scoffer wins disgrace;
>   whoever rebukes the wicked gets hurt.
> Do not rebuke ('*al tôkaḥ*) a scoffer; otherwise, he will hate you;
>   Rebuke a wise man, and he will love you.
> Instruct the wise (*tēn lĕḥākām*), and he will become wiser;
>   teach the righteous, and he will gain insight.
>
> (9:7–9, author's trans.)

While this admonition discourages rebuking the 'scoffer' and the 'wicked' (cf. 26:5), 'rebuking' the wise is mandated as a corrective that fosters appreciation, even affection and deference ('love'). Among the wise, rebuking is a sapiential exercise in reciprocity, an equal opportunity exercise. To count oneself among the wise is to be able to receive, as well as give, rebukes. The wise, unlike the wicked, respond in grateful appreciation. Here, rebuke among the wise finds a home in mutual edification rather than in a hierarchically structured pedagogy practiced from 'father' to 'son', from the 'wise' to the 'fool', from teacher to student, from Wisdom to 'simpletons', in which 'discipline' (*mûsār*) has its primary home.[23] Among the wise, the rhetoric of rebuke turns more dialogical; it serves to sustain a collegium of mutual learning, of 'iron sharpening iron' (27:17), for the wise know that wisdom is their

---

[20] See also 5:12; 10:17; 12:1; 13:18; 15:5, 32; Job 5:17.
[21] Fox, *Proverbs 1–9*, 34.
[22] E.g., Lev 26:18; 26:28; Jer 10:24; 30:11; Ps 39:12.
[23] Typical objects of the verb *ysr* include children, simpletons and scoffers (9:7; 19:18; 29:17). For the noun *mûsār*, see 1:8; 3:11 (paralleled with *tôkaḥat*); 4:1, 13; 5:12 (paralleled with *tôkaḥat*); 12:1 (paralleled with *da'at*); 22:15; 23:12, 13; 24:32.

gain even at the cost of their pride and self-certainty (a cardinal sin in the sapiential literature [Prov 3:7; 26:5, 12]). What kind of 'rebuke' is this that is given by a superior to a superior, a *tôkaḥat* among equals? Perhaps 'rebuke' may not be the best translation in the context of the wise instructing the wise. A 'rebuke' among equals is more akin to a 'dispute', particularly in the case of Job and his friends.

FROM DISPUTE TO REBUKE: THE CASE OF JOB

Job's inclusion into the so-called wisdom corpus is often questioned and for good reason: the book has closer affinities with the psalms of lament than with Proverbs and Ecclesiastes.[24] Nevertheless, the book does exhibit certain sapiential themes, concentrated particularly in chapter 28 regarding wisdom's priceless value and sapiential piety. Moreover, the book's overall search for understanding and wisdom in the face of horrific suffering, from the dialogues between Job and his friends (one could also include Job's wife's advice in 2:9) to YHWH's climactic answer, does warrant sapiential status among many scholars.[25] I would also add that Job is pedagogically fraught throughout the book.

The cycles of 'dialogues' between Job and his 'friends' have much to do with teaching and its failures, particularly as they become more disputatious. Indeed, it does not take long: diplomatic entreaties devolve into harsh rebukes traded back and forth with ever increasing vehemence. The first reference to 'rebuke' is given by Eliphaz, who pairs divine 'rebuke' with discipline (*mûsār*), implying that Job has received both and well deserves them (5:17). Job fires back one chapter later by first seeking correction from his friends: 'Teach me, and I will be silent; make me understand how I have gone astray' (6:24). Job, wise man that he is, asks for rebuke from his colleagues. Such a request, however, turns sarcastic in light of his defence, which immediately follows:

> How painful[26] are forthright words (*'imrê-yōšer*)!
>   What can your rebuke really prove?
> Do you think you can rebuke (my) words,
>   as if the speech of a despairing man were merely wind?
>   (6:25–26, author's trans.)

---

[24] For a review of the literature, see Cheung, *Wisdom Intoned*, 26–27.

[25] See Katharine J. Dell, *The Book of Job as Sceptical Literature*, BZAW 197 (Berlin, 1991), 87.

[26] The meaning of *mrṣ* ('be sick, sore') is debated here, and at least one Hebrew manuscript emends to *mlṣ* ('be smooth'), a correction or a case of graphic confusion.

Job's willingness to accept rebuke from his friends proves hollow as he rebukes his friends for even thinking they can succeed in rebuking him. To rebuke a friend whose words are painfully honest, who is genuinely in despair, is not just foolhardy; it is nothing short of a betrayal, as Job goes on to claim (v. 27). Rebuke is for correction, not for inflicting pain. It is his friends who need rebuking, so Job argues. And so the rebukes among equals ('friends') rage on throughout the rest of the dialogues: dialogues of dispute without concessions of correction.

In due course, Job claims that God will most 'certainly rebuke' his friends for their bias against him (13:10). At the same time, Job implores his friends to consider (i.e., concede to) his 'rebuke' (tôkaḥat) and 'disputations' (ribôt) in 13:6. Job wishes the same in his encounter with God, 'I would lay my case before him, and fill my mouth with rebukes (tôkāḥôt)', treating God in effect as his equal (23:4). Here, tôkaḥat refers to a well-argued case in a court of law, with God cast in the role of the defendant, because, as Job claims, an 'upright person could argue (nôkāḥ) with him' (v. 7). The heat of disputation reaches its boiling point when Eliphaz assures Job that God is the one to 'rebuke' him, not for his 'reverence' (yir'â), which would make no sense, but for his various sins, which he confidently lists for the next five verses (22:4–9).

Once the 'dialogues' reach their impasse, the interloper Elihu enters into the fray to assess that Job's friends were unable to 'rebuke' Job successfully (32:12), giving himself license to take up the pedagogical cause against Job. So the rebuking continues, from Job and his three friends to Elihu and in the end YHWH, who demands that Job's rebuke deserves an accounting: 'Anyone who rebukes (môkîaḥ) must give an answer' (40:2). Nobody rebukes YHWH without an accounting coram Deo. YHWH demands that Job 'man-up' and enter into disputational dialogue with the Deity (38:3). The irony is that YHWH hardly gives Job an opportunity to do so, and when Job is given the chance to respond, he refuses (40:3–5)

Throughout the dialogues and beyond, 'rebuke' exhibits two distinct nuances. On the one hand, it constitutes a dispute between equals, namely, Job and his friends. With this nuance, Job has the audacity to treat YHWH as an equal disputant in his 'rebuke'. On the other hand, 'rebuke', like 'discipline' (mûsār), can be deployed from superior to inferior, as from YHWH to Job. That the pedagogical versatility of 'rebuke' can traffic easily between parity and hierarchy heightens both the suspense and irony of YHWH's twofold response to Job. As Job envisioned himself engaging YHWH with 'rebukes' or disputations as his equal, YHWH engages Job with a rebuke of the highest hierarchical order to put him in his place, to which Job in the end concedes (42:6). Call it the 'pedagogy of the oppressor'. Nevertheless, as a form of pedagogy, YHWH's brutal rebuke does much more than put Job in his place. It teaches Job about the world as it is and the God who created it.

The Rebuke of Rebukes

YHWH's answer is a tempest of a rebuke, replete with rapid-fire questions and challenges. On its surface, YHWH's response serves to chasten Job and expose the limitations of his knowledge and ability (38:2; 40:2, 8–14). But never has a biblical 'rebuke' been so colourfully textured with information and insight. Through the power of divine poetry, YHWH rebukes Job by taking him on a virtual tour, as it were, through creation's far-flung domains, a mind-bending exploration into the diverse domains of cosmology, meteorology and zoology. In the best practices of the sages, YHWH's rebuke is correctional, not condemnatory. It is pedagogical. As often noted, YHWH offers no explanation for Job's personal plight. Also not offered is any condemnation of Job for having sinned, a serious concern shared by both Job and his friends (e.g., 7:21; 9:20; 10:6; 13:23). YHWH's silence on this matter is deafening: while Job is harshly rebuked for presuming to be God's 'corrector' (yissôr; 40:2), nowhere does YHWH condemn Job for having sinned, unlike Job's friends. It is Job's ignorance that YHWH admonishes, not his alleged guilt.[27]

In rebuke, YHWH plays the consummate pedagogue. Like an expert docent leading a one-man tour through a living museum, YHWH points out in profound detail the 'wonders' (niplā'ôt) of creation, to which Job testifies at the end (42:3). But creation is more than YHWH's Wunderkammern. It reflects a wisdom that Job could not recognise from his own narrow, dystopian perspective. For Job, God was all strength, specifically destructive strength exercised willy-nilly, with creation rendered fundamentally precarious(see 9:4–10; 12:13–25; 13:18–19; 26:7–14). In YHWH's answer, however, creation proves to be robust and wise, a veritable Terra sapiens (cf. Job 12:7) that teaches Job something about the Deus sapiens. One clear lesson to be learned from such a world is YHWH's preferential option for life in all its manifold

---

[27] Contra David J. A. Clines, who states that Job's encounter with God resulted in his 'ultimate humiliation' (Job 38–42, WBC 18B [Nashville, 2011], 1222). Job, however, complains that his friends have humiliated him (root: klm) ten times with their words (19:3). T. C. Ham falsely equates 'rebuke' with condemnation/humiliation and thus is forced to argue for YHWH's 'gentle' tone in Job 38 ('The Gentle Voice of God in Job 38', JBL 132 [2013]: 530–532). But YHWH's rebuke is anything but gentle.

diversity, that divine 'justice' or better 'governance' (*mišpāṭ* [40:8]) is found not in brutal force but in the 'fundamental drive toward teeming life', as YHWH intended.[28]

YHWH's answer teaches Job of creation's vastness, vitality and integrity. YHWH's world is expansively pluriform and richly pluralistic. Geographically, YHWH's creation is replete with domains and dimensions that extend far beyond Job's perceptual purview, as the first half of YHWH's answer makes clear (38:4–33). Here, YHWH turns Job's world not so much 'inside out' as outside in. The second half of YHWH's answer is populated by various wild creatures, near and far (38:39–39:30; 40:15–41:26), each one given its poetic due in YHWH's cosmic collage of life. The first animal, the lion, as with nearly every creature, is introduced with a challenge cast as a question,[29] and YHWH's question about the lion is pedagogically explosive: it effectively turns Job's own world on its head. YHWH does not challenge Job to kill the lion, as if to test his physical prowess in the face of predatory danger. Rather, YHWH challenges Job to imagine himself *providing* for the lion (38:39; cf. Ps 104:21).[30] All in all, Job learns much about these animals, about their native habitats and habits.

In YHWH's world, monstrous and marginal creatures are revealed as fully-fledged subjects unto themselves. They are YHWH's *niplā'ôt* ('wonders'; 42:3b), each described in loving detail.[31] YHWH's answer not only 'de-moralises' the world, stripping it of all notions of retributive justice, as Matitiahu Tsevat famously concluded;[32] it also fills the world with awe for Job to behold, appreciate and appropriate.

With the vast and wild creation in full view, what does Job learn specifically about the God who created it all? Often debated is the nature of the divine warrior characterisation in YHWH's answer.[33]

---

[28] J. Gerald Janzen, 'Blessing and Justice in Job: In/commensurable?', in *'When the Morning Stars Sang': Essays in Honor of Choon Leong Seow on the Occasion of His Sixty-Fifth Birthday*, ed. Scott C. Jones and Christine Roy Yoder, BZAW 500 (Berlin, 2018), 67.

[29] Exceptions include 39:13; 40:15, which possibly point to additions.

[30] For background, both literary and iconographic, see Brent A. Strawn, *What Is Stronger Than a Lion? Leonine Imagery and Metaphor in the Hebrew Bible and the Ancient Near East*, OBO 212 (Cambridge, MA, 2005), esp. 64, 161–174, 187–190.

[31] See Kathleen M. O'Connor, 'Wild, Raging Creativity: The Scene in the Whirlwind (Job 38–41)', in *A God So Near: Essays on Old Testament Theology in Honor of Patrick D. Miller*, ed. Brent A. Strawn and Nancy R. Bowen (University Park, 2003), 171–179; Brown, *Wisdom's Wonder*, 109–118.

[32] Matitiahu Tsevat, 'The Meaning of the Book of Job', *HUCA* 37 (1966): 102.

[33] For discussion and bibliography, see Brian R. Doak, *Consider Leviathan: Narratives of Nature and Self in Job* (Minneapolis, 2014), 184–189.

The key, however, lies not in *whether* it is present but in its extent and character. Warrior imagery is no doubt evident in YHWH's answer (see, e.g., 38:23, 34–35; 40:9–14, 19), but it does not run rampant as one finds in Job's own discourse prior to YHWH's rebuke (9:4–10; 12:13–25; 13:18–19; 26:7–14). Instead, the warrior script in YHWH's answer gets revised in significant ways, such as in the description of the Sea (38:8–11). The passage eschews the rhetoric of conquest and features instead the language of nurture and care. Indeed, nowhere in YHWH's description of creation's heights and depths is cosmic conflict presupposed: the 'recesses of the deep' are not trampled (v. 16), darkness is given equal play to light (v. 19), the Sea is treated as a rambunctious infant, not the purveyor of chaos and feminine agency parallels masculine agency with regards to precipitation (vv. 28–29). Nowhere is nature in a state of upheaval before the God of the Whirlwind as one finds, for example, in Nah 1:3b–6. Rather, we read primarily of nature's flourishing. Creation is, to be sure, a messy affair that entails violence and loss but never to the extent that creation's integrity is jeopardised, as Job had surmised. To the contrary, YHWH's world thrives, and it does so on the boundary between vitality and vulnerability, procreation and death, resulting in a dynamic order in which even Leviathan, the monster of chaos, plays an integral role.

In YHWH's pedagogically charged rebuke, Job must unlearn and relearn what creation is about under YHWH's providential care. Job's own creational perspective of chaos and destruction is replaced with a primarily constructive, indeed creative view of the Deity. Whereas the paired qualities of God's 'wisdom and strength' (12:13, 16) were defined by Job in terms of 'brute force' and 'craftiness',[34] they are given a more constructive context in YHWH's answer. If emphasising divine might and, by contrast, Job's powerlessness were the primary goal of YHWH's rebuke, then YHWH's answer could have simply validated what Job had already acknowledged, namely, a deity capable of infinite destructive power. Moreover, such an answer would lack all pedagogical force. Instead, the divine warrior steps back from creation, retreating, as it were, in order to highlight creation's own vital integrity for Job's edification. YHWH is a warrior, yes, but also a provider and, for Job most critically, a pedagogue – YHWH the divine docent overtakes and transforms the divine warrior. Such a powerful paradigm shift requires an equally robust pedagogy, one characterised by evocative poetry,

---

34 Tsevat, 'The Meaning of the Book of Job', 77.

arresting images, challenging questions, sarcasm and the confrontational power of rebuke. In short, a pedagogy that effects such a radical shift in perspectives requires a deity, no less, a Master Poet.

TESTIMONIAL EXPERIENCE

From the harsh pedagogy of rebuke, we move to the other extreme, its pedagogical opposite: the appeal to personal experience, the dominant pedagogical mode in Ecclesiastes but also, perhaps surprisingly, Wisdom's culminating discourse in Proverbs.

Ecclesiastes and Personal Observation

Dominated by first-person discourse, Ecclesiastes is largely a self-presentation that features the words of *qōhelet*, a sagacious character whose title means 'gatherer', whether of people or sayings, and who is identified as one who 'taught knowledge' (*limmad-da'at*; 12:9). But Qoheleth characterises himself at the outset as more than a teacher; he is the greatest of kings, having 'acquired great wisdom', surpassing all before him (1:16a). Qoheleth presents himself as the sage at the top of his game, as the one who has been at the 'business' of wisdom the longest and with the most means at his disposal. With the poignant treatise on the ravaging effects of death concluding his discourse to the 'young man' in 12:1–8, Qoheleth presents himself as the great elder of wisdom and king of pedagogues. Qoheleth's self-identified royal persona, established at the beginning of his discourse, serves to heighten and enhance his pedagogical stature (1:12).

Scholars have long recognised that Qoheleth's distinctive rhetoric is found in his repeated appeals to 'personal observation',[35] a characteristic of his testimonial style. Specifically, the most common verb associated with Qoheleth's first-person discourse is 'see' ($\sqrt{r'h}$), attested twenty-one times.[36] While his discourse is primarily observational, it is also comprehensive in its purview, beginning with his first official observation:

> I saw all the deeds done under the sun;
> and, *voila*,[37] all is futile, a chasing after wind.
> (1:14, authors trans.)[38]

---

[35] James L. Crenshaw, *Ecclesiastes: A Commentary*, OTL (Philadelphia, 1987), 28.
[36] Eccl 1:14; 2:13, 24; 3:10, 16, 22; 4:1, 4, 7, 15; 5:12, 17; 6:1; 7:15; 8:9, 10, 17; 9:11, 13; 10:5, 7.
[37] Hebrew *hinnēh*.
[38] Cf. 4:1, 4, 15; 7:15.

The ancient sage lays claim to have *seen* the totality of human conduct, given his authoritative position as king and sage, and then invites the reader to assent to his conclusion that all deeds are for naught. Such is Qoheleth's pedagogical ploy: to move seamlessly from personal observation to mandated demonstration, from 'I saw' to '*voila!*' Although a logical chasm exists between observation and conclusion, Qoheleth's appeal to personal observation lends rhetorical, if not logical, credence to his conclusion. Elsewhere, Qoheleth claims to have seen 'all the oppressions practiced under the sun' (4:1), 'all toil and all skill in work' (4:4), 'all the living' (4:15), 'everything' (*hakkōl*; 7:15) and 'all the work of God' (8:17). It is from his *all*-encompassing observational scope that the sage makes his universal, albeit unconventional, claims. Qoheleth's pedagogy begins with observational testimony and concludes with lessons for life. He is the 'analytical I' turned pedagogical.[39]

More than observation is operative in Qoheleth's pedagogy. His testimony extends from sight to action. His approach is not only experiential; it is experimental, making him perhaps the Bible's first and only 'empiricist'.[40]

> I, Qoheleth, was king over Israel in Jerusalem. And I applied my mind to inquire and to investigate by wisdom everything that is done under heaven. It is an unhappy business that God has given to human beings to be occupied with. (1:12–13, authors trans.)

In the temporary guise of King Solomon, Qoheleth sets out to conduct an analytical inquiry, something of a 'personal experiment'[41] or investigation.[42] According to Samuel Adams, 'Qoheleth undertakes a personal experiment "to seek and to search out by wisdom all that is done under heaven" (1:13)'.[43] Indeed, Adams titles the autobiographical section of

---

39 See Peter Machinist, 'The Voice of the Historian in the Ancient Near Eastern and Mediterranean World', *Int* 57 (2003): 133–135.

40 The term is used reservedly. See Michael V. Fox, 'Wisdom in Qoheleth', in *In Search of Wisdom: Essays in Memory of John G. Gammie*, ed. Leo G. Perdue, Bernard Brandon Scott and William Johnston Wiseman (Louisville, 1993), 119–121; Annette Schellenberg, *Erkenntnis als Problem: Qohelet and die atltestamentliche Diskussion um das menschliche Erkennen*, OBO 188 (Freiburg, 2002), 161–196; Stuart Weeks, *Ecclesiastes and Scepticism*, LHBOTS 541 (London, 2012), 120–125.

41 Samuel L. Adams, *Wisdom in Transition: Act and Consequence in Second Temple Instructions*, JSJSup 125 (Leiden, 2008), 105.

42 Schellenberg specifies 'induction' and 'falsification' as part of Qoheleth's 'experimental' approach (*Erkenntnis als Problem*, 175–180).

43 Adams, *Wisdom in Transition*, 105.

1:12–2:10 'Qoheleth's Royal Experiment',[44] which 'reads as the personal experiment of a critical thinker who conveys a unique set of conclusions', including 'inconsistency and death in the human experience'.[45]

In his 'experiment', Qoheleth does more than observe. He becomes his own test case, which is precisely what his royal persona affords him to do to the fullest extent (2:3). For the sake of investigation, Qoheleth the king 'made great works' (2:4a), 'built houses and planted vineyards' (v. 4b), 'bought slaves' (v. 7) and 'gathered' wealth (v. 8), all to determine that there was no lasting 'gain' (*yitrôn*) to be had, that all was, in fact, *hebel* (2:11). The investigation or 'experiment' had failed but not entirely, for there was something to be learned and taught even in the failure, namely, the pointless nature of heroic striving.[46] Qoheleth's failed 'experiment' is not merely a subversive satire of the royal annalistic successes;[47] it is a teachable moment.

Qoheleth's pedagogical style reflects a way of knowing that is grounded in personal observation leading to personally directed action, indeed 'testing' (2:1; 7:23). Only toward the end of the book does second-person discourse surface in any prevalent degree (e.g., 9:7–10; 10:20; 11:1–2, 9–10; 12:1). In short, Qoheleth's pedagogy is observational, investigative and, equally important, transparent. While Qoheleth's quest to find ultimate wisdom results in failure, it is precisely in the articulated transparency of his failure that the sage imparts his greatest wisdom: the value of a 'non-profit' (i.e., non-*yitrôn*) existence (1:3; 2:11; 3:9; 5:10, 16), the redemptive import of enjoyment (2:24–25; 3:12, 22; 5:18–19; 8:15; 9:7–9), the dangers of extreme righteousness (7:16) and perhaps his most profound truth of all: 'a living dog is better than a dead lion' (9:4).

Wisdom's Testimony in Proverbs

The only other passage in the Hebrew wisdom corpus that is thoroughly self-referential is Wisdom's culminating discourse in Proverbs 8, signalling a remarkable shift in pedagogical style from her harsh rebuke in Prov 1:20–33. Often identified generically and comparatively as an 'aretalogy', a form of self-praise associated with the goddess Isis,

---

[44] Adams, *Wisdom in Transition*, 110.

[45] Adams, *Wisdom in Transition*, 107.

[46] See Brown, 'When Wisdom Fails', 220–222.

[47] For Qoheleth's testimony as subversive satire in comparison to ancient Near Eastern royal annals, see C.-L. Seow, 'Qohelet's Autobiography', in *Fortunate the Eyes That See: Essays in Honor of David Noel Freedman in Celebration of His Seventieth Birthday*, ed. Astrid B. Beck et al. (Grand Rapids, 1995), 257–282.

Wisdom's self-praise is rife with pedagogical import.[48] As in Qoheleth's case, Wisdom casts herself as an 'I-witness' for the edification of her audience. Her personal testimony is her pedagogy. Introduced once again in her public venue (8:1–3; cf. 1:20–21), Wisdom cries out for attention, but instead of condemning her audience for their guilt, she testifies to her inestimable worth in matters of insight and judgement (8:10–11, 14–16), her discursive truth (vv. 6–9) and her moral integrity (vv. 12, 20), not to mention the material worth she offers (vv. 18–19, 21). Wisdom's self-praise serves to elicit the reader's desire for her. But she does not stop with matters of morality and material wealth. Her first-person discourse reaches its rhetorical summit in her testimony of creation (vv. 22–31), where Wisdom serves as the consummate 'I-witness' to YHWH's fashioning of creation.

Throughout her cosmic testimony, Wisdom casts herself passively before YHWH and creation. The poem opens with Wisdom placing herself at (and as) the beginning of YHWH's creative acts (vv. 22–23). Wisdom is 'created' ($\sqrt{qnh}$) by YHWH prior to the world, she testifies, thus asserting her pre-eminent status in all creation. More specifically, Wisdom is conceived in v. 22, gestated in v. 23, birthed in vv. 24–25, present during creation in v. 27 and 'playing' in vv. 30–31. The world's creation, thus, is told strictly from the standpoint of Wisdom's 'genetic' primacy. While her origin is sharply distinguished from the origins of the cosmos, Wisdom nevertheless shares an intimate bond with the 'inhabited world' (v. 31).

Although the poem nowhere suggests that Wisdom collaborates with YHWH in the task of cosmic construction, she is no passive observer. Far from being a spectator, Wisdom testifies, and in her testifying she teaches, first about herself and then about the world and the God who fashioned it. At YHWH's side before and during creation, Wisdom demonstrates that she is fully 'in the know' about the world and about YHWH. Other than YHWH, she is the one and only witness to creation, for she has remained 'beside' YHWH as creation commences and can thus tell of it with a deep sense of intimacy and joy. Wisdom's aretalogy, moreover, is a tangible testimony to her continued delight in creation and in YHWH. All the world was made for her joy and delight. Wisdom teaches that creation is her playhouse.

Yet Wisdom's self-description as a child imparts more than simply her childlike delight in and with the world. She presents something of a

---

[48] For the Egyptian background, see Schipper, *Proverbs 1–15*, 292–294.

teachable paradox: Wisdom grows in wisdom. Her status as a 'child' before YHWH at the beginning of creation establishes a bond with the reader, who was also once a child, learning and playing, exploring and delighting. Such is part of Wisdom's pedagogical ploy: first, to establish her credibility regarding her preeminent status through self-praise and second, to establish a connection with the reader, finding common ground by conceiving herself as a playing child. The latter becomes even clearer in the following admonition in which Wisdom addresses her audience as 'children' and in so doing casts herself as mother (8:32–33). By figuring herself as a child at the dawn of creation, Wisdom establishes a level of mutual identity with the child who is addressed throughout the first nine chapters, the child who serves as the 'stand in' for the reader. Unlike the father or mother, Wisdom does not embody the age that separates the generations. Rather, she serves as the vital link that bridges the generational chasm between parent and child, as well as the social domains of family and community. In stark contrast to the hierarchical protocol between father and son, the pedagogy of patriarchy, the son is urged to address wisdom as 'my sister' ('āḥōtî) and 'intimate friend' (mōdā'; 7:4), terms of endearment and intimacy.

But now that sapiential bond has turned maternal in 8:32, and so has Wisdom's discourse. Wisdom is as much a nurturer as she is a playmate, beckoning her children to come and find her. Wisdom also takes on the role of architect and host for a distinctly pedagogical purpose. In the very next chapter, Wisdom builds a house of seven pillars (9:1–2). The juxtaposition of chapters 8 and 9 in Proverbs is suggestive. By witnessing YHWH at work in creation, Wisdom comes to be a creator herself. Wisdom is not only YHWH's playmate but also YHWH's apprentice, and by the time she is grown, Wisdom is ready to ply her trade as a host-teacher. She builds a house and invites her students to come and partake of her edifying fare (9:1–6). In so doing, Wisdom instructs them about the paths of 'righteousness, justice, and equity' (see 1:3).

It is in the role of host that Wisdom sets the culinary stage for the sayings and admonitions that follow in the book (chs. 10–30). It is her edifying fare, mixed with the food and wine she serves (9:5), a multi-course meal of biblical proportions, and the only qualification for partaking is the commitment to 'lay aside immaturity, live and walk in the way of insight' (v. 6). Each proverb, thus, is a morsel to be tasted and tested, to be ingested and digested, all in order to shape and sustain the life of individuals, families and the community for the common good.

THE PEDAGOGICAL POWER OF THE PROVERB

Within the metaphorical schema of Wisdom's banquet feast, the proverbs of chapters 10–30 have their own pedagogical means of presentation.[49] For all their variety, fundamental to a biblical 'proverb' or *māšāl* is its comparative dynamic, as evidenced in the basic verbal meaning of *mšl*: 'to compare, become similar to, same as' (see Pss 28:1; 49:13; 143:7; Isa 14:10; 46:5; Job 30:19). The individual proverb invariably forges a connection between two elements, much like a metaphor. Biblical proverbs, particularly in the book of Proverbs, are typically 'two-part' or bilinear, thereby highlighting the 'pedagogical ideal' of prompting critical and creative reflection.[50]

In their collected contexts, the proverbs in Proverbs exhibit an overarching pedagogical movement from uniformity in style, as found among the antithetical sayings in the so-called Solomonic collection in 10:1–22:16, to the variety and complexity of form and poetic artistry, particularly in the use of imagery and metaphor as found in the 'Hezekian collection' (25:1–29:27) and the 'words of Agur' (30:1–33).

Certain proverbs revel in paradox, even irony, prompting greater critical reflection. Compare, for example, the following two proverbs:

A soft (*rak*) answer repels wrath;
> but a hurtful word escalates anger.
> > (15:1, author's trans.)

With patience a ruler can be won over,[51]
> and a soft (*rakkâ*) tongue shatters bones.
> > (25:15, author's trans.)

While both proverbs display their metaphorical craft (and craftiness), eliciting pause for reflection, the second fully embraces the paradoxical. In the first saying, the 'soft answer' proves strong in the face of, say, the king's 'wrath'. What is tender and delicate, like soft skin[52] or a 'green twig',[53] exhibits the strength to 'repel', to 'turn back' (*yāšîb*), the threat of aggression. Like a shield, one's 'soft answer' provides a sure defence

---

[49] See William P. Brown, 'The Didactic Power of Metaphor in the Aphoristic Sayings of Proverbs', *JSOT* 29 (2004): 133–154.

[50] Schipper, *Proverbs 1–15*, 30.

[51] Or 'seduced'. See Prov 1:10; 9:13; 16:29.

[52] E.g., Gen 18:7; 33:13, Prov 4:3; 28:54.

[53] Ezek 17:22.

against the onslaught of another's anger. Rather than giving way before wrath, the 'soft' response repels fury.

This tensive use of metaphor in 15:1 displays a hint of paradox. Much more so in 25:15, in which the 'soft tongue' does more than resist; it destroys! Like a mace or an axe, judicious speech 'shatters ($\sqrt{šbr}$) bones'. The tongue, whose softness and healing efficacy are stressed both physically and metaphorically elsewhere in Proverbs,[54] serves as a weapon that can breakdown a king's intransigent will. Far from banal, this proverb owes its evocative power to its creative use of metaphor. Such is the didactic power of a proverb. In addition to the power of speech, other themes in the collections can be traced in somewhat progressive fashion, such as wealth and poverty[55] and the power of the king,[56] from the simple to the nuanced and complex.[57]

Another level of pedagogical movement is evident from the various superscriptions of the collections in Proverbs.

1:1a	The proverbs of Solomon, son of David, king of Israel
10:1a	The proverbs of Solomon
22:17	Incline your ear and hear the words of (the) wise.
24:23	Also these (are) for[58] (the) wise.
25:1	Also these (are) proverbs of Solomon that the men of Hezekiah, king of Judah, collected.
30:1a	The words of Agur, son of Jakeh, the Massaite
31:1	The words of Lemuel, king of Massa, which his mother taught him.

The collections begin with Solomonic attribution and then proceed to the unnamed 'wise' as the origin of authorship (22:17). It is no coincidence that the collection in 22:17–24:22 draws directly from the Egyptian 'Instruction of Amenemope' (seventh–sixth century BCE).[59] In the latter half of these collections, wisdom turns international, specifically Egyptian, although it not explicitly acknowledged as such, for the 'words of the wise' reflect Yahwistic adaptation. In addition, a subtle but remarkable shift occurs in 24:23, in which the proverbs are now designated '*for* the wise', suggesting pedagogical advancement and

---

[54] See 12:8; 15:4; 16:24.

[55] See, e.g., 10:3; 22:22–23; 28:6, 11; 29:13; 31:9.

[56] Note the movement from awe to critique regarding royal power in 14:28, 35; 10:10; 19:12; 28:3, 15; 30:27, 28, 31, 32.

[57] See Brown, 'The Pedagogy of Proverbs 10:1–31:9', 150–182.

[58] Not 'of the wise' (*laḥăkāmîm*). For the syntax, see Schipper, *Proverbs 1–15*, 6–7.

[59] For the history of research, see Schipper, *Proverbs 1–15*, 1–3, 11–14.

fulfilling the curricular aim given in 1:5.[60] It is, moreover, no coincidence that the proverbial form in these latter collections has become
more varied and complex, particularly in the Hezekian collection of
25:1–29:27. Finally, the 'words of Agur' conclude these collections of
sayings, a non-Israelite figure, as also Lemuel, 'king of Massa', most
likely a tribe or region in North Arabia. The 'words of Agur', moreover,
comprise some of the most enigmatic and visually arresting sayings in
the entire book.[61] An overall, albeit not entirely linear, movement can
be discerned both at the level of the individual proverb and at the
collected, superscriptional level, namely, the movement from Israelite
to international wisdom and from proverbial simplicity to complexity.
Such is how the book of Proverbs, according to its prologue, teaches
both the 'inexperienced' and the 'wise'. Or to put it another way, the
savoury fare that Wisdom offers at her banquet table in 9:2–5 becomes,
course after course, more substantial and exotic, requiring more of, one
might say, an 'acquired taste', particularly as one digests Agur's bitter
fare. In other words, a light dessert is not on the menu. Such rich
sapiential fare ends with the 'woman of strength' ('ēšet-ḥayil) providing
food for her household (31:14–15) and, of course, doing so much more.
The book of Proverbs aptly concludes its pedagogical cuisine with an
acrostic climax, a detailed portrait of Woman Wisdom turned flesh and
blood, or 'incarnated', within the household (31:10–31). Wisdom's final
pedagogy is an elaborate teaching by example, performed acrostically
and with stunning detail. And so Proverbs ends as it began, within the
household and with the 'fear of YHWH' (1:7; 31:30).

CONCLUSION

For wisdom to be true to its nature, wisdom must be imparted, that is, it
must be teachable. From its content and perspectives to its forms and
pedagogies, wisdom's ways are many, ranging from terse proverbs,
which can easily be passed on, to the admonitory lectures the parent
expounds to the son, to the fearful rebukes of YHWH and Wisdom
herself, not to mention the testimonial reports of Qoheleth and
Wisdom. Each form is aimed at offering something worth imparting,
something edifying for the receiver. The variety of forms establishes a
pedagogical spectrum defined along the lines of relational power and

---

[60] Schipper, *Proverbs 1–15*, 6–7.
[61] See Christine Roy Yoder, 'On the Threshold of Kingship: A Study of Agur (Proverbs
30)', *Int* 63 (2009): 254–263.

hierarchy. The fearful rebukes of Wisdom and YHWH constitute one end of the spectrum. At the other end is the kind of pedagogy that establishes a personal bond, as in the case of the personal testimonials of Qoheleth and Wisdom. Such is the pedagogical versatility of the wisdom corpus. Such, indeed, is the versatility of personified Wisdom herself, exhibited in the beginning with her harsh rebuke and culminating in her gracious invitation as host, but in between displayed in her self-testimony as a child beside YHWH prior to creation. In short, the pedagogy of wisdom in the biblical corpus is multifaceted and wide ranging, and this chapter only scratches the surface. Suffice it to say, wisdom is what wisdom does, and what wisdom does is teach.

Further Reading

Adams, Samuel L. *Wisdom in Transition: Act and Consequence in Second Temple Instructions*. JSJSup 125. Leiden; Boston: 2008.

Brown, William P. 'The Pedagogy of Proverbs 10:1–31:9'. Pages 150–182 in *Character and Scripture: Moral Formation, Community, and Biblical Interpretation*. Edited by William P. Brown. Grand Rapids: 2002.

'The Didactic Power of Metaphor in the Aphoristic Sayings of Proverbs'. *JSOT* 29 (2004): 133–154.

Wisdom's Wonder: Character, Creation, and Crisis in the Bible's Wisdom Literature. Grand Rapids: 2014.

'When Wisdom Fails'. Pages 209–223 in *'When the Morning Stars Sang': Essays in Honor of Choon Leong Seow on the Occasion of His Sixty-Fifth Birthday*. Edited by Scott C. Jones and Christine Roy Yoder. BZAW 500. Berlin: 2018.

'Virtue and Its Limits in the Wisdom Corpus: Character Formation, Disruption, and Transformation'. Pages 45–64 in *The Oxford Handbook of Wisdom and the Bible*. Edited by Will Kynes. New York: 2021.

Cheung, Simon Chi-chung. *Wisdom Intoned: A Reappraisal of the Genre 'Wisdom Psalms'*. LHB OTS 613. London: 2015.

Clines, David J. A. *Job 38–42*. WBC 18B. Nashville: 2011.

Crenshaw, James L. *Education in Ancient Israel: Across the Deadening Silence*. ABRL. New York: 1998.

Dell, Katharine J. *The Book of Job as Sceptical Literature*. BZAW 197. Berlin: 1991.

The Book of Proverbs in Social and Theological Context. Cambridge: 2006.

Doak, Brian R. *Consider Leviathan: Narratives of Nature and Self in Job*. Minneapolis: 2014.

Fox, Michael V. 'Wisdom in Qoheleth'. Pages 115–131 in *In Search of Wisdom: Essays in Memory of John G. Gammie*. Edited by Leo G. Perdue, Bernard Brandon Scott and William Johnston Wiseman. Louisville: 1993.

Proverbs 1–9. AB 18A. New York: 2000.

Hatton, Peter T. H. *Contradiction in the Book of Proverbs: The Deep Water of Counsel*. Aldershot: 2008.

Melchert, Charles F. *Wise Teaching: Biblical Wisdom and Educational Ministry*. Harrisburg: 1998.

Newsom, Carol A. 'Woman and the Discourse of Patriarchal Wisdom: A Study of Proverbs 1–9'. Pages in 142–160 in *Gender and Difference in Ancient Israel*. Edited by Peggy L. Day. Minneapolis: 1989.

O'Connor, Kathleen M. 'Wild, Raging Creativity: The Scene in the Whirlwind (Job 38–41)'. Pages 171–179 in *A God So Near: Essays on Old Testament Theology in Honor of Patrick D. Miller*. Edited by Brent A. Strawn and Nancy R. Bowen. University Park: 2003.

Sandoval, Timothy J. 'Revisiting the Prologue of Proverbs'. *JBL* 126 (2007): 455–473.

The Discourse of Wealth and Poverty in the Book of Proverbs. Leiden: 2005.

Schellenberg, Annette. *Erkenntnis als Problem: Qohelet and die atltestamentliche Diskussion um das menschliche Erkennen*. OBO 188. Universitätsverlag. Freiburg: 2002.

Schipper, Bernd U. *Proverbs 1–15: A Commentary*. Hermeneia. Minneapolis: 2019.

von Rad, Gerhard. *Wisdom in Israel*. Translated by James D. Martin. Nashville: 1972.

Yoder, Christine Roy. 'Forming 'Fearers of Yahweh': Repetition and Contradiction as Pedagogy in Proverbs'. Pages 167–183 in *Seeking Out the Wisdom of the Ancients: Essays Offered to Honor Michael V. Fox on the Occasion of his Sixty-Fifth Birthday*. Edited by Ronald L. Troxel, Kelvin G. Friebel and Dennis R. Magary. Winona Lake, 2005.

'On the Threshold of Kingship: A Study of Agur (Proverbs 30)'. *Int* 63 (2009): 254–263.

23 The Wisdom Literature and Virtue Ethics

ARTHUR JAN KEEFER

VIRTUE ETHICS

The word 'virtue' has been used to describe the dispositions of those deemed 'good' by moral philosophers. Socrates spoke of virtue; Plato wrote of virtue; Aristotle and Aquinas, too, and now 'neo-Aristotelians' contend for an updated brand of moral 'virtue', what it means to be morally virtuous and how one might become that way. With each of these renditions, virtue has taken a slightly different form – so we can speak of 'Socratic virtue' and 'Aristotelian virtue' as different concepts – and yet virtue has always characterised the 'good' person, whether real or imagined, and the dispositions that make one so. Virtues are 'excellencies of character' that govern what one does and who one is.

As a normative ethical theory, 'virtue ethics' prescribes these dispositions and often embodies them in an exemplar: one ought to be, and consequently act, as the virtuous person would be and act. It is not a matter of doing one's duty but fulfilling one's function. Nor is it a matter of calculating pleasures and pains but a matter of being the kind of person who deliberates well about decisions, given all the variables. Goodness, then, takes some precedence over rightness, over obedience and over pleasure; and for virtue ethicists, this goodness is bound up with the advantage of 'faring well'.[1] Without surprise, then, virtue ethics entails a vision of the good life, of *eudaimonia*, commonly called 'flourishing', toward which it aims and in which, by the acquisition and exercise of virtue, the good life is accomplished and fulfilled.[2]

Accounting for virtue ethics when interpreting the biblical 'wisdom literature' could be done in various ways, and whilst some methodo-

---

[1] Alasdair MacIntyre, *A Short History of Ethics* (London, 1966), 84.
[2] There is, however, a lack of specificity about the contents of *eudaimonia*. See David Bostock, *Aristotle's Ethics* (Oxford, 2000), 84–85.

logical lines have been sketched, no clear-cut profile has been established. Thus, studies move forward, largely, by implicit means.[3] But two
things in this endeavour ought to be made clear. First, what is meant by
'virtue'? I have just now offered an apparently definitive definition, but
the inner workings of each virtue ethic differ with each virtue ethicist,
even if they do hold to the broad description given above. If biblical
literature is to be put into conversation with virtue ethics, then, the
exact type, and better yet, the exact intellectual sources from which
that type is derived, ought to be specified. In what follows, I use
Aristotle's idea of 'intellectual' and 'moral' virtues as laid out in his
Nicomachean Ethics (*NE*).[4] His presentation is clear and authoritative,
and his notion of virtue has been a recent starting point for interpreting
Proverbs. Second, along with the exact tradition of virtue and its
sources, we ought to be clear about just what makes someone virtuous.
Criteria for virtue are required, with which we can probe the biblical
material in order to determine if and to what extent its thought resembles virtue ethics or even in some way contains its own 'virtue ethic'. In
this chapter, I give a sense for how certain types of virtue may be found
within biblical wisdom literature, starting with the question of whether
or not we can justifiably translate any Hebrew lexemes as 'virtue'. I then
consider recent pioneering studies on virtue in Proverbs and Job and
propose some inroads for Ecclesiastes and Ben Sira, concluding with
broader reflections on 'the good' in those texts.

ḤOKMÂ AND VIRTUE

Whatever we include within the category of 'wisdom literature', it
ought to have something to do with 'wisdom'. Therefore, the Hebrew
lexemes closest to that concept will set the tone for what follows, which
ultimately asks if we can responsibly translate any biblical lexeme as
'virtue'. In one sense, biblical wisdom encompasses a whole fleet of
moral concepts. For what is 'wisdom' in Proverbs, if not to be teachable
(1:10–19), diligent (10:4), reticent (11:12), generous (11:24–26) and
self-controlled (12:16)? These concepts are effortlessly taken as ethical

---

[3] See, e.g., Jaco Gericke, *The Hebrew Bible and Philosophy of Religion*, SBLRBS 70
(Atlanta, 2012); Dru Johnson, *Epistemology and Biblical Theology: From the
Pentateuch to Mark's Gospel*, RIPBC 4 (New York, 2018), 1–10.

[4] The *NE* was a set of lecture notes from ca. 350 BCE designed for training statesmen
that covers the theory and practice of virtue within the ancient Greek *polis* or city.

qualities, and yet the question of what these qualities have to do with virtue depends on what it means to be generous and diligent and teachable. For a virtue is not just a moral action or state of being, as if we could say that because Aristotle commends generosity and Proverbs commends generosity, then the latter is speaking of virtues – this is an error similar to supposing that because the *NE* mentions what is translated 'wisdom' (*sophia*; cf. *phronēsis*) and Proverbs refers to 'wisdom' (*ḥokmâ*), then both books are referring to the same concept. A virtue ethic entails a special set of criteria for its virtues and a presupposed framework for, among other things, becoming such a person.

A misguided semantic identification between two references to 'wisdom', though, should not scare us off the terms themselves. For in the same way that biblical 'wisdom' is first a lexeme, so classical 'virtue' is first known through the language of *aretē*, which can refer to many kinds of 'goodness' or 'excellence', whether of gods, humans, animals or land (e.g., *Iliad* 9.498; 20.411). Aristotle uses the term, principally, in the context of human action to mean 'moral excellence', so that 'the happy life is the life that is lived without impediment in accordance with virtue' (*Pol.* 4.11). The LXX does not use *aretē* in this way but rather reserves it for translations of *hôd* and *tĕhillâ*, which have the sense of splendorous or praise-worthy. The Hebrew lexeme *ḥayil*, which has a broad semantic domain and often refers to one's 'strength' (e.g., Josh 1:14) or 'capability' (e.g., Exod 18:21), in several instances describes women who possess a 'strength of character'. Within biblical Hebrew, this is the sense that comes closest to 'virtue' (Ruth 3:11; Prov 12:4; 31:10). But any semantic contact is only a whisper of the possible communication that could be had between theories of virtue ethics and biblical literature.

Aquinas, in his own way, was privy to this and ventured the most extensive merger of moral philosophy and biblical literature in antiquity. For him, knowledge of God was attained in two ways: by the enquiry of human reason and by belief in those truths that exceed reason's grasp (*Summa Contra Gentiles* 1.3–9). He often worked from the basis of philosophical premises that he then supplemented with biblical material. Likewise, his biblical commentaries are infused with ancient philosophy, as his work on Job, for instance, recalls Stoic and Peripatetic views of the human passions to suggest that they accord with Job's lament, all of which he presents in a way intended to show concordance between philosophical and biblical traditions. In his discussion of virtue and vice, too, he makes particular use of biblical proverbs to explain several vicious dispositions, such as strife, anger, malice and despair.[5] Aquinas brought the Bible to bear on an Aristotelian model of virtue and, in his own complex, systematic, confessional and enduring way, integrated biblical and philosophical moral traditions. After Aquinas, many early modern moral philosophers did refer to virtue in their work, but, in the main, virtue ethics became occluded by normative theories of deontology and consequentialism and was revived only in the middle of the twentieth century thanks to the work of Elizabeth Anscombe and Alasdair MacIntyre, since then making its way into biblical scholarship.[6]

With modern biblical scholars, the use of virtue ethics primarily occurs in concentrated studies of singular biblical books, most of which will be covered in what follows, but it also crops up in expansive projects on biblical ethics, such as Bruce Birch's *Let Justice Roll Down: The Old Testament, Ethics, and Christian Life*, in which he advocates that the Old Testament, in its claim and display of human action, gives a centrality to motives, intentions and dispositions. Others, such as John Barton, have proffered virtue ethics as a promising approach to biblical ethics and yet, at times, have also pointed out the distance between these traditions.[7] Less attention has been given to the methods by which these traditions might be compared or integrated, though several possibilities have been probed, and it is perhaps on the conceptual level that an initial and patent comparison can be done.[8]

---

[5] See, e.g., *Summa Theologica* I–II 73.5; 77.2; 78.1–2; II–II 12; 14; 20.3; 30.2; 37.1; 41.2. For instance, to support the idea that discord is a sin and a vice opposed to peace, he cites Prov 6:19, where the Lord hates the one who 'sows discord among brothers' (II–II 37.1).

[6] See John Barton, 'Virtue in the Bible', *Studies in Christian Ethics* 12 (1999): 12–22; Bruce C. Birch, *Let Justice Roll Down: The Old Testament, Ethics, and Christian Life* (Louisville, 1991); Eckart Otto, 'Woher weiß der Mensch um Gut und Böse? Philosophische Annäherungen der ägyptischen und biblischen Weisheit an ein Grundproblem der Ethik', in *Recht und Ethos im Alten Testament – Gestalt und Wirkung: Festschrift für Horst Seebass zum 65. Geburtstag*, ed. S. Beyerle, G. Mayer and H. Strauß (Neukirchen-Vluyn, 1999), 207–231; William P. Brown, *Wisdom's Wonder: Character, Creation, and Crisis in the Bible's Wisdom Literature* (Grand Rapids, 2014); Christopher B. Ansberry, 'What Does Jerusalem Have to Do with Athens?: The Moral Vision of the Book of Proverbs and Aristotle's Nicomachean Ethics', *Hebrew Studies* 51 (2010): 157–173.

[7] Cf. several of Barton's treatments of the topic of virtue: *Ethics in Ancient Israel* (Oxford, 2014), 158–161; 'Ethics in the Wisdom Literature of the Old Testament', in *Perspectives on Israelite Wisdom: Proceedings of the Oxford Old Testament Seminar*, ed. J. Jarick, LHBOTS 618 (London, 2016), 24–37.

[8] See Arthur J. Keefer, *The Book of Proverbs and Virtue Ethics: Integrating the Biblical and Philosophical Traditions* (Cambridge, 2021); Gerick, *Hebrew Bible*.

In other words, one aspect of assessing ḥokmâ and virtue is that of comparing concepts – Aristotelian courage versus Proverbial courage, Thomistic hope versus Joban hope and so on – and this forms the basis of what I will present here, as respective notions of generosity, friendship and good speech, for instance, are juxtaposed with each other and their attendant ideas drawn out. I would argue that this sort of conceptual comparison is the necessary starting point for discerning any further differences or similarities within moral traditions, like explaining why Aristotle and not Proverbs focuses on one virtue over another, or how the genre of Job bears significance for interpreting its own vision of virtue or, if we do find virtues in the Bible, how they relate to the legal materials found therein. But again, conceptual comparison must not jump to conceptual identification; each concept, whilst being measured up against another, must be understood within its historical and intellectual contexts. My initial, conceptual comparison of Aristotelian virtue ethics and wisdom literature will account for the most palpable moral features of the biblical material, including moral virtue in Proverbs, intellectual virtue in Ecclesiastes, friendship in Job and the development of these features in Ben Sira.

MORAL VIRTUE IN PROVERBS

If not the mainstay of ethics in the HB, Proverbs is arguably the anchor of biblical wisdom. The book is weighted, from its first to final chapters, with references to ḥokmâ, and even when it fails to mention the concept by name, we get the sense that wise living is still the matter of concern. Beware of temptations to greed and violence (1:10–19), welcome discipline (12:1), work hard (10:4–5), speak gently (15:1), have some humility (18:12), monitor your consumption and keep company with those who do the same (23:20–21). Many of these 'instructions' are, of course, stated as observations, but when interpreted within the book as a whole and, perhaps, when read as educational literature, it becomes clear that even the most indicative sayings carry imperative force.[9] So 'a healing tongue' being 'a tree of life' is not just a matter of fact (15:4); it is a commendation to speak likewise. Far less established is the idea that these expressions reflect a sort of biblical virtue, though many have

---

[9] Arthur J. Keefer, *Proverbs 1–9 as an Introduction to the Book of Proverbs*, LHBOTS 701 (London, 2020).

called them 'virtues' in a loose sense, and some have asserted that there is a real kind of Aristotelian or Thomistic 'virtue' at play.[10]

Several scholars have taken more care with that alignment and compared Proverbs with the moral visions of Aristotle and Aquinas, drawing up criteria for virtue and coming to nuanced conclusions about the ways in which Proverbs does and does not resemble these ancient formulations of virtue. The overarching 'moral vision' of Proverbs has been, on the one hand, likened to Aristotle's and, on the other hand, likened to the views of Socrates, both arguments having especially accounted for the role of character and practical wisdom in moral conduct and the proximity of knowledge and virtue to it.[11] As for the virtues themselves, I have recently made the case that many of the moral concepts in Proverbs meet Aristotle's criteria for moral virtue, namely, that (1) virtues of action and emotion in Proverbs are identifiable through praise and blame, that (2) the vices reflect excess and deficiency in action and emotion and that (3) the virtues 'hit the mean' of these actions and emotions (NE 2.6).[12] In other words, Proverbs approves and disapproves of certain actions and emotions; when disapproved of, these actions and emotions are faults of excess or deficiency – that is, doing something too much or too little – and those that find approval in the book 'hit the mean' by being exercised 'at the right time, on the right occasion, towards the right people, for the right purpose and in the right manner' (NE 2.6.11).

The action of work, for instance, is a prime candidate for Aristotelian moral virtue in Proverbs. Praise for the one who works hard and disdain for the one who does not are heard throughout Proverbs, and both sentiments are put emphatically at the outset of its first collection of proverbs: 'A slack hand causes poverty, but the hand of the diligent makes rich. A child who gathers in summer is prudent, but a child who sleeps in harvest brings shame' (Prov 10:4–5). Declaring that the diligent person amasses wealth, embodies prudence and most likely wisdom (10:1), while the slack-handed labourer falls to poverty, shames himself and his family and is probably classed as a fool (10:1) is Proverbs' way of approving of the one and denouncing the other, expressing what Aristotle refers to as 'praise and blame'. The lazy person lies at the deficient end of the labour spectrum, failing to work enough – that is, he works too little – while the 'diligent' worker, here,

---

[10] See Brown, *Wisdom's Wonder*; Daniel J. Treier, *Proverbs and Ecclesiastes* (Grand Rapids, 2011), 66–102; James L. Crenshaw, *Old Testament Wisdom: An Introduction* (Louisville, 2010), 9–10, 224.

[11] So Ansberry, 'What Does Jerusalem'; Michael V. Fox, 'Ethics and Wisdom in the Book of Proverbs', *Hebrew Studies* 48 (2009): 75–88.

[12] Keefer, *The Book of Proverbs*.

presumably works to the right degree. For these actions to fit neatly into Aristotle's understanding of virtue and vice, Proverbs also needs to defame the person who works too much. For Aristotle's understanding of virtue is not about just doing the right action, such as working, but about doing that action in the right way, at the right time, towards the right person and so on; to work too little is a vice and to work too much is as well. A virtue – in this case, diligence – is spotted between these two poles.

Proverbs features no character that works too much, like a counterpart to the 'sluggard' who works too little, but it does condemn several forms of over-work, including the person who works too quickly: 'The plans of the diligent lead surely to abundance, but everyone who is hasty comes only to want' (Prov 21:5). Plans and diligence are distinguished here from haste, suggesting that the person at fault may attempt to obtain wealth by wicked means (e.g., 21:6) or work in an unplanned, haphazard fashion that, finally, results in no wealth at all. As far as virtue is concerned, that person errs by excess, working too much with respect to time, that is, working too quickly. Aristotle specifies that viciousness errs not only by 'amount', understood in a strictly quantitative way, but can also err with respect to purpose, manner or, in this case, timing. So the hasty worker may not be a simple 'workaholic', and when it comes to the sum of his labour, he may indeed work too little, but the point of the proverb seems to be that he works too much, or too fast, with respect to time and is condemned for it. Other errors of excess also appear in Proverbs, such as working for the wrong reasons or objects (23:4–5; 29:19), and they frame the book's teaching about work in a way that accords with Aristotle's idea of moral virtue: one should not work too little (sloth) or work too much, whether in timing (haste) or purpose (for wealth or 'empty pursuits'), but should rather work 'at the right time, on the right occasion, towards the right people, for the right purpose and in the right manner' (NE 2.6.11), which Proverbs captures in the 'virtue' of diligence.

Many of the moral concepts in Proverbs align with and are plausibly explained by such Aristotelian criteria for moral virtue, including gladness, diligence, discipline, honour, generosity, mercy, anger, dispute, fear, appetite, self-regard and four types of speech (quality, purpose, amount and timing).[13] Though not without qualification; for many actions and emotions in Proverbs, one acts in a morally virtuous way by knowing the 'mean', that action or emotion that is done or felt in the

[13] See Keefer, The Book of Proverbs.

right way, at the right time, in the right manner and so on. For example, cheer can be felt too little (sorrow; Prov 15:13), too much (levity; 25:30) or rightly (gladness; 10:1; 15:15). Disputation too falls along an Aristotelian spectrum: one can dispute too much, such as the one who sows discord (6:14; 20:3), or too little, by failing to quiet contention or drive out a scoffer (15:18; 22:10), and should ideally aim to establish peace (15:18; 16:7). But acting or feeling in a virtuous manner is, for Aristotle and perhaps for Proverbs, different from simply knowing how one ought to act or feel. Knowledge does not equate to moral virtue. In order to know the mean, one needs 'intellectual virtues', particularly 'prudence' (*phronēsis*), and whilst Proverbs may have a similar concept in mind for discerning good action (e.g., 1:4; 14:8), it is in Ecclesiastes that readers are more readily given a look at the intellectual side of Israelite wisdom. But, first, we look to Job, which features its own catalogue of virtue concepts.

FRIENDSHIP IN JOB

Many of the moral concepts that we find in Proverbs can also be found in the book of Job. By his own declaration, Job has been kind to the poor (29:12) and unsparing towards the wicked (29:17), a display and denial of mercy that accounts for its recipients and suggests that Job acts in accord with a mean state as Aristotle understands it; he shows neither too little nor too much mercy. So too, several moral categories used in Proverbs appear in Job, such as the 'wicked', varieties of human speech and implications of humility and pride (e.g., 11:4). But these actions and emotions cannot be weighed up as neatly as they were in Proverbs. For in Job they occur in a context far less abstract and emerge instead within the relationships of Job, Eliphaz, Zophar and Bildad, along with Elihu and the Lord himself. That relational context has inspired one of the most thorough works on Joban virtue.

According to Patricia Vesely, virtue ethics, with its emphasis on dispositions, intentions and perceptions, brings to the fore what Job deemed worthy of friendship. When Job speaks of his interlocutors, a set of traits are established as constitutive of a good friend, and Job 3–27 exposes several characteristics deemed virtuous in friendship: 'loyalty, compassion, courage, honesty, hospitality, and practical wisdom, as well as selfless intentions and proper perceptions'.[14] Although in that

---

[14] Vesely, *Friendship*, 130.

discourse Job is establishing such virtues through the fact that his friends lack them, Job 29–31 puts dispositions in a positive light, disclosing how Job rightly treats others, as he exercises kindness and benevolence and feels goodwill towards his community, a virtuous effort that may seem akin to Aristotle's notion of friendship but, upon closer inspection, is not. For Aristotle, friendship entails dispositions of goodwill that are reciprocated and shared by those alike in virtue and status (*NE* 8.6), which would place Job's association with the poor, the fatherless and the widow (29:12–13), for instance, outside the bounds of true Aristotelian friendship. So, according to Vesely, the book may display some virtuous dispositions, according to Job at least, but it certainly alters an Aristotelian definition of what true friendship entails.

In the case of Job as literature, any discernment of moral virtue within the book depends upon an interpretation of the whole, particularly how one relates the book's narrative and dialogue portions and thereby identifies the ethical authority of certain speakers. For Vesely, these 'virtues of friendship' are not established based upon Aristotle's criteria for moral virtue – excess, deficiency and mean-state – but rather upon post-Aristotelian definitions, that of virtues being 'persisting attitudes, those character traits we possess over a long enough time that they become part of our temperament'.[15] This definition accords with many of the conclusions about friendship in Job, although the enduring aspect of 'virtue' is only sometimes verifiable. However, what I find questionable about this approach to Job is not so much its definition for virtue as its stance on ethical authority within the book. The book's ethical system has been described as ambiguous and even, according to some scholars, ambiguous by design. Von Rad concluded that 'Right and wrong certainly cannot be counted out in such a way, piece by piece'.[16] Carol Newsom has argued that no voice in the dialogue (i.e., Job 3–41) takes final ethical authority and that the book's many genres put its judgements about piety into a 'contradictory complexity'.[17] No one character is 'right' or 'wrong'; each invites the reader into a different world of moral claims and presuppositions. The book's uniqueness and

---

[15] Vesely takes this idea from Bruce C. Birch and Larry L. Rasmussen (*Bible and Ethics in the Christian Life* [Minneapolis, 1989], 79) and also gives attention to intentions and perceptions.

[16] Gerhard von Rad, *Weisheit in Israel*, 4th ed. (Neukirchen-Vluyn, 2013), 229.

[17] Carol A. Newsom, *The Book of Job: A Contest of Moral Imaginations* (New York, 2003), 30.

mixed genre is endorsed by Vesely, but she decides upon one ethical authority, and that is Job himself. For although any 'final answer' on ethics 'would be inappropriate', it seems that the virtues of friendship are nevertheless virtues 'according to Job', representative of what it means to be a 'genuine' friend, and ultimately depend upon his word being the voice of ethical authority.[18] Hence, we can put quite a bit of weight upon his statements about friendship, as he calls his companions 'miserable comforters' (16:2) and 'worthless physicians' (13:4).

There is, of course, an exegetical basis for this: Job's own claims to innocence and perhaps a validation of them in the dialogues (e.g., Job 29–31); his matchless moral status according to the narrative portions of the book (1:1–5; 42:7–8) and concluding demonstration of it in the end (42:9–10). But the question is whether or not Job's claims about his friends – their 'virtues', intentions and perceptions – are right. Is that what God means when he says that 'you have not spoken of me what is right, as my servant Job has' (42:7)?[19] God validates the words that Job has spoken of him and decries the speech of his friends and yet the penitential action that Job performs on their behalf suggests that the friends may have indeed spoken wrongly not only of God but of Job too.[20] Therefore, while we seem assured of several things – that Job is in some way right and his friends are in many ways wrong, that Job has at least dealt with suffering in a morally exceptional way and that these parties have certainly spoken of God in opposing fashions – there remains a lingering doubt about categorically approving of Job's words and actions, especially with respect to the virtuous nature of friendship.[21] So where the debate regarding Proverbs may be about the virtuous status of its palpable moral concepts, in Job the question becomes one of how we interpret the whole in order to reach any judgement, if it

---

[18] See, e.g., Vesely, *Friendship*, 85–94.

[19] There is a *crux interpretum* in 42:7, namely, the lexeme *někônâ*, which may mean either 'correct/right' or 'honestly' and thereby imply that the norm by which their speech is measured is either external or subjective, at least to some degree. Based on the dialogue, there seems little reason to think that the friends spoke any other way but honestly about God, meaning that it is not honesty but correctness of speech at stake in this judgement.

[20] For an interpretation that stresses the consistent moral purity of Job, whilst qualifying that although he serves as an exemplar for how to deal with suffering Job may not have related to his friends rightly in every instance, see David J. A. Clines, *Job*, WBC 17, 18B (Dallas, 1989; Nashville, 2011), 65–66; 1231–1234. The question of how they could have got it right is, yet, another.

[21] See John J. Collins, 'The Friends of Job and the Task of Biblical Theology', *Int* 70 (2016): 288–292.

is indeed possible, about what is morally good or bad in the book. Both conclusions suggest that some form of discernment is at stake, whether for exercising moral virtue or recognising its source, and that concern – called 'prudence' by Aristotle – is central to Ecclesiastes.

INTELLECTUAL VIRTUE IN ECCLESIASTES

Ecclesiastes, undoubtedly, recounts a project of the intellect. Qohelet aims 'to seek and to search out by wisdom all that is done under heaven' (1:13), 'to know and to search out and to seek wisdom and the sum of things, and to know that wickedness is folly and that foolishness is madness' (7:25). He uses verbs of cognition with great frequency, claiming to 'know' (y-d-'), 'see' (r-'-h), 'find out' (m-ṣ-') and often failing to understand matters of life and faith. Qohelet's preoccupation with knowledge and knowing has not evaded interpreters, who have focused on his epistemology, especially on his method of acquiring knowledge, the limits to knowledge and the epistemological tensions of what he observes. Of this acquisition, limitation and 'contradiction' he is said to have acquired knowledge by means of independent empiricism, faced the limits of knowledge due to God, death and time and reckoned with the tensions of his knowledge by means of illusion and (mis)perception.[22] But, amidst these many epistemological considerations, scholarship on Ecclesiastes has not been concerned with virtue.

The few considerations of virtue in the book imply that Qohelet's process of obtaining knowledge cannot be considered virtuous and is, at most, redeemed by the argument that he is attempting to subvert Hellenistic epistemology.[23] What has attracted more attention is Qohelet's process of thought, which has been explained primarily as some form of rational thinking,[24] whereby Qohelet observes his world,

---

[22] See, respectively, Michael V. Fox, *A Time to Tear Down and a Time to Build Up: A Rereading of Ecclesiastes* (Grand Rapids, 1999), 76–82; Annette Schellenberg, *Erkenntnis als Problem: Qohelet und die alttestamentliche Diskussion um das menschliche Erkennen* (Göttingen, 2002); Stuart Weeks, *Ecclesiastes and Scepticism*, LHBOTS 541 (New York, 2012).

[23] Ryan P. O'Dowd, 'A Chord of Three Strands: Epistemology in Job, Proverbs and Ecclesiastes', in *The Bible and Epistemology: Biblical Soundings on the Knowledge of God*, ed. M. Healy and R. Perry (Colorado Springs, 2007), 79–83. On the subversion of autonomous Hellenism, see Craig Bartholomew, *Ecclesiastes* (Grand Rapids, 2009), 94–95, 134–135; Thomas Krüger, *Kritische Weisheit: Studien zur weisheitlichen Traditionskritik im Alten Testament* (Zürich, 1997), 146–147.

[24] See, among others, Weeks, *Ecclesiastes*, 104–131; Peter Machinist, 'Fate, miqreh, and Reason: Some Reflections on Qohelet and Biblical Thought', in *Solving Riddles and*

reckons with several alternative activities or modes of life and makes reasoned conclusions about them. Indeed, moral virtue does not seem to be the focus of Ecclesiastes. For here we are on barren scholarly terrain, and it may seem that in Ecclesiastes we are on barren moral terrain too, especially when compared to Proverbs and Job. But that does not mean that Ecclesiastes has nothing to do with virtue ethics. For Aristotle himself gave moral virtue as only one type of virtue, being also occupied by intellectual virtues, and it is my contention that the intellectual virtue of 'prudence' sheds some light on what Qohelet was thinking about and how he was thinking about it.

In the *NE*, prudence (*phronēsis*) is one of five intellectual virtues and is distinguished from science (proof by deduction based on immutable first principles), art (bringing something unnecessary into existence), intelligence (apprehending first principles) and wisdom (a combination of intelligence and scientific knowledge) (*NE* 6.1–8). Prudence is a faculty that attains truth in matters of conduct to ensure the rightness of the means we adopt to attain an end (*NE* 6.5, 9). In other words, 'Virtue ensures the rightness of the end we aim at, Prudence ensures the rightness of the means we adopt to gain that end' (*NE* 6.12.6).[25] The end that Aristotle has in mind is the good life in general (6.5.1–2), which does not entail 'things of a most exalted nature' (6.7.5); for that is the domain of *sophia* ('wisdom'). The good life takes place 'on the ground', in the realm of human action, and it takes stock of one's changing circumstances. The means of accounting for life's many variables is *phronēsis*, rightly called 'practical wisdom' or 'deliberative excellence'. The person with *phronēsis* determines the most advantageous means for achieving the good life.

Qohelet does not present a singular, accepted end for humankind and then deliberate about various means, but he does use his *ḥokmâ* in an attempt to 'see what was good for mortals to do under heaven during the few days of their life' (Eccl 2:3). This end, or 'good' (*ṭôb*), is described in various ways: it is joy/pleasure (*śimḥâ*), doing good rather than evil, partaking of and finding satisfaction in one's portion; it is life rather than death, wealth-possessions-honour and experiencing 'good' amidst

---

Untying Knots: Biblical, Epigraphic, and Semitic Studies in Honor of Jonas C. Greenfield, ed. Z. Zevit, S. Gitin and M. Sokoloff (Winona Lake, 1995), 170–173. It has been compared to a Greek 'pistis' or *argumentatio* by John Jarick, 'The Rhetorical Structure of Ecclesiastes', in *Perspectives*, 208–231.

[25] For a lengthy discussion and rebuttal of intellectualist interpretations of Aristotle, see Jessica Moss, '"Virtue Makes the Goal Right": Virtue and "Phronesis" in Aristotle's Ethics', *Phronesis* 56 (2011): 204–261.

one's toil. Much of the book is spent dismantling several notions of what that end ought to be and the means by which one might try to achieve it.[26] In terms of method (not, I think, in terms of influence), Qohelet can be deemed Aristotelian: he perceives particulars, arguably takes an end for granted (2:3),[27] deliberates about several means and decides upon a few (*NE* 3.3). He does not, however, presuppose a final end which is then left vague or undefined, as Aristotle has been accused of in his notion of *eudaimonia*. Qohelet rather makes a case for specific ends that one should pursue whilst qualifying the effectiveness of certain means by which to achieve them. Not only are certain means futile, but there are several ends that one might pursue that are themselves unattainable, or in some cases unpredictably attainable: toiling for a 'gain' (2:9–11), being wise or righteous, or even foolish, in order to outlast death and at best prolong life (2:15; 7:15; 8:12–13), working with wisdom to establish a lasting legacy (2:18–19; 8:12–15; 9:1–2) and gaining satisfaction via one or many means: loving money (5:9), expecting a lasting product (5:12–16) or being foolish (6:8). In his singularly focused study, Qohelet concludes that 'I found pleasure in all my toil', and yet 'this was my reward ... there was no gain under the sun' (2:10–11). By presenting cases and conclusions of how each of these ends, and in some cases means, evades human achievement, Qohelet demotes them and, perhaps, tries to persuade his audience that they should not strive for such ends or should not assume that the prevailing means can accomplish them.

In turn, a great deal of emphasis is laid on the ends that Qohelet deems not only attainable but acceptable: partaking of one's 'portion' (*ḥēleq*), having joy during work and life and taking satisfaction in these things, all of which are from God, bound together and not easily distinguished from each other for the reader.[28] But Qohelet not only argues for certain ends – that is, his vision of the good life – he also approves of the means that can achieve those ends. Therefore, despite its elusiveness and unreliability, one ought to use wisdom (2:12–23); one should please

---

[26] These are, of course, subject to dispute among commentators. By 'good', Qohelet could mean 'the only and highest good' (Krüger), a good that is indiscernible (Bartholomew), one that takes various descriptions (Schwienhorst-Schönberger) or one associated largely with pleasure (Fox).

[27] See discussion on 'Goods' below.

[28] See Eccl 3:12–13; 5:17–19[18–20]; 6:1–9; 8:15. Fox (*Time*, 110) is right to say, based especially on 8:15, that although one might get pleasure by means of toil, Qohelet's principle expectation is that humans have joy amidst their toil. Qohelet also seems to assume goods of living, wisdom, justice, depending on their form.

God (2:24–26) and make the most of one's 'portion' (9:7–10). Each of these is, of course, subject to life's unpredictability and unreliability, God's determination and death itself. Such are the limitations to 'faring well', and I would conclude that one's good ultimately involves living within these limitations, which accord, each in their own way, with Qohelet's endorsed ends: confining oneself to one's 'portion', finding joy and satisfaction therein and not striving to obtain it elsewhere. In the same way that one's ultimate good involves living within life's limitations, so perhaps the ends that Qohelet criticises – obtaining a 'gain', outlasting death, establishing a legacy – involve the human will to strive beyond those limitations and to expect too much from the means thought to accomplish them. So the problem is subjective and objective; humans strive beyond limitations and reality imposes them.

Aristotle's notions of ends and means, as managed by the intellectual virtue of prudence, have helped to organise the thought of Qohelet, who takes a different starting point than Aristotle but nonetheless thinks in a way reminiscent of someone with Aristotelian intellectual virtue.

VIRTUE IN BEN SIRA

In Ben Sira, we return to a work that is, upon first impression, far more like Proverbs than like Job or Ecclesiastes. Like Proverbs, its many moral concepts are a testament to moral virtue.[29] One ought to be diligent (4:29), generous (4:4), merciful (4:8–9), chary of appetitive indulgence (18:33), cheerful on most occasions (30:22, 25), humble rather than proud (3:17–20), in various ways apropos in speech (20:6, 13), having appropriate recognition of honour and shame (8:5–6) and exercising discipline towards those under one's care (7:23). The book even contains instructions that make matters of 'right time – right place' explicitly praiseworthy: 'The wise remain silent until the right moment, but a boasting fool misses the right moment' (20:7); 'Wine drunk at the proper time and in moderation is rejoicing of heart and gladness of soul' (31:28). The wise person, as Ben Sira envisions it, acts and feels in many areas of life at the right time, in the right way and

---

[29] Some comparison of Ben Sira and Stoic thought, incorporating a discussion of virtue, appears in Ursel Wicke-Reuter, 'Ben Sira und die Frühe Stoa: Zum Zusammenhang von Ethik und dem Glauben an eine göttliche Providenz', in *Ben Sira's God: Proceedings of the International Ben Sira Conference, Durham – Ushaw College 2001*, ed. Renate Egger-Wenzel, BZAW 321 (Berlin, 2002), 268–281.

towards the right people and is, for that reason, praised. We need little else for moral virtue. However, the book's patent sense of this virtue comes with an ethical form and content that is unlike Proverbs.

In many cases, Ben Sira elaborates on instruction that Proverbs only hints at, such as how a father ought to protect his daughter (42:11–14) or the extent that 'sin' and 'humility' play in life, and it makes quite a deal about matters that are absent from Proverbs, like social 'equality' and 'inequality' (10:22–25; 13:2), one's posture towards sickness and death (38:1–23) and the manner in which wisdom manifests in particular trades (38:24–39:11). Virtue is also driven inward, so that the heart itself speaks (37:14) and becomes the 'root' of one's counsel (37:17). Similarly, unprecedented tactics are employed to shape the reader's virtue, such as using empathy, based in common human experience, to motivate one to show mercy (8:5–7), moderate the appetite, act appropriately at the table (31:15) and reprove friends (19:13–17).[30] In terms of form, the book makes less use of character types and ideal portrayals of virtue and makes more of the ambiguity of ethical action, decision-making and, perhaps, of reality itself (11:25–28). As Von Rad observed, 'Sirach offers people no moral platitudes. He teaches the difficult art of finding each right aspect in the midst of ambiguous phenomena and occurrences, and of doing what is right in the sight of God'.[31] Consequently, Ben Sira's ethical vision seems as moral as it does intellectual – one must deal with the ambiguity of life and messiness of moral existence – and in this way there is substantial affinity with Ecclesiastes.[32] This suggests that, in terms of virtue, the book amplifies the depth and scope of topics addressed by Proverbs and has some bearing on the intellectual exercises of Qohelet, adding to all of this, of course, a partnership with Jewish law, ritual and ideology (4:15; 7:31; 15:1).[33]

The itemised moral virtues and the limits of moral epistemology are not the only aspects of virtue ethics within Ben Sira. For, according to Jeremy   Corley,   'More   than   any   other   biblical   book,   the

---

[30] Bradley C. Gregory, 'Empathy in the Ethical Rhetoric of Ben Sira', in *Emotions from Ben Sira to Paul*, ed. R. Egger-Wenzel and Jeremy Corley (Berlin, 2012), 103–119. Cf. Sir 8:7b and Gen 25:8; 49:29; Judg 2:10; for 'sympathy' more generally, see Job 2:11; 42:11; Ps 69:21[Eng. v. 20].

[31] Von Rad, *Weisheit*, 261.

[32] For passages in Ben Sira that touch on the themes of Ecclesiastes, see 11:10, 14, 22; 13:8; 14:3–19; 16:12; 30:16–17; 31:1–3; 37:25; 40:1.

[33] See, e.g., Friedrich Vinzenz Reiterer, 'The Theological and Philosophical Concepts of Ben Sira', in *Discovering, Deciphering and Dissenting: Ben Sira Manuscripts after 120 Years*, ed. James K. Aitken, R. Egger-Wenzel and Stefan C. Reif (Berlin, 2018), 285–315.

deuterocanonical Wisdom of Ben Sira speaks about friendship.'[34] And, indeed, Ben Sira has much to say about friends, though we might no longer agree that it says most about the topic, for with Vesely's study of friendship in Job, the deuterocanonical account of such virtue has met its match. What we have in these two books are two very different methods of addressing the question of virtuous friendship in ancient Jewish thought: Ben Sira propounding advice about 'friends' and Job displaying several relationships themselves within which judgements about friendship are levelled. So there are, then, clear commonalities within Ben Sira with Job, Ecclesiastes and Proverbs, albeit each in their own ways and with no certainty as to the extent of their influence upon Ben Sira.

There are, lastly, two other potential models of virtue in Ben Sira. First is the section that extols God and wisdom (42:15–43:33). It may rightly remind readers of Job more than Proverbs, as it accentuates the matchless power of God and his autonomy over creation, and yet it does not qualify for Aristotle's understanding of moral virtue. For it is not God's moral attributes that are praised – it is rather his bounty of knowledge, preservation of all things, works of creation and activity in nature – and, therefore, although it extols the Lord, this hymnic passage does not portray him as an exemplar of human virtue. It portrays him doing far more god-like things. Second is the section that praises the ancestors of Israel (44:1–50:24), which is less ethically removed than the first. Several figures from Jewish history are evidently esteemed for their respective deeds, whether militaristic capacities, achievements in construction, their piety or their services to the people, and they are even known as 'men of strength/virtue',[35] possessing wisdom from God that is identifiable with 'goodness' (45:26). As a whole, this section seems to take some form of a history and yet its pedagogical intent has been questioned by scholars, for it obviously polishes the character of these figures and extols the Lord's involvement in their deeds, but that does not mean that the ancestors serve as moral exemplars for Ben Sira's audience to emulate.[36] By underscoring familial memory, God's maintenance of the covenant and certain conflicts with surrounding nations,

---

[34] Jeremy Corley, 'Friendship according to Ben Sira', in *Der Einzelne und seine Gemeinschaft bei Ben Sira*, ed. R. Egger-Wenzel and Ingrid Krammer, BZAW 270 (Berlin, 1998), 65. Passages include Sir 6:5–17; 9:10–16; 12:8–12; 13:15–23; 19:6–19; 22:19–26; 25:1–11; 27:16–21 and 37:1–6.

[35] That is according to the Hebrew text:*'anšê ḥāyil*. The Greek reads 'rich men'.

[36] See such a critique in Alon Goshen-Gottstein, 'Ben Sira's Praise of the Fathers: A Canon-Conscious Reading', in *Ben Sira's God*, 235–267.

perhaps 'this portrait gallery drawn from Israel's sacred history is meant to reinforce the conviction and courage of Ben Sira's contemporaries',[37] particularly in their identity as God's chosen people rather than as individual or collective moral agents. All of this makes the significance of Sir 44:1–50:24 for a study of virtue ethics less than straightforward. That said, with such tributes at the end of the book (as we have it), which plausibly raised the people's gratitude for God, their loyalty to the covenant and courage in the face of contemporary Hellenism, Ben Sira's audience has only more reason to pursue the life of virtue prescribed throughout the book's instructional chapters.

THE GOODS AND CONTEXTS OF VIRTUE

I have tried to make plain the normative theory known as virtue ethics and how it might relate to biblical wisdom literature. This has required an explanation of 'virtue's' meaning, and it led to ways in which that concept might be used for biblical interpretation and to several proposals about how virtue ethics aligns with the biblical wisdom literature in particular. It would be appropriate to conclude by situating all of this within the recent trends of moral philosophy.

Modern moral philosophy is preoccupied with questions of 'obligation' and with certain justifications for moral choice. What ought to be done? Why is it right? And by what principle – usually what single principle – can we address these questions? Such are the kinds of queries that characterise what moral philosophers have dealt with since the Enlightenment, and the answers have been summed up neatly within two categories: for those in the Kantian tradition, individuals, being free and rational, act with a good will by adhering to duty, which is determined by its universalisability; for utilitarians, the question 'what should I do' is answered through some formulation of what produces the greatest happiness for the greatest number. This may sound reductive, but much modern moral philosophy is arguably so. For deontology and utilitarianism have narrowed moral enquiry to questions of obligation and moral action, and they have, at the same time, neglected questions about the good. Far gone too are the ancient anthropologies that saw humans as having a particular function and as being

---

[37] Patrick W. Skehan and Alexander A. Di Lella, *The Wisdom of Ben Sira: A New Translation with Notes*, AB 39 (New York, 1987), 500.

telos-oriented agents.[38] We cannot, of course, take on all of these critiques and queries here, but I can suggest that we reconsider one of the most important components of virtue. That is the question of what place goods and 'the good' have in biblical literature and whether or not they organise any part of the ethics therein. If the good was indeed such a magnet for virtue ethics, then we should expect it to draw together something of what has been discussed so far.

In Proverbs, we saw that knowledge, wisdom and growth in wise character form the overarching ends of the book, but there are also other goods that are related to these, including divine protection (Prov 2:7–8), straight paths (3:6), physical health (3:8) and material wealth (3:10). Evident too is a certain scheme of values. If, for example, one is faced with the opportunity to choose honour or riches (22:1), and wisdom or gold (16:16), we are assured that honour and wisdom are 'better than' the alternatives. To speak of a hierarchy of ends in Proverbs is possible, and its opening chapters (1–9) most likely set the agenda: receive the father's instruction and the Lord's help so that wisdom might be embraced and consequently cultivate one's wise character. From this many goods come and to this many goods lead, and this is all to say that a notion of 'the good', perhaps the 'good life', and certainly the goods of life play an integral part for ethics in Proverbs.

The book of Job too elevates good character, material prosperity and familial harmony within its narrative portions (Job 1:1–5; 42:10–17), and within its dialogues the assumption that a peaceful existence, long life and many children constitute the good life is evident (5:17–27). Even if Job cannot assent to such goods in the moment, it is not so much the content of the 'blessed' life that is under dispute for him than it is the conditions within which those goods are achieved or 'deserved'. Job does not contest the blessedness of progeny or security; he insists that such goods are no longer available to him: 'Remember that my life is a breath; my eye will never again see good' (Job 7:7). It is less a question of what is good and more a matter of accessing that good.

Qohelet, however, is concerned with the former – with what constitutes the good – and he seems to lower the standard here. For he terminates the 'good' at one's portion, having joy during one's work and life and taking satisfaction in them, as he all the while uncovers the limited access that humans have to life's great goods and even, in some cases, the goods that he has circumscribed. His inquest – to 'see what

---

[38] See Bernard Williams, *Ethics and the Limits of Philosophy* (London, 1985; repr., 2011); Alasdair MacIntyre, *After Virtue: A Study in Moral Theory*, 3rd ed. (London, 2007).

was good for mortals to do under heaven during the few days of their life' (Eccl 2:3) – apparently points to a singular 'good' that might organise the activities of life, but the good to which Qohelet here refers is not so obvious among commentators and there are at least four proposals for its interpretation: that Qohelet is referring to 'good' as the only and highest good; that whatever it is, he cannot discern it; that he refers to a good but describes it in various ways and that, although it is mostly associated with pleasure, Qohelet considers several things good throughout the book.[39] So whilst the presence of a 'supreme good' remains unclear in Ecclesiastes, there are several goods with which Qohelet reckons and orders his thought, which, as discussed above, resembles Aristotle's idea of intellectual virtue. Therefore, the good is significant and even at points determinative for the moral thought of the biblical wisdom literature, which may have more affinity with virtue ethics than with the priorities of modern moral philosophy.

Virtue ethics, then, as a textually manifested and historically situated form of moral philosophy has some affinity with the biblical wisdom literature. Such an assessment involves the particular types of 'virtue' as articulated by certain philosophers, along with the constituents and structures that make virtue ethics a distinct form of moral thought, foremost character and goods. Accounted for in this manner, virtue is not only a plausible way to interpret biblical wisdom literature but also a helpful way of construing it.

Further Reading

Ansberry, Christopher B. 'What Does Jerusalem Have to Do with Athens?: The Moral Vision of the Book of Proverbs and Aristotle's Nicomachean Ethics'. *Hebrew Studies* 51 (2010): 157–173.

Aristotle. *Nicomachean Ethics*. Translated by H. Rackham. LCL 73. London: 1934.

Barton, John. *Ethics in Ancient Israel*. Oxford: 2014.

Birch, Bruce C. *Let Justice Roll Down: The Old Testament, Ethics, and Christian Life*. Louisville: 1991.

Brown, William P. *Wisdom's Wonder: Character, Creation, and Crisis in the Bible's Wisdom Literature*. Grand Rapids: 2014.

Fox, Michael V. 'Ethics and Wisdom in the Book of Proverbs'. *Hebrew Studies* 48 (2009): 75–88.

---

[39] See, respectively, Krüger, *Kritische Weisheit*, 131; Bartholomew, *Ecclesiastes*, 250–251; Ludger Schwienhorst-Schönberger, *Kohelet*, HTKAT (Freiburg, 2011), 73–75; Fox, *Time*, 116–117, 140–143.

Gericke, Jaco. 'Axiological Assumptions in Qohelet: A Historical-Philosophical Clarification'. *Verbum et Ecclesia* 33 (2012): 1–6.

Keefer, Arthur J. *The Book of Proverbs and Virtue Ethics: Integrating the Biblical and Philosophical Traditions.* Cambridge: 2021.

Lichtheim, Miriam. *Moral Values in Ancient Egypt.* OBO 155. Göttingen: 1997.

MacIntyre, Alasdair. *A Short History of Ethics: A History of Moral Philosophy from the Homeric Age to the Twentieth Century.* London: 1966.

After Virtue: A Study in Moral Theory. 3rd ed. London: 2007.

Nasuti, Harry. 'Called into Character: Aesthetic and Ascetic Aspects of Biblical Ethics'. *CBQ* 80 (2018): 1–24.

Otto, Eckart. *Theologische Ethik des Alten Testaments.* Stuttgart: 1994.

Schellenberg, Annette. *Erkenntnis als Problem: Qohelet und die alttestamentliche Diskussion um das menschliche Erkennen.* Göttingen: 2002.

Vesely, Patricia. *Friendship and Virtue Ethics in the Book of Job.* Cambridge: 2019.

Bibliography

Adams, Samuel L. *Wisdom in Transition: Act and Consequence in Second Temple Instructions.* JSJSup 125. Leiden; Boston: 2008.

'Reassessing the Exclusivism of Ben Sira's Jewish Paideia'. Pages 47–58 in *Second Temple Jewish 'Paideia' in Context.* Edited by Jason M. Zurawski and Gabriele Boccaccini. BZNW 228. Berlin: 2017.

Albertson, R. G. 'Job and Ancient Near Eastern Wisdom Literature'. Pages 213–230 in *Scripture in Context II: More Essays on the Comparative Method.* Edited by William W. Hallo, James C. Moyer and Leo G. Perdue. Winona Lake: 1983.

Aletti, J. N. 'Seduction et parole en Proverbes I–IX'. *VT* 27 (1977): 129–144.

Alonso Schökel, Luis. 'Toward a Dramatic Reading of the Book of Job'. *Semeia* 7 (1977): 45–61.

Proverbios. Madrid: 1984.

Alster, Bendt. *Proverbs of Ancient Sumer.* 2 vols. Bethesda: 1997.

Alt, Albrecht. 'Die Weisheit Salomos'. *TLZ* 76 (1951): cols. 139–144.

Alter, Robert. *The Art of Biblical Narrative.* New York: 1981.

The Art of Biblical Poetry. New York: 1985.

Ambrose of Milan. 'Hexaemeron'. Pages 3–283 in *The Fathers of the Church.* Translated by John J. Savage. Vol. 42. New York: 1961.

Andruska, Jennifer L. *Wise and Foolish Love in the Song of Songs.* Leiden: 2019.

Annus, Amar, and Alan Lenzi. *Ludlul bēl nēmeqi: The Standard Babylonian Poem of the Righteous Sufferer.* SAACT VII. Helsinki: 2010.

Ansberry, Christopher B. 'What Does Jerusalem Have to Do with Athens?: The Moral Vision of the Book of Proverbs and Aristotle's Nicomachean Ethics'. *HS* 51 (2010): 157–173.

Anthes, R. 'Die Maat des Echnaton von Amarna'. *JAOS* 14 (1952): 1–36.

Anthonioz, Stéphanie. 'A Reflection on the Nature of Wisdom: From Psalm 1 to Mesopotamian Traditions'. Pages 43–56 in *Tracing Sapiential Traditions in Ancient Judaism.* Edited by Hindy Najman, Jean-Sébastien Rey and Eibert J. C. Tigchelaar. JSJSup 174. Leiden: 2016.

Aquinas, Thomas. *Summa Theologica.* Translated by the Fathers of the English Dominican Province. London: 1920.

Aristotle. *Nicomachean Ethics.* Translated by H. Rackham. LCL 73. London: 1934.

Arnaud, Daniel. *Recherches au pays d'Aštata, Emar VI.4: Textes de la bibliothèque, transcriptions et traductions.* Synthese 28. Paris: 1987.

'6. Textes de bibliothèque'. Pages 333–337 in *Études Ougaritiques 1. Travaux 1985–1995*. Edited by Marguerite Yon and Daniel Arnaud. Ras Shamra-Ougarit 14. Paris: 2001.

Corpus des textes de bibliothéque de Ras Shamra-Ougarit (1936–2000): En sumérien, babylonien et assyrien. AuOr Sup 23. Barcelona: 2007.

Askin, Lindsey A. 'Beyond Encomium or Eulogy: The Role of Simon the High Priest in Ben Sira'. *JAJ* 9.3 (2018): 344–365.

Scribal Culture in Ben Sira. JSJSup 184. Leiden: 2019.

Assis, Elie. 'The Alphabetic Acrostics in the Book of Lamentations'. *CBQ* 69.4 (2007): 710–724.

Assmann, Jan. *Ma'at: Gerechtigkeit und Unsterblichkeit im Alten Ägypten*. München: 1990.

Astell, Ann W. *Job, Boethius, and Epic Truth*. Ithaca: 1994.

Ayali-Darshan, Noga. 'II. Literature: Egyptian and Levantine Belles-Lettres – Links and Influences during the Bronze Age'. Pages 195–205 in *Pharaoh's Land and Beyond: Ancient Egypt and Its Neighbors*. Edited by Pearce P. Creasman and Richard H. Wilkinson. Oxford: 2017.

'"Do Not Open Your Heart to Your Wife or Servant" (Onch. 13:17): A West-Asiatic Antecedent and Its Relation to Later Wisdom Instructions'. Pages 95–103 in *Teaching Morality in Antiquity*. Edited by Takayoshi M. Oshima. ORA 29. Tübingen: 2018.

'The Sequence of Sir 4:26–27 in Light of Akkadian and Aramaic Texts from the Levant and Later Writings'. *ZAW* 130 (2018): 436–449.

Bacon, Francis. *The Twoo Bookes of Francis Bacon. Of the Proficience and Aduancement of Learning, Diuine and Humane to the King*. London: 1605.

Balentine, Samuel E. 'Job and the Priests: "He Leads Priests Away Stripped" (Job 12:19)'. Pages 42–53 in *Reading Job Intertextually*. Edited by Katharine Dell and Will Kynes. LHBOTS 574. New York: 2013.

Ballard, C. Andrew. 'The Mysteries of Paideia: "Mystery" and Education in Plato's *Symposium*, 4QInstruction, and 1 Corinthians'. Pages 243–282 in *Pedagogy in Early Judaism and Early Christianity*. Edited by K. Hogan, M. Goff and E. Wasserman. Atlanta: 2017.

Barbour, Jennifer. *The Story of Israel in the Book of Qohelet: Ecclesiastes as Cultural Memory*. Oxford Theological Monographs. New York: 2012.

Bardtke, Hans. 'Profetische Zuge im Buche Hiob'. Pages 1–10 in *Das ferne und nahe Wort: Festschrift Leonhard Rost zur Vollendung seines 70. Lebensjahres am 30. November 1966 gewidmet*. Edited by Fritz Maass. BZAW 105. Berlin: 1967.

Barns, John W. B. *Five Ramesseum Papyri*. Oxford: 1956.

Barr, James. *Biblical Words for Time*. SBT 33. London: 1962.

'The Book of Job and Its Modern Interpreters'. *BJRL* 54 (1971–1972): 28–46.

Biblical Faith and Natural Theology. Oxford: 1993.

Bartholomew, Craig G. *Reading Ecclesiastes: Old Testament Exegesis and Hermeneutical Theory*. AnBib 139. Rome: 1998.

Ecclesiastes. Grand Rapids: 2009.

Bartholomew, Craig G., and Ryan P. O'Dowd. *Old Testament Wisdom Literature: A Theological Introduction*. Downers Grove: 2018.

Barton, John. *Reading the Old Testament: Method in Biblical Study*. Rev. and enl. ed. Louisville: 1996.

'Virtue in the Bible'. *Studies in Christian Ethics* 12 (1999): 12–22.

Ethics in Ancient Israel. Oxford: 2014.

'Ethics in the Wisdom Literature of the Old Testament'. Pages 24–37 in *Perspectives on Israelite Wisdom: Proceedings of the Oxford Old Testament Seminar*. Edited by J. Jarick. LHBOTS 618. London: 2016.

Barucq, A. Le *livre des Proverbes*. *SB*. Paris: 1964.

Batten, L. W. 'The Epilogue to the Book of Job'. *AThR* 15 (1933): 125–128.

Bauer-Kayatz, Christa. *Studien zu Proverbien 1–9. Eine form- und motivgeschichtliche Untersuchung unter Einbeziehung ägyptischen Vergleichmaterials*. WMANT 22. Neukirchen-Vluyn: 1966.

Beaulieu, Paul-Alain. 'The Social and Intellectual Setting of Babylonian Wisdom Literature'. Pages 3–19 in *Wisdom Literature in Mesopotamia and Israel*. Edited by Richard J. Clifford. Atlanta: 2007.

Becker, Joachim. *Gottesfurcht im Alten Testament*. Rome: 1965.

Beckwith, Roger T. *The Old Testament Canon of the New Testament Church and Its Background in Early Judaism*. Grand Rapids: 1986.

Beentjes, Pancratius C. *The Book of Ben Sira in Hebrew: A Text Edition of All Extant Hebrew Manuscripts and a Synopsis of All Parallel Hebrew Ben Sira Texts*. VTSup 68. Leiden: 1997. Revised ed. Atlanta: 2006.

Bellinger, William H. Jr. 'Psalms and the Question of Genre'. Pages 313–325 in *The Oxford Handbook of the Psalms*. Edited by William P. Brown. Oxford: 2014.

Belousek, Darrin W. Snyder. 'God the Creator in the Wisdom of Solomon: A Theological Commentary'. 2015. www.academia.edu/15912414/God_the_Creator_in_the_Wisdom_of_Solomon_A_Theological_Commentary.

Bennema, Cornelis. 'The Strands of Wisdom Tradition in Intertestamental Judaism: Origins, Developments and Characteristics'. *TynBul* 52 (2001): 61–82.

Bentzen, Aage. *Introduction to the Old Testament*. 2 vols. Copenhagen: 1948–1949. Translation of *Indledning til det gamle Testamente*. Copenhagen: 1941.

Bergant, Dianne. 'My Beloved Is Mine and I Am His (Song 2:16): The Song of Songs and Honor and Shame'. *Semeia* 68 (1994): 23–40.

Berger, Benjamin Lyle. 'Qohelet and the Exigencies of the Absurd'. *BibInt* 9 (2001): 141–179.

Berlin, Adele. 'What Is the Book of Job About?' Pages 113–121 in *A Common Cultural Heritage: Studies on Mesopotamia and the Biblical World in Honor of Barry L. Eichler*. Edited by Grant Frame, Erle Leichty, Karen Sonik, Jeffrey H. Tigay and Steve Tinney. Bethesda: 2011.

Birch, Bruce C. *Let Justice Roll Down: The Old Testament, Ethics, and Christian Life*. Louisville: 1991.

Birch, Bruce C, and Larry L. Rasmussen. *Bible and Ethics in the Christian Life*. Minneapolis: 1989.

et al. *A Theological Introduction to the Old Testament*. Nashville: 1999.

Black, Jeremy et al. *The Literature of Ancient Sumer*. Oxford: 2004.

Boda, Mark J., Russell L. Meek and William R. Osborne, eds. *Riddles and Revelations: Explorations into the Relation between Wisdom and Prophecy in the Hebrew Bible*. London: 2018.

Boecker, Hans. *Law and the Administration of Justice in the Old Testament and the Ancient East*. Minneapolis: 1982.

Bolin, Thomas M. *Ecclesiastes and the Riddle of Authorship*. New York: 2017.

Bostock, David. *Aristotle's Ethics*. Oxford: 2000.

Boström, G. *Paronomasi i den äldre hebraisca Maschalliteraturen*. Lund: 1928.

Boström, Lennart *The God of the Sages: The Portrayal of God in the Book of Proverbs*. ConBOT 29. Stockholm: 1990.

Bottéro, Jean 'La "tenson" et la réflexion sur les choses en Mésopotamie'. Pages 7–22 in *Dispute Poems and Dialogues in the Ancient and Mediaeval Near East*. Edited by G. J. Reinink and Herman L. J. Vanstiphout. OLA 41. Leuven: 1991.

Bourdieu, Pierre. *Distinction: A Social Critique of the Judgment of Taste*. Cambridge: 1984.

Brennan Dick, Michael. 'The Legal Metaphor in Job 31'. *CBQ* 41 (1979): 37–50.

Britton-Purdy, Jedediah. 'Paleo Politics'. *The New Republic*. 1 November 2017. https://newrepublic.com/article/145444/paleo-politics-what-made-prehis toric-hunter-gatherers-give-freedom-civilization.

Brogan, T. V. F., and Fabian Gudas. 'Tone'. Pages 1293–1294 in *The New Princeton Encyclopedia of Poetry and Poetics*. Edited by Alex Preminger et al. Princeton: 1993.

Brooke, George J., and Renate Smithuis, eds. *Jewish Education from Antiquity to the Middle Ages: Studies in Honour of Philip S. Alexander*. Leiden: 2017.

Brouwer, René. *The Stoic Sage: The Early Stoics on Wisdom, Sagehood, and Socrates*. Cambridge: 2014.

Brown, Jeannine K. 'Genre Criticism and the Bible'. Pages 111–150 in *Words and the Word: Explorations in Biblical Interpretation and Literary Theory*. Edited by David G. Firth and Jamie Grant. Nottingham: 2008.

Brown, William P. *Character in Crisis: A Fresh Approach to the Wisdom Literature of the Old Testament*. Grand Rapids: 1996.

The Ethos of the Cosmos: The Genesis of Moral Imagination in the Bible. Grand Rapids: 1999.

'The Pedagogy of Proverbs 10:1–31:9'. Pages 150–182 in *Character and Scripture: Moral Formation, Community, and Biblical Interpretation*. Edited by William P. Brown. Grand Rapids: 2002.

'The Didactic Power of Metaphor in the Aphoristic Sayings of Proverbs'. *JSOT* 29 (2004): 133–154.

'"Come, O Children ... I Will Teach You the Fear of the Lord" (Psalm 34:12): Comparing Psalms and Proverbs'. Pages 85–120 in *Seeking Out the Wisdom of the Ancients: Essays Offered to Honor Michael V. Fox on the Occasion of His Sixty-Fifth Birthday*. Edited by Ronald L. Troxel, Kelvin G. Friebel and Dennis R. Magary. Winona Lake: 2005.

Wisdom's Wonder: Character, Creation, and Crisis in the Bible's Wisdom Literature. Grand Rapids; Cambridge: 2014.

'When Wisdom Fails'. Pages 209–223 in *'When the Morning Stars Sang': Essays in Honor of Choon Leong Seow on the Occasion of His Sixty-Fifth*

Birthday. Edited by Scott C. Jones and Christine Roy Yoder. BZAW 500. Berlin: 2018.

'Psalms'. Pages 67–86 in *The Wiley Blackwell Companion to Wisdom Literature*. Edited by Samuel L. Adams and Matthew Goff. Hoboken; Chichester: 2020.

'Virtue and Its Limits in the Wisdom Corpus: Character Formation, Disruption, and Transformation'. Pages 45–64 In *The Oxford Handbook of Wisdom and the Bible*. Edited by Will Kynes. New York: 2021.

Bruch, Johann. Friedrich. *Weisheits-Lehre der Hebräer: Ein Beitrag zur Geschichte der Philosophie*. Strasbourg: 1851.

Brueggemann, Walter. *In Man We Trust: The Neglected Side of Biblical Faith*. Atlanta: 1972.

Theology of the Old Testament. Minneapolis: 1997.

1 & 2 Kings. SHBC Macon: 2000.

Brueggemann, Walter A., and W. H. Bellinger Jr. *Psalms*. NCB. Cambridge: 2014.

Brunner, Helmut. *Altägyptische Weisheit*. Zürich: 1988.

Brunner-Traut, Emma. 'Die Weisheitslehre des Djedef-Hor'. *ZÄS* 76 (1940): 3–9.

Bryce, Glendon E. *A Legacy of Wisdom*. Lewisburg: 1979.

Budge, E. W. *The Teaching of Amen-Em-Apt, Son of Kanekht*. London: 1924.

Bundvad, Mette. *Time in the Book of Ecclesiastes*. Oxford Theology and Religion Monographs. Oxford: 2015.

'At Play in Potential Space'. Pages 254–273 in *Perspectives on Israelite Wisdom: Proceedings of the Oxford Old Testament Seminar*. Edited by John Jarick. London; 2016.

Burden, J. J. 'Decision by Debate: Examples of Popular Proverb Performance in the Book of Job'. *OTE* 4 (1991): 37–65.

Burke, Edmund. *A Philosophical Inquiry into the Origin of Our Ideas of the Sublime and Beautiful*. Adelaide: 2014.

Burkert, Walter. *Greek Religion*. Translated by John Raffan. Cambridge: 1985.

Burkes, Shannon. *Death in Qoheleth and Egyptian Biographies of the Late Period*. SBLDS 170. Atlanta: 1999.

Burnham, Douglas. 'Kant, Immanuel: Aesthetics'. *Internet Encyclopedia of Philosophy*. www.iep.utm.edu/kantaest/#SH2c.

Burnight, John Walton. 'The "Reversal" of *Heilsgeschichte* in Job 3'. Pages 30–41 in *Reading Job Intertextually*. Edited by Katharine Dell and Will Kynes. LHBOTS 574. New York: 2013.

Buss, Martin J. 'The Study of Forms'. Pages 1–56 in *Old Testament Form Criticism*. Edited by John H. Hayes. TUMSR 2. San Antonio: 1967.

Calduch-Benages, Núria. 'The Absence of Named Women from Ben Sira's Praise of the Ancestors'. Pages 301–317 in *Rewriting Biblical History: Essays on Chronicles and Ben Sira in Honor of Pancratius C. Beentjes*. Edited by Jeremy Corley and Harm van Grol. DCLS 7. Berlin: 2011.

Camp, Claudia V. *Wisdom and the Feminine in the Book of Proverbs*. Sheffield: 1985.

Wise, Strange and Holy: The Strange Woman and the Making of the Bible. JSOTSup 320. Sheffield: 2000.

Ben Sira and the Men Who Handle Books: Gender and the Rise of Canon-Consciousness. HBM 50. Sheffield: 2013.

Carr, David M. *Writing on the Tablet of the Heart: Origins of Scripture and Literature.* Oxford: 2005.

The Formation of the Hebrew Bible: A New Reconstruction. New York: 2011.

Cathcart, Kevin J. 'The Trees, the Beasts and the Birds: Fables, Parables and Allegories in the Old Testament'. Pages 212–221 in *Wisdom in Ancient Israel: Essays in Honour of J. A. Emerton.* Edited by John Day, R. P. Gordon and H. G. M. Williamson. Cambridge: 1995.

Ceresko, Anthony R. 'The ABCs of Wisdom in Psalm l.c.x. *VT* 35 (1985): 99–104.

Černy, J., and A. H. Gardiner. *Hieratic Ostraca.* Oxford: 1957.

Chambers, Ephraim. 'Sapiential'. Page 597 in *Cyclopædia: Or, an Universal Dictionary of Arts and Sciences.* Vol. 2. London: 1728.

Chandler, Daniel. 'An Introduction to Genre Theory'. 1997. www.aber.ac.uk/media/Documents/intgenre/chandler_genre_theory.pdf.

Cheung, Simon Chi-chung. *Wisdom Intoned: A Reappraisal of the Genre 'Wisdom Psalms'.* LHBOTS 613. New York; London: 2015.

Cheyne, T. K. *Job and Solomon: Or, the Wisdom of the Old Testament.* London: 1887.

Childs, Brevard S. *Introduction to the Old Testament as Scripture.* Philadelphia: 1979.

Christianson, Eric A. *A Time to Tell: Narrative Strategies in Ecclesiastes.* JSOTSup 280. Sheffield: 1998.

Ecclesiastes Through the Centuries. Blackwell Bible Commentary. Oxford: 2007.

Civil, Miguel. *The Farmer's Instructions: A Sumerian Agricultural Manual.* AuOr Sup. 5. Barcelona: 1994.

Clark, Rosalind. 'Seeking Wisdom in the Song of Songs'. Pages 100–112 in *Exploring Old Testament Wisdom: Literature and Themes.* Edited by David G. Firth and Lindsay Wilson. London: 2016.

Clines, David J. A. 'The Wisdom Books'. Pages 269–291 in *Creating the Old Testament: The Emergence of the Hebrew Bible.* Edited by S. Bigger. Oxford: 1989.

'Why Is There a Book of Job, and What Does It Do to You If You Read It?' Pages 122–144 in *Interested Parties: The Ideology of Writers and Readers of the Hebrew Bible.* JSOTSup 225. Sheffield: 1995.

Job. 3 vols. WBC 17–18B. Nashville: 1989–2011.

Cohen, Yoram. *The Scribes and Scholars of the City of Emar in the Late Bronze Age.* HSS 59. Winona Lake: 2009.

Wisdom from the Late Bronze Age. WAW 29. Atlanta: 2013.

'Why "Wisdom"? Copying, Studying, and Collecting Wisdom Literature in the Cuneiform World'. Pages 41–59 in *Teaching Morality in Antiquity.* Edited by Takayoshi M. Oshima. ORA 29. Tübingen: 2018.

Collins, John J. 'The Biblical Precedent for Natural Theology'. *JAAR* 45.1 (1977): 25–67.

'Wisdom Reconsidered in Light of the Scrolls'. *DSD* 4 (1997): 269–271.

Jewish Wisdom in the Hellenistic Age. Edinburgh: 1998.

'The Friends of Job and the Task of Biblical Theology'. *Int* 70 (2016): 288–292.

Introduction to the Hebrew Bible. 3rd ed. Minneapolis: 2018.

Collins, John J., Gregory Sterling and Ruth A. Clements, eds. *Sapiential Perspectives: Wisdom Literature in Light of Proceedings of the Sixth International Symposium of the Orion Center for the Study of the Dead Sea Scrolls and Associated Literature, 20–22 May, 2001*. STDJ 51. Leiden: 2004.

Coogan, Michael. *The Old Testament: A Very Short Introduction*. Oxford: 2008.

Cook, Sean E. *The Solomon Narratives in the Context of the Hebrew Bible: Told and Retold*. LHBOTS 638. London: 2017.

Corley, Jeremy. 'Friendship according to Ben Sira'. Pages 65–72 in *Der Einzelne und seine Gemeinschaft bei Ben Sira*. Edited by R. Egger-Wenzel and Ingrid Krammer. BZAW 270. Berlin: 1998.

'An Intertextual Study of Proverbs and Ben Sira'. Pages 155–182 in *Intertextual Studies in Ben Sira and Tobit: Essays in Honor of Alexander A. Di Lella, O.F.M.* Edited by Jeremy Corley and Vincent Skemp. CBQMS 38. Washington, 2005.

Corrington Streete, Gail. 'An Isis Aretalogy from Kyme in Asia Minor, First Century B.C.E.'. Pages 369–384 in *Religions of Late Antiquity in Practice*. Edited by R. Valantasis. Princeton Readings in Religions. Princeton: 2000.

Corwin, Christopher. 'Classifying Wisdom Psalms'. PhD diss., Graduate Theological Union, 1998.

Court, Simon. 'Edmund Burke and the Sublime'. *Dove Cottage & the Wordsworth Museum*. https://wordsworth.org.uk/blog/2015/03/02/edmund-burke-and-the-sublime/.

Craigie, Peter C. *Psalms 1–50*. 2nd ed. WBC 19. Nashville: 2004.

Crenshaw, James L. 'Method in Determining Wisdom Influence'. *JBL* 88 (1969): 129–142.

'Popular Questioning of the Justice of God in Ancient Israel'. *ZAW* 82 (1970): 380–395.

Prophetic Conflict: Its Effect upon Israelite Religion. BZAW 124. Berlin: 1971.

'Wisdom'. Pages 225–264 in *Old Testament Form Criticism*. Edited by J. Hayes. San Antonio: 1974.

Old Testament Wisdom: An Introduction. Atlanta: 1981.

Crenshaw, James L. ed. *Theodicy in the Old Testament*. Philadelphia; London: 1983.

A Whirlpool of Torment: Israelite Traditions of God as an Oppressive Presence. OBT 12. Philadelphia: 1984.

Ecclesiastes. OTL. Grand Rapids: 1987.

'Wisdom (1974)'. Pages 45–77 in *Urgent Advice and Probing Questions: Collected Writings on Old Testament Wisdom*. Edited by James L. Crenshaw. Macon: 1995.

Urgent Advice and Probing Questions: Collected Writings on Old Testament Wisdom. Macon: 1995.

Education in Ancient Israel: Across the Deadening Silence. ABRL. New York: 1998.

Old Testament Wisdom: An Introduction. Rev. ed. Louisville: 1998.

'Wisdom Psalms?' *CurBS* 8 (2000): 9–17.

'Gold Dust or Nuggets? A Brief Response to J. Kenneth Kuntz'. *CurBR* 1.2 (2003): 155–158.

Defending God: Biblical Responses to the Problem of Evil. Oxford: 2005.

Old Testament Wisdom: An Introduction. 3rd ed. Louisville: 2010.

Reading Job: A Literary and Theological Commentary. Macon, 2011.

Crüsemann, Frank. *Studien zur Formgeschichte von Hymnus und Danklied in Israel.* WMANT 32. Neukirchen-Vluyn: 1969.

Culler, Jonathan. *The Pursuit of Signs.* Ithaca: 1981.

Cyril of Jerusalem. 'Lecture IX. On the Words, Maker of Heaven and Earth, and of All Things Visible and Invisible'. Pages 51–56 in *Cyril of Jerusalem, Gregory Nazianzen.* Translated by Edwin Hamilton Gifford. Vol. 7 of *Nicene and Post-Nicene Fathers* 2. Edinburgh: 1893.

Davidson, Samuel. *An Introduction to the Old Testament: Critical, Historical, Theological.* 2 vols. London: 1862.

Davies, Philip. 'The False Pen of the Scribes'. Pages 117–26 in *Sense and Sensitivity: Essays on Reading the Bible in Memory of Robert Carroll.* Edited by A. Hunter and Philip Davies. JSOTSup 348. Sheffield: 2002.

Davies, Philip R., and Thomas Römer, eds. *Writing the Bible: Scribes, Scribalism and Script.* Bible World. New York: 2015.

Davison, W. T. *The Wisdom-Literature of the Old Testament.* London: 1894.

Deane-Drummond, Celia E. *Theological Ethics through a Multispecies Lens, the Evolution of Wisdom.* Oxford: 2019.

Deissler, Alfons. *Die Psalmen.* 7th ed. Düsseldorf: 1993.

Delitzsch, Franz. *Das Buch Iob.* Leipzig: 1864.

Biblical Commentary on the Proverbs of Solomon. Translated by M. G. Easton. 2 vols. Edinburgh: 1874.

Commentary on the Song of Songs and Ecclesiastes. Translated by M. G. Easton. Edinburgh: 1877.

Dell, Katharine J. *The Book of Job as Sceptical Literature.* BZAW 197. Berlin: 1991.

'Ecclesiastes as Wisdom: Consulting Early Interpreters'. *VT* 44 (1994): 301–332.

'"Green" Ideas in the Wisdom Tradition'. *SJT* 47 (1994): 423–451.

Get Wisdom Get Insight: An Introduction to Israel's Wisdom Literature. London: 2000.

'"I Will Solve My Riddle to the Music of the Lyre" (Psalm XLIX 4 [5]): A Cultic Setting for Wisdom Psalms?' *VT* 54 (2004): 445–458.

'Does the Song of Songs Have Any Connections to Wisdom?' Pages 8–26 in *Perspectives on the Song of Songs/.* Edited by Anselm C. Hagedorn. BZAW 346. Berlin: 2005.

The Book of Proverbs in Social and Theological Context. Cambridge: 2006.

'God, Creation and the Contribution of Wisdom'. Pages 60–72 in *The God of Israel.* Edited by R. P. Gordon. Cambridge: 2007.

'Job: Sceptics, Philosophers and Tragedians'. Pages 1–19 in *Das Buch Hiob und seine Interpretationen: Beiträge zum Hiob-Symposium auf dem Monte Verità vom 14.–19. August 2005.* Edited by Thomas Krüger, Manfred Oeming, Konrad Schmid and Christoph Uehlinger. ATANT 88. Zurich: 2007.

'The Significance of the Wisdom Tradition in the Ecological Debate'. Pages 56–69 in *Ecological Hermeneutics, Biblical, Historical and Theological Perspectives.* London: 2010.

'Studies of the Didactical Books of the Hebrew Bible/Old Testament'. Pages 603–624 in *Hebrew Bible/Old Testament: The History of Its Interpretation*. Vol. 3. Edited by Magno Saebø. Göttingen: 2012.

'Exploring Intertextual Links between Ecclesiastes and Genesis 1–11'. Pages 3–14 in *Reading Ecclesiastes Intertextually*. Edited by Katharine Dell and Will Kynes. LHBOTS 587. London: 2014.

'Deciding the Boundaries of "Wisdom": Applying the Concept of Family Resemblance'. Pages 145–160 in *Was There a Wisdom Tradition: New Prospects in Israelite Wisdom Studies*. Edited by Mark R. Sneed. AIL 253. Atlanta: 2015.

'Reading Ecclesiastes with the Scholars'. Pages 81–99 in *Exploring Old Testament Wisdom*. Edited by David G. Firth and Lindsay Wilson. London: 2016.

'Ecclesiastes as Mainstream Wisdom (without Job)'. Pages 43–52 in *Goochem in Mokum/Wisdom in Amsterdam: Papers on Biblical and Related Wisdom Read at the Fifteenth Joint Meeting of the Society of Old Testament Study and the Oudtestamentisch Werkgezelschap, Amsterdam July 2012*. Edited by George J. Brooke and Pierre Van Hecke. OtSt 68. Leiden: 2016.

Job, Where Shall Wisdom Be Found? London: 2017.

The Solomonic Context of 'Wisdom' and Its Influence. Oxford: 2020.

'A Wise Man Reflecting on Wisdom: Qoheleth/Ecclesiastes'. *TynBul* 71 (2020): 137–152.

The Theology of the Book of Proverbs. OTT. Cambridge: forthcoming.

Dell, Katharine, and Will Kynes, eds. *Reading Job Intertextually*. LHBOTS 574. New York: 2013.

eds. *Reading Proverbs Intertextually*. LHBOTS 629. London: 2018.

Denning-Bolle, Sara. *Wisdom in Akkadian Literature: Expression, Instruction, Dialogue*. Leiden: 1992.

Dhorme, Edouard. *A Commentary on the Book of Job*. Translated by Harold Knight. London: 1967. Translation of *Le livre de Job*. Paris: 1926.

Dijkstra, Meindert. 'The Akkado-Hurrian Bilingual Wisdom-Text RS 15.010 Reconsidered'. *UF* 25 (1993): 157–162.

Dillard, Raymond B. *2 Chronicles*. WBC 15. Waco: 1987.

Doak, Brian R. *Consider Leviathan: Narratives of Nature and Self in Job*. Minneapolis: 2014.

Dobbs-Allsopp, F. W. 'The Delight of Beauty and the Song of Songs 4:1–7'. *Int* 59.3 (2005): 260–277.

Doll, Peter. *Menschenschöpfung Und Weltschöpfung in Der Alttestamentlichen Weisheit*. SBS 117. Stuttgart: 1985.

Duguid, Ian. *The Song of Songs*. TOTC 19. Downers Grove: 2015.

Dulin, Rachel Z. '"How Sweet Is the Light": Qoheleth's Age-Centered Teachings'. *Int* 55 (2001): 260–270.

Eissfeldt, Otto. *Der Maschal im Alten Testament*. BZAW 24. Giessen: 1913.

The Old Testament: An Introduction. New York: 1965.

Ellermeier, Friedrich. *Qohelet I/1*. Herzberg am Harz: 1967.

Ellis, Teresa Ann. *Gender in the Book of Ben Sira: Divine Wisdom, Erotic Poetry, and the Garden of Eden*. BZAW 453. Berlin: 2013.

Emerton, J. A. 'The Teaching of Amenemope and Proverbs XXII 17–XXIV 22: Further Reflections on a Long-Standing Problem'. *VT* 51.4 (2001): 431–465.

Engnell, Ivan. *Critical Essays on the Old Testament*. Translated by John
    T. Willis. London: 1970.
    'The Figurative Language of the Old Testament'. Pages 242–290 in *Critical
    Essays on the Old Testament*. Translated and Edited by John T. Willis.
    London: 1970.
Enns, Peter. *Exodus Retold: Ancient Exegesis of the Departure from Egypt in
    Wis [10:]15–21 and 19:1–9*. HSM 57. Atlanta: 1997.
Eriksson, LarsOlov. *'Come, Children, Listen to Me!' Psalm 34 in the Hebrew
    Bible and in Early Christian Writings*. ConBOT 32. Uppsala: 1991.
Erman, Adolf 'Eine ägyptische Quelle der "Sprüche Salomos"'. SPAW 15 (1924):
    86–93.
Estes, Daniel J. *Handbook on the Wisdom Books and Psalms*. Grand Rapids: 2010.
Exum, J. Cheryl. 'The Poetic Genius of the Song of Songs'. Pages 78–95 in
    Perspectives on the Song of Songs/. Edited by Anselm C. Hagedorn. BZAW
    346. Berlin: 2005.
    Song of Songs. OTL. Louisville: 2005.
    'Unity, Date, Authorship and the "Wisdom" of the Song of Songs'. Pages
    53–68 in *Goochem in Mokum/ Wisdom in Amsterdam*. Edited by George
    J. Brooke and Pierre van Hecke. OtSt 68. Leiden: 2016.
Falk, Daniel K., Florentino García Martinez and Eileen Schuller, ed. *Sapiential,
    Liturgical and Poetical Texts from Qumran: Proceedings of the Third
    Meeting of the International Organization for Qumran Studies, Oslo
    1998*. Leiden: 2000.
Fichtner, Johannes. *Weisheit Salomos*. HAT II/6. Tübingen: 1938.
Fiddes, Paul S. *Seeing the World and Knowing God: Hebrew Wisdom and
    Christian Doctrine in a Late-Modern Context*. Oxford: 2013.
Fincke, Jeanette C. 'The School Curricula from Ḫattuša, Emar and Ugarit:
    A Comparison'. Pages 85–101 in *Theory and Practice of Knowledge
    Transfer: Studies in School Education in the Ancient Near East and
    Beyond. Papers Read at a Symposium in Leiden, 17–19 December 2008*.
    Edited by Wolfert S. van Egmond and Wilfred H. van Soldt. Leiden: 2012.
Firth, David G. 'The Teaching of the Psalms'. Pages 159–174 in *Interpreting the
    Psalms: Issues and Approaches*. Edited by Philip S. Johnston and David G.
    Firth. Leicester: 2005.
    'Worrying about the Wise: Wisdom in Old Testament Narrative'. Pages
    155–173 in *Exploring Old Testament Wisdom*. Edited by David G. Firth
    and Lindsay Wilson. London: 2016.
    1 & 2 Samuel: A Kingdom Comes. London: 2017.
Firth, David G., and Lindsay Wilson, eds. *Exploring Old Testament Wisdom:
    Literature and Themes*. London: 2016.
Fishbane, Michael. 'Jeremiah IV 23–26 and Job III 3–13: A Recovered Use of the
    Creation Pattern'. *VT* 21 (1971): 151–167.
Fishelov, David. *Metaphors of Genre: The Role of Analogies in Genre Theory*.
    University Park: 1993.
Fohrer, Georg. *Das Buch Hiob*. KAT 16. Gütersloh: 1963.
Fontaine, Carol. *Traditional Sayings in the Old Testament*. Sheffield: 1982.
    Smooth Words: Women, Proverbs and Performance in Biblical Wisdom.
    JSOTSup 356. Sheffield: 2002.

Forman, C. C. 'Koheleth's Use of Genesis'. *JSS* 5 (1960): 256–263.

Forti, Tova. 'The Concept of "Reward" in Proverbs: A Diachronic or Synchronic Approach?' *CurBR* 12 (2014): 129–145.

Foster, Benjamin R. *Before the Muses: An Anthology of Akkadian Literature.* 3rd ed. Bethesda: 2005.

The Epic of Gilgamesh. 2nd ed. New York; London: 2019.

Foster, Benjamin R., and Andrew R. George, 'An Old Babylonian Dialogue between a Father and His Son'. *ZA* 110 (2020): 37–61.

Fowler, Alastair. *Kinds of Literature: An Introduction to the Theory of Genres and Modes.* Oxford: 1982.

Fox, Michael V. 'Frame-Narrative and Composition in the Book of Qohelet'. *HUCA* 48 (1977): 83–106.

'Two Decades of Research in Egyptian Wisdom Literature'. *ZÄS* 107 (1980): 120–135.

The Song of Songs and the Ancient Egyptian Love Songs. Madison: 1985.

'Egyptian Onomastica and Biblical Wisdom'. *VT* 36.3 (1986): 302–310.

'Qohelet's Epistemology'. *HUCA* 58 (1987): 137–155.

Qohelet and His Contradictions. Sheffield: 1989.

'Wisdom in Qoheleth'. Pages 115–131 in *In Search of Wisdom: Essays in Memory of John G. Gammie.* Edited by Leo G. Perdue, Bernard Brandon Scott and William Johnston Wiseman. Louisville: 1993.

'World-Order and Ma'at: A Crooked Parallel'. *JANESCU* 23 (1995): 37–48.

'Ideas of Wisdom in Proverbs 1–9'. *JBL* 116.4 (1997): 613–633.

'Who Can Learn? A Dispute in Ancient Pedagogy'. Pages 62–77 in *Wisdom, You Are My Sister: Studies in Honor of Roland E. Murphy, O. Carm, on the Occasion of His Eightieth Birthday.* Edited by Michael L. Barré. Washington, 1997.

A Time to Tear Down and a Time to Build Up: A Re-reading of Ecclesiastes. Grand Rapids: 1999.

Proverbs 1–9: A New Translation with Introduction and Commentary. AB 19A. New York: 2000.

'Like Grapes of Gold Set in Silver: An Interpretation of Proverbial Clusters in Proverbs 10:1–22:16'. *HS* 44 (2003): 267–272.

'Wisdom and the Self-Presentation of Wisdom Literature'. Pages 153–172 in *Reading from Right to Left: Essays on the Hebrew Bible in Honour of David J. A. Clines.* Edited by J. Cheryl Exum and H. G. M. Williamson. Sheffield: 2003.

Ecclesiastes: The Traditional Hebrew Text with the New JPS Translation. Philadelphia: 2004.

'The Epistemology of the Book of Proverbs'. *JBL* 126 (2007): 669–684.

'Ethics and Wisdom in the Book of Proverbs'. *HS* 48 (2009): 75–88.

Proverbs 10–31: A New Translation with Introduction and Commentary. AB 18B. New Haven: 2009.

'From Amenemope to Proverbs'. *ZAW* 126.1 (2014): 76–91.

'Three Theses on Wisdom'. Pages 69–86 in *Was There a Wisdom Tradition? New Prospects in Israelite Wisdom Studies.* Edited by Mark R. Sneed. Atlanta: 2015.

'The Speaker in Job 28'. Pages 21–38 in *'When the Morning Stars Sang': Essays in Honor of Choon Leong Seow on the Occasion of His Sixty-Fifth Birthday.* Edited by Scott C. Jones and Christine Roy Yoder. BZAW 500. Berlin: 2018.

Frankfort, Henri. *Ancient Egyptian Religion*. New York: 1948; 1961.

Fraser, Peter M. *Ptolemaic Alexandria*. Vol. 1. Oxford: 1972.

Fredericks, Daniel C. *Qoheleth's Language: Re-Evaluating Its Nature and Date*. Lampeter: 1988.

Coping with Transience: Ecclesiastes on Brevity in Life. Biblical Seminar 18. Sheffield: 1993.

Fretheim, Terence E. *God and World in the Old Testament: A Relational Theology of Creation*. Nashville; Edinburgh: 2005.

Frydrych, Tomás. *Living under the Sun: Examination of Proverbs and Qoheleth*. VTSup. Leiden: 2002.

Gadamer, Hans-Georg. *Truth and Method*. 2nd rev. ed. Translated by Joel Weinsheimer and Donald G. Marshall. London: 2004.

Galling, Kurt. 'Koheleth-Studien'. *ZAW* 50 (1932): 276–299.

Gammie, John G. 'Paraenetic Literature: Toward the Morphology of a Secondary Genre'. *Semeia* 50 (1990): 41–77.

García Martínez, Florentino, and Eibert J. C. Tigchelaar. *The Dead Sea Scrolls: Study Edition*. Leiden: 1997.

Gardiner, Alan H. 'The Instruction Addressed to Kagemni and his Brethren'. *JEA* 32 (1946): 71–74.

Ancient Egyptian Onomastica. London: 1947.

Garrett, Duane A. *Proverbs, Ecclesiastes, Song of Songs*. Nashville: 1993.

Garrett, Duane, and Paul R. House. *Song of Songs/Lamentations*. WBC 23B. Nashville: 2004.

Genung, John F. *The Epic of the Inner Life Being the Book of Job*. Boston: 1891.

George, Andrew R. *Babylonian Literary Texts in the Schøyen Collection*. CUSAS 10. Bethesda: 2009.

Georgi, Dieter. 'Das Wesen der Weisheit nach der "Weisheit Salomos"'. Pages 66–81 in *Gnosis und Politik*. Religionstheorie und Politische Theologie 2. Edited by J. Taubes. Munich: 1984.

Gericke, Jaco. 'Axiological Assumptions in Qohelet: A Historical-Philosophical Clarification'. *Verbum et Ecclesia* 33 (2012): 1–6.

The Hebrew Bible and Philosophy of Religion. SBLRBS 70. Atlanta: 2012.

Gerstenberger, Erhard S. 'Non-Temple Psalms: The Cultic Setting Revisited'. Pages 338–349 in *The Oxford Handbook of the Psalms*. Edited by William P. Brown. Oxford: 2014.

Gese, Hartmut. *Lehre und Wirklichkeit der alten Weisheit: Studien zu den Sprüchen Salomos und zu dem Buche Hiob*. Tübingen: 1958.

Alttestamentliche Studien. Tübingen: 1991.

Gianto, Agustinus. 'On שׁ of Reflection in the Book of Proverbs'. Pages 157–162 in *'When the Morning Stars Sang': Essays in Honor of Choon Leong Seow on the Occasion of His Sixty-Fifth Birthday*. Edited by Scott C. Jones and Christine Roy Yoder. BZAW 500. Berlin: 2018.

Giese, Curtis. 'The Genre of Ecclesiastes as Viewed by Its Septuagint Translator and the Early Church Fathers'. PhD diss., Hebrew Union College, 1999.

Gilbert, Maurice S. J. 'The Review of History in Ben Sira 44–50 and Wisdom 10–19'. Pages 319–334 in *Rewriting Biblical History: Essays on Chronicles and Ben Sira in Honor of Pancratius C. Beentjes*. Edited by Jeremy Corley and Harm van Grol. DCLS 7. Berlin: 2011.

La Sagesse de Salomon/The Wisdom of Solomon: Recueil d'études/Selected Essays. AnBib 189. Rome: 2011.

Gillingham, Susan E. *The Poems and Psalms of the Hebrew Bible*. Oxford Bible Series. Oxford: 1994.

'The Levites and the Editorial Composition of the Psalms'. Pages 201–213 in *The Oxford Handbook of the Psalms*. Edited by William P. Brown. Oxford: 2014.

'"I Will Incline My Ear to a Proverb; I Will Solve My Riddle to the Music of the Harp" (Psalm 49.4): The Wisdom Tradition and the Psalms'. Pages 277–309 in *Perspectives on Israelite Wisdom: Proceedings of the Oxford Old Testament Seminar*. Edited by John Jarick. LHBOTS 618. London; New York: 2016.

Ginsburg, Christian D. *The Song of Songs: Translated from the Original Hebrew, with a Commentary Historical and Critical*. London: 1857.

Glicksman, Andrew T. *Wisdom of Solomon 10: A Jewish Hellenistic Reinterpretation of Early Israelite History through Sapiential Lenses*. Berlin: 2011.

Goedicke, Hans. 'Die Lehre eines Mannes für seinen Sohn'. *ZÄS* 94 (1967): 62–71.

Goering, Greg Schmidt. *Wisdom's Root Revealed: Ben Sira and the Election of Israel*. JSJSup 139. Leiden: 2009.

'Proleptic Fulfillment of the Prophetic Word: Ezekiel's Dirges over Tyre and Its Ruler'. *JSOT* 36 (2012): 483–505.

Goff, Matthew J. 'Hellenistic Instruction in Palestine and Egypt: Ben Sira and Papyrus Insinger'. *JSJ* 36.2 (2005): 147–172.

Discerning Wisdom: The Sapiential Literature of the Dead Sea Scrolls. VTSup 116. Leiden; Boston: 2007.

'Genesis 1–3 and Conceptions of Humankind in 4QInstruction, Philo and Paul'. Pages 114–125 in *Early Christian Literature and Intertextuality*. Vol. 2. Edited by C. Evans and H. D. Zacharias. London: 2009.

4QInstruction: A Commentary. WLAW 2. Atlanta: 2013.

'Scribes and Pedagogy in Ancient Israel and Second Temple Judaism'. Pages 195–212 in *The Wiley Companion to Wisdom Literature*. Edited by Samuel L. Adams and Matthew J. Goff. Hoboken; Chichester: 2020.

'The Pursuit of Wisdom at Qumran: Assessing the Classification "Wisdom Literature" and Its Application to the Dead Sea Scrolls'. Pages 617–634 in *The Oxford Handbook of Wisdom and the Bible*. New York: 2021.

Goldingay, John. 'The Arrangement of Sayings in Proverbs 10–15'. *JSOT* 61 (1994): 75–83.

Gordis, Robert. *The Book of God and Man: A Study of Job*. Chicago: 1978.

Gordley, Matthew E. *Teaching through Song in Antiquity: Didactic Hymnody among Greeks, Romans, Jews, and Christians*. WUNT II/302. Tübingen: 2011.

Goshen-Gottstein, Alon. 'Ben Sira's Praise of the Fathers: A Canon-Conscious Reading'. Pages 235–267 in *Ben Sira's God: Proceedings of the International Ben Sira Conference, Durham – Ushaw College 2001*. Edited by Renate Egger-Wenzel. BZAW 321. Berlin: 2002.

Gottlieb, Fred. 'The Creation Theme in Genesis 1, Psalm 104 and Job 38–42'. *JBQ* 44 (2016): 29–36.

Gowan, Donald E. 'God's Answer to Job: How Is It an Answer?' *HBT* 8 (1986): 85–102.

'Reading Job as a "Wisdom Script"'. *JSOT* 17 (1992): 85–95.

Gray, John. *The Book of Job: The Text of the Hebrew Bible 1*. Sheffield: 2010.

Greenstein, Edward L. 'Sages with a Sense of Humour: The Babylonian Dialogue between a Man and His Servant and the Book of Qoheleth'. Pages 55–65 in *Wisdom Literature in Mesopotamia and Israel*. Edited by Richard J. Clifford. SBL Symposium Series 36. Atlanta: 2007.

'The Problem of Evil in the Book of Job'. Pages 333–362 in *Mishneh Todah: Studies in Deuteronomy and Its Cultural Environment in Honor of Jeffrey H. Tigay*. Edited by Nili S. Fox, David A. Glatt-Gilad and Michael J. Williams. Winona Lake: 2009.

'Wisdom in Ugaritic'. Pages 69–89 in *Language and Nature: Papers Presented to John Huehnergard on the Occasion of His 60th Birthday*. Edited by Rebecca Hasselbach and Naama Pat-El. SAOC 67. Chicago: 2012.

Gregory, Bradley C. *Like an Everlasting Signet Ring: Generosity in the Book of Sirach*. DCLS 2. Berlin: 2010.

'Empathy in the Ethical Rhetoric of Ben Sira'. Pages 103–119 in *Emotions from Ben Sira to Paul*. Edited by R. Egger-Wenzel and Jeremy Corley. Berlin: 2012.

Gregory the Great. *Morals on the Book of Job*. Translated by Charles Marriott. London: 1844.

Gregory of Nyssa. *On the Inscriptions of the Psalms*. Archbishop Iakovos Library of Ecclesiastical and Historical Sources. Brookline: n.d. www.lectio-divina.org/images/nyssa/On%20the%20Inscriptions%20of%20the%20Psalms.pdf.

Grossberg, Daniel. 'Two Kinds of Sexual Relationships in the Hebrew Bible'. *HS* 35 (1994): 1–25.

Gunkel, Hermann. *Die Psalmen: Übersetzt und erklärt*. HKAT. Göttingen: 1926.

Gunkel, Hermann, and Joachim Begrich. *Introduction to Cultic Poetry: The Genres of Religious Lyric of Israel*. Repr., Macon: 1998.

Introduction to Psalms: The Genres of Religious Lyrics of Israel. Translated by James D. Nogalski. Mercer Library of Biblical Studies. Macon: 1998.

Gutiérrez, Gustavo. *On Job: God-Talk and the Suffering of the Innocent*. Maryknoll: 1987.

Habel, Norman C. 'Ezekiel 28 and the Fall of the First Man'. *CTM* 38 (1967): 516–524.

'The Symbolism of Wisdom in Proverbs 1–9'. *Int* 26 (1972): 131–157.

The Book of Job: A Commentary. OTL. Philadelphia: 1985.

Habel, Norman C., and Shirley Wurst, eds. *The Earth Story in Wisdom Traditions*. Vol. 3 of *The Earth Bible*. Sheffield: 2001.

Hallo, William W., ed. *Canonical Compositions from the Biblical World*. Vol. 1 of *The Context of Scripture*. Leiden: 1997.

Hallo, William W., and Lawson R. Younger, eds. *Context of Scripture: Canonical Compositions from the Biblical World, Volume 1*. Leiden: 2003.

Harding, James Edward. 'The Book of Job as Metaprophecy'. *SR* 39 (2010): 523–547.

Harkins, Angela K. *Reading with an 'I' to the Heavens: Looking at the Qumran Hodayot through the Lens of Visionary Traditions*. Ekstasis 3. Berlin: 2012.

Harrington, Daniel J. *Wisdom Texts from Qumran*. New York: 1996.

Hart, David Bentley. *The Beauty of the Infinite, the Aesthetics of Christian Truth*. Grand Rapids: 2003.

Hartley, John E. *The Book of Job*. NICOT. Grand Rapids: 1988.

Hatton, Peter T. H. *Contradiction in the Book of Proverbs: The Deep Waters of Counsel*. SOTSMS. Aldershot: 2008.

'A Cautionary Tale: The Acts-Consequence Construct'. *JSOT* 35 (2011): 375–384.

Hawley, Lance R. *Metaphor Competition in the Book of Job*. JAJSup. Göttingen: 2018.

Hawley, Robert. 'On the Alphabetic Scribal Curriculum at Ugarit'. Pages 57–67 in *Proceedings of the 51st Rencontre Assyriologique Internationale Held at the Oriental Institute of the University of Chicago, July 18–22, 2005*. Edited by Robert D. Biggs, Jennie Myers and Martha T. Roth. SAOC 62. Chicago: 2008.

Hays, J. Daniel. 'Has the Narrator Come to Praise Solomon or to Bury Him?: Narrative Subtlety in 1 Kings 1–11', *JSOT* 28 (2003): 149–174.

Heaton, Eric W. *The School Tradition of the Old Testament*. Oxford: 1994.

Hedlin, Kimberly Susan. 'The Book of Job in Early Modern England'. PhD diss., University of California, 2018.

Heim, Knut M. *Like Grapes of Gold Set in Silver: An Interpretation of Proverbial Clusters in Proverbs 10:1–22:16*. BZAW 273. Berlin: 2001.

Poetic Imagination in Proverbs: Variant Repetitions and the Nature of Poetry. BBRSup 4. Winona Lake: 2013.

'The Phenomenon and Literature of Wisdom'. Pages 559–593 in *Hebrew Bible/Old Testament: The History of Its Interpretation*. Vol. 3. Edited by M. Saebø. Göttingen: 2015.

Helck, W. *Die Lehre des Dw3-Htjj*. Wiesbaden: 1970.

Hempel, Charlotte, Armin Lange and Hermann Lichtenberger, eds. *The Wisdom Texts from Qumran and the Development of Sapiential Thought*. Leuven: 2002.

Hengel, Martin. *Judentum und Hellenismus: Studien zu ihrer Begegnung unter besonderer Berücksichtigung Palästinas bis zur Mitte des 2. Jh.s v. Chr.* WUNT 10. Tübingen: 1988.

Hermisson, Hans-Jürgen. *Studien zur israelitischen Spruchweisheit*. Neukirchen-Vluyn: 1968.

Hertzberg, Hans Wilhelm. *Der Prediger (Qohelet)*. Leipzig: 1932.

Heschel, Susannah. *The Aryan Jesus, Christian Theologians and the Bible in Nazi Germany*. Princeton: 2008.

Hildebrandt, Theodore A. 'Proverbial Pairs: Compositional Units in Proverbs 10–29', *JBL* 107 (1988): 207–224.

'Proverbial Strings: Cohesion in Proverbs 10'. *GTJ* 11 (1990): 171–185.

Hirsch, E. D. Jr. *Validity in Interpretation*. New Haven: 1967.

Ho, Ming Kim. *The Levite Singers in Chronicles and Their Stabilizing Role*. LHBOTS 657. London; New York: 2017.

Hogan, Karina M., Matthew Goff and Emma Wasserman, eds. *Pedagogy in Early Judaism and Early Christianity*. EJL 41. Atlanta: 2017.

Horbury, William. 'The Books of Solomon in Ancient Mysticism'. Pages 185–201 in *Reading Texts, Seeking Wisdom: Scripture and Theology*. Edited by D. F. Ford and G. Stanton. London: 2003.

Hossfeld, Frank-Lothar, and Erich Zenger. *Die Psalmen I*. NEchtB 29. Würzburg: 1993.

Huff, Barry R. 'From Societal Scorn to Divine Delight: Job's Transformative Portrayal of Wild Animals'. *Int* 73.3 (2019): 248–258.

Hunter, Alastair G. *Wisdom Literature*. London: 2006.

Hurowitz, Victor Avigdor. 'The Wisdom of Šūpê-Amēlī: A Deathbed Debate between a Father and Son'. Pages 37–45 in *Wisdom Literature in Mesopotamia and Israel*. Edited by Richard J. Clifford. SymS 36. Atlanta: 2007.

Hurvitz, Avi. 'Wisdom Vocabulary in the Hebrew Psalter: A Contribution to the Study of "Wisdom Psalms"'. *VT* 38.1 (1988): 41–51.

Wisdom Language in Biblical Psalmody (Hebrew). Jerusalem: 1991.

'"Tsadîq" = "Wise" in Biblical Hebrew and the Wisdom Connections of Psalm 37 (Hebrew)'. Pages *131–*135 in *'Sha'arei Talmon': Studies in the Bible, Qumran and the ANE presented to Shemaryahu Talmon*. Edited by Michael Fishbane and Emmanuel Tov. Winona Lake: 1992.

Ibolya, Balla. *Ben Sira on Family, Gender, and Sexuality*. DCLS 8. Berlin: 2011.

Imray, Kathryn. 'Love Is [Strong as] Death: Reading the Song of Songs through Proverbs 1–9'. *CBQ* 75 (2013): 649–665.

Ingram, Doug. *Ambiguity in Ecclesiastes*. LHBOTS 431. New York; London: 2006.

Jacobsen, Thorkild. *Treasures of Darkness: A History of Mesopotamian Religion*. New Haven; London: 1976.

Jacobson, Diane. 'Wisdom Language in the Psalms'. Pages 147–157 in *The Oxford Handbook of the Psalms*. Edited by William P. Brown. Oxford: 2014.

Janzen, J. Gerald. *Job*. IBC. Atlanta: 1985.

At the Scent of Water: The Ground of Hope in the Book of Job. Grand Rapids: 2009.

Japhet, Sara. *I & II Chronicles: A Commentary*. Louisville: 1993.

Japhet, Sara, and Barry Dov Walfish. *The Way of Lovers: The Oxford Anonymous Commentary on the Song of Songs (Bodleian Library, MS Opp. 625): An Edition of the Hebrew Text, with English Translation and Introduction*. Leiden: 2017.

Jarick, John. *1 Chronicles*. London: 2002.

'The Hebrew Book of Changes: Reflections on *hakkol hebel* and *lakkol zeman* in Ecclesiastes'. *JSOT* 90 (2008): 465–483.

'The Rhetorical Structure of Ecclesiastes'. Pages 208–231 in *Perspectives on Israelite Wisdom: Proceedings of the Oxford Old Testament Seminar*. Edited by J. Jarick. LHBOTS 618. London: 2016.

Jasnow, Richard. *A Late Period Hieratic Wisdom Text (p. Brooklyn 47.218.135)*. SAOC 52. Chicago: 1992.

Jasnow, Richard, and Karl-Theodor Zauzich. *The Ancient Egyptian Book of Thoth: A Demotic Discourse on Knowledge and Pendant to the Classical Hermetica*. 2 vols. Wiesbaden: 2005.

Jeon, Yong Ho. *Impeccable Solomon? A Study of Solomon's Faults in Chronicles*. Eugene: 2013.

Jiménez, Enrique. *The Babylonian Disputation Poems: With Editions of the Series of the Poplar, Palm and Vine, the Series of the Spider, and the Story of the Poor, Forlorn Wren*. CHANE 87. Leiden; Boston: 2017.

Jindo, Job Y. 'On the Biblical Notion of the "Fear of God" as a Condition for Human Existence'. *BibInt* 19 (2012): 433–453.

Johnson, Dru. *Epistemology and Biblical Theology: From the Pentateuch to Mark's Gospel*. RIPBC 4. New York: 2018.

Johnson, Timothy Jay. *Now My Eye Sees You: Unveiling an Apocalyptic Job*. HBM 24. Sheffield: 2009.

Johnston, Philip. *Shades of Sheol: Death and Afterlife in the Old Testament*. Leicester: 2002.

Johnston, Robert K. 'Wisdom Literature and Its Contribution to a Biblical Environmental Ethic'. Pages 66–82 in *Tending the Garden*. Edited by W. Granberg-Michaelson. Grand Rapids: 1987.

Johnstone, William. *1 and 2 Chronicles: Volume 1. 1 Chronicles 1 – 2 Chronicles 9. Israel's Place among the Nations*. LHBOTS 253. Sheffield: 1997.

Jones, Scott C. 'Job'. Pages 533–550 in *The Oxford Handbook of Wisdom and the Bible*. Edited by Will Kynes. New York: 2021.

Jurgens, Blake. 'The Figure of Solomon'. Pages 159–176 in *The Wiley Blackwell Companion to Wisdom Literature*. Edited by Samuel L. Adams and Matthew Goff. Hoboken; Chichester: 2020.

Juvan, Marko. *History and Poetics of Intertextuality*. Comparative Cultural Studies. Translated by Timothy Pogačar. Indianapolis: 2008.

Kagan, Shelly. *How to Count Animals, More or Less*. Oxford: 2019.

Kaiser, Otto. 'Jesus Sirach: Ein jüdischer Weisheitslehrer in hellenistischer Zeit'. Pages 53–69 in *Texts and Contexts of the Book of Ben Sira/Texte und Kontexte des Sirachbuches*. Edited by Gerhard Karner, Frank Ueberschaer and Burkard M. Zapff. Atlanta: 2017.

Kallen, Horace Meyer. *The Book of Job as a Greek Tragedy*. New York: 1918.

Kamano, Naoto. *Cosmology and Character: Qoheleth's Pedagogy from a Rhetorical-Critical Perspective*. BZAW 312. Berlin: 2002.

Kämmerer, Thomas R. *Šimâ milka. Induktion und Reception der mittelbaby-lonischen Dichtung von Ugarit, Emār und Tell el-'Amarna*. AOAT 251. Münster: 1998.

Kampen, John. *Wisdom Literature*. Grand Rapids: 2011.

Keefer, Arthur Jan. *Proverbs 1–9 as an Introduction to the Book of Proverbs*. LHBOTS 701. London: 2020.

—— *The Book of Proverbs and Virtue Ethics: Integrating the Biblical and Philosophical Traditions*. Cambridge: 2021.

Kellett, E. E. '"Job": An Allegory?' *ExpTim* 51 (1940): 250–251.

Kirshenblatt-Gimblett, Barbara. 'Toward a Theory of Proverb Meaning'. *Proverbium* 22 (1973): 821–827.

Klein, Jacob. 'The "Bane" of Humanity: A Lifespan of One Hundred Twenty Years'. *ASJ* 12 (1990): 57–70.

—— 'The Ballad about Early Rulers: Eastern and Western Traditions'. Pages 203–216 in *Languages and Cultures in Contact. At the Crossroads of Civilizations in the Syro-Mesopotamian Realm. Proceedings of the 42th RAI*. Edited by Karel van Lerberghe and Gabriela Voet. OLA 96. Leuven: 1999.

Kloppenborg, John S. 'Isis and Sophia in the Book of Wisdom'. *HTR* 75.1 (1982): 57–84.

Knight, Douglas, and Amy Jill-Levine. *The Meaning of the Bible: What the Jewish Scriptures and Christian Old Testament Can Teach Us.* New York: 2011.

Knoppers, Gary N. *Two Nations under God: The Deuteronomistic History of Solomon and the Dual Monarchies. Volume 1. The Reign of Solomon and the Rise of Jeroboam.* HSM 52. Atlanta: 1993.

Koch, Klaus. 'Gibt es ein Vergeltungsdogma im Alten Testament'. *ZTK* 52 (1955): 1–42.

——— *Um das Prinzip der Vergeltung in Religion und Recht des alten Testaments.* Darmstad: 1972.

——— 'Is There a Doctrine of Retribution in the Old Testament?' Pages 57–87 in *Theodicy in the Old Testament.* Edited by James L. Crenshaw. Translated by Thomas H. Trapp. London: 1983.

Koh, Yee-Von. *Royal Autobiography in the Book of Qoheleth.* Berlin: 2006.

Köhlmoos, Melanie. *Das Auge Gottes: Textstrategie im Hiobbuch.* FAT 25. Tübingen: 1999.

Koosed, Jennifer L. *(Per)Mutations of Qohelet: Reading the Body in the Book.* LHBOTS 429. London: 2006.

Korsgaard, Christine M. *Fellow Creatures: Our Obligations to the Other Animals.* Oxford: 2018.

Kramer, Samuel N. *The Sacred Marriage Rite.* Bloomington: 1969.

Kraus, Hans-Joachim. *Psalms 1–59.* Translated by Hilton C. Oswald. Minneapolis: 1988.

Krebernick, Manfred. 'Fragment einer Bilingue'. *ZA* 86 (1996): 170–176.

Krispenz, Jutta. *Spruchkompositionen im Buch Proverbia.* New York: 1989.

Kruger, Thomas. *Kritische Weisheit: Studien zur weisheitlichen Traditionskritik im Alten Testament.* Zürich: 1997.

——— 'Law and Wisdom according to Deut 4:5–8'. Pages 35–54 in *Wisdom and Torah: The Reception of the 'Torah' in the Wisdom Literature of the Second Temple Period.* Edited by Berndt U. Schipper and D. Andrew Teeter. JSJSup. Leiden: 2013.

Kuntz, J. Kenneth. 'Canonical Wisdom Psalms of Ancient Israel'. Pages 186–222 in *Rhetorical Criticism: Essays in Honour of James Muilenburg.* Edited by J. J. Jackson and M. Kessler. Pittsburgh: 1974.

——— 'Wisdom Psalms and the Shaping of the Hebrew Psalter'. Pages 144–160 in *For a Later Generation: The Transformation of Tradition in Israel, Early Judaism and Early Christianity.* Edited by R. A. Argall, B. A. Bow and R. A. Werline. Harrisburg: 2000.

Kynes, Will. *My Psalm Has Turned into Weeping: Job's Dialogue with the Psalms.* BZAW 437. Berlin: 2012.

——— 'The Trials of Job: Relitigating Job's "Good Case" in Christian Interpretation'. *SJT* 66 (2013): 174–191.

——— 'Satan'. Pages 264–267 in *The Oxford Encyclopedia of the Bible and Theology.* Edited by Samuel Balentine, Clifton Black, Katharine J. Dell, Andreas Schuele and Jerry Sumney. Oxford: 2015.

——— 'The Modern Scholarly Wisdom Tradition and the Threat of Pan-Sapientialism: A Case Report'. Pages 11–38 in *Was There a Wisdom*

Tradition? New Prospect in Israelite Wisdom Studies. Edited by Mark R. Sneed. Atlanta: 2015.

'The Nineteenth-Century Beginning of "Wisdom Literature"'. Pages 83–108 in *Perspectives on Israelite Wisdom: Proceedings of the Oxford Old Testament Seminar*. Edited by John Jarick. London: 2016.

'"Wisdom" as Mask and Mirror: Methodological Questions for "Wisdom's" Dialogue with the Canon'. Pages 19–29 in *Riddles and Revelations: Explorations into the Relation between Wisdom and Prophecy in the Hebrew Bible*. Edited by Mark J. Boda, Russell L. Meek, and William R. Osborne. London: 2018.

An Obituary for 'Wisdom Literature': The Birth, Death, and Intertextual Reintegration of a Biblical Corpus. Oxford: 2019.

Lambert, David A. 'The Book of Job in Ritual Perspective'. *JBL* 134 (2015): 557–575.

Lambert, Wilfred George. *Babylonian Wisdom Literature*. Oxford: 1960.

Landy, Francis. *Paradoxes of Paradise: Identity and Difference in the Song of Songs*. Sheffield: 1983.

Beauty and the Enigma, and Other Essays on the Hebrew Bible. Sheffield: 2001.

Lang, Bernhard. *Wisdom and the Book of Proverbs: A Hebrew Goddess Redefined*. New York: 1986.

Lange, Armin. *Weisheit und Prädestination: Weisheitliche Urodnung und Prädestination in den Textfunden von Qumran*. STDJ 18. Leiden: 1995.

'Solomon'. Page 886 in *Encyclopedia of the Dead Sea Scrolls*. Vol. 2. Edited by Lawrence H. Schiffman and James C. VanderKam. Oxford: 2000.

Lange, H. O. *Das Weisheitsbuch des Amenemope*. Copenhagen: 1925.

Lawson, R. P. *Origen: The Song of Songs Commentary and Homilies*. Westminster: 1957.

Lee, Eunny P. *The Vitality of Enjoyment in Qohelet's Theological Rhetoric*. Berlin: 2005.

Lee, Thomas R. *Studies in the Form of Sirach 44–50*. SBLDS 75. Atlanta: 1986.

Legaspi, Michael C. *Wisdom in Classical and Biblical Tradition*. New York: 2018.

Lemaire, Andre. *Les écoles et la formation de la Bible dans l'ancien Israel*. OBO 39. Freiburg; Göttingen: 1981.

Levenson, Jon D. *Creation and the Persistence of Evil: The Jewish Drama of Divine Omnipotence*. Princeton: 1988.

Lichtheim, Miriam. *Ancient Egyptian Literature*. 3 vols. Berkeley: 1973–1980.

'Observations on Papyrus Insinger'. Pages 283–306 in *Studien zu Altägyptischen Lebenslehren*. Edited by E. Hornung and O. Keel. OBO 28. Göttingen: 1979.

Late Egyptian Wisdom Literature. OBO 120. Freiburg: 1983.

'Didactic Literature'. Pages 243–262 in *Ancient Egyptian Literature: History and Forms*. Edited by A. Lopriendo. PAe. Leiden: 1996.

Moral Value in Ancient Egypt. OBO 155. Göttingen: 1997.

Limburg, James. *Encountering Ecclesiastes: A Book for Our Time*. Grand Rapids: 2006.

Linafelt, Tod. 'The Wizard of Uz: Job, Dorothy, and the Limits of the Sublime'. *BibInt* 14.1–2 (2006): 94–109.

Lloyd Miller, Marvin. *Performances of Ancient Jewish Letters: From Elephantine to MMT*. JAJSup 20. Göttingen: 2015.

Loader, James Alfred. *Polar Structures in the Book of Qohelet*. BZAW 152. Berlin: 1979.

Longman, Tremper III. *Fictional Akkadian Autobiography: A Generic and Comparative Study*. Winona Lake: 1991.

———. *Ecclesiastes*. NICOT. Grand Rapids: 1998.

———. *Song of Songs*. NICOT. Grand Rapids: 2001.

———. 'Israelite Genres in Their Ancient Near Eastern Context'. Pages 177–195 in *The Changing Face of Form Criticism in the Twenty-First Century*. Edited by Marvin A. Sweeney and E. B. Zvi. Grand Rapids: 2003.

———. *Proverbs*. BCOTWP. Grand Rapids: 2006.

———. *Job*. BCOTWP. Grand Rapids: 2012.

———. 'The "Fear of God" in the Book of Ecclesiastes'. *BBR* 25 (2015): 13–22.

———. *The Fear of the Lord Is Wisdom: A Theological Introduction to Wisdom in Israel*. Grand Rapids: 2017.

Loretz, Oswald. *Qohelet und der alte Orient: Untersuchen zu Stil und theologischer Thematik des Buches Qohelet*. Freiburg: 1964.

Lowth, Robert. *Lectures on the Sacred Poetry of the Hebrews*. Translated by G. Gregory. Boston: 1829. Translation of *De Sacra Poesi Hebraeorum: Praelectiones Academicae*. Oxford: 1753.

Lucas, Ernest, C. *Exploring the Old Testament: A Guide to the Psalms and Wisdom Literature*. Downers Grove: 2014.

———. *Proverbs*. THOTC. Grand Rapids: 2015.

Machinist, Peter. 'Fate, *miqreh*, and Reason: Some Reflections on Qohelet and Biblical Thought'. Pages 159–175 in *Solving Riddles and Untying Knots: Biblical, Epigraphic, and Semitic Studies in Honor of Jonas C. Greenfield*. Edited by Z. Zevit, S. Gitin and M. Sokoloff. Winona Lake: 1995.

MacIntyre, Alasdair. *A Short History of Ethics: A History of Moral Philosophy from the Homeric Age to the Twentieth Century*. London: 1966.

———. *After Virtue: A Study in Moral Theory*. 3rd ed. London: 2007.

Mack, Burton L. *Wisdom and the Hebrew Epic: Ben Sira's Hymn in Praise of the Fathers*. CSHJ. Chicago: 1985.

Magdalene, F. Rachel. *On the Scales of Righteousness: Neo-Babylonian Trial Law and the Book of Job*. BJS 348. Providence: 2007.

Marböck, Johannes. *Weisheit Im Wandel: Untersuchungen Zur Weisheitstheologie Bei Ben Sira*. Berlin: 1999.

———. 'Zwischen Erfahrung, Systematik und Bekenntnis: Zu Eigenart und Bedeutung der alttestamentlichen Weisheitsliteratur'. Pages 201–214 in *Weisheit und Frömmigkeit: Studien zur alttestamentlichen Literatur der Spätzeit*. Edited by Johannes Marböck. ÖBS. Frankfurt: 2006.

Marcus, David. 'A Famous Analogy of Rib-Haddi'. *JANESCU* 5 (1973): 281–286.

Mazzinghi, Luca. *Weisheit*. IEKAT. Stuttgart: 2018.

McCann, J. Clinton Jr. 'Wisdom's Dilemma: The Book of Job, the Final Form of the Book of Psalms, and the Entire Bible'. Pages 18–30 in *Wisdom, You Are*

My Sister: Studies in Honor of Roland E. Murphy, O. Carm., on the Occasion of his Eightieth Birthday. Edited by Michael L. Barré. CBQMS 29. Washington, 1997.

McKane, William. *Proverbs: A New Approach*. OTL. London: 1970.

Prophets and Wise Men. London: 1983.

McLaughlin, John L. *An Introduction to Israel's Wisdom Traditions*. Grand Rapids: 2018.

'Wisdom Influence'. Pages 409–422 in *The Oxford Handbook of Wisdom and the Bible*. Edited by Will Kynes. New York, 2021.

McNeile, Alan Hugh. *An Introduction to Ecclesiastes*. Cambridge: 1904.

Meek, Theophile J. *The Song of Songs: Introduction and Exegesis*. IB V. New York: 1956.

Meier, Sam. 'Job I–II: A Reflection of Genesis I–III'. *VT* 39 (1989): 183–193.

Meinhold, Arndt. *Die Sprüche. Teil 1: Sprüche Kapitel 1–15*. ZBK 16.1. Zürich: 1991.

Melchert, Charles F. *Wise Teaching: Biblical Wisdom and Educational Ministry*. Harrisburg: 1998.

Mettinger, Tryggve N. D. *Solomonic State Officials*. Lund: 1971.

Meyers, Carol. 'Gender Imagery in the Song of Songs.' Pages 197–212 in *The Song of Songs*. Edited by Athalya Brenner. FCB 1. Sheffield: 1993.

Mieder, Wolfgang. 'The Essence of Literary Proverb Study'. *Proverbium* 23 (1974): 888–894.

Mies, Françoise. 'Le genre littéraire du livre de Job'. *RB* 110 (2003): 336–369.

Miles, Johnny E. *God: A Biography*. New York: 1995.

Millar, Suzanna R. 'When a Straight Road Becomes a Garden Path: The "False Lead" as a Pedagogical Strategy in the Book of Proverbs'. *JSOT* 43 (2018): 67–82.

Genre and Openness in Proverbs 10:1–22:16. AIL 39. Atlanta: 2020.

'History and Wisdom Literature'. Pages 441–458 in *The Oxford Handbook of Wisdom and the Bible*. Edited by Will Kynes. New York: 2021.

Miller, Douglas B. 'Qoheleth's symbolic Use of הבל'. *JBL* 117 (1998): 437–454.

'Wisdom in the Canon: Discerning the Early Intuition'. Pages 87–113 in *Was There a Wisdom Tradition? New Prospects in Israelite Wisdom Studies*. Edited by Mark Sneed. AIL 23. Atlanta: 2015.

Miller, Shem. *Dead Sea Media Orality, Textuality, and Memory in the Scrolls from the Judean Desert*. STDJ 129. Leiden: 2019.

Montefiore, C. G. 'Notes upon the Date and Religious Value of Proverbs'. *JQR* 2 (1890): 430–453.

Montgomery, Eric R. 'A Stream from Eden: The Nature and Development of a Revelatory Tradition in the Dead Sea Scrolls'. PhD diss., McMaster University, 2013.

Morgan, Donn F. *Wisdom in the Old Testament Traditions*. Atlanta: 1981.

Morrow, William. 'Consolation, Rejection, and Repentance in Job 42:6'. *JBL* 105 (1986): 211–225.

Moss, Jessica. '"Virtue Makes the Goal Right": Virtue and "Phronesis" in Aristotle's Ethics'. *Phronesis* 56 (2011): 204–261.

Mowinckel, Sigmund. *Psalmenstudien V: Segen und Fluchen in Israels Kult und Psalmdichtung*. Amsterdam: 1923.

'Psalms and Wisdom'. Pages 205–224 in *Wisdom in Israel and in the Ancient Near East: Presented to H. H. Rowley by the Society for Old Testament Study in Association with the Editorial Board of Vetus Testamentum, in Celebration of His Sixty-Fifth Birthday, 24 March 1955*. Edited by Martin Noth and D. Winton Thomas. VTSup 3. Leiden: 1955.

Praise in Israel's Worship. Repr., Grand Rapids: 1962.

Moyise, Steve. *The Old Testament in the Book of Revelation*. JSNTSup 115. Sheffield: 1995.

Müller, Hans-Peter. 'Die weisheitliche Lehrerzählung im Alten Testament und seiner Umwelt'. *Die Welt Des Orients* 9 (1977): 77–98.

'Die Hiobrahmenerzahlung und ihre altorientalischen Parallelen als Paradigmen einer weisheitlichen Wirklichkeitswahrnahme'. Pages 21–39 in *The Book of Job*. Edited by W. A. M. Beuken. BETL 114. Leuven: 1994.

Murphy, Roland E. 'A Consideration of the Classification "Wisdom Psalms"'. Pages 156–167 in *Congress Volume Bonn 1962*. Edited by G. W. Anderson. VTSup 9. Leiden: 1962.

'Form Criticism and Wisdom Literature'. *CBQ* 31 (1969): 475–483.

Wisdom Literature: Job, Proverbs, Ruth, Canticles, Ecclesiastes, and Esther. FOTL 13. Grand Rapids: 1981.

Song of Songs: A Commentary on the Book of Canticles or the Song of Songs. Hermeneia. Minneapolis: 1990.

The Tree of Life: An Exploration of Biblical Wisdom Literature. Grand Rapids: 1990.

Proverbs. WBC 22. Nashville: 1998.

The Tree of Life: An Exploration of Biblical Wisdom Literature. 3rd ed. Grand Rapids: 2002.

Najman, Hindy. 'Jewish Wisdom in the Hellenistic Period: Towards the Study of a Semantic Constellation'. Pages 459–472 in *Is There a Text in This Cave? Studies in the Textuality of the Dead Sea Scrolls in Honour of George J. Brook*. Edited by Ariel Feldman, Maria Cioată and Charlotte Hempel. Leiden: 2017.

Najman, Hindy, Jean-Sébastien Rey and Eibert J. C. Tigchelaar, eds. *Tracing Sapiential Traditions in Ancient Judaism*. JSJSup 174. Leiden: 2016.

Nasuti, Harry. 'Called into Character: Aesthetic and Ascetic Aspects of Biblical Ethics'. *CBQ* 80 (2018): 1–24.

Newman, Judith H. 'Hybridity, Hydrology, and Hidden Transcript: Sirach 24 and the Judean Encounter with Ptolemaic Isis Worship'. Pages 157–176 in *Jewish Cultural Encounters in the Ancient Mediterranean and Near Eastern World*. Edited by Mladen Popović, Myles Schoonover and Marijn Vandenberghe. JSJSup 178. Leiden: 2017.

Before the Bible: The Liturgical Body and the Formation of Scriptures in Early Judaism. New York: 2018.

Newsom, Carol A. 'Woman and the Discourse of Patriarchal Wisdom: A Study of Proverbs 1–9'. Pages 142–160 in *Gender and Difference in Ancient Israel*. Edited by Peggy L. Day. Minneapolis: 1989.

'Job and Ecclesiastes'. Pages 177–194 in *Old Testament Interpretation: Past, Present, and Future (Essays in Honor of Gene M. Tucker)*. Edited by James Luther Mays, David L. Petersen and Kent Harold Richards. Nashville: 1995.

The Book of Job: A Contest of Moral Imaginations. Oxford: 2003.

The Self as Symbolic Space: Constructing Identity and Community at Qumran. STDJ 52. Leiden: 2004.

'Spying out the Land: A Report from Genology'. Pages 437–450 in *Seeking Out the Wisdom of the Ancients: Essays Offered to Honor Michael V. Fox on the Occasion of His Sixty-Fifth Birthday.* Edited by Ronald L. Troxel, Kelvin G. Friebel and Dennis R. Magary. Winona Lake: 2005.

'Dramaturgy and the Book of Job'. Pages 375–393 in *Das Buch Hiob und seine Interpretationen: Beiträge zum Hiob-Symposium auf dem Monte Verità vom 14.–19. August 2005.* Edited by Thomas Krüger, Manfred Oeming, Konrad Schmid and Christoph Uehlinger. ATANT 88. Zurich: 2007.

Niditch, Susan. *Oral World and Written Word: Ancient Israelite Literature.* Louisville: 1996.

Niehoff, Maren. *Philo of Alexandria: An Intellectual Biography.* New Haven: 2018.

Niehr, Herbert. 'Weisheit in den Königsepen aus Ugarit'. Pages 70–91 in *Teaching Morality in Antiquity.* Edited by Takayoshi M. Oshima. ORA 29. Tübingen: 2018.

Nissinen, Martti. 'Love Lyrics of Nabû and Tašmetu: An Assyrian Song of Songs?' Pages 585–634 in *Und Moses schrieb diese Lied auf' Studien zum Alten Testament und zum alten Orient. Festschrift für Oswald Loretz zur Vollendung seines 70. Lebensjahres.* Edited by Manfried Dietrich and Ingo Kottsieper. AOAT 250. Münster: 1998.

'Wisdom as Mediatrix in Sirach 24: Ben Sira, Love Lyrics, and Prophecy'. *Studia Orientalia Electronica* 106 (2015): 377–390.

Norrick, N. R. 'Subject Area, Terminology, Proverb Definitions, Proverb Features'. Pages 7–27 in *Introduction to Paremiology: A Comprehensive Guide to Proverb Studies.* Edited by H. Hrisztova-Gotthardt and M. Aleksa Varga. Berlin: 2015.

Nurullin, Rim. 'An Attempt at Šima Milka (Ugaritica V, 163 and Duplicates): Part I: Prologue, Instructions II, III, IV'. *Babel & Bibel* 7 (2014): 175–229.

O'Connor, Kathleen M. 'Wild, Raging Creativity: The Scene in the Whirlwind (Job 38–41)'. Pages 171–179 in *A God So Near: Essays on Old Testament Theology in Honor of Patrick D.Miller.* Edited by Brent A. Strawn and Nancy R. Bowen. Winona Lake: 2003.

O'Dowd, Ryan P. 'A Chord of Three Strands: Epistemology in Job, Proverbs and Ecclesiastes'. Pages 65–87 in *The Bible and Epistemology: Biblical Soundings on the Knowledge of God.* Edited by M. Healy and R. Perry. Milton Keynes: 2007.

The Wisdom of Torah: Epistemology in Deuteronomy and the Wisdom Literature. FRLANT 225. Göttingen: 2009.

Proverbs. Grand Rapids: 2017.

Oesterley, W. O. E. *The Book of Proverbs.* London: 1929.

Olley, John W. 'Pharaoh's Daughter, Solomon's Temple and the Palace: Another Look at the Structure of 1 Kings 1–11'. *JSOT* 27 (2003): 355–369.

Origen. *The Song of Songs: Commentary and Homilies.* Translated and annotated by R. P. Lawson. Westminster: 1957.

Osborne, William R. 'Wisdom Gets "Tyred" in the Book of Ezekiel'. Pages 109–123 in *Riddles and Revelations: Explorations into the Relation between Wisdom and Prophecy in the Hebrew Bible*. Edited by Mark J. Boda, Russell L. Meek and William R. Osborne. London: 2018.

Oshima, Takayoshi. *Babylonian Prayers to Marduk*. ORA 7. Tübingen: 2011.

Otto, Eckart. *Theologische Ethik des Alten Testaments*. Stuttgart: 1994.

'Woher weiß der Mensch um Gut und Böse? Philosophische Annäherungen der ägyptischen und biblischen Weisheit an ein Grundproblem der Ethik'. Pages 207–231 in *Recht und Ethos im Alten Testament – Gestalt und Wirkung: Festschrift für Horst Seebass zum 65. Geburtstag*. Edited by S. Beyerle, G. Mayer and H. Strauß. Neukirchen-Vluyn: 1999.

Owen, Joseph. 'Aristotle's Notion of Wisdom'. *Apeiron* 20 (1987): 1–16.

Pajunen, Mika S. *The Land to the Elect and Justice for All: Reading Psalms in the Dead Sea Scrolls in Light of 4Q381*. JAJSup 14. Göttingen: 2013.

'The Praise of God and His Name as the Core of the Second Temple Liturgy'. *ZAW* 127 (2015): 475–488.

Parker, K. I. 'Solomon as Philosopher King? The Nexus of Law and Wisdom in 1 Kings 1–11'. *JSOT* 53 (1992): 75–91.

Pelham, Abigail. 'Job as Comedy, Revisited'. *JSOT* 35 (2010): 89–112.

Contested Creations in the Book of Job, The-World-as-It-Ought-and-Ought-Not-to-Be. Leiden: 2012.

Perdue, Leo G. *Wisdom and Cult: A Critical Analysis of the Views of Cult in the Wisdom Literature of Israel and the Ancient Near East*. SBLDS 30. Missoula: 1977.

'Liminality as a Social Setting for Wisdom Instructions'. *ZAW* 93 (1981): 114–126.

Wisdom & Creation, The Theology of Wisdom Literature. Nashville: 1994.

Proverbs. IBC Louisville: 2000.

Wisdom Literature: A Theological History. Louisville: 2007.

The Sword and the Stylus: An Introduction to Wisdom in the Age of Empires. Grand Rapids: 2008.

Perry, Steven. 'Structural Patterns in Prov 10:1–22:16'. PhD diss., University of Texas at Austin, 1987.

Perry, Theodore Anthony. *Dialogues with Kohelet: The Book of Ecclesiastes*. University Park: 1993.

Petrany, Catherine. *Pedagogy, Prayer and Praise: The Wisdom of the Psalms and the Psalter*. FAT 2 83. Tübingen: 2015.

Pike, Kenneth. *Language in Relation to a Unified Theory of Human Behavior*. The Hague: 1967.

Plöger, Otto. 'Zur Auslegung der Sentenzensammlungen des Proverbienbuches'. Pages 402–416 in *Probleme biblischer Theologie: Gerhard von Rad zum 70. Geburtstag*. Edited by H. W. Wolff. Munich: 1971.

Sprüche Salomos. Neukirchen-Vluyn: 1984.

Pope, Marvin H. *El in the Ugaritic Texts*. Leiden: 1955.

Job. AB 15. 3rd ed. Garden City: 1973.

Song of Songs: A New Translation with Introduction and Commentary. AB 7C. New York: 1977.

Portier-Young, Anathea E. *Apocalypse against Empire: Theologies of Resistance in Early Judaism*. Grand Rapids; Cambridge: 2011.

Posener, Georges, 'L'exorde de l'Instruction éducative d'Amennakhte (Recherches littéraires, V)'. *Revue d'Egypte* 10 (1955): 61–72. *L'Enseignment Loyalist*. Geneva: 1976.

Poythress, Vern S. 'Analysing a Biblical Text: Some Important Linguistic Distinctions'. *SJT* 32 (1979): 113–137.

Pritchard, James B., ed. *Ancient Near Eastern Texts Relating to the Old Testament*. 3rd ed. Princeton: 1969.

Provan, Iain. W. *1 and 2 Kings*. Peabody: 1995.

Quack, Joachim Friedrich *Die Lehren des Ani*. OBO 141. Göttingen: 1994.

Quick, Laura. 'The Hidden Body as Literary Strategy in *4QWiles of the Wicked Woman* (4Q184)'. *DSD* 27 (2020): 234–256.

Rabbow, Paul. *Seelenführung: Methodik der Exerzitien in der Antike*. Munich: 1954.

Rainey, Anson F. *The El-Amarna Correspondence: A New Edition of the Cuneiform Letters from the Site of El-Amarna Based on Collations of All Extant Tablets*. Edited by William M. Schniedewind and Zipora Cochavi-Rainey. Leiden; Boston, 2015.

Reed, Annette Y. *Demons, Angels, and Writing in Ancient Judaism*. Cambridge: 2020.

Reed, Walter L. *Dialogues of the Word: The Bible as Literature according to Bakhtin*. Oxford: 1993.

Reese, James M. 'Plan and Structure in the Book of Wisdom'. *CBQ* 27 (1965): 391–399.

Hellenistic Influence on the Book of Wisdom and Its Consequences. AnBib 41. Rome: 1970.

Reiner, Erica. 'At the Fuller's'. Pages 407–411 in *Vom Alten Orient zum Alten Testament. Festschrift für Wolfram Freiherrn von Soden zum 85. Geburtstag am 19. Juni 1993*. Edited by Manfred Dietrich and Oswald Loretz. AOAT 240. Neukirchen-Vluyn: 1995.

Reiterer, Friedrich Vinzenz. 'Beobachtungen zum äußeren und inneren Exodus im Buch der Weisheit'. Pages 187–208 in *Die Rezeption des Exodusmotivs in deuterokanonischer und frühjüdischer Literatur*. DCLS 32. Edited by J. Gärtner and B. Schmitz. Berlin; Boston: 2016.

'The Theological and Philosophical Concepts of Ben Sira'. Pages 285–315 in *Discovering, Deciphering and Dissenting: Ben Sira Manuscripts after 120 Years*. Edited by James K. Aitken, R. Egger-Wenzel and Stefan C. Reif. Berlin: 2018.

Rey, Jean-Sébastien. 'Scribal Practices in the Ben Sira Hebrew Manuscript A and Codicological Remarks'. Pages 99–112 in *Texts and Contexts of the Book of Ben Sira/Texte und Kontexte des Sirachbuches*. Edited by Gerhard Karner, Frank Ueberschaer and Burkard M. Zapff. Atlanta: 2017.

Richter, Heinz. *Studien zu Hiob: Der Aufbau des Hiobbuches, dargestellt an den Gattungen des Rechtslebens*. Theologische Arbeiten 11. Berlin: 1959.

Ringgren, Helmer, and Walther Zimmerli. *Sprüche/Prediger*. Göttingen: 1962.

Rollston, Christopher A. *Writing and Literacy of Ancient Israel: Epigraphic Evidence from the Iron Age*. ABS 11. Atlanta: 2010.

Rosch, Eleanor. 'Cognitive Representations of Semantic Categories'. *Journal of Experimental Psychology: General* 104.3 (1975): 192–233.

Rousseau, Francois. 'Structure de Qohelet 1:4–11 et plan de livre'. *VT* 31 (1981): 200–217.

Rowley, Harold Henry. 'The Interpretation of the Song of Songs'. Pages 187–234 in *The Servant of the Lord and Other Essays on the Old Testament*. 2nd ed. Revised. Oxford: 1965.

Job. NCB. Rev. ed. Grand Rapids: 1976.

Ruether, Rosemary Radford. *New Woman New Earth, Sexist Ideologies & Human Liberation*. Minneapolis: 1975.

Rutz, Matthew T. *Bodies of Knowledge in Ancient Mesopotamia: The Diviners of Late Bronze Age Emar and Their Tablet Collection*. AMD 9. Leiden: 2013.

Sadgrove, Michael 'Song of Songs as Wisdom Literature'. Pages 245–248 in *Papers on the Old Testament and Related Themes*. Vol. 1 of *Studia Biblica 1978: Sixth International Congress on Biblical Studies, Oxford, 3–7 April 1978*. Edited by E. A. Livingstone. JSOTSup 11. Sheffield: 1979.

Saebø, Magne. 'From Collections to Book – A New Approach to the History of Tradition and Redaction of the Book of Proverbs'. Pages 250–258 in *Proceedings of the 9th World Congress of Jewish Studies, Jerusalem, Aug 1985*. Edited by Moshe Goshen-Gottstein and David Assaf. Jerusalem: 1986.

Salyer, Gary D. *Vain Rhetoric: Private Insight and Public Debate in Ecclesiastes*. JSOTSup 327. Sheffield: 2001.

Samet, Nili. 'Religious Redaction in Qohelet in Light of Mesopotamian Vanity Literature'. *VT* 66 (2016): 133–148.

Sander-Hansen, Constantin Emil. *Die Texte Der Metternichstele. The Text, with a German Translation and Commentary*. AAeg 7. Copenhagen: 1956.

Sanders, Jack T. *Ben Sira and Demotic Wisdom*. Chico: 1983.

Sanders, Seth L. *From Adapa to Enoch: Scribal Culture and Religious Vision in Judea and Babylonia*. Tübingen: 2017.

Sandoval, Timothy J. 'Revisiting the Prologue of Proverbs'. *JBL* 126 (2007): 455–473.

The Discourse of Wealth and Poverty in the Book of Proverbs. Leiden, 2005.

Sarna, Nahum M. 'Epic Substratum in the Prose of Job'. *JBL* 76 (1957): 13–25.

Satlow, Michael L. 'Disappearing Categories: Using Categories in the Study of Religion'. *MTSR* 17 (2005): 287–298.

Saur, Markus. 'Where Can Wisdom Be Found? New Perspectives on the Wisdom Psalms'. Pages 181–204 in *Was There a Wisdom Tradition: New Prospects in Israelite Wisdom Studies*. Edited by Mark R. Sneed. AIL 23. Atlanta: 2015.

Schäfer, Peter. *Mirror of His Beauty: Feminine Images of God from the Bible to the Early Kabbalah: Jews, Christians, and Muslims from the Ancient to the Modern World*. Princeton; Oxford: 2002.

Schams, Christine. *Jewish Scribes in the Second-Temple Period*. JSOTSup 291. Sheffield: 1998.

Schaper, Joachim. '"... denn er ist besser als das, was er anbetet" (Sapientia Salomonis 15,17): Bilderpolemik und theologische Anthropologie in der Sapientia Salomonis'. Pages 455–464 in *Was ist der Mensch, dass du seiner gedenkst? (Psalm 8,5): Aspekte einer theologischen Anthropologie.*

Festschrift für Bernd Janowski zum 65. Geburtstag. Edited by M. Bauks, K. Liess and P. Riede. Neukirchen-Vluyn: 2008.

'Νόμος and Νόμοι in the Wisdom of Solomon'. Pages 293–306 in *Wisdom and Torah: The Reception of 'Torah' in the Wisdom Literature of the Second Temple Period*. JSJSup 163. Edited by B. U. Schipper and D. A. Teeter. Leiden; Boston: 2013.

'"Out of the Iron Furnace": Exodus, Death, and the Reception History of Freedom'. *Aegyptiaca* 4 (2019): 179–187.

Schellenberg, Annette. *Erkenntnis als Problem: Qohelet and die atltestamentliche Diskussion um das menschliche Erkennen*. OBO 188. Göttingen: 2002.

'Questioning the Trend of Classifying the Song of Songs as Sapiential'. Pages 393–407 in *Nächstenliebe und Gottesfurcht: Beiträge aus alttestamentlicher, semitistischer und altorientalistischer Wissenschaft für Hans-Peter Mathys zum 65. Geburtstag*. Edited by Hanna Jenni and Markus Saur. AOAT. Münster: 2016.

Schifferdecker, Kathryn. *Out of the Whirlwind, Creation Theology in the Book of Job*. HTS. Cambridge, MA: 2008.

Schipper, Bernd U. *Israel und Ägypten in der Königszeit: Die kulturellen Kontakte von Salomo bis zum Fall Jerusalems*. OBO 170. Göttingen: 1999.

Sprüche (Proverbia). Teilband 1: Proverbien 1,1–15,33. BKAT 17.1. Göttingen: 2018.

Proverbs 1–15: A Commentary. Hermeneia. Philadelphia: 2019.

'"Teach Them Diligently to Your Son!": The Book of Proverbs and Deuteronomy'. Pages 21–34 in *Reading Proverbs Intertextually*. Edited by Katharine Dell and Will Kynes. LHBOTS 629. London: 2019.

Schmid, Hans Heinrich. *Wesen und Geschichte der Weisheit*. BZAW 101. Berlin: 1966.

Gerechtigkeit Als Weltordnung. Tübingen: 1968.

Schmid, Hartmut. *Das erste Buch der Könige*. Wuppertal: 2000.

Schmid, Konrad. 'Innerbiblische Schriftdiskussion im Hiobbuch'. Pages 241–261 in *Das Buch Hiob und seine Interpretationen: Beiträge zum Hiob-Symposium auf dem Monte Verità vom 14.–19. August 2005*. Edited by Thomas Krüger, Manfred Oeming, Konrad Schmid and Christoph Uehlinger. ATANT 88. Zurich: 2007.

Schmidt, A. Jordan. *Wisdom, Cosmos, and Cultus in the Book of Sirach*. Vol. 42 of *Deuterocanonical and Cognate Literature Studies*. Boston; Berlin: 2019.

Schmidt, Brian B., ed. *Contextualizing Israel's Sacred Writings: Ancient Literacy Orality, and Literary Production*. AIL 22. Atlanta: 2015.

Schmidt, Hans. *Die Psalmen*. HAT 15. Tübingen: 1934.

Scholnick, Sylvia Huberman. 'Lawsuit Drama in the Book of Job'. PhD diss., Brandeis University, 1975.

Schwab, George M. *The Song of Songs' Cautionary Message concerning Human Love*. StBibLit 41. New York: 2002.

Schwáb, Zoltán. *Toward an Interpretation of the Book of Proverbs: Selfishness and Secularity Reconsidered*. JTISup 7. Winona Lake: 2013.

'Is Fear of the Lord the Source of Wisdom or Vice Versa?' *VT* 63 (2013): 652–662.

Schwienhorst-Schönberger, Ludger. *Kohelet*. HThKAT. Freiburg: 2011.

Scoralick, Ruth. *Einzelspruch und Sammlung*. Berlin; New York: 1995.

Seow, Choon-Leong. 'Theology When Everything Is Out of Control'. *Int* 55.3 (2001): 237–249.

———. *Ecclesiastes: A New Translation with Introduction and Commentary*. AB 18. New Haven; London: 2008.

———. *Job 1–21: Interpretation and Commentary*. Illuminations. Grand Rapids: 2013.

Sharp, Carolyn. 'Ironic Representation, Authorial Voice, and Meaning in Qohelet'. *BibInt* 12 (2004): 37–68.

Shelton, Pauline. 'Making a Drama out of a Crisis? A Consideration of the Book of Job as a Drama'. *JSOT* 83 (1999): 69–82.

Shevka, Avi, and Pierre van Hecke. 'The Metaphor of Criminal Charge as a Paradigm for the Conflict between Job and His Friends'. *ETL* 90 (2014): 99–119.

Shupak, Nili. 'The "Sitz im Leben" of the Book of Proverbs in the Light of a Comparison of Biblical and Egyptian Wisdom Literature'. *RB* 94 (1987): 98–119.

———. *Where Can Wisdom Be Found? The Sage's Language in the Bible and in Ancient Egyptian Literature*. OBO 131. Göttingen: 1993.

———. 'Positive and Negative Human Types in the Egyptian Wisdom Literature'. Pages 245–260 in *Homeland and Exile: Biblical and Ancient Near Eastern Studies in Honour of Bustenay Oded*. Edited by G. Galil, M. Geller and A. Millard. VTSup 130. Leiden: 2009.

———. 'The Contribution of Egyptian Wisdom to the Study of Biblical Wisdom Literature'. Pages 265–304 in *Was There a Wisdom Tradition? New Prospects in Israelite Wisdom Studies*. Edited by Mark R. Sneed. Atlanta: 2015.

Siegfried, Carl. *Prediger und Hoheslied übersetzt und erklärt*. HKAT. Göttingen: 1898.

Simkins, Ronald A. 'Anthropocentrism and the Place of Humans in the Biblical Tradition'. *RelSoc Supplement 9: The Greening of the Papacy* (2013): 16–29.

Skehan, Patrick William. 'A Single Editor for the Whole Book of Proverbs'. *CBQ* 10 (1948): 115–130.

Skehan, Patrick W., and Alexander A. Di Lella. *The Wisdom of Ben Sira: A New Translation, with Notes*. AB 39. New York: 1987.

Skelton, David A. 'Sages as Singers in Sirach and the Second Temple Period'. Pages 167–182 in *Sirach and Its Contexts: The Pursuit of Wisdom and Human Flourishing: Proceedings of the Virginia Conference on the Book of Sirach and Its Contexts*. Edited by Greg Schmidt Goering, Samuel Adams, and Matthew Goff. JSJSup 196. Leiden: 2021.

———. *Singers of Wisdom: Music and Pedagogy in Ben Sira and the Second Temple Period*. JSJSup. Leiden: forthcoming.

Smil, Vaclav. *Harvesting the Biosphere: What We Have Taken from Nature*. Cambridge, MA: 2013.

Smith, Cooper. '"I Have Heard the Sound of Your Words": Allusion in the Elihu Speeches of Job 32–37'. PhD diss., Wheaton College, 2019.

Smith, David Geoffrey. *Practice of Wisdom*, Critical Pedagogy Today 5 (London 2014)

Smith, Jonathan Z. *Drudgery Divine: On the Comparison of Early Christianities and the Religions of Late Antiquity*. Chicago: 1994.

Smith, Mark S. 'The Levitical Compilation of the Psalter'. *ZAW* 103 (1991): 258–263.

Smyth, Richard. 'Nature Writing's Fascist Roots'. *NewStatesman*. 2019. www .newstatesman.com/culture/books/2019/04/eco-facism-nature-writing-nazi-far-right-nostalgia-england.

Snaith, Norman H. *The Book of Job: Its Origin and Purpose*. London: 1968.

Sneed, Mark R. '"White Trash" Wisdom: Proverbs 9 Deconstructed'. *JHS* 7 (2007): 2–10.

'Is the "Wisdom Tradition" a Tradition?' *CBQ* 73 (2011): 50–71.

The Politics of Pessimism in Ecclesiastes: A Social-Science Perspective. AIL 12. Atlanta: 2012.

'"Grasping After the Wind": The Elusive Attempt to Define and Delimit Wisdom'. Pages 39–67 in *Was There a Wisdom Tradition? New Prospects in Israelite Wisdom Studies*. Edited by Mark R. Sneed. Atlanta: 2015.

The Social World of the Sages: An Introduction to Israelite and Jewish Wisdom Literature. Minneapolis: 2015.

Sneed, Mark R. ed., *Was There a Wisdom Tradition? New Prospects in Israelite Wisdom Studies*. AIL 23. Atlanta: 2015.

'Methods, Muddles, and Modes of Literature: The Question of Influence between Wisdom and Prophecy'. Pages 30–44 in *Riddles and Revelations: Explorations into the Relation between Wisdom and Prophecy in the Hebrew Bible*. Edited by Mark J. Boda, Russell L. Meek and William R. Osborne. London: 2018.

'A Taste for Wisdom: Aesthetics, Moral Discernment, and Social Class in Proverbs'. Pages 111–126 in *Imagined Worlds and Constructed Differences in the Hebrew Bible*. Edited by Jeremiah W. Cataldo. LHBOTS 677. London: 2019.

'Inspired Sages: *Massa'* and the Confluence of Wisdom and Prophecy'. In *Scribes as Sages and Prophets*. BZAW 496. Edited by Jutta Krispenz. Berlin: 2020, 15–32.

Snell, Daniel C. *Twice-Told Proverbs and the Composition of the Book of Proverbs*. Winona Lake: 1993.

Sommer, Benjamin D. *A Prophet Reads Scripture: Allusion in Isaiah 40–66*. Stanford: 1998.

Sparks, Kenton L. *Ancient Texts for the Study of the Hebrew Bible: A Guide to the Background Literature*. Peabody: 2005.

'The Song of Songs: Wisdom for Young Jewish Women'. *CBQ* 70.2 (2008): 277–299.

'Genre Criticism'. Pages 55–94 in *Methods for Exodus*. Edited by Thomas B. Dozeman. Cambridge: 2010.

Spieckermann, Hermann. 'What Is the Place of Wisdom and Torah in the Psalter?' Pages 287–316 in *'When the Morning Stars Sang': Essays in Honor of Choon Leong Seow on the Occasion of His Sixty-Fifth Birthday*. Edited by Scott C. Jones and Christine Roy Yoder. BZAW 500. Berlin: 2018.

Steiner, George. 'Tragedy: Remorse and Justice'. *The Listener* 18 (1979): 508–510.

Stewart, Anne W. *Poetic Ethics in Proverbs: Wisdom Literature and the Shaping of the Moral Self*. New York: 2016.

Stone, Elizabeth. 'Old Man Qoheleth'. *JBR* 10 (1942): 98–102.

Sweeney, Marvin A., and Ehud B. Zvi, eds. *The Changing Face of Form Criticism in the Twenty-First Century.* Grand Rapids: 2003.

Takayoshi Oshima. *Babylonian Poems of Pious Sufferers. Ludlul bēl nēmeqi and the Babylonian Theodicy.* Tübingen: 2014.

Talmon, Shemaryahu. 'Wisdom in the Book of Esther'. *VT* 13 (1963): 419–455.

Támez, Elsa. *When the Horizons Close: Rereading Ecclesiastes.* Maryknoll: 2000.

Tanzer, Sarah. 'Response to George Nickelsburg "Wisdom and Apocalypticism in Early Judaism"'. Pages 39–50 in *Conflicted Boundaries in Wisdom and Apocalypticism.* Edited by Benjamin G. Wright and Lawrence M. Wills. SBLSymS 35. Atlanta: 2005.

Terrien, Samuel L. *The Elusive Presence: Toward a New Biblical Theology.* Religious Perspectives 26. San Francisco: 1978.

Ticciati, Susannah. *Job and the Disruption of Identity: Reading beyond Barth.* London: 2005.

Tilford, Nicole L. *Sensing World, Sensing Wisdom: The Cognitive Foundation of Biblical Metaphors.* AIL 31. Atlanta: 2017.

Toorn, Karel van der. 'The Ancient Near Eastern Literary Dialogue as a Vehicle of Critical Reflection'. Pages 59–75 in *Dispute Poems and Dialogues in the Ancient and Mediaeval Near East: Forms and Types of Literary Debates in Semitic and Related Literatures.* Edited by G. J. Reinink and H. L. J. Vanstiphout. OLA 42. Leuven: 1991.

——. *Scribal Culture and the Making of the Hebrew Bible.* Cambridge: 2007.

Topsell, Edward. *The Historie of Foure-Footed Beastes. Describing the True and Liuely Figure of Euery Beast, with a Discourse of Their Seuerall Names, Conditions, Kindes, Vertues (Both Naturall and Medicinall)* ... London: 1607.

Tov, Emanuel. 'The Biblical Texts from the Judean Desert: An Overview and Analysis'. Pages 128–154 in *Hebrew Bible, Greek Bible and Qumran: Collected Essays.* Edited by Emanuel Tov. Texts and Studies in Ancient Judaism 121. Tübingen: 2008.

Toy, C. H. *A Critical and Exegetical Commentary on the Book of Proverbs.* ICC. Edinburgh: 1899.

Treier, Daniel J. *Proverbs and Ecclesiastes.* Grand Rapids: 2011.

Tromp, Nicolas J. 'Wisdom and the Canticle: Ct., 8, 6c–7b: Text, Character, Message and Import'. Pages 88–95 in *La Sagesse de l'Ancien Testament.* Edited by Maurice Gilbert. Leuven: 1979.

Tucker, Gene M. *Form Criticism of the Old Testament.* GBS. Philadelphia: 1971.

Tull Willey, Patricia. *Remember the Former Things: The Recollection of Previous Texts in Second Isaiah.* SBLDS 161. Atlanta: 1997.

Ulrich, Eugene, ed. *The Biblical Qumran Scrolls: Transcriptions and Textual Variants.* VTSup 134. Leiden: 2010.

Uusimäki, Elisa. 'Spiritual Formation in Hellenistic Jewish Wisdom Teaching'. Pages 59–69 in *Tracing Sapiential Tradition in Ancient Judaism.* Edited by H. Najman, J.-S. Rey and E. Tigchelaar. JSJSup 174. Leiden: 2016.

——. *Turning Proverbs towards Torah: An Analysis of 4Q525.* STDJ 117. Leiden: 2016.

'The Formation of a Sage according to Ben Sira'. Pages 59–69 in *Second Temple Jewish 'Paideia' in Context*. Edited by Jason M. Zurawski and Gabriele Boccaccini. BZNW 228. Berlin: 2017.

'Maskil among the Hellenistic Jewish Sages'. *JAJ* 8 (2018): 42–68.

Van der Horst, Pieter Willem. 'From Liberation to Expulsion: The Exodus in the Earliest Jewish-Pagan Polemics'. Pages 387–396 in *Israel's Exodus in Transdisciplinary Perspective: Text, Archaeology, Culture and Geoscience*. Edited by T. E. Levy, T. Schneider and W. H. C. Propp. Cham: 2015.

Van der Lingen, Anton. '*bwʾ-Yṣ'* ("To Go out and to Come in") as a Military Term'. *VT* 42 (1992): 59–66.

Van Dijk, Johannes J. A. *La sagesse suméro-akkadienne*. Leiden: 1953.

Van Leeuwen, Raymond. *Context and Meaning in Proverbs 25–27*. SBLDS 96. Atlanta: 1988.

'Liminality and Worldview in Proverbs 1–9'. *Semeia* 50 (1990): 111–144.

'The Book of Proverbs'. Pages 17–264 in *The New Interpreters Bible*. Vol. 5. Nashville: 1997.

'Cosmos, Temple, House: Building and Wisdom in Mesopotamia and Israel'. Pages 67–92 in *Wisdom Literature in Mesopotamia and Israel*. Edited by R. J. Clifford. SBLSymS 36. Atlanta: 2007.

'Cosmos, Temple, House: Building and Wisdom in Ancient Mesopotamia and Israel' Pages 399–421 in *From the Foundations to the Crenellations: Essays on Temple Building in the Ancient Near East and Hebrew Bible*. Edited by Mark J. Boda and Jamie Novotny. AOAT 366. Münster: 2010.

Van Seters, John. 'The Creation of Man and the Creation of the King'. *ZAW* 101 (1989): 333–342.

Vayntrub, Jacqueline. 'The Book of Proverbs and the Idea of Ancient Israelite Education'. *ZAW* 128 (2016): 96–114.

Beyond Orality: Biblical Poetry in Its Own Terms. Oxford; London: 2019.

Verheij, Arian. 'Paradise Retried: On Qohelet 2:4–6'. *JSOT* 50 (1991): 113–115.

Vesely, Patricia. *Friendship and Virtue Ethics in the Book of Job*. Cambridge: 2019.

Viano, Maurizio. *The Reception of Sumerian Literature in the Western Periphery*. Antichistica 9/Studi Orientali 4. Venice: 2016.

Volten, A. *Zwei altägyptische politische Schriften*. AAeg II. Copenhagen: 1945.

Von Rad, Gerhard. 'Hiob xxxviii und die altägyptische Weisheit'. Pages 293–301 in *Wisdom in Israel and the Ancient Near East: Presented to Harold Henry Rowley by the Society for Old Testament Study, in Celebration of his Sixty-Fifth Birthday, 24 March 1955*. Edited by Martin Noth and D. Winton Thomas. VTSup 3. Leiden: 1955.

Old Testament Theology: Volume One, The History of Israel's Historical Traditions. Translated by D. M. G. Stalker. Edinburgh: 1962.

'The Joseph Narrative and Ancient Wisdom'. Pages 292–300 in *The Problem of the Hexateuch and Other Essays*. Edinburgh: 1966.

'The Theological Problem of the Old Testament Doctrine of Creation'. Pages 53–64 in *Creation in the Old Testament*. Edited by Bernhard W. Anderson. London: 1984.

Weisheit in Israel. 4th ed. Neukirchen-Vluyn: 2013 [*Wisdom in Israel*. Translated by James D. Martin. London: 1972].

Wahl, Harold-Martin *Der Gerechte Schöpfer: Eine Redaktions- Und Theologiegeschichtliche Untersuchung Der Elihureden – Hiob 32–37.* BZAW 207. Berlin: 2015.

Walsh, Carey. 'The Beasts of Wisdom: Ecological Hermeneutics of the Wild'. *BibInt* 25.2 (2017): 135–148.

Walton, John H., and Tremper Longman III. *How to Read Job.* Downers Grove: 2015.

Wasserman, Nathan. *Akkadian Love Literature of the Third and Second Millennium BCE.* Leipziger Altorientalistische Studien 4. Wiesbaden: 2016.

Watson, Francis. *Text, Church and World, Biblical Interpretation in Theological Perspective.* Edinburgh: 1994.

Watson, Wilfred G. E. 'Some Ancient Near Eastern Parallels to the Song of Songs'. Pages 253–71 in *Words Remembered Texts Renewed: Essays in Honour of John F. A. Sawyer.* Edited by John Davies, Graham Harvey and Wilfred G. E. Watson. JSOTSup 195. Sheffield: 1995.

Weeks, Stuart. *Early Israelite Wisdom.* Oxford: 2004.

'Wisdom Psalms'. Pages 292–307 in *Temple and Worship in Biblical Israel.* Edited by John Day. London: 2005.

Instruction and Imagery in Proverbs 1–9. Oxford: 2007.

An Introduction to the Study of Wisdom Literature. T&T Clark Approaches to Biblical Studies. London: 2010.

Ecclesiastes and Scepticism. LHBOTS 541. New York: 2012.

'The Limits of Form Criticism in the Study of Literature, with Reflections on Psalm 34'. Pages 15–24 in *Biblical Interpretation and Method: Essays in Honour of John Barton.* Edited by Katharine J. Dell and Paul M. Joyce. Oxford: 2013.

'Wisdom, Form and Genre'. Pages 161–177 in *Was There a Wisdom Tradition? New Prospects in Israelite Wisdom Studies.* Edited by Mark R. Sneed. AIL. Atlanta: 2015.

'Is "Wisdom Literature" a Useful Category?' Pages 3–23 in *Tracing Sapiential Traditions in Ancient Judaism.* Edited by H. Najman, J.-S. Rey and E. Tigchelaar. JSJSup 174. Leiden: 2016.

'The Place and Limits of Wisdom Revisited'. Pages 3–23 in *Perspectives on Israelite Wisdom: Proceedings of the Oxford Old Testament Seminar.* Edited by John Jarick. LHBOTS 618. London: 2016.

'Overlap? Influence? Allusion? The Importance of Asking the Right Questions'. Pages 45–54 in *Riddles and Revelations: Explorations into the Relation between Wisdom and Prophecy in the Hebrew Bible.* Edited by Mark J. Boda, Russell L. Meek and William R. Osborne. London: 2018.

A Critical and Exegetical Commentary on Ecclesiastes, Introduction and Commentary on Ecclesiastes 1.1–5.6. London; New York: 2019.

Weinfeld, Moshe. *Deuteronomy and the Deuteronomic School.* Oxford: 1972.

'Job and Its Mesopotamian Parallels – A Typological Analysis'. Pages 217–226 in *Text and Context: Old Testament and Semitic Studies for F. C. Fensham.* Edited by W. Claasen. JSOTSup 48. Sheffield: 1988.

Weiser, Artur. *The Psalms: A Commentary.* OTL. London: 1962.

Westenholz, Joan Goodnick. 'Love Lyrics from the Ancient Near East'. Pages 2471–2486 in *CANE IV.* New York: 1995.

Westermann, Claus. *The Structure of the Book of Job: A Form-Critical Analysis*. Translated by Charles A. Muenchow. Philadelphia: 1981. Translation of *Der Aufbau des Buches Hiob*. 1st ed., Tübingen: 1956; 3rd ed., Stuttgart: 1978.

Der Psalter. 4th ed. Stuttgart: 1980.

Roots of Wisdom: The Oldest Proverbs of Israel and Other Peoples. Translated by J. Daryl Charles. Louisville: 1995.

Wette, W. M. L. de. 'Beytrag zur Charakteristik des Hebraismus'. Pages 241–312 in *Studien*. Vol. 3. Edited by Carl Daub and Friedrich Creuzer. Heidelberg: 1807.

Wetzstein, J. G. 'Appendix: Remarks on the Song'. Pages 162–178 in *Commentary on the Song of Songs and Ecclesiastes*. Edited by Franz Delitzsch. Translated by M. G. Easton. Edinburgh: 1877.

Whedbee, J. William. 'The Comedy of Job'. *Semeia* 7 (1977): 1–39.

Whetter, K. S. *Understanding Genre and Medieval Romance*. Aldershot: 2008.

White Crawford, Sidnie. 'Lady Wisdom and Dame Folly at Qumran'. *DSD* 5 (1998): 355–366.

Scribes and Scrolls at Qumran. Grand Rapids: 2019.

Whybray, R. Norman. *The Succession Narrative: A Study of II Samuel 9–20; 1 Kings 1 and 2*. SBT 2/9. London: 1969.

The Intellectual Tradition in the Old Testament. Berlin: 1974.

'Yahweh-Sayings and Their Contexts in Proverbs 10,1–22,16'. Pages 153–165 in *La sagesse de l'Ancien Testament*. Edited by M. Gilbert. Leuven: 1979.

'Qoheleth, Preacher of Joy'. *JSOT* 23 (1982): 87–98.

'Thoughts on the Composition of Proverbs 10–29'. Pages 112–114 in *Priests, Prophets and Scribes*. Edited by Eugene Ulrich, John W. Wright, Robert P. Carroll and Philip R. Davies. Sheffield: 1992.

The Composition of the Book of Proverbs. Sheffield: 1994.

The Book of Proverbs: A Survey of Modern Study. Leiden: 1995.

'Wisdom, Suffering and the Freedom of God in the Book of Job'. Pages 231–245 in *In Search of True Wisdom: Essays in Old Testament Interpretation in Honour of Ronald E. Clements*. Edited by E. Ball. JSOTSup 300. Sheffield: 1999.

Wicke-Reuter, Ursel. 'Ben Sira und die Frühe Stoa: Zum Zusammenhang von Ethik und dem Glauben an eine göttliche Providenz'. Pages 268–281 in *Ben Sira's God: Proceedings of the International Ben Sira Conference, Durham – Ushaw College 2001*. Edited by Renate Egger-Wenzel. BZAW 321. Berlin: 2002.

Wildeboer, Gerrit. *Die Sprüche*. Freiburg: 1897.

Wilhelm, Gernot. 'Bemerkungen zu der akkadisch-hurritischen Bilingue aus Ugarit'. Pages 341–345 in *Literatur, Politik und Recht in Mesopotamien: Festschrift für Claus Wilcke*. Edited by Walther Sallaberger Konrad Volk and Annette Zgoll. OBC 14. Wiesbaden: 2003.

Williams, Bernard. *Ethics and the Limits of Philosophy*. London: 1985. Repr., 2011.

Williams, David S. 'Once Again: The Structure of the Narrative of Solomon's Reign'. *JSOT* 86 (1999): 49–66.

Wilson, Robert R. 'The Death of the King of Tyre: The Editorial History of Ezekiel 28'. Pages 211–218 in *Love and Death in the Ancient Near East*. Edited by John H. Marks and Robert M. Good. Guildford: 1987.

Winston, D. 'Theodicy in Ben Sira and Stoic Philosophy'. Pages 239–249 in *Of Scholars, Savants, and Their Texts*. Edited by R. Link Salinger. New York: 1989.

Witte, Markus. 'Die literarische Gattung des Buches Hiob: Robert Lowth und seine Erben'. Pages 93–123 in *Sacred Conjectures: The Context and Legacy of Robert Lowth and Jean Astruc*. Edited by John Jarick. LHBOTS 457. London: 2007.

——— 'Job in Conversation with the Torah'. Pages 81–100 in *Wisdom and Torah: The Reception of 'Torah' in the Wisdom Literature of the Second Temple Period*. Edited by Bernd Schipper and D. Andrew Teeter. JSJSup 163. Leiden: 2013.

——— 'Key Aspects and Themes in Recent Scholarship on the Book of Ben Sira'. Pages 1–31 in *Texts and Contexts of the Book of Ben Sira/Texte und Kontexte des Sirachbuches*. Edited by Gerhard Karner, Frank Ueberschaer and Burkard M. Zapff. Atlanta: 2017.

Wold, Benjamin. *4QInstruction: Divisions and Hierarchies*. Leiden: 2018.

Wolfers, David. *Deep Things out of Darkness: The Book of Job, Essays and a New Translation*. Kampen: 1995.

Woude, A. van der. 'Wisdom at Qumran'. Pages 244–256 in *Wisdom in Ancient Israel: Essays in Honour of J.A. Emerton*. Edited by J. Day, R. P. Gordon and H. G. M. Williamson. Cambridge: 1995.

Wray, Beal, and M. Lissa. *1 & 2 Kings*. AOTC. Nottingham: 2014.

Wright, Addison G. 'Riddle of the Sphinx: The Structure of the Book of Qoheleth'. *CBQ* 30 (1968): 313–334.

Wright, Benjamin G. III. 'Wisdom and Women at Qumran'. *DSD* 11 (2004): 240–261.

——— 'Ben Sira on the Sage as Exemplar'. Pages 165–182 in *Praise Israel for Wisdom and Instruction: Essays on Ben Sira and Wisdom, the Letter of Aristeas and the Septuagint*. Edited by Benjamin Wright. JSJSup 131. Leiden: 2008.

——— 'Joining the Club: A Suggestion about Genre in Early Jewish Texts'. *DSD* 17 (2010): 289–314.

——— 'Biblical Interpretation in the Book of Ben Sira'. Pages 363–388 in *A Companion to Biblical Interpretation in Early Judaism*. Edited by Matthias Henze. Grand Rapids: 2012.

——— 'Conflicted Boundaries: Ben Sira, Sage and Seer'. Pages 229–253 in *Congress Volume Helsinki 2010*. Edited by Martti Nissinen. VTSup 148. Leiden: 2012.

Wright, Benjamin G. III, and Claudia V. Camp. '"Who Has Been Tested by Gold and Found Perfect?": Ben Sira's Discourse of Riches and Poverty'. Pages 71–96 in *Praise Israel for Wisdom and Instruction: Essays on Ben Sira and Wisdom, the Letter of Aristeas and the Septuagint*. JSJSup 131. Leiden: 2008.

Wright, Benjamin G. III, and Lawrence M. Wills, eds. *Conflicted Boundaries in Wisdom and Apocalypticism*. SBLSymS 35. Atlanta: 2005.

Wright, G. E. *God Who Acts: Biblical Theology as Recital*. SBT 8. London: 1952.

Würthwein, E. *Die Weisheit Ägyptens und das Alte Testament*. Marburg: 1960.

Yoder, Christine Roy. 'Forming "Fearers of Yahweh": Repetition and Contradiction as Pedagogy in Proverbs'. Pages 167–183 in *Seeking Out the*

Wisdom of the Ancients: Essays Offered to Honor Michael V. Fox on the Occasion of his Sixty-fifth Birthday. Edited by Ronald L. Troxel, Kelvin G. Friebel and Dennis R. Magary. Winona Lake: 2005.

'Objects of our Affections: Emotions and the Moral Life in Proverbs 1–9'. Pages 73–88 in *Shaking Heaven and Earth: Essays in Honor of Walter Brueggemann and Charles Cousar*. Edited by C. R. Yoder, K. M. O'Connor, E. E. Johnson and S. P. Saunders. Louisville: 2005.

'On the Threshold of Kingship: A Study of Agur (Proverbs 30)'. *Int* 63 (2009): 254–263.

Proverbs. AOTC Nashville: 2009.

Young, Ian. *Diversity in Pre-Exilic Hebrew*. FAT 5. Tübingen: 1993.

Žába, Z. *Les Maximes de Ptaḥḥotep*. Prague: 1955.

Zahn, Molly M. 'Genre and Rewritten Scripture: A Reassessment'. *JBL* 131 (2012): 271–288.

Zimmerli, Walter. 'The Place and Limit of the Wisdom in the Framework of the Old Testament Theology'. *SJT* 17 (1964): 146–158.

Zöckler, Otto. *Die Sprüche Salomonis: Theologisch-Homiletisch Bearbeitet*. Bielefeld; Leipzig: 1867.

Zuckerman, Bruce. *Job the Silent: A Study in Historical Counterpoint*. Oxford: 1991.

Zurawski, Jason M., and Gabriele Boccaccini, eds. *Second Temple Jewish 'Paideia' in Context*. BZNW 228. Berlin: 2017.

Index

4QInstruction, 303, 306, 308–310, 312, 314–317, 321
acts-consequence, 278, 418–422, 428–429, 431–432
admonitions
  Akkadian, 376, 378
  compositions in, 221
allegory, 25, 42, 172, 176, 200, 202, 207, 213, 297, 373
ambiguity, 130, 146–149, 159–160, 184, 186, 188–189, 191, 194, 367, 374, 427, 469
Amenemope, Instruction of, 18, 38, 93, 98, 141, 154, 335, 451
animals, 10, 42, 77, 108–109, 331, 358–360, 363, 371–372, 375, 392–393, 397–398, 401, 409, 443, 457
apocalyptic, 7, 9, 26, 49, 92, 178–180, 279, 294–296, 300, 308–310, 321
Aquinas, 455, 457–458, 460
archives, 76, 81, 319, 344, 363
Aristotle, 142, 220, 241, 244, 455–463, 465–468, 470, 473
authorship, 6, 116, 140, 202, 204, 223, 286, 372, 387, 451

beauty, 11, 40, 63, 166, 253–255, 395, 402–405, 411–412
Ben Sira
  Egyptian literature and, 37, 341–342

canon, 4, 6, 8, 16–18, 20, 22–23, 32–33, 74, 82, 91, 96, 98, 100–101, 140–141, 162, 166, 170, 172–174, 176–178, 201, 203, 239, 256–257, 261–263, 283, 391, 415
character
  development of, 10, 329–330
communication, 6, 110–113, 145, 221, 225, 457

complaint, genres of, 53–55
contradictions, 7, 44–45, 102, 146–147, 184–190, 193, 198, 408, 435, 465
control, 45, 111, 165, 185, 192, 239, 326, 362, 402, 407–408, 412
creation
  theology of, 18, 27, 284, 399, 412
curricula, 5, 76, 79–82, 94

death, 6, 9, 23, 28, 87, 106, 111–113, 117–118, 144, 146, 150, 157, 187–188, 196–197, 201, 208, 262, 267, 278–280, 295–296, 310, 313, 324, 339, 352–354, 356, 358, 362, 377, 383–384, 387, 402, 404, 407–408, 411, 416–417, 430, 444–445, 447, 465–466, 468–469
dialogue, 5, 7, 26, 37, 41, 43–45, 49, 53, 55, 73, 101, 103, 111, 113, 146–147, 150, 164, 167–170, 174–175, 181–182, 188, 192, 201, 207, 213, 241, 256, 278, 295, 300, 354, 358, 370, 382, 385, 387, 427–428, 434, 436, 440–441, 463–464, 472
diatribe, 5, 36, 40–43, 55
diligence, 40, 329, 416, 461
disputation(s), 10, 30, 169, 345, 359–360, 367, 370–373, 375, 436, 441, 462

Egypt
  Kingdoms of, 9, 77, 79–81, 342, 345
  influence of, 10, 323, 333, 340, 343
Emar, 10, 81, 93, 344, 346, 348–349, 352, 354, 356, 359, 363, 369, 376, 378, 384
embodiment, 316, 320
empiricism, 170, 465
enculturation, 77, 84, 320
eschatology, 9, 286, 297, 321

ethics, 4, 11–12, 76, 94, 100, 113, 142, 329, 342, 395–397, 434, 455, 457–459, 464, 469, 471–473
eudaimonia, 455, 467
exodus narrative, 285, 294, 296
experiment, 29, 235, 430, 446–447

fables, 10, 42, 81, 345, 358–360, 371, 373–375
fear of Yahweh/the Lord, 30
form-criticism, 15, 144, 168, 180, 316
friendship, 147, 266, 268, 459, 462–465, 470
futility, 10, 196, 279, 326, 352, 367, 383–385, 430

genre
    genre realism, 226, 313
    genre theory, 15–16, 25, 28
good, the, 12, 456, 472
Gunkel, 15, 21–22, 24–25, 221–223, 225

hebel, 11, 197, 406, 409, 430, 447
history of reception, 7, 200–204
honour, 112, 421, 430, 461, 466, 468, 472
human reasoning, 36, 43–46, 55
Hurrian, 347–348
hymnody, 9, 310–311

idol polemic, 284
instruction
    transmission of, 332

Job
    date of, 166–167
    genres of, 172–173
    problems with reading, 170–172

knowledge, 8, 19, 29–30, 44, 47, 52, 73–74, 80, 91, 93, 104–106, 108, 114, 126, 128, 130–131, 151, 155–156, 158, 163, 198, 202, 212, 214, 222, 230, 241–243, 245, 248–249, 251–252, 254–255, 257, 264–266, 268–269, 272, 278, 281, 298, 300, 305, 308, 311–312, 317, 319, 321, 323, 339, 341, 366, 370, 374, 376, 379, 386–387, 392–395, 402, 424, 442, 445, 457, 460, 465–466, 470, 472
Koch, Klaus, 11, 19, 102, 159, 400, 418–420, 422–425, 428, 431–432

lament, 5, 7, 10, 25, 32, 53–55, 113, 164, 169, 172–174, 179, 182, 190, 205, 222, 256, 330, 384, 440, 457
Late Bronze Age (LBA), 10, 80, 93, 206, 344–364, 372–374, 383
leaders, 89, 121, 126, 252–256, 274, 315
life, 6, 10, 19, 27, 29, 37, 41, 47–48, 53, 67, 70, 77, 87, 101, 104–106, 108, 111–113, 120–121, 125, 137–138, 143, 146–147, 152, 156–157, 160, 167–169, 177, 184, 188, 190, 194, 196, 198, 202–203, 206, 209, 214–216, 230, 233–234, 242, 244, 247, 261–262, 264, 271, 278–280, 287, 291, 295, 297, 299–300, 304, 318, 321, 326–327, 332, 336–338, 347, 352–355, 357–358, 362, 367–368, 377, 379, 382–384, 392, 396, 399–400, 402, 406–407, 411, 414, 417, 420, 422, 425, 430–431, 433, 436, 442, 446, 449, 455, 457, 459, 465–468, 471–472
love relationship, 204, 208, 211–212, 215
Ludlul bēl nēmeqi, 174, 362, 366, 380

Ma'at, 10, 46–47, 106, 323, 328–329, 338–339, 342, 367
mebin, 308–309
Mesopotamia, 10, 45, 76, 79–80, 82, 158, 202, 204, 241, 311, 329, 344–349, 352, 355, 359–360, 362–363, 366, 369–370, 373, 376, 378, 380
moral formation, 84, 94, 435
mysticism, 296, 301

narrative
    didactic, 5, 7, 26, 36, 42–43, 55, 176–178, 213, 217
    Solomonic, 117
narrator, 7, 29, 43, 118, 120, 123, 163–164, 184–187, 190–194, 198

observation, 12, 14, 17–18, 27–28, 30–31, 44, 66, 101, 122, 124, 129–130, 160, 191, 287, 312, 326, 328, 330, 357, 417, 421, 445–447, 459
orality, 316, 319–321
order
    created, 7, 158–159
    moral, 7, 158–159, 418

pan-sapientialism, 27, 207, 239
pedagogy, 9–11, 40, 77, 84, 139, 146, 230, 264, 312, 319, 321, 323, 327–328,

330–332, 343, 436–439, 442, 444, 446–449, 452

Philo, 243, 246, 297, 300, 317–318

pneuma, 287, 289, 297

poetry, 7, 46, 48, 76, 84, 86, 97, 141, 143, 164, 175–176, 180, 203, 205, 211, 214, 222–224, 281, 369, 404, 442, 444

poverty, 9, 87, 113, 137, 146–147, 150, 160, 274–275, 310, 321, 337, 416, 421, 451, 460

power, 10, 12, 30, 46–47, 51, 79, 87, 108, 111–112, 120, 124, 156, 158, 182, 192, 194, 223, 253, 279–281, 294, 326, 338, 340, 380, 387, 398, 402–405, 411–412, 418, 430, 435–436, 442, 444, 451–452, 470

praise, genres of, 36, 46–52, 55

priests, 5, 22, 27, 50, 78, 80, 87–91, 93–94, 178, 246, 255–256, 262, 272, 328, 372

prophets, 5, 13, 17, 22, 26–27, 88–92, 94, 99, 170, 173, 179, 251, 254–255

protreptic, 5, 36, 40–43, 55

proverb(s) (also *mashal*)
    Akkadian, clusters of, 60–62, 350–351, 374

Proverbs, Book of
    Egyptian parallels and, 338–339
    literary context of, 63
    nature of, 143–150
    reception history of, 137–143
    structure of, 151–154
    themes in, 155–160

Psalms
    Wisdom, 4, 8, 13, 21, 32, 92, 99, 113, 205, 219–237, 311, 434

Qohelet, 12, 18, 29, 41, 43–44, 74, 105, 184–198, 205–206, 212, 214, 304, 318, 337, 352, 399, 404, 406–408, 410–412, 414, 418–419, 429–431, 446–447, 465–469, 472

Queen of Sheba, 124–125, 129

raz nihyeh, 9, 308–309, 314, 318

Realpolitik, 123, 132

rebuke, 11, 87, 121, 350, 434, 436–442, 445, 447, 452–453

retainer class, 79, 87, 94, 310

retribution
    doctrine of, 6, 66, 93, 101–106, 114, 168, 170, 400, 416–417, 420

reward, 7, 11, 101–103, 106, 108, 111, 159–160, 168, 172, 177, 180, 190, 268,

280, 309, 326, 329, 337, 400, 403, 414–432, 467

righteous sufferer 10, 345, 361 (also Pious Sufferer)

royal persona. *see* Qohelet

sages, 5, 14, 17–19, 22, 68, 77, 88–90, 93–94, 99, 102, 140, 158, 168, 188, 198, 223–224, 241, 243–244, 264, 311–312, 318, 326, 338, 366, 386, 400, 418, 442

sayings. *see* proverbs

school debates, 10, 385–386

schools, 4–5, 10, 14–16, 18–19, 22–24, 27, 46, 76, 79, 81–83, 99, 144, 240, 264, 319, 325, 339, 344, 348, 353, 361, 367–369, 373, 376, 385–387, 436

science, modern, 394–395

scribes (scribalism)
    Israelite, 5, 38, 82–84, 87, 94
    Sumerian, 5, 78

Second Temple Period, 21, 178, 303, 307–309, 311–312, 321

sentence literature. *see* proverbs

Septuagint, 41, 176, 203, 261, 287, 304

sloth, 461

Solomon
    reign of, 333
    wisdom of, 4–5, 9, 13, 15, 36, 41, 47–49, 55, 106, 138, 216, 272, 284, 292, 295, 301, 304–305, 307, 318, 391–392, 398–399, 403

source-criticism, 97, 118

speech, 19, 37, 52–54, 86, 127, 130, 147, 149, 164–166, 268, 271, 305, 326, 330, 338, 341, 349, 353, 355, 358, 374, 376, 382, 386, 391, 440, 451, 459, 461–462, 464, 468

spiritual exercise, 9, 286, 297–301

structure, 6–7, 9, 16, 35, 39, 47, 50–51, 63, 85, 107, 109, 137, 142, 144, 149, 151–152, 160, 185, 188–189, 194, 197–198, 208, 217, 230, 235, 245–246, 253, 286–287, 300, 309, 334, 341, 359, 369–370, 372, 380, 382, 392, 395, 473

study, 3–4, 11–12, 14, 16, 19–20, 31–33, 54, 59–61, 67–68, 70, 79, 81, 84, 94, 97–98, 142, 144, 163, 167–168, 178, 194, 204, 220, 229, 231, 236, 240, 256, 265, 270, 308–309, 311, 314, 316, 320–321, 327, 329, 331, 367, 373, 394, 456, 458, 467, 470–471

Šuruppak, 376–377, 383, 387

tabernacle, 8, 123, 127, 240, 245–250,
    252, 271
temple, 6, 8, 17, 75, 78, 80, 87, 117, 120,
    122–123, 125–128, 130–132, 158,
    222, 225, 242, 244, 246, 251–252,
    254–255, 311, 316, 327, 330, 354,
    371, 374, 377, 382, 384, 433
theodicy, 9–10, 45, 81, 104, 172, 174–175,
    177, 179, 221, 266, 280, 305, 362,
    366–367, 373, 379–383
theology
    creation, 399–401
    philosophical, 286, 290–297
    spiritual, 392–394
time, 3, 5, 7, 16, 18–19, 24, 39, 57, 64, 66,
    72, 78, 86, 92, 97, 102, 104, 124, 129,
    140, 159, 169, 184, 191, 194–198,
    201–202, 250, 252, 256, 262, 279,
    283–284, 288, 293–296, 301, 303,
    308, 312, 316, 348, 353–354,
    358–359, 364, 367–369, 371, 374,
    376, 381–382, 384–386, 393, 395,
    398, 401, 403–404, 406–407, 410,
    428, 441–442, 449, 460–463, 465,
    468, 471
Torah, 6–7, 9, 21, 25, 49, 118, 123,
    125–127, 132, 138, 140–141,
    177–178, 230, 235, 240, 243, 261,
    265, 268, 270–273, 276, 281, 284,
    306–307, 319
Tradition
    Hellenistic, 300
    Jewish, 200, 272, 281, 300

Ugarit, 10, 79, 344, 346–350, 352,
    354–356, 358, 360–363, 369,
    373–374, 378, 380, 384

variant repetitions, 62, 64, 70–71, 146,
    149–150
vernacular texts, 349–350, 357–358
versions, ancient/textual, 286, 288
virtue
    contexts of, 471–473
    moral, 72, 459–463, 465–466, 468–470
    intellectual, 459, 462, 465–468, 473

wealth, 9, 78, 87, 108, 111, 113, 121,
    124–125, 127–132, 141, 146, 160,
    164, 194, 253–255, 274–275, 305,
    337, 342, 354, 381, 384, 420–421,
    424–425, 430, 447–448, 451,
    460–461, 466, 472
wicked(ness), 11, 112, 270
wisdom
    critical, 10, 73, 345, 349, 352–358
    personification of, 9, 106, 306, 310,
        314, 321
    practical, 10, 345, 347–352, 357, 460,
        462, 466
wisdom literature
    definition of, 204–207, 367
    extent of, 15, 31–32
    problems with, 168–172
    social location of, 32
    theology of, 399–401, 412
    traditional view of, 14–19
Wisdom, Book of, 9, 283–301
Wisdom, Woman, 22, 100, 106–107, 109,
    112, 267, 270–271, 276–277, 452
worldview, 4, 14, 16, 22–23, 27, 32, 34, 37,
    66, 74–75, 90–92, 94, 111, 114, 139,
    146, 152, 157, 264, 309, 352, 394

yaḥad, 311–312, 317–319

CAMBRIDGE COMPANIONS TO RELIGION (*continued from page iii*)

THE HEBREW BIBLE/OLD TESTAMENT Edited by Stephen B. Chapman and Marvin A. Sweeney

HEBREW BIBLE AND ETHICS Edited by C. L. Crouch

THE JESUITS Edited by Thomas Worcester

JESUS Edited by Markus Bockmuehl

JUDAISM AND LAW Edited by Christine Hayes

C. S. LEWIS Edited by Robert MacSwain and Michael Ward

LIBERATION THEOLOGY Edited by Chris Rowland

MARTIN LUTHER Edited by Donald K. McKim

MEDIEVAL JEWISH PHILOSOPHY Edited by Daniel H. Frank and Oliver Leaman

MODERN JEWISH PHILOSOPHY Edited by Michael L. Morgan and Peter Eli Gordon

MOHAMMED Edited by Jonathan E. Brockup

THE NEW CAMBRIDGE COMPANION TO ST. PAUL Edited by Bruce W. Longenecker

NEW RELIGIOUS MOVEMENTS Edited by Olav Hammer and Mikael Rothstein

NEW TESTAMENT Edited by Patrick Gray

PENTECOSTALISM Edited by Cecil M. Robeck, Jr and Amos Yong

POSTMODERN THEOLOGY Edited by Kevin J. Vanhoozer

THE PROBLEM OF EVIL Edited by Chad Meister and Paul K. Moser

PURITANISM Edited by John Coffey and Paul C. H. Lim

QUAKERISM Edited by Stephen W. Angell and Pink Dandelion

THE QUR'AN Edited by Jane Dammen McAuliffe

KARL RAHNER Edited by Declan Marmion and Mary E. Hines

REFORMATION THEOLOGY Edited by David Bagchi and David C. Steinmetz

REFORMED THEOLOGY Edited by Paul T. Nimmo and David A. S. Fergusson

RELIGION AND TERRORISM Edited by James R. Lewis

RELIGIOUS EXPERIENCE Edited by Paul K. Moser and Chad Meister

RELIGIOUS STUDIES Edited by Robert A. Orsi

FREIDRICK SCHLEIERMACHER Edited by Jacqueline Mariña

SCIENCE AND RELIGION Edited by Peter Harrison

ST. PAUL Edited by James D. G. Dunn

SUFISM Edited by Lloyd Ridgeon

THE SUMMA THEOLOGIAE Edited by Philip McCosker and Denys Turner

THE TALMUD AND RABBINIC LITERATURE Edited by Charlotte E. Fonrobert and Martin S. Jaffee

THE TRINITY Edited by Peter C. Phan

HANS URS VON BALTHASAR Edited by Edward T. Oakes and David Moss

VATICAN II Edited by Richard R. Gaillardetz

JOHN WESLEY Edited by Randy L. Maddox and Jason E. Vickers

Lightning Source UK Ltd.
Milton Keynes UK
UKHW02080720123
415680UK00015B/826